Praise for this book

"*Software Requirements, Third Edition*, is the most valuable requirements guidance you will find. Wiegers and Beatty cover the entire landscape of practices that today's business analyst is expected to know. Whether you are a veteran of requirements specification or a novice on your first project, this is the book that needs to be on your desk or in your hands."

—*Gary K. Evans, Agile Coach and Use Case Expert, Evanetics, Inc.*

"It's a three-peat: Karl Wiegers and Joy Beatty score again with this third edition. From the first edition in 1999 through each successive edition, the guidance that *Software Requirements* provides has been the foundation of my requirements consulting practice. To beginning and experienced practitioners alike, I cannot recommend this book highly enough."

—*Roxanne Miller, President, Requirements Quest*

"The best book on requirements just got better! The third edition's range of new topics expands the project circumstances it covers. Using requirements in agile environments is perhaps the most significant, because everyone involved still needs to understand what a new system must do—and agile developers are now an audience who ought to have a good grasp of what's in this book."

—*Stephen Withall, author of* Software Requirement Patterns

"The third edition of *Software Requirements* is finally available—and it was worth waiting so long. Full of practical guidance, it helps readers identify many useful practices for their work. I particularly enjoy the examples and many hands-on solutions that can be easily implemented in real-life scenarios. A must-read, not only for requirements engineers and analysts but also for project managers."

—*Dr. Christof Ebert, Managing Director, Vector Consulting Services*

"Karl and Joy have updated one of the seminal works on software requirements, taking what was good and improving on it. This edition retains what made the previous versions must-have references for anyone working in this space and extends it to tackle the challenges faced in today's complex business and technology environment. Irrespective of the technology, business domain, methodology, or project type you are working in, this book will help you deliver better outcomes for your customers."

—*Shane Hastie, Chief Knowledge Engineer, Software Education*

"Karl Wiegers's and Joy Beatty's new book on requirements is an excellent addition to the literature. Requirements for large software applications are one of the most difficult business topics of the century. This new book will help to smooth out a very rough topic."

—*T. Capers Jones, VP and CTO, Namcook Analytics LLC*

"Simply put, this book is both a must-read and a great reference for anyone working to define and manage software development projects. In today's modern software development world, too often sound requirements practices are set aside for the lure of "unencumbered" agile. Karl and Joy have detailed a progressive approach to managing requirements, and detailed how to accommodate the ever-changing approaches to delivering software."

—*Mark Kulak, Software Development Director, Borland, a Micro Focus company*

"I am so pleased to see the updated book on software requirements from Karl Wiegers and Joy Beatty. I especially like the latest topic on how to apply effective requirements practices to agile projects, because it is a service that our consultants are engaged in more and more these days. The practical guide and real examples of the many different requirement practices are invaluable."

—*Doreen Evans, Managing Director of the Requirements and Business Analysis Practice for Robbins Gioia Inc.*

"As an early adopter of Karl's classic book, *Software Requirements*, I have been eagerly awaiting his new edition—and it doesn't disappoint. Over the years, IT development has undergone a change of focus from large, new, 'green-field' projects towards adoption of ready-made off-the-shelf solutions and quick-release agile practices. In this latest edition, Karl and Joy explore the implications of these new developments on the requirements process, with invaluable recommendations based not on dogma but on what works, honed from their broad and deep experience in the field."

—*Howard Podeswa, CEO, Noble Inc., and author of* The Business Analyst's Handbook

"If you are looking for a practical guide into what software requirements are, how to craft them, and what to do with them, then look no further than *Software Requirements, Third Edition*. This usable and readable text walks you through exactly how to approach common requirements-related scenarios. The incorporation of multiple stories, case studies, anecdotes, and examples keeps it engaging to read."

—*Laura Brandenburg, CBAP, Host at Bridging the Gap*

"How do you make a good requirements read better? You add content like Karl and Joy did to address incorporating product vision, tackling agility issues, covering requirements reuse, tackling packaged and outsourced software, and addressing specific user classes. You could take an outside look inside of requirements to address process and risk issues and go beyond just capturing functionality."

—*Donald J. Reifer, President, Reifer Consultants LLC*

"This new edition keeps pace with the speed of business, both in deepening the foundation of the second edition and in bringing analysts down-to-earth how-to's for addressing the surge in agile development, using features to control scope, improving elicitation techniques, and expanding modeling. Wiegers and Beatty have put together a must-read for anyone in the profession."

—*Keith Ellis, President and CEO, Enfocus Solutions Inc., and author of* Business Analysis Benchmark

Software Requirements, Third Edition

Karl Wiegers and Joy Beatty

PUBLISHED BY
Microsoft Press
A Division of Microsoft Corporation
One Microsoft Way
Redmond, Washington 98052-6399

Library of Congress Control Number: 2013942928
ISBN: 978-0-7356-7966-5

Fourth Printing: August 2015

Microsoft Press books are available through booksellers and distributors worldwide. If you need support related to this book, email Microsoft Press Book Support at mspinput@microsoft.com. Please tell us what you think of this book at *http://www.microsoft.com/learning/booksurvey*.

"Microsoft and the trademarks listed at *http://www.microsoft.com/about/legal/en/us/IntellectualProperty/ Trademarks/EN-US.aspx* are trademarks of the Microsoft group of companies. All other marks are property of their respective owners."

The example companies, organizations, products, domain names, email addresses, logos, people, places, and events depicted herein are fictitious. No association with any real company, organization, product, domain name, email address, logo, person, place, or event is intended or should be inferred.

This book expresses the author's views and opinions. The information contained in this book is provided without any express, statutory, or implied warranties. Neither the authors, Microsoft Corporation, nor its resellers, or distributors will be held liable for any damages caused or alleged to be caused either directly or indirectly by this book.

Acquisitions Editor: Devon Musgrave
Developmental Editors: Devon Musgrave and Carol Dillingham
Project Editor: Carol Dillingham
Editorial Production: Christian Holdener, S4Carlisle Publishing Services
Copyeditor: Kathy Krause
Indexer: Maureen Johnson
Cover: Twist Creative • Seattle

For Chris, yet again. Eighth time's the charm.

—K.W.

For my parents, Bob and Joanne, for a lifetime of encouragement.

—J.B.

Contents at a glance

Contents

Chapter 3   Good practices for requirements engineering   43

Chapter 4   The business analyst   61

PART II   **REQUIREMENTS DEVELOPMENT**

Chapter 11   Writing excellent requirements   203

Chapter 12   A picture is worth 1024 words   221

Chapter 29 Links in the requirements chain   491

Chapter 30 Tools for requirements engineering   503

PART V   IMPLEMENTING REQUIREMENTS ENGINEERING

Chapter 31   Improving your requirements processes   517

Chapter 32   Software requirements and risk management   537

Introduction

Despite decades of industry experience, many software organizations struggle to understand, document, and manage their product requirements. Inadequate user input, incomplete requirements, changing requirements, and misunderstood business objectives are major reasons why so many information technology projects are less than fully successful. Some software teams aren't proficient at eliciting requirements from customers and other sources. Customers often don't have the time or patience to participate in requirements activities. In many cases, project participants don't even agree on what a "requirement" is. As one writer observed, "Engineers would rather decipher the words to the Kingsmen's 1963 classic party song 'Louie Louie' than decipher customer requirements" (Peterson 2002).

The second edition of *Software Requirements* was published 10 years prior to this one. Ten years is a long time in the technology world. Many things have changed in that time, but others have not. Major requirements trends in the past decade include:

- The recognition of business analysis as a professional discipline and the rise of professional certifications and organizations, such as the International Institute of Business Analysis and the International Requirements Engineering Board.

- The maturing of tools both for managing requirements in a database and for assisting with requirements development activities such as prototyping, modeling, and simulation.

- The increased use of agile development methods and the evolution of techniques for handling requirements on agile projects.

- The increased use of visual models to represent requirements knowledge.

So, what *hasn't* changed? Two factors contribute to keeping this topic important and relevant. First, many undergraduate curricula in software engineering and computer science continue to underemphasize the importance of requirements engineering (which encompasses both requirements development and requirements management). And second, those of us in the software domain tend to be enamored with technical and process solutions to our challenges. We sometimes fail to appreciate that requirements elicitation—and much of software and systems project work in general—is primarily a human interaction challenge. No magical new techniques have come along to automate that, although various tools are available to help geographically separated people collaborate effectively.

We believe that the practices presented in the second edition for developing and managing requirements are still valid and applicable to a wide range of software projects. The creative business analyst, product manager, or product owner will thoughtfully adapt and scale the practices to best meet the needs of a particular situation. Newly added to this third edition are a chapter on handling requirements for agile projects and sections in numerous other chapters that describe how to apply and adapt the practices in those chapters to the agile development environment.

Software development involves at least as much communication as it does computing, yet both educational curricula and project activities often emphasize the computing over the communication aspect. This book offers dozens of tools to facilitate that communication and to help software practitioners, managers, marketers, and customers apply effective requirements engineering methods. The techniques presented here constitute a tool kit of mainstream "good practices," not exotic new techniques or an elaborate methodology that purports to solve all of your requirements problems. Numerous anecdotes and sidebars present stories—all true—that illustrate typical requirements-related experiences; you have likely had similar experiences. Look for the "true stories" icon, like the one to the left, next to real examples drawn from many project experiences.

Since the first edition of this book appeared in 1999, we have each worked on numerous projects and taught hundreds of classes on software requirements to people from companies and government agencies of all sizes and types. We've learned that these practices are useful on virtually any project: small projects and large, new development and enhancements, with local and distributed teams, and using traditional and agile development methods. The techniques apply to hardware and systems engineering projects, too, not just software projects. As with any other technical practice, you'll need to use good judgment and experience to learn how to make the methods work best for you. Think of these practices as tools to help ensure that you have effective conversations with the right people on your projects.

Benefits this book provides

Of all the software process improvements you could undertake, improved requirements practices are among the most beneficial. We describe practical, proven techniques that can help you to:

- Write high-quality requirements from the outset of a project, thereby minimizing rework and maximizing productivity.

- Deliver high-quality information systems and commercial products that achieve their business objectives.

- Manage scope creep and requirements changes to stay both on target and under control.

- Achieve higher customer satisfaction.

- Reduce maintenance, enhancement, and support costs.

Our objective is to help you improve the processes you use for eliciting and analyzing requirements, writing and validating requirements specifications, and managing the requirements throughout the software product development cycle. The techniques we describe are pragmatic and realistic. Both of us have used these very techniques many times, and we always get good results when we do.

Who should read this book

Anyone involved with defining or understanding the requirements for any system that contains software will find useful information here. The primary audience consists of individuals who serve as business analysts or requirements engineers on a development project, be they full-time specialists or other team members who sometimes fill the analyst role. A second audience includes the architects, designers, developers, testers, and other technical team members who must understand and satisfy user expectations and participate in the creation and review of effective requirements. Marketers and product managers who are charged with specifying the features and attributes that will make a product a commercial success will find these practices valuable. Project managers will learn how to plan and track the project's requirements activities and deal with requirements changes. Yet another audience is made up of stakeholders who participate in defining a product that meets their business, functional, and quality needs. This book will help end users, customers who procure or contract for software products, and numerous other stakeholders understand the importance of the requirements process and their roles in it.

Looking ahead

This book is organized into five parts. Part I, "Software requirements: What, why, and who," begins with some definitions. If you're on the technical side of the house, please share Chapter 2, on the customer-development partnership, with your key customers. Chapter 3 summarizes several dozen "good practices" for requirements development and management, as well as an overall process framework for requirements development. The role of the business analyst (a role that also goes by many other names) is the subject of Chapter 4.

Part II, "Requirements development," begins with techniques for defining the project's business requirements. Other chapters in Part II address how to find appropriate customer representatives, elicit requirements from them, and document user requirements, business rules, functional requirements, data requirements, and nonfunctional requirements. Chapter 12 describes numerous visual models that represent the requirements from various perspectives to supplement natural-language text, and Chapter 15 addresses the use of prototypes to reduce risk. Other chapters in Part II present ways to prioritize, validate, and reuse requirements. Part II concludes by describing how requirements affect other aspects of project work.

New to this edition, Part III contains chapters that recommend the most effective requirements approaches for various specific classes of projects: agile projects developing products of any type, enhancement and replacement projects, projects that incorporate packaged solutions, outsourced projects, business process automation projects, business analytics projects, and embedded and other real-time systems.

The principles and practices of requirements management are the subject of Part IV, with emphasis on techniques for dealing with changing requirements. Chapter 29 describes how requirements tracing connects individual requirements both to their origins and to downstream development deliverables. Part IV concludes with a description of commercial tools that can enhance the way your teams conduct both requirements development and requirements management.

The final section of this book, Part V, "Implementing requirements engineering," helps you move from concepts to practice. Chapter 31 will help you incorporate new requirements techniques into your group's development process. Common requirements-related project risks are described in Chapter 32. The self-assessment in Appendix A can help you select areas that are ripe for improvement. Two other appendices present a requirements troubleshooting guide and several sample requirements documents so you can see how the pieces all fit together.

Case studies

To illustrate the methods described in this book, we have provided examples from several case studies based on actual projects, particularly a medium-sized information system called the Chemical Tracking System. Don't worry—you don't need to know anything about chemistry to understand this project. Sample discussions among participants from the case studies are sprinkled throughout the book. No matter what kind of software your organization builds, you'll be able to relate to these dialogs.

From principles to practice

It's difficult to muster the energy needed for overcoming obstacles to change and putting new knowledge into action. As an aid for your journey to improved requirements, most chapters end with several "next steps," actions you can take to begin applying the contents of that chapter immediately. Various chapters offer suggested templates for requirements documents, a review checklist, a requirements prioritization spreadsheet, a change control process, and many other process assets. These items are available for downloading at the companion content website for this book:

http://aka.ms/SoftwareReq3E/files

Use them to jump-start your application of these techniques. Start with small improvements, but start today.

Some people will be reluctant to try new requirements techniques. Use this book to educate your peers, your customers, and your managers. Remind them of requirements-related problems encountered on previous projects, and discuss the potential benefits of trying some new approaches.

You don't need to launch a new development project to begin applying better requirements practices. Chapter 21 discusses ways to apply many of the techniques to enhancement and replacement projects. Implementing requirements practices incrementally is a low-risk process improvement approach that will prepare you for the next major project.

The goal of requirements development is to accumulate a set of requirements that are *good enough* to allow your team to proceed with design and construction of the next portion of the product at an acceptable level of risk. You need to devote enough attention to requirements to minimize the risks of rework, unacceptable products, and blown schedules. This book gives you the tools to get the right people to collaborate on developing the right requirements for the right product.

Errata & book support

We've made every effort to ensure the accuracy of this book and its companion content. Any errors that have been reported since this book was published are listed on our Microsoft Press site:

http://aka.ms/SoftwareReq3E/errata

If you find an error that is not already listed, you can report it to us through the same page.

If you need additional support, email Microsoft Press Book Support at *mspinput@microsoft.com*.

Please note that product support for Microsoft software is not offered through the addresses above.

We want to hear from you

At Microsoft Press, your satisfaction is our top priority, and your feedback our most valuable asset. Please tell us what you think of this book at:

http://aka.ms/tellpress

The survey is short, and we read every one of your comments and ideas. Thanks in advance for your input!

Stay in touch

Let's keep the conversation going! We're on Twitter: *http://twitter.com/MicrosoftPress*.

Acknowledgments

Writing a book like this is a team effort that goes far beyond the contributions from the two authors. A number of people took the time to review the full manuscript and offer countless suggestions for improvement; they have our deep gratitude. We especially appreciate the invaluable comments from Jim Brosseau, Joan Davis, Gary K. Evans, Joyce Grapes, Tina Heidenreich, Kelly Morrison Smith, and Dr. Joyce Statz. Additional review input was received from Kevin Brennan, Steven Davis, Anne Hartley, Emily Iem, Matt Leach, Jeannine McConnell, Yaaqub Mohamed, and John Parker. Certain individuals reviewed specific chapters or sections in their areas of expertise, often providing highly detailed comments. We thank Tanya Charbury, Mike Cohn, Dr. Alex Dean, Ellen Gottesdiener, Shane Hastie, James Hulgan, Dr. Phil Koopman, Mark Kulak, Shirley Sartin, Rob Siciliano, and Betsy Stockdale. We especially thank Roxanne Miller and Stephen Withall for their deep insights and generous participation.

We discussed aspects of the book's topics with many people, learning from their personal experiences and from resource materials they passed along to us. We appreciate such contributions from Jim Brosseau, Nanette Brown, Nigel Budd, Katherine Busey, Tanya Charbury, Jennifer Doyle, Gary Evans, Scott Francis, Sarah Gates, Dr. David Gelperin, Mark Kerin, Norm Kerth, Dr. Scott Meyers, John Parker, Kathy Reynolds, Bill Trosky, Dr. Ricardo Valerdi, and Dr. Ian Watson. We also thank the many people who let us share their anecdotes in our "true stories."

Numerous staff members at Seilevel contributed to the book. They reviewed specific sections, participated in quick opinion and experience surveys, shared blog material they had written, edited final chapters, drew figures, and helped us with operational issues of various sorts. We thank Ajay Badri, Jason Benfield, Anthony Chen, Kell Condon, Amber Davis, Jeremy Gorr, Joyce Grapes, John Jertson, Melanie Norrell, David Reinhardt, Betsy Stockdale, and Christine Wollmuth. Their work made ours easier. The editorial input from Candase Hokanson is greatly appreciated.

Thanks go to many people at Microsoft Press, including acquisitions editor Devon Musgrave, project editor Carol Dillingham, project editor Christian Holdener of S4Carlisle Publishing Services, copy editor Kathy Krause, proofreader Nicole Schlutt, indexer Maureen Johnson, compositor Sambasivam Sangaran, and production artists Balaganesan M., Srinivasan R., and Ganeshbabu G. Karl especially values his long-term relationship, and friendship, with Devon Musgrave and Ben Ryan.

The comments and questions from thousands of students in our requirements training classes over the years have been most helpful in stimulating our thinking about requirements issues. Our consulting experiences and the thought-provoking questions we receive from readers have kept us in touch with what practitioners struggle with on a daily basis and helped us think through some of these difficult topics. Please share your own experiences with us at *karl@processimpact.com* or *joy.beatty@seilevel.com*.

As always, Karl would like to thank his wife, Chris Zambito. And as always, she was patient and good-humored throughout the process. Karl also thanks Joy for prompting him into working on this project and for her terrific contributions. Working with her was a lot of fun, and she added a great deal of value to the book. It was great to have someone to bounce ideas off, to help make difficult decisions, and to chew hard on draft chapters before we inflicted them on the reviewers.

Joy is particularly grateful to her husband, Tony Hamilton, for supporting her writing dreams so soon again; to her daughter, Skye, for making it easy to keep her daily priorities balanced; and to Sean and Estelle for being the center of her family fun times. Joy wants to extend a special thanks to all of the Seilevel employees who collaborate to push the software requirements field forward. She particularly wants to thank two colleagues and friends: Anthony Chen, whose support for her writing this book was paramount; and Rob Sparks, for his continued encouragement in such endeavors. Finally, Joy owes a great deal of gratitude to Karl for allowing her to join him in this co-authorship, teaching her something new every day, and being an absolute joy to work with!

Software requirements: What, why, and who

CHAPTER 1

The essential software requirement

"Hello, Phil? This is Maria in Human Resources. We're having a problem with the personnel system you programmed for us. An employee just changed her name to Sparkle Starlight, and we can't get the system to accept the name change. Can you help?"

"She married some guy named Starlight?"

"No, she didn't get married, just changed her name," Maria replied. "That's the problem. It looks like we can change a name only if someone's marital status changes."

"Well, yeah, I never thought someone might just change her name. I don't remember you telling me about this possibility when we talked about the system," Phil said.

"I assumed you knew that people could legally change their name anytime they like," responded Maria. "We have to straighten this out by Friday or Sparkle won't be able to cash her paycheck. Can you fix the bug by then?"

"It's not a bug!" Phil retorted. "I never knew you needed this capability. I'm busy on the new performance evaluation system. I can probably fix it by the end of the month, but not by Friday. Sorry about that. Next time, tell me these things earlier and please write them down."

"What am I supposed to tell Sparkle?" demanded Maria. "She'll be upset if she can't cash her check."

"Hey, Maria, it's not my fault," Phil protested. "If you'd told me in the first place that you had to be able to change someone's name at any time, this wouldn't have happened. You can't blame me for not reading your mind."

Angry and resigned, Maria snapped, "Yeah, well, this is the kind of thing that makes me hate computers. Call me as soon as you get it fixed, will you?"

If you've ever been on the customer side of a conversation like this, you know how frustrating it is when a software system doesn't let you perform an essential task. You hate to be at the mercy of a developer who *might* get to your critical change request eventually. On the other hand, developers are frustrated to learn about functionality that a user expected only after they've implemented the system. It's also annoying for a developer to have his current project interrupted by a request to modify a system that does precisely what he was told it should do in the first place.

Many problems in the software world arise from shortcomings in the ways that people learn about, document, agree upon and modify the product's requirements. As with Phil and Maria, common problem areas are informal information gathering, implied functionality, miscommunicated assumptions, poorly specified requirements, and a casual change process. Various studies suggest that errors introduced during requirements activities account for 40 to 50 percent of all defects found in a software product (Davis 2005). Inadequate user input and shortcomings in specifying and managing customer requirements are major contributors to unsuccessful projects. Despite this evidence, many organizations still practice ineffective requirements methods.

Nowhere more than in the requirements do the interests of all the stakeholders in a project intersect. (See Chapter 2, "Requirements from the customer's perspective," for more about stakeholders.) These stakeholders include customers, users, business analysts, developers, and many others. Handled well, this intersection can lead to delighted customers and fulfilled developers. Handled poorly, it's the source of misunderstanding and friction that undermine the product's quality and business value. Because requirements are the foundation for both the software development and the project management activities, all stakeholders should commit to applying requirements practices that are known to yield superior-quality products.

But developing and managing requirements is hard! There are no simple shortcuts or magic solutions. On the plus side, so many organizations struggle with the same problems that you can look for techniques in common that apply to many different situations. This book describes dozens of such practices. The practices are presented as though you were building a brand-new system. However, most of them also apply to enhancement, replacement, and reengineering projects (see Chapter 21, "Enhancement and replacement projects") and to projects that incorporate commercial off-the-shelf (COTS) packaged solutions (see Chapter 22, "Packaged solution projects"). Project teams that build products incrementally by following an agile development process also need to understand the requirements that go into each increment (see Chapter 20, "Agile projects").

This chapter will help you to:

- Understand some key terms used in the software requirements domain.

- Distinguish *product* requirements from *project* requirements.

- Distinguish requirements *development* from requirements *management*.

- Be alert to several requirements-related problems that can arise.

 Important We use the terms "system," "product," "application," and "solution" interchangeably in this book to refer to any kind of software or software-containing item that you build, whether for internal corporate use, for commercial sale, or on a contract basis.

Software requirements defined

When a group of people begin discussing requirements, they often start with a terminology problem. Different observers might describe a single statement as being a user requirement, software requirement, business requirement, functional requirement, system requirement, product requirement, project requirement, user story, feature, or constraint. The names they use for various requirements deliverables also vary. A customer's definition of requirements might sound like a high-level product concept to the developer. The developer's notion of requirements might sound like a detailed user interface design to the user. This diversity of understanding leads to confusion and frustration.

Some interpretations of "requirement"

Many decades after the invention of computer programming, software practitioners still have raging debates about exactly what a "requirement" is. Rather than prolong those debates, in this book we simply present some definitions that we have found useful.

Consultant Brian Lawrence suggests that a *requirement* is "anything that drives design choices" (Lawrence 1997). This is not a bad colloquial definition, because many kinds of information fit in this category. And, after all, the whole point of developing requirements is to make appropriate design choices that will meet the customer's needs in the end. Another definition is that a requirement is a property that a product must have to provide value to a stakeholder. Also not bad, but not very precise. Our favorite definition, though, comes from Ian Sommerville and Pete Sawyer (1997):

> *Requirements are a specification of what should be implemented. They are descriptions of how the system should behave, or of a system property or attribute. They may be a constraint on the development process of the system.*

This definition acknowledges the diverse types of information that collectively are referred to as "the requirements." Requirements encompass both the user's view of the external system behavior and the developer's view of some internal characteristics. They include both the behavior of the system under specific conditions and those properties that make the system suitable—and maybe even enjoyable—for use by its intended operators.

> **Trap** Don't assume that all your project stakeholders share a common notion of what requirements are. Establish definitions up front so that you're all talking about the same things.

The pure dictionary "requirement"

Software people do not use "requirement" in the same sense as a dictionary definition of the word: something demanded or obligatory, a need or necessity. People sometimes question whether they even need to prioritize requirements, because maybe a low-priority requirement won't ever be implemented. If it isn't truly needed, then it isn't a requirement, they claim. Perhaps, but then what would you call that piece of information? If you defer a requirement from today's project to an unspecified future release, is it still considered a requirement? Sure it is.

Software requirements include a time dimension. They could be present tense, describing the current system's capabilities. Or they could be for the near-term (high priority), mid-term (medium priority), or hypothetical (low priority) future. They could even be past tense, referring to needs that were once specified and then discarded. Don't waste time debating whether or not something is a requirement, even if you know you might never implement it for some good business reason. It is.

Levels and types of requirements

Because there are so many different types of requirements information, we need a consistent set of adjectives to modify the overloaded term "requirement." This section presents definitions we will use for some terms commonly encountered in the requirements domain (see Table 1-1).

TABLE 1-1 Some types of requirements information

Term	Definition
Business requirement	A high-level business objective of the organization that builds a product or of a customer who procures it.
Business rule	A policy, guideline, standard, or regulation that defines or constrains some aspect of the business. Not a software requirement in itself, but the origin of several types of software requirements.
Constraint	A restriction that is imposed on the choices available to the developer for the design and construction of a product.
External interface requirement	A description of a connection between a software system and a user, another software system, or a hardware device.
Feature	One or more logically related system capabilities that provide value to a user and are described by a set of functional requirements.
Functional requirement	A description of a behavior that a system will exhibit under specific conditions.
Nonfunctional requirement	A description of a property or characteristic that a system must exhibit or a constraint that it must respect.
Quality attribute	A kind of nonfunctional requirement that describes a service or performance characteristic of a product.
System requirement	A top-level requirement for a product that contains multiple subsystems, which could be all software or software and hardware.
User requirement	A goal or task that specific classes of users must be able to perform with a system, or a desired product attribute.

Software requirements include three distinct levels: business requirements, user requirements, and functional requirements. In addition, every system has an assortment of nonfunctional requirements. The model in Figure 1-1 illustrates a way to think about these diverse types of requirements. As statistician George E. P. Box famously said, "Essentially, all models are wrong, but some are useful" (Box and Draper 1987). That's certainly true of Figure 1-1. This model is not all-inclusive, but it does provide a helpful scheme for organizing the requirements knowledge you'll encounter.

The ovals in Figure 1-1 represent types of requirements information, and the rectangles indicate documents in which to store that information. The solid arrows indicate that a certain type of information typically is stored in the indicated document. (Business rules and system requirements are stored separately from software requirements, such as in a business rules catalog or a system requirements specification, respectively.) The dotted arrows indicate that one type of information is the origin of or influences another type of requirement. Data requirements are not shown explicitly in this diagram. Functions manipulate data, so data requirements can appear throughout the three levels. Chapter 7, "Requirements elicitation," contains many examples of these different types of requirements information.

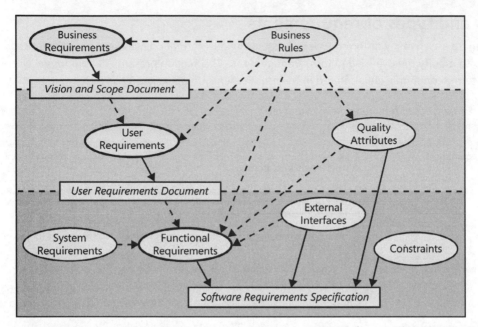

FIGURE 1-1 Relationships among several types of requirements information. Solid arrows mean "are stored in"; dotted arrows mean "are the origin of" or "influence."

> **Important** Although we will refer to requirements "documents" throughout this book, as in Figure 1-1, those do not have to be traditional paper or electronic documents. Instead, think of them simply as containers in which to store requirements knowledge. Such a container could indeed be a traditional document, or it could be a spreadsheet, a set of diagrams, a database, a requirements management tool, or some combination of these. For convenience, we will use the term "document" to refer to any such container. We will provide templates that identify the types of information to consider storing in each such grouping, regardless of what form you store it in. What you call each deliverable is less important than having your organization agree on their names, what kinds of information go into each, and how that information is organized.

Business requirements describe *why* the organization is implementing the system—the business benefits the organization hopes to achieve. The focus is on the business objectives of the organization or the customer who requests the system. Suppose an airline wants to reduce airport counter staff costs by 25 percent. This goal might lead to the idea of building a kiosk that passengers can use to check in for their flights at the airport. Business requirements typically come from the funding sponsor for a project, the acquiring customer, the manager of the actual users, the marketing department, or a product visionary. We like to record the business requirements in a *vision and scope document*. Other strategic guiding documents sometimes used for this purpose include a project charter, business case, and market (or marketing) requirements document. Specifying business requirements is the subject of Chapter 5, "Establishing the business requirements." For the purposes of this book, we are assuming that the business need or market opportunity has already been identified.

User requirements describe goals or tasks the users must be able to perform with the product that will provide value to someone. The domain of user requirements also includes descriptions of product attributes or characteristics that are important to user satisfaction. Ways to represent user requirements include use cases (Kulak and Guiney 2004), user stories (Cohn 2004), and event-response tables. Ideally, actual user representatives will provide this information. User requirements describe *what* the user will be able to do with the system. An example of a use case is "Check in for a flight" using an airline's website or a kiosk at the airport. Written as a user story, the same user requirement might read: "As a passenger, I want to check in for a flight so I can board my airplane." It's important to remember that most projects have multiple user classes, as well as other stakeholders whose needs also must be elicited. Chapter 8, "Understanding user requirements," addresses this level of the model. Some people use the broader term "stakeholder requirements," to acknowledge the reality that various stakeholders other than direct users will provide requirements. That is certainly true, but we focus the attention at this level on understanding what actual users need to achieve with the help of the product.

Functional requirements specify the behaviors the product will exhibit under specific conditions. They describe *what* the developers must implement to enable users to accomplish their tasks (user requirements), thereby satisfying the business requirements. This alignment among the three levels of requirements is essential for project success. Functional requirements often are written in the form of the traditional "shall" statements: "The Passenger shall be able to print boarding passes for all flight segments for which he has checked in" or "If the Passenger's profile does not indicate a seating preference, the reservation system shall assign a seat."

The business analyst (BA)[1] documents functional requirements in a *software requirements specification* (SRS), which describes as fully as necessary the expected behavior of the software system. The SRS is used in development, testing, quality assurance, project management, and related project functions. People call this deliverable by many different names, including business requirements document, functional spec, requirements document, and others. An SRS could be a report generated from information stored in a requirements management tool. Because it is an industry-standard term, we will use "SRS" consistently throughout this book (ISO/IEC/IEEE 2011). See Chapter 10, "Documenting the requirements," for more information about the SRS.

System requirements describe the requirements for a product that is composed of multiple components or subsystems (ISO/IEC/IEEE 2011). A "system" in this sense is not just any information system. A system can be all software or it can include both software and hardware subsystems. People and processes are part of a system, too, so certain system functions might be allocated to human beings. Some people use the term "system requirements" to mean the detailed requirements for a software system, but that's not how we use the term in this book.

A good example of a "system" is the cashier's workstation in a supermarket. There's a bar code scanner integrated with a scale, as well as a hand-held bar code scanner. The cashier has a keyboard, a display, and a cash drawer. You'll see a card reader and PIN pad for your loyalty card and credit or debit card, and perhaps a change dispenser. You might see up to three printers for your purchase

---

[1] "Business analyst" refers to the project role that has primary responsibility for leading requirements-related activities on a project. The BA role also goes by many other names. See Chapter 4, "The business analyst," for more about the business analyst role.

receipt, credit card receipt, and coupons you don't care about. These hardware devices are all interacting under software control. The requirements for the system or product as a whole, then, lead the business analyst to derive specific functionality that must be allocated to one or another of those component subsystems, as well as demanding an understanding of the interfaces between them.

Business rules include corporate policies, government regulations, industry standards, and computational algorithms. As you'll see in Chapter 9, "Playing by the rules," business rules are not themselves software requirements because they have an existence beyond the boundaries of any specific software application. However, they often dictate that the system must contain functionality to comply with the pertinent rules. Sometimes, as with corporate security policies, business rules are the origin of specific quality attributes that are then implemented in functionality. Therefore, you can trace the genesis of certain functional requirements back to a particular business rule.

In addition to functional requirements, the SRS contains an assortment of nonfunctional requirements. *Quality attributes* are also known as quality factors, quality of service requirements, constraints, and the "–ilities." They describe the product's characteristics in various dimensions that are important either to users or to developers and maintainers, such as performance, safety, availability, and portability. Other classes of nonfunctional requirements describe *external interfaces* between the system and the outside world. These include connections to other software systems, hardware components, and users, as well as communication interfaces. Design and implementation *constraints* impose restrictions on the options available to the developer during construction of the product.

If they're nonfunctional, then what are they?

For many years, the requirements for a software product have been classified broadly as either functional or nonfunctional. The functional requirements are evident: they describe the observable behavior of the system under various conditions. However, many people dislike the term "nonfunctional." That adjective says what the requirements are *not*, but it doesn't say what they *are*. We are sympathetic to the problem, but we lack a perfect solution.

Other-than-functional requirements might specify not *what* the system does, but rather *how well* it does those things. They could describe important characteristics or properties of the system. These include the system's availability, usability, security, performance, and many other characteristics, as addressed in Chapter 14, "Beyond functionality." Some people consider nonfunctional requirements to be synonymous with quality attributes, but that is overly restrictive. For example, design and implementation constraints are also nonfunctional requirements, as are external interface requirements.

Still other nonfunctional requirements address the environment in which the system operates, such as platform, portability, compatibility, and constraints. Many products are also affected by compliance, regulatory, and certification requirements. There could be localization requirements for products that must take into account the cultures, languages, laws, currencies, terminology, spelling, and other characteristics of users. Though such requirements are specified in nonfunctional terms, the business analyst typically will derive numerous bits of functionality to ensure that the system possesses all the desired behaviors and properties.

In this book, we are sticking with the term "nonfunctional requirements," despite its limitations, for the lack of a suitably inclusive alternative. Rather than worry about precisely what you call these sorts of information, just make sure that they are part of your requirements elicitation and analysis activities. You can deliver a product that has all the desired functionality but that users hate because it doesn't match their (often unstated) quality expectations.

A *feature* consists of one or more logically related system capabilities that provide value to a user and are described by a set of functional requirements. A customer's list of desired product features is not equivalent to a description of the user's task-related needs. Web browser bookmarks, spelling checkers, the ability to define a custom workout program for a piece of exercise equipment, and automatic virus signature updating in an anti-malware product are examples of features. A feature can encompass multiple user requirements, each of which implies that certain functional requirements must be implemented to allow the user to perform the task described by each user requirement. Figure 1-2 illustrates a *feature tree*, an analysis model that shows how a feature can be hierarchically decomposed into a set of smaller features, which relate to specific user requirements and lead to specifying sets of functional requirements (Beatty and Chen 2012).

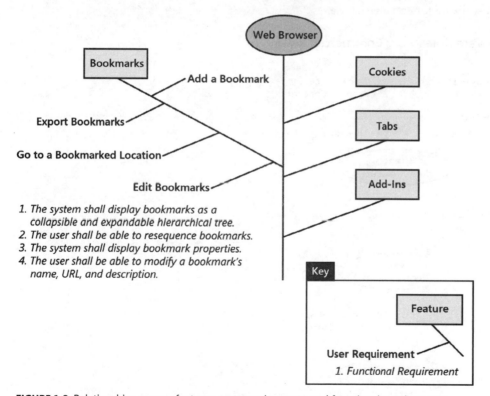

FIGURE 1-2 Relationships among features, user requirements, and functional requirements.

To illustrate some of these various kinds of requirements, consider a project to develop the next version of a text editor program. A business requirement might be "Increase non-US sales by 25 percent within 6 months." Marketing realizes that the competitive products only have English-language spelling checkers, so they decide that the new version will include a multilanguage spelling checker feature. Corresponding user requirements might include tasks such as "Select language for spelling checker," "Find spelling errors," and "Add a word to a dictionary." The spelling checker has many individual functional requirements, which deal with operations such as highlighting misspelled words, autocorrect, displaying suggested replacements, and globally replacing misspelled words with corrected words. Usability requirements specify how the software is to be localized for use with specific languages and character sets.

Working with the three levels

Figure 1-3 illustrates how various stakeholders might participate in eliciting the three levels of requirements. Different organizations use a variety of names for the roles involved in these activities; think about who performs these activities in your organization. The role names often differ depending on whether the developing organization is an internal corporate entity or a company building software for commercial use.

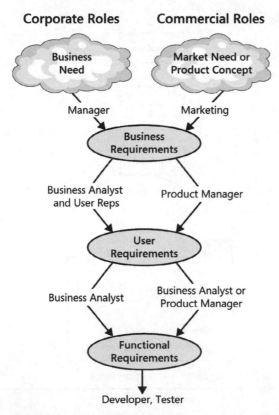

FIGURE 1-3 An example of how different stakeholders participate in requirements development.

Based on an identified business need, a market need, or an exciting new product concept, managers or marketing define the business requirements for software that will help their company operate more efficiently (for information systems) or compete successfully in the marketplace (for commercial products). In the corporate environment, a business analyst then typically works with user representatives to identify user requirements. Companies developing commercial products often identify a product manager to determine what features to include in the new product. Each user requirement and feature must align with accomplishing the business requirements. From the user requirements, the BA or product manager derives the functionality that will let users achieve their goals. Developers use the functional and nonfunctional requirements to design solutions that implement the necessary functionality, within the limits that the constraints impose. Testers determine how to verify whether the requirements were correctly implemented.

 It's important to recognize the value of recording vital requirements information in a shareable form, rather than treating it as oral tradition around the project campfire. I was on a project once that had experienced a rotating cast of development teams. The primary customer was sick to tears of having each new team come along and say, "We have to talk about your requirements." His reaction to our request was, "I already gave your predecessors my requirements. Now build me a system!" Unfortunately, no one had ever documented any requirements, so every new team had to start from scratch. To proclaim that you "have the requirements" is delusional if all you really have is a pile of email and voice mail messages, sticky notes, meeting minutes, and vaguely recollected hallway conversations. The BA must practice good judgment to determine just how comprehensive to make the requirements documentation on a given project.

Figure 1-1, shown earlier in this chapter, identified three major requirements deliverables: a vision and scope document, a user requirements document, and a software requirements specification. You do not necessarily need to create three discrete requirements deliverables on each project. It often makes sense to combine some of this information, particularly on small projects. However, recognize that these three deliverables contain different information, developed at different points in the project, possibly by different people, with different purposes and target audiences.

The model in Figure 1-1 showed a simple top-down flow of requirements information. In reality, you should expect cycles and iteration among the business, user, and functional requirements. Whenever someone proposes a new feature, user requirement, or bit of functionality, the analyst must ask, "Is this in scope?" If the answer is "yes," the requirement belongs in the specification. If the answer is "no," it does not, at least not for the forthcoming release or iteration. The third possible answer is "no, but it supports the business objectives, so it ought to be." In that case, whoever controls the project scope—the project sponsor, project manager, or product owner—must decide whether to increase the current project's or iteration's scope to accommodate the new requirement. This is a business decision that has implications for the project's schedule and budget and might demand trade-offs with other capabilities. An effective change process that includes impact analysis ensures that the right people make informed business decisions about which changes to accept and that the associated costs in time, resources, or feature trade-offs are addressed.

Product vs. project requirements

So far we have been discussing requirements that describe properties of a software system to be built. Let's call those *product* requirements. Projects certainly do have other expectations and deliverables that are not a part of the software the team implements, but that are necessary to the successful completion of the project as a whole. These are *project* requirements but not *product* requirements. An SRS houses the product requirements, but it should not include design or implementation details (other than known constraints), project plans, test plans, or similar information. Separate out such items so that requirements development activities can focus on understanding what the team intends to build. Project requirements include:

- Physical resources the development team needs, such as workstations, special hardware devices, testing labs, testing tools and equipment, team rooms, and videoconferencing equipment.

- Staff training needs.

- User documentation, including training materials, tutorials, reference manuals, and release notes.

- Support documentation, such as help desk resources and field maintenance and service information for hardware devices.

- Infrastructure changes needed in the operating environment.

- Requirements and procedures for releasing the product, installing it in the operating environment, configuring it, and testing the installation.

- Requirements and procedures for transitioning from an old system to a new one, such as data migration and conversion requirements, security setup, production cutover, and training to close skills gaps; these are sometimes called *transition requirements* (IIBA 2009).

- Product certification and compliance requirements.

- Revised policies, processes, organizational structures, and similar documents.

- Sourcing, acquisition, and licensing of third-party software and hardware components.

- Beta testing, manufacturing, packaging, marketing, and distribution requirements.

- Customer service-level agreements.

- Requirements for obtaining legal protection (patents, trademarks, or copyrights) for intellectual property related to the software.

This book does not address these sorts of project requirements further. That doesn't mean that they aren't important, just that they are out of scope for our focus on software product requirements development and management. Identifying these project requirements is a shared responsibility of the BA and the project manager. They often come up while eliciting product requirements. Project requirements information is best stored in the project management plan, which should itemize all expected project activities and deliverables.

Particularly for business applications, people sometimes refer to a "solution" as encompassing both the product requirements (which are principally the responsibility of the business analyst) and the project requirements (which are principally the responsibility of the project manager). They might use the term "solution scope" to refer to "everything that has to be done to complete the project successfully." In this book, though, we are focusing on product requirements, whether your ultimate deliverable is a commercial software product, a hardware device with embedded software, a corporate information system, contracted government software, or anything else.

Requirements development and management

Confusion about requirements terminology extends even to what to call the whole discipline. Some authors call the entire domain *requirements engineering* (our preference). Others refer to it all as *requirements management*. Still others refer to these activities as a subset of the broad domain of business analysis.

We find it useful to split requirements engineering into *requirements development* (addressed in Part II of this book) and *requirements management* (addressed in Part IV), as shown in Figure 1-4. Regardless of what development life cycle your project is following—be it pure waterfall, phased, iterative, incremental, agile, or some hybrid—these are the things you need to do regarding requirements. Depending on the life cycle, you will perform these activities at different times in the project and to varying degrees of depth or detail.

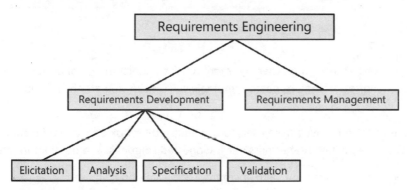

FIGURE 1-4 Subdisciplines of software requirements engineering.

Requirements development

As Figure 1-4 shows, we subdivide requirements development into *elicitation, analysis, specification,* and *validation* (Abran et al. 2004). These subdisciplines encompass all the activities involved with exploring, evaluating, documenting, and confirming the requirements for a product. Following are the essential actions in each subdiscipline.

Elicitation

Elicitation encompasses all of the activities involved with discovering requirements, such as interviews, workshops, document analysis, prototyping, and others. The key actions are:

- Identifying the product's expected user classes and other stakeholders.

- Understanding user tasks and goals and the business objectives with which those tasks align.

- Learning about the environment in which the new product will be used.

- Working with individuals who represent each user class to understand their functionality needs and their quality expectations.

Usage-centric or product-centric?

Requirements elicitation typically takes either a usage-centric or a product-centric approach, although other strategies also are possible. The usage-centric strategy emphasizes understanding and exploring user goals to derive the necessary system functionality. The product-centric approach focuses on defining features that you expect will lead to marketplace or business success. A risk with product-centric strategies is that you might implement features that don't get used much, even if they seemed like a good idea at the time. We recommend understanding business objectives and user goals first, then using that insight to determine the appropriate product features and characteristics.

Analysis

Analyzing requirements involves reaching a richer and more precise understanding of each requirement and representing sets of requirements in multiple ways. Following are the principal activities:

- Analyzing the information received from users to distinguish their task goals from functional requirements, quality expectations, business rules, suggested solutions, and other information

- Decomposing high-level requirements into an appropriate level of detail

- Deriving functional requirements from other requirements information

- Understanding the relative importance of quality attributes

- Allocating requirements to software components defined in the system architecture

- Negotiating implementation priorities

- Identifying gaps in requirements or unnecessary requirements as they relate to the defined scope

Specification

Requirements specification involves representing and storing the collected requirements knowledge in a persistent and well-organized fashion. The principal activity is:

- Translating the collected user needs into written requirements and diagrams suitable for comprehension, review, and use by their intended audiences.

Validation

Requirements validation confirms that you have the correct set of requirements information that will enable developers to build a solution that satisfies the business objectives. The central activities are:

- Reviewing the documented requirements to correct any problems before the development group accepts them.

- Developing acceptance tests and criteria to confirm that a product based on the requirements would meet customer needs and achieve the business objectives.

Iteration is a key to requirements development success. Plan for multiple cycles of exploring requirements, progressively refining high-level requirements into more precision and detail, and confirming correctness with users. This takes time and it can be frustrating. Nonetheless, it's an intrinsic aspect of dealing with the fuzzy uncertainty of defining a new software system.

> **Important** You're never going to get perfect requirements. From a practical point of view, the goal of requirements development is to accumulate a shared understanding of requirements that is *good enough* to allow construction of the next portion of the product—be that 1 percent or 100 percent of the entire product—to proceed at an acceptable level of risk. The major risk is that of having to do excessive unplanned rework because the team didn't sufficiently understand the requirements for the next chunk of work before starting design and construction.

Requirements management

Requirements management activities include the following:

- Defining the requirements baseline, a snapshot in time that represents an agreed-upon, reviewed, and approved set of functional and nonfunctional requirements, often for a specific product release or development iteration

- Evaluating the impact of proposed requirements changes and incorporating approved changes into the project in a controlled way

- Keeping project plans current with the requirements as they evolve

- Negotiating new commitments based on the estimated impact of requirements changes

- Defining the relationships and dependencies that exist between requirements

- Tracing individual requirements to their corresponding designs, source code, and tests

- Tracking requirements status and change activity throughout the project

The object of requirements management is not to stifle change or to make it difficult. It is to anticipate and accommodate the very real changes that you can always expect so as to minimize their disruptive impact on the project.

Figure 1-5 provides another view of the boundary between requirements development and requirements management. This book describes dozens of specific practices for performing requirements elicitation, analysis, specification, validation, and management.

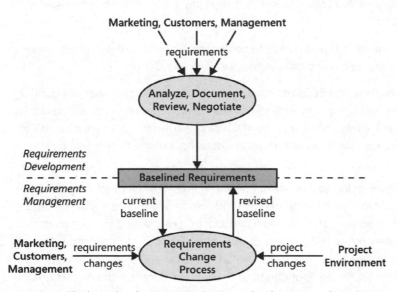

FIGURE 1-5 The boundary between requirements development and requirements management.

Every project has requirements

Frederick Brooks eloquently stated the critical role of requirements to a software project in his classic 1987 essay, "No Silver Bullet: Essence and Accidents of Software Engineering":

> *The hardest single part of building a software system is deciding precisely what to build. No other part of the conceptual work is as difficult as establishing the detailed technical requirements, including all the interfaces to people, to machines, and to other software systems. No other part of the work so cripples the resulting system if done wrong. No other part is more difficult to rectify later.*

Every software-containing system has stakeholders who rely on it. The time spent understanding their needs is a high-leverage investment in project success. If a project team does not have written representations of requirements that the stakeholders agree to, how can developers be sure to satisfy those stakeholders?

Often, it's impossible—or unnecessary—to fully specify the functional requirements before commencing design and implementation. In those cases, you can take an iterative or incremental approach, implementing one portion of the requirements at a time and obtaining customer feedback before moving on to the next cycle. This is the essence of agile development, learning just enough about requirements to do thoughtful prioritization and release planning so the team can begin delivering valuable software as quickly as possible. This isn't an excuse to write code before contemplating requirements for that next increment, though. Iterating on code is more expensive than iterating on concepts.

People sometimes balk at spending the time that it takes to write software requirements. But writing the requirements isn't the hard part. The hard part is *determining* the requirements. Writing requirements is a matter of clarifying, elaborating, and recording what you've learned. A solid understanding of a product's requirements ensures that your team works on the right problem and devises the best solution to that problem. Without knowing the requirements, you can't tell when the project is done, determine whether it has met its goals, or make trade-off decisions when scope adjustments are necessary. Instead of balking at spending time on requirements, people should instead balk at the money wasted when the project doesn't pay enough attention to requirements.

When bad requirements happen to good people

The major consequence of requirements problems is rework—doing again something that you thought was already done—late in development or after release. Rework often consumes 30 to 50 percent of your total development cost (Shull, et al. 2002; GAO 2004), and requirements errors can account for 70 to 85 percent of the rework cost (Leffingwell 1997). Some rework does add value and improves the product, but excessive rework is wasteful and frustrating. Imagine how different your life would be if you could cut the rework effort in half! Your team members could build better products faster and perhaps even go home on time. Creating better requirements is an investment, not just a cost.

It can cost far more to correct a defect that's found late in the project than to fix it shortly after its creation. Suppose it costs $1 (on a relative scale) to find and fix a requirement defect while you're still working on the requirements. If you discover that error during design instead, you have to pay the $1 to fix the requirement error, plus another $2 or $3 to redo the design that was based on the incorrect requirement. Suppose, though, that no one finds the error until a user calls with a problem. Depending on the type of system, the cost to correct a requirement defect found in operation can be $100 or more on this relative scale (Boehm 1981; Grady 1999; Haskins 2004). One of my consulting clients determined that they spent an average of $200 of labor effort to find and fix a defect in their information systems using the quality technique of software inspection, a type of peer review

(Wiegers 2002). In contrast, they spent an average of *$4,200* to fix a single defect reported by the user, an amplification factor of 21. Preventing requirements errors and catching them early clearly has a huge leveraging effect on reducing rework.

Shortcomings in requirements practices pose many risks to project success, where *success* means delivering a product that satisfies the user's functional and quality expectations at the agreed-upon cost and schedule. Chapter 32, "Software requirements and risk management," describes how to manage such risks to prevent them from derailing your project. Some of the most common requirements risks are described in the following sections.

Insufficient user involvement

Customers often don't understand why it is so essential to work hard on eliciting requirements and assuring their quality. Developers might not emphasize user involvement, perhaps because they think they already understand what the users need. In some cases it's difficult to gain access to people who will actually use the product, and user surrogates don't always understand what users really need. Insufficient user involvement leads to late-breaking requirements that generate rework and delay completion.

Another risk of insufficient user involvement, particularly when reviewing and validating the requirements, is that the business analyst might not understand and properly record the true business or customer needs. Sometimes a BA goes down the path of specifying what appears to be the "perfect" requirements, and developers implement them, but then no one uses the solution because the business problem was misunderstood. Ongoing conversations with users can help mitigate this risk, but if users don't review the requirements carefully enough, you can still have problems.

Inaccurate planning

"Here's my idea for a new product; when will you be done?" No one should answer this question until more is known about the problem being discussed. Vague, poorly understood requirements lead to overly optimistic estimates, which come back to haunt you when the inevitable overruns occur. An estimator's quick guess sounds a lot like a commitment to the listener. The top contributors to poor software cost estimation are frequent requirements changes, missing requirements, insufficient communication with users, poor specification of requirements, and insufficient requirements analysis (Davis 1995). Estimating project effort and duration based on requirements means that you need to know something about the size of your requirements and the development team's productivity. See Chapter 5 of *More about Software Requirements* (Wiegers 2006) for more about estimation based on requirements.

Creeping user requirements

As requirements evolve during development, projects often exceed their planned schedules and budgets (which are nearly always too optimistic anyway). To manage scope creep, begin with a clear statement of the project's business objectives, strategic vision, scope, limitations, and success criteria. Evaluate all proposed new features or requirements changes against this reference. Requirements *will* change and grow. The project manager should build contingency buffers into schedules so the first new requirement that comes along doesn't derail the schedule (Wiegers 2007). Agile projects take the approach of adjusting the scope for a certain iteration to fit into a defined budget and duration for the iteration. As new requirements come along, they are placed into the backlog of pending work and allocated to future iterations based on priority. Change might be critical to success, but change always has a price.

Ambiguous requirements

One symptom of ambiguity in requirements is that a reader can interpret a requirement statement in several ways (Lawrence 1996). Another sign is that multiple readers of a requirement arrive at different understandings of what it means. Chapter 11, "Writing excellent requirements," lists many words and phrases that contribute to ambiguity by placing the burden of interpretation on the reader.

Ambiguity leads to different expectations on the part of various stakeholders. Some of them are then surprised at whatever is delivered. Ambiguous requirements cause wasted time when developers implement a solution for the wrong problem. Testers who expect the product to behave differently from what the developers built waste time resolving the differences.

One way to ferret out ambiguity is to have people who represent different perspectives inspect the requirements (Wiegers 2002). As described in Chapter 17, "Validating the requirements," informal peer reviews in which reviewers simply read the requirements on their own often don't reveal ambiguities. If different reviewers interpret a requirement in different ways but it makes sense to each of them, they won't find the ambiguity. Collaborative elicitation and validation encourages stakeholders to discuss and clarify requirements as a group in a workshop setting. Writing tests against the requirements and building prototypes are other ways to discover ambiguities.

Gold plating

Gold plating takes place when a developer adds functionality that wasn't in the requirements specification (or was deemed out of scope) but which the developer believes "the users are just going to love." If users don't care about this functionality, the time spent implementing it is wasted. Rather than simply inserting new features, developers and BAs should present stakeholders with creative ideas for their consideration. Developers should strive for leanness and simplicity, not going beyond what stakeholders request without their approval.

Customers sometimes request certain features or elaborate user interfaces that look attractive but add little value to the product. Everything you build costs time and money, so you need to maximize the delivered value. To reduce the threat of gold plating, trace each bit of functionality back to its origin and its business justification so everyone knows why it's included. Make sure that what you are specifying and developing lies within the project's scope.

Overlooked stakeholders

Most products have several groups of users who might use different subsets of features, have different frequencies of use, or have varying levels of experience. If you don't identify the important user classes for your product early on, some user needs won't be met. After identifying all user classes, make sure that each has a voice, as discussed in Chapter 6, "Finding the voice of the user." Besides obvious users, think about maintenance and field support staff who have their own requirements, both functional and nonfunctional. People who have to convert data from a legacy system will have transition requirements that don't affect the ultimate product software but that certainly influence solution success. You might have stakeholders who don't even know the project exists, such as government agencies that mandate standards that affect your system, yet you need to know about them and their influence on the project.

Benefits from a high-quality requirements process

Some people mistakenly believe that time spent discussing requirements simply delays delivery by the same duration. This assumes that there's no return on investment from requirements activities. In actuality, investing in good requirements will virtually always return more than it costs.

Sound requirements processes emphasize a collaborative approach to product development that involves stakeholders in a partnership throughout the project. Eliciting requirements lets the development team better understand its user community or market, a critical success factor. Emphasizing user tasks instead of superficially attractive features helps the team avoid writing code that no one will ever execute. Customer involvement reduces the expectation gap between what the customer really needs and what the developer delivers. You're going to get the customer input eventually; it's far cheaper to reach this understanding before you build the product than after delivery. Chapter 2 addresses the nature of the customer-development partnership.

Explicitly allocating system requirements to various software, hardware, and human subsystems emphasizes a systems approach to product engineering. An effective change control process will minimize the adverse impact of requirements changes. Documented and clear requirements greatly facilitate system testing. All of these increase your chances of delivering high-quality products that satisfy all stakeholders.

No one can promise a specific return on investment from using sound requirements practices. You can go through an analytical thought process to imagine how better requirements could help your teams, though (Wiegers 2006). The cost of better requirements includes developing new procedures and document templates, training the team, and buying tools. Your greatest investment is the time your project teams actually spend on requirements engineering tasks. The potential payoff includes:

- Fewer defects in requirements and in the delivered product.

- Reduced development rework.

- Faster development and delivery.

- Fewer unnecessary and unused features.

- Lower enhancement costs.

- Fewer miscommunications.

- Reduced scope creep.

- Reduced project chaos.

- Higher customer and team member satisfaction.

- Products that do what they're supposed to do.

Even if you can't quantify all of these benefits, they are real.

Next steps

- Write down requirements-related problems that you have encountered on your current or previous project. Identify each as a requirements development or requirements management problem. Describe the root cause of each problem and its impact on the project.

- Facilitate a discussion with your team members and other stakeholders regarding requirements-related problems from your current or previous projects, their impacts, and their root causes. Pool your ideas about changes in your current requirements practices that could address these problems. The troubleshooting guide in Appendix B might be helpful.

- Map the requirements terminology and deliverables used in your organization to that shown in this chapter to see if you're covering all the categories recommended here.

- Perform a simple assessment on just a few pages of one of your requirements documents to see where your team might have some clear improvement areas. It might be most useful to have an objective outsider perform this assessment.

- Arrange a training class on software requirements for your entire project team. Invite key customers, marketing staff, managers, developers, testers, and other stakeholders to participate. Training gives project participants a common vocabulary. It provides a shared appreciation of effective techniques and behaviors so that all team members can collaborate more effectively on their mutual challenges.

CHAPTER 2

Requirements from the customer's perspective

Gerhard, a senior manager at Contoso Pharmaceuticals, was meeting with Cynthia, the manager of Contoso's IT department. "We need to build a chemical tracking information system," Gerhard began. "The system should keep track of all the chemical containers we already have in the stockroom and in laboratories. That way, the chemists can get some chemicals from someone down the hall instead of always buying a new container. This should save us a lot of money. Also, the Health and Safety Department needs to generate government reports on chemical usage and disposal with a lot less work than it takes them today. Can you build this system in time for the compliance audit in five months?"

"I see why this project is important, Gerhard," said Cynthia. "But before I can commit to a schedule, we'll need to understand the requirements for the chemical tracking system."

Gerhard was confused. "What do you mean? I just told you my requirements."

"Actually, you described some general business objectives for the project," Cynthia explained. "That doesn't give me enough information to know what software to build or how long it might take. I'd like to have one of our business analysts work with some users to understand their needs for the system."

"The chemists are busy people," Gerhard protested. "They don't have time to nail down every detail before you can start programming. Can't your people figure out what to build?"

Cynthia replied, "If we just make our best guess at what the users need to do with the system, we can't do a good job. We're software developers, not chemists. I've learned that if we don't take the time to understand the problem, nobody is happy with the results."

"We don't have time for all that," Gerhard insisted. "I gave you my requirements. Now just build the system, please. Keep me posted on your progress."

Conversations like this take place regularly in the software world. Customers who request a new system often don't understand the importance of obtaining input from actual users of the proposed system as well as other stakeholders. Marketers with a great product concept believe that they can adequately represent the interests of prospective buyers. However, there's no substitute for eliciting requirements directly from people who will actually use the product. Some agile development methods recommend that an on-site customer representative, sometimes called a product owner, work closely with the development team. As one book about agile development said, "The project is *steered* to success by the customer and programmers working in concert" (Jeffries, Anderson, and Hendrickson 2001).

Part of the requirements problem results from confusion over the different levels of requirements described in Chapter 1, "The essential software requirement": business, user, and functional. Gerhard stated some business objectives, benefits that he expects Contoso to enjoy with the help of the new chemical tracking system. Business objectives are a core element of the business requirements. However, Gerhard can't entirely describe the user requirements because he's not an intended user of the system. Users, in turn, can describe tasks they must be able to perform with the system, but they can't state all the functional requirements that developers must implement to let them accomplish those tasks. Business analysts need to collaborate with users to reach that deeper understanding.

This chapter addresses the customer-development relationship that is so critical to software project success. We propose a Requirements Bill of Rights for Software Customers and a corresponding Requirements Bill of Responsibilities for Software Customers. These lists underscore the importance of customer—and specifically end user—involvement in requirements development. This chapter also discusses the critical issue of reaching agreement on a set of requirements planned for a specific release or development iteration. Chapter 6, "Finding the voice of the user," describes various types of customers and users and ways to engage appropriate user representatives in requirements elicitation.

> ### Deliverable: Rejected
>
> I heard a sad story when I visited a corporate IT department once. The developers had recently built a new information system for use within the company. They had obtained negligible user input from the beginning. The day the developers proudly unveiled their new system, the users rejected it as completely unacceptable. This came as a shock because the developers had worked hard to satisfy what they perceived to be the users' needs. So what did they do then? They fixed it. Companies always fix the system when they get the requirements wrong, yet it always costs much more than if they had engaged user representatives from the outset.
>
> The developers hadn't planned to spend time fixing the flawed information system, of course, so the next project in the team's queue had to wait. This is a lose-lose-lose situation. The developers were chagrined, the users were unhappy because their new system wasn't available when they expected it, and the executives were upset over a lot of wasted money and the opportunity costs of delaying other projects. Extensive and ongoing customer engagement from the start could have prevented this unfortunate—but not uncommon—project outcome.

The expectation gap

Without adequate customer involvement, the inescapable outcome at the end of the project is an expectation gap, a gulf between what customers really need and what developers deliver based on what they heard at the beginning of the project (Wiegers 1996). This is shown as the dashed lines in Figure 2-1. As with the previous story, the expectation gap comes as a rude surprise to all stakeholders. In our experience, software surprises are never good news. Requirements also get out of date because of changes that occur in the business, so ongoing interactions with customers are vital.

The best way to minimize the expectation gap is to arrange frequent contact points with suitable customer representatives. These contact points can take the form of interviews, conversations, requirements reviews, user interface design walkthroughs, prototype evaluations, and—with agile development—user feedback on small increments of executable software. Each contact point affords an opportunity to close the expectation gap: what the developer builds is more closely aligned with what the customer needs.

Of course, the gap will begin to grow again immediately as development proceeds after each contact. The more frequent the contact points are, the easier it is to stay on track. As the progressively shrinking small gray triangles in Figure 2-1 illustrate, a series of such contact points will lead to a far smaller expectation gap at the end of the project and a solution that is much closer to the actual customer needs. This is why one of the guiding principles of agile development is to have ongoing conversations between developers and customers. That's an excellent principle for any project.

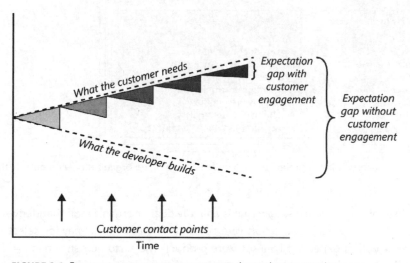

FIGURE 2-1 Frequent customer engagement reduces the expectation gap.

Who is the customer?

Before we can talk about customers, we need to discuss stakeholders. A *stakeholder* is a person, group, or organization that is actively involved in a project, is affected by its process or outcome, or can influence its process or outcome. Stakeholders can be internal or external to the project team and to the developing organization. Figure 2-2 identifies many of the potential stakeholders in these categories. Not all of these will apply to every project or situation, of course.

Stakeholder analysis is an important part of requirements development (Smith 2000; Wiegers 2007; IIBA 2009). When searching for potential stakeholders for a particular project, cast a wide net to avoid overlooking some important community. Then you can focus this candidate stakeholder list down to the core set whose input you really need, to make sure you understand all of the project's requirements and constraints so your team can deliver the right solution.

Outside the Developing Organization

Direct user	Business management	Consultant
Indirect user	Contracting officer	Compliance auditor
Acquirer	Government agency	Certifier
Procurement staff	Subject matter expert	Regulatory body
Legal staff	Program manager	Software supplier
Contractor	Beta tester	Materials supplier
Subcontractor	General public	Venture capitalist

Developing Organization

Development manager	Sales staff	Executive sponsor
Marketing	Installer	Project management office
Operational support staff	Maintainer	Manufacturing
Legal staff	Program manager	Training staff
Information architect	Usability expert	Portfolio architect
Company owner	Subject matter expert	Infrastructure support staff

Project Team

Project manager	Tester
Business analyst	Product manager
Application architect	Quality assurance staff
Designer	Documentation writer
Developer	Database administrator
Product owner	Hardware engineer
Data modeler	Infrastructure analyst
Process analyst	Business solutions architect

FIGURE 2-2 Potential stakeholders within the project team, within the developing organization, and outside the organization.

Customers are a subset of stakeholders. A *customer* is an individual or organization that derives either direct or indirect benefit from a product. Software customers could request, pay for, select, specify, use, or receive the output generated by a software product. The customers shown in Figure 2-2 include the direct user, indirect user, executive sponsor, procurement staff, and acquirer. Some stakeholders are not customers, such as legal staff, compliance auditors, suppliers, contractors, and venture capitalists. Gerhard, the manager we met earlier, represents an executive sponsor who is paying for the project. Customers like Gerhard provide the business requirements, which establish the guiding framework for the project and the business rationale for launching it. As discussed in Chapter 5, "Establishing the business requirements," business requirements describe the business objectives that the customer, company, or other stakeholders want to achieve. All other product requirements need to align with achieving those desired business outcomes.

User requirements should come from people who will actually use the product, either directly or indirectly. These users (often called *end users*) are a subset of customers. Direct users will operate the product hands-on. Indirect users might receive outputs from the system without touching it themselves, such as a warehouse manager who receives an automatic report of daily warehouse activities by email. Users can describe the tasks they need to perform with the product, the outputs they need, and the quality characteristics they expect the product to exhibit.

The case of the missing stakeholder

I know of a project that was almost finished with requirements elicitation when, while reviewing a process flow, the business analyst (BA) asked the stakeholder, "Are you sure we have the tax calculation steps correct in this flow?" The stakeholder replied, "Oh, I don't know. I don't own tax. That's the tax department." The team hadn't talked to anyone in the tax department over the course of working on the project for months. They had no idea that there even *was* a tax department. As soon as the BAs did meet with the tax department, they found a long list of missed requirements around the legal implications of how tax-related functions were implemented. The project was delayed several months as a result. Using an organization chart to search for all stakeholders who will be affected by a new system can avoid such unpleasantness.

Customers who provide the business requirements sometimes purport to speak for the actual users. They are often too far removed from the work to provide accurate user requirements, though. For corporate information systems, contract development, or custom application development, business requirements should come from the person who is ultimately accountable for the business value expected from the product. User requirements should come from people who will press the keys, touch the screen, or receive the outputs. If there is a serious disconnect between the acquiring customers who are paying for the project and the end users, major problems are guaranteed.

The situation is different for commercial software development, where the customer and the user often are the same person. Customer surrogates, such as marketing personnel or a product manager, typically attempt to determine what customers would find appealing. Even for commercial software, though, you should strive to engage end users in the process of developing user requirements, as Chapter 7, "Requirements elicitation," describes. If you don't, be prepared to read reviews pointing out product shortcomings that adequate user input could have avoided.

Conflicts can arise among project stakeholders. Business requirements sometimes reflect organizational strategies or budgetary constraints that aren't apparent to users. Users who are upset about having a new information system forced on them by management might not want to work with the software developers, viewing them as the harbingers of an undesired future. Such folks are sometimes called "loser groups" (Gause and Weinberg 1989). To manage such potential conflicts, try communication strategies about project objectives and constraints that can build buy-in and avoid debates and hard feelings.

The customer-development partnership

An excellent software product results from a well-executed design based on excellent requirements. Excellent requirements result from effective collaboration between developers and customers (in particular, actual users)—a partnership. A collaborative effort can work only when all parties involved know what they need to be successful and when they understand and respect what their collaborators need to be successful. As project pressures rise, it's easy to forget that all stakeholders share a common objective: to build a product that provides adequate business value and rewards to all stakeholders. The business analyst typically is the point person who has to forge this collaborative partnership.

The Requirements Bill of Rights for Software Customers in Table 2-1 lists 10 expectations that customers can legitimately hold regarding their interactions with BAs and developers during the project's requirements engineering activities. Each of these rights implies a corresponding responsibility on the part of the BAs or software developers. The word "you" in the rights and responsibilities refers to a customer for a software development project.

Because the flip side of a right is a responsibility, Table 2-2 lists 10 responsibilities that the customer has to BAs and developers during the requirements process. You might prefer to view these as a developer's bill of rights. If these lists aren't exactly right for your organization, modify them to suit the local culture.

TABLE 2-1 Requirements Bill of Rights for Software Customers

You have the right to
1. Expect BAs to speak your language.
2. Expect BAs to learn about your business and your objectives.
3. Expect BAs to record requirements in an appropriate form.
4. Receive explanations of requirements practices and deliverables.
5. Change your requirements.
6. Expect an environment of mutual respect.
7. Hear ideas and alternatives for your requirements and for their solution.
8. Describe characteristics that will make the product easy to use.
9. Hear about ways to adjust requirements to accelerate development through reuse.
10. Receive a system that meets your functional needs and quality expectations.

TABLE 2-2 Requirements Bill of Responsibilities for Software Customers

You have the responsibility to
1. Educate BAs and developers about your business.
2. Dedicate the time that it takes to provide and clarify requirements.
3. Be specific and precise when providing input about requirements.
4. Make timely decisions about requirements when asked.
5. Respect a developer's assessment of the cost and feasibility of requirements.
6. Set realistic requirement priorities in collaboration with developers.
7. Review requirements and evaluate prototypes.
8. Establish acceptance criteria.
9. Promptly communicate changes to the requirements.
10. Respect the requirements development process.

These rights and responsibilities apply to actual customers when the software is being developed for internal corporate use, under contract, or for a known set of major customers. For mass-market product development, the rights and responsibilities are more applicable to customer surrogates such as the product manager.

As part of project planning, the key customer and development stakeholders should review these two lists and negotiate to reach a meeting of the minds. Make sure the participants in requirements development understand and accept their responsibilities. This understanding can reduce friction later, when one party expects something that the other is not willing or able to provide.

> **Trap** Don't assume that the project participants instinctively know how to collaborate on requirements development. Take the time to discuss how those involved can work together most effectively. It's a good idea to write down how you decide to approach and manage requirements issues on the project. This will serve as a valuable communication tool throughout the project.

Requirements Bill of Rights for Software Customers

Following are 10 rights that customers can expect when it comes to requirements issues.

Right #1: To expect BAs to speak your language

Requirements discussions should center on your business needs and tasks, using business vocabulary. Consider conveying business terminology to the BAs with a glossary of terms. You shouldn't have to wade through technical jargon when talking with BAs.

Right #2: To expect BAs to learn about your business and your objectives

By interacting with you to elicit requirements, the BAs can better understand your business tasks and how the system fits into your world. This will help developers create a solution that meets your needs. Invite BAs and developers to observe what you and your colleagues do on the job. If the new system is replacing an existing one, the BAs should use the current system as you use it. This will show them how it fits into your workflow and where it can be improved. Don't just assume that the BA will already know all about your business operations and terminology (see Responsibility #1).

Right #3: To expect BAs to record requirements in an appropriate form

The BA will sort through all the information that stakeholders provide and ask follow-up questions to distinguish user requirements from business rules, functional requirements, quality goals, and other items. The ultimate deliverable from this analysis is a refined set of requirements stored in some appropriate form, such as a software requirements specification document or a requirements management tool. This set of requirements constitutes the agreement among the stakeholders about the functions, qualities, and constraints of the product to be built. Requirements should be written and organized in a way that you find easy to understand. Your review of these specifications and other requirements representations, such as visual analysis models, helps to ensure that they accurately represent your needs.

Right #4: To receive explanations of requirements practices and deliverables

Various practices can make requirements development and management both effective and efficient, and requirements knowledge can be represented in a variety of forms. The BA should explain the practices he's recommending and explain what information goes into each deliverable. For instance, the BA might create some diagrams to complement textual requirements. These diagrams might be unfamiliar to you, and they can be complex, but the notations shouldn't be difficult to understand. The BA should explain the purpose of each diagram, what the symbols mean, and how to examine the diagram for errors. If the BA doesn't offer such explanations, feel free to ask for them.

Right #5: To change your requirements

It's not realistic for BAs or developers to expect you to think of all your requirements up front or to expect those requirements to remain static throughout the development cycle. You have the right to make changes in the requirements as the business evolves, as the team gathers more input from stakeholders, or as you think more carefully about what you need. However, change always has a price. Sometimes adding a new function demands trade-offs with other functions or with the project's schedule or budget. An important part of the BA's responsibility is to assess, manage, and communicate change impacts. Work with the BA on your project to agree on a simple but effective process for handling changes.

Right #6: To expect an environment of mutual respect

The relationship between customers and developers sometimes becomes adversarial. Requirements discussions can be frustrating if the participants don't understand each other. Working together can open the eyes of the participants to the problems each group faces. Customers who participate in requirements development have the right to expect BAs and developers to treat them with respect and to appreciate the time they are investing in the project's success. Similarly, customers should demonstrate respect for the development team members as everyone collaborates toward their mutual objective of a successful project. Everyone's on the same side here.

Right #7: To hear ideas and alternatives for your requirements and for their solution

Let the BA know about ways that your existing systems don't fit well with your business processes to make sure that a new system doesn't automate ineffective or obsolete processes. That is, you want to avoid "paving the cow paths." A BA can often suggest improvements in your business processes. A creative BA also adds value by proposing new capabilities that customers haven't even envisioned.

Right #8: To describe characteristics that will make the product easy to use

You can expect BAs to ask you about characteristics of the software that go beyond your functional needs. These characteristics, or quality attributes, make the software easier or more pleasant to use, which lets users accomplish their tasks more efficiently. Users sometimes request that the product be *user-friendly* or *robust*, but such terms are too subjective to help the developers. Instead, the analyst should inquire about the specific characteristics that mean "user-friendly" or "robust" to you. Tell the BA about which aspects of your current applications seem "user-friendly" to you and which do not. If you don't discuss these characteristics with the BA, you'll be lucky if the product comes out as you hope.

Right #9: To hear about ways to adjust requirements to accelerate development through reuse

Requirements are often somewhat flexible. The BA might know of existing software components or requirements that come close to addressing some need you described. In such a case, the BA should suggest ways of modifying your requirements or avoiding unnecessary customizations so developers can reuse those components. Adjusting your requirements when sensible reuse opportunities are available saves time and money. Some requirements flexibility is essential if you want to incorporate commercial off-the-shelf (COTS) packages into the product, because they will rarely have precisely the characteristics you want.

Right #10: To receive a system that meets your functional needs and quality expectations

This is the ultimate customer right, *but* it can happen only if you clearly communicate all the information that will let developers build the right product, if developers communicate options and constraints to you, and if the parties reach agreement. Be sure to state all your assumptions and expectations; otherwise, the developers likely can't address them properly. Customers sometimes don't articulate points that they believe are common knowledge. However, validating a shared understanding across the project team is just as important as expressing something new.

Requirements Bill of Responsibilities for Software Customers

Because the counterpart to a right is a responsibility, following are 10 responsibilities that customer representatives have when it comes to defining and managing the requirements for their projects.

Responsibility #1: To educate BAs and developers about your business

The development team depends on you to educate them about your business concepts and to define business jargon. The intent is not to transform BAs into business experts but to help them understand your problems and objectives. BAs aren't likely to be aware of knowledge that you and your peers take for granted.

Responsibility #2: To dedicate the time that it takes to provide and clarify requirements

Customers are busy people; those who are involved in requirements work are often among the busiest. Nonetheless, you have a responsibility to dedicate time to workshops, interviews, and other requirements elicitation and validation activities. Sometimes the BA might think she understands a point you made, only to realize later that she needs further clarification. Please be patient with this iterative approach to developing and refining the requirements; it's the nature of complex human communication and a key to software success. The total time required is less when there is focused effort for several hours than when the time is spent in bits and pieces strung out over weeks.

Responsibility #3: To be specific and precise when providing input about requirements

It's tempting to leave the requirements vague and fuzzy because pinning down details is tedious and time consuming (or because someone wants to evade being held accountable for his decisions). At some point, though, someone must resolve the ambiguities and imprecisions. You're the best person to make those decisions. Otherwise, you're relying on the BA or developers to guess correctly. It's fine to temporarily include *to be determined* (TBD) markers in the requirements to indicate that additional exploration or information is needed. Sometimes, though, TBD is used because a specific requirement is difficult to resolve and no one wants to tackle it. Try to clarify the intent of each requirement so that the BA can express it accurately. This is the best way to ensure that the product will meet your needs.

Responsibility #4: To make timely decisions about requirements when asked

Just as a contractor does while building your fabulous dream home, the BA will ask you to make many decisions. These include resolving conflicting requests received from multiple customers, choosing between incompatible quality attributes, and evaluating the accuracy of information. Customers who are authorized to make such decisions must do so promptly when asked. Developers often can't proceed with confidence until you render your decision, so time spent waiting for an answer can delay progress. When the demands for your time start to feel onerous, remember that the system is being built for you. Business analysts are often skilled at helping people think through making decisions, so ask for their help if you get stuck.

Responsibility #5: To respect a developer's assessment of the cost and feasibility of requirements

All software functions have a cost. Developers are in the best position to estimate those costs. Some features might not be technically feasible or might be surprisingly expensive to implement. Certain requirements might demand unattainable performance in the operating environment or require access to data that isn't available to the system. The developer can be the bearer of bad news about feasibility or cost. You should respect that judgment, even if it means you might not get something you asked for in exactly the form you envisioned. Sometimes, you can rewrite requirements in a way that makes them attainable or cheaper. For example, asking for an action to take place "instantaneously" isn't feasible, but a more precise timing requirement ("within 50 milliseconds") might be achievable.

Responsibility #6: To set realistic requirement priorities in collaboration with developers

Few projects have the time and resources to implement every bit of functionality all customers want. Determining which capabilities are essential, which are useful, and which the customers can live without is an important part of requirements analysis. You have a lead role in setting requirement priorities. Developers can provide information about the cost and risk of each requirement or user story to help determine final priorities. When you establish realistic priorities, you help the developers deliver the maximum value at the lowest cost and at the right time. Collaborative prioritization is key for agile projects, so the developers can begin delivering useful software as quickly as possible.

Respect the development team's judgment as to how much of the requested functionality they can complete within the available time and resource constraints. If everything you want doesn't fit in the project box, the decision makers will have to reduce project scope based on priorities, extend the schedule, or provide additional funds or people. Simply declaring every requirement as high priority is neither realistic nor collaborative.

Responsibility #7: To review requirements and evaluate prototypes

As you'll see in Chapter 17, "Validating the requirements," peer reviews of requirements are among the most powerful software quality activities available. Having customers participate in reviews is a key way to evaluate whether the requirements demonstrate the desired characteristics of being complete, correct, and necessary. A review is also an opportunity for customer representatives to assess how well the BA's work is meeting the project's needs. Busy customers often are reluctant to devote time to a requirements review, but it's well worth their time. The BA should make requirements available to you for review in manageable chunks throughout the requirements elicitation process, not in a massive tome dumped on your desk when the requirements are "done."

It's hard to develop a good mental picture of how software will work from written requirements alone. To better understand your needs and explore the best ways to satisfy them, BAs or developers sometimes build prototypes of the intended product. Your feedback on these preliminary, partial, or exploratory implementations provides valuable information to the developers.

Responsibility #8: To establish acceptance criteria

How do developers know when they're done? How can they tell if the software they built will meet the expectations of the various customer communities? As a customer, one of your responsibilities is to establish acceptance criteria, predefined conditions that the product must satisfy to be judged acceptable. Such criteria include acceptance tests, which assess whether the product lets users perform certain of their important business operations correctly. Other acceptance criteria might address the estimated remaining defect levels, the performance of certain actions in the operating environment, or the ability to satisfy external certification requirements. Agile projects rely heavily on acceptance tests, instead of written requirements, to flesh out the details of user stories. Testers can judge whether a specified requirement was implemented correctly, but they don't always know exactly what *you* will consider an acceptable outcome.

Responsibility #9: To promptly communicate changes to the requirements

Continually changing requirements pose a serious risk to the development team's ability to deliver a high-quality product on schedule. Change is inevitable and often valuable, but the later in development a change is introduced, the greater its impact. Notify the BA as soon as you learn that you need to change a requirement. To minimize the negative impact of changes, follow the project's defined change control process. This ensures that requested changes are not lost, the impact of each change is analyzed, and all proposed changes are considered in a consistent way. As a result, the business stakeholders can make sound business decisions to incorporate appropriate changes at the right stage of the project.

Responsibility #10: To respect the requirements development process

Eliciting and specifying requirements are among the greatest challenges in software development. There's a rationale behind the BA's approach to requirements development. Although you might become frustrated, the time spent understanding requirements is an excellent investment. The process will be less painful if you respect the techniques the BAs use. Feel free to ask BAs to explain why they're requesting certain information or asking you to participate in some requirements-related activity. A mutual understanding of, and respect for, each other's approaches and needs goes a long way toward establishing an effective—perhaps even enjoyable—collaboration.

Creating a culture that respects requirements

The leader of a corporate requirements organization once posed a problem: "I'm experiencing issues in gaining agreement from some of our developers to participate in requirements development," she said. "How can I help them understand the value of their participation?" In another organization, a BA experienced a clash between developers seeking detailed input for an accounting system and an IT manager who simply wanted to brainstorm requirements without using any specific elicitation techniques. "Do readers of your book risk cultural conflict?" this BA asked me.

These questions exemplify the challenges that can arise when trying to engage BAs, developers, and customers in a collaborative requirements partnership. You'd think it would be obvious to a user that providing requirements input makes it more likely that he'll get what he needs. Developers ought to recognize that participating in the process will make their lives easier than being hit on the head by whatever requirements document flies over the proverbial wall. Obviously, not everyone is as excited about requirements as you are; if they were, they'd probably all become business analysts!

Culture clashes frequently arise when teams are working on requirements. There are those who recognize the many risks associated with trying to develop software based on minimal or telepathically communicated requirements. Then there are those who think requirements are unnecessary. It can be tough to gain business-side cooperation on projects like legacy-system replacement if users see this as unrelated to their own business problems and not worth their time. Understanding why people resist participating in requirements development is the first step to being able to address it.

It's possible that the resisters haven't been exposed to solid requirements practices. Or they might have suffered from poor implementation of requirements processes, perhaps working on a project that produced a large, incomplete, and ignored requirements specification. That would leave a bad taste in anyone's mouth. Perhaps the resisters don't understand and appreciate the value of those practices when performed effectively. They might not realize the price they have paid for having worked in a casual and unstructured environment in the past. That price mostly shows up as unexpected rework that leads to late deliveries and poor software. Such rework is buried in the daily activities of the project participants, so they don't recognize it as a serious inefficiency.

If you're trying to get developers, managers, and customers on board, make sure everyone understands the past pain the organization and its customers have experienced because of requirements problems. Find specific examples to demonstrate the impact in case individuals haven't felt the pain themselves. Express the cost in units that are meaningful to the organization, be it dollars, time, customer dissatisfaction, or lost business opportunities. Development managers aren't always aware of how badly requirements shortcomings hurt their teams' productivity. So show them how poor requirements slow down design and lead to excessive—and expensive—course corrections.

Developers are stakeholders in the project, but sometimes their input isn't solicited and they become the "victims" of the requirements that are thrust upon them. Therefore, they benefit from providing input that will make the requirements documentation as useful and meaningful as possible. I like to have developers review requirements as they are evolving. That way they know what's coming and can spot areas that need more clarity. You also need developer input when specifying internal quality attributes that aren't visible to users. Developers can offer suggestions no one else might have thought about: easier ways to do certain things; functionality that would be very time-consuming to implement; unnecessary imposed design constraints; missing requirements, such as how exceptions should be handled; and creative opportunities to take advantage of technologies.

Quality assurance staff and testers are also valuable contributors to excellent requirements. Instead of waiting until later in the project, engage these sharp-eyed people in the iterative review of requirements early on. They're likely to find many ambiguities, conflicts, and concerns with the requirements as they are developing their test cases and scenarios from the requirements. Testers can also provide input on specifying verifiable quality attribute requirements.

Resistance to process or culture change can indicate fear, uncertainty, or lack of knowledge. If you can discern the source of the resistance, you can confront it with reassurance, clarification, and education. Show people how their participation not only is in their personal best interest but also will lead to collectively better results.

The organization's leadership must understand the need for the organization to have effective business analysis and requirements engineering capabilities as strategic core competencies. Though project-specific and localized grassroots efforts are important, without management commitment, the improvements and benefits likely won't be sustained after the project ends or following a reorganization.

Identifying decision makers

There can be hundreds of decisions to make on software projects; often, they are on the critical path to being able to move ahead. You might need to resolve some conflict, accept (or reject) a proposed change, or approve a set of requirements for a specific release. Early in your project, determine who the requirements decision makers will be and how they will make decisions. My friend Chris, a seasoned project manager, pointed out, "I have found that there is usually one primary decision maker on a project, oftentimes the key sponsor within the organization. I don't rest until I have identified that person, and then I make sure he is always aware of the project's progress." There's no single correct answer as to who should make key decisions. A small group representing key areas—such as management, customers, business analysis, development, and marketing—generally works best. Chapter 28, "Change happens," describes the change control board, which serves as the decision makers for proposed requirement changes.

The decision-making group needs to identify its *decision leader* and to select a *decision rule*, which describes how they will arrive at their decisions. There are numerous decision rules to choose from, including the following (Gottesdiener 2001):

- The decision leader makes the choice, either with or without discussion with others.

- The group votes and the majority rules.

- The group votes, but the result must be unanimous to approve the decision.

- The group discusses and negotiates to reach a consensus. Everyone can live with the decision and commits to supporting it.

- The decision leader delegates authority for making the decision to one individual.

- The group reaches a decision, but some individual has veto authority over that decision.

There is no globally correct or appropriate decision rule. A single decision rule won't work in every situation, so the group must establish guidelines so they know when to vote, when to reach consensus, when to delegate, and so on. The people who will be making requirements-related decisions on each of your projects should choose a decision rule before they confront their first significant decision.

Reaching agreement on requirements

Reaching agreement on the requirements for the product to be built, or for a specific portion of it, is at the core of the customer-developer partnership. Multiple parties are involved in this agreement:

- Customers agree that the requirements address their needs.

- Developers agree that they understand the requirements and that they are feasible.

- Testers agree that the requirements are verifiable.

- Management agrees that the requirements will achieve their business objectives.

Many organizations use the act of "signing off" (why not "signing on"?) on the requirements as the mark of stakeholder approval. All participants in the requirements approval process should know exactly what sign-off means or problems could ensue. One such problem is the customer representative or manager who regards signing off on the requirements as a meaningless ritual: "I was handed a piece of paper with my name on it, so I signed on the line above my name because otherwise the developers wouldn't start coding." This can lead to future problems when that individual wants to change the requirements or when he's surprised by what is delivered: "Sure, I signed off on the requirements, but I didn't have time to read them all. I trusted you guys—you let me down!"

Equally problematic is the development manager who views sign-off as a way to freeze the requirements. Whenever a change request comes along he can protest, "But you signed off on these requirements, so that's what we're building. If you wanted something else, you should have said so."

Both of these attitudes ignore the reality that it's impossible to know all the requirements early in the project and that requirements will undoubtedly change over time. Approving a set of requirements is an appropriate action that brings closure to some stage of requirements development. However, the participants have to agree on precisely what they're saying with their signatures.

> **Important** Don't use sign-off as a weapon. Treat it as a milestone, with a clear, shared understanding of the activities that lead to sign-off and its implications for future changes. If the decision makers don't need to read every word of the requirements, select a communication technique—such as a slide presentation—that summarizes the essential elements and facilitates reaching agreement quickly.

The requirements baseline

More important than the sign-off ritual is the concept of establishing a *baseline* of the requirements agreement, a snapshot of it at a point in time (Wiegers 2006). A requirements baseline is a set of requirements that has been reviewed and agreed upon and serves as the basis for further development. Whether your team uses a formal sign-off process or some other means of reaching agreement on requirements, the subtext of that agreement should read something like this:

> *"I agree that this set of requirements represents our best understanding of the requirements for the next portion of this project and that the solution described will meet our needs as we understand them today. I agree to make future changes in this baseline through the project's defined change process. I realize that changes might require us to renegotiate cost, resource, and schedule commitments."*

Some organizations put text like this right on the signature page, so the requirement approvers know exactly what sign-off means in their world.

A shared understanding along these lines helps reduce the friction that can arise as requirements oversights are revealed or marketplace and business demands evolve over the course of the project. A meaningful baselining process gives all the major stakeholders confidence in the following ways:

- Customer management or marketing is confident that the project scope won't explode out of control, because customers manage the scope change decisions.

- User representatives have confidence that the development team will work with them to deliver the right solution, even if they didn't think of every requirement before construction began.

- Development management has confidence because the development team has a business partner who will keep the project focused on achieving its objectives and will work with development to balance schedule, cost, functionality, and quality.

- Business analysts and project managers are confident that they can manage changes to the project in a way that will keep chaos to a minimum.

- Quality assurance and test teams can confidently develop their test scripts and be fully prepared for their project activities.

After the decision makers define a baseline, the BA should place the requirements under change control. This allows the team to modify scope when necessary in a controlled way that includes analyzing the impact of each proposed change on the schedule and other success factors. Sealing the initial requirements development activities with an explicit agreement helps forge a collaborative customer-development partnership on the way to project success.

What if you don't reach agreement?

It can be hard to achieve sign-off from all the relevant stakeholders. Barriers include logistics, busy schedules, and people who are reluctant to commit and be held accountable later. If stakeholders are afraid they won't be able to make changes after they approve the requirements, they might drag their feet on the approval. This contributes to the dreaded trap of analysis paralysis. Many teams have tried sending out an email message that says, "If you don't reply by next Friday with your changes and/or sign-off, I'm going to assume you are agreeing to these requirements." That's one option, but really it equates to *not* reaching agreement. It also risks straining the relationship with those stakeholders for whom you've just assumed a tacit approval. Try to understand why they didn't feel comfortable with a sign-off and address that directly.

In such a situation, you're better off moving forward—cautiously—with the assumption that you don't have approval from the recalcitrant stakeholders. Document the fact that certain stakeholders didn't sign off on the requirements in your risk list, along with the likely impact of some of the requirements being missing or wrong. Follow up with these people as part of risk management. In a positive manner, mention that you recognize that they have not yet approved the requirements but that the project is still moving forward with those requirements as a baseline so as to not impede progress. Let them know that, if they want to change things, there's a process in place to do that. Basically, you're acting as though the stakeholder did indeed agree to the requirements, but you're managing the communications closely.

Agreeing on requirements on agile projects

Agile projects do not include a formal sign-off action. Agile projects generally maintain requirements in the form of user stories in a product backlog. The product owner and the team reach agreement on what stories will be developed in the next iteration in a planning session. The set of stories is chosen based on their priority and the team's velocity (productivity). After that set has been established and agreed to, the stories contained in the iteration are frozen. Requested changes that come in are considered for future iterations. There's no attempt on an agile project to achieve stakeholder approval on the full scope of requirements for the project up front, however. In agile projects the full set of functionality is identified over time, although the vision and other business requirements do need to be established at the outset. Chapter 20, "Agile projects," discusses how requirements are handled on agile projects.

 I once worked with a client who requested sign-off on requirements even though they were following an agile development life cycle. The team had to be creative with how to do this in a context that doesn't traditionally involve sign-offs. The BA team had worked closely with the users to elicit and review requirements in the form of user stories and other models such as process flows and state tables. We asked the users to "sign off" that, at that moment in time, there were no major requirements missing *that they knew about*, and there were no major issues with what we'd written down *that they knew about*. Because users did participate in the requirements activities, development would not be working on a solution that would be far off base. But this notion of "sign-off" also keeps open the right of the users to realize later on that they need something new or got something wrong.

In contrast to the historical notion of sign-off as meaning "approve and freeze all the requirements up front," this approach doesn't force anyone into a corner where he feels like he's signing away his life over a massive requirements document that he barely understands. Nor are customers forced to agree that the requirements are close to perfect and that everything was addressed the first time around. This version of sign-off allows the spirit of agile methods to prevail. As with the sign-off process described earlier, the essence is to reach agreement on a specific body of requirements—a baseline—to be implemented in the next construction cycle, with a clear, shared understanding of what that agreement really means.

Commonly on agile projects, the product owner publicly accepts or rejects the requirements for an iteration, which consist of a set of stories and their accompanying acceptance criteria and acceptance tests. The ultimate "sign-off" is acceptance of the working, tested software delivered from the iteration.

As consultant Nanette Brown put it, "Even in an agile environment the concept of sign-off can fill a valid function. Agile tells us to 'embrace change,' but the concept of change only exists with respect to a reference point. Even within a team where there is close communication, people can have different interpretations of current plans and status. One person's 'change' can be what another person thought was already agreed to. However, if you position a sign-off as a lightweight ceremony acknowledging that 'We are Here' I think it's fine. Just because 'We are Here' today doesn't mean we can't be somewhere else tomorrow, but at least it ensures a common understanding and point of reference."

Next steps

- Identify the customers, including end users, who are responsible for providing business and user requirements on your project. Which items from the Bill of Rights and the Bill of Responsibilities do these customers currently accept and practice? Which do they not?

- Discuss the Bill of Rights with your key customers to learn whether they feel they aren't receiving any of their rights. Discuss the Bill of Responsibilities to reach agreement as to which responsibilities they accept. Modify the Bill of Rights and the Bill of Responsibilities as appropriate so that all parties agree on how they will work together. Monitor whether the stakeholders are maintaining a balance between rights and responsibilities.

- If you're a customer participating in a software project and you don't feel that your requirements rights are being adequately respected, discuss the Bill of Rights with the project manager or the BA. Offer to do your part to satisfy the Bill of Responsibilities as you strive to build a more collaborative working relationship.

- If your organization uses a formal sign-off process, think about what it really means today. Work with development and customer (or marketing) management to reach agreement on what sign-off really ought to mean for your requirements approval process.

- Identify one example from a current or past project of not having the necessary level of customer participation. Consider what the impact of that was. See if you can quantify the risk in terms of number of late requirements changes, time spent fixing the product after delivery, or business opportunities missed. Use that experience in the future as a story to learn from and to convince others of why customer engagement is so vital.

CHAPTER 3

Good practices for requirements engineering

"Welcome to the group, Sarah," said the project manager, Kristin. "We're looking forward to having you help us with the requirements for this project. I understand that you were a business analyst in your previous job. Do you have some idea of how we should get started here?"

"Well," Sarah replied, "I was thinking I should just interview some users and see what they want. Then I'll write up what they tell me. That should give the developers a good place to start. That's mostly what we did before. Do you know some users I could talk to?"

"Hmmm. Do you think that will be good enough for this type of project?" Kristin asked. "We tried that approach before, but it didn't work out very well. I was hoping you might have some ideas about best practices from your past BA experiences that might be better than just interviewing a couple of users. Are there any particular techniques that you've found to be especially helpful?"

Sarah was rather at a loss. "I don't really know about any specific ways to approach requirements other than talking to users and trying to write clear specifications from what they say. At my last job I just did the best I could based on my business experience. Let me see what I can find out."

Every software professional needs to acquire a tool kit of techniques she can use to approach each project challenge. A practitioner who lacks such a tool kit is forced to invent an approach based on whatever seems reasonable at the moment. Such ad hoc methods rarely yield great results. Some people advocate for specific software development methodologies, packaged sets of techniques that purport to provide holistic solutions to your project challenges. However, simply following a script—a standard process that's supposed to work in every situation—doesn't work very well, either. We find it more effective to identify and apply industry best practices. The best-practice approach stocks your software tool kit with a variety of techniques you can apply to diverse problems.

The notion of best practices is debatable: who decides what is "best" and on what basis? One approach is to convene a body of industry experts to analyze projects from many organizations. These experts seek out practices whose effective performance is associated with successful projects and which are performed poorly or not at all on failed projects. Through these means, the experts reach consensus on the activities that consistently yield superior results and label them *best practices*.

Table 3-1 lists more than 50 practices, grouped into 7 categories, that can help all development teams do a better job on their requirements activities. Several of the practices contribute to more than one category, but each practice appears only once in the table. Most of these practices contribute to more effective communication among project stakeholders. Note that this chapter is titled "Good practices for requirements engineering," not "Best practices." It's doubtful whether all of these practices will ever be systematically evaluated for this purpose. Nonetheless, many other practitioners have found these techniques to be effective (Sommerville and Sawyer 1997; Hofmann and Lehner 2001; Gottesdiener 2005; IIBA 2009).

TABLE 3-1 Requirements engineering good practices

Elicitation	Analysis	Specification	Validation
■ Define vision and scope ■ Identify user classes ■ Select product champions ■ Conduct focus groups ■ Identify user requirements ■ Identify system events and responses ■ Hold elicitation interviews ■ Hold facilitated elicitation workshops ■ Observe users performing their jobs ■ Distribute questionnaires ■ Perform document analysis ■ Examine problem reports ■ Reuse existing requirements	■ Model the application environment ■ Create prototypes ■ Analyze feasibility ■ Prioritize requirements ■ Create a data dictionary ■ Model the requirements ■ Analyze interfaces ■ Allocate requirements to subsystems	■ Adopt requirement document templates ■ Identify requirement origins ■ Uniquely label each requirement ■ Record business rules ■ Specify nonfunctional requirements	■ Review the requirements ■ Test the requirements ■ Define acceptance criteria ■ Simulate the requirements

Requirements management	Knowledge	Project management
■ Establish a change control process ■ Perform change impact analysis ■ Establish baselines and control versions of requirements sets ■ Maintain change history ■ Track requirements status ■ Track requirements issues ■ Maintain a requirements traceability matrix ■ Use a requirements management tool	■ Train business analysts ■ Educate stakeholders about requirements ■ Educate developers about application domain ■ Define a requirements engineering process ■ Create a glossary	■ Select an appropriate life cycle ■ Plan requirements approach ■ Estimate requirements effort ■ Base plans on requirements ■ Identify requirements decision makers ■ Renegotiate commitments ■ Manage requirements risks ■ Track requirements effort ■ Review past lessons learned

This chapter describes each good practice briefly and provides references to other chapters in this book or to other sources where you can learn more about the technique. These practices aren't suitable for every situation, so use good judgment, common sense, and experience. Even the best practices need to be selected, applied, and adapted thoughtfully to appropriate situations by skilled business analysts. Different practices might be most appropriate for understanding the requirements for different portions of a given project. Use cases and user interface prototypes might help for the client side, whereas interface analysis is more valuable on the server side, for example.

The people who perform or take a lead role in these practices will vary from practice to practice and from project to project. The business analyst (BA) will play a major role with many of them, but not every project has a BA. The product owner could perform some of the practices on an agile project. Still other practices are the purview of the project manager. Think about who the right people in your team are to lead or participate in the practices you select for your next project.

Important None of these techniques will work if you're dealing with unreasonable people. Customers, managers, and IT people sometimes appear to be unreasonable, but perhaps they are just uninformed. They might not know why you want to use certain practices and could be uncomfortable with unfamiliar terms and activities. Try educating your collaborators about the practices, why you want to use them, and why it is important to their own goals to cooperate.

A requirements development process framework

As you saw in Chapter 1, "The essential software requirement," requirements development involves elicitation, analysis, specification, and validation. Don't expect to perform these activities in a simple linear, one-pass sequence, though. In practice, these activities are interwoven, incremental, and iterative, as shown in Figure 3-1. "Progressive refinement of detail" is a key operating phrase for requirements development, moving from initial concepts of what is needed toward further precision of understanding and expression.

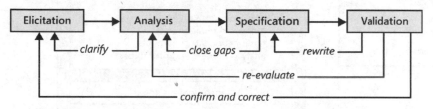

FIGURE 3-1 Requirements development is an iterative process.

If you're the BA, you'll be asking customers questions, listening to what they say, and watching what they do (elicitation). You'll process this information to understand it, classify it in various categories, and relate the customer needs to possible software requirements (analysis). Your analysis might lead you to realize that you need to clarify some requirements, so you go back and do more elicitation. You'll then structure the customer input and derived requirements as written requirement statements and diagrams (specification). While writing requirements, you might need to go back and do some additional analysis to close gaps in your knowledge. Next, you'll ask some stakeholders to confirm that what you've captured is accurate and complete and to correct any errors (validation). You'll do all this for the set of requirements that are most important and most timely for beginning software development. Validation could lead you to rewrite some unclear requirements, revisit some of your analysis activities, or even have to go back and perform additional elicitation. Then you'll move on to the next portion of the project and do it all again. This iterative process continues throughout requirements development and possibly—as with agile projects—throughout the full project duration.

Because of the diversity of software development projects and organizational cultures, there is no single, formulaic approach to requirements development. Figure 3-2 suggests a process framework for requirements development that will work, with sensible adjustments, for many projects. The business need or market opportunity is the predecessor for the process shown in Figure 3-2. These steps are generally performed approximately in numerical sequence, but the process is not strictly sequential. The first seven steps are typically performed once early in the project (although the team will need to revisit all of these activities periodically). The remaining steps are performed for each release or development iteration. Many of these activities can be performed iteratively, and they can be interwoven. For instance, you can perform steps 8, 9, and 10 in small chunks, performing a review (step 12) after each iteration.

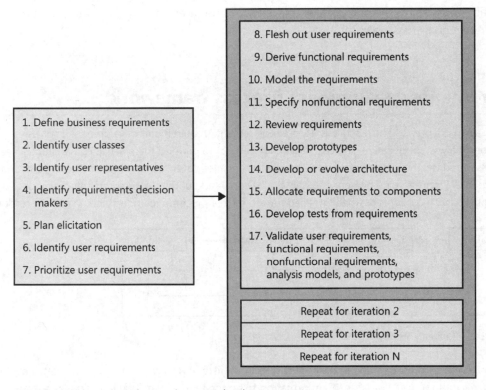

FIGURE 3-2 A representative requirements development process.

The fifth subdiscipline of requirements engineering is requirements management. Requirements management encompasses practices that help you deal with requirements after you have them in hand. These practices include version control and baselining, change control, tracking requirements status, and tracing requirements to other system elements. Requirements management will take place throughout the project's duration at a low level of intensity.

Figure 3-3 illustrates how some common software development life cycles allocate requirements effort across the product development period. The total requirements effort might not be much different for projects of comparable size that follow different life cycles, but the timing distribution of requirements work is very different. In the pure waterfall life cycle, you plan to do only one major release, so most of the requirements development effort is allocated for the beginning of the project (the solid line in Figure 3-3). This approach is still used on quite a few projects, and it is appropriate for some. But even if you plan a traditional "requirements phase" at the beginning of the project that then leads into design, you can count on having to do some additional requirements work throughout the project.

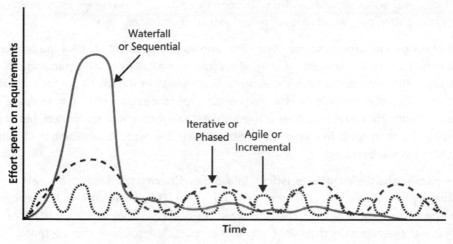

FIGURE 3-3 The distribution of requirements development effort over time varies for projects that follow different development life cycles.

Projects that follow an iterative development process, such as the Rational Unified Process (Jacobson, Booch, and Rumbaugh 1999), will work on requirements on every iteration through the development process, with a heavier emphasis in the first iteration (the dashed line in Figure 3-3). This is also the case if you are planning a series of phased releases, each of which delivers a significant fraction of the product's ultimate functionality.

Agile and other incremental development projects aim to release functionality every few weeks (Larman 2004). They will have frequent but small requirements development efforts, as shown with the dotted line in Figure 3-3. Such projects begin by doing a first cut at collecting user requirements in the form of simple user stories that describe major objectives the user wants to accomplish with the help of the system. In this approach, you need to learn enough about the stories so that you can estimate their development effort and prioritize them. Prioritizing these user requirements lets you determine which ones to allocate to specific development increments, called iterations or sprints. Those allocated requirements can be explored in further detail in a just-in-time fashion for each development cycle.

Regardless of the life cycle your project follows, you should ask yourself for each release or iteration which of the activities shown in Figure 3-2 will add value and reduce risk. After you have completed step 17 for any portion of the requirements, you're ready to commence construction of that part of the system. Repeat steps 8 through 17 with the next set of user requirements, which will lay the foundation for the subsequent release or increment.

Good practices: Requirements elicitation

Chapter 1 discussed the three levels of requirements: business, user, and functional. These come from different sources at different times during the project, have different audiences and purposes, and need to be documented in different ways. You also need to elicit nonfunctional requirements, such as quality expectations in various dimensions, from appropriate sources. Following are some practices that can help with eliciting the myriad types of requirements information.

Define product vision and project scope   The vision and scope document contains the product's business requirements. The vision statement gives all stakeholders a common understanding of the product's outcome. The scope defines the boundary between what's in and what's out for a specific release or iteration. Together, the vision and scope provide a reference against which to evaluate proposed requirements. The vision should remain relatively stable throughout the project, but each planned release or iteration needs its own scope statement. See Chapter 5, "Establishing the business requirements," for more information.

Identify user classes and their characteristics   To avoid overlooking the needs of any user community, identify the various groups of users for your product. They might differ in frequency of use, features used, privilege levels, or experience. Describe aspects of their job tasks, attitudes, location, or personal characteristics that might influence product design. Create user personas, descriptions of imaginary people who will represent particular user classes. See Chapter 6, "Finding the voice of the user," for more information.

Select a product champion for each user class   Identify an individual who can accurately serve as the literal voice of the customer for each user class. The product champion presents the needs of the user class and makes decisions on its behalf. This is easiest for internal information systems development, where your users are fellow employees. For commercial product development, build on your current relationships with major customers or beta test sites to locate appropriate product champions. See Chapter 6 for more information.

Conduct focus groups with typical users   Convene groups of representative users of your previous products or of similar products. Collect their input on both functionality and quality characteristics for the product under development. Focus groups are particularly valuable for commercial product development, for which you might have a large and diverse customer base. Unlike product champions, focus groups generally do not have decision-making authority. See Chapter 7, "Requirements elicitation," for more information.

Work with user representatives to identify user requirements   Explore with your user representatives the tasks they need to accomplish with the software and the value they're trying to achieve. User requirements can be expressed in the form of use cases, user stories, or scenarios. Discuss the interactions between the users and the system that will allow them to complete each task. See Chapter 8, "Understanding user requirements," for more information.

Identify system events and responses   List the external events that the system can experience and its expected response to each event. There are three classes of external events. Signal events are control signals or data received from external hardware devices. Temporal, or time-based, events trigger a response, such as an external data feed that your system generates at the same time every night. Business events trigger use cases in business applications. See Chapter 12, "A picture is worth 1024 words," for more information.

Hold elicitation interviews Interviews can be performed one-on-one or with a small group of stakeholders. They are an effective way to elicit requirements without taking too much stakeholder time because you meet with people to discuss only the specific requirements that are important to them. Interviews are helpful to separately elicit requirements from people in preparation for workshops where those people come together to resolve any conflicts. See Chapter 7 for more information.

Hold facilitated elicitation workshops Facilitated requirements-elicitation workshops that permit collaboration between analysts and customers are a powerful way to explore user needs and to draft requirements documents (Gottesdiener 2002). Such workshops are sometimes called Joint Application Design, or JAD, sessions (Wood and Silver 1995). See Chapter 7 for more information.

Observe users performing their jobs Watching users perform their business tasks establishes a context for their potential use of a new application. Simple process flow diagrams can depict the steps and decisions involved and show how different user groups interact. Documenting the business process flow will help you identify requirements for a solution that's intended to support that process. See Chapter 7 for more information.

Distribute questionnaires Questionnaires are a way to survey large groups of users to determine what they need. Questionnaires are useful with any large user population but are particularly helpful with distributed groups. If questions are well written, questionnaires can help you quickly determine analytical information about needs. Additional elicitation efforts can then be focused according to the questionnaire results. See Chapter 7 for more information.

Perform document analysis Existing documentation can help reveal how systems currently work or what they are supposed to do. Documentation includes any written information about current systems, business processes, requirements specifications, competitor research, and COTS (commercial off-the-shelf) package user manuals. Reviewing and analyzing the documents can help identify functionality that needs to remain, functionality that isn't used, how people do their jobs currently, what competitors offer, and what vendors say their software should do. See Chapter 7 for more information.

Examine problem reports of current systems for requirement ideas Problem reports and enhancement requests from users provide a rich source of ideas for capabilities to include in a later release or in a new product. Help desk and support staff can provide valuable input into the requirements for future development work.

Reuse existing requirements If customers request functionality similar to that already present in an existing product, see whether the requirements (and the customers!) are flexible enough to permit reusing or adapting the existing software components. Projects often can reuse those requirements that comply with an organization's business rules, such as security requirements, and requirements that conform to government regulations, such as accessibility requirements. Other good candidates for reuse include glossaries, data models and definitions, stakeholder profiles, user class descriptions, and personas. See Chapter 18, "Requirements reuse," for more information.

Good practices: Requirements analysis

Requirements analysis involves refining the requirements to ensure that all stakeholders understand them and scrutinizing them for errors, omissions, and other deficiencies. Analysis includes decomposing high-level requirements into appropriate levels of detail, building prototypes, evaluating feasibility, and negotiating priorities. The goal is to develop requirements of sufficient quality and precision that managers can construct realistic project estimates and technical staff can proceed with design, construction, and testing.

It is very valuable to represent some of the requirements in multiple ways—for example, in both textual and visual forms, or in the forms of both requirements and tests (Wiegers 2006). These different views will reveal insights and problems that no single view can provide. Multiple views also help all stakeholders arrive at a common understanding—a shared vision—of what they will have when the product is delivered.

Model the application environment   The context diagram is a simple analysis model that shows how the new system fits into its environment. It defines the boundaries and interfaces between the system being developed and external entities, such as users, hardware devices, and other systems. An ecosystem map shows the various systems in the solution space that interact with each other and the nature of their interconnections (Beatty and Chen 2012). See Chapter 5 for more information.

Create user interface and technical prototypes   When developers or users aren't certain about the requirements, construct a prototype—a partial, possible, or preliminary implementation—to make the concepts and possibilities more tangible. Prototypes allow developers and users to achieve a mutual understanding of the problem being solved, as well as helping to validate requirements. See Chapter 15, "Risk reduction through prototyping," for more information.

Analyze requirement feasibility   The BA should work with developers to evaluate the feasibility of implementing each requirement at acceptable cost and performance in the intended operating environment. This allows stakeholders to understand the risks associated with implementing each requirement, including conflicts and dependencies with other requirements, dependencies on external factors, and technical obstacles. Requirements that are technically infeasible or overly expensive to implement can perhaps be simplified and still contribute to achieving the project's business objectives.

Prioritize the requirements   It's important to prioritize requirements to ensure that the team implements the highest value or most timely functionality first. Apply an analytical approach to determine the relative implementation priority of product features, use cases, user stories, or functional requirements. Based on priority, determine which release or increment will contain each feature or set of requirements. Adjust priorities throughout the project as new requirements are proposed and as customer needs, market conditions, and business goals evolve. See Chapter 16, "First things first: Setting requirements priorities," for more information.

Create a data dictionary   Definitions of the data items and structures associated with the system reside in the data dictionary. This enables everyone working on the project to use consistent data definitions. As requirements are developed, the data dictionary should define data items from the problem domain to facilitate communication between the customers and the development team. See Chapter 13, "Specifying data requirements," for more information.

Model the requirements   An analysis model is a diagram that depicts requirements visually, in contrast to the textual representation of a list of functional requirements. Models can reveal incorrect, inconsistent, missing, and superfluous requirements. Such models include data flow diagrams, entity-relationship diagrams, state-transition diagrams, state tables, dialog maps, decision trees, and others (Beatty and Chen 2012). See Chapters 5, 12, and 13 for more information about modeling.

Analyze interfaces between your system and the outside world   All software systems have connections to other parts of the world through external interfaces. Information systems have user interfaces and often exchange data with other software systems. Embedded systems involve interconnections between software and hardware components. Network-connected applications have communication interfaces. Analyzing these helps make sure that your application will fit smoothly into its environment. See Chapter 10, "Documenting the requirements," for more information.

Allocate requirements to subsystems   The requirements for a complex product that contains multiple subsystems must be apportioned among the various software, hardware, and human subsystems and components. An example of such a product is an access system to a secure building that includes magnetic or optical badges, scanners, video cameras and recorders, door locks, and human guards. See Chapter 26, "Embedded and other real-time systems projects," for more information.

Good practices: Requirements specification

The essence of requirements specification is to document requirements of different types in a consistent, accessible, and reviewable way that is readily understandable by the intended audiences. You can record the business requirements in a vision and scope document. User requirements typically are represented in the form of use cases or user stories. Detailed software functional and nonfunctional requirements are recorded in a software requirements specification (SRS) or an alternative repository, such as a requirements management tool.

Adopt requirement document templates   Adopt standard templates for documenting requirements in your organization, such as the vision and scope document template in Chapter 5, the use case template in Chapter 8, and the SRS template in Chapter 10. The templates provide a consistent structure for recording various groups of requirements-related information. Even if you don't store the requirements in traditional document form, the template will remind you of the various kinds of requirements information to explore and record.

Identify requirement origins   To ensure that all stakeholders know why every requirement is needed, trace each one back to its origin. This might be a use case or some other customer input, a high-level system requirement, or a business rule. Recording the stakeholders who are affected by each requirement tells you whom to contact when a change is requested. Requirement origins can be identified through traceability links or by defining a requirement attribute for this purpose. See Chapter 27, "Requirements management practices," for more information on requirement attributes.

Uniquely label each requirement Define a convention for giving each requirement a unique identifying label. The convention must be robust enough to withstand additions, deletions, and changes made in the requirements over time. Labeling the requirements permits requirements traceability and the recording of changes made. See Chapter 10 for more information.

Record business rules Business rules include corporate policies, government regulations, standards, and computational algorithms. Document your business rules separately from a project's requirements because they typically have an existence beyond the scope of a specific project. That is, treat business rules as an enterprise-level asset, not a project-level asset. Some rules will lead to functional requirements that enforce them, so define traceability links between those requirements and the corresponding rules. See Chapter 9, "Playing by the rules," for more information.

Specify nonfunctional requirements It's possible to implement a solution that does exactly what it's supposed to do but does not satisfy the users' quality expectations. To avoid that problem, you need to go beyond the functionality discussion to understand the quality characteristics that are important to success. These characteristics include performance, reliability, usability, modifiability, and many others. Customer input on the relative importance of these quality attributes lets the developer make appropriate design decisions. Also, specify external interface requirements, design and implementation constraints, internationalization issues, and other nonfunctional requirements. See Chapter 14, "Beyond functionality," for more information.

Good practices: Requirements validation

Validation ensures that the requirements are correct, demonstrate the desired quality characteristics, and will satisfy customer needs. Requirements that seem fine when you read them might turn out to have ambiguities and gaps when developers try to work with them. You must correct these problems if the requirements are to serve as a reliable foundation for design and for final system testing and user acceptance testing. Chapter 17, "Validating the requirements," discusses this topic further.

Review the requirements Peer review of requirements, particularly the type of rigorous review called inspection, is one of the highest-value software quality practices available (Wiegers 2002). Assemble a small team of reviewers who represent different perspectives (such as analyst, customer, developer, and tester), and carefully examine the written requirements, analysis models, and related information for defects. Informal preliminary reviews during requirements development are also valuable. It's important to train the team members in how to perform effective requirements reviews and to adopt a review process for your organization. See Chapter 17 for more information.

Test the requirements Tests constitute an alternative view of the requirements. Writing tests requires you to think about how to tell if the expected functionality was correctly implemented. Derive tests from the user requirements to document the expected behavior of the product under specified conditions. Walk through the tests with customers to ensure that they reflect user expectations. Map the tests to the functional requirements to make sure that no requirements have been overlooked and that all have corresponding tests. Use the tests to verify the correctness of analysis models and prototypes. Agile projects often create acceptance tests in lieu of detailed functional requirements. See Chapter 17 for more information.

Define acceptance criteria   Ask users to describe how they will determine whether the solution meets their needs and is fit for use. Acceptance criteria include a combination of the software passing a defined set of acceptance tests based on user requirements, demonstrating satisfaction of specific nonfunctional requirements, tracking open defects and issues, having infrastructure and training in place for a successful rollout, and more. See Chapter 17 for more information.

Simulate the requirements   Commercial tools are available that allow a project team to simulate a proposed system either in place of or to augment written requirements specifications. Simulation takes prototyping to the next level, by letting BAs work with users to rapidly build executable mock-ups of a system. Users can interact with the simulated system to validate requirements and make design choices, making the requirements come to life before they are cast into the concrete of code. Simulation is not a substitute for thoughtful requirements elicitation and analysis, but it does provide a powerful supplement.

Good practices: Requirements management

After you have the initial requirements for a body of work in hand, you must cope with the inevitable changes that customers, managers, marketing, the development team, and others request during development. Effective change management demands a process for proposing changes, evaluating their potential cost and impact on the project, and making sure that appropriate stakeholders make sensible business decisions about which proposed changes to incorporate.

Well-established configuration management practices are a prerequisite for effective requirements management. The same version control tools that you use to control your code base can manage your requirements documents. Even better, store requirements in a requirements management tool, which provides many capabilities to perform these practices.

Establish a requirements change control process   Rather than stifling change or hoping changes don't happen, accept the fact that they will and establish a mechanism to prevent rampant changes from causing chaos. Your change process should define how requirements changes are proposed, analyzed, and resolved. Manage all proposed changes through this process. Defect-tracking tools can support the change control process. Charter a small group of project stakeholders as a change control board (CCB) to evaluate proposed requirements changes, decide which ones to accept, and set implementation priorities or target releases. See Chapter 28, "Change happens," for more information.

Perform impact analysis on requirements changes   Impact analysis is an important element of the change process that helps the CCB make informed business decisions. Evaluate each proposed requirement change to assess the effect it will have on the project. Use the requirements traceability matrix to identify the other requirements, design elements, source code, and tests that you might need to modify. Identify the tasks required to implement the change and estimate the effort needed to perform those tasks. See Chapter 28 for more information.

Establish baselines and control versions of requirements sets   A baseline defines a set of agreed-upon requirements, typically for a specific release or iteration. After the requirements have been baselined, changes should be made only through the project's change control process. Give every version of the requirements specification a unique identifier to avoid confusion between drafts and baselines and between previous and current versions. See Chapter 2, "Requirements from the customer's perspective," and Chapter 27 for more information.

Maintain a history of requirements changes   Retain a history of the changes made to individual requirements. Sometimes you need to revert to an earlier version of a requirement or want to know how a requirement came to be in its current form. Record the dates that requirements were changed, the changes that were made, who made each change, and why. A version control tool or requirements management tool can help with these tasks.

Track the status of each requirement   Establish a repository with one record for each discrete requirement of any type that affects implementation. Store key attributes about each requirement, including its status (such as proposed, approved, implemented, or verified), so you can monitor the number of requirements in each status category at any time. Tracking the status of each requirement as it moves through development and system testing provides insight into overall project status. See Chapter 27 for more information.

Track requirements issues   When busy people are working on a complex project, it's easy to lose sight of the many issues that arise, including questions about requirements that need resolution, gaps to eradicate, and issues arising from requirements reviews. Issue-tracking tools can keep these items from falling through the cracks. Assign a single owner to each issue. Monitor the status of requirement issues to determine the overall state of the requirements. See Chapter 27 for more information.

Maintain a requirements traceability matrix   It's often valuable—and sometimes required—to assemble a set of links that connect each functional requirement to the design and code elements that implement it and the tests that verify it. Such a *requirements traceability matrix* is helpful for confirming that all requirements are implemented and verified. It's also useful during maintenance when a requirement has to be modified. The requirements traceability matrix can also connect functional requirements to the higher-level requirements from which they were derived and to other related requirements. Populate this matrix during development, not at the end. Tool support is essential on all but the smallest projects. See Chapter 29, "Links in the requirements chain," for more information.

Use a requirements management tool   Commercial requirements management tools let you store various types of requirements in a database. Such tools help you implement and automate many of the other requirements management practices described in this section. See Chapter 30, "Tools for requirements engineering," for more information.

Good practices: Knowledge

Various team members might perform the role of business analyst on a given project, but few software practitioners receive formal training in requirements engineering. Business analysis is a specialized and challenging role, with its own body of knowledge (IIBA 2009). As with all technical disciplines, there is no substitute for experience. It isn't reasonable to expect all people to be instinctively competent at the communication-intensive tasks of requirements engineering. Training can increase the proficiency and comfort level of those who serve as analysts, but it can't compensate for absent interpersonal skills or a lack of interest in the role.

Train business analysts   All team members who will perform BA tasks, whether they have the job title "business analyst" or not, should receive training in requirements engineering. Business analyst specialists need several days of training in the diverse activities that BAs typically perform. This will give them a solid foundation on which to build through their own experiences and advanced training. In addition to having an extensive tool kit of techniques, the skilled analyst is patient and well organized, has effective interpersonal and communication skills, and understands the application domain. See Chapter 4, "The business analyst," for more information about this important role.

Educate stakeholders about requirements   The most effective requirements training classes have an audience that spans multiple project functional areas, not just BAs. Users who will participate in software development should receive one or two days of education about requirements so they understand terminology, key concepts and practices, and why this is such an important contributor to project success. Development managers and customer managers will also find this information useful. Bringing together the various stakeholders for a class on software requirements can be an effective team-building activity. All parties will better appreciate the challenges their counterparts face and what the participants require from each other for the whole team to succeed. Some users who have attended our requirements classes have said that they came away with more sympathy for the software developers.

Educate developers about the application domain   To help give developers a basic understanding of the application domain, arrange a seminar on the customer's business activities, terminology, and objectives for the product being created. This can reduce confusion, miscommunication, and rework down the road. "Day-in-the-life" experiences in which developers accompany users to see how they perform their jobs are sound investments. You might also match each developer with a "user buddy" for the life of the project to translate jargon and explain business concepts. The product champion could play this role, as described in Chapter 6.

Define a requirements engineering process   Document the steps your organization follows to elicit, analyze, specify, validate, and manage requirements. Providing guidance on how to perform the key steps will help analysts do a consistently good job. It will also make it easier to plan each project's requirements development and management tasks, schedule, and required resources. The project manager should incorporate requirements activities as discrete tasks in the project plan. See Chapter 31, "Improving your requirements processes," for more information.

Create a glossary   A glossary that defines specialized terms from the application domain will minimize misunderstandings. Include synonyms, acronyms or abbreviations, terms that can have multiple meanings, and terms that have both domain-specific and everyday meanings. A glossary could be a reusable enterprise-level asset. Developing a glossary could be an activity for new team members, because they will be the ones most confused by the unfamiliar terminology. See Chapter 10 for more information on the glossary.

Good practices: Project management

Software project management approaches are tightly coupled to a project's requirements processes. The project manager should base project schedules, resources, and commitments on the requirements that are to be implemented. An alternative strategy is to timebox development cycles, such that the team estimates the scope of the work they can fit into an iteration of fixed duration. This is the approach taken by agile development projects. Scope is regarded as negotiable within the schedule. This transforms scope creep into "scope choice"—the product owner can ask for anything and as much as he wants, but he must prioritize it, and the team quits developing when they run out of time. Then the team plans a subsequent release for the remaining requirements.

Select an appropriate software development life cycle   Your organization should define several development life cycles that are appropriate for various types of projects and different degrees of requirements uncertainty (Boehm and Turner 2004). Each project manager should select and adapt the life cycle that best suits her project. Include requirements activities in your life cycle definitions. When possible, specify and implement sets of functionality incrementally so that you can deliver useful software to the customer as early as possible (Larman 2004; Schwaber 2004; Leffingwell 2011).

Plan requirements approach   Each project team should plan how it will handle its requirements development and management activities. An elicitation plan helps ensure that you identify and obtain input from appropriate stakeholders at the right stages of the project using the most appropriate techniques. The BA and project manager should work together to ensure that tasks and deliverables related to requirements engineering appear in the project management plan. See Chapter 7 for more information.

Estimate requirements effort   Stakeholders often want to know how long it's going to take to develop the requirements for a project and what percentage of their total effort should be devoted to requirements development and management. Naturally, this depends on many factors. Consider the factors that would indicate that you should spend either more or less time than average to ensure the requirements lay a solid foundation for development (Wiegers 2006). See Chapter 19, "Beyond requirements development," for more information.

Base project plans on requirements   Develop plans and schedules for your project iteratively as the scope and detailed requirements become clear. Begin by estimating the effort needed to develop the user requirements from the initial product vision and project scope. Early cost and schedule estimates based on fuzzy requirements will be highly uncertain, but you can improve the estimates as your understanding of the requirements improves. On agile projects, the timeboxed nature of iterations means that planning involves adjusting the scope to fit within the fixed schedule and resource constraints. See Chapter 19, "Beyond requirements development," and Chapter 20, "Agile projects," for more information.

Identify requirements decision makers   Software development involves making many decisions. Conflicting user inputs must be resolved, commercial package components must be selected, change requests must be evaluated, and on and on. Because so many decisions involve requirements issues, it's essential for the project team to identify and empower its requirements decision makers, preferably before they confront their first significant decision. See Chapter 2 for more information.

Renegotiate project commitments when requirements change   A project team makes commitments to deliver specific sets of requirements within a particular schedule and budget. As you incorporate new requirements into the project, evaluate whether you can still achieve the current commitments with the available resources. If not, communicate the project realities to management and negotiate new, realistically achievable commitments (Wiegers 2007; Fisher, Ury, and Patton 2011). You might also need to renegotiate commitments as requirements evolve from their fuzzy beginnings with initial implementation estimates to clear, validated requirements.

Analyze, document, and manage requirements-related risks   Unanticipated events and conditions can wreak havoc on an unprepared project. Identify and document risks related to requirements as part of the project's risk-management activities. Brainstorm approaches to mitigate or prevent these risks, implement the mitigation actions, and track their progress and effectiveness. See Chapter 32, "Software requirements and risk management," for more information.

Track the effort spent on requirements   To improve your ability to estimate the resources needed for requirements work on future projects, record the effort your team expends on requirements development and management activities (Wiegers 2006). Monitor the effect that your requirements activities have on the project to help judge the return on your investment in requirements engineering. See Chapter 27 for more information.

Review lessons learned regarding requirements on other projects   A learning organization conducts periodic retrospectives to collect lessons learned from completed projects or from earlier iterations of the current project (Kerth 2001; Derby and Larsen 2006; Wiegers 2007). Studying the lessons learned from previous requirements experiences can help project managers and business analysts steer a more confident course in the future.

Getting started with new practices

Table 3-2 groups the requirements engineering good practices described in this chapter by the relative value they can contribute to most projects and their relative difficulty of implementation. These classifications are not absolute; your experiences might be different. Although all the practices can be beneficial, you might begin with those practices that have a high impact on project success and are relatively easy to implement.

TABLE 3-2 Implementing requirements engineering good practices

Value	Difficulty		
	High	**Medium**	**Low**
High	■ Define a requirements engineering process ■ Base plans on requirements ■ Renegotiate commitments	■ Train business analysts ■ Plan requirements approach ■ Select product champions ■ Identify user requirements ■ Hold elicitation interviews ■ Specify nonfunctional requirements ■ Prioritize requirements ■ Define vision and scope ■ Establish a change control process ■ Review the requirements ■ Allocate requirements to subsystems ■ Use a requirements management tool ■ Record business rules	■ Educate developers about application domain ■ Adopt requirement document templates ■ Identify user classes ■ Model the application environment ■ Identify requirement origins ■ Establish baselines and control versions of requirements sets ■ Identify requirements decision makers
Medium	■ Maintain a requirements traceability matrix ■ Hold facilitated elicitation workshops ■ Estimate requirements effort ■ Reuse existing requirements	■ Educate stakeholders about requirements ■ Conduct focus groups ■ Create prototypes ■ Analyze feasibility ■ Define acceptance criteria ■ Model the requirements ■ Analyze interfaces ■ Perform change impact analysis ■ Select an appropriate life cycle ■ Identify system events and responses ■ Manage requirements risks ■ Review past lessons learned ■ Track requirements effort	■ Create a data dictionary ■ Observe users performing their jobs ■ Test the requirements ■ Track requirements status ■ Perform document analysis ■ Track requirements issues ■ Uniquely label each requirement ■ Create a glossary
Low		■ Distribute questionnaires ■ Maintain change history ■ Simulate the requirements	■ Examine problem reports

Don't try to apply all of these techniques on your next project. Instead, think of these good practices as new items for your requirements tool kit. You can begin to use certain practices, such as those dealing with change management, no matter where your project is in its development cycle. Elicitation practices will be more useful when you begin the next project or iteration. Still others might not fit your current project, organizational culture, or resource availability. Chapter 31 and Appendix A describe ways to evaluate your organization's current requirements engineering practices. Chapter 31 will help you devise a road map for implementing selected improvements in your requirements process based on the practices described in this chapter. Incorporate the adoption of new requirements techniques into your organization's software process improvement activities, relying on change leadership to facilitate the piloting, rollout, and adoption of better practices. Just make sure that each of your development teams tries something new and better at each opportunity.

Next steps

- Go back to the requirements-related problems you identified from the Next Steps in Chapter 1. Identify good practices from this chapter that might help with each problem you identified. Group the practices into high, medium, and low impact in your organization. Identify any barriers to implementing each practice in your organization or culture. Who can help you break down those barriers? Can you pick one activity to begin performing better than you already are?

- Determine how you would assess the benefits from the practices that you think would be most valuable. Would you find fewer requirements defects late in the game, reduce unnecessary rework, better meet project schedules, achieve higher customer satisfaction or product sales, or enjoy other advantages?

- List all the requirements good practices you identified in the first step. For each, indicate your project team's current level of capability: expert, proficient, novice, or unfamiliar. If your team is not at least proficient in any of those practices, ask someone on your project to learn more about the practice and to share what he learns with the rest of the team.

CHAPTER 4

The business analyst

Molly is a senior business analyst in an insurance company, where she has worked for seven years. Her manager recently told her that, because of her stellar performance over the course of her career, he wanted her to help build a stronger BA career path for the rest of the department. He asked Molly for ideas of what to look for when hiring new BAs and how to train the ones already on the team. Molly was flattered. She reflected on her own career path to see if she could replicate any of her formative experiences.

Molly received a degree in computer science from a university whose curriculum did not discuss requirements; the focus was on the technical aspects of software development. Her first career was as an enterprise software developer. Within a year she knew it was not the job for her. Molly spent most of her time stuck in a cubicle writing code, desperately wanting to talk to other people. Over the next couple of years, she evolved her role into one of a BA, though she was still called a developer. She eventually convinced her manager to give her the more appropriate title and formally redefine her role. Molly also took a basic class on software requirements to learn the fundamentals. Then she got herself assigned to projects where she could try different practices and learn from more experienced mentors. Within a couple more years, she was able to develop a requirements process for her company. Molly had become the resident business analysis expert.

Molly recognizes that she shouldn't expect a specific educational background when hiring new business analysts. She'll focus on interviewing for the most important BA soft skills. Her training development program will emphasize the fundamentals of business analysis and how to apply the critical soft skills. Finally, she will establish a mentoring program for junior BAs.

Explicitly or implicitly, someone performs the role of business analyst (BA) on every software project. A business analyst enables change in an organizational context by defining needs and recommending solutions that deliver value to stakeholders. The analyst elicits and analyzes others' perspectives, transforms the information collected into a requirements specification, and communicates the information to other stakeholders. The analyst helps stakeholders find the difference between what they say they want and what they really need. She educates, questions, listens, organizes, and learns. It's a tough job.

This chapter looks at the vital functions the BA performs, the skills and knowledge an effective analyst needs, and how you might develop such people in your organization (Wiegers 2000; IIBA 2011). Ralph Young (2004) proposes a job description for a requirements analyst, and you can also access a sample BA job description from the companion content for this book.

The business analyst role

The business analyst is the individual who has the primary responsibility to elicit, analyze, document, and validate the needs of the project stakeholders. The analyst serves as the principal interpreter through which requirements flow between the customer community and the software development team, as shown in Figure 4-1. Many other communication pathways also are used, so the analyst isn't solely responsible for information exchange on the project. The BA plays a central role in collecting and disseminating *product* information, whereas the project manager takes the lead in communicating *project* information.

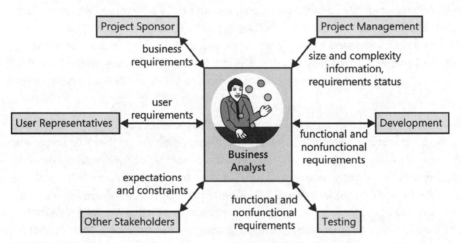

FIGURE 4-1 The business analyst bridges communication between customer and development stakeholders.

Business analyst is a project role, not necessarily a job title. Synonyms for *business analyst* include *requirements analyst, systems analyst, requirements engineer, requirements manager, application analyst, business systems analyst, IT business analyst*, and simply *analyst*. These job titles are used inconsistently from organization to organization. One or more dedicated specialists could perform the role on a given project or it could be assigned to team members who also perform other project functions. These team members include project manager, product manager, product owner, subject matter expert (SME), developer, and sometimes even user.

It's important to note that when a person who has another project role also serves as the business analyst, he is doing two distinct jobs. Consider a project manager who is also the BA on a project. A project manager needs to create and manage plans, including schedules and resource needs, based on work that BAs define. The project manager must help manage scope and deal with schedule changes as scope evolves. He might perform the project management role one minute, then change hats to execute the analyst practices the next. But these are distinct roles, requiring somewhat different skill sets.

In organizations that develop consumer products, the analyst role is often the product manager's or marketing staff's responsibility. Essentially, the product manager acts as a BA, often with additional emphasis on understanding the market landscape and anticipating external users' needs. If the project has both a product manager and a BA, typically the product manager focuses on the external market and user demands, and the BA converts those into functional requirements.

Agile projects need business analysis skills, too. There will likely be a project role such as a product owner who performs some of the traditional BA tasks. Some teams find it helpful to have someone in an analyst role as well (Cohn 2010). The BA can help represent the users and understand their needs, while performing the additional BA activities described later in the chapter. Regardless of the job title, the person performing the analyst tasks must have the skills, knowledge, and personality to perform the role well.

> **Trap** Don't assume that any talented developer or knowledgeable user can automatically be an effective business analyst without training, resource materials, and coaching.

 A talented analyst can make the difference between a project that succeeds and one that struggles. One company discovered that they could inspect requirements specifications written by experienced analysts twice as fast as those written by novices because they contained fewer defects. In the popular Cocomo II model for project estimation, analyst experience and capability have a great influence on a project's effort and cost (Boehm et al. 2000). Using highly experienced analysts can reduce the project's overall effort by one-third compared to similar projects with inexperienced analysts.

The business analyst's tasks

The analyst must first understand the business objectives for the project and then define user, functional, and quality requirements that allow teams to estimate and plan the project and to design, build, and verify the product. The BA is also a leader and a communicator, turning vague customer notions into clear specifications that guide the software team's work. This section describes some of the typical activities that you might perform while wearing an analyst's hat.

Define business requirements   Your work as a BA begins when you help the business or funding sponsor, product manager, or marketing manager define the project's business requirements. You might suggest a template for a vision and scope document (see Chapter 5, "Establishing the business requirements") and work with those who hold the vision to help them express it clearly.

Plan the requirements approach   The analyst should develop plans to elicit, analyze, document, validate, and manage requirements throughout the project. Work closely with the project manager to ensure these plans align with the overall project plans and will help achieve the project goals.

Identify project stakeholders and user classes   Work with the business sponsors to select appropriate representatives for each user class (see Chapter 6, "Finding the voice of the user"), enlist their participation, and negotiate their responsibilities. Explain what you would like from your customer collaborators and agree on an appropriate level of engagement from each one.

Elicit requirements   A proactive analyst helps users articulate the system capabilities they need to meet their business objectives by using a variety of information-gathering techniques. See Chapter 7, "Requirements elicitation," and Chapter 8, "Understanding user requirements," for further discussion.

Analyze requirements   Look for derived requirements that are a logical consequence of what the customers requested and for implicit requirements that the customers seem to expect without saying so. Use requirements models to recognize patterns, identify gaps in the requirements, reveal conflicting requirements, and confirm that all requirements specified are within scope. Work with stakeholders to determine the necessary level of detail for specifying user and functional requirements.

Document requirements   The analyst is responsible for documenting requirements in a well-organized and well-written manner that clearly describes the solution that will address the customer's problem. Using standard templates accelerates requirements development by reminding the BA of topics to discuss with the user representatives.

Communicate requirements   You must communicate the requirements effectively and efficiently to all parties. The BA should determine when it is helpful to represent requirements by using methods other than text, including various types of visual analysis models (discussed in Chapters 5, 12, and 13), tables, mathematical equations, and prototypes (discussed in Chapter 15, "Risk reduction through prototyping"). Communication is not simply a matter of putting requirements on paper and tossing them over a wall. It involves ongoing collaboration with the team to ensure that they understand the information you are communicating.

Lead requirements validation   The BA must ensure that requirement statements possess the desired characteristics that are discussed in Chapter 11, "Writing excellent requirements," and that a solution based on the requirements will satisfy stakeholder needs. Analysts are the central participants in reviews of requirements. You should also review designs and tests that were derived from the requirements to ensure that the requirements were interpreted correctly. If you are creating acceptance tests in place of detailed requirements on an agile project, those should also be reviewed.

Facilitate requirements prioritization   The analyst brokers collaboration and negotiation among the various stakeholders and the developers to ensure that they make sensible priority decisions in alignment with achieving business objectives.

Manage requirements   A business analyst is involved throughout the entire software development life cycle, so she should help create, review, and execute the project's requirements management plan. After establishing a requirements baseline for a given product release or development iteration, the BA's focus shifts to tracking the status of those requirements, verifying their satisfaction in the product, and managing changes to the requirements baseline. With input from various colleagues, the analyst collects traceability information that connects individual requirements to other system elements.

Essential analyst skills

It isn't reasonable to expect people to serve as analysts without sufficient training, guidance, and experience. They won't do a good job, and they'll find the experience frustrating. The job includes many "soft skills" that are more people-oriented than technical. Analysts need to know how to use a variety of elicitation techniques and how to represent information in forms other than natural-language text. An effective BA combines strong communication, facilitation, and interpersonal skills with technical and business domain knowledge and the right personality for the job. Patience and a genuine desire to work with people are key success factors. The skills described in this section are particularly important. Young (2004) provides a comprehensive table of skills that are appropriate for junior-level, mid-level, and senior-level requirements analysts.

Listening skills   To become proficient at two-way communication, learn how to listen effectively. Active listening involves eliminating distractions, maintaining an attentive posture and eye contact, and restating key points to confirm your understanding. You need to grasp what people are saying and also to read between the lines to detect what they might be hesitant to say. Learn how your collaborators prefer to communicate, and avoid imposing your personal filter of understanding on what you hear from the customers. Watch for unstated assumptions that underlie either what you hear from others or your own interpretation.

Interviewing and questioning skills   Most requirements input comes through discussions, so the BA must be able to interact with diverse individuals and groups about their needs. It can be intimidating to work with senior managers and with highly opinionated or aggressive individuals. You need to ask the right questions to surface essential requirements information. For example, users naturally focus on the system's normal, expected behaviors. However, much code gets written to handle exceptions. Therefore, you must also probe to identify error conditions and determine how the system should respond. With experience, you'll become skilled in the art of asking questions that reveal and clarify uncertainties, disagreements, assumptions, and unstated expectations (Gause and Weinberg 1989).

Thinking on your feet   Business analysts always need to be aware of the existing information and to process new information against it. They need to spot contradictions, uncertainty, vagueness, and assumptions so they can discuss them in the moment if appropriate. You can try to script the perfect set of interview questions; however, you'll always need to ask something you could not have foreseen. You need to draft good questions, listen clearly to the responses, and quickly come up with the next smart thing to say or ask. Sometimes you won't be asking a question but rather giving an appropriate example in context to help your stakeholder formulate the next answer.

Analytical skills   An effective business analyst can think at both high and low levels of abstraction and knows when to move from one to another. Sometimes, you must drill down from high-level information into details. In other situations, you'll need to generalize from a specific need that one user described to a set of requirements that will satisfy multiple stakeholders. BAs need to understand complex information coming from many sources and to solve hard problems related to that information. They need to critically evaluate the information to reconcile conflicts, separate user "wants" from the underlying true needs, and distinguish solution ideas from requirements.

Systems thinking skills   Although a business analyst must be detail-oriented, he must also see the big picture. The BA must check requirements against what he knows about the whole enterprise, the business environment, and the application to look for inconsistencies and impacts. The BA needs to understand the interactions and relationships among the people, processes, and technology related to the system (IIBA 2009). If a customer requests a requirement for his functional area, the BA needs to judge whether the requirement affects other parts of the system in unobvious ways.

Learning skills   Analysts must learn new material quickly, whether it is about new requirements approaches or the application domain. They need to be able to translate that knowledge into practice efficiently. Analysts should be efficient and critical readers because they have to wade through a lot of material and grasp the essence quickly. You do not have to be an expert in the domain, so don't hesitate to ask clarifying questions. Be honest about what you don't know. It's okay not to know it all, but it's not okay to hide your ignorance.

Facilitation skills   The ability to facilitate requirements discussions and elicitation workshops is a vital analyst capability. Facilitation is the act of leading a group towards success. Facilitation is essential when collaboratively defining requirements, prioritizing needs, and resolving conflicts. A neutral facilitator who has strong questioning, observational, and facilitation skills can help a group build trust and improve the sometimes tense relationship between business and IT staff. Chapter 7 presents guidelines for facilitating requirements elicitation activities.

Leadership skills   A strong analyst can influence a group of stakeholders to move in a certain direction to accomplish a common goal. Leadership requires understanding a variety of techniques to negotiate agreements among project stakeholders, resolve conflicts, and make decisions. The analyst should create a collaborative environment, fostering trust among the various stakeholder groups who might not understand each other's motivations, needs, and constraints.

Observational skills   An observant analyst will detect comments made in passing that might turn out to be significant. By watching a user perform her job or use a current application, a good observer can detect subtleties that the user might not think to mention. Strong observational skills sometimes expose new areas for elicitation discussions, thereby revealing additional requirements.

Communication skills   The principal deliverable from requirements development is a set of written requirements that communicates information effectively among customers, marketing, managers, and technical staff. The analyst needs a solid command of the language and the ability to express complex ideas clearly, both in written form and verbally. You must be able to write for multiple audiences, including customers who have to validate the requirements and developers who need clear, precise requirements for implementation. A BA needs to speak clearly, adapting to local terminology and to regional differences in dialect. Also, a BA must be able to summarize and present information at the level of detail the target audience needs.

Organizational skills   BAs must contend with a vast array of jumbled information gathered during elicitation and analysis. Coping with rapidly changing information and structuring all the bits into a coherent whole demands exceptional organizational skills and the patience and tenacity to make sense from ambiguity and disarray. As an analyst, you need to be able to set up an information architecture to support the project information as it grows throughout the project (Beatty and Chen 2012).

Modeling skills   Models ranging from the venerable flowchart through structured analysis models (data flow diagram, entity-relationship diagram, and similar diagrams) to Unified Modeling Language (UML) notations should be part of every analyst's repertoire (Beatty and Chen 2012). Some will be useful when communicating with users, others when communicating with developers, and still others purely for analysis to help the BA improve the requirements. The BA will need to know when to select specific models based on how they add value. Also, he'll need to educate other stakeholders on the value of using these models and how to read them. See Chapters 5, 12, and 13 for overviews of several types of analysis models.

Interpersonal skills   Analysts must be able to get people with competing interests to work together as a team. An analyst should feel comfortable talking with individuals in diverse job functions and at all levels of the organization. A BA should speak the language of the audience she is talking to, not using technical jargon with business stakeholders. She might need to work with virtual teams whose members are separated by geography, time zones, cultures, or native languages. A BA should be easy to communicate with and be clear and consistent when communicating with team members.

Creativity   The BA is not merely a scribe who records whatever customers say. The best analysts invent potential requirements for customers to consider (Robertson 2002). They conceive innovative product capabilities, imagine new markets and business opportunities, and think of ways to surprise and delight their customers. A really valuable BA finds creative ways to satisfy needs that users didn't even know they had. Analysts can offer new ideas because they are not as close as users to the problem being solved. Analysts have to be careful to avoid gold-plating the solution, though; don't simply add new requirements to the specification without customer approval.

Practicing what you teach

An experienced BA and developer once saved me from myself. I was talking to my friend and colleague Tanya about a software service I thought I needed for my website. I told her that I needed some kind of script that could intercept certain email messages I received and parse certain information out of them. I didn't know how to write such a script, so I asked Tanya how she would suggest proceeding.

Tanya replied, "Excuse me, Karl, but I don't think that's your real requirement. Your real requirement is to get the information you need in some other way besides manually reading and processing emails as they arrive in your inbox." She was exactly correct. I had fallen into the oh-so-common trap of a user attempting to specify a solution as a requirement. Fortunately, this observant BA detected my mistake. Tanya stepped back a bit and immediately grasped the underlying issue. When you do that, you almost always find that there are multiple ways you could solve the problem, some of which might be better than the first one that popped into your head. My smart friend Tanya reminded me how important it is for the skillful BA to dig below a presented solution and really understand the user's objectives.

Essential analyst knowledge

In addition to having specific capabilities and personal characteristics, business analysts need a breadth of knowledge, much of which is gained through experience. They need to understand contemporary requirements engineering practices and how to apply them in the context of various software development life cycles. They might need to educate and persuade those who are not familiar with established requirements practices. The effective analyst has a rich tool kit of techniques available and knows when—and when not—to use each one.

BAs need to thread requirements development and management activities through the entire project life span. An analyst with a sound understanding of project management, development life cycles, risk management, and quality engineering can help prevent requirements issues from torpedoing the project. In a commercial development setting, the BA will benefit from knowledge of product management concepts. BAs benefit from a basic level of knowledge about the architecture and operating environment, so that they can engage in technical conversations about priorities and nonfunctional requirements.

Knowledge of the business, the industry, and the organization are powerful assets for an effective BA (IIBA 2009). The business-savvy analyst can minimize miscommunications with users. Analysts who understand the organization and business domains often detect unstated assumptions and implicit requirements. They can suggest ways that users could improve their business processes or propose valuable functionality that no other stakeholder thought of. Understanding the industry domain can be particularly helpful in a commercial environment so analysts can offer marketplace and competitive product analysis.

The making of a business analyst

Great business analysts are grown from diverse backgrounds of education and work experience, so they will likely have gaps in their knowledge and skill sets. All analysts should decide which of the knowledge and skills described in this chapter pertain to their situation and actively seek to fill their own gaps. The International Institute of Business Analysis (IIBA) describes the competencies that entry-level, junior, intermediate, and senior business analysts should exhibit across the common BA activities (IIBA 2011). All new BAs will benefit from mentoring and coaching from those who have more experience, perhaps in the form of an apprenticeship. Let's explore how people with different backgrounds might move into the analyst role and see some of the challenges and risks they'll face.

The former user

Corporate IT departments often have business analysts who migrated into that role after working on the business side as a user of information systems. These individuals understand the business and the work environment, so they can easily gain the trust of their former colleagues. They speak the user's language, and they know the existing systems and business processes.

On the downside, former users who are now BAs might know little about software engineering or how to communicate with technical people. If they aren't familiar with modeling techniques, they will express all information in textual form. Users who become BAs need to learn more about the technical side of software development so they can represent information in the most appropriate forms for their multiple audiences.

Some former users believe they understand what is needed better than current users do, so they don't solicit or respect input from those who will actually use the new system. Recent users can be stuck in the here-and-now of the current ways of working, such that they don't see opportunities to improve business processes with the help of a new information system. It's also easy for a former user to think of requirements strictly from a user interface perspective. Focusing on solution ideas can impose unnecessary design constraints and often fails to solve the real problem.

From medical technologist to business analyst

The senior manager of a medical devices division in a large company had a problem. "Two years ago, I hired three medical technologists into my division to represent our customers' needs," he said. "They've done a great job, but they're no longer current in medical technology, so they can't speak accurately for what our customers need today. What's a reasonable career path for them now?"

This manager's former medical technologists were good candidates to become business analysts. Although they weren't up on the latest happenings in the hospital laboratory, they could still communicate with other med techs. Spending two years in a product development environment gave them a good appreciation for how it works. They needed some additional training in requirements-writing techniques, but these employees had accumulated a range of valuable experiences that could make them effective analysts. These former users did indeed transition into the BA role successfully.

The former developer or tester

Project managers who lack a dedicated BA often expect a developer to do the job. Unfortunately, the skills and personality needed for requirements development aren't the same as those needed for software development. Some developers have little patience with users, preferring to work with the code and promote the glamour of technology. Of course, many other developers do recognize the criticality of the requirements process and can work as analysts when necessary. Those who enjoy collaborating with customers to understand the needs that drive software development are good candidates to specialize in business analysis.

The developer-turned-analyst might need to learn more about the business domain. Developers can easily lapse into technical thinking and jargon, focusing on the software to be built instead of the customers' needs. They'll need to get up to speed on current best practices for requirements engineering. Developers will benefit from training and mentoring in the diverse soft skills that the best analysts master, as described earlier in this chapter.

Testers aren't commonly asked to perform the analyst role. However, a tester often has an analytical mindset that can lend itself to being a good BA. Testers are already used to thinking about exceptions and how to break things, a useful skill for finding gaps in requirements. As with a former developer, a tester will have to learn about good requirements engineering practices. She might also need to become more knowledgeable about the business domain.

The former (or concurrent) project manager

Project managers are sometimes asked to also fill the role of business analyst, probably because they have some of the same skills and domain knowledge required. This can be an effective role change. Project managers will already be used to working with the appropriate teams, understanding the organization and business domains, and demonstrating strong communication skills. They will likely be good at listening, negotiation, and facilitation. They should have strong organizational and writing skills as well.

However, the former project manager will have to learn more about requirements engineering practices. It is one thing to set up a plan, allocate resources, and coordinate the activities of analysts and other team members. It is a very different matter to perform the business analyst role yourself. Former project managers must learn to focus on understanding the business needs and prioritizing those within existing project schedules, rather than focusing on timelines, resources, and budget constraints. They will need to develop the analysis, modeling, and interviewing skills that are less important for project managers but are essential to BA success.

The subject matter expert

Young (2001) recommends that the business analyst be an application domain expert or a SME, as opposed to being a typical user: "SMEs can determine, based on their experience, whether the requirements are reasonable, how they extend the existing system, how the proposed architecture should be designed, and the impacts on users, among other areas." Some product development organizations hire expert users of their products who have extensive domain experience into their companies to serve either as analysts or as user surrogates.

There are risks here, though, too. The business analyst who is a domain expert might specify the system's requirements to suit his own preferences, rather than addressing the legitimate needs of the various user classes. He might have blinders on when thinking about requirements and be less creative in proposing new ideas. SMEs are expert in their understanding of the "as-is" system; they sometimes have difficulty imagining the "to-be" system. It often works better to have a BA from the development team work with the SME, who then serves as a key user representative or product champion. The product champion is described in Chapter 6.

The rookie

Becoming a business analyst is a good entry point into the information technology arena for someone right out of school or coming from a completely unrelated job. The new graduate will have little, if any, relevant experience or knowledge. He will likely be hired into the BA role because he demonstrates many of the skills required to be a good analyst. An advantage of hiring a novice as a BA is that he will have few preconceived notions about how requirements processes should work.

Because he lacks related experience and knowledge, a new graduate will have much to learn about how to execute the BA tasks and the intricacies of the practices. The recent graduate also needs to learn enough about the software development process to understand the challenges that developers, testers, and other team members face so he can collaborate effectively with them. Mentoring can reduce the learning curve for a novice BA and instill good habits from the outset.

No matter what his background, a creative business analyst can apply it to enhance his effectiveness. The analyst needs to gain the knowledge and skills he is lacking, build on any past experiences, and practice performing the BA tasks to become more proficient. All of these help create the well-rounded BA (Figure 4-2).

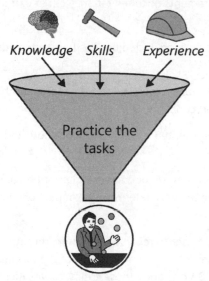

The well-rounded BA

FIGURE 4-2 Knowledge, skills, and experience feed into creating an effective business analyst.

The analyst role on agile projects

On projects using agile development methods, the business analyst functions still need to be performed, but the individual who does them might not be called a BA. Some agile approaches have a key team member called the *product owner*. The person in that role might perform some of the traditional business analysis activities, as well as providing the product vision, communicating constraints, prioritizing the product backlog of remaining work, and making the ultimate decisions about the product (Cohn 2010). Other projects maintain a business analyst role separate from the product owner. Additionally, other team members, such as developers, perform portions of the analyst role. The point is that, regardless of the project's development approach, the tasks associated with the BA role still have to get done. The team will benefit from having members who possess the skills associated with business analysts.

Often, in an organization moving toward an agile development approach, the BA finds herself unsure as to how she can most effectively contribute to the project. In the spirit of agile development, the analyst has to be willing to step out of a preconceived role of "business analyst" and fill in where needed to help deliver a successful product. Ellen Gottesdiener (2009) offers a detailed list of how traditional business analyst activities can be adapted to an agile environment. Following are a few suggestions for a BA to apply her skills on an agile project:

- Define a lightweight, flexible requirements process and adapt it as the project warrants.

- Ensure that requirements documentation is at the right level: not too little and not too much. (Many BAs tend to document everything in specifications to the nth degree. Some purists suggest agile projects should have little or no requirements documentation. Neither extreme is ideal.)

- Help determine the best approach to document the backlog, including whether story cards or more formal tools are most appropriate.

- Apply facilitation and leadership skills to ensure that stakeholders are talking to one another frequently about requirements needs, questions, and concerns.

- Help validate that customer needs are accurately represented in the product backlog, and facilitate backlog prioritization.

- Work with customers when they change their minds about requirements and priorities, and help record those changes. Work with the rest of the team to determine the impact of changes on iteration contents and release plans.

There is a lot of value in having a role such as a product owner to represent the users throughout development. However, the person filling the product owner role might not have all of the business analysis skills or time to perform all the related activities. A BA can bring those critical capabilities to the team.

Creating a collaborative team

Software projects sometimes experience strained relationships among analysts, developers, users, managers, and marketing. The parties don't always trust each other's motivations or appreciate each other's needs and constraints. In reality, though, the producers and consumers of a software product share common objectives. For corporate information systems development, all parties work for the same company, so they all benefit from improvements to the corporate bottom line. For commercial products, happy customers generate revenue for the producer and satisfaction for the developers.

The business analyst has the major responsibility for forging a collaborative relationship among the user representatives and other project stakeholders. An effective analyst appreciates the challenges that both business and technical stakeholders face and demonstrates respect for his or her collaborators at all times. The analyst steers the project participants toward a requirements agreement that leads to a win-win-win outcome in the following ways:

- Customers are delighted with the product.

- The developing organization is happy with the business outcomes.

- All team members are proud of the good work they did on a challenging and rewarding project.

Next steps

- Complete a self-assessment of your BA skills or compare your own skills and knowledge with those described in this chapter to identify areas for further development. The IIBA's self-assessment is a good tool for this purpose (IIBA 2010). Create a personal roadmap to close the gaps.

- For any skills gaps, select two specific areas for improvement and begin closing those gaps immediately by reading, practicing, finding a mentor, or taking a class.

- Evaluate your current knowledge about the business, industry, and organization in which you're working and identify subject matter expertise to develop further. Find an article about that subject or an expert from whom you can learn more.

CHAPTER 5

Establishing the business requirements

Karen is a business analyst on a project to implement a new online product catalog for the company's customer service representatives. The drafted SRS is going through review when the marketing manager says he wants to add a "Like this product" feature. Karen's first instinct is to push back; there is already concern about meeting schedules with the current requirements set. But then she realizes that maybe that's a smart feature to add, because customer service representatives can promote the most-liked products with other customers. Before she elicits and documents functional requirements for this feature, she needs an objective analysis about whether this feature should be added to the scope or not.

When she explains to the marketing manager the need to analyze this request further, he responds, "Well, soon the developers are going to be in there changing code anyway. How hard is it to add just one tiny feature?" Karen's analysis determines that the proposed feature lies outside the project's scope: it won't contribute to the business objectives to reduce the customer service representatives' average call time, and it wouldn't be simple to implement. Karen needs to be able to clearly articulate why the feature isn't in scope to the marketing manager, who doesn't have the business objectives readily in mind.

As you saw in Chapter 1, "The essential software requirement," business requirements represent the top of the requirements chain. They define the vision of the solution and the scope of the project that will implement the solution. The user requirements and functional requirements must align with the context and objectives that the business requirements establish. Requirements that don't help the project achieve its business objectives shouldn't be implemented.

A project without a clearly defined and well-communicated direction invites disaster. Project participants can unwittingly work at cross-purposes if they have different objectives and priorities. The stakeholders will never agree on the requirements if they lack a common understanding of the project's business objectives. Without this understanding up front, project deadlines will likely be missed and budgets will likely be overrun as the team struggles to deliver the right product.

This chapter describes the vision and scope document, a deliverable that contains the project's business requirements. Figure 5-3 later in this chapter suggests a template for the vision and scope document. But before we get to the template, let's see just what we mean by "business requirements."

Defining business requirements

"Business requirements" refers to a set of information that, in the aggregate, describes a need that leads to one or more projects to deliver a solution and the desired ultimate business outcomes. Business opportunities, business objectives, success metrics, and a vision statement make up the business requirements.

Business requirements issues must be resolved before the functional and nonfunctional requirements can be fully specified. A statement of the project's scope and limitations helps greatly with discussions of proposed features and target releases. The business requirements provide a reference for making decisions about proposed requirement changes and enhancements. We recommend displaying the business objectives, vision, and scope highlights in every requirements elicitation session so the team can quickly judge whether a proposed requirement is in or out of scope.

Identifying desired business benefits

The business requirements set the context for, and enable the measurement of, the benefits the business hopes to achieve from undertaking a project. Organizations should not initiate any project without a clear understanding of the value it will add to the business. Set measurable targets with business objectives, and then define success metrics that allow you to measure whether you are on track to meet those objectives.

Business requirements might come from funding sponsors, corporate executives, marketing managers, or product visionaries. However, it can be challenging to identify and communicate the business benefits. Team members sometimes aren't exactly sure what the project is intended to accomplish. Sometimes, sponsors don't want to set objectives in a measurable fashion and then be held accountable for achieving them. There could be multiple important stakeholders who don't agree on what the objectives should be. The business analyst can ensure that the right stakeholders are setting the business requirements and facilitate elicitation, prioritization, and conflict resolution. Karl Wiegers (2006) suggests some questions that the BA can ask to help elicit business requirements.

The business benefit has to represent a true value for the project's sponsors and to the product's customers. For example, simply merging two systems into one is not a reasonable business objective. Customers don't care if they are using an application that involves 1, 5, or even 10 systems. They care about issues like increasing revenue and decreasing costs. Merging two systems might be part of the solution, but it is rarely the true business objective. Regulatory and legal compliance projects also have clear business objectives. Often the objectives are phrased as risk avoidance, possibly to avoid getting sued or being put out of business.

Product vision and project scope

Two core elements of the business requirements are the vision and the scope. The *product vision* succinctly describes the ultimate product that will achieve the business objectives. This product could serve as the complete solution for the business requirements or as just a portion of the solution. The vision describes what the product is about and what it ultimately could become. It provides the context for making decisions throughout the product's life, and it aligns all stakeholders in a common direction. The *project scope* identifies what portion of the ultimate product vision the current project or development iteration will address. The statement of scope draws the boundary between what's in and what's out for this project.

Important The product vision ensures that we all know where we are hoping to go eventually. The project scope ensures that we are all talking about the same thing for the immediate project or iteration.

Make sure the vision solves the problem

In one of our training courses, we give students a business problem and a corresponding business objective. Throughout the exercise, we periodically provide additional details about the requirements. At each step, we ask the students to conceive a solution to the problem, given the information they have. By the end of the exercise, all of the students' solution ideas are similar, but rarely do any of them actually solve the original problem!

This mimics what we see on real projects. Teams might set clear objectives and then specify, develop, and test the system, without checking against the objectives along the way. A stakeholder might come up with a "shiny" new feature she wants implemented. The team adds it because it seems reasonable and interesting. However, months down the road, the delivered system doesn't solve the original problem, despite all of its cool features.

The vision applies to the product as a whole. The vision should change relatively slowly as a product's strategic positioning or a company's business objectives evolve over time. The scope pertains to a specific project or iteration that will implement the next increment of the product's functionality, as shown in Figure 5-1. Scope is more dynamic than vision because the stakeholders adjust the contents of each release within its schedule, budget, resource, and quality constraints. Scope for the current release should be clear, but the scope of future releases will be fuzzier the farther out you look. The team's goal is to manage the scope of a specific development or enhancement project as a defined subset of the strategic vision for the product.

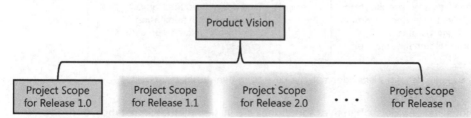

FIGURE 5-1 The product vision encompasses the scope for each planned release, which is less well defined the farther out you look.

Interlocking scopes

A federal government agency is undertaking a massive five-year information system development effort. The agency defined the business objectives and vision for this system early in the process; they won't change substantially over the next few years. The agency has planned 15 releases of portions of the ultimate system, each created by a separate project team and having its own scope description. Some projects will run in parallel, because certain of them are relatively independent of each other and some have longer timelines than others. Each scope description must align with the overall product vision and interlock with the scope for the other projects to ensure that nothing is inadvertently omitted and that lines of responsibility are clear.

Conflicting business requirements

Business requirements collected from multiple sources might conflict. Consider a kiosk that will be used by a retail store's customers. Figure 5-2 shows the likely business interests of the kiosk developer, retailer, and customer as we envision how each of these stakeholders hopes the kiosk will provide an advantage over their current way of doing business.

The Kiosk Developers
- Generate revenue by leasing or selling the kiosk to the retailer
- Sell consumables to customers through the kiosk
- Attract retailers to the brand
- Make a wide variety of products or services available

The Retailer
- Maximize revenue from the available floor space
- Attract new customers to the store
- Increase sales to existing customers
- Increase profit margins
- Little kiosk maintenance required

The Customer
- Broad selection of products or services available
- Find desired products quickly
- Spend less time purchasing
- Easy-to-understand purchasing process

FIGURE 5-2 Stakeholders for a kiosk don't always have congruent business interests.

The various stakeholders' objectives sometimes are in alignment. For instance, both the kiosk developers and the customers want to have a wide variety of products or services available through the kiosk. However, some business objectives could conflict. The customer wants to spend less time purchasing goods and services, but the retailer would prefer to have customers linger in the store and spend more money. The tension among stakeholders with different goals and constraints can lead to clashing business requirements. The project's decision makers must resolve these conflicts before the analyst can detail the kiosk's requirements. The focus should be on delivering the maximum business value to the primary stakeholders. It's easy to be distracted by superficial product characteristics that don't really address the business objectives.

The project's decision makers shouldn't expect the software team to resolve conflicts among various stakeholders. As more constituencies with diverse interests climb aboard, scope will grow. Uncontrolled scope creep, in which stakeholders overstuff the new system in an attempt to satisfy every interest, can cause the project to topple under its own weight. A BA can help by surfacing potential areas of conflict and differing assumptions, flagging conflicting business objectives, noting when requested features don't achieve those objectives, and facilitating conflict resolution. Resolving such issues is often a political and power struggle, which lies outside the scope of this book.

Long-duration projects often experience a change in decision makers partway through. If this happens to you, immediately revisit the baselined business requirements with the new decision makers. They need to be aware of the existing business requirements, which they might want to modify. If so, the project manager will have to adjust budgets, schedules, and resources, while the BA might need to work with stakeholders to update user and functional requirements and reset their priorities.

Vision and scope document

The *vision and scope document* collects the business requirements into a single deliverable that sets the stage for the subsequent development work. Some organizations create a project charter (Wiegers 2007) or a business case document that serves a similar purpose. Organizations that build commercial software often create a market (or marketing) requirements document (MRD). An MRD might go into more detail about the target market segments and the issues that pertain to commercial success.

The owner of the vision and scope document is the project's executive sponsor, funding authority, or someone in a similar role. A business analyst can work with this individual to articulate the business requirements and write the vision and scope document. Input to the business requirements should come from people who have a clear sense of why they are undertaking the project. These individuals might include the customer or development organization's senior management, a product visionary, a product manager, a subject matter expert, or members of the marketing department.

Figure 5-3 suggests a template for a vision and scope document; the sections that follow describe each of the template headings in more detail. As with any template, adapt this to meet the specific needs of your own projects. If you already have recorded some of this information elsewhere, do not duplicate it in the vision and scope document. Some elements of the vision and scope document might be reusable from project to project, such as business objectives, business risks, and stakeholder profiles. Appendix C includes an example vision and scope document written according to this template.

```
1. Business requirements
   1.1 Background
   1.2 Business opportunity
   1.3 Business objectives
   1.4 Success metrics
   1.5 Vision statement
   1.6 Business risks
   1.7 Business assumptions and dependencies
2. Scope and limitations
   2.1 Major features
   2.2 Scope of initial release
   2.3 Scope of subsequent releases
   2.4 Limitations and exclusions
3. Business context
   3.1 Stakeholder profiles
   3.2 Project priorities
   3.3 Deployment considerations
```

FIGURE 5-3 Suggested template for a vision and scope document.

The vision and scope document only defines the scope at a high level; the scope details are represented by each release baseline that the team defines. Major new projects should have both a complete vision and scope document and an SRS. (See Chapter 10, "Documenting the requirements," for an SRS template.) Each iteration, release, or enhancement project for an evolving product can include its own scope statement in that project's requirements documentation, rather than creating a separate vision and scope document.

Template tactics

Templates provide a consistent way to organize information from one project to the next. They help me remember information that I might overlook if I started with a blank piece of paper.

I don't fill out a template from top to bottom. Instead, I populate the various sections as I accumulate information during the course of the project. Empty sections highlight gaps in our current knowledge. Suppose one section of my document template is titled "Business risks." Partway through the project, I realize this section is empty. Does the project really have no business risks? Have we identified some business risks but stored them someplace else? Or have we not yet worked with appropriate stakeholders to identify possible risks? Blank sections in the template help me conduct a richer exploration for important project information. If there are common questions you ask to elicit content for a section, consider embedding those in the appropriate section of the template, perhaps in the form of hidden text, for others to reuse.

I use the term "shrink to fit" when working with templates. I begin with a rich template with many categories that might be important. Then I condense it down to just what I need for each situation. Suppose that a certain section of the template—business risks, say—doesn't pertain to the current project. I can remove that section from my document or I can retain the heading but leave the contents blank. Both options run the risk that a reader will notice the hole and question whether there are indeed any business risks. The best solution is to put an explicit message in that section: "No business risks have been identified."

If certain sections of a template rarely get used, delete them. You might want to create a small set of templates for use on different types of projects, such as SRS templates suitable for use on large, new development projects; small websites; and enhancement projects. Even if you store your requirements in some repository other than a traditional document, a template can help you consider all the requirements information you need to accumulate for your project.

One project manager described the benefits his team received from adopting requirements document templates: "They are time consuming to fill in. The first couple of times I created them, I was surprised at the amount of detail required to make them useful, and then the amount of work taken to review and tidy up the documents, cleaning up any ambiguities, filling in gaps, etc. *But* it's worth it. The first two products that were developed after introducing the documents came in on time and were of much higher quality than before."

1. Business requirements

Projects are launched in the belief that creating or changing a product will provide worthwhile benefits for someone and a suitable return on investment. The business requirements describe the primary benefits that the new system will provide to its sponsors, buyers, and users. Business requirements directly influence which user requirements to implement and in what sequence.

1.1 Background

Summarize the rationale and context for the new product or for changes to be made to an existing one. Describe the history or situation that led to the decision to build this product.

1.2 Business opportunity

For a corporate information system, describe the business problem that is being solved or the process being improved, as well as the environment in which the system will be used. For a commercial product, describe the business opportunity that exists and the market in which the product will be competing. This section could include a comparative evaluation of existing products, indicating why the proposed product is attractive and the advantages it provides. Describe the problems that cannot currently be solved without the envisioned solution. Show how it aligns with market trends, technology evolution, or corporate strategic directions. List any other technologies, processes, or resources required to provide a complete customer solution.

Describe the needs of typical customers or of the target market. Present customer problems that the new product will address. Provide examples of how customers would use the product. Define any known critical interface or quality requirements, but omit design or implementation specifics.

1.3 Business objectives

Summarize the important business benefits the product will provide in a quantitative and measurable way. Platitudes ("become recognized as a world-class <whatever>") and vaguely stated improvements ("provide a more rewarding customer experience") are neither helpful nor verifiable. Table 5-1 presents some simplified examples of both financial and nonfinancial business objectives (Wiegers 2007).

TABLE 5-1 Examples of financial and nonfinancial business objectives

Financial	Nonfinancial
▪ Capture a market share of X% within Y months. ▪ Increase market share in country W from X% to Y% within Z months. ▪ Reach a sales volume of X units or revenue of $Y within Z months. ▪ Achieve X% return on investment within Y months. ▪ Achieve positive cash flow on this product within Y months. ▪ Save $X per year currently spent on a high-maintenance legacy system. ▪ Reduce monthly support costs from $X to $Y within Z months. ▪ Increase gross margin on existing business from X% to Y% within 1 year.	▪ Achieve a customer satisfaction measure of at least X within Y months of release. ▪ Increase transaction-processing productivity by X% and reduce data error rate to no more than Y%. ▪ Develop an extensible platform for a family of related products. ▪ Develop specific core technology competencies. ▪ Be rated as the top product for reliability in published product reviews by a specified date. ▪ Comply with specific federal and state regulations. ▪ Receive no more than X service calls per unit and Y warranty calls per unit within Z months after shipping. ▪ Reduce turnaround time to X hours on Y% of support calls.

Organizations generally undertake a project to solve a problem or exploit an opportunity. A business objectives model shows a hierarchy of related business problems and measurable business objectives (Beatty and Chen 2012). The problems describe what is keeping the business from meeting their goals at present, whereas the objectives define ways to measure achievement of those goals. Problems and objectives are intertwined: understanding one can reveal the other.

Given a set of business objectives, ask, "What is keeping us from achieving the goal?" to identify a more detailed business problem. Or work backward by asking, "Why do we care about that goal?" to better understand the top-level business problem or opportunity. Given a business problem, ask, "How will we assess whether the problem is solved?" to identify the measurable objective. The process is iterative, cycling through the hierarchy of problems and objectives until you see a list of features emerge that would help solve the problems and meet the objectives.

A conversation between a business analyst and an executive sponsor to identify business problems and objectives might look similar to the one in Figure 5-4. This illustration is for the Chemical Tracking System project at Contoso Pharmaceuticals that was introduced in Chapter 2, "Requirements from the customer's perspective." From the executive's responses to these questions, the BA could construct a business objectives model for the Chemical Tracking System, as shown in Figure 5-5.

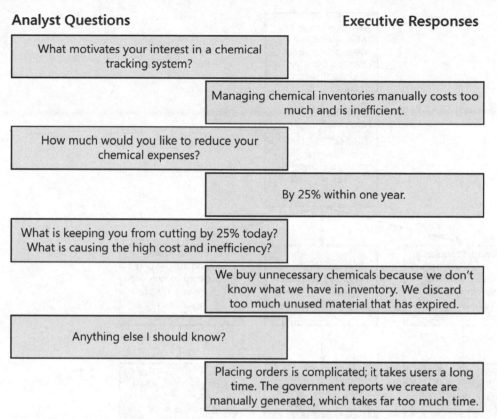

Analyst Questions

What motivates your interest in a chemical tracking system?

How much would you like to reduce your chemical expenses?

What is keeping you from cutting by 25% today? What is causing the high cost and inefficiency?

Anything else I should know?

Executive Responses

Managing chemical inventories manually costs too much and is inefficient.

By 25% within one year.

We buy unnecessary chemicals because we don't know what we have in inventory. We discard too much unused material that has expired.

Placing orders is complicated; it takes users a long time. The government reports we create are manually generated, which takes far too much time.

FIGURE 5-4 Example of a conversation between a business analyst and an executive sponsor.

1.4 Success metrics

Specify the indicators that stakeholders will use to define and measure success on this project (Wiegers 2007). Identify the factors that have the greatest impact on achieving that success, including factors both within and outside the organization's control.

Business objectives sometimes cannot be measured until well after a project is complete. In other cases, achieving the business objectives might be dependent on projects beyond your current one. However, it's still important to evaluate the success of an individual project. Success metrics indicate whether a project is on track to meet its business objectives. The metrics can be tracked during testing or shortly after product release. For the Chemical Tracking System, one success metric might be the same as Business Objective 3 in Figure 5-5 to "Reduce time spent ordering chemicals to 10 minutes on 80 percent of orders," because you can measure the average order time during testing or soon after release. Another success metric might relate to Business Objective 2 with a timeline that can be measured much earlier than a year after release, such as "Track 60 percent of commercial chemical containers and 50 percent of proprietary chemicals within 4 weeks."

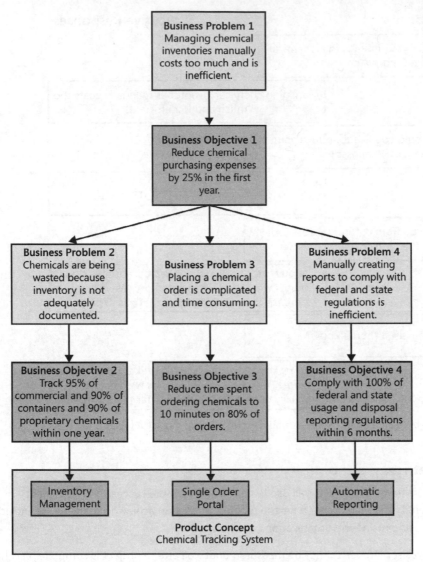

FIGURE 5-5 Example business objectives model for the Chemical Tracking System.

 Important Choose your success metrics wisely. Make sure they measure what is important to your business, not just what is easy to measure. A success metric to "Reduce product development costs by 20 percent" is easy to measure. It might also be easy to achieve by laying off employees or investing less in innovation. However, these might not be the intended outcomes of the objectives.

1.5 Vision statement

Write a concise vision statement that summarizes the long-term purpose and intent of the product. The vision statement should reflect a balanced view that will satisfy the expectations of diverse stakeholders. It can be somewhat idealistic but should be grounded in the realities of existing or anticipated markets, enterprise architectures, corporate strategic directions, and resource limitations. The following keyword template works well for crafting a product vision statement (Moore 2002):

- *For* [target customer]
- *Who* [statement of the need or opportunity]
- *The* [product name]
- *Is* [product category]
- *That* [major capabilities, key benefit, compelling reason to buy or use]
- *Unlike* [primary competitive alternative, current system, current business process]
- *Our product* [statement of primary differentiation and advantages of new product]

Here's a sample vision statement for the Chemical Tracking System, with the keywords in boldface:

> *For scientists **who** need to request containers of chemicals, **the** Chemical Tracking System **is** an information system **that** will provide a single point of access to the chemical stockroom and to vendors. The system will store the location of every chemical container within the company, the quantity of material remaining in it, and the complete history of each container's locations and usage. This system will save the company 25 percent on chemical costs in the first year of use by allowing the company to fully exploit chemicals that are already available within the company, dispose of fewer partially used or expired containers, and use a standard chemical purchasing process. **Unlike** the current manual ordering processes, **our product** will generate all reports required to comply with federal and state government regulations that require the reporting of chemical usage, storage, and disposal.*

Crafting the product vision

I use the vision statement in my own consulting work. One longtime client and I work together very well, but occasionally Bill asks me to undertake a new project that's a little different. If we aren't exactly sure what he wants me to do, I ask him to write a vision statement. Bill always grumbles a bit because he knows that this will force him to think carefully about exactly what outcome he is expecting. But Bill's vision statement invariably gives me a clear idea of just what we are trying to accomplish so we can work efficiently together. It's well worth the time it takes.

You might have several key stakeholders write their vision statements separately, rather than doing it as a group exercise. Comparing their vision statements is a good way to spot different understandings about the project's objectives. And it's never too late to write a vision statement. Even if the project is under way, crafting a vision statement can help keep the rest of the project work on track and in focus. Though drafting a vision statement is quick, crafting the *right* vision statement and reaching agreement among the key stakeholders will take more time.

1.6 Business risks

Summarize the major business risks associated with developing—or not developing—this product. Risk categories include marketplace competition, timing issues, user acceptance, implementation issues, and possible negative impacts on the business. Business risks are not the same as project risks, which often include resource availability concerns and technology factors. Estimate the potential loss from each risk, the likelihood of it occurring, and any potential mitigation actions. See Chapter 32, "Software requirements and risk management," for more about this topic.

1.7 Business assumptions and dependencies

An *assumption* is a statement that is believed to be true in the absence of proof or definitive knowledge. Business assumptions are specifically related to the business requirements. Incorrect assumptions can potentially keep you from meeting your business objectives. For example, an executive sponsor might set a business objective that a new website will increase revenue by $100,000 per month. To establish this revenue target, the sponsor made some assumptions, perhaps that the new site will attract 200 additional unique visitors per day and that each visitor will spend an average of $17. If the new site does not attract enough visitors with a high enough average sale per visitor, the project might not achieve its business objective. If you learn that certain assumptions are wrong, you might have to change scope, adjust the schedule, or launch other projects to achieve the objectives.

Record any assumptions that the stakeholders made when conceiving the project and writing their vision and scope document. Often, one party's assumptions are not shared by others. If you write them down and review them, you can avoid possible confusion and aggravation in the future.

Record any major dependencies the project has on external factors. Examples are pending industry standards or government regulations, deliverables from other projects, third-party suppliers, or development partners. Some business assumptions and dependencies might turn into risks that the project manager must monitor regularly. Broken dependencies are a common source of project delays. Note the impact of an assumption not being true, or the impact of a broken dependency, to help stakeholders understand why it is critical.

2. Scope and limitations

When a chemist invents a new reaction that transforms one kind of chemical into another, he writes a paper that includes a "Scope and limitations" section, which describes what the reaction will and will not do. Similarly, a software project should define its scope and limitations. You need to state both what the solution being developed *is* and what it *is not*.

Many projects suffer from scope creep—rampant growth as more and more functionality gets stuffed into the product. The first step to controlling scope creep is to define the project's scope. The scope describes the concept and range of the proposed solution. The limitations itemize certain capabilities that the product will *not* include that some people might assume will be there. The scope and limitations help to establish realistic stakeholder expectations because customers sometimes request features that are too expensive or that lie outside the intended project scope.

Scope can be represented in numerous ways (see "Scope representation techniques" later in this chapter). At the highest level, scope is defined when the customer decides which business objectives to target. At a lower level, scope is defined at the level of features, user stories, use cases, or events and responses to include. Scope ultimately is defined through the set of functional requirements planned for implementation in a specific release or iteration. At each level, the scope must stay within the bounds of the level above it. For example, in-scope user requirements must map to the business objectives, and functional requirements must map to user requirements that are in scope.

Blue-sky requirements

A manager at a product development company that suffered near-catastrophic scope creep once told me ruefully, "We blue-skied the requirements too much." She meant that any idea anyone had was included in the requirements. This company had a solid product vision, but they didn't manage the scope by planning a series of releases and deferring some suggested features to later (perhaps infinitely later) releases. The team finally released an overinflated product after four years of development. It can be valuable to jot down the blue-sky requirements for future consideration. However, thoughtful scope management and an incremental development approach would have let the team ship a useful product much earlier.

2.1 Major features

List the product's major features or user capabilities, emphasizing those that distinguish it from previous or competing products. Think about how users will use the features, to ensure that the list is complete and that it does not include unnecessary features that sound interesting but don't provide customer value. Give each feature a unique and persistent label to permit tracing it to other system elements. You might include a feature tree diagram, as described later in this chapter.

2.2 Scope of initial release

Summarize the capabilities that are planned for inclusion in the initial product release. Scope is often defined in terms of features, but you can also define scope in terms of user stories, use cases, use case flows, or external events. Also describe the quality characteristics that will let the product provide the intended benefits to its various user classes. To focus the development effort and maintain a reasonable project schedule, avoid the temptation to include every feature that any potential customer might eventually want in release 1.0. Bloatware and slipped schedules are common outcomes of such insidious scope stuffing. Focus on those features that will provide the most value, at the most acceptable cost, to the broadest community, in the earliest time frame.

As an illustration, a recent project team decided that users had to be able to run their package delivery business with the first release of the software application. Version 1 didn't have to be fast, pretty, or easy to use, but it had to be reliable; this focus drove everything the team did. The initial release accomplished the basic objectives of the system. Future releases will include additional features, options, and usability aids. Be careful not to neglect nonfunctional requirements in the initial release, though. The ones that directly affect architecture are particularly critical to establish from the outset. Rearchitecting to try to fix quality deficiencies can be almost as expensive as a total rewrite. See Chapter 14, "Beyond functionality," for more about software quality attributes.

2.3 Scope of subsequent releases

If you envision a staged evolution of the product, or if you are following an iterative or incremental life cycle, build a release roadmap that indicates which functionality chunks will be deferred and the desired timing of later releases. Subsequent releases let you implement additional use cases and features, as well as enriching the capabilities of the initial ones. The farther out you look, the fuzzier these future scope statements will be and the more they will change over time. Expect to shift functionality from one planned release to another and to add unanticipated capabilities. Short release cycles provide frequent opportunities for learning based on customer feedback.

2.4 Limitations and exclusions

List any product capabilities or characteristics that a stakeholder might expect but that are not planned for inclusion in the product or in a specific release. List items that were cut from scope, so the scope decision is not forgotten. Maybe a user requested that she be able to access the system from her phone while away from her desk, but this was deemed to be out of scope. State that explicitly in this section: "The new system will not provide mobile platform support."

3. Business context

This section presents profiles of major stakeholder categories, management's priorities for the project, and a summary of some factors to consider when planning deployment of the solution.

3.1 Stakeholder profiles

Stakeholders are the people, groups, or organizations that are actively involved in a project, are affected by its outcome, or are able to influence its outcome (Smith 2000; IIBA 2009; PMI 2013). The stakeholder profiles describe different categories of customers and other key stakeholders for the project. You needn't describe every stakeholder group, such as legal staff who must check for compliance with pertinent laws on a website development project. Focus on different types of customers, target market segments, and the various user classes within those segments. Each stakeholder profile should include the following information:

- The major value or benefit that the stakeholder will receive from the product. Stakeholder value could be defined in terms of:

  - Improved productivity.

- Reduced rework and waste.

- Cost savings.

- Streamlined business processes.

- Automation of previously manual tasks.

- Ability to perform entirely new tasks.

- Compliance with pertinent standards or regulations.

- Improved usability compared to current products.

■ Their likely attitudes toward the product.

■ Major features and characteristics of interest.

■ Any known constraints that must be accommodated.

You might include a list of key stakeholders by name for each profile or an organization chart that shows the relationships among the stakeholders within the organization.

3.2 Project priorities

To enable effective decision making, the stakeholders must agree on the project's priorities. One way to approach this is to consider the five dimensions of features, quality, schedule, cost, and staff (Wiegers 1996). Each dimension fits in one of the following three categories on any given project:

■ **Constraint**   A limiting factor within which the project manager must operate

■ **Driver**   A significant success objective with limited flexibility for adjustment

■ **Degree of freedom**   A factor that the project manager has some latitude to adjust and balance against the other dimensions

The project manager's challenge is to adjust the degrees of freedom to achieve the project's success drivers within the limits imposed by the constraints. Suppose marketing suddenly demands that you release the product one month earlier than scheduled. How do you respond? Do you:

■ Defer certain requirements to a later release?

■ Shorten the planned system test cycle?

■ Demand overtime from your staff or hire contractors to accelerate development?

■ Shift resources from other projects to help out?

The project priorities drive the actions you take when such eventualities arise. Realistically, when change happens, you need to have conversations with the key stakeholders to determine the most appropriate actions to take based on the change requested. For example, marketing might want to add features or shorten a timeline, but perhaps they are willing to defer certain features in exchange. See Appendix C for an example of how to document these project priorities.

> **Important** Not all of the five dimensions can be constraints, and they cannot all be drivers. The project manager needs some degrees of freedom to be able to respond appropriately when requirements or project realities change.

3.3 Deployment considerations

Summarize the information and activities that are needed to ensure an effective deployment of the solution into its operating environment. Describe the access that users will require to use the system, such as whether the users are distributed over multiple time zones or located close to each other. State when the users in various locations need to access the system. If infrastructure changes are needed to support the software's need for capacity, network access, data storage, or data migration, describe those changes. Record any information that will be needed by people who will be preparing training or modifying business processes in conjunction with deployment of the new solution.

Scope representation techniques

The models described in this section can be used to represent project scope in various ways. You don't need to create all of these models; consider which ones provide the most useful insight for each project. The models can be included in the vision and scope document or stored elsewhere and referenced as needed.

The purpose of tools such as the context diagram, ecosystem map, feature tree, and event list is to foster clear and accurate communication among the project stakeholders. That clarity is more important than dogmatically adhering to the rules for a "correct" diagram. We strongly recommend, though, that you adopt the notations illustrated in the following examples as standards for drawing the diagrams. For example, in a context diagram, suppose you were to use a triangle to represent the system instead of a circle, and ovals rather than rectangles for external entities. Your colleagues would have difficulty reading a diagram that follows your personal preferences rather than a team standard.

Context diagrams, ecosystem maps, feature trees, and event lists are the most common ways to represent scope visually. However, other techniques are also used. Identifying affected business processes also can help define the scope boundary. Use case diagrams can depict the scope boundary between use cases and actors (see Chapter 8, "Understanding user requirements").

Context diagram

The scope description establishes the boundary and connections between the system you're developing and everything else in the universe. The *context diagram* visually illustrates this boundary. It identifies *external entities* (also called *terminators*) outside the system that interface to it in some way, as well as data, control, and material *flows* between the terminators and the system. The context diagram is the top level in a data flow diagram developed according to the principles of structured analysis (Robertson and Robertson 1994), but it's a useful model for all projects.

Figure 5-6 illustrates a portion of the context diagram for the Chemical Tracking System. The entire system is depicted as a single circle; the context diagram deliberately provides no visibility into the system's internal objects, processes, or data. The "system" inside the circle could encompass any combination of software, hardware, and human components. Therefore, it could include manual operations as part of the entire system. The external entities in the rectangles can represent user classes (Chemist, Buyer), organizations (Health and Safety Department), other systems (Training Database), or hardware devices (Bar Code Reader). The arrows on the diagram represent the flow of data (such as a request for a chemical) or physical items (such as a chemical container) between the system and its external entities.

You might expect to see chemical vendors shown as an external entity in this diagram. After all, the company will route orders to vendors for fulfillment, the vendors will send chemical containers and invoices to Contoso Pharmaceuticals, and Contoso's purchasing department will pay the vendors. However, those processes take place outside the scope of the Chemical Tracking System, as part of the operations of the purchasing and receiving departments. Their absence from the context diagram makes it clear that this system is not directly involved in placing orders with the vendors, receiving the products, or paying the bills.

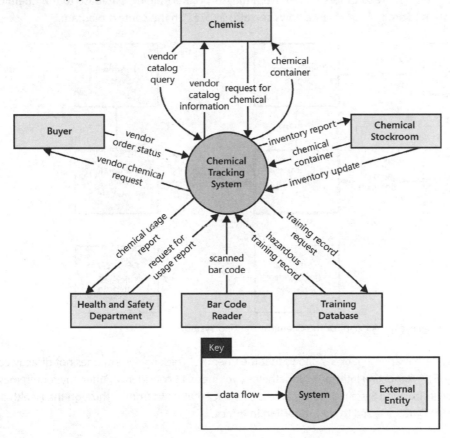

FIGURE 5-6 Partial context diagram for the Chemical Tracking System.

Ecosystem map

An *ecosystem map* shows all of the systems related to the system of interest that interact with one another and the nature of those interactions (Beatty and Chen 2012). An ecosystem map represents scope by showing all the systems that interconnect and that therefore might need to be modified to accommodate your new system. Ecosystem maps differ from context diagrams in that they show other systems that have a relationship with the system you're working on, including those without direct interfaces. You can identify the affected systems by determining which ones consume data from your system. When you reach the point that your project does not affect any additional data, you've identified the scope boundary of systems that participate in the solution.

Figure 5-7 is a partial ecosystem map for the Chemical Tracking System. The systems are all shown in boxes (such as the Purchasing System or Receiving System). In this example, the primary system we are working on is shown in a bold box (Chemical Tracking System), but if all systems have equal status in your solution, you can use the same box style for all of them. The lines show interfaces between systems (for instance, the Purchasing System interfaces to the Chemical Tracking System). Lines with arrows and labels show that major pieces of data are flowing from one system to another (for instance, "training records" are passed from the Corporate Training Database to the Chemical Tracking System). Some of these same flows can also appear on the context diagram.

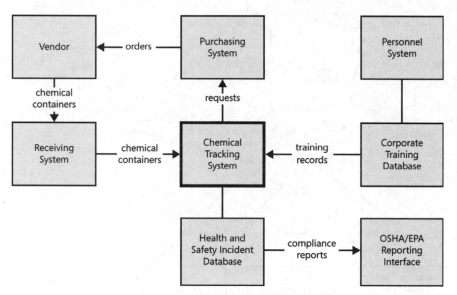

FIGURE 5-7 Partial ecosystem map for the Chemical Tracking System.

The ecosystem map in Figure 5-7 shows that the Chemical Tracking System does not directly connect to the OSHA/EPA Reporting Interface. Nonetheless, you need to consider whether any requirements in the Chemical Tracking System arise because of the data that flows from it, through the Health and Safety Incident Database, and to that reporting interface.

Feature tree

A *feature tree* is a visual depiction of the product's features organized in logical groups, hierarchically subdividing each feature into further levels of detail (Beatty and Chen 2012). The feature tree provides a concise view of all of the features planned for a project, making it an ideal model to show to executives who want a quick glance at the project scope. A feature tree can show up to three levels of features, commonly called level 1 (L1), level 2 (L2), and level 3 (L3). L2 features are subfeatures of L1 features, and L3 features are subfeatures of L2 features.

Figure 5-8 shows a partial feature tree for the Chemical Tracking System. The main branch of the tree in the middle represents the product being implemented. Each feature has its own line or "branch" coming off that central main branch. The gray boxes represent the L1 features, such as Order Chemicals and Inventory Management. The lines coming off an L1 branch are L2 features: Search and Chemical Request are subfeatures of Order Chemicals. The branches off an L2 branch are the L3 features: Local Lab Search is a subfeature of Search.

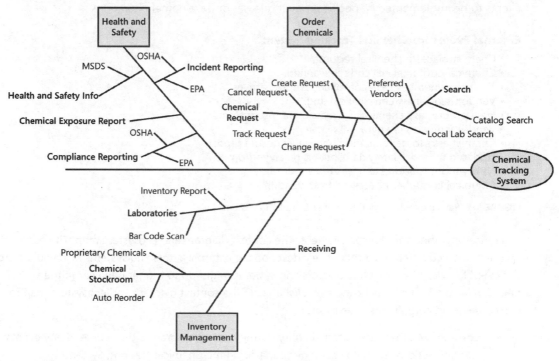

FIGURE 5-8 Partial feature tree for the Chemical Tracking System.

When planning a release or an iteration, you can define its scope by selecting a specific set of features and subfeatures to be implemented (Nejmeh and Thomas 2002; Wiegers 2006). You could implement a feature in its entirety in a specific release, or you could implement only a portion of it by choosing just certain L2 and L3 subfeatures. Future releases could enrich these rudimentary implementations by adding more L2 and L3 subfeatures until each feature is fully implemented in the final product. So the scope of a particular release consists of a defined set of L1, L2, and/or L3 features chosen from the feature tree. You can mark up a feature tree diagram to illustrate these feature allocations across releases by using colors or font variations. Alternatively, you can create a feature roadmap table that lists the subfeatures planned for each release (Wiegers 2006).

Event list

An *event list* identifies external events that could trigger behavior in the system. The event list depicts the scope boundary for the system by naming possible business events triggered by users, time-triggered (temporal) events, or signal events received from external components, such as hardware devices. The event list only names the events; the functional requirements that describe how the system responds to the events would be detailed in the SRS by using event-response tables. See Chapter 12, "A picture is worth 1024 words," for more information about event-response tables.

Figure 5-9 is a partial event list for the Chemical Tracking System. Each item in the list states what triggers the event ("Chemist" does something or the "Time to" do something arrives), as well as identifying the event action. An event list is a useful scoping tool because you can allocate certain events to be implemented in specific product releases or development iterations.

External Events for Chemical Tracking System
- Chemist places a chemical request.
- Chemical container bar code is scanned.
- Time to generate OSHA compliance report arrives.
- Vendor issues new chemical catalog.
- New proprietary chemical is accessioned into system.
- Vendor indicates chemical is backordered.
- Chemist asks to generate his chemical exposure report.
- Updated material safety datasheet is received from EPA.
- New vendor is added to preferred vendor list.
- Chemical container is received from vendor.

FIGURE 5-9 Partial event list for the Chemical Tracking System.

Notice how the event list complements the context diagram and ecosystem map. The context diagram and ecosystem map collectively describe the external actors and systems involved, whereas the event list identifies what those actors and systems might do to trigger behavior in the system being specified. You can check the event list against the context diagram and ecosystem map for correctness and completeness, as follows:

- Consider whether each external entity on the context diagram is the source of any events: "Do any actions by Chemists trigger behavior in the Chemical Tracking System?"

- Consider whether any systems in the ecosystem map lead to events for your system.

- For each event, consider whether you have corresponding external entities in the context diagram or systems in the ecosystem map: "If a chemical container can be received from a vendor, does Vendor appear in the context diagram and/or ecosystem map?"

If you find a disconnect, consider whether the model is missing an element. In this case, Vendor did not appear on the context diagram because the Chemical Tracking System doesn't interface directly to vendors. However, Vendor is included in the ecosystem map.

Keeping the scope in focus

A scope definition is a structure, not a straitjacket. The business requirements and an understanding of how customers will use the product provide valuable tools for dealing with scope change. Scope change isn't a bad thing if it helps you steer the project toward satisfying evolving customer needs. The information in the vision and scope document lets you assess whether proposed requirements are appropriate for inclusion in the project. You can modify the scope for a future iteration or for an entire project if it's done consciously, by the right people, for the right business reasons, and with understanding and acceptance of the tradeoffs.

Remember, whenever someone requests a new requirement, the analyst needs to ask, "Is this in scope?" One response might be that the proposed requirement is clearly out of scope. Perhaps it's interesting, but it should be addressed in a future release or by another project. Another possibility is that the request obviously lies within the defined project scope. You can incorporate new in-scope requirements in the current project if they are of high priority relative to the other requirements that were already committed. Including new requirements often involves making a decision to defer or cancel other planned requirements, unless you're willing to extend the project's duration.

The third possibility is that the proposed new requirement is out of scope, but it's such a good idea that the scope should be broadened to accommodate it, with corresponding changes in budget, schedule, and/or staff. That is, there's a feedback loop between the user requirements and the business requirements. This will require that you update the vision and scope document, which should have been placed under change control at the time it was baselined. Keep a record of why requirements were rejected; they have a way of reappearing. Chapter 27, "Requirements management practices," describes how to use a requirement attribute to track rejected or deferred requirements.

Using business objectives to make scoping decisions

The business objectives are the most important factor to consider when making scope decisions. Determine which proposed features or user requirements add the most value with respect to the business objectives; schedule those for the early releases. When a stakeholder wants to add functionality, consider how the suggested changes will contribute to achieving the business objectives. For example, a business objective to generate maximum revenue from a kiosk implies the early implementation of features that sell more products or services to the customer. Glitzy features that appeal to only a few technology-hungry customers and don't contribute to the primary business objective shouldn't have high priority.

If possible, quantify the contribution the feature makes towards the business objectives, so that people can make scoping decisions on the basis of facts rather than emotions (Beatty and Chen 2012). Will a specific feature contribute roughly $1,000, $100,000, or $1,000,000 toward a business objective? When an executive requests a new feature that he thought of over the weekend, you can use quantitative analysis to help determine if adding it is the right business decision.

Assessing the impact of scope changes

When the project's scope increases, the project manager usually will have to renegotiate the planned budget, resources, schedule, and/or staff. Ideally, the original schedule and resources will accommodate a certain amount of change because of thoughtfully included contingency buffers (Wiegers 2007). Otherwise, you'll need to re-plan after requirements changes are approved.

A common consequence of scope change is that completed activities must be reworked in response to the changes. Quality often suffers if the allocated resources or time are not increased when new functionality is added. Documented business requirements make it easier to manage legitimate scope growth as the marketplace or business needs change. They also help a harried project manager to justify saying "no"—or at least "not yet"—when influential people try to stuff more features into an overly constrained project.

Vision and scope on agile projects

Managing scope on an agile project, in which development is performed in a series of fixed timebox iterations, takes a different approach. The scope of each iteration consists of user stories selected from a dynamic product backlog, based on their relative priority and the estimated delivery capacity of the team for each timebox. Instead of trying to fight scope creep, the team prioritizes new requirements against existing items in the backlog and allocates them to future iterations. The number of iterations—and hence the overall project duration—still depends on the total amount of functionality to be implemented, but the scope of each iteration is controlled to ensure timely completion. Alternatively, some agile projects fix the overall project duration, yet are willing to modify the scope. The number of iterations might remain the same, but the scope addressed in remaining iterations changes according to the relative priorities of existing and newly defined user stories.

The team can define a high-level roadmap of iterations at the beginning of the project, but the user story allocation for an iteration will be performed at the beginning of each iteration. Referencing the business requirements as the team sets the scope for each iteration helps to ensure that the project delivers a product that meets the business objectives. The same strategy can be used on any project that follows a timeboxed development process (see the "Scope management and timeboxed development" sidebar).

Scope management and timeboxed development

Enrique, a project manager at Litware, Inc., had to deliver a web-enabled version of Litware's flagship portfolio-management software. It would take about two years to fully supplant the mature application, but Litware needed a web presence right away. Enrique selected a timeboxed development approach, promising to release a new version every 90 days. His marketing team carefully prioritized the product's requirements. The SRS for each quarterly release included a committed set of new and enhanced features, as well as a list of lower-priority "stretch" requirements to be implemented as time permitted. Enrique's team didn't incorporate every stretch requirement into each release, but they did ship a stable release every three months through this schedule-driven approach to scope management. Schedule and quality are normally constraints on a timeboxed project, and scope is a degree of freedom.

Although agile projects might not create a formal vision and scope document, the contents from the template in Figure 5-3 are both relevant and essential to delivering a successful product. Many agile projects conduct an upfront planning iteration (iteration zero) to define the overarching product vision and other business requirements for the project.

Business requirements need to be defined for all software projects, regardless of their development approach. The business objectives describe the expected value coming out of the project, and on an agile project, they are used to help prioritize the backlog to deliver the most business value in the earliest iterations. Success metrics should be defined so that as iterative releases go live, the success can be measured and the rest of the backlog adjusted accordingly. A vision statement describes the long-term plan for what the product will be after all iterations are complete.

Using business objectives to determine completion

How do you know when you can stop implementing functionality? Traditionally, a project manager manages the project towards completion. However, a business analyst is intimately familiar with the business objectives and can help determine when the desired value has been delivered, implying that the work is done.

If you begin with a clear vision for the solution, and if each release or iteration is scoped to deliver just a portion of the total functionality, then you will be done when you complete the preplanned iterations. The completed iterations should have led to a fully realized product vision that meets the business objectives.

However, particularly in iterative development approaches, the end point might be vague. Within each iteration, scope is defined for that iteration. As the project continues, the backlog of uncompleted work dwindles. It's not always necessary to implement the entire set of remaining functionality. It's critical to have clear business objectives so that you can move toward satisfying those objectives incrementally as information becomes available. The project is complete when the success metrics indicate that you have a good chance of meeting the business objectives. Vague business objectives will guarantee an open-ended project with no way to know when you're done. Funding sponsors don't like it because they don't know how to budget, schedule, or plan for such projects. Customers don't like it because they might receive a solution that is delivered on time and on budget but that doesn't provide the value they need. But that might just be the risk of working on products that cannot be clearly defined at the outset, unless you refine the business objectives partway through the project.

Focus on defining clear business requirements for all of your projects. Otherwise, you are just wandering about aimlessly hoping to accomplish something useful without any way to know if you're reaching your destination.

Next steps

- Ask several stakeholders for your project each to write a vision statement using the keyword template described in this chapter. See how similar the visions are. Rectify any disconnects and come up with a unified vision statement that all those stakeholders agree to.

- Whether you're near the launch of a new project or in the midst of construction, document the business requirements by using the template in Figure 5-3. Or, simply create a business objectives model, and have the rest of the team review it. This might reveal that your team doesn't share a common understanding of the project's objectives or scope. Correct that problem now; it will be even more difficult to correct if you wait. This activity will also suggest ways to modify the template to best meet the needs of your organization's projects.

- Write down the measurable business objectives for your project in a format that can be shared easily in meetings throughout the project's duration. Take it to your next requirements-related meeting and see if the team finds the reminder to be useful.

CHAPTER 6

Finding the voice of the user

Jeremy walked into the office of Ruth Gilbert, the director of the Drug Discovery Division at Contoso Pharmaceuticals. Ruth had asked the information technology team that supported Contoso's research organization to build a new application to help the research chemists accelerate their exploration for new drugs. Jeremy was assigned as the business analyst for the project. After introducing himself and discussing the project in broad terms, Jeremy said to Ruth, "I'd like to talk with some of your chemists to understand their requirements for the system. Who might be some good people to start with?"

Ruth replied, "I did that same job for five years before I became the division director three years ago. You don't really need to talk to any of my people; I can tell you everything you need to know about this project."

Jeremy was concerned. Scientific knowledge and technologies change quickly, so he wasn't sure if Ruth could adequately represent the current and future needs for users of this complex application. Perhaps there were some internal politics going on that weren't apparent and there was a good reason for Ruth to create a buffer between Jeremy and the actual users. After some discussion, though, it became clear that Ruth didn't want any of her people involved directly with the project.

"Okay," Jeremy agreed reluctantly. "Maybe I can start by doing some document analysis and bring questions I have to you. Can we set up a series of interviews for the next couple of weeks so I can understand the kinds of things you expect your scientists to be able to do with this new system?"

"Sorry, I'm swamped right now," Ruth told him. "I can give you a couple of hours in about three weeks to clarify things you're unsure about. Just go ahead and start writing the requirements. When we meet, then you can ask me any questions you still have. I hope that will let you get the ball rolling on this project."

If you share our conviction that customer involvement is a critical factor in delivering excellent software, you will ensure that the business analyst (BA) and project manager for your project will work hard to engage appropriate customer representatives from the outset. Success in software requirements, and hence in software development, depends on getting the voice of the user close to the ear of the developer. To find the voice of the user, take the following steps:

- Identify the different classes of users for your product.

- Select and work with individuals who represent each user class and other stakeholder groups.

- Agree on who the requirements decision makers are for your project.

Customer involvement is the best way to avoid the expectation gap described in Chapter 2, "Requirements from the customer's perspective," a mismatch between the product that customers expect to receive and what developers build. It's not enough simply to ask a few customers or their manager what they want once or twice and then start coding. If developers build exactly what customers initially request, they'll probably have to build it again because customers often don't know what they really need. In addition, the BAs might not be talking to the right people or asking the right questions.

The features that users present as their "wants" don't necessarily equate to the functionality they need to perform their tasks with the new product. To gain a more accurate view of user needs, the business analyst must collect a wide range of user input, analyze and clarify it, and specify just what needs to be built to let users do their jobs. The BA has the lead responsibility for recording the new system's necessary capabilities and properties and for communicating that information to other stakeholders. This is an iterative process that takes time. If you don't invest the time to achieve this shared understanding—this common vision of the intended product—the certain outcomes are rework, missed deadlines, cost overruns, and customer dissatisfaction.

User classes

People often talk about "the user" for a software system as though all users belong to a monolithic group with similar characteristics and needs. In reality, most products of any size appeal to a diversity of users with different expectations and goals. Rather than thinking of "the user" in singular, spend some time identifying the multiple user classes and their roles and privileges for your product.

Classifying users

Chapter 2 described many of the types of stakeholders that a project might have. As shown in Figure 6-1, a user class is a subset of the product's users, which is a subset of the product's customers, which is a subset of its stakeholders. An individual can belong to multiple user classes. For example, an application's administrator might also interact with it as an ordinary user at times. A product's users might differ—among other ways—in the following respects, and you can group users into a number of distinct *user classes* based on these sorts of differences:

- Their access privilege or security levels (such as ordinary user, guest user, administrator)

- The tasks they perform during their business operations

- The features they use

- The frequency with which they use the product

- Their application domain experience and computer systems expertise

- The platforms they will be using (desktop PCs, laptop PCs, tablets, smartphones, specialized devices)

- Their native language
- Whether they will interact with the system directly or indirectly

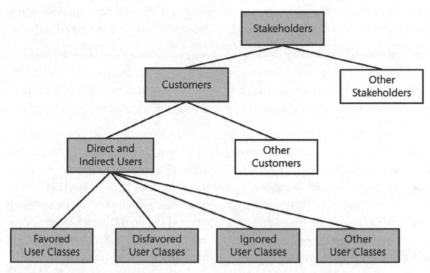

FIGURE 6-1 A hierarchy of stakeholders, customers, users, and user classes.

It's tempting to group users into classes based on their geographical location or the kind of company they work in. One company that creates software used in the banking industry initially considered distinguishing users based on whether they worked in a large commercial bank, a small commercial bank, a savings and loan institution, or a credit union. These distinctions really represent different market segments, though, not different user classes.

A better way to identify user classes is to think about the tasks that various users will perform with the system. All of those types of financial institutions will have tellers, employees who process loan applications, business bankers, and so forth. The individuals who perform such activities—whether they are job titles or simply roles—will have similar functional needs for the system across all of the financial institutions. Tellers all have to do more or less the same things, business bankers do more or less the same things, and so on. More logical user class names for a banking system therefore might include teller, loan officer, business banker, and branch manager. You might discover additional user classes by thinking of possible use cases, user stories, and process flows and who might perform them.

Certain user classes could be more important than others for a specific project. Favored user classes are those whose satisfaction is most closely aligned with achieving the project's business objectives. When resolving conflicts between requirements from different user classes or making priority decisions, favored user classes receive preferential treatment. This doesn't mean that the customers who are paying for the system (who might not be users at all) or those who have the most political clout should necessarily be favored. It's a matter of alignment with the business objectives.

Disfavored user classes are groups who aren't supposed to use the product for legal, security, or safety reasons (Gause and Lawrence 1999). You might build in features to deliberately make it hard for disfavored users to do things they aren't supposed to do. Examples include access security mechanisms, user privilege levels, antimalware features (for non-human users), and usage logging. Locking a user's account after four unsuccessful login attempts protects against access by the disfavored user class of "user impersonators," albeit at the risk of inconveniencing forgetful legitimate users. If my bank doesn't recognize the computer I'm using, it sends me an email message with a one-time access code I have to enter before I can log on. This feature was implemented because of the disfavored user class of "people who might have stolen my banking information."

You might elect to ignore still other user classes. Yes, they will use the product, but you don't specifically build it to suit them. If there are any other groups of users that are neither favored, disfavored, nor ignored, they are of equal importance in defining the product's requirements.

Each user class will have its own set of requirements for the tasks that members of the class must perform. There could be some overlap between the needs of different user classes. Tellers, business bankers, and loan officers all might have to check a bank customer's account balance, for instance. Different user classes also could have different quality expectations, such as usability, that will drive user interface design choices. New or occasional users are concerned with how easy the system is to learn. Such users like menus, graphical user interfaces, uncluttered screen displays, wizards, and help screens. As users gain experience with the system, they become more interested in efficiency. They now value keyboard shortcuts, customization options, toolbars, and scripting facilities.

> **Trap** Don't overlook indirect user classes. They won't use your application themselves, instead accessing its data or services through other applications or through reports. Your customer once removed is still your customer.

User classes need not be human beings. They could be software agents performing a service on behalf of a human user, such as bots. Software agents can scan networks for information about goods and services, assemble custom news feeds, process your incoming email, monitor physical systems and networks for problems or intrusions, or perform data mining. Internet agents that probe websites for vulnerabilities or to generate spam are a type of disfavored non-human user class. If you identify these sorts of disfavored user classes, you might specify certain requirements not to meet their needs but rather to thwart them. For instance, website tools such as CAPTCHA that validate whether a user is a human being attempt to block such disruptive access by "users" you want to keep out.

Remember, users are a subset of customers, which are a subset of stakeholders. You'll need to consider a much broader range of potential sources of requirements than just direct and indirect user classes. For instance, even though the development team members aren't end users of the system they're building, you need their input on internal quality attributes such as efficiency, modifiability, portability, and reusability, as described in Chapter 14, "Beyond functionality." One company found that every installation of their product was an expensive nightmare until they introduced an "installer" user class so they could focus on requirements such as the development of a customization architecture for their product. Look well beyond the obvious end users when you're trying to identify stakeholders whose requirements input is necessary.

Identifying your user classes

Identify and characterize the different user classes for your product early in the project so you can elicit requirements from representatives of each important class. A useful technique for this is a collaboration pattern developed by Ellen Gottesdiener called "expand then contract" (Gottesdiener 2002). Start by asking the project sponsor who he expects to use the system. Then brainstorm as many user classes as you can think of. Don't get nervous if there are dozens at this stage; you'll condense and categorize them later. It's important not to overlook a user class, which can lead to problems later when someone complains that the delivered solution doesn't meet her needs. Next, look for groups with similar needs that you can either combine or treat as a major user class with several subclasses. Try to pare the list down to about 15 or fewer distinct user classes.

One company that developed a specialized product for about 65 corporate customers initially regarded each company as a distinct user with unique needs. Grouping their customers into just six user classes greatly simplified their requirements challenges. Donald Gause and Gerald Weinberg (1989) offer much advice about casting a wide net to identify potential users, pruning the user list, and seeking specific users to participate in the project.

Various analysis models can help you identify user classes. The external entities shown outside your system on a context diagram (see Chapter 5, "Establishing the business requirements") are candidates for user classes. A corporate organization chart can also help you discover potential users and other stakeholders (Beatty and Chen 2012). Figure 6-2 illustrates a portion of the organization chart for Contoso Pharmaceuticals. Nearly all of the potential users for the system are likely to be found somewhere in this chart. While performing stakeholder and user analysis, study the organization chart to look for:

- Departments that participate in the business process.

- Departments that are affected by the business process.

- Departments or role names in which either direct or indirect users might be found.

- User classes that span multiple departments.

- Departments that might have an interface to external stakeholders outside the company.

Organization chart analysis reduces the likelihood that you will overlook an important class of users within that organization. It shows you where to seek potential representatives for specific user classes, as well as helping determine who the key requirements decision makers might be. You might find multiple user classes with diverse needs within a single department. Conversely, recognizing the same user class in multiple departments can simplify requirements elicitation. Studying the organization chart helps you judge how many user representatives you'll need to work with to feel confident that you thoroughly understand the broad user community's needs. Also try to understand what type of information the users from each department might supply based on their role in the organization and their department's perspective on the project.

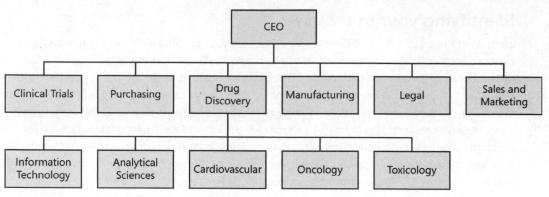

FIGURE 6-2 A portion of the organization chart for Contoso Pharmaceuticals.

Document the user classes and their characteristics, responsibilities, and physical locations in the software requirements specification (SRS) or in a requirements plan for your project. Check that information against any information you might already have about stakeholder profiles in the vision and scope document to avoid conflicts and duplication. Include all pertinent information you have about each user class, such as its relative or absolute size and which classes are favored. This will help the team prioritize change requests and conduct impact assessments later on. Estimates of the volume and type of system transactions help the testers develop a usage profile for the system so that they can plan their verification activities. The project manager and business analyst of the Chemical Tracking System discussed in earlier chapters identified the user classes and characteristics shown in Table 6-1.

TABLE 6-1 User classes for the Chemical Tracking System

Name	Number	Description
Chemists (favored)	Approximately 1,000 located in 6 buildings	Chemists will request chemicals from vendors and from the chemical stockroom. Each chemist will use the system several times per day, mainly for requesting chemicals and tracking chemical containers into and out of the laboratory. The chemists need to search vendor catalogs for specific chemical structures imported from the tools they use for drawing structures.
Buyers	5	Buyers in the purchasing department process chemical requests. They place and track orders with external vendors. They know little about chemistry and need simple query facilities to search vendor catalogs. Buyers will not use the system's container-tracking features. Each buyer will use the system an average of 25 times per day.
Chemical stockroom staff	6 technicians, 1 supervisor	The chemical stockroom staff manages an inventory of more than 500,000 chemical containers. They will supply containers from three stockrooms, request new chemicals from vendors, and track the movement of all containers into and out of the stockrooms. They are the only users of the inventory-reporting feature. Because of their high transaction volume, features that are used only by the chemical stockroom staff must be automated and efficient.
Health and Safety Department staff (favored)	1 manager	The Health and Safety Department staff will use the system only to generate predefined quarterly reports that comply with federal and state chemical usage and disposal reporting regulations. The Health and Safety Department manager will request changes in the reports periodically as government regulations change. These report changes are of the highest priority, and implementation will be time critical.

Consider building a catalog of user classes that recur across multiple applications. Defining user classes at the enterprise level lets you reuse those user class descriptions in future projects. The next system you build might serve the needs of some new user classes, but it probably will also be used by user classes from your earlier systems. If you do include the user-class descriptions in the project's SRS, you can incorporate entries from the reusable user-class catalog by reference and just write descriptions of any new groups that are specific to that application.

User personas

To help bring your user classes to life, consider creating a *persona* for each one, a description of a representative member of the user class (Cooper 2004; Leffingwell 2011). A persona is a description of a hypothetical, generic person who serves as a stand-in for a group of users having similar characteristics and needs. You can use personas to help you understand the requirements and to design the user experience to best meet the needs of specific user communities.

A persona can serve as a placeholder when the BA doesn't have an actual user representative at hand. Rather than having progress come to a halt, the BA can envision a persona performing a particular task or try to assess what the persona's preferences would be, thereby drafting a requirements starting point to be confirmed when an actual user is available. Persona details for a commercial customer include social and demographic characteristics and behaviors, preferences, annoyances, and similar information. Make sure the personas you create truly are representative of their user class, based on market, demographic, and ethnographic research.

Here's an example of a persona for one user class on the Chemical Tracking System:

> Fred, 41, has been a chemist at Contoso Pharmaceuticals since he received his Ph.D. 14 years ago. He doesn't have much patience with computers. Fred usually works on two projects at a time in related chemical areas. His lab contains approximately 300 bottles of chemicals and gas cylinders. On an average day, he'll need four new chemicals from the stockroom. Two of these will be commercial chemicals in stock, one will need to be ordered, and one will come from the supply of proprietary Contoso chemical samples. On occasion, Fred will need a hazardous chemical that requires special training for safe handling. When he buys a chemical for the first time, Fred wants the material safety data sheet emailed to him automatically. Each year, Fred will synthesize about 20 new proprietary chemicals to go into the stockroom. Fred wants a report of his chemical usage for the previous month to be generated automatically and sent to him by email so that he can monitor his chemical exposure.

As the business analyst explores the chemists' requirements, he can think about Fred as the archetype of this user class and ask himself, "What would Fred need to do?" Working with a persona makes the requirements thought process more tangible than if you simply contemplate what a whole faceless group of people might want. Some people choose a random human face of the appropriate gender to make a persona seem even more real.

Dean Leffingwell (2011) suggests that you design the system to make it easy for the individual described in your persona to use the application. That is, you focus on meeting that one (imaginary) person's needs. Provided you've created a persona that accurately represents the user class, this should help you do a good job of satisfying the needs and expectations of the whole class. As one colleague related, "On a project for servicing coin-operated vending machines, I introduced Dolly the Serviceperson and Ralph the Warehouse Supervisor. We wrote scenarios for them and they became part of the project team—virtually."

Connecting with user representatives

Every kind of project—corporate information systems, commercial applications, embedded systems, websites, contracted software—needs suitable representatives to provide the voice of the user. These users should be involved throughout the development life cycle, not just in an isolated requirements phase at the beginning of the project. Each user class needs someone to speak for it.

It's easiest to gain access to actual users when you're developing applications for deployment within your own company. If you're developing commercial software, you might engage people from your beta-testing or early-release sites to provide requirements input much earlier in the development process. (See the "External product champions" section later in this chapter). Consider setting up focus groups of current users of your products or your competitors' products. Instead of just guessing at what your users might want, ask some of them.

One company asked a focus group to perform certain tasks with various digital cameras and computers. The results indicated that the company's camera software took too long to perform the most common operation because of a design decision that was made to accommodate less likely scenarios as well. The company changed their next camera to reduce customer complaints about speed.

Be sure that the focus group represents the kinds of users whose needs should drive your product development. Include both expert and less experienced customers. If your focus group represents only early adopters or blue-sky thinkers, you might end up with many sophisticated and technically difficult requirements that few customers find useful.

Figure 6-3 illustrates some typical communication pathways that connect the voice of the user to the ear of the developer. One study indicated that employing more kinds of communication links and more direct links between developers and users led to more successful projects (Keil and Carmel 1995). The most direct communication occurs when developers can talk to appropriate users themselves, which means that the developer is also performing the business analyst role. This can work on very small projects, provided the developer involved has the appropriate BA skills, but it doesn't scale up to large projects with thousands of potential users and dozens of developers.

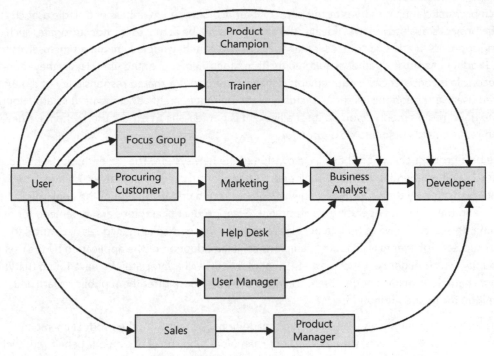

FIGURE 6-3 Some possible communication pathways between the user and the developer.

As in the children's game "Telephone," intervening layers between the user and the developer increase the chance of miscommunication and delay transmission. Some of these intervening layers add value, though, as when a skilled BA works with users or other participants to collect, evaluate, refine, and organize their input. Recognize the risks that you assume by using marketing staff, product managers, subject matter experts, or others as surrogates for the actual voice of the user. Despite the obstacles to—and the cost of—optimizing user representation, your product and your customers will suffer if you don't talk to the people who can provide the best information.

The product champion

Many years ago I worked in a small software development group that supported the scientific research activities at a major corporation. Each of our projects included a few key members of our user community to provide the requirements. We called these people *product champions* (Wiegers 1996). The product champion approach provides an effective way to structure that all-important customer-development collaborative partnership discussed in Chapter 2.

Each product champion serves as the primary interface between members of a single user class and the project's business analyst. Ideally, the champions will be actual users, not surrogates such as funding sponsors, marketing staff, user managers, or software developers imagining themselves to be users. Product champions gather requirements from other members of the user classes they represent and reconcile inconsistencies. Requirements development is thus a shared responsibility of the BA and selected users, although the BA should actually write the requirements documents. It's hard enough to write good requirements if you do it for a living; it is not realistic to expect users who have never written requirements before to do a good job.

The best product champions have a clear vision of the new system. They're enthusiastic because they see how it will benefit them and their peers. Champions should be effective communicators who are respected by their colleagues. They need a thorough understanding of the application domain and the solution's operating environment. Great product champions are in demand for other assignments, so you'll have to build a persuasive case for why particular individuals are critical to project success. For example, product champions can lead adoption of the application by the user community, which might be a success metric that managers will appreciate. We have found that good product champions made a huge difference in our projects, so we offer them public reward and recognition for their contributions.

Our software development teams enjoyed an additional benefit from the product champion approach. On several projects, we had excellent champions who spoke out on our behalf with their colleagues when the customers wondered why the software wasn't done yet. "Don't worry about it," the champions told their peers and their managers. "I understand and agree with the software team's approach to software engineering. The time we're spending on requirements will help us get the system we really need and will save time in the long run." Such collaboration helps break down the tension that can arise between customers and development teams.

The product champion approach works best if each champion is fully empowered to make binding decisions on behalf of the user class he represents. If a champion's decisions are routinely overruled by others, his time and goodwill are being wasted. However, the champions must remember that they are not the sole customers. Problems arise when the individual filling this critical liaison role doesn't adequately communicate with his peers and presents only his own wishes and ideas.

External product champions

When developing commercial software, it can be difficult to find product champions from outside your company. Companies that develop commercial products sometimes rely on internal subject matter experts or outside consultants to serve as surrogates for actual users, who might be unknown or difficult to engage. If you have a close working relationship with some major corporate customers, they might welcome the opportunity to participate in requirements elicitation. You might give external product champions economic incentives for their participation. Consider offering them discounts on the product or paying for the time they spend working with you on requirements. You still face the challenge of how to avoid hearing only the champions' requirements and overlooking the needs of other stakeholders. If you have a diverse customer base, first identify core requirements that are common to all customers. Then define additional requirements that are specific to individual corporate customers, market segments, or user classes.

Another alternative is to hire a suitable product champion who has the right background. One company that developed a retail point-of-sale and back-office system for a particular industry hired three store managers to serve as full-time product champions. As another example, my longtime family doctor, Art, left his medical practice to become the voice-of-the-physician at a medical software company. Art's new employer believed that it was worth the expense to hire a doctor to help the company build software that other doctors would accept. A third company hired several former employees from one of their major customers. These people provided valuable domain expertise as well as insight into the politics of the customer organization. To illustrate an alternative engagement model, one company had several corporate customers that used their invoicing systems extensively. Rather than bringing in product champions from the customers, the developing company sent BAs to the customer sites. Customers willingly dedicated some of their staff time to helping the BAs get the right requirements for the new invoicing system.

Anytime the product champion is a former or simulated user, watch out for disconnects between the champion's perceptions and the current needs of real users. Some domains change rapidly, whereas others are more stable. Regardless, if people aren't operating in the role anymore, they simply might have forgotten the intricacies of the daily job. The essential question is whether the product champion, no matter what her background or current job, can accurately represent the needs of today's real users.

Product champion expectations

To help the product champions succeed, document what you expect your champions to do. These written expectations can help you build a case for specific individuals to fill this critical role. Table 6-2 identifies some activities that product champions might perform (Wiegers 1996). Not every champion will do all of these; use this table as a starting point to negotiate each champion's responsibilities.

TABLE 6-2 Possible product champion activities

Category	Activities
Planning	<ul><li>Refine the scope and limitations of the product.</li><li>Identify other systems with which to interact.</li><li>Evaluate the impact of the new system on business operations.</li><li>Define a transition path from current applications or manual operations.</li><li>Identify relevant standards and certification requirements.</li></ul>
Requirements	<ul><li>Collect input on requirements from other users.</li><li>Develop usage scenarios, use cases, and user stories.</li><li>Resolve conflicts between proposed requirements within the user class.</li><li>Define implementation priorities.</li><li>Provide input regarding performance and other quality requirements.</li><li>Evaluate prototypes.</li><li>Work with other decision makers to resolve conflicts among requirements from different stakeholders.</li><li>Provide specialized algorithms.</li></ul>

Category	Activities
Validation and verification	■ Review requirements specifications. ■ Define acceptance criteria. ■ Develop user acceptance tests from usage scenarios. ■ Provide test data sets from the business. ■ Perform beta testing or user acceptance testing.
User aids	■ Write portions of user documentation and help text. ■ Contribute to training materials or tutorials. ■ Demonstrate the system to peers.
Change management	■ Evaluate and prioritize defect corrections and enhancement requests. ■ Dynamically adjust the scope of future releases or iterations. ■ Evaluate the impact of proposed changes on users and business processes. ■ Participate in making change decisions.

Multiple product champions

One person can rarely describe the needs for all users of an application. The Chemical Tracking System had four major user classes, so it needed four product champions selected from the internal user community at Contoso Pharmaceuticals. Figure 6-4 illustrates how the project manager set up a team of BAs and product champions to elicit the right requirements from the right sources. These champions were not assigned full time, but each one spent several hours per week working on the project. Three BAs worked with the four product champions to elicit, analyze, and document their requirements. (One BA worked with two product champions because the Buyer and the Health and Safety Department user classes were small and had few requirements.) One of the BAs assembled all the input into a unified SRS.

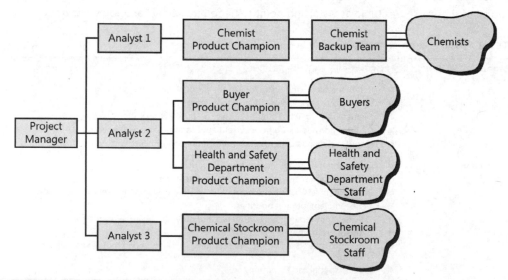

FIGURE 6-4 Product champion model for the Chemical Tracking System.

We didn't expect a single person to provide all the diverse requirements for the hundreds of chemists at Contoso. Don, the product champion for the Chemist user class, assembled a backup team of five chemists from other parts of the company. They represented subclasses within the broad Chemist user class. This hierarchical approach engaged additional users in requirements development while avoiding the expense of massive workshops or dozens of individual interviews. Don always strove for consensus. However, he willingly made the necessary decisions when agreement wasn't achieved so the project could move ahead. No backup team was necessary when the user class was small enough or cohesive enough that one individual truly could represent the group's needs.[1]

The voiceless user class

A business analyst at Humongous Insurance was delighted that an influential user, Rebecca, agreed to serve as product champion for the new claims processing system. Rebecca had many ideas about the system features and user interface design. Thrilled to have the guidance of an expert, the development team happily complied with her requests. After delivery, though, they were shocked to receive many complaints about how hard the system was to use.

Rebecca was a power user. She specified usability requirements that were great for experts, but the 90 percent of users who *weren't* experts found the system unintuitive and difficult to learn. The BA didn't recognize that the claims processing system had at least two user classes. The large group of non–power users was disenfranchised in the requirements and user interface design processes. Humongous paid the price in an expensive redesign. The BA should have engaged at least one more product champion to represent the large class of nonexpert users.

Selling the product champion idea

Expect to encounter resistance when you propose the idea of having product champions on your projects. "The users are too busy." "Management wants to make the decisions." "They'll slow us down." "We can't afford it." "They'll run amok and scope will explode." "I don't know what I'm supposed to do as a product champion." Some users won't want to cooperate on a project that will make them change how they work or might even threaten their jobs. Managers are sometimes reluctant to delegate authority for requirements to ordinary users.

Separating business requirements from user requirements alleviates some of these discomforts. As an actual user, the product champion makes decisions at the user requirements level within the scope boundaries imposed by the business requirements. The management sponsor retains the authority to make decisions that affect the product vision, project scope, business-related priorities, schedule, or budget. Documenting and negotiating each product champion's role and responsibilities give candidate champions a comfort level about what they're being asked to do. Remind management that a product champion is a key contributor who can help the project achieve its business objectives.

---

[1] There's an interesting coda to this story. Years after I worked on this project, a man in a class I was teaching said he had worked at the company that Contoso Pharmaceuticals had contracted to build the Chemical Tracking System. The developers found that the requirements specification we created using this product champion model provided a solid foundation for the development work. The system was delivered successfully and was used at Contoso for many years.

If you encounter resistance, point out that insufficient user involvement is a leading cause of software project failure. Remind the protesters of problems they've experienced on previous projects that trace back to inadequate user input. Every organization has horror stories of new systems that didn't satisfy user needs or failed to meet unstated usability or performance expectations. You can't afford to rebuild or discard systems that don't measure up because no one understood the requirements. Product champions provide one way to get that all-important customer input in a timely way, not at the end of the project when customers are disappointed and developers are tired.

Product champion traps to avoid

The product champion model has succeeded in many environments. It works only when the product champions understand and sign up for their responsibilities, have the authority to make decisions at the user requirements level, and have time available to do the job. Watch out for the following potential problems:

- Managers override the decisions that a qualified and duly authorized product champion makes. Perhaps a manager has a wild new idea at the last minute, or thinks he knows what the users need. This behavior often results in dissatisfied users and frustrated product champions who feel that management doesn't trust them.

- A product champion who forgets that he is representing other customers and presents only his own requirements won't do a good job. He might be happy with the outcome, but others likely won't be.

- A product champion who lacks a clear vision of the new system might defer decisions to the BA. If all of the BA's ideas are fine with the champion, the champion isn't providing much help.

- A senior user might nominate a less experienced user as champion because she doesn't have time to do the job herself. This can lead to backseat driving from the senior user who still wishes to strongly influence the project's direction.

Beware of users who purport to speak for a user class to which they do not belong. Rarely, an individual might actively try to block the BA from working with the ideal contacts for some reason. On the Chemical Tracking System, the product champion for the chemical stockroom staff—herself a former chemist—initially insisted on providing what she thought were the needs of the chemist user class. Unfortunately, her input about current chemist needs wasn't accurate. It was difficult to convince her that this wasn't her job, but the BA didn't let her intimidate him. The project manager lined up a separate product champion for the chemists, who did a great job of collecting, evaluating, and relaying that community's requirements.

User representation on agile projects

Frequent conversations between project team members and appropriate customers are the most effective way to resolve many requirements issues and to flesh out requirements specifics when they are needed. Written documentation, however detailed, is an incomplete substitute for these ongoing communications. A fundamental tenet of Extreme Programming, one of the early agile development methods, is the presence of a full-time, on-site customer for these discussions (Jeffries, Anderson, and Hendrickson, 2001).

Some agile development methods include a single representative of stakeholders called a *product owner* in the team to serve as the voice of the customer (Schwaber 2004; Cohn 2010; Leffingwell 2011). The product owner defines the product's vision and is responsible for developing and prioritizing the contents of the product backlog. (The *backlog* is the prioritized list of user stories—requirements—for the product and their allocation to upcoming iterations, called sprints in the agile development method called Scrum.) The product owner therefore spans all three levels of requirements: business, user, and functional. He essentially straddles the product champion and business analyst functions, representing the customer, defining product features, prioritizing them, and so forth. Ultimately, someone does have to make decisions about exactly what capabilities to deliver in the product and when. In Scrum, that's the product owner's responsibility.

The ideal state of having a single product owner isn't always practical. We know of one company that was implementing a package solution to run their insurance business. The organization was too big and complex to have one person who understood everything in enough detail to make all decisions about the implementation. Instead, the customers selected a product owner from each department to own the priorities for the functionality used by that department. The company's CIO served as the lead product owner. The CIO understood the entire product vision, so he could ensure that the departments were on track to deliver that vision. He had responsibility for decision making when there were conflicts between department-level product owners.

The premises of the on-site customer and close customer collaboration with developers that agile methods espouse certainly are sound. In fact, we feel strongly that *all* development projects warrant this emphasis on user involvement. As you have seen, though, all but the smallest projects have multiple user classes, as well as numerous additional stakeholders whose interests must be represented. In many cases it's not realistic to expect a single individual to be able to adequately understand and describe the needs of all relevant user classes, nor to make all the decisions associated with product definition. Particularly with internal corporate projects, it will generally work better to use a representative structure like the product champion model to ensure adequate user engagement.

The product owner and product champion schemes are not mutually exclusive. If the product owner is functioning in the role of a business analyst, rather than as a stakeholder representative himself, he could set up a structure with one or more product champions to see that the most appropriate sources provide input. Alternatively, the product owner could collaborate with one or more business analysts, who then work with stakeholders to understand their requirements. The product owner would then serve as the ultimate decision maker.

"On-sight" customer

I once wrote programs for a research scientist who sat about 10 feet from my desk. John could provide instantaneous answers to my questions, provide feedback on user interface designs, and clarify our informally written requirements. One day John moved to a new office, around the corner on the same floor of the same building, about 100 feet away. I perceived an immediate drop in my programming productivity because of the cycle time delay in getting John's input. I spent more time fixing problems because sometimes I went down the wrong path before I could get a course correction. There's no substitute for having the right customers continuously available to the developers both on-site and "on-sight." Beware, though, of too-frequent interruptions that make it hard for people to refocus their attention on their work. It can take up to 15 minutes to reimmerse yourself into the highly productive, focused state of mind called *flow* (DeMarco and Lister 1999).

An on-site customer doesn't guarantee the desired outcome. My colleague Chris, a project manager, established a development team environment with minimal physical barriers and engaged two product champions. Chris offered this report: "While the close proximity seems to work for the development team, the results with product champions have been mixed. One sat in our midst and still managed to avoid us all. The new champion does a fine job of interacting with the developers and has truly enabled the rapid development of software." There is no substitute for having the right people, in the right role, in the right place, with the right attitude.

Resolving conflicting requirements

Someone must resolve conflicting requirements from different user classes, reconcile inconsistencies, and arbitrate questions of scope that arise. The product champions or product owner can handle this in many, but likely not all, cases. Early in the project, determine who the decision makers will be for requirements issues, as discussed in Chapter 2. If it's not clear who is responsible for making these decisions or if the authorized individuals abdicate their responsibilities, the decisions will fall to the developers or analysts by default. Most of them don't have the necessary knowledge and perspective to make the best business decisions, though. Analysts sometimes defer to the loudest voice they hear or to the person highest on the food chain. Though understandable, this is not the best strategy. Decisions should be made as low in the organization's hierarchy as possible by well-informed people who are close to the issues.

Table 6-3 identifies some requirements conflicts that can arise on projects and suggests ways to handle them. The project's leaders need to determine who will decide what to do when such situations arise, who will make the call if agreement is not reached, and to whom significant issues must be escalated when necessary.

TABLE 6-3 Suggestions for resolving requirements disputes

Disagreement between	How to resolve
Individual users	Product champion or product owner decides
User classes	Favored user class gets preference
Market segments	Segment with greatest impact on business success gets preference
Corporate customers	Business objectives dictate direction
Users and user managers	Product owner or product champion for the user class decides
Development and customers	Customers get preference, but in alignment with business objectives
Development and marketing	Marketing gets preference

> **Trap** Don't justify doing whatever any customer demands because "The customer is always right." We all know the customer is *not* always right (Wiegers 2011). Sometimes, a customer is unreasonable, uninformed, or in a bad mood. The customer always has a point, though, and the software team must understand and respect that point.

These negotiations don't always turn out the way the analyst might hope. Certain customers might reject all attempts to consider reasonable alternatives and other points of view. We've seen cases where marketing never said no to a customer request, no matter how infeasible or expensive. The team needs to decide who will be making decisions on the project's requirements before they confront these types of issues. Otherwise, indecision and the revisiting of previous decisions can stall the project in endless wrangling. If you're a BA caught in this dilemma, rely on your organizational structure and processes to work through the disagreements. But, as we've cautioned before, there aren't any easy solutions if you're working with truly unreasonable people.

Next steps

- Relate Figure 6-3 to the way you hear the voice of the user in your own environment. Do you encounter any problems with your current communication links? Identify the shortest and most effective communication paths that you can use to elicit user requirements in the future.

- Identify the different user classes for your project. Which ones are favored? Which, if any, are disfavored? Who would make a good product champion for each important user class? Even if the project is already underway, the team likely would benefit from having product champions involved.

- Starting with Table 6-2, define the activities you would like your product champions to perform. Negotiate the specific contributions with each candidate product champion and his or her manager.

- Determine who the decision makers are for requirements issues on your project. How well does your current decision-making approach work? Where does it break down? Are the right people making decisions? If not, who should be doing it? Suggest processes that the decision makers should use for reaching agreement on requirements issues.

CHAPTER 7

Requirements elicitation

"Good morning, Maria. I'm Phil, the business analyst for the new employee information system we're going to build for you. Thanks for agreeing to be the product champion for this project. Your input will help us a lot. So, can you tell me what you want?"

"Hmmm, what do I want?" mused Maria. "I hardly know where to start. The new system should be a lot faster than the old one. And you know how the old system crashes if an employee has a really long name and we have to call the help desk and ask them to enter the name for us? The new system should take long names without crashing. Also, a new law says we can't use Social Security numbers for employee IDs anymore, so we'll have to change all of the IDs when the new system goes in. Oh, yes, it'd be great if I could get a report of how many hours of training each employee has had so far this year."

Phil dutifully wrote down everything Maria said, but his head was spinning. Maria's desires were so scattered that he wasn't sure he was getting all her requirements. He had no idea if Maria's needs aligned with the project's business objectives. And he didn't know exactly what to do with all these bits of information. Phil wasn't sure what to ask next.

The heart of requirements development is *elicitation*, the process of identifying the needs and constraints of the various stakeholders for a software system. Elicitation is not the same as "gathering requirements." Nor is it a simple matter of transcribing exactly what users say. Elicitation is a collaborative and analytical process that includes activities to collect, discover, extract, and define requirements. Elicitation is used to discover business, user, functional, and nonfunctional requirements, along with other types of information. Requirements elicitation is perhaps the most challenging, critical, error-prone, and communication-intensive aspect of software development.

Engaging users in the elicitation process is a way to gain support and buy-in for the project. If you're the business analyst, try to understand the thought processes behind the requirements the users state. Walk through the processes that users follow to make decisions about their work, and extract the underlying logic. Make sure that everyone understands why the system must perform certain functions. Look for proposed requirements that reflect obsolete or ineffective business processes or rules that should *not* be incorporated into a new system.

The BA must create an environment conducive to a thorough exploration of the product being specified. To facilitate clear communication, use the vocabulary of the business domain instead of forcing customers to understand technical jargon. Record significant application domain terms in a glossary, rather than assuming that all participants share the same definitions. Customers must understand that a discussion about possible functionality is not a commitment to include it in the product. Brainstorming and imagining the possibilities is a separate matter from analyzing priorities, feasibility, and the constraining realities. It's never too early for stakeholders to prioritize their blue-sky wish lists to avoid defining an enormous project that never delivers anything useful.

The output of requirements development is a common understanding of the needs held by the diverse project stakeholders. When the developers understand those needs, they can explore alternative solutions to address them. Elicitation participants should resist the temptation to design the system until they understand the problem. Otherwise, they can expect to do considerable design rework as the requirements become better defined. Emphasizing user tasks rather than user interfaces, and focusing on true needs more than on expressed desires, help keep the team from being sidetracked by prematurely specifying design details.

As Figure 7-1 shows, the nature of requirements development is cyclic. You will do some elicitation, study what you learned, write some requirements, perhaps determine that you are missing some information, perform additional elicitation, and so forth. Don't expect to just hold a couple of elicitation workshops and then declare victory and move on.

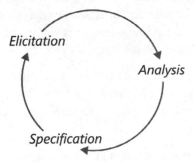

Elicitation

Analysis

Specification

FIGURE 7-1 The cyclic nature of requirements elicitation, analysis, and specification.

This chapter describes a variety of effective elicitation techniques, including when to use each one, as well as tips and challenges for each. The rest of the chapter describes the overall elicitation process, from planning elicitation activities to organizing the session outputs. Later in the chapter, we offer cautions about a few traps to watch out for during elicitation, and specific suggestions for identifying missing requirements. Figure 7-2 depicts the activities for a single requirements elicitation session. Before we walk through this process, though, let's explore some of the requirements elicitation techniques you might find valuable.

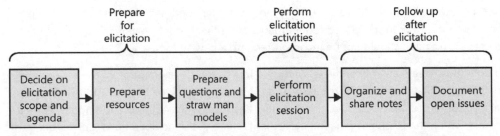

FIGURE 7-2 Activities for a single requirements elicitation session.

Requirements elicitation techniques

Numerous elicitation techniques can be employed on software projects. In fact, no project team should expect to use only one elicitation technique. There are always many types of information to be discovered, and different stakeholders will prefer different approaches. One user might be able to clearly articulate how he uses the system, whereas you might need to observe another performing her job to reach the same level of understanding.

Elicitation techniques include both facilitated activities, in which you interact with stakeholders to elicit requirements, and independent activities, in which you work on your own to discover information. Facilitated activities primarily focus on discovering business and user requirements. Working directly with users is necessary because user requirements encompass the tasks that users need to accomplish with the system. To elicit business requirements, you will need to work with people such as the project sponsor. The independent elicitation techniques supplement requirements that users present and reveal needed functionality that end users might not be aware of. Most projects will use a combination of both facilitated and independent elicitation activities. Each technique offers a different exploration of the requirements or might even reveal completely different requirements. The following sections describe several techniques commonly used to elicit requirements.

Interviews

The most obvious way to find out what the users of a software system need is to ask them. Interviews are a traditional source of requirements input for both commercial products and information systems, across all software development approaches. Most BAs will facilitate some form of individual or small-group interviews to elicit requirements on their projects. Agile projects make extensive use of interviews as a mechanism to get direct user involvement. Interviews are easier to schedule and lead than large-group activities such as requirements workshops.

If you are new to an application domain, interviews with experts can help you get up to speed quickly. This will allow you to prepare draft requirements and models to use in other interviews or in workshops. If you can establish rapport with the interviewees, they will feel safer when sharing their thoughts one-on-one or in a small group than in a larger workshop, particularly about touchy topics. It's also easier to get user buy-in about participating in the project or reviewing existing requirements during a one-on-one or small-group interview than in a large group setting. Interviews are appropriate for eliciting business requirements from executives who do not have a lot of time to meet.

For guidance on how to conduct user interviews, see Ian Alexander and Ljerka Beus-Dukic (2009) and Howard Podeswa (2009). A few suggestions for conducting interviews follow. These are useful tips for conducting elicitation workshops as well.

Establish rapport   To begin an interview, introduce yourself if the attendees don't already know you, review the agenda, remind attendees of the session objectives, and address any preliminary questions or concerns attendees have.

Stay in scope   As with any elicitation session, keep the discussion focused on its objective. Even when you are talking with just one person or a small group, there's a chance the interview will go off topic.

Prepare questions and straw man models ahead of time   Prepare for interviews by drafting any materials you can beforehand, such as a list of questions to guide the conversation. Draft materials will give your users a starting point to think from. People can often critique content more easily than they can create it. Preparing questions and drafting straw man models are described further in the "Preparing for elicitation" section later in this chapter.

Suggest ideas   Rather than simply transcribing what customers say, a creative BA proposes ideas and alternatives during elicitation. Sometimes users don't realize the capabilities developers can provide; they might get excited when you suggest functionality that will make the system especially valuable. When users truly can't express what they need, perhaps you can watch them work and suggest ways to automate portions of the job (see the "Observations" section later in this chapter). BAs can think outside the mental box that limits people who are too close to the problem domain.

Listen actively   Practice the techniques of active listening (leaning forward, showing patience, giving verbal feedback, and inquiring when something is unclear) and paraphrasing (restating the main idea of a speaker's message to show your understanding of that message).

Workshops

Workshops encourage stakeholder collaboration in defining requirements. Ellen Gottesdiener (2002) defines a requirements workshop as "a structured meeting in which a carefully selected group of stakeholders and content experts work together to define, create, refine, and reach closure on deliverables (such as models and documents) that represent user requirements." Workshops are facilitated sessions with multiple stakeholders and formal roles, such as a facilitator and a scribe. Workshops often include several types of stakeholders, from users to developers to testers. They are used to elicit requirements from multiple stakeholders concurrently. Working in a group is more effective for resolving disagreements than is talking to people individually. Also, workshops are helpful when quick elicitation turnaround is needed because of schedule constraints.

According to one authority, "Facilitation is the art of leading people through processes toward agreed-upon objectives in a manner that encourages participation, ownership, and productivity from all involved" (Sibbet 1994). The facilitator plays a critical role in planning the workshop, selecting participants, and guiding them to a successful outcome. Business analysts frequently facilitate elicitation workshops. When a team is getting started with new approaches to requirements elicitation, consider having an outside facilitator or a second BA facilitate the initial workshops. This way the lead BA can devote his full attention to the discussion. If the sole BA is also acting as facilitator, she needs to be mindful of when she is speaking as a facilitator and when she is participating in the discussion. A scribe assists the facilitator by capturing the points that come up during the discussion. It's extremely challenging to facilitate, scribe, and participate simultaneously and do a good job on all three.

Workshops can be resource intensive, sometimes requiring numerous participants for several days at a time. They must be well planned to avoid wasting time. Minimize wasted time by coming into a workshop with drafts of materials prepared ahead of time. For example, you might draft use cases that can be reviewed as a group rather than having the entire group draft them together. Rarely does it make sense to start a workshop with a completely blank slate. Use other elicitation techniques prior to the workshops, and then bring the stakeholders together to work through only the necessary areas.

General facilitation practices apply to requirements elicitation (Schwarz 2002). A definitive resource specific to facilitating requirements elicitation workshops is Gottesdiener's *Requirements by Collaboration* (2002). She describes a wealth of techniques and tools for workshop facilitation. Following are a few tips for conducting effective elicitation workshops, many of which also apply to interviews.

Establish and enforce ground rules   The workshop participants should agree on some basic operating principles. Examples include starting and ending on time; returning from breaks promptly; silencing electronic devices; holding one conversation at a time; expecting everyone to contribute; and focusing comments and criticisms on issues rather than individuals. After the rules are set, ensure that participants follow them.

Fill all of the team roles   A facilitator must make sure that the following tasks are covered by people in the workshop: note taking, time keeping, scope management, ground rule management, and making sure everyone is heard. A scribe might record what's going on, while someone else watches the clock.

Plan an agenda   Each workshop needs a clear plan, as discussed in the "Preparing for elicitation" section later in this chapter. Create the plan and workshop agenda ahead of time, and communicate them to participants so they know the objectives and what to expect and can prepare accordingly.

Stay in scope   Refer to the business requirements to confirm whether proposed user requirements lie within the current project scope. Keep each workshop focused on the right level of abstraction for that session's objectives. Groups easily dive into distracting detail during requirements discussions. Those discussions consume time that the group should spend on developing a higher-level understanding of user requirements; the details will come later. The facilitator will have to reel in the elicitation participants periodically to keep them on topic.

> **Trap** Watch out for off-topic discussions, such as design explorations, during elicitation sessions. Keep the participants focused on the session's objectives, while assuring them that they'll have future opportunities to work through other issues that arise.

Use parking lots to capture items for later consideration   An array of random but important information will surface during elicitation discussions: quality attributes, business rules, user interface ideas, and more. Organize this information on flipcharts—parking lots—so you don't lose it and to demonstrate respect for the participant who brought it up. Don't be distracted into discussing off-topic details unless they turn out to be showstoppers. Describe what will happen with the parking lot issues following the meeting.

Timebox discussions   Consider allocating a fixed period of time to each discussion topic. The discussion might need to be completed later, but timeboxing helps avoid the trap of spending far more time than intended on the first topic and neglecting other important topics entirely. When closing a timeboxed discussion, summarize status and next steps before leaving the topic.

Keep the team small but include the right stakeholders   Small groups can work much faster than larger teams. Elicitation workshops with more than five or six active participants can become mired in side trips, concurrent conversations, and bickering. Consider running multiple workshops in parallel to explore the requirements of different user classes. Workshop participants could include the product champion and other user representatives, perhaps a subject matter expert, a BA, a developer, and a tester. Knowledge, experience, and the authority to make decisions are qualifications for participating in elicitation workshops.

Too many cooks

Requirements elicitation workshops that involve too many participants can slow to a contentious crawl. My colleague Debbie was frustrated at the sluggish progress of the first use case workshop she facilitated for a website project. The 12 participants held extended discussions of unnecessary details and couldn't agree on how each use case ought to work. The team's progress accelerated nicely when Debbie reduced the number of participants to about six who represented the key roles of analyst, customer, system architect, developer, and visual designer. The workshop lost some input by using the smaller team, but the rate of progress more than compensated for that loss. The workshop participants should exchange information off-line with colleagues who don't attend and then bring the collected input to the workshops.

Keep everyone engaged   Sometimes certain participants will stop contributing to the discussion. These people might be frustrated for a variety of reasons. Perhaps their input isn't being taken seriously because other participants don't find their concerns interesting, or maybe they don't want to disrupt the work that the group has completed so far. Perhaps the stakeholder who has withdrawn is deferring to more aggressive participants or a domineering analyst. The facilitator must read the body language (lack of eye contact, fidgeting, sighing, checking the clock), understand why someone has tuned out of the process, and try to re-engage the person. Visual cues are absent when you are facilitating via a teleconference, so you have to listen carefully to learn who is not participating and the tones being used. You might ask these silent individuals directly if they have any thoughts about the discussion they'd like to share. The facilitator must ensure that everyone is heard.

Focus groups

A focus group is a representative group of users who convene in a facilitated elicitation activity to generate input and ideas on a product's functional and quality requirements. Focus group sessions must be interactive, allowing all users a chance to voice their thoughts. Focus groups are useful for exploring users' attitudes, impressions, preferences, and needs (IIBA 2009). They are particularly valuable if you are developing commercial products and don't have ready access to end users within your company.

When conflicts erupt

Differing perspectives, priorities, and personalities can lead to conflict and even anger within a group. If this happens, deal with it immediately. Look for nonverbal clues showing conflict or anger and try to understand the cause. When the group is clear on the reason for the conflict, you might be able to find a solution to it (if one is needed).

If an individual simply will not participate in a productive way, talk with him privately to determine whether his presence will prevent the group from moving forward. If so, you might need to thank the person for his time and continue without him. Sometimes this will not be an option and you need to simply abandon the session or topic completely for now. Conflict management is a complex skill to develop and there are numerous resources on this (Fisher, Ury, and Patton 2011; Patterson et al. 2011).

I once scheduled a session to elicit business requirements from a new director of sales. He was known to have an antagonistic personality, so I came to the meeting prepared to really listen to and understand his desires. In the very first minute of the meeting, he started yelling at me, asking why we were holding this meeting at all. He said, "Who are you to think you have a right to ask me about my business objectives?" I took a deep breath and a long pause. Then I tried to explain why I needed to understand his business objectives—that without them, the team would be guessing at what we needed to develop to meet the customers' desires, and he would be sorely disappointed with the results. And as fast as he got mad, he got over it. Without hesitation, he started rattling off his business objectives. Thankfully my scribe was there to catch them because I was still a bit taken aback by the whole exchange.

Often, you will have a large and diverse user base to draw from, so select the focus group members carefully. Include users who have used previous versions or products similar to the one you're implementing. Either select a pool of users who are of the same type (and hold multiple focus groups for the different user classes) or select a pool representing the full spectrum of user classes so everyone is equally represented.

Focus groups must be facilitated. You will need to keep them on topic, but without influencing the opinions being expressed. You might want to record the session so you can go back and listen carefully to comments. Do not expect quantitative analysis from focus groups, but rather a lot of subjective feedback that can be further evaluated and prioritized as requirements are developed. Elicitation sessions with focus groups benefit from many of the same tips described previously for workshops. Participants in focus groups normally do not have decision-making authority for requirements.

Observations

When you ask users to describe how they do their jobs, they will likely have a hard time being precise—details might be missing or incorrect. Often this is because tasks are complex and it's hard to remember every minute detail. In other cases, it is because users are so familiar with executing a task that they can't articulate everything they do. Perhaps the task is so habitual that they don't even think about it. Sometimes you can learn a lot by observing exactly how users perform their tasks.

Observations are time consuming, so they aren't suitable for every user or every task. To avoid disrupting the users' regularly assigned work activities, limit each observation time to two hours or less. Select important or high-risk tasks and multiple user classes for observations. If you use observations in agile projects, have the user demonstrate only the specific tasks related to the forthcoming iteration.

Observing a user's workflow in the task environment allows the BA to validate information collected from other sources, to identify new topics for interviews, to see problems with the current system, and to identify ways that the new system can better support the workflow. The BA must abstract and generalize beyond the observed user's activities to ensure that the requirements captured apply to the user class as a whole, not just to that individual. A skillful BA can also often suggest ideas for improving the user's current business processes.

Watch me bake a cake

To demonstrate the power of observations, tell some friends the steps to bake a cake from a mix. You'll likely remember the steps to turn on the oven, get out the necessary dishes and utensils, add each ingredient, mix the ingredients, prepare the pan, put the batter in the pan, bake it, and pull it out of the oven when done. But when you told your friends to add each ingredient, did you remember to say to open the bag with the mix in it? Did you remember to say to crack the eggshell, add only the contents of the egg, and discard the shell? These seemingly obvious steps might not be so obvious to someone who has never baked before.

Observations can be silent or interactive. Silent observations are appropriate when busy users cannot be interrupted. Interactive observations allow the BA to interrupt the user mid-task and ask a question. This is useful to understand immediately why a user made a choice or to ask him what he was thinking about when he took some action. Document what you observe for further analysis after the session. You might also consider video recording the session, if policies allow, so you can refresh your memory later.

 I was developing a call-center application for customer service representatives (CSRs) who were used to having to page through printed catalogs to find products that customers wanted to order. The BA team met with several CSRs to elicit use cases for the new application. Each one said how difficult it was to have to flip through multiple catalogs to find exactly what product a customer was referring to. Each BA sat with a different CSR while the CSRs took orders over the phone. We saw the difficulty they faced by watching them first try to find the catalog by date, then try to locate the right product. The observation sessions helped us understand what features they would need in an online product catalog.

Questionnaires

Questionnaires are a way to survey large groups of users to understand their needs. They are inexpensive, making them a logical choice for eliciting information from large user populations, and they can be administered easily across geographical boundaries. The analyzed results of questionnaires can be used as an input to other elicitation techniques. For example, you might use a questionnaire to identify users' biggest pain points with an existing system, then use the results to discuss prioritization with decision makers in a workshop. You can also use questionnaires to survey commercial product users for feedback.

Preparing well-written questions is the biggest challenge with questionnaires. Many tips are available for writing questionnaires (Colorado State University 2013), and we suggest the most important ones here:

- Provide answer options that cover the full set of possible responses.

- Make answer choices both mutually exclusive (no overlaps in numerical ranges) and exhaustive (list all possible choices and/or have a write-in spot for a choice you didn't think of).

- Don't phrase a question in a way that implies a "correct" answer.

- If you use scales, use them consistently throughout the questionnaire.

- Use closed questions with two or more specific choices if you want to use the questionnaire results for statistical analysis. Open-ended questions allows users to respond any way they want, so it's hard to look for commonalities in the results.

- Consider consulting with an expert in questionnaire design and administration to ensure that you ask the right questions of the right people.

- Always test a questionnaire before distributing it. It's frustrating to discover too late that a question was phrased ambiguously or to realize that an important question was omitted.

- Don't ask too many questions or people won't respond.

System interface analysis

Interface analysis is an independent elicitation technique that entails examining the systems to which your system connects. System interface analysis reveals functional requirements regarding the exchange of data and services between systems (IIBA 2009). Context diagrams and ecosystem maps (see Chapter 5, "Establishing the business requirements") are an obvious choice to begin finding interfaces for further study. In fact, if you find an interface that has associated requirements and that is *not* represented in one of these diagrams, the diagrams are incomplete.

For each system that interfaces with yours, identify functionality in the other system that might lead to requirements for your system. These requirements could describe what data to pass to the other system, what data is received from it, and rules about that data, such as validation criteria. You might also discover existing functionality that you do *not* need to implement in your system. Suppose you thought you needed to implement validation rules for a shopping-cart order in an e-commerce website before passing it to an order-management system. Through system interface analysis, you might learn that multiple systems pass orders to the order-management system, which performs the validation, so you don't need to build this function.

User interface analysis

User interface (UI) analysis is an independent elicitation technique in which you study existing systems to discover user and functional requirements. It's best to interact with the existing systems directly, but if necessary you can use screen shots. User manuals for purchased packaged-software implementations often contain screen shots that will work fine as a starting point. If there is no existing system, you might be able to look at user interfaces of similar products.

When working with packaged solutions or an existing system, UI analysis can help you identify a complete list of screens to help you discover potential features. By navigating the existing UI, you can learn about the common steps users take in the system and draft use cases to review with users. UI analysis can reveal pieces of data that users need to see. It's a great way to get up to speed on how an existing system works (unless you need a lot of training to do so). Instead of asking users how they interact with the system and what steps they take, perhaps you can reach an initial understanding yourself.

Do not assume that certain functionality is needed in the new system just because you found it in an existing one. Furthermore, do not assume that because the UI looks or flows a certain way in the current system that it must be implemented that way in the future system.

Document analysis

Document analysis entails examining any existing documentation for potential software requirements. The most useful documentation includes requirements specifications, business processes, lessons-learned collections, and user manuals for existing or similar applications. Documents can describe corporate or industry standards that must be followed or regulations with which the product must comply. When replacing an existing system, past documentation can reveal functionality that might need to be retained, as well as obsolete functionality. For packaged-solution implementations, the vendor documentation mentions functionality that your users might need, but you might have to further explore just how to implement it in the target environment. Comparative reviews point out shortcomings in other products that you could address to gain a competitive advantage. Problem reports and enhancement requests collected from users by help desk and field support personnel can offer ideas for improving the system in future releases.

Document analysis is a way to get up to speed on an existing system or a new domain. Doing some research and drafting some requirements beforehand reduces the elicitation meeting time needed. Document analysis can reveal information people don't tell you, either because they don't think of it or because they aren't aware of it. For example, if you are building a new call-center application, you might find some complicated business logic described in the user manual for an existing application. Perhaps users don't even know about this logic. You can use the results of this analysis as input to user interviews.

A risk with this technique is that the available documents might not be up to date. Requirements might have changed without the specifications being updated, or functionality might be documented that is not needed in a new system.

Planning elicitation on your project

Early in a project, the business analyst should plan the project's approach to requirements elicitation. Even a simple plan of action increases the chance of success and sets realistic expectations for the stakeholders. Only by gaining explicit commitment on elicitation resources, schedule, and deliverables can you avoid having participants pulled away to do other work. An elicitation plan includes the techniques you'll use, when you plan to use them, and for what purpose. As with any plan, use it as a guide and reminder throughout the project, but realize that you might need to change the plan throughout the project. Your plan should address the following items:

- **Elicitation objectives** Plan the elicitation objectives for the entire project and the objectives for each planned elicitation activity.

- **Elicitation strategy and planned techniques** Decide which techniques to use with different stakeholder groups. You might use some combination of questionnaires, workshops, customer visits, individual interviews, and other techniques, depending on the access you have to stakeholders, time constraints, and your knowledge of the existing system.

- **Schedule and resource estimates** Identify both customer and development participants for the various elicitation activities, along with estimates of the effort and calendar time required. You might only be able to identify the user classes and not specific individuals up front, but that will allow managers to begin planning for upcoming resource needs. Estimate the BA time, including time to prepare for elicitation and to perform follow-up analysis.

- **Documents and systems needed for independent elicitation** If you are conducting document, system interface, or user interface analysis, identify the materials needed to ensure that you have them when you need them.

- **Expected products of elicitation efforts** Knowing you are going to create a list of use cases, an SRS, an analysis of questionnaire results, or quality attribute specifications helps ensure that you target the right stakeholders, topics, and details during elicitation.

- **Elicitation risks** Identify factors that could impede your ability to complete the elicitation activities as intended, estimate the severity of each risk, and decide how you can mitigate or control it. See Chapter 32, "Software requirements and risk management," for more on risk management. See Appendix B, "Requirements troubleshooting guide," for symptoms, root causes, and possible solutions for common elicitation problems.

Many BAs have their "go-to" elicitation technique—commonly interviews and workshops—and do not think to use other techniques that might reduce resource needs or increase the quality of the information discovered. Rarely will a BA get the best results by using only one elicitation technique on a project. Elicitation techniques apply across the spectrum of development approaches. The selection of elicitation techniques should be based on the characteristics of the project.

Figure 7-3 suggests the elicitation techniques that are most likely to be useful for various types of projects. Select the row or rows that represent characteristics of your project and read to the right to see which elicitation techniques are most likely to be helpful (marked with an X). For instance, if you're developing a new application, you're likely to get the best results with a combination of stakeholder interviews, workshops, and system interface analysis. Most projects can make use of interviews and workshops. Focus groups are more appropriate than workshops for mass-market software because you have a large external user base but limited access to representatives. These suggestions for elicitation techniques are just that—suggestions. For instance, you might conclude that you do want to apply user interface analysis on mass-market software projects.

	Interviews	Workshops	Focus groups	Observations	Questionnaires	System interface analysis	User interface analysis	Document analysis
Mass-market software	x		x		x			
Internal corporate software	x	x	x	x		x		x
Replacing existing system	x	x		x		x	x	x
Enhancing existing system	x	x				x	x	x
New application	x	x				x		
Packaged software implementation	x	x		x		x		x
Embedded systems	x	x				x		x
Geographically distributed stakeholders	x	x			x			

FIGURE 7-3 Suggested elicitation techniques by project characteristic.

Preparing for elicitation

Facilitated elicitation sessions require preparation to make the best use of everyone's time. The larger the group participating in the session, the more important preparation is. Figure 7-4 highlights the activities to prepare for a single requirements elicitation session.

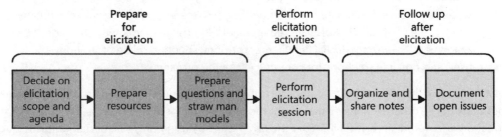

FIGURE 7-4 Activities to prepare for a single elicitation session.

Prepare for each session by deciding on the scope of the session, communicating an agenda, preparing questions, and drafting materials that might be useful during the session. The following tips will help you prepare for elicitation.

Plan session scope and agenda   Decide on the scope of the elicitation session, taking into account how much time is available. You might define the session scope by using a set of topics or questions, or you might list a specific set of process flows or use cases to be explored. Align the scope of the session with the overall project scope defined in the business requirements so you can keep the conversation on topic. The agenda should itemize what topics will be covered, the available time for each topic, and targeted objectives. Share the session agenda with stakeholders in advance.

Prepare resources   Schedule the physical resources needed, such as rooms, projectors, teleconference numbers, and videoconferencing equipment. Also, schedule the participants, being sensitive to time zone differences if you are not all in the same location. For geographically dispersed groups, change the schedule each time you meet so the sessions do not always inconvenience the same people in a particular part of the world. Collect documentation from various sources. Gain access to systems as necessary. Take online training to learn about existing systems.

Learn about the stakeholders   Identify the relevant stakeholders for the session (see Chapter 6, "Finding the voice of the user"). Learn about the stakeholders' cultural and regional preferences for meetings. If some of the participants are not native speakers of the language in which the session will be conducted, consider providing them with supporting documentation, such as slides, ahead of time so they can read ahead or follow along. The slides can list specific questions you will be asking or simply provide context for the session that you might also verbally explain. Avoid creating an "us" versus "them" tension.

Prepare questions   Go into every facilitated elicitation session with a set of prepared questions. Use areas of uncertainty in straw man models (described in the next section) as a source of questions. If you are preparing for an interview or workshop, use results from other elicitation techniques to identify unresolved questions. There are many sources of suggested questions for elicitation (Wiegers 2006; Miller 2009).

Phrase your questions to avoid leading customers down an unintended path or toward a specific answer. As an analyst, you must probe beneath the surface of the requirements the customers present to understand their true needs. Simply asking users, "What do you want?" generates a mass of random information that leaves the analyst floundering. "What do you need to do?" is a much better question. Asking "why" several times can move the discussion from a presented solution to a solid understanding of the problem that needs to be solved. Ask open-ended questions to help you understand the users' current business processes and to see how the new system could improve their performance.

Imagine yourself learning the user's job, or actually do the job under the user's direction. What tasks would you perform? What questions would you have? Another approach is to play the role of an apprentice learning from a master user. The user you are interviewing then guides the discussion and describes what he views as the important topics for discussion.

Probe around the exceptions. What could prevent the user from successfully completing a task? How should the system respond to various error conditions? Ask questions that begin with "What else could . . . ," "What happens when . . . ," "Would you ever need to . . . ," "Where do you get . . . ," "Why do you (or don't you) . . . ," and "Does anyone ever . . ." Document the source of each requirement so that you can obtain further clarification if needed and trace development activities back to specific customer origins.

As with any improvement activity, dissatisfaction with the current situation provides excellent fodder for the new and improved future state. When you're working on a replacement project for a legacy system, ask the users, "What three things annoy you the most about the existing system?" This question surfaces expectations that the users hold for the follow-on system.

You won't have—nor do you need—a perfect script going into an interview or a workshop. The prepared questions are to help you if you get stuck. The questions should seem natural and comfortable—like a conversation, not an interrogation. Five minutes into a session, you might realize that you missed an important area for discussion. Be ready to abandon your questions if needed. At the end of your session, ask "Is there anything else you expected me to ask?" to try to surface issues you just didn't think of.

Prepare straw man models   Analysis models can be used during elicitation sessions to help users provide better requirements. Some of the most useful models are use cases and process flows because they closely align with how people think about doing their jobs. Create straw man, or draft, models ahead of your elicitation sessions. A straw man serves as a starting point that helps you learn about the topic and inspires your users to think of ideas. It is easier to revise a draft model than to create one from scratch.

If you are new to the project's domain, it might be hard to create a draft model on your own. Use other elicitation techniques to glean enough knowledge to work from. Read existing documents, examine existing systems for models you can reuse as a starting point, or hold a one-on-one interview with a subject matter expert to learn enough to get started. Then tell the group you're working with, "This model will probably be wrong. Please tear it apart and tell me how it should look. You won't hurt my feelings."

Performing elicitation activities

Figure 7-5 highlights the activity to perform elicitation in a single requirements elicitation session.

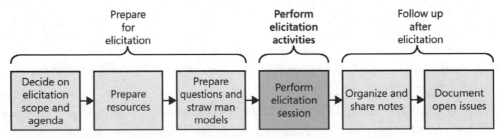

FIGURE 7-5 The perform elicitation activities step for a single elicitation session.

Executing the elicitation activity itself is relatively obvious—if you are interviewing, you talk to people; if you are performing document analysis, you read the document. However, when facilitating an elicitation activity, the following tips might be useful.

Educate stakeholders   Teach your stakeholders about your elicitation approach and why you chose it. Explain the exploration techniques you'll be using, such as use cases or process flows, and how they can help stakeholders provide better requirements. Also describe how you will capture their information and send them materials for review after the session.

Take good notes   Assign someone who isn't actively participating in the discussion to be the scribe, responsible for taking accurate notes. Session notes should contain an attendee list, invitees who did not attend, decisions made, actions to be taken and who is responsible for each, outstanding issues, and the high points of key discussions. Unfortunately, BAs sometimes hold facilitated elicitation sessions without a dedicated scribe and have to fill the role themselves. If you're in this situation, be prepared to write shorthand, type fast, or use a recording device (if the participants agree). Audio pens can translate handwritten notes to electronic form and tie them to the recorded audio discussion. You can also use whiteboards and paper on the walls and photograph them.

Prepare questions ahead of time to eliminate some of the on-the-spot thinking necessary to keep the conversation going. Come up with a shorthand notation to capture a question that comes to mind while someone is talking, so you can quickly flip back to it when you have an opportunity. Don't try to capture diagrams in complicated diagramming software; just photograph sketched diagrams or draw quickly by hand.

Exploit the physical space   Most rooms have four walls, so use them during facilitation to draw diagrams or create lists. If there aren't whiteboards available, attach big sheets of paper to the walls. Have sticky notes and markers available. Invite other participants to get up and contribute to the wall as well; moving around helps to keep people engaged. Gottesdiener (2002) refers to this technique as the "Wall of Wonder" collaboration pattern. If there are existing artifacts to look at (such as straw man models, existing requirements, or existing systems), project them on the wall.

Facilitating collaborative sessions with participants in multiple locations requires more creativity. You can use online conferencing tools to share slides and permit interactions. If several participants are in the same room, use videoconferencing tools to show remote participants what's on the walls and whiteboards.

Stakeholders on the move

I once facilitated a workshop to elicit process flows for a semiconductor fabrication plant with a dozen engineers. I started out by working at the whiteboard, drawing the flows as we talked. Each time we completed a flow, I'd stop to photograph it before moving on to the next. Half a day into the first session, one of the engineers asked if he could have a turn at the whiteboard. I happily handed him the marker. He had learned the flowchart notation, and since he was already an expert in the system, he could easily draw the flow on the board. He then walked us through it, asking his peers at each step to validate or correct it. He was leading the process, which allowed me to focus on asking probing questions and taking notes. Soon, all the engineers were passing the marker around, so everyone got a turn.

If it's culturally appropriate, use toys to stimulate participants' minds or give them something to do with their hands. Simple toys can help inspire ideas. One team held a brainstorming session to establish the business objectives for their project. To start the day, I gave every participant some modeling clay and asked them to model their product vision using the clay—with no more instruction than that. It woke them up, got them thinking creatively, and they had some fun with it. We transitioned that energy into actually writing down a real vision for the product.

Following up after elicitation

After each elicitation activity is complete, there's still a lot to do. You need to organize and share your notes, document open issues, and classify the newly gathered information. Figure 7-6 highlights the activities to follow up after a single requirements elicitation session.

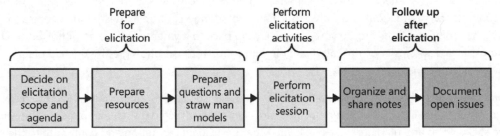

FIGURE 7-6 Activities to follow up after an elicitation session.

Organizing and sharing the notes

If you led an interview or workshop, organizing your notes probably requires more effort than if you organized information as you encountered it during an independent elicitation activity. Consolidate your input from multiple sources. Review and update your notes soon after the session is complete, while the content is still fresh in your mind.

Editing the elicitation notes is a risk. You might be incorrectly remembering what something meant, thereby unknowingly changing the meaning. Keep a set of the raw notes to refer to later if necessary. Soon after each interview or workshop, share the consolidated notes with the participants and ask them to review them to ensure that they accurately represent the session. Early review is essential to successful requirements development because only those people who supplied the requirements can judge whether they were captured correctly. Hold additional discussions to resolve any inconsistencies and to fill in any blanks. Consider sharing the consolidated notes with other project stakeholders who weren't present in the session, so that they are aware of progress. This gives them the opportunity to flag any issues or concerns immediately.

Documenting open issues

During elicitation activities, you might have encountered items that need to be further explored at a later date or knowledge gaps you need to close. Or you might have identified new questions while reviewing your notes. Examine any parking lots from elicitation sessions for issues that are still open and record them in an issue-tracking tool. For each issue, record any relevant notes related to resolving the issues, progress already made, an owner, and a due date. Consider using the same issue-tracking tool that the development and testing teams use.

Classifying customer input

Don't expect your customers to present a succinct, complete, and well-organized list of their needs. Analysts must classify the myriad bits of requirements information they hear into various categories so that they can document and use it appropriately. Figure 7-7 illustrates nine such categories. During elicitation activities, make quick notations in your notes if you detect that some bit of information is one of these types. For example, write "DD" in a little circle if you recognize a data definition.

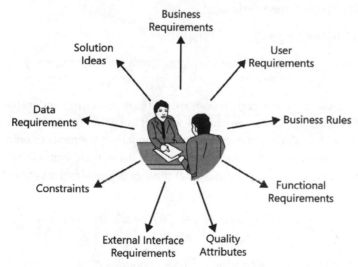

FIGURE 7-7 Classifying customer input.

As with many categorizations, the information gathered might not fit precisely into these nine buckets. You will probably have pieces of information left over after this classification. Anything that doesn't fit into one of these categories might be:

- A project requirement not related to the software development, such as the need to train users on the new system.

- A project constraint, such as a cost or schedule restriction (as opposed to the design or implementation constraints described in this chapter).

- An assumption or a dependency.

- Additional information of a historical, context-setting, or descriptive nature.

- Extraneous information that does not add value.

Elicitation participants won't simply tell you, "Here comes a business requirement." As an analyst, you need to determine what type of information each provided statement you hear represents. The following discussion suggests some phrases to listen for that will help you in this classification process.

Business requirements Anything that describes the financial, marketplace, or other business benefit that either customers or the developing organization wish to gain from the product is a business requirement (see Chapter 5). Listen for statements about the value that buyers or users of the software will receive, such as these:

- "Increase market share in region X by Y percent within Z months."

- "Save $X per year on electricity now wasted by inefficient units."

User requirements General statements of user goals or business tasks that users need to perform are user requirements, most typically represented as use cases, scenarios, or user stories (see Chapter 8, "Understanding user requirements"). A user who says, "I need to <do something>" is probably describing a user requirement, as in the following examples:

- "I need to print a mailing label for a package."

- "As the lead machine operator, I need to calibrate the pump controller first thing every morning."

Business rules When a customer says that only certain users can perform an activity under specific conditions, he might be presenting a business rule (see Chapter 9, "Playing by the rules"). These aren't software requirements as they stand, but you might derive some functional requirements to enforce the rules. Phrases such as "Must comply with . . . ," "If <some condition is true>, then <something happens>," or "Must be calculated according to . . . " suggest that the user is describing a business rule. Here are some examples:

- "A new client must pay 30 percent of the estimated consulting fee and travel expenses in advance."

- "Time-off approvals must comply with the company's HR vacation policy."

Functional requirements Functional requirements describe the observable behaviors the system will exhibit under certain conditions and the actions the system will let users take. Here are some examples of functional requirements as you might hear them from users:

- "If the pressure exceeds 40.0 psi, the high-pressure warning light should come on."

- "The user must be able to sort the project list in forward and reverse alphabetical order."

These statements illustrate how users typically present functional requirements, but they don't represent good ways to write functional requirements. The BA will need to craft these into more precise specifications. See Chapter 11, "Writing excellent requirements," for guidance on writing good functional requirements.

Quality attributes Statements that describe how well the system does something are quality attributes (see Chapter 14, "Beyond functionality"). Listen for words that describe desirable system characteristics: fast, easy, user-friendly, reliable, secure. You'll need to work with the users to understand just what they mean by these ambiguous and subjective terms so that you can write clear, verifiable quality goals. The following examples suggest what quality attributes might sound like when described by users:

- "The mobile software must respond quickly to touch commands."

- "The shopping cart mechanism has to be simple to use so my new customers don't abandon the purchase."

External interface requirements Requirements in this category describe the connections between your system and the rest of the universe. The SRS template in Chapter 10, "Documenting the requirements," includes sections for interfaces to users, hardware, and other software systems. Phrases such as "Must read signals from . . . ," "Must send messages to . . . ," "Must be able to read files in <format>," and "User interface elements must conform to <a standard>" indicate that the customer is describing an external interface requirement. Following are some examples:

- "The manufacturing execution system must control the wafer sorter."

- "The mobile app should send the check image to the bank after I photograph the check I'm depositing."

Constraints Design and implementation constraints legitimately restrict the options available to the developer (see Chapter 14). Devices with embedded software often must respect physical constraints such as size, weight, and interface connections. Phrases that indicate that the customer is describing a design or implementation constraint include: "Must be written in <a specific programming language>," "Cannot exceed <some limit>," and "Must use <a specific user interface control>." The following are examples of constraints that a customer might present:

- "Files submitted electronically cannot exceed 10 MB in size."

- "The browser must use 256-bit encryption for all secure transactions."

As with functional requirements, don't just transcribe the user's statement of a constraint. Ask why the constraint exists, confirm its validity, and record the rationale for including it as a requirement.

Data requirements Customers are presenting a data requirement whenever they describe the format, data type, allowed values, or default value for a data element; the composition of a complex business data structure; or a report to be generated (see Chapter 13, "Specifying data requirements"). Some examples of data requirements are as follows:

- "The ZIP code has five digits, followed by an optional hyphen and four digits that default to 0000."

- "An order consists of the customer's identity, shipping information, and one or more products, each of which includes the product number, number of units, unit price, and total price."

Solution ideas   Many "requirements" from users are really solution ideas. Someone who describes a specific way to interact with the system to perform some action is suggesting a solution. The business analyst needs to probe below the surface of a solution idea to get to the real requirement. Repeatedly asking "why" the user needs it to work this way will likely reveal the true need (Wiegers 2006). For instance, passwords are just one of several possible ways to implement a security requirement. Two other examples of solution ideas are the following:

- "Then I select the state where I want to send the package from a drop-down list."

- "The phone has to allow the user to swipe with a finger to navigate between screens."

In the first example, the phrase *from a drop-down list* indicates that this is a solution idea because it's describing a specific user interface control. The prudent BA will ask, "Why from a drop-down list?" If the user replies, "That just seemed like a good way to do it," then the real requirement is something like, "The system shall permit the user to specify the state where he wants to send the package." But maybe the user says, "We do the same thing in several other places and I want it to be consistent. Also, the drop-down list prevents the user from entering invalid data." These are legitimate reasons to specify a specific solution. Recognize, though, that embedding a solution in a requirement imposes a design constraint on that requirement: it limits the requirement to being implemented in only one way. This isn't necessarily wrong or bad; just make sure the constraint is there for a good reason.

Classifying the customer input is just the beginning of the process to create requirements specifications. You still need to assemble the information into clearly stated and well-organized requirements collections. As you work through the information, craft clear individual requirements and store them in the appropriate sections of the team's document templates or repository. Make additional passes through this information to ensure that each statement demonstrates the characteristics of high-quality requirements as described in Chapter 11. As you process your elicitation notes, mark the items complete as you store them in the right place.

How do you know when you're done?

No simple signal will indicate when you've completed requirements elicitation. In fact, you'll never be entirely done, particularly if you are deliberately implementing a system incrementally, as on agile projects. As people muse in the shower each morning and talk with their colleagues, they'll generate ideas for additional requirements and want to change some of the ones they already have. The following cues suggest that you're reaching the point of diminishing returns on requirements elicitation, at least for now. Perhaps you are done if:

- The users can't think of any more use cases or user stories. Users tend to identify user requirements in sequence of decreasing importance.

- Users propose new scenarios, but they don't lead to any new functional requirements. A "new" use case might really be an alternative flow for a use case you've already captured.

- Users repeat issues they already covered in previous discussions.

- Suggested new features, user requirements, or functional requirements are all deemed to be out of scope.

- Proposed new requirements are all low priority.

- The users are proposing capabilities that might be included "sometime in the lifetime of the product" rather than "in the specific product we're talking about right now."

- Developers and testers who review the requirements for an area raise few questions.

Amalgamating requirements input from numerous users is difficult without using a structured organizing scheme, such as use cases or the sections in an SRS template. Despite your best efforts to discover *all* the requirements, you won't, so expect to make changes as construction proceeds. Remember, your goal is to accumulate a shared understanding of requirements that is good enough to let construction of the next release or increment proceed at an acceptable level of risk.

Some cautions about elicitation

Skill in conducting elicitation discussions comes with experience and builds on training in interviewing, group facilitation, conflict resolution, and similar activities. However, a few cautions will decrease the learning curve.

Balance stakeholder representation   Collecting input from too few representatives or hearing the voice of only the loudest, most opinionated customer is a problem. It can lead to overlooking requirements that are important to certain user classes or to including requirements that don't represent the needs of a majority of the users. The best balance involves a few product champions who can speak for their respective user classes, with each champion backed up by other representatives from the same user class.

Define scope appropriately   During requirements elicitation, you might find that the project scope is improperly defined, being either too large or too small. If the scope is too large, you'll accumulate more requirements than are needed to deliver adequate business and customer value, and the elicitation process will drag on. If the project is scoped too small, customers will present needs that are clearly important yet just as clearly lie beyond the limited scope currently established for the project. The current scope could be too small to yield a satisfactory product. Eliciting user requirements therefore can lead to modifying the product vision or the project scope.

Avoid the requirements-versus-design argument   It's often stated that requirements are about *what* the system has to do, whereas *how* the solution will be implemented is the realm of design. Although attractively concise, this is an oversimplification. Requirements elicitation should indeed focus on the *what*, but there's a gray area—not a sharp line—between analysis and design (Wiegers 2006). Hypothetical *how*s help to clarify and refine the understanding of what users need. Analysis models, screen sketches, and prototypes help to make the needs expressed during elicitation more tangible and to reveal errors and omissions. Make it clear to users that these screens and prototypes are illustrative only, not necessarily the ultimate solution.

Research within reason The need to do exploratory research sometimes disrupts elicitation. An idea or a suggestion arises, but extensive research is required to assess whether it should even be considered for the product. Treat these explorations of feasibility or value as project tasks in their own right. Prototyping is one way to explore such issues. If your project requires extensive research, use an incremental development approach to explore the requirements in small, low-risk portions.

Assumed and implied requirements

You will never document 100 percent of the requirements for a system. But the requirements you *don't* specify pose a risk that the project might deliver a solution different from what stakeholders expect. Two likely culprits behind missed expectations are assumed and implied requirements:

- *Assumed requirements* are those that people expect without having explicitly expressed them. What you assume as being obvious might not be the same as assumptions that various developers make.

- *Implied requirements* are necessary because of another requirement but aren't explicitly stated. Developers can't implement functionality they don't know about.

To reduce these risks, try to identify knowledge gaps waiting to be filled with implied and assumed requirements. Ask, "What are we assuming?" during elicitation sessions to try to surface those hidden thoughts. If you come across an assumption during requirements discussions, record it and confirm its validity. People often assume that things have to be the way they've always been because they're so familiar with an existing system or business process. If you're developing a replacement system, review the previous system's features to determine whether they're truly required in the replacement.

To identify implied requirements, study the results of initial elicitation sessions to identify areas of incompleteness. Does a vague, high-level requirement need to be fleshed out so the stakeholders all understand it? Is a requirement that might be part of a logical set (say, saving an incomplete web form) lacking its counterpart (retrieving a saved form for further work)? You might need to re-interview some of the same stakeholders to have them look for missing requirements (Rose-Coutré 2007). Also, think of new stakeholders who know the topic and can spot gaps.

Read between the lines to identify features or characteristics the customers expect to be included without having said so. Ask *context-free questions*, high-level and open-ended questions that elicit information about global characteristics of both the business problem and the potential solution (Gause and Weinberg 1989). The customer's response to questions such as "What kind of precision is required in the product?" or "Can you help me understand why you don't agree with Miguel's reply?" can lead to insights that questions with standard yes/no or A/B/C answers do not.

No assumed requirements

I once encountered a development team that was implementing a content portal that was intended to do many things, including upload, edit, and publish content to a website. There were approximately 1,000 pieces of existing content, organized in a hierarchy. The content management team assumed that users would be able to navigate the hierarchy to quickly find a specific piece of content. They did not specify requirements regarding the user interface navigation. However, when the developers implemented the user interface to navigate to content, they organized all of the content in a single level, not hierarchically, and showed only 20 items per screen. To find a specific piece of content, a user might have to navigate through as many as 50 screens. A little more specification and dialogue between developers and the content management team could have avoided considerable rework.

Finding missing requirements

Missing requirements constitute a common type of requirement defect. Missing requirements are hard to spot because they're invisible! The following techniques will help you detect previously undiscovered requirements:

- Decompose high-level requirements into enough detail to reveal exactly what is being requested. A vague, high-level requirement that leaves much to the reader's interpretation will lead to a gap between what the requester has in mind and what the developer builds.

- Ensure that all user classes have provided input. Make sure that each user requirement has at least one identified user class who will receive value from the requirement.

- Trace system requirements, user requirements, event-response lists, and business rules to their corresponding functional requirements to make sure that all the necessary functionality was derived.

- Check boundary values for missing requirements. Suppose that one requirement states, "If the price of the order is less than $100, the shipping charge is $5.95" and another says, "If the price of the order is more than $100, the shipping charge is 6 percent of the total order price." But what's the shipping charge for an order with a price of exactly $100? It's not specified, so a requirement is missing, or at least poorly written.

- Represent requirements information in more than one way. It's difficult to read a mass of text and notice the item that's absent. Some analysis models visually represent requirements at a high level of abstraction—the forest, not the trees. You might study a model and realize that there should be an arrow from one box to another; that missing arrow represents a missing requirement. Analysis models are described in Chapter 12, "A picture is worth 1024 words."

- Sets of requirements with complex Boolean logic (ANDs, ORs, and NOTs) often are incomplete. If a combination of logical conditions has no corresponding functional requirement, the developer has to deduce what the system should do or chase down an answer. "Else" conditions frequently are overlooked. Represent complex logic by using decision tables or decision trees to cover all the possible situations, as described in Chapter 12.

- Create a checklist of common functional areas to consider for your projects. Examples include error logging, backup and restore, access security, reporting, printing, preview capabilities, and configuring user preferences. Periodically compare this list with the functions you've already specified to look for gaps.

- A data model can reveal missing functionality. All data entities that the system will manipulate must have corresponding functionality to create them, read them from an external source, update current values, and/or delete them. The acronym CRUD is often used to refer to these four common operations. Make sure you can identify functionality in your application to perform these operations on all of your entities that need them (see Chapter 13).

> **Trap** Watch out for the dreaded *analysis paralysis*, spending too much time on requirements elicitation in an attempt to avoid missing any requirements.

You'll likely never discover all of the requirements for your product, but nearly every software team can do a better job of requirements elicitation by applying the practices described in this chapter.

Next steps

- Think about requirements that were found late on your last project. Why were they overlooked during elicitation? How could you have discovered each of these requirements earlier? What would that have been worth to your organization?

- Select a portion of any documented customer input on your project or a section from the SRS. Classify every item in that requirements fragment into the categories shown in Figure 7-7. If you find items that were organized incorrectly, move them to the correct place in your requirements documentation.

- List the requirements elicitation techniques used on your previous or current project. Which ones worked well? Why? Which ones did not work so well? Why not? Identify elicitation techniques that you think would work better and decide how you'd apply them next time. Identify any barriers you might encounter to making those techniques work, and brainstorm ways to overcome those barriers.

CHAPTER 8

Understanding user requirements

The Chemical Tracking System (CTS) project was holding its first requirements elicitation workshop to learn what chemists would need to do with the system. The participants included a business analyst, Lori; the product champion for the chemists, Tim; two other chemist representatives, Sandy and Peter; and the lead developer, Ravi.

"Tim, Sandy, and Peter have identified 14 use cases that chemists would need to perform using the Chemical Tracking System," Lori told the group. "You said the use case called 'Request a Chemical' is top priority and Tim already wrote a brief description for it, so let's begin there. Tim, how do you visualize the process to request a chemical with the system?"

"First," said Tim, "you should know that only people who have been authorized by their lab managers are allowed to request chemicals."

"Okay, that sounds like a business rule," Lori replied. "I'll start a list of business rules because we'll probably find others. It looks like we'll have to verify that the user is on the approved list." Lori then guided the group through a discussion of how they envisioned creating a request for a new chemical. She used flipcharts and sticky notes to collect information about preconditions, postconditions, and the interactions between the user and the system. Lori asked how a session would be different if the user were requesting a chemical from a vendor rather than from the stockroom. She asked what could go wrong and how the system should handle each error condition. After about 30 minutes, the group had a solid handle on how a user would request a chemical. They moved on to the next use case.

A necessary prerequisite to designing software that meets user needs is to understand what the users intend to do with it. Some teams take a product-centric approach. They focus on defining the features to implement in the software, with the hope that those features will appeal to prospective customers. In most cases, though, you're better off taking a user-centric and usage-centric approach to requirements elicitation. Focusing on users and their anticipated usage helps reveal the necessary functionality, avoids implementing features that no one will use, and assists with prioritization.

User requirements are found in the second level of requirements that you saw in Figure 1-1 in Chapter 1, "The essential software requirement." They lie between the business requirements that set the objectives for the project and the functional requirements that describe what developers must implement. This chapter addresses two of the most commonly employed techniques for exploring user requirements: use cases and user stories.

Analysts have long employed usage scenarios to elicit user requirements (Alexander and Maiden 2004). The usage-centered perspective was formalized into the use case approach to requirements modeling (Jacobson et al. 1992; Cockburn 2001; Kulak and Guiney 2004). More recently, proponents of agile development introduced the concept of a "user story," a concise statement that articulates a user need and serves as a starting point for conversations to flesh out the details (Cohn 2004).

Both use cases and user stories shift from the product-centric perspective of requirements elicitation to discussing what *users* need to accomplish, in contrast to asking users what they want the *system* to do. The intent of this approach is to describe tasks that users will need to perform with the system, or user-system interactions that will result in a valuable outcome for some stakeholder. That understanding leads the BA to derive the necessary functionality that must be implemented to enable those usage scenarios. It also leads to tests to verify whether the functionality was implemented correctly. Usage-centric elicitation strategies will bring you closer to understanding the user's requirements on many classes of projects than any other technique we have used.

Use cases and user stories work well for exploring the requirements for business applications, websites, kiosks, and systems that let a user control a piece of hardware. However, they are inadequate for understanding the requirements of certain types of applications. Applications such as batch processes, computationally intensive systems, business analytics, and data warehousing might have just a few use cases. The complexity of these applications lies in the computations performed, the data found and compiled, or the reports generated, not in the user-system interactions.

Nor are use cases and user stories sufficient for specifying many embedded and other real-time systems. Consider an automated car wash. The driver of the car has just one goal—to wash the car—with perhaps a few options: underbody spray, sealer wax, polish. However, the car wash has a lot going on. It has a drive mechanism to move your car; numerous motors, pumps, valves, switches, dials, and lights; and timers or sensors to control the activation of these physical components. You also have to worry about diagnostic functionality, such as notifying the operator when a tank of liquid is nearly empty, as well as fault detection and safety requirements. What happens if the drive mechanism fails while a car is in the tunnel, or if the motor on a blower fails? A requirements technique often used for real-time systems is to list the external events to which the system must react and the corresponding system responses. See Chapter 12, "A picture is worth 1024 words," for more about event analysis.

Use cases and user stories

A *use case* describes a sequence of interactions between a system and an external actor that results in the actor being able to achieve some outcome of value. The names of use cases are always written in the form of a verb followed by object. Select strong, descriptive names to make it evident from the name that the use case will deliver something valuable for some user. Table 8-1 lists some sample use cases from a variety of applications.

TABLE 8-1 Sample use cases from various applications

Application	Sample use case
Chemical tracking system	Request a Chemical Print Material Safety Data Sheet Change a Chemical Request Check Status of an Order Generate Quarterly Chemical-Usage Reports
Airport check-in kiosk	Check in for a Flight Print Boarding Passes Change Seats Check Luggage Purchase an Upgrade
Accounting system	Create an Invoice Reconcile an Account Statement Enter a Credit Card Transaction Print Tax Forms for Vendors Search for a Specific Transaction
Online bookstore	Update Customer Profile Search for an Item Buy an Item Track a Shipped Package Cancel an Unshipped Order

As used on agile development projects, a user story is a "short, simple description of a feature told from the perspective of the person who desires the new capability, usually a user or customer of the system" (Cohn 2010). User stories often are written according to the following template, although other styles also are used:

> As a <type of user>, I want <some goal> so that <some reason>.

Using this template provides an advantage over the even shorter use case name because, although they both state the user's goal, the user story also identifies the user class and the rationale behind the request for that system capability. These are valuable additions. The user class—which need not be a human being—in a user story corresponds to the primary actor in a use case (described later in this chapter). The rationale could be provided in the brief description of the use case. Table 8-2 shows how we could state some of the use cases from Table 8-1 in the form of user stories.

TABLE 8-2 Some sample use cases and corresponding user stories

Application	Sample use case	Corresponding user story
Chemical tracking system	Request a Chemical	As a chemist, I want to request a chemical so that I can perform experiments.
Airport check-in kiosk	Check in for a Flight	As a traveler, I want to check in for a flight so that I can fly to my destination.
Accounting system	Create an Invoice	As a small business owner, I want to create an invoice so that I can bill a customer.
Online bookstore	Update Customer Profile	As a customer, I want to update my customer profile so that future purchases are billed to a new credit card number.

At this level, use cases look much like user stories. Both are focused on understanding what different types of users need to accomplish through interactions with a software system. However, the two processes move in different directions from these similar starting points, as illustrated in Figure 8-1. Both approaches can also produce other deliverables, such as visual analysis models, but Figure 8-1 illustrates the core distinction.

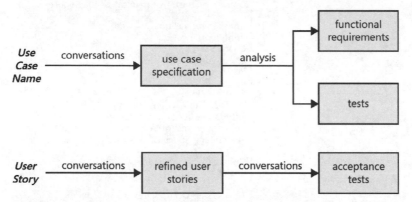

FIGURE 8-1 How user requirements lead to functional requirements and tests with the use case approach and the user story approach.

With use cases, the next step is for the BA to work with user representatives to understand how they imagine a dialog taking place with the system to perform the use case. The BA structures the information collected according to a use case template; you'll see an example later in the chapter. The template contains numerous spaces in which to store information that can provide a rich understanding of the use case, its variants, and related information. It's not necessary to fully complete the template if the developers can get the information they need from a briefer specification, but referring to the template during elicitation will help the participants discover all the pertinent information. From the use case specification, the BA can derive the functional requirements that developers must implement, and a tester can identify tests to judge whether the use case was properly implemented. Developers might implement an entire use case in a single release or iteration. Alternatively, they might implement just a portion of a particular use case initially, either for size or priority reasons, and then implement additional parts in future releases.

As employed on agile projects, a user story serves as a placeholder for future conversations that need to take place on a just-in-time basis among developers, customer representatives, and a business analyst (if one is working on the project). Those conversations reveal the additional information that developers must know to be able to implement the story. Refining the user stories through conversations leads to a collection of smaller, focused stories that describe individual chunks of system functionality. User stories that are too large to implement in one agile development iteration (called *epics*) are split into smaller stories that can be implemented within a single iteration. See Chapter 20, "Agile projects," for more about epics and user stories.

Rather than specifying functional requirements, agile teams typically elaborate a refined user story into a set of acceptance tests that collectively describe the story's "conditions of satisfaction." Thinking about tests at this early stage is an excellent idea for all projects, regardless of their development approach. Test thinking helps you identify variations of the basic user story (or use case), exception conditions that must be handled, and nonfunctional requirements such as performance and security considerations. If the developer implements the necessary code to satisfy the acceptance tests—and hence to meet conditions of satisfaction—the user story is considered to be correctly implemented.

User stories provide a concise statement of a user's needs. Use cases dive further into describing how the user imagines interacting with the system to accomplish his objective. The use case should not get into design specifics, just into the user's mental image about the interaction. User stories offer the advantage of simplicity and conciseness, but there is a tradeoff. Use cases provide project participants with a structure and context that a collection of user stories lacks. They provide an organized way for the BA to lead elicitation discussions beyond simply collecting a list of things that users need to achieve with the system as a starting point for planning and discussion.

Not everyone is convinced that user stories are an adequate requirements solution for large or more demanding projects (Gilb and Gilb 2011). You can examine each element of a use case (flows, preconditions, postconditions, and so on) to look for pertinent functional and nonfunctional requirements and to derive tests. This helps you avoid overlooking any requirements that developers must implement to let users perform the use case. But user stories do not replicate that structure and rigor, so it's easier for the team to miss some acceptance tests. A BA or developer must have experience in effective user story development to avoid overlooking relevant functionality. A use-case analysis might reveal that several use cases involve similar exceptions (or other commonalities) that could perhaps be implemented as a single consistent error-handling strategy within the application. Such commonalities are more difficult to discern with a collection of user stories.

For more information about how to elicit and apply user stories when exploring user requirements, see Cohn (2004), Cohn (2010), or Leffingwell (2011). The rest of this chapter will focus on the use case technique, pointing out similarities and contrasts with the user story approach where appropriate.

The use case approach

As mentioned earlier, a use case describes a sequence of interactions between a system and an external actor that results in some outcome that provides value to the actor. An *actor* is a person (or sometimes another software system or a hardware device) that interacts with the system to perform a use case. For example, the Chemical Tracking System's "Request a Chemical" use case involves an actor named *Requester*. There is no CTS user class named Requester. Both chemists and members of the chemical stockroom staff may request chemicals, so members of either user class may perform the Requester role. Following are some questions you might ask to help user representatives identify actors:

- Who (or what) is notified when something occurs within the system?

- Who (or what) provides information or services to the system?

- Who (or what) helps the system respond to and complete a task?

Use case diagrams provide a high-level visual representation of the user requirements. Figure 8-2 shows a partial use case diagram for the CTS, using the Unified Modeling Language (UML) notation (Booch, Rumbaugh, and Jacobson 1999; Podeswa 2010). The box frame represents the system boundary. Arrows from each actor (stick figure) connect to the use cases (ovals) with which the actor interacts. An arrow from an actor to a use case indicates that he is the *primary actor* for the use case. The primary actor initiates the use case and derives the main value from it. An arrow goes from a use case to a *secondary actor*, who participates somehow in the successful execution of the use case. Other software systems often serve as secondary actors, contributing behind the scenes to the use case execution. The Training Database is just such a secondary actor in Figure 8-2. This system gets involved when a Requester is requesting a hazardous chemical that requires the Requester to have been trained in how to safely handle such dangerous materials.

Compare this use case diagram to the context diagram shown earlier in Figure 5-6 in Chapter 5, "Establishing the business requirements." Both define the scope boundary between objects that lie outside the system and things inside the system. In the use case diagram, the box separates some internal aspects of the system—use cases—from the external actors. The context diagram also depicts objects that lie outside the system, but it provides no visibility into the system internals. The arrows in a context diagram indicate the flow of data, control signals, or physical materials (if you defined the "system" to include manual processes) across the system boundary. In contrast, the arrows in a use case diagram simply indicate the connections between actors and use cases in which they participate; they do not represent a flow of any kind. As with all forms of requirements representations, all readers of the models you create must have a consistent understanding of the notations used.

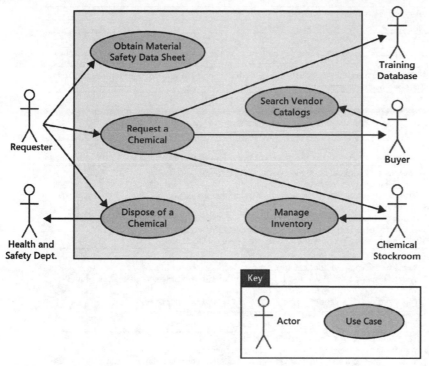

FIGURE 8-2 Partial use case diagram for the Chemical Tracking System.

Use cases and usage scenarios

A use case describes a discrete, standalone activity that an actor can perform to achieve some outcome of value. A use case might encompass a number of related activities having a common goal. A *scenario* is a description of a single instance of usage of the system. A use case is therefore a collection of related usage scenarios, and a scenario is a specific instance of a use case. When exploring user requirements, you can begin with a general use case statement and develop more specific usage scenarios, or you can generalize from a specific scenario example to the broader use case.

Figure 8-3 shows a comprehensive use case template filled in with an example drawn from the Chemical Tracking System. Appendix C shows more sample use cases written according to this template. As with all templates, you don't complete this from top to bottom, and you don't necessarily need all of the template information for every use case. The template is simply a structure in which to store the information you encounter during a use case discussion in an organized and consistent fashion. The template reminds you of all the information you should contemplate regarding each use case. If information that belongs in the template already exists somewhere else, simply point to it to include that information by reference. For instance, don't incorporate the actual text of each business rule that affects the use case in the template; just list the identifiers for the relevant business rules so the reader can find that information when necessary.

ID and Name:	UC-4 Request a Chemical		
Created By:	Lori	Date Created:	8/22/13
Primary Actor:	Requester	Secondary Actors:	Buyer, Chemical Stockroom, Training Database
Description:	The Requester specifies the desired chemical to request by entering its name or chemical ID number or by importing its structure from a chemical drawing tool. The system either offers the Requester a container of the chemical from the chemical stockroom or lets the Requester order one from a vendor.		
Trigger:	Requester indicates that he wants to request a chemical.		
Preconditions:	PRE-1. User's identity has been authenticated. PRE-2. User is authorized to request chemicals. PRE-3. Chemical inventory database is online.		
Postconditions:	POST-1. Request is stored in the CTS. POST-2. Request was sent to the Chemical Stockroom or to a Buyer.		
Normal Flow:	**4.0 Request a Chemical from the Chemical Stockroom** 1. Requester specifies the desired chemical. 2. System lists containers of the desired chemical that are in the chemical stockroom, if any. 3. System gives Requester the option to View Container History for any container. 4. Requester selects a specific container or asks to place a vendor order (see 4.1). 5. Requester enters other information to complete the request. 6. System stores the request and notifies the Chemical Stockroom.		
Alternative Flows:	**4.1 Request a Chemical from a Vendor** 1. Requester searches vendor catalogs for the chemical (see 4.1.E1). 2. System displays a list of vendors for the chemical with available container sizes, grades, and prices. 3. Requester selects a vendor, container size, grade, and number of containers. 4. Requester enters other information to complete the request. 5. System stores the request and notifies the Buyer.		
Exceptions:	**4.1.E1 Chemical Is Not Commercially Available** 1. System displays message: No vendors for that chemical. 2. System asks Requester if he wants to request another chemical (3a) or to exit (4a). 3a. Requester asks to request another chemical. 3b. System starts normal flow over. 4a. Requester asks to exit. 4b. System terminates use case.		
Priority:	High		
Frequency of Use:	Approximately 5 times per week by each chemist, 200 times per week by chemical stockroom staff		
Business Rules:	BR-28, BR-31		
Other Information:	The system must be able to import a chemical structure in the standard encoded form from any of the supported chemical drawing packages.		
Assumptions:	Imported chemical structures are assumed to be valid.		

FIGURE 8-3 Partial specification of the Chemical Tracking System's "Request a Chemical" use case.

The essential elements of a use case are the following:

- A unique identifier and a succinct name that states the user goal

- A brief textual description that describes the purpose of the use case

- A trigger condition that initiates execution of the use case

- Zero or more preconditions that must be satisfied before the use case can begin

- One or more postconditions that describe the state of the system after the use case is successfully completed

- A numbered list of steps that shows the sequence of interactions between the actor and the system—a dialog—that leads from the preconditions to the postconditions

Use case labeling convention

Use case specifications consist of numerous small packets of information: normal and alternative flows, exceptions, preconditions and postconditions, and so on. The example in Figure 8-3 illustrates a simple labeling convention that can help keep these elements straight. Each use case has a sequence number and a meaningful name that reflects the user's goal: UC-4 Request a Chemical. The identifier for the normal flow for this use case is 4.0. Alternative flows are identified by incrementing the number to the right of the decimal, so the first alternative flow is 4.1, a second would be 4.2, and so on. Both the normal flow and alternative flows can have their own exceptions. The first exception on the normal flow of use case number 4 would be labeled 4.0.E1. The second exception for the first alternative flow for this use case would be 4.1.E2.

Preconditions and postconditions

Preconditions define prerequisites that must be met before the system can begin executing the use case. The system should be able to test all preconditions to see if it's possible to proceed with the use case. Preconditions could describe the system state (for a use case to withdraw cash from an automated teller machine, the ATM must contain money), but they don't describe the user's intent ("I need some cash").

When the system detects the trigger event that indicates that a user wants to execute a particular use case, the system says to itself (though not necessarily to the user!), "Hold on a moment while I check these preconditions." The trigger event itself is not one of the preconditions. If the preconditions are all satisfied, the system can begin executing the use case; otherwise, it cannot. Checking preconditions can prevent some errors that might otherwise take place if the system knows at the outset that it can't successfully complete the use case but proceeds anyway. If the ATM is empty, it shouldn't let a user even begin a withdrawal transaction. This is a way to make your applications more robust. Users aren't likely to be aware of all of a use case's preconditions, so the BA might need to get some input from other sources.

Postconditions describe the state of the system after the use case executed successfully. Postconditions can describe:

- Something observable to the user (the system displayed an account balance).

- Physical outcomes (the ATM has dispensed money and printed a receipt).

- Internal system state changes (the account has been debited by the amount of a cash withdrawal, plus any transaction fees).

Many postconditions are evident to the user, because they reflect the outcome that delivers user value: "I've got my cash!" However, no user will ever tell a BA that the system should reduce its record of the amount of cash remaining in the ATM by the amount the user just withdrew. Users neither know nor care about such internal housekeeping details. But developers and testers need to know about them, which means that the BA needs to discover those—perhaps by working with a subject matter expert—and record them as additional postconditions.

Normal flows, alternative flows, and exceptions

One scenario is identified as the *normal flow* of events for the use case. It's also called the main flow, basic flow, normal course, primary scenario, main success scenario, sunny-day scenario, and happy path. The normal flow for the "Request a Chemical" use case is to request a chemical that's available in the chemical stockroom. As Figure 8-3 illustrates, the normal flow is written as a numbered list of steps, indicating which entity—the system or a specific actor—performs each step.

Other success scenarios within the use case are called *alternative flows* or *secondary scenarios*. Alternative flows deliver the same business outcome (sometimes with variations) as the normal flow but represent less common or lower-priority variations in the specifics of the task or how it is accomplished. The normal flow can branch off into an alternative flow at some decision point in the dialog sequence; it might (or might not) rejoin the normal flow later. The steps in the normal flow indicate where the user can branch into an alternative flow. A user who says, "The default should be. . ." is describing the normal flow of the use case. A statement such as "The user should also be able to request a chemical from a vendor" suggests an alternative flow, shown as 4.1 in Figure 8-3, which branches from step 4 in the normal flow.

Recall that user stories are concise statements of user needs, in contrast to the richer description that a use case provides. In the agile world, a user story sometimes covers the same scope as an entire use case, but in other cases a user story represents just a single scenario or alternative flow. If an agile development team were discussing requirements for the CTS, they might come up with user stories such as the following:

As a chemist, I want to request a chemical so that I can perform experiments.

As a chemist, I want to request a chemical from the Chemical Stockroom so that I can use it immediately.

As a chemist, I want to request a chemical from a vendor because I don't trust the purity of any of the samples available in the Chemical Stockroom.

The first of these three stories corresponds to the use case as a whole. The second and third user stories represent the normal flow of the use case and the first alternative flow, from Figure 8-3.

Conditions that have the potential to prevent a use case from succeeding are called *exceptions*. Exceptions describe anticipated error conditions that could occur during execution of the use case and how they are to be handled. In some cases, the user can recover from an exception, perhaps by re-entering some data that was incorrect. In other situations, though, the use case must terminate without reaching its success conditions. One exception for the "Request a Chemical" use case is "Chemical Is Not Commercially Available," labeled as 4.1.E1 in Figure 8-3. If you don't specify exception handling during requirements elicitation, there are two possible outcomes:

- Each developer will make his best guess at how to deal with the exceptions he sees, leading to inconsistent error handling throughout the application and less robust software.

- The system will fail when a user hits the error condition because no one thought about it.

It's a safe bet that system crashes aren't on the user's list of requirements.

Some error conditions could affect multiple use cases or multiple steps in a use case's normal flow. Examples are a loss of network connectivity, a database failure partway through an operation, or a physical device failure such as a paper jam. Treat these as additional functional requirements to be implemented, instead of repeating them as exceptions for all the potentially affected use cases. The goal is not to force-fit all known functionality into a use case. You're employing usage-centric elicitation to try to discover as much of the essential system functionality as you can.

You won't necessarily implement every alternative flow that you identify for a use case. You might defer some to later iterations or releases. However, you *must* implement the exceptions that can prevent the flows that you do implement from succeeding. Experienced programmers know that handling exceptions represents a lot of the coding effort. Overlooked exceptions are a common source of missing requirements. Specifying exception conditions during requirements elicitation helps teams build robust products. The steps in the normal flow indicate where known exceptions could take place, pointing to the section in the use case template for how the system should handle the exception.

Agile projects employing the user story approach address exceptions through the acceptance tests they create for each story. The third user story above pertained to requesting a chemical from a vendor. Conversations about this story might raise questions such as, "What if the chemical you want is not commercially available from any vendor?" This could lead to an acceptance test like, "If the chemical isn't found in any available vendor catalogs, show a message to that effect." As with any good testing approach, the set of acceptance tests for a user story must cover both expected behavior and things that could go wrong.

Although many use cases can be described in simple prose, a flowchart or a UML activity diagram is a useful way to visually represent the logic flow in a complex use case, as illustrated in Figure 8-4. Flowcharts and activity diagrams show the decision points and conditions that cause a branch from the normal flow into an alternative flow.

In the example in Figure 8-3, the actor's ultimate goal—to request a chemical—is the same in both situations. Therefore, requesting a chemical from the stockroom or from a vendor are two scenarios within the same use case, not separate use cases. Some of the steps in an alternative flow will be the same as those in the normal flow, but certain unique actions are needed to accomplish the alternative path. This alternative flow might allow the user to search vendor catalogs for a desired chemical, then rejoin the normal flow and continue with the requesting process back at step 4.

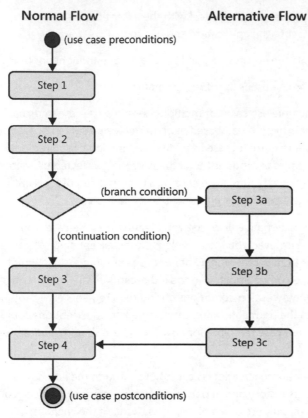

Normal Flow   **Alternative Flow**

(use case preconditions)

Step 1

Step 2

(branch condition) → Step 3a

(continuation condition)

Step 3b

Step 3

Step 4 ← Step 3c

(use case postconditions)

FIGURE 8-4 An activity diagram illustrating the step sequence in the normal and alternative flows of a use case.

Dressing the use cases

You don't always need a comprehensive use case specification. Cockburn (2001) describes *casual* and *fully dressed* use case templates. A casual use case is simply a textual narrative of the user goal and interactions with the system, perhaps just the "Description" section from Figure 8-3. The completed template in Figure 8-3 illustrates a fully dressed use case. And, of course, you can do anything in between. Nor must you document all of your use cases to the same degree of detail. Sometimes, the use case name and short description suffice to convey the functionality to implement. Other times, you can simply list the alternative flows and exceptions but not elaborate them further. In some cases, though, the team will benefit from a more comprehensive specification of a complex use case. Fully dressed use cases are valuable when:

- User representatives are not closely engaged with the development team throughout the project.

- The application is complex and system failures carry a high risk.

- The use cases represent novel requirements with which the developers are not familiar.

- The use cases are the most detailed requirements that the developers will receive.

- You intend to develop comprehensive test cases based on the user requirements.

- Collaborating remote teams need a detailed, shared group memory.

Instead of being dogmatic about how much detail to include in a use case, remember your goal: to understand the user's objectives well enough to enable developers to proceed at low risk of having to do rework.

Extend and include

You can show two types of relationships, called *extend* and *include,* between use cases in a use case diagram. Figure 8-3 showed that the normal flow for the "Request a Chemical" use case is to request a chemical from the Chemical Stockroom; an alternative flow is to request a chemical from a vendor. In the use case diagram in Figure 8-2, the Buyer has a use case called "Search Vendor Catalogs." Suppose you wanted to let the Requester execute that same "Search Vendor Catalog" use case as an option when requesting a chemical, as part of the alternative flow processing. A use case diagram can show that a standalone use case like "Search Vendor Catalogs" *extends* the normal flow into an alternative flow, as illustrated in Figure 8-5 (Armour and Miller 2001).

FIGURE 8-5 An example of the use case *extend* relationship for the Chemical Tracking System.

Sometimes several use cases share a common set of steps. To avoid duplicating these steps in each such use case, you can define a separate use case that contains the shared functionality and indicate that the other use cases *include* that subordinate use case. This is analogous to calling a common subroutine in a computer program. Consider an accounting software package. Two use cases are "Pay a Bill" and "Reconcile Credit Card," both of which might involve the user writing a check to make the payment. You can create a separate use case called "Write a Check" that contains the common steps involved in writing the check. The two transaction use cases both include the "Write a Check" use case, as shown with the notation in Figure 8-6. "Write a Check" is a standalone use case, because that's another task someone might perform with the accounting software.

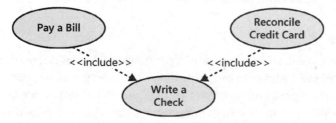

FIGURE 8-6 An example of the use case *include* relationship for an accounting application.

> **Trap** Don't have protracted debates with your colleagues over when, how, and whether to use the extend and include relationships. One author of a book on use cases told me that *extend* and *include* are best discussed by friends over beer.

Aligning preconditions and postconditions

In many applications, the user can chain together a sequence of use cases into a "macro" use case that describes a larger task. Some use cases for an e-commerce website might be "Search Catalog," "Add Item to Shopping Cart," and "Pay for Items in Shopping Cart." If you could perform each of these activities independently, they are individual use cases. That is, you could have one session with the website in which you just searched the catalog, a second session in which you just added an item to your shopping cart without searching (perhaps by typing in the product number), and a third session in which you paid for the items in the shopping cart (implying that your cart must persist across logon sessions). However, you might also be able to perform all three activities in sequence as a single large use case called "Buy Product," as shown in Figure 8-7. The description of the "Buy Product" use case could simply say to perform each of those other three use cases in turn: "Search Catalog," "Add Item to Shopping Cart," and then "Pay for Items in Shopping Cart."

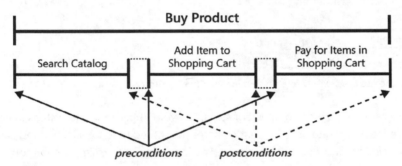

FIGURE 8-7 Preconditions and postconditions define the boundaries of the individual use cases that can be chained together to perform a larger task.

To make this process work, each use case must leave the system in a state that enables the user to commence the next use case immediately. That is, the postconditions of one use case must satisfy the preconditions of the next one in the sequence. Similarly, in a transaction-processing application such as an ATM, each use case must leave the system in a state that permits the next transaction to begin.

Use cases and business rules

Use cases and business rules are intertwined. Some business rules constrain which roles can perform all or parts of a use case. Perhaps only users who have certain privilege levels can perform specific alternative flows. That is, the rule might impose preconditions that the system must test before letting the user proceed. Business rules can influence specific steps in the normal flow by defining valid input values or dictating how computations are to be performed. Suppose an airline charges a premium for passengers who want certain preferred seats. If the passenger executes a use case to select a new seat on the airline's website, the relevant business rules would change the passenger's airfare if he chooses one of those seats. When specifying a use case, record the identifiers of any known business rules that affect the use case, and indicate which part of the use case each rule affects.

 While you are exploring use cases you might uncover pertinent business rules. When the chemists who participated in requirements elicitation for the Chemical Tracking System discussed the use case to view an order stored in the system, one of them said, "Fred shouldn't be able to see my orders, and I don't want to see Fred's orders." That is, they came up with a business rule: a user may view only chemical orders that he placed. Sometimes you invent business rules during elicitation and analysis, sometimes your discussions reveal relevant rules that already exist in the organization, and sometimes you already know about existing rules that the system will have to respect.

Identifying use cases

You can identify use cases in several ways (Ham 1998; Larman 1998):

- Identify the actors first, then lay out the business processes being supported by the system, and define the use cases for activities where actors and systems interact.

- Create a specific scenario to illustrate each business process, then generalize the scenarios into use cases and identify the actors involved in each one.

- Using a business process description, ask, "What tasks must the system perform to complete this process or convert the inputs into outputs?" Those tasks might be use cases.

- Identify the external events to which the system must respond, then relate these events to participating actors and specific use cases.

- Use a CRUD analysis to identify data entities that require use cases to create, read, update, delete, or otherwise manipulate them (see Chapter 13, "Specifying data requirements").

- Examine the context diagram and ask, "What objectives do each of these external entities want to achieve with the help of the system?"

The CTS team followed the first approach, using the process described in the next several sections of this chapter. The three business analysts facilitated a series of two-hour use case elicitation workshops, which were held twice a week. They chose to use workshops for elicitation partly because none of them had tried the use case method before, so they needed to learn together. Also, they saw the value of group synergy in the workshop format over individual interviews. Members of the various user classes participated in separate, parallel workshops, working with different BAs. This worked well because only a few use cases were common to multiple user classes. Each workshop included the user class's product champion, other selected user representatives, and a developer. Participating in elicitation workshops gives developers early insight into the product they will be expected to build. Developers also serve as the voice of reality when infeasible requirements are suggested.

Prior to beginning the workshops, each BA asked the users to think of tasks they would need to perform with the new system. Each of these tasks became a candidate use case. This is a bottom-up approach to use case elicitation, which complements the top-down strategy of identifying all the business processes the system will support and gleaning use cases from those. Comparing the lists of use cases generated from these different thought processes reduces the chance of overlooking one.

A few candidates were judged to be out of scope and weren't pursued. As the group explored the remaining in-scope use cases in the workshops, they found that some of them were related scenarios that could be consolidated into a single, more general use case. The group also discovered additional use cases beyond those in the initial set. Expect to perform these sorts of adjustments as you go along.

Some users proposed use cases that were not phrased as tasks, such as "Material Safety Data Sheet." A use case's name should indicate a goal the user wants to accomplish, so you need to start with a verb. Does the user want to request, view, print, download, order, revise, delete, or create a material safety data sheet? Sometimes a suggested use case was just a single step the actor would perform as part of process, such as "Scan Bar Code." The BA needs to learn what objective the user has in mind that involves scanning a bar code. The BA might ask, "When you scan the bar code on the chemical container, what are you trying to accomplish?" Suppose the reply is, "As a chemist, I need to scan the container's bar code so I can log the chemical into my laboratory." (Note how this is stated in the style of a user story.) The real use case, therefore, is "Log Chemical into Lab." Scanning the bar code label is just one step in the interaction between the actor and the system that logs the chemical into the lab.

Don't dive into high-resolution analysis of the first use case that someone proposes. Learn just enough about each use case so the team can prioritize them and do an initial allocation of use cases, or portions thereof, to forthcoming releases or iterations. Then you can begin exploring the highest-priority use cases, those that are allocated to the next development cycle, so developers can begin implementing them as soon as possible. Lower-priority use cases can wait for detailing until just before they're scheduled to be implemented. This is the same strategy you would pursue when working with user stories on an agile project.

> **Trap** Don't try to force every requirement to fit into a use case. Use cases can reveal most—but probably not all—of the functional requirements. If the BA already knows of certain functionality that must be implemented, there's little value in creating a use case simply to hold that functionality.

Exploring use cases

The participants in the CTS elicitation workshops began each use case discussion by identifying the actor who would benefit from the use case and writing the short description. Estimating the frequency of use provided an early indicator of concurrent usage and capacity requirements. Then they began defining the preconditions and postconditions, which are the boundaries of the use case; all use case steps take place between these boundaries. The preconditions and postconditions were adjusted as more information surfaced during the discussion.

Next, the BA asked the participants how they envisioned interacting with the system to perform the task. The resulting sequence of actor actions and system responses became the normal flow for the use case. Although each participant had a different mental image of what the future user interface would look like, the group reached a common vision of the essential steps in the actor-system dialog.

Staying in bounds

While reviewing a use case whose normal flow had eight steps, I realized that the postconditions were satisfied after step 5. Steps 6, 7, and 8 therefore were unnecessary, being outside the boundary of the use case. Similarly, a use case's preconditions must be satisfied prior to commencing step 1 of the normal flow. When you review a use case flow, make sure that its preconditions and postconditions properly frame it.

The BA captured the actor actions and their corresponding system responses on sticky notes, which he placed on a flipchart sheet. Sticky notes work well for such workshops. It's easy to move them around, group them together, and replace them as the discussion progresses. Another way to conduct such a workshop is to project a use case template onto a large screen from a computer and populate the template during the discussion. The elicitation team developed similar dialogs for the alternative flows and exceptions. Many exceptions were discovered when the analyst asked questions similar to "What should happen if the database isn't online at that moment?" or "What if the chemical isn't commercially available?" The workshop is also a good time to discuss the user's expectations of quality, such as response times and availability, security requirements, and UI design constraints.

After the workshop participants described each use case and no one proposed additional variations, exceptions, or other information, they moved on to another one. They didn't try to cover all the use cases in one marathon workshop or to pin down every detail of every use case they discussed. Instead, they explored the use cases in layers, beginning with the broad strokes for the top-priority use cases and iteratively refining them just prior to implementation.

Figure 8-8 shows the sequence of work products created during the CTS use case elicitation process. Following the workshop, the analyst documented each use case by using the template illustrated in Figure 8-3, using his judgment to decide how complete the template needed to be for each use case.

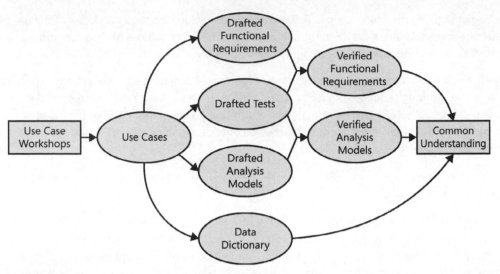

FIGURE 8-8 Use case elicitation work products.

When writing the steps in the use case flows, avoid language that refers to specific user interface interactions. "Requester specifies the desired chemical" is nicely general and UI-independent. It allows for multiple ways to accomplish the user's intention of indicating the chemical to be requested: enter a chemical ID number, import a chemical structure from a file, draw the structure on the screen with the mouse (or a stylus on a tablet), or select a chemical from a list. Proceeding too quickly into specific interaction details constrains the thinking of the workshop participants.

Use cases often involve some additional information or requirements that do not fit within any of the template sections. Use the "Other Information" section to record pertinent performance and other quality requirements, constraints, and external interface knowledge. Eventually, all this information should find a home in the SRS or other elements of your requirements documentation. Also note any information that might not be visible to the users, such as the need for one system to communicate behind the scenes with another to complete the use case.

Validating use cases

The process in Figure 8-8 shows that after each workshop, the BAs on the Chemical Tracking System derived software functional requirements from the use cases. (For more about this, see the next section, "Use cases and functional requirements.") The BAs also drew some analysis models, such as a state-transition diagram that showed all possible chemical request statuses and the permitted status changes. Multiple use cases can manipulate a chemical request, so the diagram pulls together information and operations that span several use cases. Chapter 12 illustrates several analysis models for the CTS; the state-transition diagram is in Figure 12-3.

A day or two after each workshop, the BA gave the use cases and functional requirements to the workshop participants, who reviewed them prior to the next workshop. These informal reviews revealed many errors: previously undiscovered alternative flows, new exceptions, incorrect functional requirements, and missing dialog steps. The team quickly learned to allow at least one day between successive workshops. The mental relaxation that comes after a day or two away allows people to examine their earlier work from a fresh perspective. One BA who held daily workshops found that the participants had difficulty spotting errors in the materials they reviewed because the information was too fresh in their minds. They mentally recited the recent discussion and didn't see the errors.

> **Trap** Don't wait until requirements specification is complete to solicit review feedback from users, developers, and other stakeholders. Early reviews help improve the subsequent requirements work.

Early in requirements development, the Chemical Tracking System's test lead began creating conceptual tests—independent of implementation and user-interface specifics—from the use cases (Collard 1999). These tests helped the team reach a shared understanding of how the system should behave in specific scenarios. The tests let the BAs verify whether they had derived the functionality needed to let users perform each use case. During the final elicitation workshop, the participants walked through the tests together to be sure they agreed on how the use cases should work.

Early conceptual test thinking like this is much cheaper and faster than writing code, building part of the system, executing tests, and only then discovering problems with requirements. It is analogous to the agile approach of fleshing out user stories with acceptance tests, but the CTS team wrote both functional requirements and tests. Comparing the two revealed errors in both before any code was written. Chapter 17, "Validating the requirements," discusses generating tests from requirements.

The CTS team created multiple representations of the requirements they identified: a list of functional requirements, a set of corresponding tests, and analysis models, all based on use cases. Comparing these alternative views of the requirements is a powerful quality technique (Wiegers 2006). The team used the tests to verify the functional requirements, looking for tests that couldn't be "executed" with the set of requirements and for requirements that were not covered by tests.

If you create just a single representation, or view, of the requirements, you must trust it. You have nothing to compare it against to look for errors, gaps, and different interpretations. Agile project teams do not typically document functional requirements, preferring to create acceptance tests. Although thinking about testing during requirements exploration is an excellent idea on every project, it still leaves you with only a single representation of the requirements that you must trust as being correct. Similarly, traditional project teams that create only a set of functional requirements and leave testing until later in the project have only one representation. You'll get the best results with a judicious combination of written requirements, tests, analysis models, and prototypes.

Use cases and functional requirements

Software developers don't implement business requirements or user requirements. They implement functional requirements, specific bits of system behavior. Some practitioners regard the use cases as being the functional requirements. However, we have seen many organizations get into trouble when they simply pass their use cases to developers for implementation. Use cases describe the user's perspective, looking at the externally visible behavior of the system. They don't contain all the information that a developer needs to write the software. The user of an ATM doesn't know about any back-end processing involved, such as communicating with the bank's computer. This detail is invisible to the user, yet the developer needs to know about it. Developers who receive even fully dressed use cases often have many questions. To reduce this uncertainty, consider having a BA explicitly specify the functional requirements necessary to implement each use case (Arlow 1998).

Many functional requirements fall right out of the dialog steps between the actor and the system. Some are obvious, such as "The system shall assign a unique sequence number to each request." There is no point in duplicating those elsewhere if they're clear from the use case. Other functional requirements don't appear in the use case description. For instance, the way use cases are typically documented does not specify what the system should do if a precondition is *not* satisfied. This is an example of how use cases often do not provide all the necessary information for a developer to know what to build. The BA must derive those missing requirements and communicate them to developers and testers (Wiegers 2006). This analysis to get from the user's view of the requirements to the developer's view is one of the many ways the BA adds value to a project.

The Chemical Tracking System employed the use cases primarily as a tool to reveal the necessary functional requirements. The analysts wrote only casual descriptions of the less complex use cases. They then derived all the functional requirements that, when implemented, would allow an actor to perform the use case, including alternative flows and exception handlers. The analysts documented these functional requirements in the SRS, which was organized by product feature.

You can document the functionality associated with a use case in several ways. None of the following methods is perfect, so select the approach that best fits with how you want to document and manage your project's software requirements.

Use cases only

One possibility is to include the functional requirements along with each use case specification, if they aren't already evident. You'll still need to document nonfunctional requirements and any functionality that's not associated with a use case. Additionally, several use cases might need the same functional requirement. If five use cases require that the user's identity be authenticated, you don't want to write five different blocks of code for that purpose. Rather than duplicate them, cross-reference functional requirements that appear in multiple use cases. The use cases could be collected in a user requirements document.

Use cases and functional requirements

Another option is to write fairly simple use cases and document the functional requirements derived from each one in an SRS or a requirements repository. In this approach, you should establish traceability between the use cases and their associated functional requirements. That way, if a use case changes, you can quickly find the affected functional requirements. The best way to manage the traceability is with a requirements management tool.

Functional requirements only

One more option is to organize your functional requirements by use case or by feature, and include both the use cases and the functional requirements in the SRS or requirements repository. This is the approach that the CTS team used, and we've done the same on several website development projects. We wrote most of our use cases in very concise form, not completing the full template from Figure 8-3. The details were then specified through a set of functional requirements. This approach doesn't result in a separate user requirements document.

Use cases and tests

If you write both detailed use case specifications and functional requirements, you might notice some duplication, particularly around the normal flow. There is little value in writing the same requirement twice. So another strategy is to write fairly complete use case specifications, but then write acceptance tests to determine if the system properly handles the basic behavior of the use case, alternative success paths, and the various things that could go wrong.

Use case traps to avoid

As with any software engineering technique, there are many ways to go astray when applying the use case approach (Lilly 2000; Kulak and Guiney 2004). Watch out for the following traps:

- **Too many use cases** If you're caught in a use case explosion, you might not be writing them at the appropriate level of abstraction. Don't create a separate use case for every possible scenario. You'll typically have many more use cases than business requirements and features, but many more functional requirements than use cases.

- **Highly complex use cases** I once reviewed a use case with four dense pages of dialog steps, with a lot of embedded logic and branching conditions. It was incomprehensible. I've heard of even longer use cases, going on page after page. You can't control the complexity of the business tasks, but you can control how you represent them in use cases. Select one success path through the use case and call that the normal flow. Use alternative flows for the other logic branches that lead to success, and use exceptions to handle branches that lead to failure. You might have many alternatives, but each one will be short and easy to understand. If a flow exceeds 10 to 15 steps in length, confirm whether it truly describes just a single scenario. Don't arbitrarily split a legitimately long flow just because it has a lot of steps, though.

- **Including design in the use cases** Use cases should focus on what the users need to accomplish with the system's help, not on how the screens will look. Emphasize the conceptual interactions between the actors and the system. For example, say "System presents choices" instead of "System displays drop-down list." Don't let the UI design drive the requirements exploration. Use screen sketches and dialog maps (see Chapter 12) to help visualize the actor-system interactions, not as firm design specifications.

- **Including data definitions in the use cases**   Use case explorations naturally stimulate data discussions, thinking about what data elements serve as inputs and outputs during the interaction. Some use case authors include definitions of the pertinent data elements right in the use case specification. This makes it difficult for people to find the information because it isn't obvious which use case contains each data definition. It can also lead to duplicate definitions, which get out of sync when one instance is changed and others are not. Store data definitions in a project-wide data dictionary and data model, as discussed in Chapter 13.

- **Use cases that users don't understand**   If users can't relate a use case to their business processes or goals, there's a problem. Write use cases from the user's perspective, not the system's point of view, and ask users to review them. Keep the use cases as simple as you can while still achieving the goal of clear and effective communication.

Benefits of usage-centric requirements

The power of both use cases and user stories comes from their user-centric and usage-centric perspective. The users will have clearer expectations of what the new system will let them do than if you take a feature-centric approach. The customer representatives on several Internet development projects found that use cases clarified their notions of what visitors to their websites should be able to do. Use cases help BAs and developers understand the user's business. Thinking through the actor-system dialogs reveals ambiguity and vagueness early in the development process, as does generating tests from the use cases.

Overspecifying the requirements up front and trying to include every conceivable function can lead to implementing unnecessary requirements. The usage-centric approach leads to functionality that will allow the user to perform certain known tasks. This helps prevent "orphan functionality" that seems like a good idea but that no one uses because it doesn't relate directly to user goals.

Developing user requirements helps with requirements prioritization. The highest-priority functional requirements are those that originate in the top-priority user requirements. A use case or user story could be of high priority for several reasons:

- It describes part of a core business process that the system enables.

- Many users will use it frequently.

- A favored user class requested it.

- It's required for regulatory compliance.

- Other system functions depend on its presence.

> **Trap** Don't spend a lot of time detailing use cases that won't be implemented for months or years. They're likely to change or disappear before construction begins.

There are technical benefits to use cases, too. They reveal some of the important domain objects and their responsibilities to each other. Developers using object-oriented design methods can turn use cases into object models such as class and sequence diagrams. As business processes change over time, the tasks that are embodied in specific user requirements will change. If you've traced functional requirements, designs, code, and tests back to their parent user requirements—the voice of the user—it will be easier to cascade those changes through the entire system.

Next steps

- Write several use cases for your current project by using the template in Figure 8-3. Include alternative flows and exceptions. Identify the functional requirements that will allow the user to successfully complete each use case. Check whether your project's requirements repository already includes all those requirements.

- If your organization is considering adopting agile practices, then try writing one use case as a user story or set of user stories to assess the differences between the two approaches.

- Walk through a use case, trying to derive the necessary functional requirements at each step and from the preconditions, postconditions, business rules, and other requirements.

- Review the use case with customers to make sure the steps are correct, that variations from the normal flow have been considered, and that exceptions have been anticipated and handled in a way the customers think is sensible.

CHAPTER 9

Playing by the rules

"Hi, Tim, this is Jackie. I'm having a problem requesting a chemical with the Chemical Tracking System. My lab manager suggested that I ask you about it. He said you were the product champion who provided many of the requirements for this system."

"Yes, that's correct," Tim replied. "What's the problem?"

"I need to get some more phosgene for those dyes that I make for my research project," said Jackie, "but the system won't accept my request. It says I haven't taken a training class in handling hazardous chemicals in more than a year. What's that all about? I've been using phosgene for years with no problem. Why can't I get some more?"

"You're probably aware that Contoso requires an annual refresher class in the safe handling of hazardous chemicals," Tim pointed out. "This is a corporate policy based on OSHA regulations. The Chemical Tracking System just enforces it. I know the stockroom guys used to give you whatever you wanted, but they can't do that anymore. Sorry about the inconvenience, but you'll have to take the refresher training before the system will let you request more phosgene."

Every organization operates according to an extensive set of policies, laws, and industry standards. Industries such as banking, aviation, and medical device manufacture must comply with volumes of government regulations. Such controlling principles are known collectively as *business rules* or *business logic*. Business rules often are enforced through manual implementation of policies and procedures. In many cases, though, software applications also need to enforce these rules.

Most business rules originate outside the context of any specific software application. The corporate policy requiring annual training in handling hazardous chemicals applies even if all chemical purchasing and dispensing is done manually. Standard accounting practices were in use long before the digital computer was invented. Because business rules are a property of the business, they are not in themselves software requirements. However, business rules are a rich source of requirements because they dictate properties the system must possess to conform to the rules. As Figure 1-1 in Chapter 1, "The essential software requirement" showed, business rules can be the origin of several types of requirements. Table 9-1 illustrates and provides examples of how business rules influence several types of requirements.

TABLE 9-1 How business rules can influence various types of software requirements

Requirement type	Illustration of business rules' influence	Example
Business requirement	Government regulations can lead to necessary business objectives for a project.	*The Chemical Tracking System must enable compliance with all federal and state chemical usage and disposal reporting regulations within five months.*
User requirement	Privacy policies dictate which users can and cannot perform certain tasks with the system.	*Only laboratory managers are allowed to generate chemical exposure reports for anyone other than themselves.*
Functional requirement	Company policy is that all vendors must be registered and approved before an invoice will be paid.	*If an invoice is received from an unregistered vendor, the Supplier System shall email the vendor editable PDF versions of the supplier intake form and the W-9 form.*
Quality attribute	Regulations from government agencies, such as OSHA and EPA, can dictate safety requirements, which must be enforced through system functionality.	*The system must maintain safety training records, which it must check to ensure that users are properly trained before they can request a hazardous chemical.*

People sometimes confuse business *rules* with business *processes* or business *requirements*. As you saw in Chapter 5, "Establishing the business requirements," a business *requirement* states a desirable outcome or a high-level objective of the organization that builds or procures a software solution. Business requirements serve as the justification for undertaking a project. A business *process* describes a series of activities that transform inputs into outputs to achieve a specific result. Information systems frequently automate business processes, which could lead to efficiencies and other benefits that achieve stated business requirements. Business *rules* influence business processes by establishing vocabulary, imposing restrictions, triggering actions, and governing how computations are carried out. The same business rule could apply to multiple manual or automated processes, which is one reason why it's best to treat business rules as a separate set of information.

Not all companies treat their essential business rules as the valuable enterprise asset they are. Certain departments might document their local rules, but many companies lack a unified effort to document business rules in a common repository accessible to the IT organization. Treating this vital information as corporate folklore leads to numerous problems. If business rules are not properly documented and managed, they exist only in the heads of select individuals. A BA needs to know who to call to learn about rules that affect his project. Individuals can have conflicting understandings of the rules, which can lead to different software applications enforcing the same business rule inconsistently or overlooking it entirely. Having a master repository of business rules makes it easier for all projects that are affected by certain rules to learn about them and implement them in a consistent fashion.

> **Trap** Having undocumented business rules known only to certain experts results in a knowledge vacuum when those experts leave the organization.

As an example, your organization likely has security policies that control access to information systems. Such policies might state the minimum and maximum length and the allowed characters in passwords, dictate the frequency of required password changes, state how many failed login attempts a user gets before his account is locked, and the like. Applications that the organization develops should apply these policies—these business rules—consistently. Tracing each rule into the code that implements it makes it easier to update systems to comply with changes in the rules, such as altering the required frequency of password changes. It also facilitates code reuse across projects.

A business rules taxonomy

The Business Rules Group (2012) provides definitions for business rules from the perspectives of both the business and its information systems:

- From the business perspective: "A business rule is guidance that there is an obligation concerning conduct, action, practice, or procedure within a particular activity or sphere." (There ought to be an explicit motivation for the rule, as well as enforcement methods and an understanding of what the consequences would be if the rule were broken.)

- From the information system perspective: "A business rule is a statement that defines or constrains some aspect of the business. It is intended to assert business structure or to control or influence the behavior of the business."

Whole methodologies have been developed based on the discovery and documentation of business rules and their implementation in automated business rules systems (von Halle 2002; Ross 1997; Ross and Lam 2011). Unless you're building a system that is heavily rules-driven, you don't need an elaborate methodology. Simply identify and document the rules that pertain to your system and link them to the specific requirements that implement them.

Numerous classification schemes have been proposed for organizing business rules (Ross 2001; Morgan 2002; von Halle 2002; von Halle and Goldberg 2010). The simple taxonomy shown in Figure 9-1, with five types of rules, will work for most situations. A sixth category is *terms*, defined words, phrases, and abbreviations that are important to the business. You could group terms with factual business rules. A glossary is another convenient place to define terms.

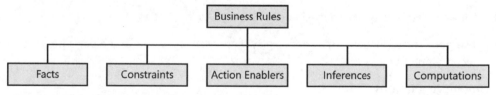

FIGURE 9-1 A simple business rule taxonomy.

Recording the business rules in a consistent way is more important than having heated arguments about precisely how to classify each one. However, a taxonomy is helpful to identify business rules you might not have thought of otherwise. Classifying the rules also gives you an idea of how you might apply them in a software application. For instance, constraints often lead to system functionality that enforces the restrictions, and action enablers lead to functionality to make something happen under certain conditions. Let's see some examples of these five kinds of business rules.

Facts

Facts are simply statements that are true about the business at a specified point in time. A fact describes associations or relationships between important business terms. Facts about data entities that are important to the system might appear in data models. (See Chapter 13, "Specifying data requirements," for more about data modeling.) Examples of facts include the following:

- Every chemical container has a unique bar code identifier.

- Every order has a shipping charge.

- Sales tax is not computed on shipping charges.

- Nonrefundable airline tickets incur a fee when the purchaser changes the itinerary.

- Books taller than 16 inches are shelved in the library's Oversize section.

Of course, there are countless facts floating around about businesses. Collecting irrelevant facts can bog down business analysis. Even if they're true, it might not be obvious how the development team is to use the information. Focus on facts that are in scope for the project, rather than trying to amass a complete collection of business knowledge. Try to connect each fact to the context diagram's inputs and outputs, to system events, to known data objects, or to specific user requirements.

Constraints

A constraint is a statement that restricts the actions that the system or its users are allowed to perform. Someone describing a constraining business rule might say that certain actions *must* or *must not* or *may not* be performed, or that *only* certain people or roles can perform particular actions. Following are some examples of constraints with various origins.

Organizational policies

- A loan applicant who is less than 18 years old must have a parent or a legal guardian as cosigner on the loan.

- A library patron may have a maximum of 10 items on hold at any time.

- Insurance correspondence may not display more than four digits of the policyholder's Social Security number.

Government regulations

- All software applications must comply with government regulations for usage by visually impaired persons.

- Airline pilots must receive at least 8 continuous hours of rest in every 24-hour period.

- Individual federal income tax returns must be postmarked by midnight on the first business day after April 14 unless an extension has been granted.

Industry standards

- Mortgage loan applicants must satisfy the Federal Housing Authority qualification standards.

- Web applications may not contain any HTML tags or attributes that are deprecated according to the HTML 5 standard.

> ## So many constraints
>
> Software projects have many kinds of constraints. Project managers must work within schedule, staff, and budget limitations. Such project-level constraints belong in the project management plan. Product design and implementation constraints represent imposed conditions that one might otherwise expect to be left to the discretion of the people building the solution. Such restrictions on the developer's choices belong in the SRS or design specification. Certain business rules impose constraints on the way the business operates; these should be stored in a business rules repository. Whenever these constraints are reflected in the software requirements, indicate the pertinent rule as the rationale for each such derived requirement.

Constraining business rules can convey implications for software development even if they don't translate directly into functionality. Consider a retail store's policy that only supervisors and managers are allowed to issue cash refunds larger than $50. If you're developing a point-of-sale application for use by store employees, this rule implies that each user must have a privilege level. The software must check to see if the current user is of sufficiently high privilege level to perform certain actions, such as opening the cash register drawer so a cashier can issue a refund to a customer.

Because many constraint-type business rules deal with which types of users can perform which functions, a concise way to document such rules is with a roles and permissions matrix (Beatty and Chen 2012). Figure 9-2 illustrates such a matrix for various users of a public library's information system. The roles have been separated into employees and non-employees. The system functions are grouped into system operations, operations dealing with patron records, and operations involving individual library items. An X in a cell indicates that the role named in the column has permission to perform the operation shown in the row.

Action enablers

A rule that triggers some activity if specific conditions are true is an *action enabler*. A person could perform the activity in a manual process. Alternatively, the rule might lead to specifying software functionality that makes an application exhibit the correct behavior when the system detects the triggering event. The conditions that lead to the action could be a complex combination of true and false values for multiple individual conditions. A decision table (described in Chapter 12, "A picture is worth 1024 words") provides a concise way to document action-enabling business rules that involve extensive logic. A statement in the form "If <some condition is true or some event takes place>, then

<something happens>" is a clue that someone might be describing an action enabler. Following are some examples of action-enabling business rules for the Chemical Tracking System:

- If the chemical stockroom has containers of a requested chemical in stock, then offer existing containers to the requester.

- On the last day of a calendar quarter, generate the mandated OSHA and EPA reports on chemical handling and disposal for that quarter.

- If the expiration date for a chemical container has been reached, then notify the person who currently possesses that container.

Businesses often develop policies that are intended to enhance their commercial success. Consider how an online bookstore might use the following business rules to try to stimulate impulse purchases after a customer has asked to buy a specific product:

- If the customer ordered a book by an author who has written multiple books, then offer the author's other books to the customer before completing the order.

- After a customer places a book into the shopping cart, display related books that other customers also bought when they bought this one.

Roles and Permissions Matrix	Employee	Administrator	Circulation Staff	Library Aide	Non-Employee	Volunteer	Patron
System Operations							
Log in to library system		X	X	X			
Set up new staff members		X					
Print hold pick list		X	X	X			
Patron Records							
View a patron record		X	X				
Edit a patron record		X	X				
View your own patron record		X	X	X		X	X
Issue a library card		X	X				
Accept a fine payment		X	X				
Item Operations							
Search the library catalog		X	X	X		X	X
Check out an item		X	X				
Check in an item		X	X	X		X	
Route an item to another branch		X	X	X		X	
Put an item on hold		X	X	X		X	X

FIGURE 9-2 Constraining business rules sometimes can be represented in a roles and permissions matrix.

Overruled by constraints

I recently redeemed some of my frequent-flyer miles on Blue Yonder Airlines to buy a ticket for my wife, Chris. When I attempted to finalize the purchase, BlueYonder.com said that it had encountered an error and couldn't issue the ticket. It told me to call the airline immediately. The reservation agent I (finally!) spoke with told me that the airline couldn't issue a mileage award ticket through the mail or by email because Chris and I have different last names. I had to go to the airport ticket counter and show identification to have the ticket issued.

This incident resulted from a constraining business rule that probably went something like this: "If the passenger has a different last name from the mileage redeemer, then the redeemer must pick up the ticket in person." This is probably for fraud prevention. The software driving the Blue Yonder website enforces the rule, but in a way that resulted in usability shortcomings and customer inconvenience. Rather than simply telling me about the issue with different last names and what I needed to do, the system displayed an alarming error message. It wasted my time and the reservation agent's time with an unnecessary phone call. Poorly thought-out business rule implementations can adversely affect your customer and hence your business.

Inferences

Sometimes called *inferred knowledge* or a *derived fact*, an *inference* creates a new fact from other facts. Inferences are often written in the "if/then" pattern also found in action-enabling business rules, but the "then" clause of an inference simply provides a piece of knowledge, not an action to be taken. Some examples of inferences are:

- If a payment is not received within 30 calendar days after it is due, then the account is delinquent.

- If the vendor cannot ship an ordered item within five days of receiving the order, then the item is considered back-ordered.

- Chemicals with an LD_{50} toxicity lower than 5 mg/kg in mice are considered hazardous.

Computations

The fifth class of business rules defines *computations* that transform existing data into new data by using specific mathematical formulas or algorithms. Many computations follow rules that are external to the enterprise, such as income tax withholding formulas. Following are a few examples of computational business rules written in text form.

- The domestic ground shipping charge for an order that weighs more than two pounds is $4.75 plus 12 cents per ounce or fraction thereof.

- The total price for an order is the sum of the price of the items ordered, less any volume discounts, plus state and county sales taxes for the location to which the order is being shipped, plus the shipping charge, plus an optional insurance charge.

- The unit price is reduced by 10 percent for orders of 6 to 10 units, by 20 percent for orders of 11 to 20 units, and by 30 percent for orders of more than 20 units.

Representing the details of computations in natural language like this can be wordy and confusing. As an alternative, you could represent these in some symbolic form, such as a mathematical expression or in a table of rules that is clearer and easier to maintain. Table 9-2 represents the previous unit-price discount computation rule in a clearer fashion.

TABLE 9-2 Using a table to represent computational business rules

ID	Number of units purchased	Percent discount
DISC-1	1 through 5	0
DISC-2	6 through 10	10
DISC-3	11 through 20	20
DISC-4	More than 20	30

Trap Watch out for boundary value overlaps when you are writing a set of business rules or requirements that define ranges. It's easy to inadvertently define ranges like 1–5, 5–10, and 10–20, which introduces ambiguity about which range the values of exactly 5 and 10 fit into.

Atomic business rules

Suppose you walk up to your friendly local librarian with a question. "How long can I check out a DVD for?" you ask. The librarian replies, "You can check out a DVD or Blu-ray Disc for one week, and you may renew it up to two times for three days each, but only if another patron hasn't placed a hold on it." The librarian's answer is based on the library's business rules. However, her answer combines several rules into a single statement. Composite business rules like this can be hard to understand and maintain. It's also hard to confirm that all possible conditions are covered. If several functionality segments trace back to this complex rule, it can be time-consuming to find and modify the appropriate code when just one part of the rule changes in the future.

A better strategy is to write your business rules at the atomic level, rather than combining multiple details into a single rule. This keeps your rules short and simple. It also facilitates reusing the rules, modifying them, and combining them in various ways. To write inferred knowledge and action-enabling business rules in an atomic way, don't use "or" logic on the left-hand side of an "if/then" construct, and avoid "and" logic on the right-hand side (von Halle 2002). You might break that complex library rule down into several atomic business rules, as shown in Table 9-3. (Chapter 10, "Documenting the requirements," describes the hierarchical labeling notation illustrated in Table 9-3.) These business rules are called *atomic* because they can't be decomposed further. You will likely end up with many atomic business rules, and your functional requirements will depend on various combinations of them.

TABLE 9-3 Some atomic business rules for a library

ID	Rule
Video.Media.Types	DVD discs and Blu-ray Discs are video items.
Video.Checkout.Duration	Video items may be checked out for one week at a time.
Renewal.Video.Times	Video items may be renewed up to two times.
Renewal.Video.Duration	Renewing a checked-out video item extends the due date by three days.
Renewal.HeldItem	A patron may not renew an item that another patron has on hold.

To illustrate how using atomic business rules facilitates maintenance, when the next generation video technology comes along, or the library purges all of its DVD discs, the library could just update the Video.Media.Types rule and none of the others are affected.

Documenting business rules

Because business rules can influence multiple applications, organizations should manage their rules as enterprise-level assets. A simple business rules catalog will suffice initially. If you're using a requirements management tool, you can store business rules as a requirement type, provided they are accessible to all of your software projects. Large organizations or those whose operations and information systems are heavily business-rule driven should establish a database of business rules. Commercial rule-management tools become valuable if your rules catalog outgrows a solution using a word processor, spreadsheet, Wiki, or other collaboration tool. Some business-rule management systems contain rules engines, which can automate the implementation of the rules in your applications. The Business Rules Group (2012) maintains a list of products for managing business rules. As you identify new rules while working on an application, add them to the catalog rather than embedding them in the documentation for that specific application or—worse—only in its code. Rules related to safety, security, finance, or regulatory compliance pose the greatest risk if they are not managed and enforced appropriately.

> **Trap** Don't make your business rules catalog more complex than necessary. Use the simplest form of documenting business rules that ensures that your development teams will use them effectively. The business should own the rules repository, not the IT department or the project team.

As you gain experience with identifying and documenting business rules, you can apply structured templates for defining rules of different types (Ross 1997; von Halle 2002). These templates describe patterns of keywords and clauses that structure the rules in a consistent fashion. They also facilitate storing the rules in a database, a commercial business-rule management tool, or a business rules engine. Sets of related rules can also be represented by using tools such as decision trees and decision tables (particularly when complex logic is involved) and roles and permissions matrices. To begin, though, try the simple format illustrated in Table 9-4 (Kulak and Guiney 2004).

TABLE 9-4 Some sample business rules catalog entries

ID	Rule definition	Type of rule	Static or dynamic	Source
ORDER-5	If the customer ordered a book by an author who has written multiple books, then offer the author's other books to the customer before completing the order.	Action enabler	Static	Marketing policy XX
ACCESS-8	All website images must include alternative text to be used by electronic reading devices to meet accessibility requirements for visually impaired users.	Constraint	Static	ADA Standards for Accessible Design
DISCOUNT-13	A discount is calculated based on the size of the current order, as defined in Table BR-060.	Computation	Dynamic	Corporate pricing policy XX

Giving each business rule a unique identifier lets you link requirements back to a specific rule. For instance, some templates for use cases contain a field for business rules that influence the use case. Instead of including the rule definition in the use case description, simply enter the identifiers for the relevant rules. Each ID serves as a pointer to the master instance of the business rule. This way you don't have to worry about the use case specification becoming obsolete if the rule changes.

The "Type of rule" column identifies each business rule as being a fact, constraint, action enabler, inference, or computation. The "Static or dynamic" column indicates how likely the rule is to change over time. This information is helpful to developers. If they know that certain rules are subject to periodic change, they can structure the software to make the affected functionality or data easy to update. Income tax calculations change at least every year. If the developer structures the income tax information into tables or a database, rather than hard-coding it into the software, it's a lot easier to update those values when necessary. It's safe to hard-code laws of nature, such as calculations based on the laws of thermodynamics; laws of humans are much more volatile.

The laws of separation

Air traffic control (ATC) systems must ensure minimum separation between aircraft in four dimensions—altitude, lateral, longitudinal, and time—to avoid collisions. The on-board aircraft systems, pilots, controllers on the ground, and the ATC system itself need to assemble flight path and speed information from hundreds of sources to anticipate when one plane might get dangerously close to another. Many business rules govern the minimum legal separation distances and times. These rules are dynamic: they change periodically as technology improves (GPS positioning versus radar, for example) and regulations are updated. This implies that the system needs to be able to accept a new set of rules on a regular schedule, validate the rules' self-consistency and completeness, and switch over to using the new rules at the same time the pilots and controllers do. One ATC project initially hard-coded the current set of such business rules into their software, thinking of them as being static. Major rework was required when the stakeholders realized the need to cope with periodic changes in these safety-critical rules.

The final column in Table 9-4 identifies the source of each rule. Sources of business rules include corporate and management policies, subject matter experts and other individuals, and documents such as government laws and regulations. Knowing the source helps people know where to go if they need more information about the rule or need to learn about changes.

Discovering business rules

Just as asking "What are your requirements?" doesn't help much when eliciting user requirements, asking users "What are your business rules?" doesn't get you very far. Sometimes you invent business rules as you go along, sometimes they come up during requirements discussions, and sometimes you need to hunt for them. Barbara von Halle (2002) describes a comprehensive process for discovering business rules. Following are several common places and ways to look for rules (Boyer and Mili 2011):

- "Common knowledge" from the organization, often collected from individuals who have worked with the business for a long time and know the details of how it operates.

- Legacy systems that embed business rules in their requirements and code. This requires reverse-engineering the rationale behind the requirements or code to understand the pertinent rules. This sometimes yields incomplete knowledge about the business rules.

- Business process modeling, which leads the analyst to look for rules that can affect each process step: constraints, triggering events, computational rules, and relevant facts.

- Analysis of existing documentation, including requirements specifications from earlier projects, regulations, industry standards, corporate policy documents, contracts, and business plans.

- Analysis of data, such as the various states that a data object can have and the conditions under which a user or a system event can change the object's state. These authorizations could also be represented as a roles and permissions matrix like the one shown earlier in Figure 9-2 to provide information about rules regarding user privilege levels and security.

- Compliance departments in companies building systems subject to regulation.

Just because you found some business rules in these various sources doesn't mean they necessarily apply to your current project or that they are even still valid. Computational formulas implemented in the code of legacy applications could be obsolete. Be sure to confirm whether rules gleaned from older documents and applications need to be updated. Assess the scope of applicability of rules you discover. Are they local to the project, or do they span a business domain or the entire enterprise?

Often, project stakeholders already know about business rules that will influence the application. Certain employees sometimes deal with particular types or classes of rules. If that's the case in your environment, find out who those people are and bring them into the discussion. The BA can glean business rules during elicitation activities that also define other requirements artifacts and models. During interviews and workshops, the BA can ask questions to probe around the rationale for the requirements and constraints that users present. These discussions frequently surface business rules as the underlying rationale. Figure 9-3 shows several potential origins of rules. It also suggests some questions a BA can ask when discussing various requirements issues with users.

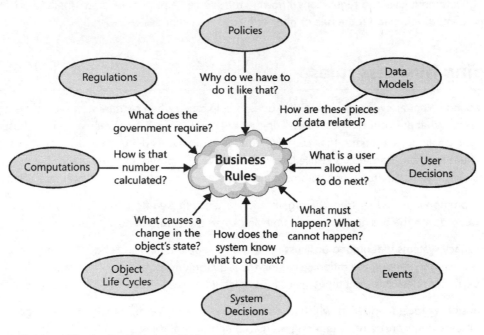

FIGURE 9-3 Discovering business rules by asking questions from different perspectives.

Business rules and requirements

After identifying and documenting business rules, determine which ones must be implemented in the software. Business rules and their corresponding functional requirements sometimes look a lot alike. However, the rules are external statements of policy that must be enforced in software, thereby driving system functionality. Every BA must decide which rules pertain to his application, which ones must be enforced in the software, and how to enforce them.

Recall the constraint rule from the Chemical Tracking System requiring that training records be current before a user can request a hazardous chemical. The analyst would derive different functional requirements to comply with this rule depending on whether the training records database is accessible to the Chemical Tracking System. If it is, the system can look up the user's training record and decide whether to accept or reject the request. If the records aren't available online, though, the system might store the chemical request temporarily and send a message to the training coordinator, who could approve or reject the request. The rule is the same in either situation, but the software functionality—the actions to take when the business rule is encountered during execution—varies depending on the system's environment.

As another illustration, consider the following rules:

- Rule #1 (action enabler): "If the expiration date for a chemical container has been reached, then notify the person who currently possesses that container."

- Rule #2 (fact): "A container of a chemical that can form explosive decomposition products expires one year after its manufacture date."

Rule #1 serves as the origin for a system feature called "Notify chemical owner of expiration." Additional rules like #2 would help the system determine which containers will have expiration dates and thus require notifying their owners at the right time. For instance, an opened can of ether becomes unsafe because it can form explosive byproducts in the presence of oxygen. Based on such rules, it's clear that the Chemical Tracking System must monitor the status of chemical containers that have expiration dates and inform the right people to return the containers for safe disposal. The BA might derive some functional requirements for that feature such as the following:

Expired.Notify.Before   *If the status of a chemical container that has an expiration date is not Disposed, the system shall notify the container's current owner one week before the date the container expires.*

Expired.Notify.Date   *If the status of a chemical container that has an expiration date is not Disposed, the system shall notify the container's current owner on the date the container expires.*

Expired.Notify.After   *If the status of a chemical container that has an expiration date is not Disposed, the system shall notify the container's current owner one week after the date the container expires.*

Expired.Notify.Manager   *If the status of a chemical container that has an expiration date is not Disposed, the system shall notify the manager of the container's current owner two weeks after the date the container expires.*

Whenever you encounter a set of very similar requirements like these, consider laying them out in the form of a table instead of a list (Wiegers 2006). This is more compact and easier to review, understand, and modify. It also provides a more concise way to label the requirements, because the table has to show just the suffixes to append to the parent requirement's label. Here's an alternative representation for the preceding four functional requirements:

Expired.Notify   *If the status of a chemical container that has an expiration date is not Disposed, the system shall notify the individuals shown in the following table at the times indicated.*

Requirement ID	Who to notify	When to notify
.Before	Container's current owner	One week before expiration date
.Date	Container's current owner	On expiration date
.After	Container's current owner	One week after expiration date
.Manager	Manager of container's current owner	Two weeks after expiration date

Tying everything together

To prevent redundancy, don't duplicate rules from your business rules catalog in the requirements documentation. Instead, refer back to specific rules as being the source of certain functionality or algorithms. You can define the links between a functional requirement and its parent business rules in several ways; following are three possibilities.

- If you are using a requirements management tool, create a requirement attribute called "Origin" and indicate the rules as being the origin of derived functional requirements. (See Chapter 27, "Requirements management practices.")

- Define traceability links between functional requirements and the connected business rules in a requirements traceability matrix or a requirements mapping matrix (Beatty and Chen 2012). This is easiest when the business rules are stored in the same repository as the requirements. (See Chapter 29, "Links in the requirements chain.")

- If the business rules and requirements are stored in word processing or spreadsheet files, define hyperlinks from business rule ID references in the requirements back to the descriptions of the business rules stored elsewhere. Be aware that hyperlinks are prone to breaking if the location of the rules collection changes.

These links keep the requirements current with rule changes because the requirements simply point to the master instance of the rule. If the rule changes, you can search for the linked rule ID to find requirements—or implemented functionality—you might need to change. Using links like this facilitates reusing the same rule in multiple places and projects, because the rules are not buried in the documentation for any single application. However, a developer reading the SRS will need to follow the cross-referenced link to access the rule details. This is the trade-off that results when you elect not to duplicate information (Wiegers 2006).

As with so many aspects of requirements engineering, there is no simple, perfect solution to managing business rules that works in all situations. But after you begin actively looking for, recording, and applying business rules, the rationale behind your application development choices will become clearer to all stakeholders.

Next steps

- Try to identify at least one of each business rule type from the taxonomy in Figure 9-1 for your current project.

- Begin populating a business rules catalog with the rules that pertain to your current project. Classify the rules according to the scheme in Figure 9-1 and note the origin of each rule.

- Set up a traceability matrix to indicate which functional requirements enforce each business rule you identified.

- Identify the rationale behind each of your functional requirements to discover other, implicit business rules.

CHAPTER 10

Documenting the requirements

At the launch of a large project to build a commercial software company's next-generation flagship product, a senior manager convened about 60 employees in a daylong off-site "voice-of-the-customer workshop." These employees worked with facilitators to generate ideas for the new product. The manager compiled the results of these brainstorming sessions into a 100-page document. He called this a requirements specification, but in fact it was nothing more than a pile of information.

The information from the brain dump by all these smart people wasn't classified into various categories, organized logically, analyzed, or otherwise processed into anything that described a proposed software solution. Developers could not have gleaned what they needed to know about the new product from this massive collection of ideas. Certainly there were nuggets of valuable requirements buried among all the chaff. But simply collecting raw ideas and needs into a long list isn't an effective way to document and communicate software requirements.

Clear and effective communication is the core principle of requirements development—communication from people with needs to people who can conceive solutions, then to people who can implement and verify those solutions. A skilled business analyst will choose the most effective way to communicate each type of requirements information to each audience.

The result of requirements development is a documented agreement among stakeholders about the product to be built. As you saw in earlier chapters, the vision and scope document contains the business requirements, and user requirements can be captured in the form of use cases or user stories. The product's functional and nonfunctional requirements often are stored in a software requirements specification, or SRS, which is delivered to those who must design, build, and verify the solution. Recording requirements in an organized fashion that key project stakeholders can review helps ensure that they know what they're agreeing to.

This chapter addresses the purpose, structure, and contents of the SRS. We will describe the SRS as being a document, but it doesn't have to be in the form of a traditional word-processing document. In fact, documents pose numerous limitations:

- It's difficult to store descriptive attributes along with the requirements.

- Change management is clumsy.

- It's difficult to retain historical versions of the requirements.

- It's not easy to subset out a portion of requirements that are allocated to a particular iteration or keep track of those that were once approved but then deferred or canceled.

- It's hard to trace requirements to other development artifacts.

- Duplicating a requirement that logically fits in multiple places causes maintenance issues.

As alternatives, you might store information in a spreadsheet (which has many of the same limitations as a document), a Wiki, a database, or a requirements management (RM) tool (see Chapter 30, "Tools for requirements engineering"). Think of these as different possible repositories or containers for requirements information. No matter what form of requirements repository you use, you still need the same kinds of information. The SRS template described here is a helpful reminder of information to collect and how you might organize it.

Not everyone agrees that it's worth the time to document requirements. And on exploratory or highly volatile projects where you're not sure what solution you'll end up with, trying to keep up with changes in the requirements details adds little value. However, the cost of recording knowledge is small compared to the cost of acquiring that knowledge or regenerating it at some point in the future. The acts of specification and modeling help project participants think through and precisely state important things that a verbal discussion can leave ambiguous. If you are *100 percent certain* that no stakeholders will ever need a specific piece of information beyond the duration of their own short-term memories, then you don't need to record it. Otherwise, store it in some kind of a group memory.

You will never get perfect requirements. Remember that you are writing requirements for certain audiences. The amount of detail, the kinds of information you provide, and the way you organize it should all be intended to meet the needs of your audiences. Analysts quite naturally write requirements from their own point of view, but really they should write them to be most meaningful to those who have to understand the requirements and do work based on them. This is why it's important to have representatives of those audiences review the requirements to make sure they'll meet their needs.

Progressive refinement of detail is a key principle for effective requirements development. On most projects it's neither realistic nor necessary to pin down every requirement detail early in the project. Instead, think in terms of layers. You need to learn just enough about the requirements to be able to roughly prioritize them and allocate them to forthcoming releases or iterations. Then you can detail groups of requirements in a just-in-time fashion to give developers enough information so they can avoid excessive and unnecessary rework.

Don't expect even the finest requirements documentation to replace ongoing discussions throughout the project. Keep the communication lines open among the BA, development team, customer representatives, and other stakeholders so that they can quickly address the myriad issues that will arise.

> **Trap** Do not rely on telepathy and clairvoyance as substitutes for solid requirements specification practices. They don't work, even though they seem to be the technical foundation for some software projects.

You can represent software requirements in several ways, including:

- Well-structured and carefully written natural language.

- Visual models that illustrate transformational processes, system states and changes between them, data relationships, logic flows, and the like.

- Formal specifications that define requirements by using mathematically precise specification languages.

Formal specifications provide the greatest rigor and precision, but few software developers—and even fewer customers—are familiar with them. Most projects don't demand this level of formality, but I'd certainly hope that the designers of high-risk systems like nuclear power plant control systems use formal specification methods. Structured natural language, augmented with visual models and other representation techniques (such as tables, mock-ups, photographs, and mathematical expressions), remains the most practical way for most software projects to document their requirements. The rest of this chapter addresses how you might organize the information in a software requirements specification. Chapter 11, "Writing excellent requirements," describes characteristics of high-quality requirements and offers many suggestions for how to write them.

The software requirements specification

The software requirements specification goes by many names in various organizations, although organizations do not use these terms in the same way. It is sometimes called a *business requirements document* (BRD), *functional specification, product specification, system specification*, or simply *requirements document*. Because "software requirements specification" is an industry-standard term, that's what we'll call it here (ISO/IEC/IEEE 2011).

The SRS states the functions and capabilities that a software system must provide, its characteristics, and the constraints that it must respect. It should describe as completely as necessary the system's behaviors under various conditions, as well as desired system qualities such as performance, security, and usability. The SRS is the basis for subsequent project planning, design, and coding, as well as the foundation for system testing and user documentation. However, it should not contain design, construction, testing, or project management details other than known design and implementation constraints. Even people working on agile projects need the kind of information found in a good SRS. They don't ordinarily collect all this information in a cohesive deliverable, but an SRS template provides a convenient reminder of what kinds of knowledge to explore. This chapter concludes with a section that describes how agile projects typically handle requirements specification.

Important A single requirements deliverable often cannot meet the needs of all audiences. Some people need to know just the business objectives, others want only a high-level big picture, still others want to see just the user's perspective, and yet others need all the details. This is one reason why we advocate creating the deliverables we call the vision and scope document, user requirements document, and software requirements specification. Don't expect all of your user representatives to read the detailed SRS, and don't expect developers to learn all they need from a set of use cases or user stories.

Numerous audiences rely on the SRS:

- Customers, the marketing department, and sales staff need to know what product they can expect to be delivered.

- Project managers base their estimates of schedule, effort, and resources on the requirements.

- Software development teams need to know what to build.

- Testers use it to develop requirements-based tests, test plans, and test procedures.

- Maintenance and support staff use it to understand what each part of the product is supposed to do.

- Documentation writers base user manuals and help screens on the SRS and the user interface design.

- Training personnel use the SRS and user documentation to develop educational materials.

- Legal staff ensures that the requirements comply with applicable laws and regulations.

- Subcontractors base their work on—and can be legally held to—the specified requirements.

If a desired capability or quality doesn't appear somewhere in the requirements agreement, no one should expect it to appear in the product.

How many specifications?

Most projects will create just one software requirements specification. This isn't practical for large projects, though. Large systems projects often write a system requirements specification, followed by separate software and perhaps hardware requirements specifications (ISO/IEC/IEEE 2011). One company was building a very complex process control application, with more than 100 people working for multiple years. This project had about 800 high-level requirements in its system requirements specification. The project was divided into 20 subprojects, each of which had its own software requirements specification with perhaps 800 or 900 requirements derived from the system requirements. This makes for a lot of documentation, but a large project becomes unmanageable if you don't take a divide-and-conquer approach.

At the other extreme, another company created just a single guiding document for each medium-sized project, which they called simply "The Spec." The Spec contained every piece of known information about the project: requirements, estimates, project plans, quality plans, test plans, tests, everything. Change management and version control on such an all-inclusive document is a nightmare. Nor is the information level in such an all-inclusive document suitable for each audience for requirements information.

A third company that began to adopt agile development practices stopped writing any formal documentation. Instead, they wrote user stories for a large project on sticky notes that they placed on their office walls. Unfortunately for one project, the adhesive on the sticky notes gradually failed. A couple of months into the project, it was normal for no-longer-sticky notes to flutter to the ground as someone walked by the wall.

Still another company took an intermediate approach. Although their projects weren't huge and could be specified in just 40 to 60 pages, some team members wanted to subdivide the SRS into as many as 12 separate documents: one SRS for a batch process, one for the reporting engine, and one for each of 10 reports. A document explosion like this causes headaches because it's hard to keep changes to them synchronized and to make sure the right people get all the information they need efficiently.

A better alternative for all of these situations is to store the requirements in a requirements management tool, as described in Chapter 30. An RM tool also helps greatly with the problem of whether to create a single SRS or multiple specifications for a project that plans multiple product releases or development iterations (Wiegers 2006). The SRS for any one portion of the product or for a given iteration then is just a report generated from the database contents based on certain query criteria.

You don't have to write the SRS for the entire product before beginning development, but you should capture the requirements for each increment before building that increment. Incremental development is appropriate when you want to get some functionality into the users' hands quickly. Feedback from using the early increments will shape the rest of the project. However, every project should baseline an agreement for each set of requirements before the team implements them. *Baselining* is the process of transitioning an SRS under development into one that has been reviewed and approved. Working from an agreed-upon set of requirements minimizes miscommunication and unnecessary rework. See Chapter 2, "Requirements from the customer's perspective," and Chapter 27, "Requirements management practices," for more about baselining.

It's important to organize and write the SRS so that the diverse stakeholders can understand it. Keep the following readability suggestions in mind:

- Use an appropriate template to organize all the necessary information.

- Label and style sections, subsections, and individual requirements consistently.

- Use visual emphasis (bold, underline, italics, color, and fonts) consistently and judiciously. Remember that color highlighting might not be visible to people with color blindness or when printed in grayscale.

- Create a table of contents to help readers find the information they need.

- Number all figures and tables, give them captions, and refer to them by number.

- If you are storing requirements in a document, define your word processor's cross-reference facility rather than hard-coded page or section numbers to refer to other locations within a document.

- If you are using documents, define hyperlinks to let the reader jump to related sections in the SRS or in other files.

- If you are storing requirements in a tool, use links to let the reader navigate to related information.

- Include visual representations of information when possible to facilitate understanding.

- Enlist a skilled editor to make sure the document is coherent and uses a consistent vocabulary and layout.

Labeling requirements

Every requirement needs a unique and persistent identifier. This allows you to refer to specific requirements in a change request, modification history, cross-reference, or requirements traceability matrix. It also enables reusing the requirements in multiple projects. Uniquely identified requirements facilitate collaboration between team members when they're discussing requirements, as in a peer review meeting. Simple numbered or bulleted lists aren't adequate for these purposes. Let's look at the advantages and shortcomings of several requirements-labeling methods. Select whichever technique makes the most sense for your situation.

Number 8, with a bullet

I was chatting with my seatmate on a long airplane flight once. It turned out that Dave was also in the software business. I mentioned that I had some interest in requirements. Dave pulled an SRS out of his briefcase. I don't know if he carried one with him everywhere he went for emergency purposes or what. I saw that the requirements in his document were organized hierarchically, but they were all in bulleted list form. He had up to eight levels of bullet hierarchy in some places. They all used different symbols—○, ■, ◆, ✓, ❑, ⇨, and the like—but they had no labels more meaningful than those simple symbols. It's impossible to refer to a bulleted item or to trace it to a design element, code segment, or test.

Sequence number

The simplest approach gives every requirement a unique sequence number, such as UC-9 or FR-26. Commercial requirements management tools assign such an identifier when a user adds a new requirement to the tool's database. The prefix indicates the requirement type, such as *FR* for *functional requirement*. A number is not reused if a requirement is deleted, so you don't have to worry about a reader confusing the original FR-26 with a new FR-26. This simple numbering approach doesn't provide any logical or hierarchical grouping of related requirements, the number doesn't imply any kind of ordering, and the labels give no clue as to what each requirement is about. It does make it easy to retain a unique identifier if you move requirements around in a document.

Hierarchical numbering

In the most commonly used convention, if the functional requirements appear in section 3.2 of your SRS, they will all have labels that begin with 3.2. More digits indicate a more detailed, lower-level requirement, so you know that 3.2.4.3 is a child requirement of 3.2.4. This method is simple, compact, and familiar. Your word processor can probably assign the numbers automatically. Requirements management tools generally also support hierarchical numbering.

However, hierarchical numbering poses some problems. The labels can grow to many digits in even a medium-sized SRS. Numeric labels tell you nothing about the intent of a requirement. If you are using a word processor, typically this scheme does not generate persistent labels. If you insert a new requirement, the numbers of the following requirements in that section all will be incremented. Delete or move a requirement, and the numbers following it in that section will be decremented. Delete, insert, merge, or move whole sections, and a lot of labels change. These changes disrupt any references to those requirements elsewhere in the system.

> **Trap** A BA once told me in all seriousness, "We don't let people insert requirements—it messes up the numbering." Don't let ineffective practices hamper your ability to work effectively and sensibly.

An improvement over hierarchical numbering is to number the major sections of the requirements hierarchically and then identify individual functional requirements in each section with a short text code followed by a sequence number. For example, the SRS might contain "Section 3.5—Editor Functions," and the requirements in that section could be labeled ED-1, ED-2, and so forth. This approach provides some hierarchy and organization while keeping the labels short, somewhat meaningful, and less positionally dependent. It doesn't totally solve the sequence number problem, though.

Hierarchical textual tags

Consultant Tom Gilb (1988) suggests a text-based hierarchical tagging scheme for labeling individual requirements. Consider this requirement: "The system shall ask the user to confirm any request to print more than 10 copies." This requirement might be tagged Print.ConfirmCopies. This indicates that it is part of the print function and relates to the number of copies to print. Hierarchical textual tags are structured, meaningful, and unaffected by adding, deleting, or moving other requirements. The sample SRS in Appendix C illustrates this labeling technique, as do other examples throughout the book. This method also is suitable for labeling business rules if you're maintaining them manually, rather than in a dedicated business rules repository or tool.

Using hierarchical textual tags like this helps solve another problem. With any hierarchical organization you have parent-child relationships between requirements. If the parent is written as a functional requirement, the relationship between the children and the parent can be confusing. A good convention is to write the parent requirement to look like a title, a heading, or a feature name, rather than looking like a functional requirement in itself. The children requirements of that parent, in the aggregate, deliver the capability described in the parent. Following is an example that contains a heading and four functional requirements.

Product: Ordering products from the website

.Cart	The website shall use a shopping cart to contain products a Customer selects to purchase.
.Discount	The shopping cart shall provide one discount code field. Each discount code provides either a specific discount percentage or a fixed dollar discount amount on specific items in the cart.
.Error	If the Customer enters an invalid discount code, the website shall display an error message.
.Shipping	The shopping cart shall add a shipping charge if a Customer orders a physical product that must be mailed.

The full unique ID of each requirement is built by appending each line's label to the parent labels above it. The **Product** statement is written as a heading, not as a discrete requirement. The first functional requirement is tagged **Product.Cart**. The full ID for the third requirement is **Product.Discount.Error**. This hierarchical scheme avoids the maintenance problems with the hierarchical numbering, but the tags are longer and you do have to think of meaningful names for them, perhaps building from the name of the relevant feature. It can be challenging to maintain uniqueness, especially if you have multiple people working on the set of requirements. You can simplify the scheme by combining the hierarchical naming technique with a sequence number suffix for small sets of requirements: Product.Cart.01, Product.Cart.02, and so on. Many schemes can work.

Dealing with incompleteness

Sometimes you know that you lack a piece of information about a specific requirement. Use the notation *TBD* (to be determined) to flag these knowledge gaps. Plan to resolve all TBDs before implementing a set of requirements. Any uncertainties that remain increase the risk of a developer or a tester making errors and having to perform rework. When the developer encounters a TBD, he might make his best guess—which won't always be correct—instead of tracking down the requirement's originator to resolve it. If you must proceed with construction of the next product increment while TBDs remain, either defer implementing the unresolved requirements or design those portions of the product to be easily modifiable when the open issues are resolved. Record TBDs and other requirements questions in an issues list. As the number of open issues dwindles, the requirements are stabilizing. Chapter 27 further describes managing and resolving open issues.

> **Trap** TBDs won't resolve themselves. Number the TBDs, record who is responsible for resolving each issue and by when, review their status at regular checkpoints, and track them to closure.

User interfaces and the SRS

Incorporating user interface designs in the SRS has both benefits and drawbacks. On the plus side, exploring possible user interfaces with paper prototypes, working mock-ups, wireframes, or simulation tools makes the requirements tangible to both users and developers. As discussed in Chapter 15, "Risk reduction through prototyping," these are powerful techniques for eliciting and validating requirements. If the product's users have expectations of how portions of the product might look and feel—and hence could be disappointed if their expectations weren't fulfilled—those expectations belong in the realm of requirements.

On the negative side, screen images and user interface architectures describe solutions and might not truly be requirements. Including them in the SRS makes the document larger, and big requirements documents frighten some people. Delaying baselining of the SRS until the UI design is complete can slow down development and try the patience of people who are already concerned about spending too much time on requirements. Including UI design in the requirements can result in the visual design driving the requirements, which often leads to functional gaps. The people who write the requirements aren't necessarily well qualified for designing user interfaces. Additionally, after stakeholders see a user interface in an SRS (or anywhere else), they will not "unsee" it. Early visualization can clarify requirements, but it can also lead to resistance to improving the UI over time.

 Screen layouts don't replace written user and functional requirements. Don't expect developers to deduce the underlying functionality and data relationships from screen shots. One Internet development company repeatedly got in trouble because the team routinely went directly from signing a contract with a client into an eight-hour visual design workshop. They never sufficiently understood what a user would be able to do at each website they built, so they spent a lot of time fixing the sites after delivery.

If you really do want to implement certain functionality with specific UI controls and screen layouts, it's both appropriate and important to include that information in the SRS as design constraints. Design constraints restrict the choices available to the user interface designer. Just make sure that you don't impose constraints unnecessarily, prematurely, or for the wrong reasons. If the SRS is specifying an enhancement to an existing system, it often makes sense to include screen displays exactly as they are to be implemented. The developers are already constrained by the current reality of the existing system, so it's possible to know up front just how the modified—and perhaps also the new—displays should look.

A sensible balance is to include conceptual images—I call them sketches, no matter how nicely drawn they are—of selected displays in the requirements without demanding that the implementation precisely follow those models. See Figure 10-1 for a sample webpage sketch. Incorporating such sketches in the SRS helpfully communicates another view of the requirements, but makes it clear that the sketches are not the committed screen designs. For example, a preliminary sketch of a complex dialog box will illustrate the intent behind a group of requirements, but a visual designer might turn it into a tabbed dialog box to improve usability.

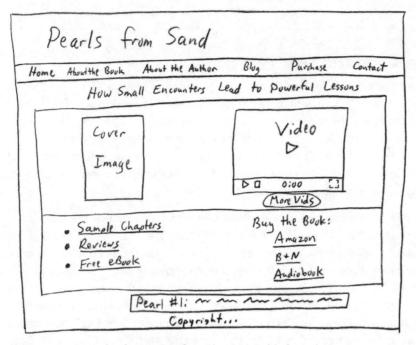

FIGURE 10-1 Example of a user interface "sketch" suitable for inclusion in a requirements document.

Teams working on projects that have many screens might find it more manageable to document the user interface design specifics in a separate user interface specification or by using UI design tools or prototyping tools. Use techniques such as display-action-response models to describe screen element names, their properties, and their behavior in detail (Beatty and Chen 2012).

A software requirements specification template

Every software development organization should adopt one or more standard SRS templates for its projects. Various SRS templates are available (for example: ISO/IEC/IEEE 2011; Robertson and Robertson 2013). If your organization tackles various kinds or sizes of projects, such as new, large system development as well as minor enhancements to existing systems, adopt an SRS template for each major project class. See the "Template tactics" sidebar in Chapter 5, "Establishing the business requirements," for some thoughts about how to use document templates effectively.

Figure 10-2 illustrates an SRS template that works well for many types of projects. Appendix C contains a sample SRS that follows this template. This template, with usage guidance embedded in each section, is available for downloading from this book's companion content website. Some people format such guidance text as "hidden text" in Microsoft Word. That way, you can leave the prompts in the document. If you want a memory jogger, just turn on nonprinting characters to see the information.

1. **Introduction**

    1.1 Purpose
    1.2 Document conventions
    1.3 Project scope
    1.4 References

2. **Overall description**

    2.1 Product perspective
    2.2 User classes and characteristics
    2.3 Operating environment
    2.4 Design and implementation constraints
    2.5 Assumptions and dependencies

3. **System features**

    3.x System feature X
        3.x.1 Description
        3.x.2 Functional requirements

4. **Data requirements**

    4.1 Logical data model
    4.2 Data dictionary
    4.3 Reports
    4.4 Data acquisition, integrity, retention, and disposal

5. **External interface requirements**

    5.1 User interfaces
    5.2 Software interfaces
    5.3 Hardware interfaces
    5.4 Communications interfaces

6. **Quality attributes**

    6.1 Usability
    6.2 Performance
    6.3 Security
    6.4 Safety
    6.x [others]

7. **Internationalization and localization requirements**

8. **Other requirements**

Appendix A: Glossary

Appendix B: Analysis models

FIGURE 10-2 Proposed template for a software requirements specification.

Sometimes a piece of information could logically be recorded in several template sections. Pick one section and use it consistently for that kind of information on your project. Avoid duplicating information in multiple sections even if it could logically fit in more than one (Wiegers 2006). Cross-references and hyperlinks can help readers find the information they need.

When you create requirements documents, use effective version control practices and tools to make sure all readers know which version they are reading. Include a revision history to provide a record of changes made in the document, who made each change, when it was made, and the reason for it (see Chapter 27). The rest of this section describes the information to include in each section of the SRS.

Important You can incorporate material by reference to other existing project documents instead of duplicating information in the SRS. Hyperlinks between documents are one way to do this, as are traceability links defined in a requirements management tool. A risk with hyperlinks is that they can break if the document folder hierarchy changes. Chapter 18, "Requirements reuse," discusses several techniques for reusing existing requirements knowledge.

1. Introduction

The introduction presents an overview to help the reader understand how the SRS is organized and how to use it.

1.1 Purpose

Identify the product or application whose requirements are specified in this document, including the revision or release number. If this SRS pertains to only part of a complex system, identify that portion or subsystem. Describe the different types of reader that the document is intended for, such as developers, project managers, marketing staff, users, testers, and documentation writers.

1.2 Document conventions

Describe any standards or typographical conventions used, including the meaning of specific text styles, highlighting, or notations. If you are manually labeling requirements, you might specify the format here for anyone who needs to add one later.

1.3 Project scope

Provide a short description of the software being specified and its purpose. Relate the software to user or corporate goals and to business objectives and strategies. If a separate vision and scope or similar document is available, refer to it rather than duplicating its contents here. An SRS that specifies an incremental release of an evolving product should contain its own scope statement as a subset of the long-term strategic product vision. You might provide a high-level summary of the major features the release contains or the significant functions that it performs.

1.4 References

List any documents or other resources to which this SRS refers. Include hyperlinks to them if they are in a persistent location. These might include user interface style guides, contracts, standards, system requirements specifications, interface specifications, or the SRS for a related product. Provide enough information so that the reader can access each reference, including its title, author, version number, date, source, storage location, or URL.

2. Overall description

This section presents a high-level overview of the product and the environment in which it will be used, the anticipated users, and known constraints, assumptions, and dependencies.

2.1 Product perspective

Describe the product's context and origin. Is it the next member of a growing product line, the next version of a mature system, a replacement for an existing application, or an entirely new product? If this SRS defines a component of a larger system, state how this software relates to the overall system and identify major interfaces between the two. Consider including visual models such as a context diagram or ecosystem map (described in Chapter 5) to show the product's relationship to other systems.

2.2 User classes and characteristics

Identify the various user classes that you anticipate will use this product, and describe their pertinent characteristics. (See Chapter 6, "Finding the voice of the user.") Some requirements might pertain only to certain user classes. Identify the favored user classes. User classes represent a subset of the stakeholders described in the vision and scope document. User class descriptions are a reusable resource. If a master user class catalog is available, you can incorporate user class descriptions by simply pointing to them in the catalog instead of duplicating information here.

2.3 Operating environment

Describe the environment in which the software will operate, including the hardware platform; operating systems and versions; geographical locations of users, servers, and databases; and organizations that host the related databases, servers, and websites. List any other software components or applications with which the system must peacefully coexist. If extensive technical infrastructure work needs to be performed in conjunction with developing the new system, consider creating a separate infrastructure requirements specification to detail that work.

2.4 Design and implementation constraints

There are times when a certain programming language must be used, a particular code library that has already had time invested to develop it needs to be used, and so forth. Describe any factors that will restrict the options available to the developers and the rationale for each constraint. Requirements that incorporate or are written in the form of solution ideas rather than needs are imposing design constraints, often unnecessarily, so watch out for those. Constraints are described further in Chapter 14, "Beyond functionality."

2.5 Assumptions and dependencies

An *assumption* is a statement that is believed to be true in the absence of proof or definitive knowledge. Problems can arise if assumptions are incorrect, are obsolete, are not shared, or change, so certain assumptions will translate into project risks. One SRS reader might assume that the product will conform to a particular user interface convention, whereas another might assume something different. A developer might assume that a certain set of functions will be custom-written for this application, whereas the business analyst might assume that they will be reused from a previous project, and the project manager might expect to procure a commercial function library. The assumptions to include here are those related to system functionality; business-related assumptions appear in the vision and scope document, as described in Chapter 5.

Identify any *dependencies* the project or system being built has on external factors or components outside its control. For instance, if Microsoft .NET Framework 4.5 or a more recent version must be installed before your product can run, that's a dependency.

3. System features

The template in Figure 10-2 shows functional requirements organized by system feature, which is just one possible way to arrange them. Other organizational options include arranging functional requirements by functional area, process flow, use case, mode of operation, user class, stimulus, and response. Hierarchical combinations of these elements are also possible, such as use cases within user classes. There is no single right choice; select a method of organization that makes it easy for readers to understand the product's intended capabilities. We'll describe the feature scheme as an example.

3.x System feature X

State the name of the feature in just a few words, such as "3.1 Spell Check." Repeat section 3.x with its subsections 3.x.1 and 3.x.2 for each system feature.

3.x.1 Description

Provide a short description of the feature and indicate whether it is of high, medium, or low priority. (See Chapter 16, "First things first: Setting requirement priorities.") Priorities often are dynamic, changing over the course of the project. If you're using a requirements management tool, define a requirement attribute for priority. Requirement attributes are discussed in Chapter 27 and requirements management tools in Chapter 30.

3.x.2 Functional requirements

Itemize the specific functional requirements associated with this feature. These are the software capabilities that must be implemented for the user to carry out the feature's services or to perform a use case. Describe how the product should respond to anticipated error conditions and to invalid inputs and actions. Uniquely label each functional requirement, as described earlier in this chapter. If you're using a requirements management tool, you can create multiple attributes for each functional requirement, such as rationale, origin, and status.

4. Data requirements

Information systems provide value by manipulating data. Use this section of the template to describe various aspects of the data that the system will consume as inputs, process in some fashion, or create as outputs. Chapter 13, "Specifying data requirements," addresses this topic in more detail. Stephen Withall (2007) describes many patterns for documenting data (also known as information) requirements precisely.

4.1 Logical data model

As described in Chapter 13, a data model is a visual representation of the data objects and collections the system will process and the relationships between them. Numerous notations exist for data modeling, including entity-relationship diagrams and UML class diagrams. You might include a data model for the business operations being addressed by the system, or a logical representation for the data that the system will manipulate. This is not the same thing as an implementation data model that will be realized in the form of database design.

4.2 Data dictionary

The data dictionary defines the composition of data structures and the meaning, data type, length, format, and allowed values for the data elements that make up those structures. Commercial data modeling tools often include a data dictionary component. In many cases, you're better off storing the data dictionary as a separate artifact, rather than embedding it in the middle of an SRS. That also increases its reusability potential in other projects. Chapter 13 discusses the data dictionary.

4.3 Reports

If your application will generate any reports, identify them here and describe their characteristics. If a report must conform to a specific predefined layout, you can specify that here as a constraint, perhaps with an example. Otherwise, focus on the logical descriptions of the report content, sort sequence, totaling levels, and so forth, deferring the detailed report layout to the design stage. Chapter 13 offers guidance on specifying reports.

4.4 Data acquisition, integrity, retention, and disposal

If relevant, describe how data is acquired and maintained. For instance, when starting a data inventory feed, you might need to do an initial dump of all the inventory data to the receiving system and then have subsequent feeds that consist only of changes. State any requirements regarding the need to protect the integrity of the system's data. Identify any specific techniques that are necessary, such as backups, checkpointing, mirroring, or data accuracy verification. State policies the system must enforce for either retaining or disposing of data, including temporary data, metadata, residual data (such as deleted records), cached data, local copies, archives, and interim backups.

5. External interface requirements

This section provides information to ensure that the system will communicate properly with users and with external hardware or software elements. Reaching agreement on external and internal system interfaces has been identified as a software industry best practice (Brown 1996). A complex system with multiple subcomponents should create a separate interface specification or system architecture specification. The interface documentation could incorporate material from other documents by reference. For instance, it could point to a hardware device manual that lists the error codes that the device could send to the software.

Interface wars

Two software teams collaborated to build the A. Datum Corporation's flagship product. The knowledge base team built a complex inference engine in C++, and the applications team implemented the user interface in Java. The two subsystems communicated through an application programming interface (API). Unfortunately, the knowledge base team periodically modified the API, with the consequence that the complete system would not build and execute correctly. The applications team needed several hours to diagnose each problem they discovered and determine the root cause as being an API change. These changes were not agreed upon by the two teams, were not communicated to all affected parties, and were not coordinated with corresponding modifications in the Java code. A change in an interface *demands* communication with the person, group, or system on the other side of that interface. The interfaces glue your system components—including the users—together, so document the interface details and synchronize necessary modifications through your project's change control process.

5.1 User interfaces

Describe the logical characteristics of each user interface that the system needs. Some specific characteristics of user interfaces could appear in section 6.1 Usability. Some possible items to address here are:

- References to user interface standards or product line style guides that are to be followed

- Standards for fonts, icons, button labels, images, color schemes, field tabbing sequences, commonly used controls, branding graphics, copyright and privacy notices, and the like

- Screen size, layout, or resolution constraints

- Standard buttons, functions, or navigation links that will appear on every screen, such as a help button

- Shortcut keys

- Message display and phrasing conventions

- Data validation guidelines (such as input value restrictions and when to validate field contents)

- Layout standards to facilitate software localization

- Accommodations for users who are visually impaired, color blind, or have other limitations

5.2 Software interfaces

Describe the connections between this product and other software components (identified by name and version), including other applications, databases, operating systems, tools, libraries, websites, and integrated commercial components. State the purpose, formats, and contents of the messages, data, and control values exchanged between the software components. Specify the mappings of input and output data between the systems and any translations that need to be made for the data to get from one system to the other. Describe the services needed by or from external software components and the nature of the inter-component communications. Identify data that will be exchanged between or shared across software components. Specify nonfunctional requirements affecting the interface, such as service levels for response times and frequencies, or security controls and restrictions. Some of this information might be specified as data requirements in section 4 or as interoperability requirements in section 6, Quality attributes.

5.3 Hardware interfaces

Describe the characteristics of each interface between the software components and hardware components, if any, of the system. This description might include the supported device types, the data and control interactions between the software and the hardware, and the communication protocols to be used. List the inputs and outputs, their formats, their valid values or ranges, and any timing issues developers need to be aware of. If this information is extensive, consider creating a separate interface specification document. For more about specifying requirements for systems containing hardware, see Chapter 26, "Embedded and other real-time systems projects."

5.4 Communications interfaces

State the requirements for any communication functions the product will use, including email, web browser, network protocols, and electronic forms. Define any pertinent message formatting. Specify communication security and encryption issues, data transfer rates, handshaking, and synchronization mechanisms. State any constraints around these interfaces, such as whether certain types of email attachments are acceptable or not.

6. Quality attributes

This section specifies nonfunctional requirements other than constraints, which are recorded in section 2.4, and external interface requirements, which appear in section 5. These quality requirements should be specific, quantitative, and verifiable. Indicate the relative priorities of various attributes, such as ease of use over ease of learning, or security over performance. A rich specification notation such as Planguage clarifies the needed levels of each quality much better than can simple descriptive statements (see the "Specifying quality requirements with Planguage" section in Chapter 14). Chapter 14 presents more information about these quality attribute requirements and many examples.

6.1 Usability

Usability requirements deal with ease of learning, ease of use, error avoidance and recovery, efficiency of interactions, and accessibility. The usability requirements specified here will help the user interface designer create the optimum user experience.

6.2 Performance

State specific performance requirements for various system operations. If different functional requirements or features have different performance requirements, it's appropriate to specify those performance goals right with the corresponding functional requirements, rather than collecting them in this section.

6.3 Security

Specify any requirements regarding security or privacy issues that restrict access to or use of the product. These could refer to physical, data, or software security. Security requirements often originate in business rules, so identify any security or privacy policies or regulations to which the product must conform. If these are documented in a business rules repository, just refer to them.

6.4 Safety

Specify requirements that are concerned with possible loss, damage, or harm that could result from use of the product. Define any safeguards or actions that must be taken, as well as potentially dangerous actions that must be prevented. Identify any safety certifications, policies, or regulations to which the product must conform.

6.x [Others]

Create a separate section in the SRS for each additional product quality attribute to describe characteristics that will be important either to customers or to developers and maintainers. Possibilities include availability, efficiency, installability, integrity, interoperability, modifiability, portability, reliability, reusability, robustness, scalability, and verifiability. Chapter 14 describes a procedure for focusing on those attributes that are of most importance to a particular project.

7. Internationalization and localization requirements

Internationalization and localization requirements ensure that the product will be suitable for use in nations, cultures, and geographic locations other than those in which it was created. Such requirements might address differences in currency; formatting of dates, numbers, addresses, and telephone numbers; language, including national spelling conventions within the same language (such as American versus British English), symbols used, and character sets; given name and family name order; time zones; international regulations and laws; cultural and political issues; paper sizes used; weights and measures; electrical voltages and plug shapes; and many others. Internationalization and localization requirements could well be reusable across projects.

8. [Other requirements]

Define any other requirements that are not covered elsewhere in the SRS. Examples are legal, regulatory, or financial compliance and standards requirements; requirements for product installation, configuration, startup, and shutdown; and logging, monitoring, and audit trail requirements. Instead of just combining these all under "Other," add any new sections to the template that are pertinent to your project. Omit this section if all your requirements are accommodated in other sections. Transition requirements that are necessary for migrating from a previous system to a new one could be included here if they involve software being written (as for data conversion programs), or in the project management plan if they do not (as for training development or delivery).

Appendix A: Glossary

Define any specialized terms that a reader needs to know to understand the SRS, including acronyms and abbreviations. Spell out each acronym and provide its definition. Consider building a reusable enterprise-level glossary that spans multiple projects and incorporating by reference any terms that pertain to this project. Each SRS would then define only those terms specific to an individual project that do not appear in the enterprise-level glossary. Note that data definitions belong in the data dictionary, not the glossary.

Appendix B: Analysis models

This optional section includes or points to pertinent analysis models such as data flow diagrams, feature trees, state-transition diagrams, or entity-relationship diagrams. (See Chapter 12, "A picture is worth 1024 words.") Often it's more helpful for the reader if you incorporate certain models into the relevant sections of the specification instead of collecting them at the end.

Requirements specification on agile projects

Projects following agile development life cycles take a variety of approaches to specifying requirements that differ from the method just described. As you saw in Chapter 8, "Understanding user requirements," many agile projects employ user stories during elicitation. Each user story is a statement of a user need or functionality that will be valuable to the user or purchaser of the system (Cohn 2004; Cohn 2010). Teams might begin specification on agile projects by writing just enough information for each user story so that the stakeholders have a general understanding of what the story is about and can prioritize it relative to other stories. This allows the team to begin planning allocations of specific stories to iterations. The team might aggregate a group of related stories into a "minimally marketable feature" that needs to be fully implemented prior to a product release so the feature delivers the expected customer value.

User stories are accumulated and prioritized into a dynamic *product backlog* that evolves throughout the project. Large stories that encompass significant functionality that cannot be implemented within a single iteration are subdivided into smaller stories, which are allocated to multiple iterations for implementation. (See Chapter 20, "Agile projects.") User stories can be recorded on something as simple as index cards, instead of in a traditional document. Some agile teams record their stories in a story management tool, whereas others don't retain them at all following implementation.

As the team gets into each iteration, conversations among the product owner, people performing the business analyst role, developers, testers, and users will flesh out the details of each story allocated to the iteration. That is, specification involves the progressive refinement of detail at the right stage of the project, which is a good practice on any project. Those details generally correspond to what we have identified as functional requirements in the SRS. However, agile projects often represent those details in the form of user acceptance tests that describe how the system will behave if the story is properly implemented. The tests for a story are conducted during the iteration in which the story is implemented and in future iterations for regression testing. As with all tests, they should cover exception conditions as well as the expected behavior. These acceptance tests can be written on cards as well or recorded in a more persistent form, such as in a testing tool. Tests should be automated to assure rapid and complete regression testing. If the team elects to discard the original user stories, then the only persistent documentation of the requirements is likely to be the acceptance tests, if they are stored in a tool.

Similarly, nonfunctional requirements can be written on cards not as user stories but as constraints (Cohn 2004). Alternatively, teams might specify nonfunctional requirements that are associated with a specific user story in the form of acceptance criteria or tests, such as to demonstrate achievement of specific quality attribute goals. As an example, security tests might demonstrate that certain users are permitted to access the functionality described in a particular user story but that the system blocks access for other users. The agile team is not precluded from using other methods to represent requirements knowledge, such as analysis models or a data dictionary. They should select whatever representation techniques are customary and appropriate for their culture and project.

It's up to each project team to choose the most appropriate forms for specifying its software requirements. Remember the overarching goal of requirements development: to accumulate a shared understanding of requirements that is *good enough* to allow construction of the next portion of the product to proceed at an acceptable level of risk. The appropriate level of formality and detail in which to document requirements depends on factors including the following:

- The extent to which just-in-time informal verbal and visual communication between customers and developers can supply the necessary details to permit the correct implementation of each user requirement

- The extent to which informal communication methods can keep the team effectively synchronized across time and space

- The extent to which it is valuable or necessary to retain requirements knowledge for future enhancement, maintenance, application reengineering, verification, statutory and audit mandates, product certification, or contractual satisfaction

- The extent to which acceptance tests can serve as effective replacements for descriptions of the expected system capabilities and behaviors

- The extent to which human memories can replace written representations

No matter what type of product the team is building, what development life cycle they are following, or what elicitation techniques the BA is using, effective requirements specification is an essential key to success. There are many ways to achieve this. Just remember that when you don't specify high-quality requirements, the resulting software is like a box of chocolates: you never know what you're going to get.

Next steps

- Review your project's set of requirements against the template in Figure 10-2 to see if you have requirements from all the sections that pertain to your project. This chapter is less about populating a specific template and more about ensuring that you accumulate the necessary information for a successful project; the template is a helpful reminder.

- If your organization doesn't already have a standard SRS template, convene a small working group to adopt one. Begin with the template in Figure 10-2 and adapt it to best meet the needs of your organization's projects and products. Agree on a convention for labeling individual requirements.

- If you are storing your requirements in some form other than in a traditional document, such as in a requirements management tool, study the SRS template in Figure 10-2 and see if there are any categories of requirements information that you are not currently eliciting and recording. Modify your repository to incorporate those categories so the repository can serve as a reminder for future requirements elicitation activities.

Writing excellent requirements

"Hi, Gautam. This is Ruth calling from the Austin branch. We got that latest drop of the website software for the online music store. I wanted to ask you about the song preview feature. That's not working the way I had in mind."

Gautam replied, "Let me find the requirements you sent for that. Here they are. The user story said, 'As a Customer, I want to listen to previews of the available songs so I can decide which ones to buy.' My notes say that when we discussed this, you said each song sample should be 30 seconds long and that it should use our built-in MP3 player so the customer didn't have to wait for another player to launch. Isn't that working correctly?"

"Well, yes, that all works fine," said Ruth, "but there are a couple of problems. I can click on the play icon to start the sample, but I don't have any way to pause it or stop it. I'm forced to listen to the entire 30-second sample. Also, all the samples start at the beginning of the song. Some songs have long introductions so you really can't hear what they're like from just the beginning. The sample should start somewhere in the middle of those songs so people could hear what they're really like. And the sample starts playing at full volume and then stops abruptly. If the customer's speakers are up pretty loud this could be startling. I think it would be better if we fade in and fade out on each sample."

Gautam was a little frustrated. "I wish you had told me all of this when we spoke earlier. You didn't give me much to go on so I just had to make my best guess. I can do all that, but it's going to take a few more days."

The best requirements repository in the world is useless if it doesn't contain high-quality information. This chapter describes desirable characteristics of requirements and of requirements documents. It presents numerous guidelines for writing requirements, along with many examples of flawed requirements and suggestions for improving them. These recommendations apply to the requirements that are created for any project following any development life cycle. The requirements authors on each project need to judge the appropriate level of precision and detail for their requirements, but there's no substitute for clear communication.

Characteristics of excellent requirements

How can you tell good requirements from those with problems? This section describes several characteristics that individual requirement statements should exhibit, followed by desirable characteristics of the requirements set as a whole (Davis 2005; ISO/IEC/IEEE 2011). The best way to tell whether your requirements possess these desired attributes is to have several stakeholders review them. Different stakeholders will spot different kinds of problems. Chapter 17, "Validating the requirements," describes the use of checklists to remind reviewers of common requirements errors.

Characteristics of requirement statements

In an ideal world, every individual business, user, functional, and nonfunctional requirement would exhibit the qualities described in the following sections.

Complete

Each requirement must contain all the information necessary for the reader to understand it. In the case of functional requirements, this means providing the information the developer needs to be able to implement it correctly. If you know you're lacking certain information, use *TBD* (to be determined) as a standard flag to highlight these gaps, or log them in an issue-tracking system to follow up on later. Resolve all TBDs in each portion of the requirements before the developers proceed with construction of that portion.

Correct

Each requirement must accurately describe a capability that will meet some stakeholder's need and must clearly describe the functionality to be built. You'll have to go to the source of the requirement to check its correctness. This might be a user who supplied the initial requirement, a higher-level system requirement, a use case, a business rule, or another document. A low-level requirement that conflicts with its parent is not correct. To assess the correctness of user requirements, user representatives or their close surrogates should review them.

Feasible

It must be possible to implement each requirement within the known capabilities and limitations of the system and its operating environment, as well as within project constraints of time, budget, and staff. A developer who participates during elicitation can provide a reality check on what can and cannot be done technically and what can be done only at excessive cost or effort. Incremental development approaches and proof-of-concept prototypes are two ways to evaluate requirement feasibility. If a requirement needs to be cut because it is not be feasible, understand the impact on the project vision and scope.

Necessary

Each requirement should describe a capability that provides stakeholders with the anticipated business value, differentiates the product in the marketplace, or is required for conformance to an external standard, policy, or regulation. Every requirement should originate from a source that has the authority to provide requirements. Trace functional and nonfunctional requirements back to specific voice-of-the-user input, such as a use case or user story. You should be able to relate each requirement to a business objective that clearly indicates why it's necessary. If someone asks why a particular requirement is included, there should be a good answer.

Prioritized

Prioritize business requirements according to which are most important to achieving the desired value. Assign an implementation priority to each functional requirement, user requirement, use case flow, or feature to indicate how essential it is to a particular product release. If all requirements are equally important, the project manager doesn't know how best to respond to schedule overruns, personnel losses, or new requirements that come along. Requirements prioritization should be a collaborative activity involving multiple stakeholder perspectives. Chapter 16, "First things first: Setting requirement priorities," discusses prioritization in further detail.

Unambiguous

Natural language is prone to two types of ambiguity. One type I can spot myself, when I can think of more than one way to interpret a given requirement. The other type of ambiguity is harder to catch. That's when different people read the requirement and come up with different interpretations of it. The requirement makes sense to each of them but means something different to each of them. Inspections are a good way to spot ambiguities (Wiegers 2002). A formal peer review such as an inspection (as opposed to just passing out the requirements to individuals to examine on their own) provides an opportunity for each participant to compare his understanding of each requirement to someone else's. "Comprehensible" is related to "unambiguous": readers must understand what each requirement is saying. Chapter 17 describes the software peer review process.

You'll never remove all the ambiguity from requirements—that's the nature of human language. Most of the time, reasonable people can draw the right conclusions from even a slightly fuzzy requirement. Getting a little help from your colleagues through reviews will clean up a lot of the worst issues, though.

Verifiable

Can a tester devise tests or other verification approaches to determine whether each requirement is properly implemented? If a requirement isn't verifiable, deciding whether it was correctly implemented becomes a matter of opinion, not objective analysis. Requirements that are incomplete, inconsistent, infeasible, or ambiguous are also unverifiable. Testers are good at examining requirements for verifiability. Include them in your requirements peer reviews to catch problems early.

Characteristics of requirements collections

It's not enough to have excellent individual requirement statements. Sets of requirements that are grouped into a baseline for a specific release or iteration should exhibit the characteristics described in the following sections, whether they are recorded in an SRS document, a requirements management tool, a set of user stories and acceptance tests, or any other form.

Complete

No requirement or necessary information should be absent. In practice, you'll never document *every* single requirement for any system. There are always some assumed or implied requirements, although they carry more risk than explicitly stated requirements. Missing requirements are hard to spot because they aren't there! The section "Avoiding incompleteness" later in this chapter suggests some ways to identify missing requirements. Any specification that contains TBDs is incomplete.

Consistent

Consistent requirements don't conflict with other requirements of the same type or with higher-level business, user, or system requirements. If you don't resolve contradictions between requirements before diving into construction, the developers will have to deal with them. Recording the originator of each requirement lets you know who to talk to if you discover conflicts. It can be hard to spot inconsistencies when related information is stored in different locations, such as in a vision and scope document and in a requirements management tool.

Modifiable

You can always rewrite a requirement, but you should maintain a history of changes made to each requirement, especially after they are baselined. You also need to know about connections and dependencies between requirements so you can find all the ones that must be changed together. Modifiability dictates that each requirement be uniquely labeled and expressed separately from others so you can refer to it unambiguously. See Chapter 10, "Documenting the requirements," for various ways to label requirements.

To facilitate modifiability, avoid stating requirements redundantly. Repeating a requirement in multiple places where it logically belongs makes the document easier to read but harder to maintain (Wiegers 2006). The multiple instances of the requirement all have to be modified at the same time to avoid generating inconsistencies. Cross-reference related items in the SRS to help keep them synchronized when making changes. Storing individual requirements just once in a requirements management tool solves the redundancy problem and facilitates reuse of common requirements across multiple projects. Chapter 18, "Requirements reuse," offers several strategies for reusing requirements.

Traceable

A traceable requirement can be linked both backward to its origin and forward to derived requirements, design elements, code that implements it, and tests that verify its implementation. Note that you don't actually have to define all of these trace links for a requirement to have the properties that make it traceable. Traceable requirements are uniquely labeled with persistent identifiers. They are written in a structured, fine-grained way, not in long narrative paragraphs. Avoid combining multiple requirements together into a single statement, because the different requirements might trace to different development components. Chapter 29, "Links in the requirements chain," addresses requirements tracing.

You're never going to create a perfect specification in which *all* requirements demonstrate *all* of these ideal attributes. But if you keep these characteristics in mind when you write and review the requirements, you'll produce better requirements specifications and better software.

Guidelines for writing requirements

There is no formulaic way to write excellent requirements; the best teachers are experience and feedback from the recipients of your requirements. Receiving constructive feedback from colleagues with sharp eyes is a great help because you can learn where your writing did and didn't hit the mark. This is why peer reviews of requirements documents are so critical. To get started with reviews, buddy up with a fellow business analyst and begin exchanging requirements for review. You'll learn from seeing how another BA writes requirements, and you'll improve the team's collective work by discovering errors and improvement opportunities as early as possible. The following sections provide numerous tips for writing requirements—particularly functional requirements—that readers can clearly understand. Benjamin Kovitz (1999), Ian Alexander and Richard Stevens (2002), and Karl Wiegers (2006) present many other recommendations and examples for writing good requirements.

When we say "writing requirements," people immediately think of writing textual requirements in natural language. It's better to mentally translate the phrase "writing requirements" to "representing requirements knowledge." In many cases, alternative representation techniques can present information more effectively than can straight text (Wiegers 2006). The BA should choose an appropriate mix of communication methods that ensures a clear, shared understanding of both the stakeholder needs and the solution to be built.

The sample requirements presented here can always be improved upon, and there are always equivalent ways to state them. Two important goals of writing requirements are that:

- Anyone who reads the requirement comes to the same interpretation as any other reader.

- Each reader's interpretation matches what the author intended to communicate.

These outcomes are more important than purity of style or conforming dogmatically to some arbitrary rule or convention.

System or user perspective

You can write functional requirements from the perspective of either something the system does or something the user can do. Because effective communication is the overarching goal, it's fine to intermingle these styles, phrasing each requirement in whichever style is clearer. State requirements in a consistent fashion, such as "The system shall" or "The user shall," followed by an action verb, followed by the observable result. Specify the trigger action or condition that causes the system to perform the specified behavior. A generic template for a requirement written from the system's perspective is (Mavin et al. 2009):

[optional precondition] [optional trigger event] the system shall [expected system response].

This template is from the Easy Approach to Requirements Syntax (EARS). EARS also includes additional template constructs for event-driven, unwanted behavior, state-driven, optional, and complex requirements. Following is an example of a simple functional requirement that describes a system action using this template:

If the requested chemical is found in the chemical stockroom, the system shall display a list of all containers of the chemical that are currently in the stockroom.

This example includes a precondition, but not a trigger. Some requirement writers would omit the phrase "the system shall" from this requirement. They argue that, because the requirements are describing system behavior, there's no need to repetitively say "the system shall" do this or that. In this example, deleting "the system shall" is not confusing. Sometimes, though, it's more natural to phrase the requirement in terms of a user's action, not from the system's perspective. Including the "shall" and writing in the active voice makes it clear what entity is taking the action described.

When writing functional requirements from the user's perspective, the following general structure works well (Alexander and Stevens 2002):

The [user class or actor name] shall be able to [do something] [to some object] [qualifying conditions, response time, or quality statement].

Alternative phrasings are "The system shall let (or allow, permit, or enable) the [a particular user class name] to [do something]." Following is an example of a functional requirement written from the user's perspective:

The Chemist shall be able to reorder any chemical he has ordered in the past by retrieving and editing the order details.

Notice how this requirement uses the name of the user class—Chemist—in place of the generic "user." Making the requirement as explicit as possible reduces the possibility of misinterpretation.

Writing style

Writing requirements isn't like writing either fiction or other types of nonfiction. The writing style you might have learned in school in which you present the main idea, then supporting facts, then the conclusion, doesn't work well. Adjust your writing style to put the punch line—the statement of need or functionality—first, followed by supporting details (rationale, origin, priority, and other requirement attributes). This structure helps readers who are just skimming through a document, while still being useful for those thorough readers who need all the details. Including tables, structured lists, diagrams, and other visual elements helps to break up a monotonous litany of functional requirements and provides richer communication to those who learn best in different ways.

Nor are requirements documents the place to practice your creative writing skills. Avoid interleaving passive and active voice in an attempt to make the material more interesting to read. Don't use multiple terms for the same concept just to achieve variety (customer, account, patron, user, client). Being easy to read and understand is an essential element of well-written requirements; being interesting is, frankly, less important. If you are not a skilled writer, you should expect that your readers might not understand what you intend to convey. Keep the tips that follow in mind as you craft your requirements statements for maximum communication effectiveness.

Clarity and conciseness   Write requirements in complete sentences using proper grammar, spelling, and punctuation. Keep sentences and paragraphs short and direct. Write requirements in simple and straightforward language appropriate to the user domain, avoiding jargon. Define specialized terms in a glossary.

Another good guideline is to write concisely. Phrases like "needs to provide the user with the capability to" can be condensed to "shall." For each piece of information in the requirements set, ask yourself, "What would the reader do with this information?" If you aren't certain that some stakeholder would find that information valuable, perhaps you don't need it. Clarity is more important than conciseness, though.

Precisely stated requirements increase the chance of people receiving what they expect; less specific requirements offer the developer more latitude for interpretation. Sometimes that lack of specificity is fine, but in other cases it can lead to too much variability in the outcome. If a developer who reviews the SRS isn't clear on the customer's intent, consider including additional information to reduce the risk of problems later on.

The keyword "shall"   A traditional convention is to use the keyword "shall" to describe some system capability. People sometimes object to the word "shall." "That's not how people talk," they protest. So what? "Shall" statements clearly indicate the desired functionality, consistent with your overarching objective of clear and effective communication. You might prefer to say "must," "needs to," or something similar, but be consistent. I sometimes read specifications that contain a random and confusing mix of requirements verbs: shall, must, may, might, will, would, should, could, needs to, has to, should provide, and others. I never know if there are differences between the meanings of these or not. Nuances between different verbs also make the document far more difficult for cross-cultural teams to interpret consistently. You're better off sticking with a keyword such as "shall."

Some requirement authors deliberately use different verbs to imply subtle distinctions. They use certain keywords to connote priority: "shall" means required, "should" means desired, and "may" means optional (ISO/IEC/IEEE 2011). We regard such conventions as dangerous. It's clearer to always say "shall" or "must" and explicitly assign high, medium, or low priority to each requirement. Also, priorities will change as iterations proceed, so don't tie them to the phrasing of the requirements. Today's "must" could become tomorrow's "should." Other authors use "shall" to indicate a requirement and "will" to denote a design expectation. Such conventions run the risk of some readers not understanding the distinctions between words people use interchangeably in everyday conversation; they are best avoided.

> **Trap** One witty consultant suggested that you mentally replace each instance of "should" with "probably won't." Would the resulting requirement be acceptable? If not, replace "should" with something more precise.

Active voice Write in the active voice to make it clear what entity is taking the action described. Much business and scientific writing is in the passive voice, but it is never as clear and direct as using the active voice. The following requirement is written in passive voice:

Upon product upgrade shipment, the serial number will be updated on the contract line.

The phrasing "will be updated" is indicative of passive voice. It denotes the recipient of the action (serial number) but not the performer of the action. That is, this phrasing offers no clue as to who or what updates the serial number. Will the system do that automatically, or is the user expected to update the serial number? Rephrasing this requirement into active voice makes the actor explicit and also clarifies the triggering event:

When Fulfillment confirms that they shipped a product upgrade, the system shall update the customer's contract with the new product serial number.

Individual requirements Avoid writing long narrative paragraphs that contain multiple requirements. Readers shouldn't have to glean the individual requirements embedded in a mass of free-flowing descriptive language. Clearly distinguish individual requirements from background or contextual information. Such information is valuable to readers, but they need to unambiguously recognize the actual requirement statements. I once reviewed a large requirements specification written in the form of long paragraphs. I could read a full page and understand it, but I had to work hard to pick out the discrete requirements. Other readers might well come to different conclusions of exactly what requirements were lurking in that mass of text.

Words such as "and," "or," "additionally," or "also" in a requirement suggest that several requirements might have been combined. This doesn't mean you can't use "and" in a requirement; just make sure the conjunction is joining two parts of a single requirement instead of two separate requirements. If you would use different tests to verify the two parts, split the sentence into separate requirements.

Avoid using "and/or" in a requirement; it leaves the interpretation up to the reader, as in this case:

The system must permit search by order number, invoice number, and/or customer purchase order number.

This requirement would permit the user to enter one, two, or three numbers at once when performing a single search. That might not be what's intended.

The words "unless," "except," and "but" also indicate the presence of multiple requirements:

The Buyer's credit card on file shall be charged for payment, unless the credit card has expired.

Failing to specify what happens when the "unless" clause is true is a common source of missing requirements. Split this into two requirements to address the behavior for the two conditions of the credit card being active and expired:

If the Buyer's credit card on file is active, the system shall charge the payment to that card.

and

If the Buyer's credit card on file has expired, the system shall allow the Buyer to either update the current credit card information or enter a new credit card for payment.

Level of detail

Requirements need to be specified at a level of precision that provides developers and testers with just enough information to properly implement them.

Appropriate detail   An important part of requirements analysis is to decompose a high-level requirement into sufficient detail to clarify it and flesh it out. There's no single correct answer to the commonly asked question, "How detailed should the requirements be?" Provide enough specifics to minimize the risk of misunderstanding, based on the development team's knowledge and experience. The fewer the opportunities for ongoing discussion about requirements issues, the more specifics you need to record in the requirements set. If a developer can think of several possible ways to satisfy a requirement and all are acceptable, the specificity and detail are about right. You should include more detail when (Wiegers 2006):

- The work is being done for an external client.

- Development or testing will be outsourced.

- Project team members are geographically dispersed.

- System testing will be based on requirements.

- Accurate estimates are needed.

- Requirements traceability is needed.

It's safe to include less detail when:

- The work is being done internally for your company.

- Customers are extensively involved.

- Developers have considerable domain experience.

- Precedents are available, as when a previous application is being replaced.

- A package solution will be used.

Consistent granularity   Requirement authors often struggle to find the right level of granularity for writing functional requirements. It's not necessary to specify all of your requirements to the same level of detail. For example, you might go into more depth in an area that presents higher risk than others. Within a set of related requirements, though, it's a good idea to try to write functional requirements at a consistent level of granularity.

A helpful guideline is to write individually testable requirements. The count of testable requirements has even been proposed as a metric for software product size (Wilson 1995). If you can think of a small number of related test cases to verify that a requirement was correctly implemented, it's probably at an appropriate granularity. If you envision numerous and diverse tests, perhaps several requirements are combined and ought to be separated.

I've seen requirement statements in the same SRS that varied widely in their scope. For instance, the following two functions were split out as separate requirements:

1. *The system shall interpret the keystroke combination Ctrl+S as File Save.*

2. *The system shall interpret the keystroke combination Ctrl+P as File Print.*

These requirements are very fine-grained. They will need few tests for verification of correct behavior. You can imagine a tediously long list of similar requirements, which would better be expressed in the form of a table that lists all the keystroke shortcuts and how the system interprets them.

However, that same SRS also contained a functional requirement that seemed rather large in scope:

The product shall respond to editing directives entered by voice.

This single requirement—seemingly no larger or smaller than all the others in the SRS—stipulated the inclusion of a complex speech-recognition subsystem—virtually an entire product in its own right! Verifying this one requirement in the working system could require hundreds of tests. The requirement as stated here could be appropriate at the high level of abstraction found in a vision statement or a market requirements document, but the speech-recognition requirement clearly demands much more functionality detail.

Representation techniques

Readers' eyes glaze over when confronting a dense mass of turgid text or a long list of similar-looking requirements. Consider the most effective way to communicate each requirement to the intended audience. Some alternatives to the natural language requirements that we're used to are lists, tables, visual analysis models, charts, mathematical formulas, photographs, sound clips, and video clips. These won't suffice as substitutes for written requirements in many cases, but they serve as excellent supplemental information to enhance the reader's understanding.

I once saw a set of requirements that fit the following pattern:

The Text Editor shall be able to parse <format> documents that define <jurisdiction> laws.

There were 3 possible values for *<format>* and 4 possible values for *<jurisdiction>*, for a total of 12 similar requirements. The SRS did indeed contain 12 such requirements, but one of the combinations was missing and another was duplicated. You can prevent such errors by representing these types of requirements in a table, which is more compact and less boring than a requirements list. The generic requirement could be stated as:

Editor.DocFormat   *The Text Editor shall be able to parse documents in several formats that define laws in the jurisdictions shown in Table 11-1.*

TABLE 11-1 Requirements for parsing documents

Jurisdiction	Tagged format	Untagged format	ASCII format
Federal	.1	.2	.3
State	.4	.5	.6
Territorial	.7	N/A	.8
International	.9	.10	.11

The cells in the table contain only the suffix to append to the master requirement's identifier. For example, the third requirement in the top row expands to:

> **Editor.DocFormat.3**   *The Text Editor shall be able to parse ASCII documents that define federal laws.*

If any of the combinations don't have a corresponding functional requirement for some logical reason, put *N/A* (not applicable) in that table cell. This is much clearer than omitting the irrelevant combination from the long list and then having a reader wonder why there is no requirement for parsing documents containing territorial laws in the untagged format. This technique also ensures completeness in the requirements set—if there's something in every cell, you know you haven't missed any.

Avoiding ambiguity

Requirements quality is in the eye of the reader, not the author. The analyst might believe that a requirement he has written is crystal clear, free from ambiguities and other problems. However, if a reader has questions, the requirement needs additional work. Peer reviews are the best way to find places where the requirements aren't clearly understood by all the intended audiences. This section describes several common sources of requirements ambiguity.

Fuzzy words   Use terms consistently and as defined in the glossary. Watch out for synonyms and near-synonyms. I know of one project where four different terms were used to refer to the same item in a single requirements document. Pick a single term and use it consistently, placing synonyms in the glossary so people who are accustomed to calling the item by a different name see the connection.

If you use a pronoun to refer to something mentioned earlier, make sure the antecedent is crystal clear. Adverbs introduce subjectivity and hence ambiguity. Avoid words like *reasonably, appropriately, generally, approximately, usually, systematically,* and *quickly* because the reader won't be sure how to interpret them.

Ambiguous language leads to unverifiable requirements, so avoid using vague and subjective terms. Table 11-2 lists many such terms, along with suggestions for how to remove the ambiguity. Some of these words might be acceptable in business requirements, but not in user requirements or specific functional requirements that are attempting to describe the solution to be built.

TABLE 11-2 Some ambiguous terms to avoid in requirements

Ambiguous terms	Ways to improve them
acceptable, adequate	Define what constitutes acceptability and how the system can judge this.
and/or	Specify whether you mean "and," "or," or "any combination of" so the reader doesn't have to guess.
as much as practicable	Don't leave it up to the developers to determine what's practicable. Make it a TBD and set a date to find out.
at least, at a minimum, not more than, not to exceed	Specify the minimum and maximum acceptable values.
best, greatest, most	State what level of achievement is desired and the minimum acceptable level of achievement.
between, from X to Y	Define whether the end points are included in the range.
depends on	Describe the nature of the dependency. Does another system provide input to this system, must other software be installed before your software can run, or does your system rely on another to perform some calculations or provide other services?
efficient	Define how efficiently the system uses resources, how quickly it performs specific operations, or how quickly users can perform certain tasks with the system.
fast, quick, rapid	Specify the minimum acceptable time in which the system performs some action.
flexible, versatile	Describe the ways in which the system must be able to adapt to changing operating conditions, platforms, or business needs.
i.e., e.g.	Many people are unclear about which of these means "that is" (i.e., meaning that the full list of items follows) and which means "for example" (e.g., meaning that just some examples follow). Use words in your native language, not confusing Latin abbreviations.
improved, better, faster, superior, higher quality	Quantify how much better or faster constitutes adequate improvement in a specific functional area or quality aspect.
including, including but not limited to, and so on, etc., such as, for instance	List all possible values or functions, not just examples, or refer the reader to the location of the full list. Otherwise, different readers might have different interpretations of what the whole set of items being referred to contains or where the list stops.
in most cases, generally, usually, almost always	Clarify when the stated conditions or scenarios do not apply and what happens then. Describe how either the user or the system can distinguish one case from the other.
match, equals, agree, the same	Define whether a text comparison is case sensitive and whether it means the phrase "contains," "starts with," or is "exact." For real numbers, specify the degree of precision in the comparison.
maximize, minimize, optimize	State the maximum and minimum acceptable values of some parameter.
normally, ideally	Identify abnormal or non-ideal conditions and describe how the system should behave in those situations.
optionally	Clarify whether this means a developer choice, a system choice, or a user choice.
probably, ought to, should	Will it or won't it?
reasonable, when necessary, where appropriate, if possible, as applicable	Explain how either the developer or the user can make this judgment.
robust	Define how the system is to handle exceptions and respond to unexpected operating conditions.

Ambiguous terms	Ways to improve them
seamless, transparent, graceful	What does "seamless" or "graceful" mean to the user? Translate the user's expectations into specific observable product characteristics.
several, some, many, few, multiple, numerous	State how many, or provide the minimum and maximum bounds of a range.
shouldn't, won't	Try to state requirements as positives, describing what the system will do.
state-of-the-art	Define what this phrase means to the stakeholder.
sufficient	Specify how much of something constitutes sufficiency.
support, enable	Define exactly what functions the system will perform that constitute "supporting" some capability.
user-friendly, simple, easy	Describe system characteristics that will satisfy the customer's usage needs and usability expectations.

The A/B construct   Many requirements specifications include expressions in the form "A/B," in which two related (or synonymous, or opposite) terms are combined with a slash. Such expressions frequently are ambiguous. Here's an example:

> *The system shall provide automated information collection of license key data for a mass release from the Delivery/Fulfillment Team.*

This sentence could be interpreted in several ways:

- The name of the team is Delivery/Fulfillment.

- Delivery and fulfillment are synonyms.

- Some projects call the group a Delivery Team; others call it a Fulfillment Team.

- Either the Delivery Team or the Fulfillment Team can do a mass release, so the slash means "or."

- The Delivery Team and the Fulfillment Team jointly do a mass release, so the slash means "and."

Sometimes authors use the A/B construct because they aren't sure exactly what they have in mind. Unfortunately, this means that each reader gets to interpret the requirement to mean whatever he thinks it ought to mean. It's better to decide exactly what you intend to say and choose the right words.

Boundary values   Many ambiguities occur at the boundaries of numerical ranges in both requirements and business rules. Consider the following:

> *Vacation requests of up to 5 days do not require approval. Vacation requests of 5 to 10 days require supervisor approval. Vacation requests of 10 days or longer require management approval.*

This phrasing makes it unclear as to which category vacation requests of exactly 5 days and exactly 10 days belong. It gets even more confusing if fractions are involved, like 5.5 days of vacation. The words "through," "inclusive," and "exclusive" make it totally clear whether the endpoints of the numerical range lie inside or outside the range:

> *Vacation requests of 5 or fewer days do not require approval. Vacation requests of longer than 5 days through 10 days require supervisor approval. Vacation requests of longer than 10 days require management approval.*

Negative requirements   People sometimes write requirements that say what the system *will not* do rather than what it *will* do. How do you implement a don't-do-this requirement? Double and triple negatives are particularly tricky to decipher. Try to rephrase negative requirements into a positive sense that clearly describes the restricting behavior. Here's an example:

Prevent the user from activating the contract if the contract is not in balance.

Consider rephrasing this double negative ("prevent" and "not in balance") as a positive statement:

The system shall allow the user to activate the contract only if the contract is in balance.

Instead of using negative requirements to indicate that certain functionality is out of scope, include the restriction in the Limitations and Exclusions section of the vision and scope document, as described in Chapter 5, "Establishing the business requirements." If a specific requirement was once in scope but then removed, you don't want to lose sight of it—it might come back someday. If you are maintaining requirements in a document, use strikethrough formatting to indicate a deleted requirement. The best way to handle such deleted requirements is with a requirements status attribute in a requirements management tool (see Chapter 27, "Requirements management practices," for more about requirements attributes and status tracking).

Avoiding incompleteness

We don't know of any way to be certain that you've found every requirement. Chapter 7, "Requirements elicitation," suggests several ways to identify missing requirements. Focusing elicitation on user tasks rather than system features can help avoid overlooking functionality. Also, using analysis models can help you spot missing requirements (see Chapter 12, "A picture is worth 1024 words").

Symmetry   Symmetrical operations are a common source of missing requirements. I once found the following requirement in an SRS I was reviewing:

The user must be able to save the contract at any point during manual contract setup.

Nowhere in the rest of the specification did I find a requirement to allow the user to retrieve an incomplete but saved contract to work on it further: perhaps a requirement was missing. Nor was it clear whether the system should validate the data entries in the incomplete contract before saving it. An implied requirement? Developers need to know.

Complex logic   Compound logical expressions often leave certain combinations of decision values undefined. Consider this requirement:

If the Premium plan is not selected and proof of insurance is not provided, the customer should automatically default into the Basic plan.

This requirement refers to two binary decisions, whose combinations lead to four possible outcomes. However, the specification only addressed this one combination. It didn't say what should happen if:

■ The Premium plan is selected and proof of insurance is not provided.

- The Premium plan is selected and proof of insurance is provided.

- The Premium plan is not selected and proof of insurance is provided.

The reader is forced to conclude that the system doesn't take any action for those three other conditions. That might be correct, but it's better to make such conclusions explicit rather than implicit. Use decision tables or decision trees to represent complex logic and ensure that you have not missed any variants.

Missing exceptions   Each requirement that states how the system should work when everything is correct should also have accompanying requirements as necessary to describe how the system should respond when exceptions occur. Consider the following requirement:

> *If the user is working in an existing file and chooses to save the file, the system shall save it with the same name.*

This requirement alone does not indicate what the system should do if it's unable to save the file with the same name. An appropriate second requirement to go with the first might be:

> *If the system is unable to save a file using a specific name, the system shall give the user the option to save it with a different name or to cancel the save operation.*

Sample requirements, before and after

This chapter opened with several characteristics of high-quality requirements. Requirements that don't exhibit these characteristics cause confusion, wasted effort, and rework later, so strive to correct any problems early. Following are several functional requirements adapted from real projects that are less than ideal. Examine each statement for those quality characteristics to see whether you can spot the problems. Verifiability is a good starting point. If you can't devise tests to tell whether the requirement was correctly implemented, it's probably ambiguous or lacks necessary information.

For each example, we present some observations about the problems with these requirements and suggested improvements. Additional reviews would no doubt improve them further, but at some point you need to write software. More examples of rewriting poor requirements are available from Ivy Hooks and Kristin Farry (2001), Al Florence (2002), Ian Alexander and Richard Stevens (2002), and Karl Wiegers (2006). Note that pulling requirements out of context like this shows them at their worst. These might well make more sense in their original environment. We also assume that business analysts (and all other team members) come to work each day to do the best job they can, based on what they know at the moment, so we're not picking on the original authors here.

> **Trap** Watch out for analysis paralysis. All of the sample "after" requirements in this chapter can be improved further, but you can't spend forever trying to perfect the requirements. Remember, your goal is to write requirements that are *good enough* to let your team proceed with design and construction at an acceptable level of risk.

Example 1 *The Background Task Manager shall provide status messages at regular intervals not less than every 60 seconds.*

What are the status messages? Under what conditions and in what fashion are they provided to the user? If displayed on the screen, how long do they remain visible? Is it okay if they just flash up for half a second? The timing interval is not clear, and the word "every" just muddles the issue. One way to evaluate a requirement is to see whether a ludicrous but legitimate interpretation is all right with the user. If not, the requirement needs more work. In this example, is the interval between status messages supposed to be *at least* 60 seconds, so providing a new message once per year is okay? Alternatively, if the intent is to have *at most* 60 seconds elapse between messages, would one millisecond be too short an interval? These extreme interpretations might be consistent with the original requirement, but they certainly aren't what the user had in mind. Because of these problems, this requirement is not verifiable.

Here's one way to rewrite the preceding requirement to address those shortcomings, after we get some more information from the customer:

1. The Background Task Manager (BTM) shall display status messages in a designated area of the user interface.

1.1. The BTM shall update the messages every 60 plus or minus 5 seconds after background task processing begins.

1.2. The messages shall remain visible continuously during background processing.

1.3. The BTM shall display the percent of the background task that is completed.

1.4. The BTM shall display a "Done" message when the background task is completed.

1.5. The BTM shall display a message if the background task has stalled.

Rewriting a flawed requirement often makes it longer because information was missing. Splitting this into multiple child requirements makes sense because each will demand separate tests. This also makes each one individually traceable. There would likely be additional status messages that the BTM might display. If those are documented someplace else, such as in an interface specification, incorporate that information here by reference instead of replicating it. Listing the messages in a table of conditions and corresponding messages would be more concise than writing numerous functional requirements.

The revised requirements don't specify how the status messages will be displayed, just "in a designated area of the user interface." Such wording defers the placement of the messages to being a design issue, which is fine in many cases. If you specify the display location in the requirements, it becomes a design constraint placed on the developer. Unnecessarily constrained design options frustrate the programmers and can result in a suboptimal product design.

Suppose, though, that we're adding this functionality to an existing application whose user interface already contains a status bar, where users are accustomed to seeing important messages. For consistency with the rest of the application it would make perfect sense to stipulate that the BTM's status messages shall appear in the status bar. That is, you might deliberately impose the design constraint for a very good reason.

Example 2 *Corporate project charge numbers should be validated online against the master corporate charge number list, if possible.*

The phrase "if possible" is ambiguous. Does it mean "if it's technically feasible" (a question for the developer) or "if the master charge number list can be accessed at run time"? If you aren't sure whether a requested capability can be delivered, use TBD to indicate that the issue is unresolved. After investigation, either the TBD goes away or the requirement goes away. This requirement doesn't specify what to do when the validation either passes or fails. Also, avoid imprecise words such as "should." Here's a revised version of this requirement:

> *At the time the requester enters a charge number, the system shall display an error message if the charge number is not in the master corporate charge number list.*

A related requirement would address the exception condition of the master corporate charge number list not being available at the time the validation was attempted.

Example 3 *The device tester shall allow the user to easily connect additional components, including a pulse generator, a voltmeter, a capacitance meter, and custom probe cards.*

This requirement is for a product containing embedded software that's used to test several kinds of measurement devices. The word "easily" implies a usability requirement, but it is neither measurable nor verifiable. "Including" doesn't make it clear whether this is the complete list of external devices that must be connected to the tester. Perhaps there are many others that we don't know about. Consider the following alternative requirements, which contain some intentional design constraints:

> *1. The device tester shall incorporate a USB port to allow the user to connect any measurement device that has a USB connection.*

> *2. The USB port shall be installed on the front panel to permit a trained operator to connect a measurement device in 10 seconds or less.*

A business analyst shouldn't rewrite requirements in a way that imposes design constraints on his own initiative. Instead, detect the flawed requirements and discuss them with the appropriate stakeholders so they can be clarified.

Example 4 *The system must check for inconsistencies in account data between the Active Account Log and the Account Manager archive. The logic that is used to generate these comparisons should be based on the logic in the existing consistency checker tool. In other words, the new code does not need to be developed from scratch. The developers should utilize the current consistency checker code as the foundation. However, additional logic must be added to identify which database is the authoritative source. The new functionality will include writing data to holding tables to indicate how/where to resolve inconsistencies. Additionally, the code should also check for exception scenarios against the security tools database. Automated email alerts should be sent to the Security Compliance Team whenever discrepancies are found.*

This is a good one for you to practice on. We'll point out some of the problems with this paragraph, and you might want to try rewriting it in an improved form, making some assumptions as necessary to fill in the gaps. Following are some issues you might want to correct.

- There are numerous requirements in here that should be split out individually.

- If the comparison logic is "based on" logic in the existing consistency checker tool, exactly what portion of the code can be reused and how does it need to be changed? What functions are different between the new system and the existing tool? What "additional logic" must be added? How exactly can the system determine "which database is the authoritative source"?

- The new functionality "includes" writing data to holding tables; is that all, or is other functionality "included" that isn't explicitly stated?

- Clarify what "how/where" means when resolving inconsistencies.

- "Should" is used in several places.

- What's the relationship between an "exception scenario" and a "discrepancy"? If they're synonyms, pick one term and stick with it. A glossary might clarify whether these are the same or how they are related.

- What information should the system send to the Security Compliance Team when it detects a discrepancy?

As we said earlier, you're never going to get perfect requirements. But an experienced BA can nearly always help make requirements better.

Next steps

- Hold a discussion with your customers, developers, and testers to evaluate the current level of requirements documentation on your project to determine if more or less detail is needed in specific areas and how best to represent those requirements.

- Examine a page of functional requirements from your project's requirements set to see whether each statement exhibits the characteristics of excellent requirements. Look for any of the types of problems described in this chapter. Rewrite any requirements that don't measure up.

- Convene three to six project stakeholders to inspect the SRS for your project (Wiegers 2002). Make sure each requirement demonstrates the desirable characteristics discussed in this chapter. Look for conflicts between different requirements in the specification, for missing requirements, and for missing sections of the SRS. Ensure that the defects you find are corrected in the SRS and in any downstream work products based on those requirements.

CHAPTER 12

A picture is worth 1024 words

The Chemical Tracking System (CTS) project team was holding its first detailed requirements review. The participants were Dave (project manager), Lori (business analyst), Helen (lead developer), Ramesh (test lead), Tim (product champion for the chemists), and Roxanne (product champion for the chemical stockroom staff). Tim began by saying, "I read the whole document. Most of the requirements seemed okay to me, but I had a hard time digesting the long lists of requirements in a few sections. I'm not sure whether we identified all the steps in the chemical request process."

"It was hard for me to think of all the tests that I'll need to cover the status changes for a request," Ramesh added. "I found a bunch of requirements sprinkled throughout the document about the status changes, but I couldn't tell whether any were missing. A couple of requirements seemed to conflict."

Roxanne had a similar problem. "I got confused when I read about the way I would actually request a chemical," she said. "I had trouble visualizing the sequence of steps I would go through."

After the reviewers raised several other concerns, Lori concluded, "It looks like this document doesn't tell us everything we need to know about the system. I'll create some diagrams to help us visualize the requirements and see whether that clarifies these problem areas. Thanks for the feedback."

As requirements authority Alan Davis pointed out, no single view of the requirements provides a complete understanding (Davis 1995). You need a combination of textual and visual requirements representations at different levels of abstraction to paint a full picture of the intended system. Requirements views can include functional requirements lists, tables, visual analysis models, user interface prototypes, acceptance tests, decision trees, decision tables, photographs, videos, and mathematical expressions (Wiegers 2006). Ideally, different people will create various requirements representations. The business analyst might write the functional requirements and draw some models, whereas the user interface designer builds a prototype and the test lead writes test cases. Comparing the requirements representations created through diverse thought processes and diverse notations reveals inconsistencies, ambiguities, assumptions, and omissions that are difficult to spot from any single view.

Diagrams communicate certain types of information more efficiently than text can. Pictures help bridge language and vocabulary barriers among team members. The BA initially might need to explain the purpose of the models and the notations used to other stakeholders. There are many different diagrams and modeling techniques to choose from to create visual representations of the requirements. This chapter introduces several requirements modeling techniques, with illustrations and pointers to other sources for further details.

Modeling the requirements

Business analysts might hope to find one technique that pulls everything together into a holistic depiction of a system's requirements. Unfortunately, there is no such all-encompassing diagram. In fact, if you could model the entire system in a single diagram, that diagram would be just as unusable as a long list of requirements on its own. An early goal of structured systems analysis was to replace the classical functional specification with diagrams and notations that are more formal than narrative text. However, experience has shown that analysis models should augment—rather than replace—a requirements specification written in natural language. Developers and testers still benefit from the detail and precision that written requirements offer.

Visual requirements models can help you identify missing, extraneous, and inconsistent requirements. Given the limitations of human short-term memory, analyzing a list of one thousand requirements for inconsistencies, duplication, and extraneous requirements is nearly impossible. By the time you reach the fifteenth requirement, you have likely forgotten the first few that you read. You're unlikely to find all of the errors simply by reviewing the textual requirements.

Visual requirements models described in this book include:

- Data flow diagrams (DFDs)

- Process flow diagrams such as swimlane diagrams

- State-transition diagrams (STDs) and state tables

- Dialog maps

- Decision tables and decision trees

- Event-response tables

- Feature trees (discussed in Chapter 5, "Establishing the business requirements")

- Use case diagrams (discussed in Chapter 8, "Understanding user requirements")

- Activity diagrams (also discussed in Chapter 8)

- Entity-relationship diagrams (ERDs) (discussed in Chapter 13, "Specifying data requirements")

The notations presented here provide a common, industry-standard language for project participants to use. Inventing your own modeling notations presents more risk of misinterpretation than if you adopt standard notations.

These models are useful for elaborating and exploring the requirements, as well as for designing software solutions. Whether you are using them for analysis or for design depends on the timing and the intent of the modeling. Used for requirements analysis, these diagrams let you model the problem domain or create conceptual representations of the new system. They depict the logical aspects of the problem domain's data components, transactions and transformations, real-world objects, and changes in system state. You can base the models on the textual requirements to represent them from different perspectives, or you can derive functional requirements from high-level models that are based on user input. During design, models represent how you intend to implement the system: the actual database to create, the object classes to instantiate, and the code modules to develop. Because analysis and design diagrams use the same notations, clearly identify each one you draw as being an analysis model (the concepts) or a design model (what you intend to build).

The analysis modeling techniques described in this chapter are supported by a variety of commercial modeling tools, requirements management tools, and drawing tools such as Microsoft Visio. Specialized modeling tools provide several benefits over general-purpose drawing tools. First, they make it easy to improve the diagrams through iteration. You'll almost never get a model right the first time through, so iteration is a key to modeling success. Tools can also enforce the rules for each modeling method they support. They can identify syntax errors and inconsistencies that people who review the diagrams might not see. Requirements management tools that support modeling allow you to trace requirements to the models. Some tools link multiple diagrams together and to their related functional and data requirements. Using a tool with standard symbols can help you keep the models consistent with each other.

We hear arguments against using requirements models that range from "Our system is too complex to model" to "We have a tight project schedule; there is no time to model the requirements." A model is simpler than the system you are modeling. If you cannot handle the complexity of the model, how will you be able to handle the complexity of the system? Creating most models doesn't require significantly more time than you would spend writing the requirements statements and analyzing them for issues. Any extra time spent using requirements analysis models should be more than made up for by catching requirements errors prior to building the system. Models, or portions of models, can sometimes be reused from one project to another, or at least serve as a straw-man starting point for requirements elicitation on a subsequent project.

From voice of the customer to analysis models

By listening carefully to how customers present their requirements, the business analyst can pick out keywords that translate into specific model elements. Table 12-1 suggests possible mappings from customers' word choices into model components, which are described later in this chapter. As you evolve customer input into written requirements and models, you should be able to link each model component to a specific user requirement.

TABLE 12-1 Relating the customer's voice to analysis model components

Type of word	Examples	Analysis model components
Noun	People, organizations, software systems, data elements, or objects that exist	■ External entities, data stores, or data flow (DFD) ■ Actors (use case diagram) ■ Entities or their attributes (ERD) ■ Lanes (swimlane diagram) ■ Objects with states (STD)
Verb	Actions, things a user or system can do, or events that can take place	■ Processes (DFD) ■ Process steps (swimlane diagram) ■ Use cases (use case diagram) ■ Relationships (ERD) ■ Transitions (STD) ■ Activities (activity diagram) ■ Events (event-response table)
Conditional	Conditional logic statements, such as if/then	■ Decisions (decision tree, decision table, or activity diagram) ■ Branching (swimlane diagram or activity diagram)

Building on the Chemical Tracking System example, consider the following paragraph of user needs supplied by the product champion who represented the Chemist user class. Significant unique nouns are highlighted in **bold,** verbs are in *italics*, and conditional statements are in ***bold italics***; look for these keywords in the analysis models shown later in this chapter. For the sake of illustration, some of the models show information that goes beyond that contained in the following paragraph, whereas other models depict just part of the information presented here:

> A **chemist** or a member of the **chemical stockroom staff** can *place* a **request** for one or more **chemicals** ***if the user is an authorized requester***. The request can be *fulfilled* either by *delivering* a **container** of the chemical that is already in the chemical stockroom's **inventory** or by placing an **order** for a new container of the chemical with an outside **vendor**. ***If the chemical is hazardous***, the chemical can be delivered only ***if the user is trained***. The **person** placing the request must be able to *search* **vendor catalogs** online for specific chemicals while *preparing* his request. The system needs to *track* the **status** of every chemical request from the time it is prepared until the request is either fulfilled or *canceled*. It also needs to track the **history** of every chemical container from the time it is *received* at the **company** until it is fully *consumed* or *disposed* of.

> **Trap** Don't assume that customers already know how to read analysis models, but don't conclude that they're unable to understand them, either. Include a key and explain the purpose and notations of each model to your product champions. Walk through a sample model to help them learn how to review each type of diagram.

Selecting the right representations

Rarely does a team need to create a complete set of analysis models for an entire system. Focus your modeling on the most complex and riskiest portions of the system and on those portions most subject to ambiguity or uncertainty. Safety-critical, security-critical, and mission-critical system elements are good candidates for modeling because the impact of defects in those areas is so severe. Also choose models to use together to help ensure all of the models are complete. For example, examining the data objects in a DFD can uncover missing entities in an ERD. Considering all the processes in a DFD might identify useful swimlane diagrams to create. There are suggestions throughout the rest of the chapter on which models complement each other well in this fashion.

Table 12-2, adapted from Karl Wiegers' work (2006), suggests which representation techniques to use based on what type of information you are trying to show, analyze, or discover. Joy Beatty and Anthony Chen (2012) provide additional suggestions about what requirements models to create based on project phases, characteristics of the project, and the target audience(s) for the models. The rest of this chapter describes some of the most commonly used models from this table that are not covered elsewhere in the book.

TABLE 12-2 Choosing the most appropriate representation techniques

Information depicted	Representation techniques
System external interfaces	■ *The context diagram* and *use case diagram* identify objects outside the system that connect to it. The context diagram and *data flow diagrams* illustrate the system inputs and outputs at a high level of abstraction. The *ecosystem map* identifies possible systems that interact, but includes some that do not interface directly as well. *Swimlane diagrams* show what happens in the interactions between systems. ■ External interface details can be recorded in input and output *file formats* or *report layouts*. Products that include both software and hardware components often have *interface specifications* with data attribute definitions, perhaps in the form of an application programming interface or specific input and output signals for a hardware device.
Business process flow	■ A top-level *data flow diagram* represents how a business process handles data at a high level of abstraction. *Swimlane diagrams* show the roles that participate in executing the various steps in a business process flow. ■ Refined levels of *data flow diagrams* or *swimlane diagrams* can represent business process flows in considerable detail. Similarly, *flowcharts* and *activity diagrams* can be used at either high or low levels of abstraction, although most commonly they are used to define the details of a process.
Data definitions and data object relationships	■ The *entity-relationship diagram* shows the logical relationships between data objects (entities). *Class diagrams* show the logical connections between object classes and the data associated with them. ■ The *data dictionary* contains detailed definitions of data structures and individual data items. Complex data objects are progressively broken down into their constituent data elements.

Information depicted	Representation techniques
System and object states	■ *State-transition diagrams* and *state tables* represent a high-abstraction view of the possible states of a system or object and the changes between states that can take place under certain circumstances. These models are helpful when multiple use cases can manipulate (and change the state of) certain objects. ■ Some analysts create an *event-response table* as a scoping tool, identifying external events that help define the product's scope boundary. You can also specify individual functional requirements with an event-response table by detailing how the system should behave in response to each combination of external event and system state. ■ *Functional requirements* provide the details that describe exactly what user and system behaviors lead to status changes.
Complex logic	■ A *decision tree* shows the possible outcomes from a set of related decisions or conditions. A *decision table* identifies the unique functional requirements associated with the various combinations of true and false outcomes for a series of decisions or conditions.
User interfaces	■ The *dialog map* provides a high-level view of a proposed or actual user interface, showing the various display elements and possible navigation pathways between them. ■ *Storyboards* and *low-fidelity prototypes* flesh out the dialog map by showing what each screen will contain without depicting precise details. *Display-action-response models* describe the display and behavior requirements of each screen. ■ *Detailed screen layouts* and *high-fidelity prototypes* show exactly how the display elements will look. *Data field definitions* and *user interface control descriptions* provide additional detail.
User task descriptions	■ *User stories*, *scenarios*, and *use case specifications* describe user tasks in various levels of detail. ■ *Swimlane diagrams* illustrate the business process or interplay between multiple actors and the system. *Flowcharts* and *activity diagrams* visually depict the flow of the use case dialog and branches into alternative flows and exceptions. ■ *Functional requirements* provide detailed descriptions of how the system and user will interact to achieve valuable outcomes. *Test cases* provide an alternative low-abstraction view, describing exactly what system behavior to expect under specific conditions of inputs, system state, and actions.
Nonfunctional requirements (quality attributes, constraints)	■ Quality attributes and constraints are usually written in the form of *natural language text*, but that often results in a lack of precision and completeness. Chapter 14, "Beyond functionality" describes a definitive technique for precisely specifying nonfunctional requirements called *Planguage* (Gilb 2005).

Data flow diagram

The *data flow diagram* is the basic tool of structured analysis (DeMarco 1979; Robertson and Robertson 1994). A DFD identifies the transformational processes of a system, the collections (stores) of data or physical materials that the system manipulates, and the flows of data or material between processes, stores, and the outside world. Data flow modeling takes a functional decomposition approach to systems analysis, breaking complex problems into progressive levels of detail. This works well for transaction-processing systems and other function-intensive applications. Through the addition of control flow elements, the DFD technique has been extended to permit modeling of real-time systems (Hatley, Hruschka, and Pirbhai 2000).

DFDs provide a big-picture view of how data moves through a system, which other models don't show well. Various people and systems execute processes that use, manipulate, and produce data, so any single use case or swimlane diagram can't show you the full life cycle of a piece of data. Also, multiple pieces of data might be pulled together and transformed by a process (for example, shopping cart contents plus shipping information plus billing information are transformed into an order object). Again, this is hard to show in other models. However, DFDs do not suffice as a sole modeling technique. The details about how the data is transformed are better shown by steps in a process using use cases or swimlane diagrams.

Beatty and Chen (2012) suggest tips for creating DFDs and using DFDs for requirements analysis. This tool is often used when interviewing customers, because it's easy to scribble a DFD on a whiteboard while discussing how the user's business operates. DFDs can be used as a technique to identify missing data requirements. The data that flows between processes, data stores, and external entities should also be modeled in ERDs and described in the data dictionary. Also, a DFD gives context to the functional requirements regarding how the user performs specific tasks, such as requesting a chemical.

Data flow diagrams can represent systems over a wide range of abstraction. High-level DFDs provide a holistic, bird's-eye view of the data and processing components in a multistep activity, which complements the precise, detailed view embodied in the functional requirements. The context diagram in Figure 5-6 in Chapter 5 represents the highest level of abstraction of the DFD. The context diagram represents the entire system as a single black-box process, depicted as a circle (a *bubble*). It also shows the *external entities*, or terminators, that connect to the system, and the data or material flows between the system and the external entities. Flows on a context diagram often represent complex data structures, which are defined in the data dictionary.

You can elaborate the context diagram into a level 0 DFD (the highest level of a data flow model), which partitions the system into its major processes. Figure 12-1 shows a partial level 0 DFD for the Chemical Tracking System. This model uses the Yourdon-DeMarco DFD notation. There are alternative notations that use slightly different symbols.

The single circle that represented the entire Chemical Tracking System on the context diagram has been subdivided into six major processes (the process bubbles). As with the context diagram, the external entities are shown in rectangles. All data flows (arrows) from the context diagram also appear on the level 0 DFD. In addition, the level 0 diagram contains several *data stores*, depicted as a pair of parallel horizontal lines, which are internal to the system and therefore do not appear on the context diagram. A flow from a bubble to a store indicates that data is being placed into the store, a flow out of the store shows a read operation, and a bidirectional arrow between a store and a bubble indicates an update operation.

Each process that appears as a separate bubble on the level 0 diagram can be further expanded into a separate DFD to reveal more detail about its functioning. The BA continues this progressive refinement until the lowest-level diagrams contain only primitive process operations that can be clearly represented in narrative text, pseudocode, a swimlane diagram, or an activity diagram. The functional requirements will define precisely what happens within each primitive process. Each level of the DFD must be balanced and consistent with the level above it so that all the input and output flows on the child diagram match up with flows on its parent. Complex data structures in the high-level diagrams might be split into their constituent elements, as defined in the data dictionary, on the lower-level DFDs.

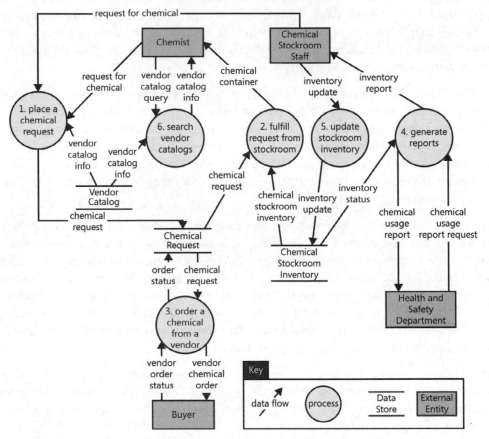

FIGURE 12-1 Partial level 0 data flow diagram for the Chemical Tracking System.

Figure 12-1 looks complex at first glance. However, if you examine the immediate environment of any one process, you will see the data items that it consumes and produces and their sources and destinations. To see exactly how a process uses the data items, you'll need to either draw a more detailed child DFD or refer to the functional requirements for that part of the system.

Following are several conventions for drawing data flow diagrams. Not everyone adheres to the same conventions (for example, some BAs show external entities only on the context diagram), but we find them helpful. Using the models to enhance communication among the project participants is more important than dogmatic conformance to these principles.

■ Processes communicate through data stores, not by direct flows from one process to another. Similarly, data cannot flow directly from one store to another or directly between external entities and data stores; it must pass through a process bubble.

■ Don't attempt to imply the processing sequence using the DFD.

- Name each process as a concise action: verb plus object (such as "generate reports"). Use names that are meaningful to the customers and pertinent to the business or problem domain.

- Number the processes uniquely and hierarchically. On the level 0 diagram, number each process with an integer. If you create a child DFD for process 3, number the processes in that child diagram 3.1, 3.2, and so on.

- Don't show more than 8 to 10 processes on a single diagram or it will be difficult to draw, change, and understand. If you have more processes, introduce another layer of abstraction by grouping related processes into a higher-level process.

- Bubbles with flows that are only coming in or only going out are suspect. The processing that a DFD bubble represents normally requires both input and output flows.

When customer representatives review a DFD, they should make sure that all the known and relevant data-manipulating processes are represented and that processes have no missing or unnecessary inputs or outputs. DFD reviews often reveal previously unrecognized user classes, business processes, and connections to other systems.

Modeling problems, not software

I once served as the IT representative on a team that was doing some business process reengineering. Our goal was to reduce the time that it took to make a new chemical available for use in a product by a factor of 10. The reengineering team included the following representatives of the various functions involved in chemical commercialization:

- The synthetic chemist who first makes the new chemical (he's a real person, but a synthetic chemist)

- The scale-up chemist who develops a process for making large batches of the chemical

- The analytical chemist who devises techniques for analyzing the chemical's purity

- The patent attorney who applies for patent protection

- The health and safety representative who obtains government approval to use the chemical in consumer products

The team worked together to invent a new process that we believed would greatly accelerate the chemical commercialization activity and modeled it in a swimlane diagram. Then, I interviewed the person on the reengineering team who was responsible for each process step. I asked each owner two questions: "What information do you need to perform this step?" and "What information does this step produce that we should store?" When correlating the answers for all process steps, I found steps that needed data that no one had available. Other steps produced data that no one needed. We fixed all those problems.

Next, I drew a data flow diagram to illustrate the new chemical commercialization process and an entity-relationship diagram (Chapter 13) to model the data relationships. A data dictionary (Chapter 13) defined all our data items. These analysis models served as useful communication tools to help the team members arrive at a common understanding of the new process. The models would also be a valuable starting point to scope and specify the requirements for software applications that supported portions of the process.

Swimlane diagram

Swimlane diagrams provide a way to represent the steps involved in a business process or the operations of a proposed software system. They are a variation of flowcharts, subdivided into visual subcomponents called *lanes*. The lanes can represent different systems or actors that execute the steps in the process. Swimlane diagrams are most commonly used to show business processes, workflows, or system and user interactions. They are similar to UML activity diagrams. Swimlane diagrams are sometimes called *cross-functional diagrams*.

Swimlane diagrams can show what happens inside the process bubbles from DFDs. They help tie together the functional requirements that enable users to perform specific tasks. They can also be used to perform detailed analysis to identify the requirements that support each process step (Beatty and Chen 2012).

The swimlane diagram is one of the easiest models for stakeholders to understand because the notation is simple and commonly used. Drafting business processes in swimlane diagrams can be a good starting point for elicitation conversations, as is described in Chapter 24, "Business process automation projects." Swimlane diagrams can contain additional shapes, but the most commonly used elements are:

- Process steps, shown as rectangles.

- Transitions between process steps, shown as arrows connecting pairs of rectangles.

- Decisions, shown as diamonds with multiple branches leaving each diamond. The decision choices are shown as text labels on each arrow leaving a diamond.

- Swimlanes to subdivide the process, shown as horizontal or vertical lines on the page. The lanes are most commonly roles, departments, or systems. They show who or what is executing the steps in a given lane.

Figure 12-2 shows a partial swimlane diagram for the CTS. The swimlanes in this example are roles or departments, showing which group executes each step in the business process to order a chemical from a vendor. To identify functional requirements, you can start at the first box, "Create a chemical request," and think about what functionality the system must have to support that step, as well as the data requirements for a "chemical request." A later step to "Receive and approve invoice" might trigger the team to identify requirements for what it means to process an invoice. How is the invoice received? What is its format? Is the invoice processing manual, or does the system automate some or all of it? Does the data from the invoice get pushed to other systems?

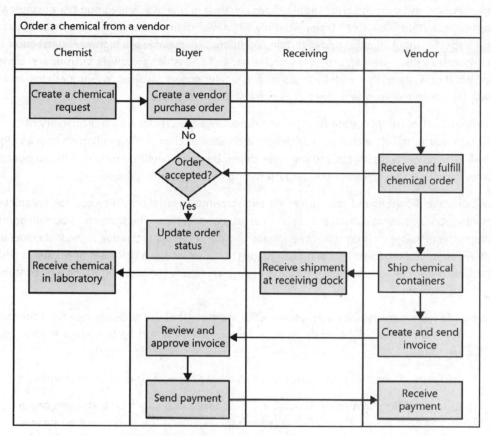

FIGURE 12-2 Partial swimlane diagram for a process in the Chemical Tracking System.

A complete business process might not fit entirely within the scope of a software system. Notice that the Receiving department appears in the swimlane as part of the process, but it is not found in the context diagram or the DFD because the Receiving department will never interact with the CTS directly. Reviewing the ecosystem map shown in Figure 5-7 (shown earlier, in Chapter 5) triggered the team to realize that Receiving had a place in this business process, though. The team also reviewed the data inputs to and outputs from this process bubble in the DFD (process 3 in Figure 12-1) to ensure that both models consumed and produced the same data, correcting any errors they found. This illustrates the power of modeling, creating multiple representations using different thought processes to gain a richer understanding of the system you're building.

State-transition diagram and state table

Software systems involve a combination of functional behavior, data manipulation, and state changes. Real-time systems and process control applications can exist in one of a limited number of states at any given time. A state change can take place only when well-defined criteria are satisfied, such as receiving a specific input stimulus under certain conditions. An example is a highway intersection that incorporates vehicle sensors, protected turn lanes, and pedestrian crosswalk buttons and signals. Many information systems deal with business objects—sales orders, invoices, inventory items, and the like—with life cycles that involve a series of possible states, or statuses.

Describing a set of complex state changes in natural language creates a high probability of overlooking a permitted state change or including a disallowed change. Depending on how an SRS is organized, requirements that pertain to the state-driven behavior might be sprinkled throughout it. This makes it difficult to reach an overall understanding of the system's behavior.

State-transition diagrams and *state tables* are two state models that provide a concise, complete, and unambiguous representation of the states of an object or system. The state-transition diagram (STD) shows the possible transitions between states visually. A related technique is the *state machine diagram* included in the Unified Modeling Language (UML), which has a richer set of notations and which models the states an object goes through during its lifetime (Ambler 2005). The STD contains three types of elements:

- Possible system states, shown as rectangles. Some notations use circles to represent the state (Beatty and Chen 2012). Either circles or rectangles work fine; just be consistent in what you choose to use.

- Allowed state changes or *transitions*, shown as arrows connecting pairs of rectangles.

- Events or conditions that cause each transition to take place, shown as text labels on each transition arrow. The label might identify both the event and the corresponding system response.

The STD for an object that passes through a defined life cycle will have one or more termination states, which represent the final status values that an object can have. Termination states have transition arrows coming in, but none going out. Customers can learn to read an STD with just a little coaching about the notation—it's just boxes and arrows.

Recall from Chapter 8 that a primary function of the Chemical Tracking System is to permit actors called Requesters to place requests for chemicals, which can be fulfilled either from the chemical stockroom's inventory or by placing orders to outside vendors. Each request will pass through a series of states between the time it's created and the time it's either fulfilled or canceled (the two termination states). Thus, an STD models the life cycle of a chemical request, as shown in Figure 12-3.

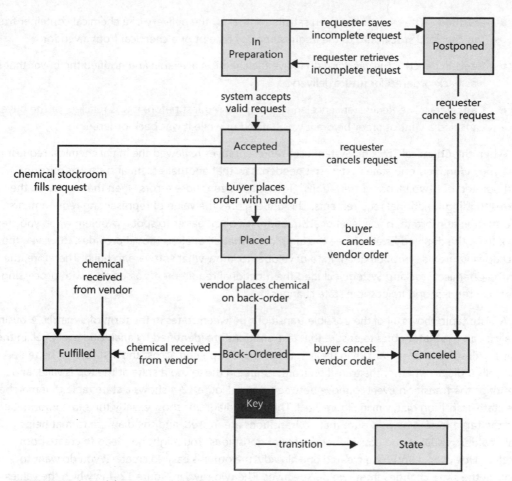

FIGURE 12-3 A partial state-transition diagram for a chemical request in the Chemical Tracking System.

This STD shows that an individual request can take on one of the following seven possible states:

- **In Preparation**   The Requester is creating a new request, having initiated that function from some other part of the system.

- **Postponed**   The Requester saved a partial request for future completion without either submitting the request to the system or canceling the request operation.

- **Accepted**   The Requester submitted a completed chemical request and the system accepted it for processing.

- **Placed**   The request must be satisfied by an outside vendor and a buyer has placed an order with the vendor.

- **Fulfilled** The request has been satisfied, either by the delivery of a chemical container from the chemical stockroom to the Requester or by receipt of a chemical from a vendor.

- **Back-ordered** The vendor didn't have the chemical available and notified the buyer that it was back-ordered for future delivery.

- **Canceled** The Requester canceled an accepted request before it was fulfilled, or the buyer canceled a vendor order before it was fulfilled or while it was back-ordered.

When the Chemical Tracking System user representatives reviewed the initial chemical request STD, they identified one state that wasn't needed, saw that another essential state was missing, and pointed out two incorrect transitions. No one had seen those errors when they reviewed the corresponding functional requirements. This underscores the value of representing requirements information at more than one level of abstraction. It's often easier to spot a problem when you step back from the detailed level and see the big picture that an analysis model provides. However, the STD doesn't provide enough detail for a developer to know what software to build. Therefore, the SRS for the Chemical Tracking System included the functional requirements associated with processing a chemical request and its possible state changes.

A state table shows all of the possible transitions between states in the form of a matrix. A business analyst can use state tables to ensure that all transitions are identified by analyzing every cell in the matrix. All states are written down the first column and repeated across the first row of the table. The cells indicate whether the transition from a state on the left to a state at the top is valid, and identifies the transition event to move between states. Figure 12-4 shows a state table that matches the state-transition diagram in Figure 12-3. These two diagrams show exactly the same information, but the table format helps ensure that no transitions are missed, and the diagram format helps stakeholders visualize the possible sequences of transitions. You might not need to create both models. However, if you have created one already, the other is easy to create, if you do want to analyze the state changes from two perspectives. The two rows in Figure 12-4 in which the values are all "no" are both termination states; when the chemical request is in either the Fulfilled or the Canceled state, it cannot transition out of it.

The state-transition diagram and state table provide a high-level viewpoint that spans multiple use cases or user stories, each of which might perform a transition from one state to another. The state models don't show the details of the processing that the system performs; they show only the possible state changes that result from that processing. They help developers understand the intended behavior of the system. The models facilitate early testing because testers can derive tests from the STD that cover all allowed transition paths. Both models are useful for ensuring that all the required states and transitions have been correctly and completely described in the functional requirements.

	In preparation	Postponed	Accepted	Placed	Back-Ordered	Fulfilled	Canceled
In Preparation	no	user saves incomplete request	system accepts valid request	no	no	no	no
Postponed	user retrieves incomplete request	no	no	no	no	no	no
Accepted	no	no	no	buyer places order with vendor	no	chemical stockroom fills request	requester cancels request
Placed	no	no	no	no	vendor places chemical on back-order	chemical received from vendor	buyer cancels vendor order
Back-Ordered	no	no	no	no	no	chemical received from vendor	buyer cancels vendor order
Fulfilled	no	no	no	no	no	no	no
Canceled	no	no	no	no	no	no	no

FIGURE 12-4 State table for a chemical request in the Chemical Tracking System.

Dialog map

The *dialog map* represents a user interface design at a high level of abstraction. It shows the dialog elements in the system and the navigation links among them, but it doesn't show the detailed screen designs. A user interface can be regarded as a series of state changes. Only one dialog element (such as a menu, workspace, dialog box, line prompt, or touch screen display) is available at any given time for user input. The user can navigate to certain other dialog elements based on the action he takes at the active input location. The number of possible navigation pathways can be large in a complex system, but the number is finite and the options are usually known. A dialog map is really just a user interface modeled in the form of a state-transition diagram (Wasserman 1985; Wiegers 1996). Larry Constantine and Lucy Lockwood (1999) describe a similar technique called a *navigation map*, which includes a richer set of notations for representing different types of interaction elements and context transitions. A *user interface flow* is similar to a dialog map but shows the navigation paths between user interface screens in a swimlane diagram format (Beatty and Chen 2012).

A dialog map allows you to explore hypothetical user interface concepts based on your understanding of the requirements. Users and developers can study a dialog map to reach a common vision of how the user might interact with the system to perform a task. Dialog maps are also useful for modeling the visual architecture of a website. Navigation links that you build into the website appear as transitions on the dialog map. Of course, the user has additional navigation options through the browser's Back and Forward buttons, as well as the URL input field, but the dialog map does not show those. Dialog maps are related to system storyboards, which also include a short description of each screen's purpose (Leffingwell and Widrig 2000).

Dialog maps capture the essence of the user–system interactions and task flow without bogging the team down in detailed screen layouts. Users can trace through a dialog map to find missing, incorrect, or unnecessary navigations, and hence missing, incorrect, or unnecessary requirements. The abstract, conceptual dialog map formulated during requirements analysis serves as a guide during detailed user interface design.

Just as in ordinary state-transition diagrams, the dialog map shows each dialog element as a state (rectangle) and each allowed navigation option as a transition (arrow). The condition that triggers user interface navigation is shown as a text label on the transition arrow. There are several types of trigger conditions:

- A user action, such as pressing a function key, clicking on a hyperlink, or making a gesture on a touch screen.

- A data value, such as an invalid user input value that triggers an error message display

- A system condition, such as detecting that a printer is out of paper

- Some combination of these, such as typing a menu option number and pressing the Enter key

Dialog maps look a bit like flowcharts, but they serve a different purpose. A flowchart explicitly shows the processing steps and decision points, but not the user interface displays. In contrast, the dialog map does *not* show the processing that takes place along the transition lines that connect one dialog element to another. The branching decisions (usually user choices) are hidden behind the display screens that are shown as rectangles on the dialog map, and the conditions that lead to displaying one screen or another appear in the labels on the transitions.

To simplify the dialog map, omit global functions such as pressing the F1 key to bring up a help display from each dialog element. The SRS section on user interfaces should specify that this functionality will be available, but showing lots of help-screen boxes on the dialog map clutters the model while adding little value. Similarly, when modeling a website, you needn't include standard navigation links that will appear on each page in the site. You can also omit the transitions that reverse the flow of a webpage navigation sequence because the web browser's Back button handles that navigation.

A dialog map is an excellent way to represent the interactions between an actor and the system that a use case describes. The dialog map can depict alternative flows as branches off the normal flow. I found that sketching dialog map fragments on a whiteboard was helpful during use case elicitation workshops in which a team explored the sequence of actor actions and system responses that would lead to task completion. For use cases and process flows that are already complete, compare them to dialog maps to ensure that all the functions needed to execute the steps can be accessed in the UI navigation.

Chapter 8 presented a use case for the Chemical Tracking System called "Request a Chemical." The normal flow for this use case involved requesting a chemical container from the chemical stockroom's inventory. An alternative flow was to request the chemical from a vendor. The user placing the request wanted the option to view the history of the available stockroom containers of that chemical before selecting one. Figure 12-5 shows a dialog map for this fairly complex use case. The entry point for this dialog map is the transition line that begins with a solid black circle, "ask to place a request." The user would enter this portion of the application's user interface from some other part of the UI along that line. Exit points for the dialog map to return to some other portion of the UI are the transition lines ending with a solid black circle inside another circle, "cancel entire request" and "OK; exit request function."

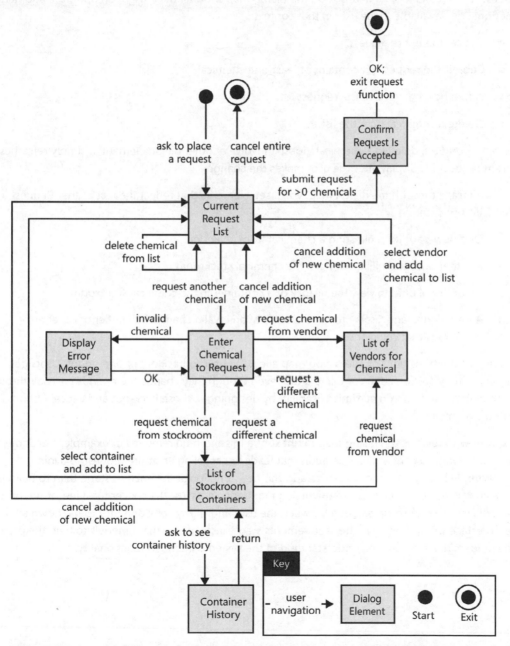

FIGURE 12-5 A partial dialog map for the "Request a Chemical" use case from the Chemical Tracking System.

This diagram might look complicated at first, but if you trace through it one line and one box at a time, it's not difficult to understand. The user initiates this use case by asking to place a request for a chemical from some menu in the Chemical Tracking System. In the dialog map, this action brings the user to the box called "Current Request List," along the arrow in the upper-left part of the dialog map. That box represents the main workspace for this use case, a list of the chemicals in the user's current request. The arrows leaving that box on the dialog map show all the navigation options—and hence functionality—available to the user in that context:

- Cancel the entire request.

- Submit the request if it contains at least one chemical.

- Add a new chemical to the request list.

- Delete a chemical from the list.

The last operation, deleting a chemical, doesn't involve another dialog element; it simply refreshes the current request list display after the user makes the change.

As you trace through this dialog map, you'll see elements that reflect the rest of the "Request a Chemical" use case:

- One flow path for requesting a chemical from a vendor

- Another path for fulfillment from the chemical stockroom

- An optional path to view the history of a container in the chemical stockroom

- An error message display to handle entry of an invalid chemical identifier or other error conditions that could arise

Some of the transitions on the dialog map allow the user to back out of operations. Users get annoyed if they are forced to complete a task even though they change their minds partway through it. The dialog map lets you maximize usability by designing in those back-out and cancel options at strategic points.

A user who reviews this dialog map might spot a missing requirement. For example, a cautious user might want to confirm the operation that leads to canceling an entire request to avoid inadvertently losing data. It costs less to add this new function at the analysis stage than to build it into a completed product. Because the dialog map represents just the conceptual view of the possible elements involved in the interaction between the user and the system, don't try to pin down all the user interface design details at the requirements stage. Instead, use these models to help the project stakeholders reach a common understanding of the system's intended functionality.

Decision tables and decision trees

A software system is often governed by complex logic, with various combinations of conditions leading to different system behaviors. For example, if the driver presses the accelerate button on a car's cruise control system and the car is currently cruising, the system increases the car's speed, but if the car isn't cruising, the input is ignored. Developers need functional requirements that describe what the system should do under all possible combinations of conditions. However, it's easy to overlook a condition, which results in a missing requirement. These gaps are hard to spot by reviewing a textual specification.

Decision tables and decision trees are two alternative techniques for representing what the system should do when complex logic and decisions come into play (Beatty and Chen 2012). A *decision table* lists the various values for all the factors that influence the behavior and indicates the expected system action in response to each combination of factors. The factors can be shown either as statements with possible conditions of true and false, as questions with possible answers of yes and no, or as questions with more than two possible values.

Figure 12-6 shows a decision table for the logic that governs whether the Chemical Tracking System should accept or reject each request for a new chemical. Four factors influence this decision:

- Whether the user who is creating the request is authorized to request chemicals

- Whether the chemical is available either in the chemical stockroom or from a vendor

- Whether the chemical is on the list of hazardous chemicals that require special training in safe handling

- Whether the user who is creating the request has been trained in handling this type of hazardous chemical

Requirement Number					
Condition	1	2	3	4	5
User is authorized	F	T	T	T	T
Chemical is available	—	F	T	T	T
Chemical is hazardous	—	—	F	T	T
Requester is trained	—	—	—	F	T
Action					
Accept request			X		X
Reject request	X	X		X	

FIGURE 12-6 Sample decision table for the Chemical Tracking System.

Each of these four factors has two possible conditions, true or false. In principle, this gives rise to 2^4, or 16, possible true/false combinations, for a potential of 16 distinct functional requirements. In practice, though, many of the combinations lead to the same system response. If the user isn't authorized to request chemicals, then the system won't accept the request, so the other conditions are irrelevant (shown as dashes in the cells in the decision table). The table shows that only five distinct functional requirements arise from the various combinations.

Figure 12-7 shows a decision tree that represents this same logic. The five boxes indicate the five possible outcomes of either accepting or rejecting the chemical request. Both decision tables and decision trees are useful ways to document requirements (or business rules) to avoid overlooking any combinations of conditions. Even a complex decision table or tree is easier to read than a mass of repetitious textual requirements.

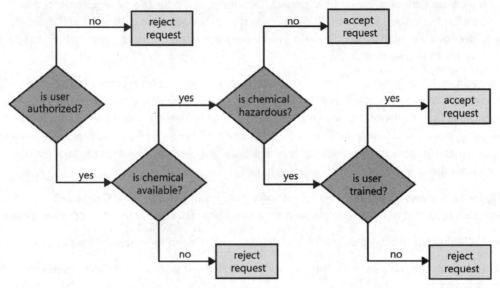

FIGURE 12-7 Sample decision tree for the Chemical Tracking System.

Event-response tables

Use cases and user stories aren't always helpful or sufficient for discovering the functionality that developers must implement (Wiegers 2006). This is particularly true for real-time systems. Consider a complex highway intersection with numerous traffic lights and pedestrian walk signals. There aren't many use cases for a system like this. A driver might want to proceed through the light or to turn left or right. A pedestrian wants to cross the road. Perhaps an emergency vehicle wants to be able to turn the traffic signals green in its direction so it can speed its way to people who need help. Law enforcement might have cameras at the intersection to photograph the license plates of red-light violators. This information alone isn't enough for developers to build the correct functionality.

Another way to approach user requirements is to identify the external events to which the system must respond. An *event* is some change or activity that takes place in the user's environment that stimulates a response from the software system (Wiley 2000). An *event-response table* (also called an *event table* or an *event list*) itemizes all such events and the behavior the system is expected to exhibit in reaction to each event. There are three classes of system events, as shown in Figure 12-8:

- **Business event** A business event is an action by a human user that stimulates a dialog with the software, as when the user initiates a use case. The event-response sequences correspond to the steps in a use case or swimlane diagram.

- **Signal event**   A signal event is registered when the system receives a control signal, data reading, or interrupt from an external hardware device or another software system, such as when a switch closes, a voltage changes, another application requests a service, or a user swipes his finger on a tablet's screen.

- **Temporal event**   A temporal event is time-triggered, as when the computer's clock reaches a specified time (say, to launch an automatic data export operation at midnight) or when a preset duration has passed since a previous event (as in a system that logs the temperature read by a sensor every 10 seconds).

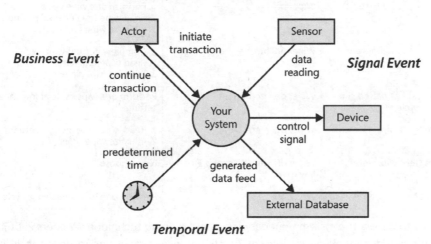

FIGURE 12-8 Systems respond to business, signal, and temporal events.

Event analysis works especially well for specifying real-time control systems. To identify events, consider all the states associated with the object you are analyzing, and identify any events that might transition the object into those states. Review context diagrams for any external entities that might initiate an action (trigger an event) or require an automatic response (need a temporal event triggered). Table 12-3 contains a sample event-response table that partially describes the behavior of an automobile's windshield wipers. Other than event 6, which is a temporal event, these are all signal events. Note that the expected response depends not only on the event but also on the state of the system at the time the event takes place. For instance, events 4 and 5 in Table 12-3 result in slightly different behaviors depending on whether the wipers were on at the time the user set the wiper control to the intermittent setting. A response could simply alter some internal system information or it could result in an externally visible result. Other information you might want to add to an event-response table includes:

- The event frequency (how many times the event takes place in a given time period, or a limit to how many times it can occur).

- Data elements that are needed to process the event.

- The state of the system after the event responses are executed (Gottesdiener 2005).

TABLE 12-3 Partial event-response table for an automobile windshield-wiper system

ID	Event	System state	System response
1	Set wiper control to low speed	Wiper off, on high speed, or on intermittent	Set wiper motor to low speed
2	Set wiper control to high speed	Wiper off, on low speed, or on intermittent	Set wiper motor to high speed
3	Set wiper control to off	Wiper on high speed, low speed, or intermittent	1. Complete current wipe cycle 2. Turn wiper motor off
4	Set wiper control to intermittent	Wiper off	1. Perform one wipe cycle 2. Read wipe time interval setting 3. Initialize wipe timer
5	Set wiper control to intermittent	Wiper on low speed or on high speed	1. Complete current wipe cycle 2. Read wipe time interval setting 3. Initialize wipe timer
6	Wipe time interval has passed since completing last cycle	Wiper on intermittent	Perform one wipe cycle at low speed setting
7	Change intermittent wiper interval	Wiper on intermittent	1. Read wipe time interval setting 2. Initialize wipe timer
8	Change intermittent wiper interval	Wiper off, on high speed, or on low speed	No response
9	Immediate wipe signal received	Wiper off	Perform one low-speed wipe cycle

Listing the events that cross the system boundary is a useful scoping technique (Wiegers 2006). An event-response table that defines every possible combination of event, state, and response, including exception conditions, can serve as part of the functional requirements for that portion of the system. You might model the event-response table in a decision table to ensure that all possible combinations of events and system states are analyzed. However, the BA must supply additional functional and nonfunctional requirements. How many cycles per minute does the wiper perform on the slow and fast wipe settings? Is the intermittent setting continuously variable, or does it have discrete settings? What are the minimum and maximum delay times between intermittent wipes? If you omit this sort of information, the developer has to track it down or make the decisions himself. Remember, the goal is to specify the requirements precisely enough that a developer knows what to build and a tester can determine if it was built correctly.

Notice that the events listed in Table 12-3 describe the essence of the event, not the specifics of the implementation. Table 12-3 shows nothing about how the windshield wiper controls look or how the user manipulates them. The designer could satisfy these requirements with anything from traditional stalk-mounted wiper controls to recognition of spoken commands: "wipers on," "wipers faster," "wipe once." Writing requirements at the essential level like this avoids imposing unnecessary design constraints. However, record any known design constraints to guide the designer's thinking.

A few words about UML diagrams

Many projects use object-oriented analysis, design, and development methods. *Objects* typically correspond to real-world items in the business or problem domain. They represent individual instances derived from a generic template called a *class*. Class descriptions encompass both attributes (data) and the operations that can be performed on the attributes. A *class diagram* is a graphical way to depict the classes identified during object-oriented analysis and the relationships among them (see Chapter 13).

Products developed using object-oriented methods don't demand unique requirements development approaches. This is because requirements development focuses on what the users need to do with the system and the functionality it must contain, not with how it will be constructed. Users don't care about objects or classes. However, if you know that you're going to build the system using object-oriented techniques, it can be helpful to begin identifying classes and their attributes and behaviors during requirements analysis. This facilitates the transition from analysis to design, because the designer maps the problem-domain objects to the system's objects and further details each class's attributes and operations.

The standard object-oriented modeling language is the Unified Modeling Language (Booch, Rumbaugh, and Jacobson 1999). The UML is primarily used for creating design models. At the level of abstraction that's appropriate for requirements analysis, several UML models can be useful (Fowler 2003; Podeswa 2010):

- Class diagrams, to show the object classes that pertain to the application domain; their attributes, behavior, and properties; and relations among classes. Class diagrams can also be used for data modeling, as illustrated in Chapter 13, but this limited application doesn't fully exploit the semantic capabilities of a class diagram.

- Use case diagrams, to show the relationships between actors external to the system and the use cases with which they interact (see Chapter 8).

- Activity diagrams, to show how the various flows in a use case interlace, or which roles perform certain actions (as in a swimlane diagram), or to model the flow of business processes. See Chapter 8 for a simple example.

- State (or state machine) diagrams, to represent the different states a system or data object can take on and the allowed transitions between the states.

Modeling on agile projects

All projects should exploit requirements models to analyze their requirements from a variety of perspectives, no matter what the project's development approach is. The choice of models used across different development approaches will likely be the same. The difference in how traditional and agile projects perform modeling is related to when the models are created and the level of detail in them.

For example, you might draft a level 0 DFD early in an agile project. Then, during an iteration, you could draw more detailed DFDs to cover the scope of that iteration only. Also, you might create models in a less persistent or less perfected format on an agile project than on a traditional project. You might sketch an analysis model on a whiteboard and photograph it, but not store it with formal requirements documentation or in a modeling tool. As user stories are implemented, models can be updated (perhaps using color to indicate completeness), which shows what is being implemented in an iteration and reveals additional user stories that are needed to complete the picture.

The key point in using analysis models on agile projects—or really, on any project—is to focus on creating only the models you need, only when you need them, and only to the level of detail you need to make sure project stakeholders adequately understand the requirements. User stories won't always be sufficient to capture the level of detail and precision necessary for an agile project (Leffingwell 2011). Do not rule out the use of any models just because you are working on an agile project.

A final reminder

Each of the modeling techniques described in this chapter has its strengths and its limitations. No one particular view will be sufficient to represent all aspects of the system. Also, they overlap in the views they provide, so you won't need to create every kind of diagram for your project. For instance, if you create an ERD and a data dictionary, you probably won't need to create a class diagram. Keep in mind that you draw analysis models to provide a level of understanding and communication that goes beyond what textual requirements or any other single view of the requirements can provide.

Next steps

- Practice using the modeling techniques described in this chapter by documenting the design of an existing system. For example, draw a dialog map for an automated teller machine or for a website that you use.

- On your current or next project, select a modeling technique that complements the textual requirements. Sketch the model on paper or a whiteboard once or twice to make sure you're on the right track, and then use a modeling tool that supports the notation you're using. Try to create at least one model you haven't used before.

- Try creating a visual model collaboratively with other stakeholders. Use whiteboards or sticky notes to encourage their participation.

- List the external events that could stimulate your system to behave in specific ways. Create an event-response table that shows the state the system is in when each event is received and how the system is to respond.

CHAPTER 13

Specifying data requirements

Long ago I led a software project on which the three developers sometimes inadvertently used different variable names, lengths, and validation criteria for the same data item. In fact, I used different lengths for the variable that held the user's name in two programs I wrote myself. Bad things can happen when you interconvert data of different lengths. You can overwrite other data, pick up stray pad characters at the end, have unterminated character strings, and even overwrite program code, eventually causing a crash. Bad things.

Our project suffered from the lack of a data dictionary—a shared repository that defines the meaning, composition, data type, length, format, and allowed values for data elements used in the application. As soon as the team began defining and managing our data in a more disciplined way, all of those problems disappeared.

Computer systems manipulate data in ways that provide value to customers. Although they were not shown explicitly in the three-level requirements model in Figure 1-1 in Chapter 1, "The essential software requirement," data requirements pervade the three levels. Anywhere there are functions, there is data. Whether the data represents pixels in a video game, packets in a cell phone call, your company's quarterly sales figures, your bank account activity, or anything else, software functionality is specified to create, modify, display, delete, process, and use data. The business analyst should begin collecting data definitions as they pop up during requirements elicitation.

A good place to start is with the input and output flows on the system's context diagram. These flows represent major data elements at a high level of abstraction, which the BA can refine into details as elicitation progresses. Nouns that users mention during requirements elicitation often indicate important data entities: chemical request, requester, chemical, status, usage report. This chapter describes ways to explore and represent the data that's important to your application's users, along with ways to specify any reports or dashboards your application needs to generate.

Modeling data relationships

Just as the data flow diagram described in Chapter 12, "A picture is worth 1024 words," illustrates the processes that take place in a system, a data model depicts the system's data relationships. A data model provides the high-level view of the system's data; the data dictionary provides the detailed view.

A commonly used data model is the *entity-relationship diagram* or ERD (Robertson and Robertson 1994). If your ERD represents logical groups of information from the problem domain and their interconnections, you're using the ERD as a requirements analysis tool. An analysis ERD helps you understand and communicate the data components of the business or the system, without implying that the product will necessarily even include a database. When you create an ERD during design, you're defining the logical or physical (implementation) structure of the system's database. That implementation view extends or completes the understanding of the system begun during analysis and optimizes its realization in, say, a relational database environment.

Entities could represent physical items (including people) or aggregations of data that are important to the business you're analyzing or to the system you intend to build. Entities are named as singular nouns and are shown in rectangles in an ERD. Figure 13-1 illustrates a portion of the entity-relationship diagram for the Chemical Tracking System, using the Peter Chen notation, one of several common ERD modeling notations. Notice that the entities named Chemical Request, Vendor Catalog, and Chemical Stockroom Inventory appeared as data stores in the data flow diagram in Figure 12-1 in Chapter 12. Other entities represent actors who interact with the system (Requester), physical items that are part of the business operations (Chemical Container), and blocks of data that weren't shown in the level 0 DFD but that would appear on a lower-level DFD (Container History, Chemical). During physical database design of a relational database, entities normally become tables.

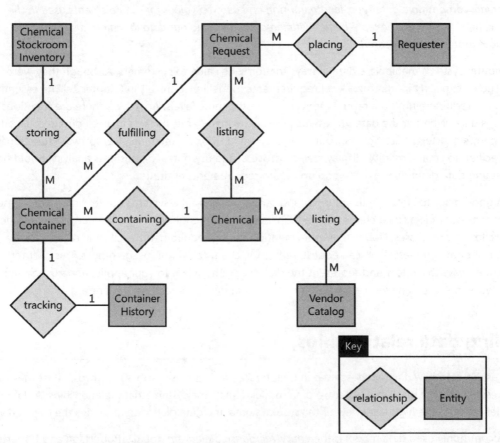

FIGURE 13-1 Partial entity-relationship diagram for the Chemical Tracking System.

Each entity is described by one or more *attributes*; individual instances of an entity will have different attribute values. For example, the attributes for each chemical include a unique chemical identifier, its chemical name, and a graphical representation of its chemical structure. The data dictionary contains the precise definitions of those attributes, which helps ensure that entities in the ERD and their corresponding data stores in the DFD are defined identically.

The diamonds in the ERD represent *relationships*, which identify the logical linkages between pairs of entities. Relationships are named in a way that describes the nature of the connection. For example, the relationship between the Chemical Request and the Requester is a *placing* relationship. You can read the relationship as either "a Chemical Request is placed by a Requester" (left-to-right, passive voice) or as "a Requester places a Chemical Request" (right-to-left, active voice). Some conventions would have you label the relationship diamond "is placed by," which makes sense only if you read the diagram from left to right. If you happened to redraw the diagram such that relative positions of Requester and Chemical Request were reversed, then the "is placed by" relationship name would be incorrect when read left to right: "a Requester is placed by a Chemical Request" is wrong. It's better to name the relationship "placing" and then just restate "placing" in whichever way is grammatically logical—"places" or "is placed by"—when you read the statement.

When you ask customers to review an ERD, ask them to check whether the relationships shown are all correct and appropriate. Also ask them to identify any missing entities or any possible relationships between entities that the model doesn't show.

The *cardinality*, or multiplicity, of each relationship is shown with a number or letter on the lines that connect entities and relationships. Different ERD notations use different conventions to represent cardinality; the example in Figure 13-1 illustrates one common approach. Because each Requester can place multiple requests, there's a one-to-many relationship between Requester and Chemical Request. This cardinality is shown with a *1* on the line connecting Requester and the *placing* relationship and an *M* (for many) on the line connecting Chemical Request and the *placing* relationship. Other possible cardinalities are one-to-one (every Chemical Container is tracked by a single Container History) and many-to-many (every Vendor Catalog lists many Chemicals, and some Chemicals are listed in multiple Vendor Catalogs). If you know that a more precise cardinality exists than simply *many* (one person has exactly two biological parents), you can show the specific number or range of numbers instead of the generic *M*.

Alternative ERD notations use different symbols on the lines connecting entities and relationships to indicate cardinality. In the James Martin notation illustrated in Figure 13-2, the entities still appear as rectangles, but the relationship between them is labeled on the line that connects the entities. The vertical line next to Chemical Stockroom Inventory indicates a cardinality of 1, and the crow's foot symbol next to Chemical Container indicates a cardinality of many. The circle next to the crow's foot means that the Chemical Stockroom Inventory stores zero or more Chemical Containers.

FIGURE 13-2 One alternative notation for an entity-relationship diagram.

Other data modeling conventions are available besides the various ERD notations. Teams that are applying object-oriented development methods will draw UML class diagrams, which show the data attributes for individual classes (which correspond to entities in the ERD), the logical links between classes, and the cardinalities of those links. Figure 13-3 illustrates a fragment of a class diagram for the Chemical Tracking System. It shows the one-to-many relationship between a Requester and a Chemical Request, each of which is a "class" shown in a rectangle. The "1..* notation means "one or more;" several other cardinality (or multiplicity) notations also can be used in class diagrams (Ambler 2005). Note that the class diagram also lists the attributes associated with each class in the middle section of the rectangle. Figure 13-3 shows just a simplified version of the class diagram notation. When class diagrams are used for object-oriented analysis or design, the bottommost section of a class rectangle (empty in this example) normally shows the operations, or behaviors, that an object of the class can perform. For data modeling, though, that third section of the class rectangle is left empty.

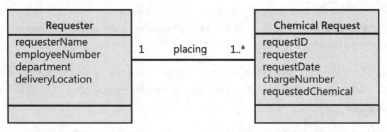

FIGURE 13-3 Portion of a UML class diagram for the Chemical Tracking System.

It's not important which notation you select for drawing a data model. What *is* important is that everyone involved with the project (and ideally, everyone in the organization) who creates such models follows the same notation conventions, and that everyone who has to use or review the models knows how to interpret them.

Of course, the system must also contain the functionality that does something useful with the data. The relationships between entities often reveal such functionality. Figure 13-1 showed that there is a "tracking" relationship between the entities Chemical Container and Container History. Therefore, you'll need some functionality—perhaps captured in the form of a use case, a user story, or a process flow—to give the user access to the history for a given chemical container. As you analyze your project requirements with the help of the data models, you might even discover unneeded data that came up in the discussion but that isn't used anywhere.

The data dictionary

A *data dictionary* is a collection of detailed information about the data entities used in an application. Collecting the information about composition, data types, allowed values, and the like into a shared resource identifies the data validation criteria, helps developers write programs correctly, and minimizes integration problems. The data dictionary complements the project glossary, which defines application domain or business terms, abbreviations, and acronyms. We recommend keeping the data dictionary and the glossary separate.

During requirements analysis, the information in the data dictionary represents data elements and structures of the application domain (Beatty and Chen 2012). This information feeds into design in the form of database schemas, tables, and attributes, which ultimately lead to variable names in programs. The time you invest in creating a data dictionary will be more than repaid by avoiding the mistakes that can result when project participants have different understandings of the data. If you keep the data dictionary current, it will remain a valuable tool throughout the system's operational life and beyond. If you don't, it might falsely suggest out-of-date information, and team members will no longer trust it. Maintaining a data dictionary is a serious investment in quality. Data definitions often are reusable across applications, particularly within a product line. Using consistent data definitions across the enterprise reduces integration and interface errors. When possible, refer to existing standard data definitions from a repository of enterprise knowledge, using a smaller, project-specific set to close the gaps.

 As opposed to sprinkling data definitions throughout the project documentation, a separate data dictionary makes it easy to find the information you need. It also helps avoid redundancies and inconsistencies. I once reviewed some use case specifications that identified the data elements that made up certain data structures. Unfortunately, these compositions weren't the same in all the places where they appeared. Such inconsistency forces a developer or tester to track down which—if any—of the definitions is correct. Maintaining the integrity of the replicated data structures as they evolve is also difficult. Compiling or consolidating such information so that there is only one instance of each definition that is readily accessible by all stakeholders solves these problems.

Figure 13-4 illustrates a portion of the data dictionary for the Chemical Tracking System. The notations used are described in the following paragraphs. Organize the entries in the data dictionary alphabetically to make it easy for readers to find what they need.

Data Element	Description	Composition or Data Type	Length	Values
Chemical Request	request for a new chemical from either the Chemical Stockroom or a vendor	Request ID + Requester + Request Date + Charge Number + 1:10{Requested Chemical}		
Delivery Location	the place to which requested chemicals are to be delivered	Building + Lab Number + Lab Partition		
Number of Containers	number of containers of a given chemical and size being requested	Positive integer	3	
Quantity	amount of chemical in the requested container	numeric	6	
Quantity Units	units associated with the quantity of chemical requested	alphabetic characters	10	grams, kilograms, milligrams, each
Request ID	unique identifier for a request	integer	8	system-generated sequential integer, beginning with 1

Data Element	Description	Composition or Data Type	Length	Values
Requested Chemical	description of the chemical being requested	Chemical ID + Number of Containers + Grade + <u>Quantity</u> + Quantity Units + (Vendor)		
Requester	information about the individual who placed a chemical request	Requester Name + Employee Number + Department + Delivery Location		
Requester Name	name of the employee who submitted the request	alphabetic characters	40	can contain blanks, hyphens, periods, apostrophes

FIGURE 13-4 Partial data dictionary for the Chemical Tracking System.

Entries in the data dictionary can represent the following types of data elements.

Primitive A primitive data element is one for which no further decomposition is possible or necessary. Primitives defined in Figure 13-4 are Number of Containers, Quantity, Quantity Units, Request ID, and Requester Name. You can use other columns in the data dictionary to describe each primitive's data type, length, numerical range, list of allowed values (as with Quantity Units), and other pertinent attributes.

Structure A data structure (or a record) is composed of multiple data elements. Data structures shown in Figure 13-4 are Chemical Request, Delivery Location, Requested Chemical, and Requester. The "Composition or Data Type" column in the data dictionary is a place to list the elements that make up the structure, separating the elements with plus (+) signs. Structures also can incorporate other structures: the Requester structure includes the Delivery Location structure. Data elements that appear in a structure must also have definitions in the data dictionary.

If an element in a data structure is optional (a value doesn't have to be supplied by the user or the system), enclose it in parentheses. In the Requested Chemical structure, the Vendor data element is optional because the person submitting the request might not know or care which vendor supplies the chemical.

Hyperlinks are useful in such a data dictionary layout (although storing the information in a tool that permits defining such links is even better). As an illustration, the data item called Quantity in the Requested Chemical data structure in Figure 13-4 is shown as a hyperlink. The reader could click on that link and jump to the definition of Quantity elsewhere in the data dictionary. Navigation links are very helpful in an extensive data dictionary that could span many pages, or even multiple documents if a project's data dictionary incorporates some definitions from an enterprise-wide data dictionary. It's a good idea to include hyperlinks for all items found in the "Composition or Data Type" column that are defined in the data dictionary.

Repeating group   If multiple instances of a particular data element can appear in a structure, enclose that item in curly braces. Show the allowed number of possible repeats in the form minimum:maximum in front of the opening curly brace. As an example, Requested Chemical in the Chemical Request structure is a repeating group that appears as *1:10{Requested Chemical}*. This shows that a chemical request must contain at least one chemical but may not contain more than 10 chemicals. If the maximum number of instances in a repeating field is unlimited, use "n" to indicate this. For example, "3:n{something}" means that the data structure being defined must contain at least three instances of the "something" and there is no upper limit on the number of instances of that "something."

Precisely defining data elements is harder than it might appear. Consider a data type as simple as *alphabetic characters*, as is indicated for the Requester Name entry in Figure 13-4. Is a name case-sensitive, such that "Karl" is different from "karl"? Should the system convert text to all uppercase or all lowercase, retain the case in a looked-up or user-entered value, or reject an input that doesn't match the expected case? Can any characters other than the 26 letters in the English alphabet be used, such as blanks, hyphens, periods, or apostrophes, all of which might appear in names? Is only the English alphabet permitted, or can alphabets with diacritical marks—tilde (~), umlaut (¨), accent (´), grave (`), cedilla (‚)—be used? Such precise definitions are essential for the developer to know exactly how to validate entered data. The formats to be used for displaying data elements introduce yet another level of variability. There are many ways to show timestamps and dates, for example, with different conventions used in different countries. Stephen Withall (2007) describes many considerations to keep in mind when specifying various data types.

Data analysis

When performing data analysis, you can map various information representations against one another to find gaps, errors, and inconsistencies. The entities in your entity-relationship diagram are likely defined in the data dictionary. The data flows and stores in your DFD are probably found somewhere in your ERD, as well as in the data dictionary. The display fields found in a report specification also should appear in the data dictionary. During data analysis, you can compare these complementary views to identify errors and further refine your data requirements.

A CRUD matrix is a rigorous data analysis technique for detecting missing requirements. *CRUD* stands for *Create, Read, Update,* and *Delete*. A CRUD matrix correlates system actions with data entities to show where and how each significant data entity is created, read, updated, and deleted. (Some people add an *L* to the matrix to indicate that the entity appears as a *List* selection, *M* to indicate moving data from one location to another, and perhaps a second *C* to indicate copying data. We'll stick with CRUD here for simplicity.) Depending on the requirements approaches you are using, you can examine various types of correlations, including the following:

- Data entities and system events (Ferdinandi 2002; Robertson and Robertson 2013)

- Data entities and user tasks or use cases (Lauesen 2002)

- Object classes and use cases (Armour and Miller 2001)

Figure 13-5 illustrates an entity/use case CRUD matrix for a portion of the Chemical Tracking System. Each cell indicates how the use case in the leftmost column uses each data entity shown in the other columns. The use case can create, read, update, or delete the entity. After creating a CRUD matrix, see whether any of these four letters do not appear in any of the cells in a column. For instance, if an entity is updated but never created, where does it come from?

Entity Use Case	Order	Chemical	Requester	Vendor Catalog
Place Order	C	R	R	R
Change Order	U, D		R	R
Manage Chemical Inventory		C, U, D		
Report on Orders	R	R	R	
Edit Requesters			C, U	

FIGURE 13-5 Sample CRUD matrix for the Chemical Tracking System.

Notice that none of the cells under the column labeled Requester (the person who places an order for a chemical) contains a *D*. That is, none of the use cases in Figure 13-5 can delete a Requester from the list of people who have ordered chemicals. There are three possible interpretations:

1. Deleting a Requester is not an expected function of the Chemical Tracking System.

2. We are missing a use case that deletes a Requester.

3. The "Edit Requesters" use case (or some other use case) is incomplete. It's supposed to permit the user to delete a Requester, but that functionality is missing from the use case at present.

We don't know which interpretation is correct, but the CRUD analysis is a powerful way to detect missing requirements.

Specifying reports

Many applications generate reports from one or more databases, files, or other information sources. Reports can consist of traditional tabular presentations of rows and columns of data, charts and graphs of all types, or any combination. Exploring the content and format of the reports needed is an important aspect of requirements development. Report specification straddles requirements (what information goes into the report and how it is organized) and design (what the report should look like). This section suggests specific aspects of reports to ask about and information to record. A template for specifying reports also is included.

Eliciting reporting requirements

If you're a BA working with customers on defining reporting requirements for an information system, consider asking questions like the following:

- What reports do you currently use? (Some reports from an existing system, or manually generated reports from the business, will need to be replicated in the new system.)

- Which existing reports need to be modified? (A new or revised information system project provides an opportunity to update reports that don't fully meet current needs.)

- Which reports are currently generated but are not used? (Perhaps you don't need to build those into the new system.)

- Can you describe any departmental, organizational, or government standards to which reports must conform, such as to provide a consistent look and feel or to comply with a regulation? (Obtain copies of those standards and examples of current reports that meet them.)

Withall (2007) describes a pattern and template for specifying report requirements. Joy Beatty and Anthony Chen (2012) also offer extensive guidance for specifying reports. Following are some questions to explore for each customer-requested report. The first set of questions deals with the context for the report and its usage:

- What is the name of the report?

- What is the purpose or business intent of the report? How do the recipients of the report use the information? What decisions will be made from the report, and by whom?

- Is the report generated manually? If so, how frequently and by which user classes?

- Is the report generated automatically? If so, how frequently and what are the triggering conditions or events?

- What are the typical and maximum sizes of the report?

- Is there a need for a dashboard that would display several reports and/or graphs? If so, must the user be able to drill down or roll up any of the dashboard elements?

- What is the disposition of the report after it is generated? Is it displayed on the screen, sent to a recipient, exported to a spreadsheet, or printed automatically? Is it stored or archived somewhere for future retrieval?

- Are there security, privacy, or management restrictions that limit the access of the report to specific individuals or user classes, or which restrict the data that can be included in the report depending on who is generating it? Identify any relevant business rules concerning security.

The following questions will elicit information about the report itself:

- What are the sources of the data and the selection criteria for pulling data from the repository?

- What parameters are selectable by the user?

- What calculations or other data transformations are required?

- What are the criteria for sorting, page breaks, and totals?

- How should the system respond if no data is returned in response to a query when attempting to generate this report?

- Should the underlying data of the report be made available to the user for ad hoc reporting?

- Can this report be used as a template for a set of similar reports?

Report specification considerations

The following suggestions might be useful as the BA explores reporting requirements.

Consider other variations   When a user requests a specific report, the BA could suggest variations on that theme to see if altering or augmenting the report would add business value. One variation is simply sequencing the data differently, such as providing order-by capability on data elements beyond those the user initially requested. Consider providing the user with tools to specify the column sequence. Another type of variation is to summarize or drill down. A summarized report aggregates detailed results into a more concise, higher-level view. "Drill down" means to produce a report that displays the supporting details that fed into the summary data.

Find the data   Ensure that the data necessary to populate the report is available to the system. Users think in terms of generating the outputs they want, which implies certain inputs and sources that will make the necessary data available. This analysis might reveal previously unknown requirements to access or generate the needed data. Identify any business rules that will be applied to compute the output data.

Anticipate growth   Users might request particular reports based on their initial conceptions of how much data or how many parameters might be involved. As systems grow over time, an initial report layout that worked well with small quantities of data might prove intractable. For instance, a columnar layout for a certain number of company divisions would fit nicely on one page. But doubling the number of company divisions might lead to awkward page breaks or the need to scroll a displayed report horizontally. You might need to change the layout from portrait to landscape mode or to transpose the information shown from columnar layout to rows.

Look for similarities   Multiple users—or even the same user—might request similar, but not identical, reports. Look for opportunities to merge these variations into a single report that provides flexibility to meet diverse needs without requiring redundant development and maintenance effort. Sometimes the variations can be handled with parameters to provide the necessary user flexibility.

Distinguish static and dynamic reports   Static reports print out or display data as of a point in time. Dynamic reports provide an interactive, real-time view of data. As underlying data changes, the system updates the report display automatically. My accounting software has this feature. If I'm looking at an expense report and then enter a new check I recently wrote, the displayed expense report updates immediately. Indicate which type of report you are requesting and tailor the requirements accordingly.

Prototype reports   It's often valuable to create a mock-up of the report that illustrates a possible approach to stimulate user feedback, or to use a similar existing report to illustrate the desired layout. Generating such a prototype while discussing requirements can lead the elicitation participants to impose design constraints, which might or might not be desirable. Other times, the developer will create a sample report layout during design and solicit customer feedback. Use plausible data in the mock-up to make the prototype experience realistic for the users who evaluate it.

A report specification template

Figure 13-6 suggests a template for specifying reports. Some of these report elements will be determined during requirements elicitation; others will be established during design. The requirements might specify the report contents, whereas the design process establishes the precise layout and formatting. Existing reporting standards might address some of the items in the template.

Not all of these elements and questions will pertain to every report. Also, there is considerable variation in where elements might be placed. The report title could appear just on the top of the first page or as a header on every page. Use the information in Figure 13-6 as a guide to help the BA, customers, developers, and testers understand the requirements and design constraints for each report.

Report Element	Element Description
Report ID	Number, code, or label used to identify or classify the report
Report Title	■ Name of the report ■ Positioning of the title on the page ■ Include query parameters used to generate the report (such as date range)?
Report Purpose	Brief description of the project, background, context, or business need that led to this report
Decisions Made from Report	The business decisions that are made using information in the report
Priority	The relative priority of implementing this reporting capability
Report Users	User classes who will generate the report or use it to make decisions
Data Sources	The applications, files, databases, or data warehouses from which data will be extracted
Frequency and Disposition	■ Is the report static or dynamic? ■ How frequently is the report generated: weekly, monthly, on demand? ■ How much data is accessed, or how many transactions are included, when the report is generated? ■ What conditions or events trigger generation of the report? ■ Will the report be generated automatically? Is manual intervention required? ■ Who will receive the report? How is it made available to them (displayed in an application, sent in email, printed, viewed on a mobile device)?

Report Element	Element Description
Latency	■ How quickly must the report be delivered to users when requested? ■ How current must the data be when the report is run?
Visual Layout	■ Landscape or portrait ■ Paper size (or type of printer) to be used for hard-copy reports ■ If the report includes graphs, define the type(s) of each graph, its appearance, and parameters: titles, axis scaling and labels, data sources, and so on
Header and Footer	The following items are among those that could be positioned somewhere in the report header or footer. For each element included, specify the location on the page and its appearance, including font face, point size, text highlighting, color, case, and text justification. When a title or other content exceeds its allocated space, should it be truncated, word-wrapped to the next line, or what? ■ Report title ■ Page numbering and format (such as "Page x" or "Page x of y") ■ Report notes (such as "The report excludes employees who worked for the company for less than one month.") ■ Report run timestamp ■ Name of the person who generated the report ■ Data source(s), particularly in a data warehousing application that consolidates data from multiple sources ■ Report begin and end dates ■ Organization identification (company name, department, logo, other graphics) ■ Confidentiality statement or copyright notice
Report Body	■ Record selection criteria (logic for what data to select and what to exclude) ■ Fields to include ■ User-specified text or parameters to customize field labels ■ Column and row heading names and formats: text, font, size, color, highlighting, case, justification ■ Column and row layout of data fields, or graph positioning and parameters for charts or graphs ■ Display format for each field: font, size, color, highlighting, case, justification, alignment, numeric rounding, digits and formatting, special characters ($, %, commas, decimals, leading or trailing pad characters) ■ How numeric and text field overflows should be handled ■ Calculations or other transformations that are performed to generate the data displayed ■ Sort criteria for each field ■ Filter criteria or parameters used to restrict the report query prior to running the report ■ Grouping and subtotals, including formatting of totals or subtotal breakout rows ■ Paging criteria
End-of-Report Indicator	Appearance and position of any indicator that appears at the end of the report
Interactivity	■ If the report is dynamic or is generated interactively, what options should the user have to modify the contents or appearance of the initially generated report (expand and collapse views, link to other reports, drill down to data sources)? ■ What is the expected persistence of report settings between usage sessions?
Security Access Restrictions	Any limitations regarding which individuals, groups, or organizations are permitted to generate or view the report or which data they are permitted to select for inclusion

FIGURE 13-6 A report specification template.

Dashboard reporting

A *dashboard* is a screen display or printed report that uses multiple textual and/or graphical representations of data to provide a consolidated, multidimensional view of what is going on in an organization or a process. Companies often use dashboards to pull together information about sales, expenses, key performance indicators (KPIs), and the like. Stock trading applications display a bewildering (to the novice) array of charts and data that the skilled eye can scan and process at a glance. Certain displays in a dashboard might be dynamically updated in real time as input data changes. Figure 13-7 shows a hypothetical reporting dashboard for a charitable foundation.

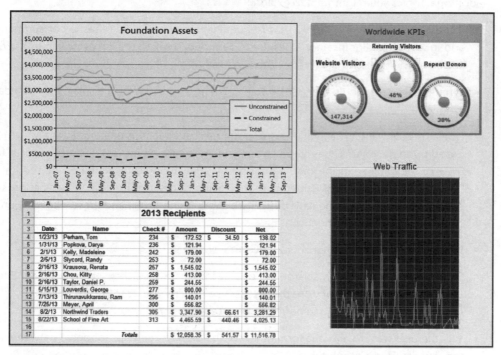

FIGURE 13-7 Hypothetical reporting dashboard for a charitable foundation.

Specifying the requirements for a dashboard involves the following sequence of elicitation and analysis activities. Many of these steps are also useful when specifying individual reports, as described earlier in the chapter.

- Determine what information the dashboard users need for making specific decisions or choices. Understanding how the presented data will be used helps you choose the most appropriate display techniques.

- Identify the sources of all the data to be presented so you can ensure that the application has access to those feeds and you know whether they are static or dynamic.

- Choose the most appropriate type of display for each set of related data. Should it appear as a simple table of data, a modifiable spreadsheet containing formulas, blocks of text, bar chart, pie chart, line chart, video display, or one of many other ways to present information?

- Determine the optimal layout and relative sizing of the various displays in the dashboard, based on how the user will absorb and apply the information.

- Specify the details of each display in the dashboard. That is, treat each of them as a separate mini-report. The questions listed in the "Eliciting reporting requirements" section earlier in this chapter and the template in Figure 13-6 will be helpful for this discussion. Following are some additional topics you might want to explore:

  - If the displayed data is dynamic, how frequently must the data be refreshed or augmented, and in what way? For instance, does the current data scroll to the left as new information is added to the right end of a fixed-width window?

  - What parameters should the user be able to change to customize a display, such as a date range?

  - Does the user want any conditional formatting to have sections of a display change based upon the data? This is helpful when you are creating progress or status reports: use green if the data meets the criteria for "good," yellow to indicate "caution," and red for "Whoa, this is messed up!" Remember, when using colors in a display, also use patterns to accommodate viewers who have difficulty distinguishing colors and those who print and distribute the display in monochrome.

  - Which displays will need horizontal or vertical scrollbars?

  - Should the user be able to enlarge any display in the dashboard to see more detail? Should she be able to minimize or close displays to free up screen space? In what ways do the user's customizations need to persist across usage sessions?

  - Will the user want to alter the form of any of the displays, perhaps to toggle between a tabular view and a graphical view?

  - Will the user want to drill down in any of the displays to see a more detailed report or the underlying data?

Prototyping a dashboard is an excellent way to work with stakeholders to ensure that the layout and presentation styles used will meet their needs. You can sketch out possible display components on sticky notes and have the stakeholders move them around until they find a layout they like. Iteration is a key both to refining the requirements and to exploring design alternatives.

As usual with requirements specification, the amount of detail to provide when specifying reports or dashboards depends on who makes decisions about their appearance and when those decisions are made. The more of these details you're willing to delegate to the designer, the less information you need to supply in requirements. And, as always, close collaboration among the BA, user representatives, and developers will help ensure that everyone is happy with the outcome.

Next steps

- Take a moderately complex data object from your application and define it and its components using the data dictionary notation presented in this chapter.

- Create an entity-relationship diagram for a portion of your application's data objects. If you don't have a data modeling tool available, a tool such as Microsoft Visio will get you started.

- For practice, specify one of your application's existing reports according to the specification template shown in Figure 13-6. Adjust the template as necessary to suit the nature of the reports that you create for your applications.

CHAPTER 14

Beyond functionality

"Hi, Sam, this is Clarice. I'm presenting a class in the new training room today, but the heating system is terribly loud. I'm practically shouting over the fan and I'm getting hoarse. You're the maintenance supervisor. Why is this system so loud? Is it broken?"

"It's working normally," Sam replied. "The heating system in that room meets the requirements the engineers gave me. It circulates the right amount of air per minute, it controls the temperature to within half a degree from 60 to 85 degrees, and it has all the requested profile programming capabilities. Nobody said anything about noise, so I bought the cheapest system that satisfied the requirements."

Clarice said, "The temperature control is fine. But this is a training room! The students can hardly hear me. We're going to have to install a PA system or get a quieter heating system. What do you suggest?"

Sam wasn't much help. "Clarice, the system meets all the requirements I was given," he repeated. "If I'd known that noise levels were so important, I could have bought a different unit, but now it would be really expensive to replace it. Maybe you can use some throat lozenges so you don't lose your voice."

There's more to software success than just delivering the right functionality. Users also have expectations, often unstated, about *how well* the product will work. Such expectations include how easy it is to use, how quickly it executes, how rarely it fails, how it handles unexpected conditions—and perhaps, how loud it is. Such characteristics, collectively known as *quality attributes, quality factors, quality requirements, quality of service requirements*, or the "*–ilities*," constitute a major portion of the system's nonfunctional requirements. In fact, to many people, quality attributes are synonymous with nonfunctional requirements, but that's an oversimplification. Two other classes of nonfunctional requirements are constraints (discussed at the end of this chapter) and external interface requirements (discussed in Chapter 10, "Documenting the requirements"). See the sidebar "If they're nonfunctional, then what are they?" in Chapter 1, "The essential software requirement," for more about the term "nonfunctional requirements."

People sometimes get hung up on debating whether a particular need is a functional or a nonfunctional requirement. The categorization matters less than making sure you identify the requirement. This chapter will help you detect and specify nonfunctional requirements you might not have found otherwise.

Quality attributes can distinguish a product that merely does what it's supposed to from one that delights its users. Excellent products reflect an optimum balance of competing quality characteristics.

If you don't explore the customers' quality expectations during elicitation, you're just lucky if the product satisfies them. Disappointed users and frustrated developers are the more typical outcome.

Quality attributes serve as the origin of many functional requirements. They also drive significant architectural and design decisions. It's far more costly to re-architect a completed system to achieve essential quality goals than to design for them at the outset. Consider the many security updates that vendors of operating systems and commonly used applications issue periodically. Some additional work on security at development time might avoid a lot of cost and user inconvenience.

> ### You can't make me
>
> Quality attributes can make or break the success of your product. One large company spent millions of dollars to replace a green-screen call center application with a fancy Windows-based version. After all that investment, the call center representatives refused to adopt the new system because it was too hard to navigate. These power users lost all of the keyboard shortcuts that helped them use the old system efficiently. Now they had to use a mouse to get around in the app, which was slower for them. The corporate leaders first tried the hard-line approach: "We'll just mandate that they have to use the new app," they said. But the call center staff still resisted. What are you going to do? These people are taking customer orders, so the company isn't going to literally turn off the old system if they won't use the new one and risk losing all those orders. Users hate to have their productivity impaired by a "new and improved" system. The development team had to redesign the user interface and add the old keyboard shortcuts before the users would accept the new software, delaying the release by months.

Software quality attributes

Several dozen product characteristics can be called quality attributes, although most project teams need to carefully consider only a handful of them. If developers know which of these characteristics are most crucial to success, they can select appropriate design and construction approaches to achieve the quality goals. Quality attributes have been classified according to a wide variety of schemes (DeGrace and Stahl 1993; IEEE 1998; ISO/IEC 2007; Miller 2009; ISO/IEC 2011). Some authors have constructed extensive hierarchies that group related attributes into several major categories.

One way to classify quality attributes distinguishes those characteristics that are discernible through execution of the software (external quality) from those that are not (internal quality) (Bass, Clements, and Kazman 1998). External quality factors are primarily important to users, whereas internal qualities are more significant to development and maintenance staff. Internal quality attributes indirectly contribute to customer satisfaction by making the product easier to enhance, correct, test, and migrate to new platforms.

Table 14-1 briefly describes several internal and external aspects of quality that every project should consider. Certain attributes are of particular importance on certain types of projects:

- Embedded systems: performance, efficiency, reliability, robustness, safety, security, usability (see Chapter 26, "Embedded and other real-time systems projects")

- Internet and corporate applications: availability, integrity, interoperability, performance, scalability, security, usability

- Desktop and mobile systems: performance, security, usability

In addition, different parts of a system might need to emphasize different quality attributes. Performance could be critical for certain components, with usability being paramount for others. Your environment might have other unique quality attributes that aren't covered here. For example, gaming companies might want to capture emotional requirements for their software (Callele, Neufeld, and Schneider 2008).

Section 6 of the SRS template described in Chapter 10 is devoted to quality attributes. If some quality requirements are specific to certain features, components, functional requirements, or user stories, associate those with the appropriate item in the requirements repository.

TABLE 14-1 Some software quality attributes

External quality	Brief description
Availability	The extent to which the system's services are available when and where they are needed
Installability	How easy it is to correctly install, uninstall, and reinstall the application
Integrity	The extent to which the system protects against data inaccuracy and loss
Interoperability	How easily the system can interconnect and exchange data with other systems or components
Performance	How quickly and predictably the system responds to user inputs or other events
Reliability	How long the system runs before experiencing a failure
Robustness	How well the system responds to unexpected operating conditions
Safety	How well the system protects against injury or damage
Security	How well the system protects against unauthorized access to the application and its data
Usability	How easy it is for people to learn, remember, and use the system

Internal quality	Brief description
Efficiency	How efficiently the system uses computer resources
Modifiability	How easy it is to maintain, change, enhance, and restructure the system
Portability	How easily the system can be made to work in other operating environments
Reusability	To what extent components can be used in other systems
Scalability	How easily the system can grow to handle more users, transactions, servers, or other extensions
Verifiability	How readily developers and testers can confirm that the software was implemented correctly

Exploring quality attributes

In an ideal universe, every system would exhibit the maximum possible value for all its attributes. The system would be available at all times, would never fail, would supply instantaneous results that are always correct, would block all attempts at unauthorized access, and would never confuse a user. In reality, there are trade-offs and conflicts between certain attributes that make it impossible to simultaneously maximize all of them. Because perfection is unattainable, you have to determine which attributes from Table 14-1 are most important to your project's success. Then you can craft specific quality objectives in terms of these essential attributes so designers can make appropriate choices.

Different projects will demand different sets of quality attributes for success. Jim Brosseau (2010) recommends the following practical approach for identifying and specifying the most important attributes for your project. He provides a spreadsheet to assist with the analysis at *www.clarrus.com/resources/articles/software-quality-attributes*.

Step 1: Start with a broad taxonomy

Begin with a rich set of quality attributes to consider, such as those listed in Table 14-1. This broad starting point reduces the likelihood of overlooking an important quality dimension.

Step 2: Reduce the list

Engage a cross-section of stakeholders to assess which of the attributes are likely to be important to the project. (See Figure 2-2 in Chapter 2, "Requirements from the customer's perspective," for an extensive list of possible project stakeholders.) An airport check-in kiosk needs to emphasize usability (because most users will encounter it infrequently) and security (because it has to handle payments). Attributes that don't apply to your project need not be considered further. Record the rationale for deciding that a particular quality attribute is either in or out of consideration.

Recognize, though, that if you don't specify quality goals, no one should be surprised if the product doesn't exhibit the expected characteristics. This is why it's important to get input from multiple stakeholders. In practice, some of the attributes will clearly be in scope, some will clearly be out of scope, and only a few will require discussion about whether they are worth considering for the project.

Step 3: Prioritize the attributes

Prioritizing the pertinent attributes sets the focus for future elicitation discussions. Pairwise ranking comparisons can work efficiently with a small list of items like this. Figure 14-1 illustrates how to use Brosseau's spreadsheet to assess the quality attributes for an airport check-in kiosk. For each cell at the intersection of two attributes, ask yourself, "If I could have only one of these attributes, which would I take?" Entering a less-than sign (<) in the cell indicates that the attribute in the row is more important; a caret symbol (^) points to the attribute at the top of the column as being more important. For instance, comparing availability and integrity, I conclude that integrity is more important. The passenger can always check in with the desk agent if the kiosk isn't operational (albeit, perhaps with a long line of fellow travelers). But if the kiosk doesn't reliably show the correct data, the passenger will be very unhappy. So I put a caret in the cell at the intersection of availability and integrity, pointing up to integrity as being the more important of the two.

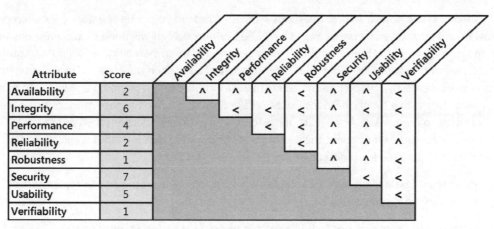

FIGURE 14-1 Sample quality attribute prioritization for an airport check-in kiosk.

The spreadsheet calculates a relative score for each attribute, shown in the second column. In this illustration, security is most important (with a score of 7), closely followed by integrity (6) and usability (5). Though the other factors are indeed important to success—it's not good if the kiosk isn't available for travelers to use or if it crashes halfway through the check-in process—the fact is that not all quality attributes can have top priority.

The prioritization step helps in two ways. First, it lets you focus elicitation efforts on those attributes that are most strongly aligned with project success. Second, it helps you know how to respond when you encounter conflicting quality requirements. In the airport check-in kiosk example, elicitation would reveal a desire to achieve specific performance goals, as well as some specific security goals. These two attributes can clash, because adding security layers can slow down transactions. However, because the prioritization exercise revealed that security is more important (with a score of 7) than performance (with a score of 4), you should bias the resolution of any such conflicts in favor of security.

> **Trap** Don't neglect stakeholders such as maintenance programmers and technical support staff when exploring quality attributes. Their quality priorities could be very different from those of other users. Quality priorities also can vary from one user class to another. If you encounter conflicts, then the approach is doing exactly what it was intended to do: expose these conflicts so you can work through them early in the development life cycle, where conflicts can be resolved with minimal cost and grief.

Step 4: Elicit specific expectations for each attribute

The comments users make during requirements elicitation supply some clues about the quality characteristics they have in mind for the product. The trick is to pin down just what the users are thinking when they say the software must be user-friendly, fast, reliable, or robust. Questions that explore the users' expectations can lead to specific quality requirements that help developers create a delightful product.

Users won't know how to answer questions such as "What are your interoperability requirements?" or "How reliable does the software have to be?" The business analyst will need to ask questions that guide the users' thought processes through an exploration of interoperability, reliability, and other attributes. Roxanne Miller (2009) provides extensive lists of suggested questions to use when eliciting quality requirements; this chapter also presents many examples. When planning an elicitation session, a BA should start with a list of questions like Miller's and distill it down to those questions that are most pertinent to the project. As an illustration, following are a few questions a BA might ask to understand user expectations about the performance of a system that manages applications for patents that inventors have submitted:

1. What would be a reasonable or acceptable response time for retrieval of a typical patent application in response to a query?

2. What would users consider an unacceptable response time for a typical query?

3. How many simultaneous users do you expect on average?

4. What's the maximum number of simultaneous users that you would anticipate?

5. What times of the day, week, month, or year have much heavier usage than usual?

Sending a list of questions like these to elicitation participants in advance gives them an opportunity to think about or research their answers so they don't have to answer a barrage of questions off the tops of their heads. A good final question to ask during any such elicitation discussion is, "Is there anything I haven't asked you that we should discuss?"

Consider asking users what would constitute *unacceptable* performance, security, or reliability. That is, specify system properties that would violate the user's quality expectations, such as allowing an unauthorized user to delete files (Voas 1999). Defining unacceptable characteristics lets you devise tests that try to force the system to demonstrate those characteristics. If you can't force them, you've probably achieved your quality goals. This approach is particularly valuable for safety-critical applications, in which a system that violates reliability or safety tolerances poses a risk to life or limb.

Another possible elicitation strategy is to begin with the quality goals that stakeholders have for the system under development (Alexander and Beus-Dukic 2009). A stakeholder's quality goal can be decomposed to reveal both functional and nonfunctional subgoals—and hence requirements—which become both more specific and easier to measure through the decomposition.

Step 5: Specify well-structured quality requirements

Simplistic quality requirements such as "The system shall be user-friendly" or "The system shall be available 24x7" aren't useful. The former is far too subjective and vague; the latter is rarely realistic or necessary. Neither is measurable. Such requirements provide little guidance to developers. So the final step is to craft specific and verifiable requirements from the information that was elicited regarding each quality attribute. When writing quality requirements, keep in mind the useful SMART mnemonic—make them *Specific, Measurable, Attainable, Relevant,* and *Time-sensitive.*

Quality requirements need to be measurable to establish a precise agreement on expectations among the BA, the customers, and the development team. If it's not measurable, there is little point in specifying it, because you'll never be able to determine if you've achieved a desired goal. If a tester can't test a requirement, it's not good enough. Indicate the scale or units of measure for each attribute and the target, minimum, and maximum values. The notation called Planguage described later in this chapter helps with this sort of precise specification. It might take a few discussions with users to pin down clear, measurable criteria for assessing satisfaction of a quality requirement.

Suzanne and James Robertson (2013) recommend including *fit criteria*—"a quantification of the requirement that demonstrates the standard the product must reach"—as part of the specification of every requirement, both functional and nonfunctional. This is excellent advice. Fit criteria describe a measurable way to assess whether each requirement has been implemented correctly. They help designers select a solution they believe will meet the goal, and they help testers evaluate the results.

Instead of inventing your own way to document unfamiliar requirements, look for an existing requirement pattern to follow. A pattern provides guidance about how to write a particular type of requirement, along with a template you can populate with the specific details for your situation. Stephen Withall (2007) provides numerous patterns for specifying quality requirements, including performance, availability, flexibility, scalability, security, user access, and installability. Following patterns like these will help even novice BAs write sound quality requirements.

Defining quality requirements

This section describes each of the quality attributes in Table 14-1 and presents some sample quality requirements from various projects. Soren Lauesen (2002) and Roxanne Miller (2009) provide many additional examples of well-specified quality attribute requirements. As with all requirements, it's a good idea to record the origin of each quality requirement and the rationale behind the stated quality goals if these are not obvious. The rationale is important in case questions arise about the need for a specific goal or whether the cost is justifiable. That type of source information has been omitted from the examples presented in this chapter.

External quality attributes

External quality attributes describe characteristics that are observed when the software is executing. They profoundly influence the user experience and the user's perception of system quality. The external quality attributes described in this chapter are availability, installability, integrity, interoperability, performance, reliability, robustness, safety, security, and usability.

Availability

Availability is a measure of the planned up time during which the system's services are available for use and fully operational. Formally, availability equals the ratio of up time to the sum of up time and down time. Still more formally, availability equals the mean time between failures (MTBF) for the system divided by the sum of the MTBF and the mean time to repair (MTTR) the system after a failure is encountered. Scheduled maintenance periods also affect availability. Availability is closely related to reliability and is strongly affected by the maintainability subcategory of modifiability.

Certain tasks are more time-critical than others. Users become frustrated—even irate—when they need to get essential work done and the functionality they need isn't available. Ask users what percentage of up time is really needed or how many hours in a given time period the system must be available. Ask whether there are any time periods for which availability is imperative to meet business or safety objectives. Availability requirements are particularly complex and important for websites, cloud-based applications, and applications that have users distributed throughout many time zones. An availability requirement might be stated like the following:

> AVL-1. The system shall be at least 95 percent available on weekdays between 6:00 A.M. and midnight Eastern Time, and at least 99 percent available on weekdays between 3:00 P.M. and 5:00 P.M. Eastern Time.

As with many of the examples presented in this chapter, this requirement is somewhat simplified. It doesn't define the level of performance that constitutes being *available*. Is the system considered available if only one person can use it on the network in a degraded mode? Probably not.

Availability requirements are sometimes stipulated contractually as a service level agreement. Service providers might have to pay a penalty if they do not satisfy such agreements. Such requirements must precisely define exactly what constitutes a system being available (or not) and could include statements such as the following:

> AVL-2. Down time that is excluded from the calculation of availability consists of maintenance scheduled during the hours from 6:00 P.M. Sunday Pacific Time, through 3:00 A.M. Monday Pacific Time.

The cost of quality

Beware of specifying 100 percent as the expected value of a quality attribute such as reliability or availability. It will be impossible to achieve and expensive to strive for. Life-critical applications such as air traffic control systems do have very stringent—and legitimate—availability demands. One such system had a "five 9s" requirement, meaning that the system must be available 99.999 percent of the time. That is, the system could be down no more than 5 minutes and 15 seconds per year. This one requirement contributed to perhaps 25 percent of the system costs. It virtually doubled the hardware costs because of the redundancy required, and it introduced very complex architectural elements to handle a hot backup and failover strategy for the system.

When eliciting availability requirements, ask questions to explore the following issues (Miller 2009):

- What portions of the system are most critical for being available?

- What are the business consequences of the system being unavailable to its users?

- If scheduled maintenance must be performed periodically, when should it be scheduled? What is the impact on system availability? What are the minimum and maximum durations of the maintenance periods? How are user access attempts to be managed during the maintenance periods?

- If maintenance or housekeeping activities must be performed while the system is up, what impact will they have on availability and how can that impact be minimized?

- What user notifications are necessary if the system becomes unavailable?

- What portions of the system have more stringent availability requirements than others?

- What availability dependencies exist between functionality groups (such as not accepting credit card payment for purchases if the credit-card authorization function is not available)?

Installability

Software is not useful until it is installed on the appropriate device or platform. Some examples of software installation are: downloading apps to a phone or tablet; moving software from a PC onto a web server; updating an operating system; installing a huge commercial system, such as an enterprise resource planning tool; downloading a firmware update into a cable TV set-top box; and installing an end-user application onto a PC. Installability describes how easy is it to perform these operations correctly. Increasing a system's installability reduces the time, cost, user disruption, error frequency, and skill level needed for an installation operation. Installability addresses the following activities:

- Initial installation

- Recovery from an incomplete, incorrect, or user-aborted installation

- Reinstallation of the same version

- Installation of a new version

- Reverting to a previous version

- Installation of additional components or updates

- Uninstallation

A measure of a system's installability is the mean time to install the system. This depends on a lot of factors, though: how experienced the installer is, how fast the destination computer is, the medium from which the software is being installed (Internet download, local network, CD/DVD), manual steps needed during the installation, and so forth. The Testing Standards Working Party provides a detailed list of guidelines and considerations for installability requirements and installability testing at *www.testingstandards.co.uk/installability_guidelines.htm*. Following are some sample installability requirements:

> *INS-1. An untrained user shall be able to successfully perform an initial installation of the application in an average of 10 minutes.*

> *INS-2. When installing an upgraded version of the application, all customizations in the user's profile shall be retained and converted to the new version's data format if needed.*

INS-3. The installation program shall verify the correctness of the download before beginning the installation process.

INS-4. Installing this software on a server requires administrator privileges.

INS-5. Following successful installation, the installation program shall delete all temporary, backup, obsolete, and unneeded files associated with the application.

Following are examples of some questions to explore when eliciting installability requirements:

- What installation operations must be performed without disturbing the user's session?

- What installation operations will require a restart of the application? Of the computer or device?

- What should the application do upon successful, or unsuccessful, installation?

- What operations should be performed to confirm the validity of an installation?

- Does the user need the capability to install, uninstall, reinstall, or repair just selected portions of the application? If so, which portions?

- What other applications need to be shut down before performing the installation?

- What authorization or access privileges does the installer need?

- How should the system handle an incomplete installation, such as one interrupted by a power failure or aborted by the user?

Integrity

Integrity deals with preventing information loss and preserving the correctness of data entered into the system. Integrity requirements have no tolerance for error: the data is either in good shape and protected, or it is not. Data needs to be protected against threats such as accidental loss or corruption, ostensibly identical data sets that do not match, physical damage to storage media, accidental file erasure, or data overwriting by users. Intentional attacks that attempt to deliberately corrupt or steal data are also a risk. Security sometimes is considered a subset of integrity, because some security requirements are intended to prevent access to data by unauthorized users. Integrity requirements should ensure that the data received from other systems matches what is sent and vice versa. Software executables themselves are subject to attack, so their integrity also must be protected.

Data integrity also addresses the accuracy and proper formatting of the data (Miller 2009). This includes concerns such as formatting of fields for dates, restricting fields to the correct data type or length, ensuring that data elements have valid values, checking for an appropriate entry in one field when another field has a certain value, and so on. Following are some sample integrity requirements:

INT-1. After performing a file backup, the system shall verify the backup copy against the original and report any discrepancies.

INT-2. The system shall protect against the unauthorized addition, deletion, or modification of data.

INT-3. The Chemical Tracking System shall confirm that an encoded chemical structure imported from third-party structure-drawing tools represents a valid chemical structure.

INT-4. The system shall confirm daily that the application executables have not been modified by the addition of unauthorized code.

Some factors to consider when discussing integrity requirements include the following (Withall 2007):

- Ensuring that changes in the data are made either entirely or not at all. This might mean backing out of a data change if a failure is encountered partway through the operation.

- Ensuring the persistence of changes that are made in the data.

- Coordinating changes made in multiple data stores, particularly when changes have to be made simultaneously (say, on multiple servers) and at a specific time (say, at 12:00 A.M. GMT on January 1 in several locations).

- Ensuring the physical security of computers and external storage devices.

- Performing data backups. (At what frequency? Automatically and/or on demand? Of what files or databases? To what media? With or without compression and verification?)

- Restoring data from a backup.

- Archiving of data: what data, when to archive, for how long, with what deletion requirements.

- Protecting data stored or backed up in the cloud from people who aren't supposed to access it.

Interoperability

Interoperability indicates how readily the system can exchange data and services with other software systems and how easily it can integrate with external hardware devices. To assess interoperability, you need to know which other applications the users will employ in conjunction with your product and what data they expect to exchange. Users of the Chemical Tracking System were accustomed to drawing chemical structures with several commercial tools, so they presented the following interoperability requirement:

IOP-1. The Chemical Tracking System shall be able to import any valid chemical structure from the ChemDraw (version 13.0 or earlier) and MarvinSketch (version 5.0 or earlier) tools.

You might prefer to state this as an external interface requirement and define the information formats that the Chemical Tracking System can import. You could also define several functional requirements that deal with the import operation. Identifying and documenting such requirements is more important than exactly how you classify them.

> **Trap** Don't store the same requirement in several places, even if it logically fits. That's an invitation to generate an inconsistency if you change, for example, an interoperability requirement but forget to change the same information that you also recorded as a functional or external interface requirement.

Interoperability requirements might dictate that standard data interchange formats be used to facilitate exchanging information with other software systems. Such a requirement for the Chemical Tracking System was:

> *IOP-2. The Chemical Tracking System shall be able to import any chemical structure encoded using the SMILES (simplified molecular-input line-entry system) notation.*

Thinking about the system from the perspective of quality attributes sometimes reveals previously unstated requirements. The users hadn't expressed this chemical structure interoperability need when we were discussing either external interfaces or system functionality. As soon as the BA asked about other systems to which the Chemical Tracking System had to connect, though, the product champion immediately mentioned the two chemical structure drawing packages.

Following are some questions you can use when exploring interoperability requirements:

- To what other systems must this one interface? What services or data must they exchange?

- What standard data formats are necessary for data that needs to be exchanged with other systems?

- What specific hardware components must interconnect with the system?

- What messages or codes must the system receive and process from other systems or devices?

- What standard communication protocols are necessary to enable interoperability?

- What externally mandated interoperability requirements must the system satisfy?

Performance

Performance is one of the quality attributes that users often will bring up spontaneously. Performance represents the responsiveness of the system to various user inquiries and actions, but it encompasses much more than that, as shown in Table 14-2. Withall (2007) provides patterns for specifying several of these classes of performance requirements.

Poor performance is an irritant to the user who's waiting for a query to display results. But performance problems can also represent serious risks to safety, such as when a real-time process control system is overloaded. Stringent performance requirements strongly affect software design strategies and hardware choices, so define performance goals that are appropriate for the operating environment. All users want their applications to run instantly, but the real performance requirements will be different for a spell-check feature than for a missile's radar guidance system. Satisfying performance requirements can be tricky because they depend so much upon external factors such as the speed of the computer being used, network connections, and other hardware components.

TABLE 14-2 Some aspects of performance

Performance dimension	Example
Response time	Number of seconds to display a webpage
Throughput	Credit card transactions processed per second
Data capacity	Maximum number of records stored in a database
Dynamic capacity	Maximum number of concurrent users of a social media website
Predictability in real-time systems	Hard timing requirements for an airplane's flight-control system
Latency	Time delays in music recording and production software
Behavior in degraded modes or overloaded conditions	A natural disaster leads to a massive number of emergency telephone system calls

When documenting performance requirements, also document their rationale to guide the developers in making appropriate design choices. For instance, stringent database response time demands might lead the designers to mirror the database in multiple geographical locations. Specify the number of transactions per second to be performed, response times, and task scheduling relationships for real-time systems. You could also specify memory and disk space requirements, concurrent user loads, or the maximum number of rows stored in database tables. Users and BAs might not know all this information, so plan to collaborate with various stakeholders to research the more technical aspects of quality requirements. Following are some sample performance requirements:

> *PER-1. Authorization of an ATM withdrawal request shall take no more than 2.0 seconds.*

> *PER-2. The anti-lock braking system speed sensors shall report wheel speeds every 2 milliseconds with a variation not to exceed 0.1 millisecond.*

> *PER-3. Webpages shall fully download in an average of 3 seconds or less over a 30 megabits/second Internet connection.*

> *PER-4. At least 98 percent of the time, the trading system shall update the transaction status display within 1 second after the completion of each trade.*

Performance is an external quality attribute because it can be observed only during program execution. It is closely related to the internal quality attribute of *efficiency*, which has a big impact on the user-observed performance.

Reliability

The probability of the software executing without failure for a specific period of time is known as reliability (Musa 1999). Reliability problems can occur because of improper inputs, errors in the software code itself, components that are not available when needed, and hardware failures. Robustness and availability are closely related to reliability. Ways to specify and measure software reliability include the percentage of operations that are completed correctly, the average length of time the system runs before failing (mean time between failures, or MTBF), and the maximum acceptable probability of a failure during a given time period. Establish quantitative reliability requirements based on how severe the impact would be if a failure occurred and whether the cost of maximizing reliability is justifiable. Systems that require high reliability should also be designed for high verifiability to make it easier to find defects that could compromise reliability.

My team once wrote some software to control laboratory equipment that performed day-long experiments using scarce, expensive chemicals. The users required the software component that actually ran the experiments to be highly reliable. Other system functions, such as logging temperature data periodically, were less critical. A reliability requirement for this system was

> REL-1. No more than 5 experimental runs out of 1,000 can be lost because of software failures.

Some system failures are more severe than others. A failure might force the user to re-launch an application and recover data that was saved. This is annoying but not catastrophic. Failures that result in lost or corrupted data, such as when an attempted database transaction fails to commit properly, are more severe. Preventing errors is better than detecting them and attempting to recover from them.

Like many other quality attributes, reliability is a lagging indicator: you can't tell if you've achieved it until the system has been in operation for awhile. Consider the following example:

> REL-2. The mean time between failures of the card reader component shall be at least 90 days.

There's no way to tell if the system has satisfied this requirement until at least 90 days have passed. However, you can tell if the system has *failed* to demonstrate sufficient reliability if the card reader component fails more than once within a 90-day period.

Following are some questions to ask user representatives when you're eliciting reliability requirements:

- How would you judge whether this system was reliable enough?

- What would be the consequences of experiencing a failure when performing certain operations with the system?

- What would you consider to be a critical failure, as opposed to a nuisance?

- Under what conditions could a failure have severe repercussions on your business operations?

- No one likes to see a system crash, but are there certain parts of the system that absolutely have to be super-reliable?

- If the system goes down, how long could it stay offline before it significantly affects your business operations?

Understanding reliability requirements lets architects, designers, and developers take actions that they think will achieve the necessary reliability. From a requirements perspective, one way to make a system both reliable and robust is to specify exception conditions and how they are to be handled. Badly handled exceptions can convey an impression of poor reliability and usability to users. A website that blanks out the information a user had entered in a form when it encounters a single bad input value is exasperating. No user would ever specify that behavior as being acceptable. Developers can make systems more reliable by practicing defensive programming techniques, such as testing all input data values for validity and confirming that disk write operations were completed successfully.

Robustness

A customer once told a company that builds measurement devices that its next product should be "built like a tank." The developing company therefore adopted—slightly tongue-in-cheek—the new quality attribute of "tankness." Tankness is a colloquial way of saying *robustness*. Robustness is the degree to which a system continues to function properly when confronted with invalid inputs, defects in connected software or hardware components, external attack, or unexpected operating conditions. Robust software recovers gracefully from problem situations and is forgiving of user mistakes. It recovers from internal failures without adversely affecting the end-user experience. Software errors are handled in a way the user perceives as reasonable, not annoying. Other attribute terms associated with robustness are *fault tolerance* (are user input errors caught and corrected?), *survivability* (can the camera experience a drop from a certain height without damage?), and *recoverability* (can the PC resume proper operation if it loses power in the middle of an operating system update?).

When eliciting robustness requirements, ask users about error conditions the system might encounter and how the system should react. Think about ways to detect possible faults that could lead to a system failure, report them to the user, and recover from them if the failure occurs. Make sure you understand when one operation (such as preparing data for transmission) must be completed correctly before another can begin (sending the data to another computer system). One example of a robustness requirement is

> ROB-1. If the text editor fails before the user saves the file, it shall recover the contents of the file being edited as of, at most, one minute prior to the failure the next time the same user launches the application.

A requirement like this might lead a developer to implement checkpointing or periodic autosave to minimize data loss, along with functionality to look for the saved data upon startup and restore the file contents. You wouldn't want to stipulate the precise mechanism in a robustness requirement, though. Leave those technical decisions to developers.

Mea culpa

While writing this chapter, I had a software robustness experience. I was printing a draft chapter and put my computer into sleep mode before the printing was complete, thinking that the data had all been spooled to the printer. It hadn't. How would the print spooler recover from my error when I woke the computer up? Would the spooler terminate and not print the rest of the file, resume printing where it left off, reprint the entire job, or what? It reprinted the entire job, although I would have preferred that it would just continue printing. I wasted some paper, but at least the spooler recovered from my user error and kept going.

I once led a project to develop a reusable software component called the Graphics Engine, which interpreted data files that defined graphical plots and rendered the plots on a designated output device. Several applications that needed to generate plots invoked the Graphics Engine. Because the developers had no control over the data that these applications fed into the Graphics Engine, robustness was an essential quality. One of our robustness requirements was

> ROB-2. All plot description parameters shall have default values specified, which the Graphics Engine shall use if a parameter's input data is missing or invalid.

With this requirement, the program wouldn't crash if, for example, an application requested an unsupported line style. The Graphics Engine would supply the default solid line style and continue executing. This would still constitute a product failure because the end user didn't get the desired output. But designing for robustness reduced the severity of the failure from a program crash to generating an incorrect line style, an example of fault tolerance.

Safety

Safety requirements deal with the need to prevent a system from doing any injury to people or damage to property (Leveson 1995; Hardy 2011). Safety requirements might be dictated by government regulations or other business rules, and legal or certification issues could be associated with satisfying such requirements. Safety requirements frequently are written in the form of conditions or actions the system must not allow to occur.

People are rarely injured by exploding spreadsheets. However, hardware devices controlled by software can certainly pose a risk to life and limb. Even some software-only applications can have unobvious safety requirements. An application to let people order meals from a cafeteria might include a safety requirement like the following:

> SAF-1. The user shall be able to see a list of all ingredients in any menu items, with ingredients highlighted that are known to cause allergic reactions in more than 0.5 percent of the North American population.

Web browser capabilities like parental controls that disable access to certain features or URLs could be considered as solutions to either safety or security requirements. It's more common to see safety requirements written for systems that include hardware, such as the following examples:

SAF-2. If the reactor vessel's temperature is rising faster than 5°C per minute, the Chemical Reactor Control System shall turn off the heat source and signal a warning to the operator.

SAF-3. The therapeutic radiation machine shall allow irradiation only if the proper filter is in place.

SAF-4. The system shall terminate any operation within 1 second if the measured tank pressure exceeds 90 percent of the specified maximum pressure.

When eliciting safety requirements you might need to interview subject matter experts who are very familiar with the operating environment or people who have thought a lot about project risks. Consider asking questions like the following:

- Under what conditions could a human be harmed by the use of this product? How can the system detect those conditions? How should it respond?

- What is the maximum allowed frequency of failures that have the potential to cause injury?

- What failure modes have the potential of causing harm or property damage?

- What operator actions have the potential of inadvertently causing harm or property damage?

- Are there specific modes of operation that pose risks to humans or property?

Security

Security deals with blocking unauthorized access to system functions or data, ensuring that the software is protected from malware attacks, and so on. Security is a major issue with Internet software. Users of e-commerce systems want their credit card information to be secure. Web surfers don't want personal information or a record of the sites they visit to be used inappropriately. Companies want to protect their websites against denial-of-service or hacking attacks. As with integrity requirements, security requirements have no tolerance for error. Following are some considerations to examine when eliciting security requirements:

- User authorization or privilege levels (ordinary user, guest user, administrator) and user access controls (the roles and permissions matrix that was illustrated in Figure 9-2 can be a useful tool)

- User identification and authentication (password construction rules, password change frequency, security questions, forgotten logon name or password procedures, biometric identification, account locking after unsuccessful access attempts, unrecognized computer)

- Data privacy (who can create, see, change, copy, print, and delete what information)

- Deliberate data destruction, corruption, or theft

- Protection against viruses, worms, Trojan horses, spyware, rootkits, and other malware

- Firewall and other network security issues

- Encryption of secure data

- Building audit trails of operations performed and access attempts

Following are some examples of security requirements. It's easy to see how you could design tests to verify that these requirements are correctly implemented.

> *SEC-1. The system shall lock a user's account after four consecutive unsuccessful logon attempts within a period of five minutes.*

> *SEC-2. The system shall log all attempts to access secure data by users having insufficient privilege levels.*

> *SEC-3. A user shall have to change the temporary password assigned by the security officer to a previously unused password immediately following the first successful logon with the temporary password.*

> *SEC-4. A door unlock that results from a successful security badge read shall keep the door unlocked for 8.0 seconds, with a tolerance of 0.5 second.*

> *SEC-5. The resident antimalware software shall quarantine any incoming Internet traffic that exhibits characteristics of known or suspected virus signatures.*

> *SEC-6. The magnetometer shall detect at least 99.9 percent of prohibited objects, with a false positive rate not to exceed 1 percent.*

Security requirements often originate from business rules, such as corporate security policies, as the following example illustrates:

> *SEC-7. Only users who have Auditor access privileges shall be able to view customer transaction histories.*

Try to avoid writing security requirements with embedded design constraints. Specifying passwords for access control is an example. The real requirement is to restrict access to the system to authorized users; passwords are merely one way (albeit the most common way) to accomplish that objective. Depending on which user authentication method is chosen, this security requirement will lead to specific functional requirements that implement the authentication method.

Following are some questions to explore when eliciting security requirements:

- What sensitive data must be protected from unauthorized access?

- Who is authorized to view sensitive data? Who, specifically, is not authorized?

- Under what business conditions or operational time frames are authorized users allowed to access functionality?

- What checks must be performed to confirm that the user is operating the application in a secure environment?

- How frequently should virus software scan for viruses?

- Is there a specific user authentication method that must be used?

Usability

Usability addresses the myriad factors that constitute what people describe colloquially as *user-friendliness, ease of use,* and *human engineering.* Analysts and developers shouldn't talk about "friendly" software but rather about software that's designed for effective and unobtrusive usage. Usability measures the effort required to prepare input for a system, operate it, and interpret its outputs.

Software usability is a huge topic with a considerable body of literature (for example: Constantine and Lockwood 1999; Nielsen 2000; Lazar 2001; Krug 2006; Johnson 2010). Usability encompasses several subdomains beyond the obvious ease of use, including ease of learning; memorability; error avoidance, handling, and recovery; efficiency of interactions; accessibility; and ergonomics. Conflicts can arise between these categories. For instance, ease of learning can be at odds with ease of use. The actions a designer might take to make it easy for a new or infrequent user to employ the system can be irritating impediments to a power user who knows exactly what he wants to do and craves efficiency. Different features within the same application might also have different usability goals. It might be important to be able to enter data very efficiently, but also to be able to easily figure out how to generate a customized report. Table 14-3 illustrates some of these usability design approaches; you can see the possible conflict if you optimize for one aspect of usability over another inappropriately for specific user classes.

Important The key goal for usability—as well as for other quality attributes—is to balance the usability optimally for the whole spectrum of users, not just for a single community. This might mean that certain users aren't as happy with the result as they'd like to be. User customization options can broaden the application's appeal.

TABLE 14-3 Possible design approaches for ease of learning and ease of use

Ease of learning	Ease of use
Verbose prompts	Keyboard shortcuts
Wizards	Rich, customizable menus and toolbars
Visible menu options	Multiple ways to access the same function
Meaningful, plain-language messages	Autocompletion of entries
Help screens and tooltips	Autocorrection of errors
Similarity to other familiar systems	Macro recording and scripting capabilities
Limited number of options and widgets displayed	Ability to carry over information from a previous transaction
	Automatically fill in form fields
	Command-line interface

As with the other quality attributes, it is possible to measure many aspects of "user-friendliness." Usability indicators include:

- The average time needed for a specific type of user to complete a particular task correctly.

- How many transactions the user can complete correctly in a given time period.

- What percentage of a set of tasks the user can complete correctly without needing help.

- How many errors the user makes when completing a task.

- How many tries it takes the user to accomplish a particular task, like finding a specific function buried somewhere in the menus.

- The delay or wait time when performing a task.

- The number of interactions (mouse clicks, keystrokes, touch-screen gestures) required to get to a piece of information or to accomplish a task.

Just tell me what's wrong

Usability shortcomings can be exasperating. I recently tried to report a problem using a website's feedback form. I received an error message that "no special characters were allowed" but the website did not tell me which characters in my text were causing the problem. Obviously, the software knew what the bad characters were because it detected them. Showing me a generic error message instead of offering precise feedback didn't help me solve the problem. I eventually figured out that the software was objecting to the presence of quotation marks in my message. It never occurred to me that quotation marks would be considered a special character; "special character" is vague and ambiguous. To help developers determine how best to satisfy a user's usability expectations, the BA should write specific usability requirements, and developers should provide precise error feedback whenever possible.

To explore their usability expectations, the business analysts on the Chemical Tracking System asked their product champions questions such as "How many steps would you be willing to go through to request a chemical?" and "How long should it take you to complete a chemical request?" These are simple starting points toward defining the many characteristics that will make the software easy to use. Discussions about usability can lead to measurable goals such as the following:

> USE-1. A trained user shall be able to submit a request for a chemical from a vendor catalog in an average of three minutes, and in a maximum of five minutes, 95 percent of the time.

Inquire whether the new system must conform to any user interface standards or conventions, or whether its user interface needs to be consistent with those of other frequently used systems. You might state such a usability requirement in the following way:

> USE-2. All functions on the File menu shall have shortcut keys defined that use the Control key pressed simultaneously with one other key. Menu commands that also appear in Microsoft Word shall use the same default shortcut keys that Word uses.

Such consistency of usage can help avoid those frustrating errors that occur when your fingers perform an action by habit that has some different meaning in an application you don't use frequently. Ease-of-learning goals also can be quantified and measured, as the following example indicates:

> USE-3. 95 percent of chemists who have never used the Chemical Tracking System before shall be able to place a request for a chemical correctly with no more than 15 minutes of orientation.

Carefully specifying requirements for the diverse dimensions of usability can help designers make the choices that distinguish delighted users from those who use an application with frowns on their faces or, worse, those who refuse to use it at all.

Internal quality attributes

Internal quality attributes are not directly observable during execution of the software. They are properties that a developer or maintainer perceives while looking at the design or code to modify it, reuse it, or move it to another platform. Internal attributes can indirectly affect the customer's perception of the product's quality if it later proves difficult to add new functionality or if internal inefficiencies result in performance degradation. The following sections describe quality attributes that are particularly important to software architects, developers, maintainers, and other technical staff.

Efficiency

Efficiency is closely related to the external quality attribute of performance. Efficiency is a measure of how well the system utilizes processor capacity, disk space, memory, or communication bandwidth. If a system consumes too much of the available resources, users will encounter degraded performance.

Efficiency—and hence performance—is a driving factor in systems architecture, influencing how a designer elects to distribute computations and functions across system components. Efficiency requirements can compromise the achievement of other quality attributes. Consider minimum hardware configurations when defining efficiency, capacity, and performance goals. To allow engineering margins for unanticipated conditions and future growth (thereby influencing scalability), you might specify something like the following:

> EFF-1. At least 30 percent of the processor capacity and memory available to the application shall be unused at the planned peak load conditions.

EFF-2. The system shall provide the operator with a warning message when the usage load exceeds 80 percent of the maximum planned capacity.

Users won't state efficiency requirements in such technical terms; instead, they will think in terms of response times or other observations. The BA must ask the questions that will surface user expectations regarding issues such as acceptable performance degradation, demand spikes, and anticipated growth. Examples of such questions are:

- What is the maximum number of concurrent users now and anticipated in the future?

- By how much could response times or other performance indicators decrease before users or the business suffer adverse consequences?

- How many operations must the system be able to perform simultaneously under both normal and extreme operating conditions?

Modifiability

Modifiability addresses how easily the software designs and code can be understood, changed, and extended. Modifiability encompasses several other quality attribute terms that relate to different forms of software maintenance, as shown in Table 14-4. It is closely related to verifiability. If developers anticipate making many enhancements, they can choose design approaches that maximize the software's modifiability. High modifiability is critical for systems that will undergo frequent revision, such as those being developed by using an incremental or iterative life cycle.

TABLE 14-4 Some aspects of modifiability

Maintenance type	Modifiability dimensions	Description
Corrective	Maintainability, understandability	Correcting defects
Perfective	Flexibility, extensibility, and augmentability	Enhancing and modifying functionality to meet new business needs and requirements
Adaptive	Maintainability	Modifying the system to function in an altered operating environment without adding new capabilities
Field support	Supportability	Correcting faults, servicing devices, or repairing devices in their operating environment

Ways to measure modifiability include the average time required to add a capability or fix a problem, and the percentage of fixes that are made correctly. The Chemical Tracking System included the following modifiability requirement:

MOD-1. A maintenance programmer experienced with the system shall be able to modify existing reports to conform to revised chemical-reporting regulations from the federal government with 10 hours or less of development effort.

On the Graphics Engine project, we knew we would be doing frequent software surgery to satisfy evolving user needs. Being experienced developers ourselves, we adopted design guidelines such as the following to guide developers in writing the code to enhance the program's understandability and hence maintainability:

MOD-2. Function calls shall not be nested more than two levels deep.

Such design guidelines should be stated carefully to discourage developers from taking silly actions that conform to the letter, but not the intent, of the goal. The BA should work with maintenance programmers to understand what properties of the code would make it easy for them to modify it or correct defects.

Hardware devices containing embedded software often have requirements for supportability in the field. Some of these lead to software design choices, whereas others influence the hardware design. The following is an example of the latter:

SUP-1. A certified repair technician shall be able to replace the scanner module in no more than 10 minutes.

Supportability requirements might also help make the user's life easier, as this example illustrates:

SUP-2. The printer shall display an error message if replacement ink cartridges were not inserted in the proper slots.

Portability

The effort needed to migrate software from one operating environment to another is a measure of portability. Some practitioners include the ability to internationalize and localize a product under the heading of portability. The design approaches that make software portable are similar to those that make it reusable. Portability has become increasingly important as applications must run in multiple environments, such as Windows, Mac, and Linux; iOS and Android; and PCs, tablets, and phones. Data portability requirements are also important.

Portability goals should identify those portions of the product that must be movable to other environments and describe those target environments. One product for analyzing chemicals ran in two very different environments. One version ran in a laboratory where a PhD chemist used the software to control several analytical instruments. The second version ran in a handheld device to be used in the field, such as at an oil pipeline, by someone who had much less technical education. The core capabilities of the two versions were largely the same. Such a product needs to be designed from the outset to work in both kinds of environments with the minimum amount of development work. If developers know about the customers' expectations of portability, they can select development approaches that will enhance the product's portability appropriately. Following are some sample portability requirements:

POR-1. Modifying the iOS version of the application to run on Android devices shall require changing no more than 10 percent of the source code.

POR-2. The user shall be able to port browser bookmarks to and from Firefox, Internet Explorer, Opera, Chrome, and Safari.

POR-3. The platform migration tool shall transfer customized user profiles to the new installation with no user action needed.

When you are exploring portability, questions like the following might be helpful:

- What different platforms will this software need to run on, both now and in the future?

- What portions of the product need to be designed for greater portability than other portions?

- What data files, program components, or other elements of the system need to be portable?

- By making the software more portable, what other quality attributes might be compromised?

Reusability

Reusability indicates the relative effort required to convert a software component for use in other applications. Reusable software must be modular, well documented, independent of a specific application and operating environment, and somewhat generic in capability. Numerous project artifacts offer the potential for reuse, including requirements, architectures, designs, code, tests, business rules, data models, user class descriptions, stakeholder profiles, and glossary terms (see Chapter 18, "Requirements reuse"). Making software reusable is facilitated by thorough specification of requirements and designs, rigorous adherence to coding standards, a maintained regression suite of test cases, and a maintained standard library of reusable components.

Reusability goals are difficult to quantify. Specify which elements of the new system need to be constructed in a manner that facilitates their reuse, or stipulate the reusable components that should be created as a spin-off from the project. Following are some examples:

REU-1. The chemical structure input functions shall be reusable at the object code level in other applications.

REU-2. At least 30 percent of the application architecture shall be reused from the approved reference architectures.

REU-3. The pricing algorithms shall be reusable by future store-management applications.

Consider discussing the following questions when you are trying to learn about reusability requirements for your project:

- What existing requirements, models, design components, data, or tests could be reused in this application?

- What functionality available in related applications might meet certain requirements for this application?

- What portions of this application offer good potential for being reused elsewhere?

- What special actions should be taken to facilitate making portions of this application reusable?

Scalability

Scalability requirements address the ability of the application to grow to accommodate more users, data, servers, geographic locations, transactions, network traffic, searches, and other services without compromising performance or correctness. Scalability has both hardware and software implications. Scaling up a system could mean acquiring faster computers, adding memory or disk space, adding servers, mirroring databases, or increasing network capacity. Software approaches might include distributing computations onto multiple processors, compressing data, optimizing algorithms, and other performance-tuning techniques. Scalability is related to modifiability and to robustness, because one category of robustness has to do with how the system behaves when capacity limits are approached or exceeded. Following are some examples of scalability requirements:

> SCA-1. The capacity of the emergency telephone system must be able to be increased from 500 calls per day to 2,500 calls per day within 12 hours.

> SCA-2. The website shall be able to handle a page-view growth rate of 30 percent per quarter for at least two years without user-perceptible performance degradation.

> SCA-3. The distribution system shall be able to accommodate up to 20 new warehouse centers.

The business analyst might not have a good sense of future expansion plans for a specific application. She might need to work with the project sponsor or subject matter experts to get a sense of how much the user base, data volume, or other parameters could grow over time. The following questions could be helpful during those discussions:

- What are your estimates for the number of total and concurrent users the system must be able to handle over the next several months, quarters, or years?

- Can you describe how and why data capacity demands of the system might grow in the future?

- What are the minimum acceptable performance criteria that must be satisfied regardless of the number of users?

- What growth plans are available regarding how many servers, data centers, or individual installations the system might be expected to run on?

No, wait, please don't go!

"Cyber Monday" is a marketing term for the Monday following Thanksgiving every November. It has become a traditional day for consumers to shop at online sales for the holiday season. When this custom took root in the mid-2000s, many e-commerce websites weren't prepared to handle the spikes in traffic and transactions from customers shopping for bargains. Servers crashed, passwords weren't recognized, and purchases took too long to be completed. Many shoppers abandoned the online stores they were trying to access and found someplace else to shop, perhaps never to return. Cybercriminals made out, well, like bandits, as traffic was diverted to their look-alike websites that stole shoppers' personal information.

These problems reveal an intertwined mass of unsatisfied software quality requirements. Because of inadequate scalability, systems experienced reliability problems as websites were overwhelmed with visitors, which led to reduced availability. Better software has a direct impact on a company's financial bottom line.

Verifiability

More narrowly referred to as *testability*, verifiability refers to how well software components or the integrated product can be evaluated to demonstrate whether the system functions as expected. Designing for verifiability is critical if the product has complex algorithms and logic, or if it contains subtle functionality interrelationships. Verifiability is also important if the product will be modified often, because it will undergo frequent regression testing to determine whether the changes damaged any existing functionality. Systems with high verifiability can be tested both effectively and efficiently. Designing software for verifiability means making it easy to place the software into the desired pretest state, to provide the necessary test data, and to observe the result of the test. Here are some examples of verifiability requirements:

> *VER-1. The development environment configuration shall be identical to the test configuration environment to avoid irreproducible testing failures.*

> *VER-2. A tester shall be able to configure which execution results are logged during testing.*

> *VER-3. The developer shall be able to set the computational module to show the interim results of any specified algorithm group for debugging purposes.*

Because my team and I knew that we'd have to test the Graphics Engine many times while it was repeatedly enhanced, we included the following design guideline to enhance verifiability:

> *VER-4. The maximum cyclomatic complexity of a module shall not exceed 20.*

Cyclomatic complexity is a measure of the number of logic branches in a source code module. Adding more branches and loops to a module makes it harder to understand, to test, and to maintain. The project wasn't going to be a failure if some module had a cyclomatic complexity of 24, but documenting such guidelines helped the developers achieve a desired quality objective.

Defining verifiability requirements can be difficult. Explore questions like the following:

- How can we confirm that specific calculations are giving the expected results?

- Are there any portions of the system that do not yield deterministic outputs, such that it could be difficult to determine if they were working correctly?

- Is it possible to come up with test data sets that have a high probability of revealing any errors in the requirements or in their implementation?

- What reference reports or other outputs can we use to verify that the system is producing its outputs correctly?

Specifying quality requirements with Planguage

You can't evaluate a product to judge whether it satisfies vague quality requirements. Unverifiable quality requirements are no better than unverifiable functional requirements. Simplistic quality and performance goals can be unrealistic. Specifying a subsecond response time for a database query might be fine for a simple lookup in a local database but unrealistic for a six-way join of relational tables residing on geographically separated servers.

To address the problem of ambiguous and incomplete nonfunctional requirements, Tom Gilb (1997; 2005) developed *Planguage*, a language with a rich set of keywords that permits precise statements of quality attributes and other project goals (Simmons 2001). Following is an example of how to express a performance requirement using just a few of the many Planguage keywords. Expressed in traditional form, this requirement might read: "At least 95 percent of the time, the system shall take no more than 8 seconds to display any of the predefined accounting reports."

- **TAG** Performance.Report.ResponseTime

- **AMBITION** Fast response time to generate accounting reports on the base user platform.

- **SCALE** Seconds of elapsed time between pressing the Enter key or clicking OK to request a report and the beginning of the display of the report.

- **METER** Stopwatch testing performed on 30 test reports that represent a defined usage operational profile for a field office accountant.

- **GOAL** No more than 8 seconds for 95 percent of reports. ←Field Office Manager

- **STRETCH** No more than 2 seconds for predefined reports, 5 seconds for all reports.

- **WISH** No more than 1.5 seconds for all reports.

- **base user platform DEFINED** Quad-core processor, 8GB RAM, Windows 8, QueryGen 3.3 running, single user, at least 50 percent of system RAM and 70 percent of system CPU capacity free, network connection speed of at least 30 Mbps.

Each requirement receives a unique *tag,* or label, using the hierarchical naming convention that was described in Chapter 10. The *ambition* states the purpose or objective of the system that leads to this requirement. *Scale* defines the units of measurement and *meter* describes how to make the measurements. All stakeholders need to have the same understanding of what "performance" means. Suppose that a user interprets the measurement to be from the time that he presses the Enter key until the complete report appears, rather than until the beginning of the report display, as stated in the example. The developer might claim that the requirement is satisfied, whereas the user insists that it is not. Unambiguous quality requirements and measurements prevent these sorts of debates.

One advantage of Planguage is that you can specify several target values for the quantity being measured. The *goal* criterion is the minimum acceptable achievement level. The requirement isn't satisfied unless every *goal* condition is completely satisfied, so make sure the goals are justifiable in terms of real business needs. An alternative way to state the *goal* requirement is to define the *fail* (another Planguage keyword) condition: "More than 8 seconds on more than 5 percent of all reports." The *stretch* value describes a more desirable performance objective, and the *wish* value represents the ideal outcome. Consider showing the origin of performance goals. The "←" notation following the *goal* criterion shows that it came from the Field Office Manager. Any specialized terms in the Planguage statement are *defined* to make them clear to the reader. This example provides a definition of something called the Base User Platform on which the test is to be conducted.

Planguage includes many additional keywords to provide flexibility and precision in specifying unambiguous quality attribute requirements, and even business objectives. Specifying multiple levels of achievement yields a far richer statement of a quality requirement than a simple black-and-white, yes-or-no construct can. The drawback to using Planguage is that the resulting requirements are much bulkier than simple quality requirement statements. However, the richness of information provided outweighs this inconvenience. Even if you don't write the quality requirements using the full Planguage formalism, using the keywords to think through exactly what people mean by "fast" will yield much more precise and shared expectations.

Quality attribute trade-offs

Certain attribute combinations have inescapable trade-offs. Users and developers must decide which attributes are more important than others, and they must respect those priorities when they make decisions. The technique described earlier in "Step 3: Prioritize the attributes" can help with this analysis. Figure 14-2 illustrates some typical interrelationships among the quality attributes from Table 14-1, although you might encounter exceptions to these (Charette 1990; Glass 1992; IEEE 1998). A plus sign in a cell indicates that increasing the attribute in the corresponding row usually has a positive effect on the attribute in the column. For example, design approaches that increase a software component's portability also make the software easier to connect to other software components, easier to reuse, and easier to test.

	Availability	Efficiency	Installability	Integrity	Interoperability	Modifiability	Performance	Portability	Reliability	Reusability	Robustness	Safety	Scalability	Security	Usability	Verifiability
Availability								+			+					
Efficiency	+			−	−	+	−			−			+		−	
Installability	+							+					+			
Integrity			−		−	−			−			+	+		−	−
Interoperability	+		−	−		−	+	+	+	−		−				
Modifiability	+		−				−	+	+			+				+
Performance		+			−	−		−	−		−		−			
Portability		−		+	−	−			+					−	−	+
Reliability	+	−		+		+	−				+	+		+	+	+
Reusability		−		−	+	+	−	+						−		+
Robustness	+	−	+	+	+		−		+			+	+	+		
Safety		−	+	+		−			+					+	−	−
Scalability	+	+		+		+	+	+	+							
Security	+			+	+		−	−	+		+				−	−
Usability		−	+				−	−	+		+					−
Verifiability	+		+	+	+			+	+		+			+	+	

FIGURE 14-2 Positive and negative relationships among selected quality attributes.

A minus sign in a cell means that increasing the attribute in that row generally adversely affects the attribute in the column. An empty cell indicates that the attribute in the row has little effect on the attribute in the column. Performance and efficiency have a negative impact on several other attributes. If you write the tightest, fastest code you can, using coding tricks and relying on execution side effects, it's likely to be hard to maintain and enhance. It also could be harder to port to other platforms if you've tuned the code for a specific operating environment. Similarly, systems that optimize ease of use or that are designed to be reusable and interoperable with other software or hardware components often incur a performance penalty. Using the general-purpose Graphics Engine component described earlier in the chapter to generate plots resulted in poorer performance compared with the old applications that incorporated custom graphics code. You have to balance the possible performance (or other) reductions against the anticipated benefits of your proposed solution to ensure that you're making sensible trade-offs.

The matrix in Figure 14-2 isn't symmetrical because the effect that increasing attribute A has on attribute B isn't necessarily the same as the effect that increasing B will have on A. Figure 14-2 shows that designing the system to increase performance doesn't necessarily have any effect on security. However, increasing security likely will hurt performance because the system must go through more layers of user authentications, encryption, and malware scanning.

To reach the optimum balance of product characteristics, you must identify, specify, and prioritize the pertinent quality attributes during requirements elicitation. As you define the important quality attributes for your project, use Figure 14-2 to avoid making commitments to conflicting goals. Following are some examples:

- Don't expect to maximize usability if the software must run on multiple platforms with minimal modification (portability). Different platforms and operating systems impose different constraints and offer different usability characteristics.

- It's hard to completely test the integrity requirements of highly secure systems. Reused generic components could compromise security mechanisms.

- Highly robust code could exhibit reduced performance because of the data validations and error checking that it performs.

As usual, overconstraining system expectations or defining conflicting requirements makes it impossible for the developers to fully satisfy the requirements.

Implementing quality attribute requirements

Designers and programmers will have to determine the best way to satisfy each quality requirement. Although these are nonfunctional requirements, they can lead to derived functional requirements, design guidelines, or other types of technical information that will produce the desired product characteristics. Table 14-5 indicates the likely categories of technical information that different types of quality attributes will generate. For example, a medical device with stringent availability and reliability requirements might include a backup battery power supply (architecture), along with functional requirements to indicate when the product is operating on battery power, when the battery is getting low, and so forth. This translation from external or internal quality requirements into corresponding technical information is part of the requirements analysis and high-level design processes.

TABLE 14-5 Translating quality attributes into technical specifications

Quality attributes	Likely technical information category
Installability, integrity, interoperability, reliability, robustness, safety, security, usability, verifiability	Functional requirement
Availability, efficiency, modifiability, performance, reliability, scalability	System architecture
Interoperability, security, usability	Design constraint
Efficiency, modifiability, portability, reliability, reusability, scalability, verifiability, usability	Design guideline
Portability	Implementation constraint

Business analysts who lack development experience might not appreciate the technical implications of quality requirements. Therefore, the BA should engage the right stakeholders who have knowledge of these implications and learn from those collaborations. Consider scalability, which can be profoundly affected by architecture and design choices. Scalability requirements might lead the developer to retain performance buffers (disk space, CPU consumption, network bandwidth) to accommodate potential growth without degrading system performance unacceptably. Scalability expectations can affect the hardware and operating environment decisions that developers make. This is why it's important to elicit and document scalability requirements early on so developers can ensure that the product can grow as expected and still exhibit acceptable performance. This is also one reason why it's important to involve developers early in requirements elicitation and reviews.

Constraints

A constraint places restrictions on the design or implementation choices available to the developer. Constraints can be imposed by external stakeholders, by other systems that interact with the one you're building or maintaining, or by other life cycle activities for your system, such as transition and maintenance. Other constraints result from existing agreements, management decisions, and technical decisions (ISO/IEC/IEEE 2011). Sources of constraints include:

- Specific technologies, tools, languages, and databases that must be used or avoided.

- Restrictions because of the product's operating environment or platform, such as the types and versions of web browsers or operating-systems that will be used.

- Required development conventions or standards. (For instance, if the customer's organization will be maintaining the software, the organization might specify design notations and coding standards that a subcontractor must follow.)

- Backward compatibility with earlier products and potential forward compatibility, such as knowing which version of the software was used to create a specific data file.

- Limitations or compliance requirements imposed by regulations or other business rules.

- Hardware limitations such as timing requirements, memory or processor restrictions, size, weight, materials, or cost.

- Physical restrictions because of the operating environment or because of characteristics or limitations of the users.

- Existing interface conventions to be followed when enhancing an existing product.

- Interfaces to other existing systems, such as data formats and communication protocols.

- Restrictions because of the size of the display, as when running on a tablet or phone.

- Standard data interchange formats used, such as XML, or RosettaNet for e-business.

These sorts of constraints often are imposed from external sources and must be respected. Constraints can be imposed inadvertently, though. It's common for users to present "requirements" that are actually solution ideas that describe one particular way the user envisions meeting a need. The BA must detect when a requirement includes a solution idea like this and distinguish the underlying need from the constraint that the solution imposes. Perhaps the solution the user has in mind is in fact the ideal way to solve the problem, in which case the constraint is perfectly legitimate. More often, the real need is hidden, and the BA must work with the user to articulate the thoughts that led to the presented solution. Asking "why" a few times generally will lead to that real requirement.

Some people say that quality attributes *are* constraints. We prefer to think of certain quality requirements as being the origin of some design or implementation constraints. As Table 14-5 indicated, interoperability and usability requirements are potential sources of design constraints. Portability often imposes implementation constraints to make sure the application can easily be moved from one platform or operating environment to another. For instance, some compilers define an *integer* as being 32 bits long, and others define it as 64 bits. To satisfy a portability requirement, a developer might symbolically define a data type called *WORD* as a 32-bit unsigned integer and use the WORD data type instead of the compiler's default integer data type. This ensures that all compilers will treat data items of type WORD in the same way, which helps to make the system work predictably in different operating environments.

Following are some examples of constraints. You can see how these restrict the options available to the architect, designer, and developer.

> CON-1. The user clicks at the top of the project list to change the sort sequence. *[specific user interface control imposed as a design constraint on a functional requirement]*

> CON-2. Only open source software available under the GNU General Public License may be used to implement the product. *[implementation constraint]*

> CON-3. The application must use Microsoft .NET framework 4.5. *[architecture constraint]*

> CON-4. ATMs contain only $20 bills. *[physical constraint]*

> CON-5. Online payments may be made only through PayPal. *[design constraint]*

> CON-6. All textual data used by the application shall be stored in the form of XML files. *[data constraint]*

Note that some of these constraints exist to comply with some perhaps-unstated quality expectation. Ask why each constraint is imposed to try to reach that underlying quality requirement. Why must open-source software be used, as stated in CON-2? Perhaps because of a desire for increased modifiability, so that's the requirement that leads to the constraint. Why must a specific version of .NET be used, per CON-3? Perhaps because of an implicit portability or reliability requirement. Remember, a constraint is a perceived solution; asking "why" can lead you to the requirement for which it is thought to be a solution.

Handling quality attributes on agile projects

It can be difficult and expensive to retrofit desired quality characteristics into a product late in development or after delivery. That's why even agile projects that develop requirements and deliver functionality in small increments need to specify significant quality attributes and constraints early in the project. This allows developers to make appropriate architectural and design decisions as a foundation for the desired quality characteristics. Nonfunctional requirements need to have priority alongside user stories; you can't defer their implementation until a later iteration.

It's possible to specify quality attributes in the form of stories:

> *As a help desk technician, I want the knowledge base to respond to queries within five seconds so the customer doesn't get frustrated and hang up.*

However, quality requirements are not implemented in the same discrete way as user stories. They can span multiple stories and multiple iterations. Nor are they always readily divisible into smaller chunks to be implemented across multiple iterations like user stories.

Developers need to keep nonfunctional requirements in mind as they consider the implications of implementing individual user stories. As more functionality is added through a series of iterations, the system's efficiency and hence performance can deteriorate. Specify performance goals and begin performance testing with early iterations, so you can become aware of concerns early enough to take corrective actions.

As you saw in Table 14-5, some quality attributes are the source of derived functionality. On an agile project, quality requirements can spawn new items for the product backlog. Consider the following security requirement:

> *As an account owner, I want to prevent unauthorized users from accessing my account so I don't lose any money.*

This requirement would lead the product owner or business analyst on the project to derive multiple user stories that describe the security-related functionality. These stories can be added to the backlog and planned for implementation in specific iterations in the usual fashion. Understanding these requirements up front ensures that the team implements the security requirements at the right time.

As with user stories, it's possible to write acceptance tests for quality attributes. This is a way to quantify the quality attributes. If a performance goal is stated simply as "The knowledge base must return search results quickly," you can't write tests to define what constitutes "quickly." A better acceptance test would be:

> *Keyword search of the knowledge base takes less than 5 seconds, and preferably less than 3 seconds, to return a result.*

Acceptance tests written in this form can present several acceptable levels of satisfaction for the requirement, much like the Goal, Stretch, and Wish keywords used in Planguage, as discussed earlier in this chapter. You could use the Planguage keywords Scale and Meter to define more precisely what exactly is meant by "return a result" and how to perform the test and evaluate the results.

Part of accepting an iteration as being complete is to assess whether the pertinent nonfunctional requirements are satisfied. Often there is a range of acceptable performance, with some outcomes more desirable than others. As it does for any other software development approach, satisfying quality requirements can distinguish delight from disappointment on agile projects.

Next steps

- Identify several quality attributes from Table 14-1 that might be important to users on your current project. Formulate a few questions about each attribute that will help your users articulate their expectations. Based on the user responses, write one or two specific requirements for each important attribute.

- Examine several documented quality requirements for your project to see if they are verifiable. If not, rewrite them so you could assess whether the expected quality outcomes were achieved in the product.

- Revisit the section titled "Exploring quality attributes" in this chapter and try the spreadsheet approach described to rank-order your important quality attributes. Are the trade-offs between attributes being made on your project in agreement with this priority analysis?

- Rewrite several of the quality attribute examples in this chapter by using Planguage, making assumptions when necessary for the sake of illustration. Can you state those quality requirements with more precision and less ambiguity by using Planguage?

- Examine your users' quality expectations for the system for possible conflicts and resolve them. The favored user classes should have the most influence on making the necessary trade-off choices.

- Trace your quality attribute requirements to the functional requirements, design and implementation constraints, or architectural and design choices that implement them.

CHAPTER 15

Risk reduction through prototyping

"Sharon, today I'd like to talk with you about the requirements that the buyers in the Purchasing Department have for the new Chemical Tracking System," began Lori, the business analyst. "Can you tell me what you want to be able to do with the system?"

"I'm not sure what to say," replied Sharon with a puzzled expression. "I can't describe what I need, but I'll know it when I see it."

The phrase IKIWISI—"I'll know it when I see it"—chills the blood of business analysts. It conjures an image of the development team having to make their best guess at the right software to build, only to have users tell them, "Nope, that's not right; try again." To be sure, envisioning a future software system and articulating its requirements is hard. People have difficulty describing their needs without having something tangible in front of them to contemplate; critiquing is much easier than conceiving.

Software prototyping takes a tentative step into the solution space. It makes the requirements more real, brings use cases to life, and closes gaps in your understanding of the requirements. Prototyping puts a mock-up or an initial slice of a new system in front of users to stimulate their thinking and catalyze the requirements dialog. Early feedback on prototypes helps stakeholders arrive at a shared understanding of the system's requirements, which reduces the risk of customer dissatisfaction.

Even if you apply the requirements development practices described in earlier chapters, portions of your requirements might still be uncertain or unclear to customers, developers, or both. If you don't correct these problems, an expectation gap between a user's vision of the product and a developer's understanding of what to build is guaranteed. Prototyping is a powerful way to introduce those all-important customer contact points that can reduce the expectation gap described in Chapter 2, "Requirements from the customer's perspective." It's hard to visualize exactly how software will behave by reading textual requirements or studying analysis models. Users are more willing to try out a prototype (which is fun) than to read an SRS (which is tedious). When you hear *IKIWISI* from your users, think about what you can provide that would help them articulate their needs or help you better understand what they have in mind (Boehm 2000). Prototypes are also a valuable tool for requirements validation. A business analyst can have users interact with prototypes to see if a product based on the prototype would truly meet their needs.

The word *prototype* has multiple meanings, and participants in a prototyping activity can hold very different expectations. A prototype airplane actually flies—it's the first instance of a new type of airplane. In contrast, a software prototype is only a portion or a model of a real system—it might not do anything useful at all. Software prototypes can be static designs or working models; quick sketches or highly detailed screens; visual displays or full slices of functionality; or simulations (Stevens et al. 1998; Constantine and Lockwood 1999).

This chapter describes how prototyping provides value to the project and different kinds of prototypes you might create for different purposes. It also offers guidance on how to use them during requirements development, as well as ways to make prototyping an effective part of your software engineering process.

Prototyping: What and why

A software *prototype* is a partial, possible, or preliminary implementation of a proposed new product. Prototypes can serve three major purposes, and that purpose must be made clear from the very beginning:

- **Clarify, complete, and validate requirements**   Used as a requirements tool, the prototype assists in obtaining agreement, finding errors and omissions, and assessing the accuracy and quality of the requirements. User evaluation of the prototype points out problems with requirements and uncovers overlooked requirements, which you can correct at low cost before you construct the actual product. This is especially helpful for parts of the system that are not well understood or are particularly risky or complex.

- **Explore design alternatives**   Used as a design tool, a prototype lets stakeholders explore different user interaction techniques, envision the final product, optimize system usability, and evaluate potential technical approaches. Prototypes can demonstrate requirements feasibility through working designs. They're useful for confirming the developer's understanding of the requirements before constructing the actual solution.

- **Create a subset that will grow into the ultimate product**   Used as a construction tool, a prototype is a functional implementation of a subset of the product, which can be elaborated into the complete product through a sequence of small-scale development cycles. This is a safe approach only if the prototype is carefully designed with eventual release intended from the beginning.

The primary reason for creating a prototype is to resolve uncertainties early in the development process. You don't need to prototype the entire product. Focus on high-risk areas or known uncertainties to decide which parts of the system to prototype and what you hope to learn from the prototype evaluations. A prototype is useful for revealing and resolving ambiguity and incompleteness in the requirements. Users, managers, and other nontechnical stakeholders find that prototypes give them something concrete to contemplate while the product is being specified and designed. For each prototype you create, make sure you know—and communicate—why you're creating it, what you expect to learn from it, and what you'll do with the prototype after you've had people evaluate it.

Because of the risk of confusion, it's important to put some descriptors in front of the word "prototype" so the project participants understand why and when you might create one type of prototype or another. This chapter describes three classes of prototype attributes, each of which has two alternatives:

- **Scope** A mock-up prototype focuses on the user experience; a proof-of-concept prototype explores the technical soundness of a proposed approach.

- **Future use** A throwaway prototype is discarded after it has been used to generate feedback, whereas an evolutionary prototype grows into the final product through a series of iterations.

- **Form** A paper prototype is a simple sketch drawn on paper, a whiteboard, or in a drawing tool. An electronic prototype consists of working software for just part of the solution.

Each prototype you create will possess a specific combination of these attributes. For instance, you could devise a throwaway paper mock-up having simple drawings of possible screens. Or you might build an evolutionary electronic proof-of-concept, working software that demonstrates a desired technical capability that you can then grow into a deliverable product. Certain combinations don't make sense, though. For instance, you couldn't create an evolutionary paper proof of concept.

Mock-ups and proofs of concept

When people say "software prototype," they are usually thinking about a *mock-up* of a possible user interface. A mock-up is also called a *horizontal prototype*. Such a prototype focuses on a portion of the user interface; it doesn't dive into all the architectural layers or into detailed functionality. This type of prototype lets you explore some specific behaviors of the intended system, with the goal of refining the requirements. The mock-up helps users judge whether a system based on the prototype will let them do their job in a reasonable way.

A mock-up implies behavior without actually implementing it. It displays the facades of user interface screens and permits some navigation between them, but it contains little or no real functionality. Think of the set for a Western movie: the cowboy walks into the saloon and then walks out of the livery stable, yet he doesn't have a drink and he doesn't see a horse because there's nothing behind the false fronts of the buildings.

Mock-ups can demonstrate the functional options the user will have available, the look and feel of the user interface (colors, layout, graphics, controls), and the navigation structure. The navigations might work, but at certain points the user might see only a message that describes what would really be displayed or will find that some controls don't do anything. The information that appears in response to a database query could be faked or constant, and report contents are hardcoded. If you create a mock-up, try to use actual data in sample displays and outputs. This enhances the validity of the prototype as a model of the real system, but be sure to make it clear to the prototype evaluators that the displays and outputs are simulated, not live.

A mock-up doesn't perform any useful work, although it looks as if it should. The simulation is often good enough to let the users judge whether any functionality is missing, wrong, or unnecessary. Some prototypes represent the developer's concept of how a specific use case might be implemented. User evaluations of the prototype can point out alternative flows for the use case, missing interaction steps, additional exceptions, overlooked postconditions, and pertinent business rules.

When working with a throwaway mock-up prototype, the user should focus on broad requirements and workflow issues without becoming distracted by the precise appearance of screen elements (Constantine 1998). Don't worry at this stage about exactly where the screen elements will be positioned, fonts, colors, or graphics. The time to explore the specifics of user interface design is after you've clarified the requirements and determined the general structure of the interface. With an evolutionary mock-up, building in those refinements moves the user interface closer to being releasable.

A *proof of concept*, also known as a *vertical prototype*, implements a slice of application functionality from the user interface through all the technical services layers. A proof-of-concept prototype works like the real system is supposed to work because it touches on all levels of the system implementation. Develop a proof of concept when you're uncertain whether a proposed architectural approach is feasible and sound, or when you want to optimize algorithms, evaluate a proposed database schema, confirm the soundness of a cloud solution, or test critical timing requirements. To make the results meaningful, such prototypes are constructed by using production tools in a production-like operating environment. A proof of concept is also useful for gathering information to improve the team's ability to estimate the effort involved in implementing a specific user story or block of functionality. Agile development projects sometimes refer to a proof-of-concept prototype as a "spike."

I once worked with a team that wanted to implement an unusual client/server architecture as part of a transitional strategy from a mainframe-centric world to an application environment based on networked UNIX servers and workstations (Thompson and Wiegers 1995). A proof-of-concept prototype that implemented just a bit of the user interface client (on a mainframe) and the corresponding server functionality (on a UNIX workstation) allowed us to evaluate the communication components, performance, and reliability of our proposed architecture. The experiment was a success, as was the ultimate implementation based on that architecture.

Throwaway and evolutionary prototypes

Before constructing a prototype, make an explicit and well-communicated decision as to whether the prototype is exploratory only or will become part of the delivered product. Build a *throwaway prototype* to answer questions, resolve uncertainties, and improve requirements quality (Davis 1993). Because you'll discard the prototype after it has served its purpose, build it as quickly and cheaply as you can. The more effort you invest in the prototype, the more reluctant the project participants are to discard it and the less time you will have available to build the real product.

You don't have to throw the prototype away if you see merit in keeping it for possible future use. However, it won't be incorporated into the delivered product. For this reason, you might prefer to call it a *nonreleasable prototype*.

When developers build a throwaway prototype, they ignore solid software construction techniques. A throwaway prototype emphasizes quick implementation and modification over robustness, reliability, performance, and long-term maintainability. For this reason, you must not allow low-quality code from a throwaway prototype to migrate into a production system. If you do, the users and the maintainers will suffer the consequences for the life of the product.

A throwaway prototype is most appropriate when the team faces uncertainty, ambiguity, incompleteness, or vagueness in the requirements, or when they have difficulty envisioning the system from the requirements alone. Resolving these issues reduces the risks of proceeding with construction. A prototype that helps users and developers visualize how the requirements might be implemented can reveal gaps in the requirements. It also lets users judge whether the requirements will enable the necessary business processes.

> **Trap** Don't make a throwaway prototype more elaborate than is necessary to meet the prototyping objectives. Resist the temptation—or the pressure from users—to keep adding more capabilities to the prototype.

A *wireframe* is a particular approach to throwaway prototyping commonly used for custom user interface design and website design. You can use wireframes to reach a better understanding of three aspects of a website:

- The conceptual requirements

- The information architecture or navigation design

- The high-resolution, detailed design of the pages

The pages sketched when exploring conceptual requirements in the first type of wireframe need not resemble the final screens. This wireframe is useful for working with users to understand the types of activities they might want to perform at the screen. Paper prototypes can work fine for this purpose, as described later in this chapter. The second type of wireframe need not involve page designs at all. The analysis model called the dialog map, described in Chapter 12, "A picture is worth 1024 words," is an excellent tool for exploring and iterating on page navigation for a website. The third type of wireframe gets into the details of what the final pages would look like.

In contrast to a throwaway prototype, an *evolutionary prototype* provides a solid architectural foundation for building the product incrementally as the requirements become clear over time (McConnell 1996). Agile development provides an example of evolutionary prototyping. Agile teams construct the product through a series of iterations, using feedback on the early iterations to adjust the direction of future development cycles. This is the essence of evolutionary prototyping.

In contrast to the quick-and-dirty nature of throwaway prototyping, an evolutionary prototype must be built with robust, production-quality code from the outset. Therefore, an evolutionary prototype takes longer to create than a throwaway prototype that simulates the same system capabilities. An evolutionary prototype must be designed for easy growth and frequent enhancement, so developers must emphasize software architecture and solid design principles. There's no room for shortcuts in the quality of an evolutionary prototype.

Think of the first iteration of an evolutionary prototype as a pilot release that implements an initial portion of the requirements. Lessons learned from user acceptance testing and initial usage lead to modifications in the next iteration. The full product is the culmination of a series of evolutionary prototyping cycles. Such prototypes quickly get useful functionality into the hands of the users. Evolutionary prototypes work well for applications that you know will grow over time, but that can be valuable to users without having all the planned functionality implemented. Agile projects often are planned such that they could stop development at the end of an iteration and still have a product that is useful for customers, even though it is incomplete.

Evolutionary prototyping is well suited for web development projects. On one such project, my team created a series of four prototypes, based on requirements that we developed from a use case analysis. Several users evaluated each prototype, and we revised each one based on their responses to questions we posed. The revisions following the fourth prototype evaluation resulted in the production website.

Figure 15-1 illustrates several possible ways to combine the various prototypes. For example, you can use the knowledge gained from a series of throwaway prototypes to refine the requirements, which you might then implement incrementally through an evolutionary prototyping sequence. An alternative path through Figure 15-1 uses a throwaway mock-up to clarify the requirements prior to finalizing the user interface design, while a concurrent proof-of-concept prototyping effort validates the architecture and core algorithms. What you *cannot* do successfully is turn the deliberately low quality of a throwaway prototype into the maintainable robustness that a production system demands. In addition, working prototypes that appear to get the job done for a handful of concurrent users likely won't scale up to handle thousands of users without major architectural changes. Table 15-1 summarizes some typical applications of throwaway, evolutionary, mock-up, and proof-of-concept prototypes.

TABLE 15-1 Typical applications of software prototypes

	Throwaway	Evolutionary
Mock-up	■ Clarify and refine user and functional requirements. ■ Identify missing functionality. ■ Explore user interface approaches.	■ Implement core user requirements. ■ Implement additional user requirements based on priority. ■ Implement and refine websites. ■ Adapt system to rapidly changing business needs.
Proof of concept	■ Demonstrate technical feasibility. ■ Evaluate performance. ■ Acquire knowledge to improve estimates for construction.	■ Implement and grow core multi-tier functionality and communication layers. ■ Implement and optimize core algorithms. ■ Test and tune performance.

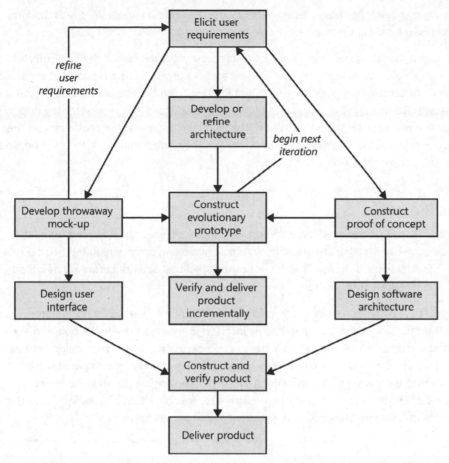

FIGURE 15-1 Several possible ways to incorporate prototyping into the software development process.

Paper and electronic prototypes

You don't always need an executable prototype to resolve requirements uncertainties. A *paper prototype* (sometimes called a *low-fidelity prototype*) is a cheap, fast, and low-tech way to explore how a portion of an implemented system might look (Rettig 1994). Paper prototypes help you test whether users and developers hold a shared understanding of the requirements. They let you take a tentative and low-risk step into a possible solution space prior to developing production code. A similar deliverable is called a *storyboard* (Leffingwell and Widrig 2000). Use low-fidelity prototypes to explore functionality and flow, and use high-fidelity prototypes to determine precise look and feel.

Paper prototypes involve tools no more sophisticated than paper, index cards, sticky notes, and whiteboards. The designer sketches ideas of possible screens without worrying about exactly where the controls appear and what they look like. Users willingly provide feedback on designs drawn on a piece of paper, although they're sometimes less eager to critique a lovely computer-based prototype in which it appears the developer has invested a lot of work. Developers, too, might resist making substantial changes in a carefully crafted electronic prototype.

When a low-fidelity prototype is being evaluated, someone plays the role of the computer while a user walks through an evaluation scenario. The user initiates actions by saying aloud what she would like to do at a specific screen: "I'm going to select Print Preview from the File menu." The person simulating the computer then displays the piece of paper or index card that represents the display that would appear when the user takes that action. The user can judge whether that is indeed the expected response and whether the item displayed contains the correct elements. If it's wrong, you simply take a blank page or index card and try again.

Off to see the wizard

A development team that designed large commercial photocopiers once lamented to me that their previous copier had a usability problem. A common copying activity required five discrete steps, which the users found clumsy. "I wish we'd prototyped that activity before we designed the copier," one developer said wistfully.

How do you prototype a product as complex as a photocopier? First, buy a refrigerator. Write *COPIER* on the side of the box that it came in. Have someone sit inside the box, and ask a user to stand outside the box and simulate doing copier activities. The person inside the box responds in the way he expects the copier to respond, and the user representative observes whether that response is what he has in mind. A simple, fun prototype like this—sometimes called a *Wizard of Oz prototype*—stimulates the early user feedback that effectively guides the development team's design decisions. Plus, you get to keep the refrigerator.

No matter how efficient your prototyping tools are, sketching displays on paper or a whiteboard is faster. Paper prototyping facilitates rapid iteration, and iteration is a key success factor in requirements development. Paper prototyping is an excellent technique for refining the requirements prior to designing detailed user interfaces, constructing an evolutionary prototype, or undertaking traditional design and construction activities. It also helps the development team manage customer expectations.

Numerous tools are available if you decide to build an electronic throwaway prototype. They range from simple drawing tools such as Microsoft Visio and Microsoft PowerPoint to commercial prototyping tools and graphical user interface builders. Tools also are available specifically for creating website wireframes. Such tools will let you easily implement and modify user interface components, regardless of how inefficient the temporary code behind the interface is. Of course, if you're building an evolutionary prototype, you must use production development tools from the outset. Because tools and their vendors change so rapidly, we won't suggest specific ones here.

Various tools are commercially available that let you simulate your application before you build it. Application simulation lets you quickly assemble screen layouts, user interface controls, navigation flow, and functionality into something that closely resembles the product you think you need to build. The ability to iterate on the simulation provides a valuable mechanism for interacting with user representatives to clarify requirements and revise your thinking about the solution.

With any kind of prototyping—paper prototypes, wireframes, electronic prototypes, or simulations—the business analyst must be careful not get drawn into high-precision user interface designs prematurely. Prototype evaluators often offer feedback like "Can this text be a little darker red?", "Let's move this box up just a little," or "I don't like that font." Unless the purpose of the prototype is to perform detailed screen or webpage design, those sorts of comments are just distractions. The color, font, and box positioning are immaterial if the application doesn't properly support the users' business tasks. Until you're sure you have a rich understanding of the necessary functionality, focus the prototyping efforts on refining requirements, not visual designs.

Working with prototypes

Figure 15-2 shows one possible sequence of development activities that moves from use cases to detailed user interface design with the help of a throwaway prototype. Each use case description includes a sequence of actor actions and system responses, which you can model by using a dialog map to depict a possible user interface architecture. A throwaway prototype or a wireframe elaborates the dialog elements into specific screens, menus, and dialog boxes. When users evaluate the prototype, their feedback might lead to changes in the use case descriptions (if, say, an alternative flow is discovered) or to changes in the dialog map. After the requirements are refined and the screens sketched, each user interface element can be optimized for usability. These activities don't need to be performed strictly sequentially. Iterating on the use case, the dialog map, and the wireframe is the best way to quickly reach an acceptable and agreed-upon approach to user interface design.

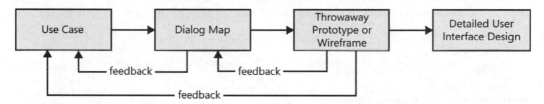

FIGURE 15-2 Activity sequence from use cases to user interface design using a throwaway prototype.

This progressive refinement approach is cheaper than leaping directly from use case descriptions to a complete user interface implementation and then discovering major issues that necessitate extensive rework. You only need to perform as many steps in this sequence as are necessary to acceptably reduce the risk of going wrong on the user interface design. If your team is confident that they understand the requirements, that the requirements are sufficiently complete, and that they have a good handle on the right UI to build, then there's little point in prototyping. Also, you can focus prototyping on user requirements that have a big risk of error or a big impact if there is a problem. One project performed an e-commerce website redesign for a major corporation that would be used by millions of users. The team prototyped the core elements of the website, including the online catalog, shopping cart, and checkout process, to make sure they got those right the first time. They spent less time exploring exception paths and less commonly used scenarios.

To help make this whole process more tangible, let's look at an actual example, a small website to promote a book, a memoir of life lessons called *Pearls from Sand*. The author of the book (Karl, actually) thought of several things that visitors should be able to do at the website, each of which is a use case. There are additional use cases for other user classes (Table 15-2).

TABLE 15-2 Some use cases for PearlsFromSand.com

User class	Use case
Visitor	Get Information about the Book Get Information about the Author Read Sample Chapters Read the Blog Contact the Author
Customer	Order a Product Download an Electronic Product Request Assistance with a Problem
Administrator	Manage the Product List Issue a Refund to a Customer Manage the Email List

The next step was to think of the pages the website should provide and imagine the navigation pathways between them. The final website might not implement all of these pages separately. Some pages might be condensed together; others might function as pop-ups or other modifications of a single page. Figure 15-3 illustrates a portion of a dialog map that illustrates a conceptual page architecture. Each box represents a page that would contribute to providing the services identified in the use cases. The arrows represent links to enable navigation from one page to another. While drawing a dialog map, you might discover new actions a user would want to perform. While working through a use case, you might find ways to simplify and streamline the user's experience.

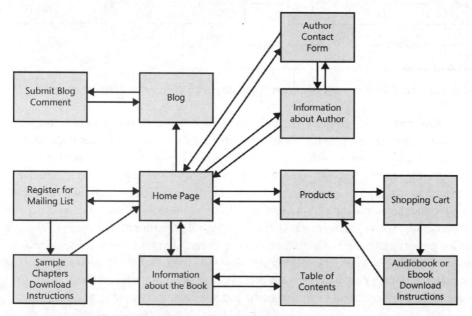

FIGURE 15-3 Partial dialog map for PearlsFromSand.com.

The next step was to construct a throwaway prototype or a wireframe of selected pages to work out the visual design approach. Each of these can be a hand-drawn sketch on paper (see the example in Figure 10-1 in Chapter 10, "Documenting the requirements"), a simple line drawing, or a mock-up created with a dedicated prototyping or visual design tool. The wireframe illustrated in Figure 15-4 was drawn by using PowerPoint in just a few minutes. Such a simple diagram is a tool to work with user representatives to understand the broad strokes of what sort of page layout and cosmetic features would make the pages easy to understand and use.

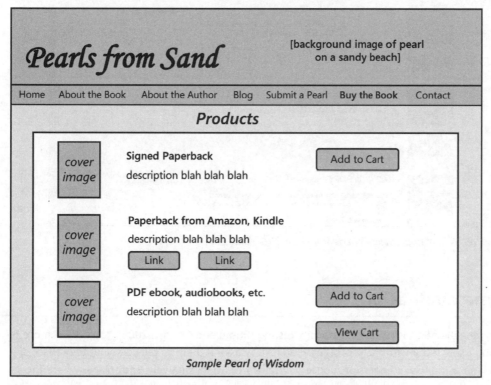

FIGURE 15-4 Sample wireframe of one page for PearlsFromSand.com.

Finally, the fourth step illustrated in Figure 15-2 is to create a detailed user interface screen design. Figure 15-5 shows one final page from the PearlsFromSand.com website, the culmination of the requirements analysis and prototyping activities that came before. This iterative approach to user interface design leads to better results than diving immediately into high-resolution page design without having a clear understanding of what members of various user classes will want to do when they visit a website.

FIGURE 15-5 A final implemented page from PearlsFromSand.com.

Prototype evaluation

Prototype evaluation is related to usability testing (Rubin and Chisnell 2008). You'll learn more by watching users work with the prototype than just by asking them to tell you what they think of it. Watch where the user's fingers or mouse pointer try to go instinctively. Spot places where the prototype conflicts with the behavior of other applications that the evaluators use. The evaluator might try incorrect keyboard shortcuts or have to "mouse around" hunting for the correct menu option. Look for the furrowed brow that indicates a puzzled user who can't determine what to do next, how to navigate to a desired destination, or how to take a side trip to another part of the application. See if the prototype has any dead ends, as happens sometimes when a user submits a form on a website.

Have the right people evaluate the prototype from the appropriate perspectives. Include members of multiple user classes, both experienced and inexperienced. When you present the prototype to the evaluators, stress that it addresses only a portion of the functionality; the rest will be implemented when the actual system is developed.

> **Trap** As with any usability testing, watch out for omitting members of significant user classes from the prototype evaluation. A novice user might love a prototype for its apparent ease of use, but a more experienced or power user could hate the way it slows him down. Make sure both groups are represented.

To improve the evaluation of user interface prototypes, create scripts that guide the users through a series of operations and ask specific questions to elicit the information you seek. This supplements a general invitation to "tell me what you think of this prototype." Derive the evaluation scripts from the use cases, user stories, or features that the prototype addresses. The script asks evaluators to perform specific tasks, working through the parts of the prototype that have the most uncertainty. At the end of each task, and possibly at intermediate points, the script presents specific task-related questions. You might also ask general questions like the following:

- Does the prototype implement the functionality in the way you expected?

- What functionality is missing from the prototype?

- Can you think of any possible error conditions that the prototype doesn't address?

- Are any unnecessary functions present?

- How logical and complete does the navigation seem to you?

- Are there ways to simplify any of the tasks that require too many interaction steps?

- Were you ever unsure of what to do next?

Ask evaluators to share their thoughts aloud as they work with the prototype so that you understand what they're thinking and can detect any issues that the prototype handles poorly. Create a nonjudgmental environment in which the evaluators feel free to express their thoughts, ideas, and concerns. Avoid coaching users on the "right" way to perform some function with the prototype.

Document what you learn from the prototype evaluation. Use the information from a mock-up prototype to refine the requirements. If the evaluation led to some user-interface design decisions, such as the selection of specific interaction techniques, record those conclusions and how you arrived at them. Decisions that lack the accompanying thought processes tend to be revisited repeatedly. For a proof of concept, document the evaluations you performed and their results, culminating in the decisions you made about the technical approaches explored. Resolve any conflicts between the specified requirements and the prototype.

Risks of prototyping

Creating even a simple prototype costs time and money. Although prototyping reduces the risk of software project failure, it poses its own risks, some of which are explained in this section.

Pressure to release the prototype

The biggest risk is that a stakeholder will see a running throwaway prototype and conclude that the product is nearly completed. "Wow, it looks like you're almost done!" says the enthusiastic prototype evaluator. "This looks great. Can you just finish this up and give it to me?"

In a word: NO! A throwaway prototype is never intended for production use, no matter how much it looks like the real thing. It is merely a model, a simulation, an experiment. Unless there's a compelling business motivation to achieve a marketplace presence immediately (and management accepts the resulting high maintenance burden and risk of annoyed users), resist the pressure to deliver a throwaway prototype. Delivering this prototype will likely delay the project's completion because the design and code were intentionally created without regard to quality or durability. Expectation management is a key to successful prototyping. Everyone who sees the prototype must understand its purpose and its limitations. Be clear about why you are creating specific kinds of prototypes, decide what their ultimate fate will be, and communicate this clearly to those stakeholders who are involved with them.

Don't let the fear of premature delivery pressure dissuade you from creating prototypes, though. Make it clear to those who see the prototype that you will not release it as production software. One way to control this risk is to use paper, rather than electronic, prototypes. No one who evaluates a paper prototype will think the product is nearly done! Another option is to use prototyping tools that are different from those used for actual development. No one will mistake a navigable PowerPoint mock-up or a simple wireframe for the real thing. This will help you resist pressure to "just finish up" the prototype and ship it. Leaving the prototype looking a bit rough and unpolished also mitigates this risk. Some of the many tools available for creating wireframes allow for the quick development of a high-fidelity user interface. This increases the likelihood of people expecting that the software is almost done, and it adds to the pressure to transform a throwaway prototype into an evolutionary one.

One developer cobbled together an executable prototype of a user interface with a shocking pink motif. As he explained it, "When we showed the customers the first couple of iterations with this color scheme, NO ONE thought this was a close-to-finished product. I actually retained that abomination for an additional iteration just to avoid falling into some of these prototyping risk traps."

Distraction by details

Another risk of prototyping is that users become fixated on details about how the user interface will look and operate. When working with real-looking prototypes, it's easy for users to forget that they should be primarily concerned with conceptual issues at the requirements stage. Limit the prototype to the displays, functions, and navigation options that will let you clear up uncertain requirements.

Baby with the bath water

I once consulted at a company where a senior manager had banned prototyping. He had seen projects in which customers pressured developers into delivering throwaway prototypes prematurely as the final product, with predictable results. The prototypes did not handle user errors or bad input data well, did not cover all the options users wanted, and were difficult to maintain and enhance. These unpleasant experiences led the senior manager to conclude that prototyping could only lead to trouble.

As you've seen in this chapter, delivering to customers a prototype that was intended to be discarded and calling it a product certainly will cause problems. Nonetheless, prototyping offers a range of powerful techniques that can contribute substantially to building the right product. Rather than dismissing prototyping as a dangerous method to be avoided, it's important to make sure everyone involved understands the various kinds of prototypes, why a particular prototype is being created, and how the results will be used.

Unrealistic performance expectations

A third risk is that users will infer the expected performance of the final product from the prototype's performance. You won't be evaluating a mock-up in the intended production environment, though. You might have built it using tools or languages that differ in efficiency from the production development tools, such as interpreted scripts versus compiled code. A proof-of-concept prototype might not use tuned algorithms, or it could lack security layers that will reduce the ultimate performance. If evaluators see the prototype respond instantaneously to a simulated database query using hard-coded sample query results, they might expect the same fabulous performance in the production software with an enormous distributed database. Consider building in time delays to more realistically simulate the expected behavior of the final product—and perhaps to make the prototype look even less ready for immediate delivery. You might put a message on the screen to clearly state that this is not necessarily representative of the final system.

In agile development and other evolutionary prototyping situations, be sure to design a robust and extendable architecture and craft high-quality code from the beginning. You're building production software, just a small portion at a time. You can tune up the design through refactoring in later iterations, but don't substitute refactoring in the future for thinking about design today.

Investing excessive effort in prototypes

Finally, beware of prototyping activities that consume so much effort that the development team runs out of time and is forced to deliver the prototype as the product or to rush through a haphazard product implementation. This can happen when you are prototyping the whole solution rather than only the most uncertain, high-risk, or complex portions. Treat a prototype as an experiment. You're testing the hypothesis that the requirements are sufficiently defined and the key human-computer interface and architectural issues are resolved so that design and construction can proceed. Do just enough prototyping to test the hypothesis, answer the questions, and refine the requirements.

Prototyping success factors

Software prototyping provides a powerful set of techniques that can minimize development schedules, ensure customer satisfaction, and produce high-quality products. To make prototyping an effective part of your requirements process, follow these guidelines:

- Include prototyping tasks in your project plan. Schedule time and resources to develop, evaluate, and modify the prototypes.

- State the purpose of each prototype before you build it, and explain what will happen with the outcome: either discard (or archive) the prototype, retaining the knowledge it provided, or build upon it to grow it into the ultimate solution. Make sure those who build the prototypes and those who evaluate them understand these intentions.

- Plan to develop multiple prototypes. You'll rarely get them right on the first try, which is the whole point of prototyping!

- Create throwaway prototypes as quickly and cheaply as possible. Invest the minimum amount of effort that will answer questions or resolve requirements uncertainties. Don't try to perfect a throwaway prototype.

- Don't include input data validations, defensive coding techniques, error-handling code, or extensive code documentation in a throwaway prototype. It's an unnecessary investment of effort that you're just going to discard.

- Don't prototype requirements that you already understand, except to explore design alternatives.

- Use plausible data in prototype screen displays and reports. Evaluators can be distracted by unrealistic data and fail to focus on the prototype as a model of how the real system might look and behave.

- Don't expect a prototype to replace written requirements. A lot of behind-the-scenes functionality is only implied by the prototype and should be documented in an SRS to make it complete, specific, and traceable. Screen images don't give the details of data field definitions and validation criteria, relationships between fields (such as UI controls that appear only if the user makes certain selections in other controls), exception handling, business rules, and other essential bits of information.

Thoughtfully applied and skillfully executed, prototypes serve as a valuable tool to help with requirements elicitation, requirements validation, and that tricky translation from needs into solutions.

Next steps

- Identify a portion of your project that exhibits confusion about requirements or is a high-risk area of functionality. Sketch out a portion of a possible user interface that represents your understanding of the requirements and how they might be implemented—a paper prototype. Have some users walk through your prototype to simulate performing a usage scenario. Identify places where the initial requirements were incomplete or incorrect. Modify the prototype accordingly and walk through it again to confirm that the shortcomings are corrected.

- Summarize this chapter for your prototype evaluators to help them understand the rationale behind the prototyping activities and to help them have realistic expectations for the outcome.

- If your product is a hardware device, think of a way you can physically simulate it so users can interact with it to validate and flesh out their requirements.

CHAPTER 16

First things first: Setting requirement priorities

After most of the user requirements for the Chemical Tracking System were identified, the project manager, Dave, and the business analyst, Lori, met with two of the product champions. Tim represented the chemist community and Roxanne spoke for the chemical stockroom staff.

Dave said, "Now that we have a general idea of the main capabilities you want, we need to think about allocating some of the user stories you've identified to the first few iterations. It's important that we agree on where to start so you can begin getting some value from the system as quickly as possible. Let's do a first-cut prioritization on these user stories so we know what's most important to you. Then we can learn more about exactly what you expect from each of those initial capabilities."

Tim was puzzled. "Why do you need the requirements prioritized? They're all important, or we wouldn't have given them to you."

Lori, the BA, explained, "We know they're all important, but we need to address the most urgent requirements in the first few iterations. We're asking you to help us distinguish the requirements that must be included initially from those that can wait for later iterations. Can you think of certain functionality that would provide the greatest immediate value to chemists or other user classes?"

"I know that the reports that the Health and Safety Department needs to generate for the government have to be available soon or the company will get in trouble," Roxanne pointed out. "We can use our current inventory system for a few more months if we have to."

Tim added, "I promised the online catalog search function to the chemists as a way for this system to save them time. Can we please start on that right away? It doesn't have to be perfect, but we want to get access to the catalogs as quickly as we can."

Tim and Roxanne realized that, because the project couldn't deliver every desired feature at the same time, it would be better if everyone could agree on the set to implement first. They continued sorting their user stories into a top-priority category for early implementation and others that could wait a while.

Few software projects deliver all the capabilities that all stakeholders want by the targeted initial delivery date. Every project with resource limitations needs to define the relative priorities of the requested product capabilities. Prioritization, also called *requirements triage* (Davis 2005), helps reveal competing goals, resolve conflicts, plan for staged or incremental deliveries, control scope creep, and make the necessary trade-off decisions. This chapter discusses the importance of prioritizing requirements, describes several prioritization techniques, and presents a spreadsheet tool for prioritization analysis based on value, cost, and risk.

Why prioritize requirements?

When customer expectations are high and timelines are short, you need to make sure the product delivers the most critical or valuable functionality as early as possible. Prioritization is a way to deal with competing demands for limited resources. Establishing the relative priority of each product capability lets you plan construction to provide the highest value at the lowest cost. Because prioritization is relative, you can begin prioritization as soon as you discover your second requirement.

Sometimes customers don't like to prioritize requirements, thinking that they won't ever get the ones that are low priority. Well, if you aren't going to get everything you'd like, as is often the case, you should make sure that you *do* get the capabilities that are most important to achieving your business objectives. Sometimes developers don't like to prioritize requirements because it gives the impression that they can't do it all. The reality is that they can't, at least not all at once. Prioritization helps the project deliver the maximum business value as quickly as possible within the project constraints.

Prioritization is a critical strategy for agile or other projects that develop products through a series of fixed-schedule timeboxes. Project teams can populate their product backlog with user stories, features, business processes, and defect stories (bugs awaiting correction). Customers prioritize the stories in the backlog and select which ones they'd like to have implemented in each development iteration. Developers estimate the effort involved with implementing each story and judge how many of these stories they can fit into each iteration, based on their empirically demonstrated delivery capacity as measured by the team's velocity. As new stories are proposed, customers assess their priorities against the contents of the backlog, thus dynamically adjusting scope for the upcoming iterations. All projects should do this to ensure that the team is always working on those capabilities that will get useful software in the users' hands as soon as possible.

On every project, a project manager must balance the desired project scope against the constraints of schedule, budget, staff, and quality goals (Wiegers 1996). One way to accomplish this is to drop—or to defer to a later release—low-priority requirements when new, more essential requirements are accepted or when other project conditions change. That is, prioritization is a dynamic and ongoing process. If customers don't distinguish their requirements by importance and urgency, project managers must make these decisions on their own. Not surprisingly, customers might not agree with a project manager's priorities; therefore, customers must indicate which requirements are needed initially and which can wait. Establish priorities early in the project, when you have more flexibility for achieving a successful project outcome, and revisit them periodically.

It's difficult enough to get any one customer to decide which of his requirements are top priority. Achieving consensus among multiple customers with diverse expectations is even harder.

People naturally have their own interests at heart and aren't eager to compromise their needs for someone else's benefit. However, contributing to requirements prioritization is one of the customer's responsibilities in the customer-development partnership, as was discussed in Chapter 2, "Requirements from the customer's perspective." More than simply defining the sequence of requirements implementation, discussing priorities helps to clarify the customers' expectations.

Some prioritization pragmatics

Even a medium-sized project can have dozens of user requirements and hundreds of functional requirements, too many to classify analytically and consistently. To keep it manageable, choose an appropriate level of abstraction for the prioritization—features, use cases, user stories, or functional requirements. Within a use case, some alternative flows could have a higher priority than others. You might decide to do an initial prioritization at the feature level and then to prioritize the functional requirements within certain features separately. This will help you to distinguish the core functionality from refinements that can be deferred or cut entirely. As was described in Chapter 5, "Establishing the business requirements," feature prioritization feeds directly into scope and release planning. Don't lose sight of the low-priority requirements, although there's no point in analyzing them further just yet. Their priority might change later, and knowing about them now will help the developers plan for future enhancements.

Various stakeholders need to participate in prioritization, representing customers, project sponsors, project management, development, and perhaps other perspectives. You really need one ultimate decision maker when stakeholders can't agree. A good starting point is for the prioritization participants to agree upon a set of criteria to use for judging whether one requirement has higher priority than another. The prioritization can include considerations of customer value, business value, business or technical risk, cost, difficulty of implementation, time to market, regulatory or policy compliance, competitive marketplace advantage, and contractual commitments (Gottesdiener 2005). Alan Davis (2005) indicates that successful prioritization requires an understanding of six issues:

- The needs of the customers

- The relative importance of requirements to the customers

- The timing at which capabilities need to be delivered

- Requirements that serve as predecessors for other requirements and other relationships among requirements

- Which requirements must be implemented as a group

- The cost to satisfy each requirement

Customers place a high priority on those functions that provide the greatest business or usability benefit. However, after a developer points out the cost, difficulty, technical risk, or trade-offs associated with a specific requirement, the customers might conclude that it isn't as essential as they first thought. The developer might also decide to implement certain lower-priority functions early on because of their effect on the system's architecture, laying the foundation to implement future functionality efficiently without major restructuring. Some functionality must have high priority because it is required to meet regulatory demands for the application. As with all aspects of requirements development, the overarching business objectives that led to launching the project in the first place should drive priority decisions.

Certain requirements must be implemented together or in a specific sequence. It makes no sense to implement a redo edit capability in release 1 but not implement the corresponding undo capability until some months later. Similarly, suppose you implement just the normal flow of a particular use case in release 1, deferring the lower-priority alternative flows to some later date. That's fine, but you must also implement the corresponding exception handlers at the same time you implement each success flow. Otherwise, you could end up writing code to, say, accept credit card payments without checking to see if the card is valid, rejecting cards that were reported stolen, or handling other exceptions.

Games people play with priorities

The knee-jerk response to a request for customers to set priorities sometimes is, "I need all these features. Just make it happen." They feel that every requirement should be ranked as high priority, and they might not recognize that prioritization will help to ensure the project's success. Start by explaining that all things cannot be done simultaneously, so you want to make sure you work on the right things first. It can be difficult to persuade customers to discuss priorities if they know that low-priority requirements might never be implemented. One developer told me that it wasn't politically acceptable in his company to say that a requirement had low priority. Therefore, the priority categories they adopted were "high," "super-high," and "incredibly high." Another developer who was filling the BA role claimed that priorities weren't necessary: if he wrote something in the SRS, he intended to build it. That doesn't address the issue of *when* each piece of functionality gets built, though.

I recently visited one company that had great difficulty getting their projects done on time. Although management claimed that there would be multiple releases of applications so lower-priority requirements could wait, in reality each project delivered just a single release. Consequently, the stakeholders all knew that they only had one shot to get all the functionality they needed. Every requirement, therefore, became high priority, overloading the team's capacity to deliver.

In reality, some system capabilities are more essential than others from the perspective of satisfying business objectives. This becomes apparent during the all-too-common "rapid descoping phase" late in the project, when nonessential features are jettisoned to ensure that the critical capabilities ship on schedule. At that point, people are clearly making priority decisions, but in a panicked state. Setting priorities early in the project and reassessing them in response to changing customer preferences, market conditions, and business events lets the team spend time wisely on high-value activities. Implementing most of a feature before you conclude that it isn't necessary is wasteful and frustrating.

If left to their own devices, customers will establish perhaps 85 percent of the requirements as high priority, 10 percent as medium, and 5 percent as low. This doesn't give the project manager much flexibility. If all requirements truly are of top priority, your project has a high risk of not being fully successful. Scrub the requirements to eliminate any that aren't essential and to simplify those that are unnecessarily complex. One study found that nearly two-thirds of the features developed in software systems are rarely or never used (The Standish Group 2009). To encourage customers to acknowledge that some requirements have lower priority, the analyst can ask questions such as the following:

- Is there some other way to satisfy the need that this requirement addresses?

- What would the consequences be of omitting or deferring this requirement?

- What effect would it have on the project's business objectives if this requirement weren't implemented for several months?

- Why might a customer be unhappy if this requirement were deferred to a later release?

- Is having this feature worth delaying release of all of the other features with this same priority?

> **Important** If you go through a prioritization process and all of the requirements come out with about the same priority, you really haven't prioritized them at all.

When you evaluate priorities, look at the connections and interrelationships among requirements and their alignment with the project's business objectives. The management team on one large commercial project displayed impatience over the analyst's insistence on prioritizing the requirements. The managers pointed out that often they can do without a particular feature but that another feature might need to be beefed up to compensate. If they deferred too many requirements, the resulting product wouldn't achieve the projected revenue.

Conflicts arise among stakeholders who are convinced that *their* requirements are the most important. As a general rule, members of the favored user classes should get preference in the case of competing priorities. This is one reason to identify and assess your user classes early in the project.

Some prioritization techniques

On a small project, the stakeholders should be able to agree on requirement priorities informally. Large or contentious projects with many stakeholders demand a more structured approach that removes some of the emotion, politics, and guesswork from the process. Several analytical and mathematical techniques have been proposed to assist with requirements prioritization. These methods involve estimating the relative value and relative cost of each requirement. The highest priority requirements are those that provide the largest fraction of the total product value at the smallest fraction of the total cost (Karlsson and Ryan 1997; Jung 1998). This section discusses several techniques people use for prioritizing requirements. Simpler is better, provided the technique is effective.

> **Trap** Avoid "decibel prioritization," in which the loudest voice heard gets top priority, and "threat prioritization," in which stakeholders holding the most political power always get what they demand.

In or out

The simplest of all prioritization methods is to have a group of stakeholders work down a list of requirements and make a binary decision: is it in, or is it out? Keep referring to the project's business objectives to make this judgment, paring the list down to the bare minimum needed for the first release. Then, when implementation of that release is under way, you can go back to the previously "out" requirements and go through the process again for the next release.

Pop goes the requirement

I once facilitated a workshop that had six stakeholders in the room and four more on the phone. We had 400 requirements to prioritize. We opted to decide simply if each was in or out, then figured we'd deal with the "out" ones for the next release. We blocked off several hours in this room to grind through the list. One executive stakeholder had the final prioritization decision when there were conflicts. Shortly into this meeting, he realized that the day was going to be long and monotonous. He decided to have some fun. Every time the team cut a requirement, he made an explosion sound, like blowing up the requirement. It was a fun way to cut scope.

Pairwise comparison and rank ordering

People sometimes try to assign a unique priority sequence number to each requirement. Rank ordering a list of requirements involves making pairwise comparisons between all of them so you can judge which member of each pair has higher priority. Figure 14-1 in Chapter 14, "Beyond functionality," illustrated the use of a spreadsheet to perform just such a pairwise comparison of quality attributes; the same strategy could be applied to a set of features, user stories, or any other set of requirements of the same type. Performing such comparisons becomes unwieldy for more than a couple of dozen requirements. It could work at the granularity level of features, but not for all the functional requirements for a system as a whole.

In reality, rank ordering all of the requirements by priority is overkill. You won't be implementing all of these in individual releases; instead, you'll group them together in batches by release or development timebox. Grouping requirements into features, or into small sets of requirements that have similar priority or that otherwise must be implemented together, is sufficient.

Three-level scale

A common prioritization approach groups requirements into three categories. No matter how you label them, if you're using three categories they boil down to high, medium, and low priority. Such prioritization scales are subjective and imprecise. To make the scale useful, the stakeholders must agree on what each level means in the scale they use.

One way to assess priority is to consider the two dimensions of *importance* and *urgency* (Covey 2004). Every requirement can be considered as being either important to achieving business objectives or not so important, and as being either urgent or not so urgent. This is a relative assessment among a set of requirements, not an absolute binary distinction. As Figure 16-1 shows, these alternatives yield four possible combinations, which you can use to define a priority scale:

- *High-priority* requirements are both important (customers need the capability) and urgent (customers need it in the next release). Alternatively, contractual or compliance obligations might dictate that a specific requirement must be included, or there might be compelling business reasons to implement it promptly. If you can wait to implement a requirement in a later release without adverse consequences, then it is not high priority per this definition.

- *Medium-priority* requirements are important (customers need the capability) but not urgent (they can wait for a later release).

- *Low-priority* requirements are neither important (customers can live without the capability if necessary) nor urgent (customers can wait, perhaps forever).

- Requirements in the fourth quadrant appear to be urgent to some stakeholder, perhaps for political reasons, but they really aren't important to achieving the business objectives. Don't waste your time working on these, because they don't add sufficient value to the product. If they aren't important, either set them to low priority or scrub them entirely.

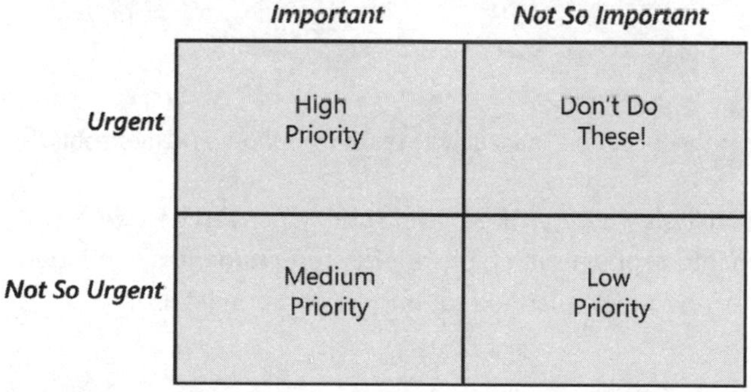

	Important	*Not So Important*
Urgent	High Priority	Don't Do These!
Not So Urgent	Medium Priority	Low Priority

FIGURE 16-1 Requirements prioritization based on importance and urgency.

Include the priority of each requirement as an attribute of the requirement in the user requirements documents, the SRS, or the requirements database. Establish a convention so that the reader knows whether the priority assigned to a high-level requirement is inherited by all its subordinate requirements or whether every individual functional requirement is to have its own priority attribute.

Sometimes, particularly on a large project, you might want to perform prioritization iteratively. Have the team rate requirements as high, medium, or low priority. If the number of high-priority requirements is excessive and you're not convinced that they all really *must* be delivered in the next release, perform a second-level partitioning of the high-priority ones into three groups. You could call them high, higher, and highest if you like, so people don't lose sight of the fact that they were originally designated as being important. The requirements rated "highest" become your new group of top-priority requirements. Group the "high" and "higher" requirements in with your original medium-priority group (Figure 16-2). Taking a hard line on the criterion of "must be in the next release or that release is not shippable" helps keep the team focused on the truly high-priority capabilities.

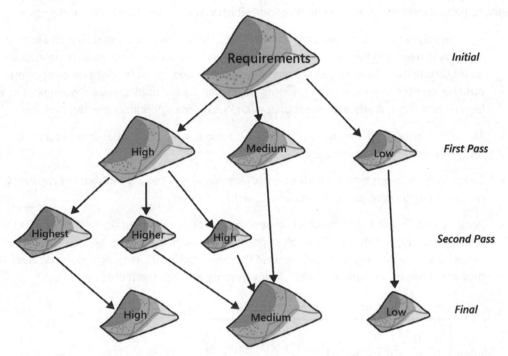

FIGURE 16-2 Multipass prioritization keeps the focus on a manageable set of top-priority requirements.

When performing a prioritization analysis with the three-level scale, you need be aware of requirement dependencies. You'll run into problems if a high-priority requirement is dependent on another that is ranked lower in priority and hence planned for implementation later on.

MoSCoW

The four capitalized letters in the MoSCoW prioritization scheme stand for four possible priority classifications for the requirements in a set (IIBA 2009):

- **M**ust: The requirement must be satisfied for the solution to be considered a success.

- **S**hould: The requirement is important and should be included in the solution if possible, but it's not mandatory to success.

- **C**ould: It's a desirable capability, but one that could be deferred or eliminated. Implement it only if time and resources permit.

- **W**on't: This indicates a requirement that will not be implemented at this time but could be included in a future release.

The MoSCoW scheme changes the three-level scale of high, medium, and low into a four-level scale. It doesn't offer any rationale for making the decision about how to rate the priority of a given requirement compared to others. MoSCoW is ambiguous as to timing, particularly when it comes to the "Won't" rating. "Won't" could mean either "not in the next release" or "not ever." Such distinctions must be made clear so that all stakeholders share a common understanding of the implications of a particular priority rating. The three-level scale described previously, which relies on analysis of the two dimensions of importance and urgency, and focuses specifically on the forthcoming release or development timebox, is a crisper way to think about priorities. We don't recommend MoSCoW.

MoSCoW in practice

One consultant described how a client company actually practiced the MoSCoW method on its projects. "All the action centers around getting an 'M' for almost every feature or requirement that is captured," he said. "If something is not an 'M' it will almost certainly not get built. Although the original intent may have been to prioritize, users have long since figured out to never submit something that does not have an 'M' associated with it. Do they understand the nuanced differences between S, C, and W? I have no idea. But they have figured out the implications of these rankings. They treat them all the same and understand their meaning to be 'not happening any time soon'."

$100

Prioritization is about thoughtfully allocating limited resources to achieve the maximum benefit from the investment an organization makes in a project. One way to make prioritization more tangible is to cast it in terms of an actual resource: money. In this case, it's just play money, but money nonetheless.

Give the prioritization team 100 imaginary dollars to work with. Team members allocate these dollars to "buy" items that they would like to have implemented from the complete set of candidate requirements. They weight the higher-priority requirements more heavily by allocating more dollars to them. If one requirement is three times as important to a stakeholder as another requirement, she would assign perhaps nine dollars to the first requirement and three dollars to the second. But 100 dollars is all the prioritizers get—when they are out of money, nothing else can be implemented, at least not in the release they are currently focusing on. One approach is to have different participants in the prioritization process perform their own dollar allocations, then add up the total number of dollars assigned to each requirement to see which ones collectively come out as having the highest priority.

The hundred-dollar approach is not a bad way to get a group of people to think in terms of allocating resources based on priority. However, Davis (2005) points out several ways that participants can "game" the process to skew the results. For instance, if you really, REALLY want a particular requirement, you might give it all 100 of your dollars to try to float it to the top of the list. In reality, you'd never accept a system that possessed just that single requirement, though. Nor does this scheme take into account any concern about the relative amount of effort needed to implement each of those requirements. If you could get three requirements each valued at $10 for the same effort as one valued at $15, you're likely better off with the three. The scheme is based solely on the perceived value of certain requirements to a particular set of stakeholders, a limitation of many prioritization techniques.

Another prioritization technique is based on real money, not play money. In Joy Beatty and Anthony Chen's (2012) *objective chain* technique, you assign an estimated dollar value that represents how much each proposed feature contributes to achieving the project's business objectives. You can then compare the relative value of features to one another and select which ones to implement first.

Prioritization based on value, cost, and risk

When the stakeholders can't agree on requirement priorities through the other relatively informal techniques, it might be useful to apply a more analytical method. A definitive, rigorous way to relate customer value to proposed product features is with a technique called Quality Function Deployment, or QFD (Cohen 1995). Few software organizations seem to be willing to undertake the rigor of QFD, although a structured prioritization method adapted from QFD has proven to be helpful.

Table 16-1 illustrates a spreadsheet model to help estimate the relative priorities for a set of requirements. This technique was ranked in the top tier of effectiveness in a comparative evaluation of 17 requirements prioritization methods (Kukreja et al. 2012). The Microsoft Excel spreadsheet is available in the companion content for this book. The example in Table 16-1 lists several features from (what else?) the Chemical Tracking System. This scheme borrows from the QFD concept of basing customer value on both the *benefit* provided to the customer if a specific product feature is present and the *penalty* paid if that feature is absent (Pardee 1996). A feature's attractiveness is directly proportional to the value it provides and inversely proportional to its *cost* and the technical *risk* associated with implementing it. All other things being equal, those features with the highest risk-adjusted value/cost ratio should have the highest priority. This approach distributes a set of estimated priorities across a continuum, rather than grouping them into just a few discrete levels.

TABLE 16-1 Sample prioritization matrix for the Chemical Tracking System

Relative weights	2	1		1		0.5		
Feature	Relative benefit	Relative penalty	Total value	Value %	Relative cost	Cost %	Relative risk	Risk %	Priority
1. Print a material safety data sheet.	2	4	8	5.2	1	2.7	1	3.0	1.22
2. Query status of a vendor order.	5	3	13	8.4	2	5.4	1	3.0	1.21
3. Generate a chemical stockroom inventory report.	9	7	25	16.1	5	13.5	3	9.1	0.89
4. See history of a specific chemical container.	5	5	15	9.7	3	8.1	2	6.1	0.87
5. Search vendor catalogs for a specific chemical.	9	8	26	16.8	3	8.1	8	24.2	0.83
6. Maintain a list of hazardous chemicals.	3	9	15	9.7	3	8.1	4	12.1	0.68
7. Change a pending chemical request.	4	3	11	7.1	3	8.1	2	6.1	0.64
8. Generate a laboratory inventory report.	6	2	14	9.0	4	10.8	3	9.1	0.59
9. Check training database for hazardous chemical training record.	3	4	10	6.5	4	10.8	2	6.1	0.47
10. Import chemical structures from structure drawing tools.	7	4	18	11.6	9	24.3	7	21.2	0.33
Totals	53	49	155	100.0	37	100.0	33	100.0	

Apply this prioritization scheme to discretionary requirements, those that aren't obviously top priority. For instance, you wouldn't include in this analysis items that implement the product's core business functions, key product differentiators, or items required for regulatory compliance. After you've identified those features that absolutely must be included for the product to be releasable, use the model in Table 16-1 to scale the relative priorities of the remaining capabilities. Typical participants in the prioritization process include:

- The project manager or business analyst, who leads the process, arbitrates conflicts, and adjusts prioritization data received from the other participants if necessary.

- Customer representatives, such as product champions, a product manager, or a product owner, who supply the benefit and penalty ratings.

- Development representatives, who provide the cost and risk ratings.

Follow these steps to use this prioritization model (it's more complicated to explain than to use):

1. List in the spreadsheet all the features, use cases, use case flows, user stories, or functional requirements that you want to prioritize against each other. We've used features in the example. All the items must be at the same level of abstraction—don't mix functional requirements with features, use cases, or user stories. Certain features might be logically linked (you'd implement feature B only if feature A were included) or have dependencies (feature A must be implemented before feature B). For those, include only the driving feature in the analysis. This model will work with up to several dozen items before it becomes unwieldy. If you have more than that, group related items together to create a manageable list. You can apply the method hierarchically. After you perform an initial prioritization on, for example, features, you can apply it again within a feature to prioritize its individual subfeatures or functional requirements.

2. Have the customer representatives estimate the relative benefit each feature would provide to the customer or to the business on a scale of 1 to 9. A rating of 1 indicates that no one would find it useful; 9 means that it would be extremely valuable. These benefit ratings indicate alignment of the features with the product's business objectives.

3. Estimate the relative penalty that the customer or the business would suffer if each feature were *not* included. Again, use a scale of 1 to 9. A rating of 1 means that no one will be upset if it's absent; 9 indicates a serious downside. Requirements with both a low benefit and a low penalty add cost but little value. Sometimes a feature could have a fairly low value, if not many customers will use it, but a high penalty if your competitor's product boasts that feature and the customers expect it to be there—even if they don't personally plan to use it! Marketing people sometimes call these "checkbox features": you need to say you have it, even if few people really care. When assigning penalty ratings, consider what might happen if you do not include the capability:

   - Would your product suffer in comparison with other products that do have that capability?

   - Would there be any legal or contractual consequences?

   - Would you be violating some government or industry standard?

   - Would users be unable to perform some necessary or expected functions?

   - Would it be a lot harder to add that capability later as an enhancement?

   - Would problems arise because marketing promised a feature to some customers?

4. The spreadsheet calculates the total value for each feature as the sum of its benefit and penalty scores (weighted as described later in the chapter). The spreadsheet sums the values for all the features and calculates the percentage of the total value that comes from each of the features (the Value % column). Note that this is not the percentage of total value for the entire product, just for the set of features you're prioritizing against each other here.

5. Have developers estimate the relative cost of implementing each feature, again on a scale of 1 (quick and easy) to 9 (time-consuming and expensive). The spreadsheet will calculate the percentage of the total cost that each feature contributes. Developers estimate the cost ratings based on the feature's complexity, the extent of user interface work required, the potential ability to reuse existing code, the amount of testing needed, and so forth. Agile teams could base these cost ratings on the number of story points they've assigned to each user story. (See Chapter 19, "Beyond requirements development," for more about estimation on agile projects.)

6. Similarly, have developers rate the relative technical (not business) risk associated with each feature on a scale of 1 to 9. Technical risk is the probability of *not* getting the feature right on the first try. A rating of 1 means you can program it in your sleep. A 9 indicates serious concerns about feasibility, the lack of necessary expertise on the team, the use of unfamiliar tools and technologies, or concern about the amount of complexity hidden within the requirement. The spreadsheet will calculate the percentage of the total risk that comes from each feature.

7. After you've entered all the estimates into the spreadsheet, it will calculate a priority value for each feature by using the following formula:

$$priority = \frac{value\ \%}{cost\ \% + risk\ \%}$$

8. Finally, sort the list of features in descending order by calculated priority, the rightmost column. The features at the top of the list have the most favorable balance of value, cost, and risk and thus—all other factors being equal—should have highest priority. Discussions that focus on those features at the top of the list will let you refine that preliminary ranking into a priority sequence that stakeholders can agree on, even if not everyone gets exactly what they want.

By default, the benefit, penalty, cost, and risk terms are weighted equally. You can change the relative weights for the four factors in the top row of the spreadsheet, to reflect the thought process by which your team makes priority decisions. In Table 16-1, all benefit ratings are weighted twice as heavily as the corresponding penalty ratings, penalty and cost are weighted the same, and risk has half the weight of the cost and penalty terms. To drop a term out of the model, set its weight to zero.

When using this spreadsheet model with prioritization participants, you might want to hide certain columns that appear in Table 16-1: Total value, Value %, Cost %, and Risk %. These show intermediate results from the calculations that could just be a distraction. Hiding them will let the customers focus on the four rating categories and the calculated priority values.

Or, we could arm wrestle

One company that introduced a requirements prioritization procedure based on this spreadsheet found that it helped a project team to break through an impasse. Several stakeholders had different opinions about which features were most important on a large project; the team was deadlocked. The spreadsheet analysis made the priority assessment more objective and less emotionally charged, enabling the team to agree on some conclusions and move ahead.

Consultant Johanna Rothman (2000) reported that, "I have suggested this spreadsheet to my clients as a tool for decision-making. Although the ones who tried it have never completely filled out the spreadsheet, they found the discussion it stimulated extremely helpful in deciding the relative priorities of the different requirements." That is, you can use the framework of benefit, penalty, cost, and risk to guide discussions about priorities. This is more valuable than working completely through the spreadsheet analysis and relying exclusively on the calculated priority sequence. Because requirements and their priorities can change with time, use the spreadsheet tool throughout the project to help manage the backlog of work remaining to be done.

This priority model's usefulness is limited by the team's ability to estimate the benefit, penalty, cost, and risk for each item. Therefore, use the calculated priorities only as a guideline. Stakeholders should review the completed spreadsheet to agree on the ratings and the resulting sorted priority sequence. If you aren't sure whether you can trust the results, consider calibrating this model for your own use with a set of implemented requirements from a previous project. Adjust the weighting factors until the calculated priority sequence correlates well with your after-the-fact evaluation of how important the requirements in your calibration set really were. This will give you some confidence in using the tool as a predictive model of how you make priority decisions on your projects.

Trap Don't over-interpret small differences in calculated priority numbers. This semi-quantitative method is not mathematically rigorous. Group together sets of requirements that have approximately the same calculated priority numbers.

Different stakeholders often have conflicting ideas about the relative benefit of a specific requirement or the penalty of omitting it. The prioritization spreadsheet includes a variant that accommodates input from several user classes or other stakeholder groups. In the Multiple Stakeholders worksheet tab in the downloadable spreadsheet, duplicate the Relative Benefit and Relative Penalty columns so that you have a set for each stakeholder who's contributing to the analysis. Then assign a weighting factor to each stakeholder, giving higher weights to favored user classes than to groups who have less influence on the project's decisions. Have each stakeholder representative provide his own benefit and penalty ratings for each feature. The spreadsheet will incorporate the stakeholder weights when it calculates the final value scores.

This model can also help you to make trade-off decisions when you're evaluating proposed requirements additions. Add the new requirements to the prioritization spreadsheet and see how their priorities align with those of the existing requirements baseline so you can choose an appropriate implementation sequence.

You don't always need to use a method this elaborate. Keep your prioritization process as simple as possible, but no simpler. Strive to move prioritization away from the political and emotional arena into a forum in which stakeholders can make honest assessments. This will give you a better chance of building products that deliver the maximum business value with the minimum cost.

Next steps

- Reevaluate the requirements in your backlog for an upcoming release, using the definitions in Figure 16-1 to distinguish requirements that truly must be included in that release from those that could wait if necessary. Does this make you change any of your priorities?

- Apply the spreadsheet model illustrated in Table 16-1 to prioritize 10 or 15 features, use cases, or user stories from a recent project. How well do the calculated priorities compare with the priorities you had determined by some different method? How well do they compare with your subjective sense of the proper priorities?

- If the model's priorities don't match what you think is right, analyze which part of the model isn't giving sensible results. Try using different weighting factors for benefit, penalty, cost, and risk. Adjust the model until it provides results consistent with what you expect. Otherwise, you can't trust its predictive capability.

- After you've calibrated the prioritization model, apply it to a new project. Incorporate the calculated priorities into the decision-making process. See whether this yields results that the stakeholders find more satisfying than those from their previous prioritization approach.

- Try one new prioritization technique today that you have not used before. For example, if you use MoSCoW already, try using the three-level method to see how it compares.

CHAPTER 17

Validating the requirements

Barry, a test lead, was the moderator for an inspection meeting whose participants were carefully examining a software requirements specification for problems. The meeting included representatives from two user classes, a developer named Jeremy, and Trish, the business analyst who wrote the SRS. One requirement stated, "The system shall provide unattended terminal timeout security of workstations accessing the training system." Jeremy presented his interpretation of this requirement to the rest of the group. "This requirement says the system will automatically log off the current user of any workstation logged into the training system if there hasn't been any activity within a certain period of time."

Hui-Lee, one of the product champions, chimed in. "How does the system determine that the terminal is unattended? Is it like a screen saver, so if there isn't any mouse or keyboard activity for several minutes, it logs the user off? That could be annoying if the user was just talking to someone briefly."

Trish added, "The requirement doesn't say anything about logging off the user. I assumed that timeout security meant a logoff, but maybe the user just has to retype her password to keep going."

Jeremy was confused also. "Does this mean any workstation that can connect to the training system, or just workstations that are actively logged into the system at the moment? How long of a timeout period are we talking about? Maybe there's a security guideline for this kind of thing."

Barry made sure that the inspection recorder had captured all these concerns accurately. He followed up with Trish after the meeting to ensure that she understood all of the issues so she could resolve them.

Most software developers have experienced the frustration of being presented with requirements that were ambiguous or incomplete. If they can't get the information they need, the developers have to make their own interpretations, which aren't always correct. As you saw in Chapter 1, "The essential software requirement," it costs far more to correct a requirement error after implementation than to correct one found during requirements development. One study found that it took an average of 30 minutes to fix a defect discovered during the requirements phase. In contrast, 5 to 17 hours were needed to correct a defect identified during system testing (Kelly, Sherif, and Hops 1992). Clearly, any measures you can take to detect errors in the requirements specifications will save time and money.

On many projects, testing is a late-stage activity. Requirements-related problems linger in the product until they're finally revealed through time-consuming system testing or—worse—by the end user. If you start your test planning and test-case development in parallel with requirements development, you'll detect many errors shortly after they're introduced. This prevents them from doing further damage and minimizes your development and maintenance costs.

Figure 17-1 illustrates the V model of software development. It shows test activities beginning in parallel with the corresponding development activities. This model indicates that acceptance tests are derived from the user requirements, system tests are based on the functional requirements, and integration tests are based on the system's architecture. This model is applicable whether the software development activities being tested are for the product as a whole, a particular release, or a single development increment.

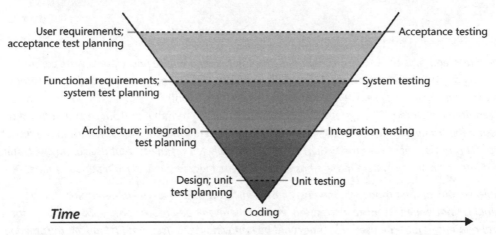

FIGURE 17-1 The V model of software development incorporates early test planning and test design.

As we will discuss later in the chapter, you can use the tests to validate each of these requirement types during requirements development. You can't actually execute any tests during requirements development because you don't have any running software yet. However, conceptual (that is, implementation-independent) tests based on the requirements will reveal errors, ambiguities, and omissions in your requirements and models before the team writes any code.

Project participants sometimes are reluctant to spend time reviewing and testing requirements. Their intuition tells them that inserting time into the schedule to improve requirements quality would delay the planned ship date by that same duration. However, this expectation assumes a zero return on your investment in requirements validation. In reality, that investment can actually *shorten* the delivery schedule by reducing the rework required and by accelerating system integration and testing (Blackburn, Scudder, and Van Wassenhove 1996). Better requirements lead to higher product quality and customer satisfaction, which reduce the product's lifetime costs for maintenance, enhancement, and customer support. Investing in requirements quality usually saves you much more than you spend.

Various techniques can help you to evaluate the correctness and quality of your requirements (Wallace and Ippolito 1997). One approach is to quantify each requirement so that you can think of a way to measure how well a proposed solution satisfies it. Suzanne and James Robertson (2013) use the term *fit criteria* to describe such quantifications. This chapter addresses the validation techniques of formal and informal requirements reviews, developing tests from requirements, and having customers define their acceptance criteria for the product.

Validation and verification

Requirements validation is the fourth component of requirements development, along with elicitation, analysis, and specification. Some authors use the term "verification" for this step. In this book, we've adopted the terminology of the *Software Engineering Body of Knowledge* (Abran et al. 2004) and refer to this aspect of requirements development as "validation." Verifying requirements to ensure that they have all the desired properties of high-quality requirements is also an essential activity. Precisely speaking, validation and verification are two different activities in software development. *Verification* determines whether the product of some development activity meets its requirements (doing the thing right). *Validation* assesses whether a product satisfies customer needs (doing the right thing).

Extending these definitions to requirements, verification determines whether you have written the requirements right: your requirements have the desirable properties described in Chapter 11, "Writing excellent requirements." Validation of requirements assesses whether you have written the right requirements: they trace back to business objectives. These two concepts are closely intertwined. For simplicity in this chapter, we talk about validating the requirements, but the techniques we describe contribute both to having the correct requirements and to having high-quality requirements.

Validating requirements allows teams to build a correct solution that meets the stated business objectives. Requirements validation activities attempt to ensure that:

- The software requirements accurately describe the intended system capabilities and properties that will satisfy the various stakeholders' needs.

- The software requirements are correctly derived from the business requirements, system requirements, business rules, and other sources.

- The requirements are complete, feasible, and verifiable.

- All requirements are necessary, and the entire set is sufficient to meet the business objectives.

- All requirements representations are consistent with each other.

- The requirements provide an adequate basis to proceed with design and construction.

Validation isn't a single discrete phase that you perform after eliciting and documenting all the requirements. Some validation activities, such as incremental reviews of the growing requirements set, are threaded throughout the iterative elicitation, analysis, and specification processes. Other activities, such as formal inspections, provide a final quality gate prior to baselining a set of requirements. Include requirements validation activities as tasks in your project plan. Of course, you can validate only requirements that have been documented, not implicit requirements that exist only in someone's mind.

Reviewing requirements

Anytime someone other than the author of a work product examines the product for problems, a *peer review* is taking place. Reviewing requirements is a powerful technique for identifying ambiguous or unverifiable requirements, requirements that aren't defined clearly enough for design to begin, and other problems.

Different kinds of peer reviews go by a variety of names (Wiegers 2002). Informal reviews are useful for educating other people about the product and collecting unstructured feedback. However, they are not systematic, thorough, or performed in a consistent way. Informal review approaches include:

- A *peer deskcheck*, in which you ask one colleague to look over your work product.

- A *passaround*, in which you invite several colleagues to examine a deliverable concurrently.

- A *walkthrough*, during which the author describes a deliverable and solicits comments on it.

Informal reviews are good for catching glaring errors, inconsistencies, and gaps. They can help you spot statements that don't meet the characteristics of high-quality requirements. But it's hard for a reviewer to catch all of the ambiguous requirements on his own. He might read a requirement and think he understands it, moving on to the next without a second thought. Another reviewer might read the same requirement, arrive at a different interpretation, and also not think there is an issue. If these two reviewers never discuss the requirement, the ambiguity will go unnoticed until later in the project.

Formal peer reviews follow a well-defined process. A formal requirements review produces a report that identifies the material examined, the reviewers, and the review team's judgment as to whether the requirements are acceptable. The principal deliverable is a summary of the defects found and the issues raised during the review. The members of a formal review team share responsibility for the quality of the review, although authors ultimately are responsible for the quality of the deliverables they create.

The best-established type of formal peer review is called an *inspection*. Inspection of requirements documents is one of the highest-leverage software quality techniques available. Several companies have avoided as many as 10 hours of labor for every hour they invested in inspecting requirements documents and other software deliverables (Grady and Van Slack 1994). A 1,000 percent return on investment is not to be sneezed at.

If you're serious about maximizing the quality of your software, your teams will inspect most of their requirements. Detailed inspection of large requirements sets is tedious and time consuming. Nonetheless, the teams I know who have adopted requirements inspections agree that every minute they spent was worthwhile. If you don't have time to inspect everything, use risk analysis to differentiate those requirements that demand inspection from less critical, less complex, or less novel material for which an informal review will suffice. Inspections are not cheap. They're not even that much fun. But they are cheaper—and more fun—than the alternative of expending lots of effort and customer goodwill fixing problems found much later on.

The closer you look, the more you see

On the Chemical Tracking System project, the user representatives informally reviewed their latest contribution to the growing SRS after each elicitation workshop. These quick reviews uncovered many errors. After elicitation was complete, one of the BAs combined the input from all user classes into a single SRS of about 50 pages plus several appendices. Two BAs, one developer, three product champions, and one tester then inspected this full SRS in three two-hour inspection meetings held over the course of a week. The inspectors found 223 additional errors, including dozens of major defects. All the inspectors agreed that the time they spent grinding through the SRS, one requirement at a time, saved the project team countless more hours in the long run.

The inspection process

Michael Fagan developed the inspection process at IBM (Fagan 1976; Radice 2002), and others have extended or modified his method (Gilb and Graham 1993; Wiegers 2002). Inspection has been recognized as a software industry best practice (Brown 1996). Any software work product can be inspected, including requirements, design documents, source code, test documentation, and project plans.

Inspection is a well-defined multistage process. It involves a small team of participants who carefully examine a work product for defects and improvement opportunities. Inspections serve as a quality gate through which project deliverables must pass before they are baselined. There are several forms of inspection, but any one of them is a powerful quality technique. The following description is based on the Fagan inspection technique.

Participants

Ensure that you have all of the necessary people in an inspection meeting before proceeding. Otherwise you might correct issues only to find out later that someone important disagrees with the change. The participants in an inspection should represent four perspectives (Wiegers 2002):

- **The author of the work product and perhaps peers of the author**   The business analyst who wrote the requirements document provides this perspective. Include another experienced BA if you can, because he'll know what sorts of requirements-writing errors to look for.

- **People who are the sources of information that fed into the item being inspected**   These participants could be actual user representatives or the author of a predecessor specification. In the absence of a higher-level specification, the inspection must include customer representatives, such as product champions, to ensure that the requirements describe their needs correctly and completely.

- **People who will do work based on the item being inspected** For an SRS, you might include a developer, a tester, a project manager, and a user documentation writer because they will detect different kinds of problems. A tester is most likely to catch an unverifiable requirement; a developer can spot requirements that are technically infeasible.

- **People who are responsible for interfacing systems that will be affected by the item being inspected** These inspectors will look for problems with the external interface requirements. They can also spot ripple effects, in which changing a requirement in the SRS being inspected affects other systems.

Try to limit the team to seven or fewer inspectors. This might mean that some perspectives won't be represented in every inspection. Large teams easily get bogged down in side discussions, problem solving, and debates over whether something is really an error. This reduces the rate at which they cover the material during the inspection and increases the cost of finding each defect.

The author's manager normally should not attend an inspection meeting, unless the manager is actively contributing to the project and his presence is acceptable to the author. An effective inspection that reveals many defects might create a bad impression of the author to a hypercritical manager. Also, the manager's presence might stifle discussion from other participants.

Inspection roles

All participants in an inspection, including the author, look for defects and improvement opportunities. Some of the inspection team members perform the following specific roles during the inspection (Wiegers 2002).

Author The author created or maintains the work product being inspected. The author of a requirements document is usually the business analyst who elicited customer needs and wrote the requirements. During informal reviews such as walkthroughs, the author often leads the discussion. However, the author takes a more passive role during an inspection. The author should not assume any of the other assigned roles—moderator, reader, or recorder. By not having an active role, the author can listen to the comments from other inspectors, respond to—but not debate—their questions, and think. This way the author can often spot errors that other inspectors don't see.

Moderator The moderator plans the inspection with the author, coordinates the activities, and facilitates the inspection meeting. The moderator distributes the materials to be inspected, along with any relevant predecessor documents, to the participants a few days before the inspection meeting. Moderator responsibilities include starting the meeting on time, encouraging contributions from all participants, and keeping the meeting focused on finding major defects rather than resolving problems or being distracted by minor stylistic issues and typos. The moderator follows up on proposed changes with the author to ensure that the issues that came out of the inspection were addressed properly.

Reader   One inspector is assigned the role of reader. During the inspection meeting, the reader paraphrases the requirements and model elements being examined one at a time. The other participants then point out potential defects and issues that they see. By stating a requirement in her own words, the reader provides an interpretation that might differ from that held by other inspectors. This is a good way to reveal an ambiguity, a possible defect, or an assumption. It also underscores the value of having someone other than the author serve as the reader. In less formal types of peer reviews, the reader role is omitted, with the moderator walking the team through the work product and soliciting comments on one section at a time.

Recorder   The recorder uses standard forms to document the issues raised and the defects found during the meeting. The recorder should review aloud or visually share (by projecting or sharing in a web conference) what he wrote to confirm its accuracy. The other inspectors should help the recorder capture the essence of each issue in a way that clearly communicates to the author the location and nature of the issue so he can address it efficiently and correctly.

Entry criteria

You're ready to inspect a requirements document when it satisfies specific prerequisites. These *entry criteria* set some clear expectations for authors to follow while preparing for an inspection. They also keep the inspection team from spending time on issues that should be resolved prior to the inspection. The moderator uses the entry criteria as a checklist before deciding to proceed with the inspection. Following are some suggested inspection entry criteria for requirements documents:

❑ The document conforms to the standard template and doesn't have obvious spelling, grammatical, or formatting issues.

❑ Line numbers or other unique identifiers are printed on the document to facilitate referring to specific locations.

❑ All open issues are marked as TBD (to be determined) or accessible in an issue-tracking tool.

❑ The moderator didn't find more than three major defects in a ten-minute examination of a representative sample of the document.

Inspection stages

An inspection is a multistep process, as illustrated in Figure 17-2. You can inspect small sets of requirements at a time—perhaps those allocated to a specific development iteration—thereby eventually covering the full requirements collection. The purpose of each inspection process stage is summarized briefly in this section.

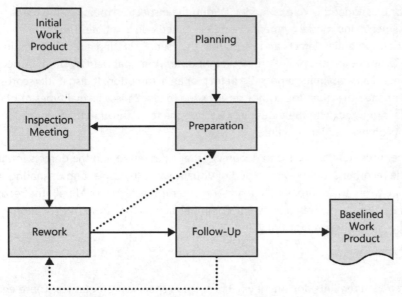

FIGURE 17-2 Inspection is a multistep process. The dotted lines indicate that portions of the inspection process might be repeated if reinspection is necessary because of extensive rework.

Planning   The author and moderator plan the inspection together. They determine who should participate, what materials the inspectors should receive prior to the inspection meeting, the total meeting time needed to cover the material, and when the inspection should be scheduled. The number of pages reviewed per hour has a large impact on how many defects are found (Gilb and Graham 1993). As Figure 17-3 shows, proceeding through a requirements document slowly reveals the most defects. (An alternative interpretation of this frequently reported relationship is that the inspection slows down if you encounter a lot of defects. It's not totally clear which is cause and which is effect.) Because no team has infinite time available for requirements inspections, select an appropriate inspection rate based on the risk of overlooking major defects. Two to four pages per hour is a practical guideline, although the optimum rate for maximum defect-detection effectiveness is about half that rate (Gilb and Graham 1993). Adjust this rate based on the following factors:

- The team's previous inspection data, showing inspection effectiveness as a function of rate

- The amount of text on each page

- The complexity of the requirements

- The likelihood and impact of having errors remain undetected

- How critical the material being inspected is to project success

- The experience level of the person who wrote the requirements

Preparation   Prior to the inspection meeting, the author should share background information with inspectors so they understand the context of the items being inspected and know the author's objectives for the inspection. Each inspector then examines the product to identify possible defects and issues, using the checklist of typical requirements defects described later in this chapter or other analysis techniques (Wiegers 2002). Up to 75 percent of the defects found by an inspection are discovered during preparation, so don't omit this step (Humphrey 1989). The techniques described in the "Finding missing requirements" section in Chapter 7, "Requirements elicitation," can be helpful during preparation. Plan on spending at least half as much time on individual preparation as is scheduled for the team inspection meetings.

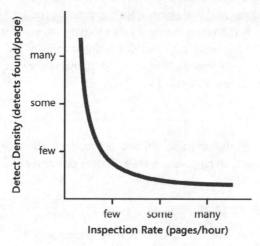

FIGURE 17-3 The number of defects found depends on the inspection rate.

> **Trap** Don't proceed with an inspection meeting if the participants haven't already examined the work product on their own. Ineffective meetings can lead to the erroneous conclusion that inspections are a waste of time.

Inspection meeting During an inspection meeting, the reader leads the other inspectors through the document, describing one requirement at a time in his own words. As inspectors bring up possible defects and other issues, the recorder captures them in the action item list for the requirements author. The purpose of the meeting is to identify as many major defects as possible. The inspection meeting shouldn't last more than about two hours; tired people aren't effective inspectors. If you need more time to cover all the material, schedule additional meetings.

After examining all the material, the team decides whether to accept the requirements document as is, accept it with minor revisions, or indicate that major revision is needed. An outcome of "major revision needed" could suggest that the requirements development process has some shortcomings or that the BA who wrote the requirements needs additional training. Consider holding a retrospective to explore how the process can be improved prior to the next specification activity (Kerth 2001). If major revisions are necessary, the team might elect to re-examine portions of the product that require extensive rework, as shown by the dotted line between Rework and Preparation in Figure 17-2.

Sometimes inspectors report only superficial and cosmetic issues. In addition, inspectors are easily sidetracked into discussing whether an issue really is a defect, debating questions of project scope, and brainstorming solutions to problems. These activities can be useful, but they distract attention from the core objective of finding significant defects and improvement opportunities.

Rework   Nearly every quality control activity reveals some defects. The author should plan to spend some time reworking the requirements following the inspection meeting. Uncorrected requirement defects will be expensive to fix down the road, so this is the time to resolve the ambiguities, eliminate the fuzziness, and lay the foundation for a successful development project.

Follow-up   In this final inspection step, the moderator or a designated individual works with the author to ensure that all open issues were resolved and that errors were corrected properly. Follow-up brings closure to the inspection process and enables the moderator to determine whether the inspection's exit criteria have been satisfied. The follow-up step might reveal that some of the modifications made were incomplete or not performed correctly, leading to additional rework, as shown by the dotted line between Follow-up and Rework in Figure 17-2.

Exit criteria

Your inspection process should define the exit criteria that must be satisfied before the moderator declares the full inspection process (not just the meeting) complete. Here are some possible exit criteria for requirements inspections:

❑   All issues raised during the inspection have been addressed.

❑   Any changes made in the requirements and related work products were made correctly.

❑   All open issues have been resolved, or each open issue's resolution process, target date, and owner have been documented.

Defect checklist

To help reviewers look for typical kinds of errors in the products they review, develop a defect checklist for each type of requirements document your projects create. Such checklists call the reviewers' attention to historically frequent requirement problems. Checklists serve as reminders. Over time, people will internalize the items and look for the right issues in each review out of habit. Figure 17-4 illustrates a requirements review checklist, which is included with the companion content for this book. If you create particular requirements representations or models, you might expand the items in the checklist to be more thorough for those. Business requirements, such as a vision and scope document, might warrant their own checklist. Cecilie Hoffman and Rebecca Burgess (2009) provide several detailed review checklists, including one to validate software requirements against business requirements.

No one can remember all the items on a long checklist. If there are more than six or eight items on the list, a reviewer will likely have to do multiple passes through the material to look for everything on the list; most reviewers won't bother. Pare the lists to meet your organization's needs, and modify the items to reflect the problems that people encounter most often with your own requirements. Some studies have shown that giving reviewers specific defect-detection responsibilities—providing structured thought processes or scenarios to help them hunt for particular kinds of errors—is more effective than simply handing all reviewers the same checklist and hoping for the best (Porter, Votta, and Basili 1995).

Completeness

❑ Do the requirements address all known customer or system needs?
❑ Is any needed information missing? If so, is it identified as TBD?
❑ Have algorithms intrinsic to the functional requirements been defined?
❑ Are all external hardware, software, and communication interfaces defined?
❑ Is the expected behavior documented for all anticipated error conditions?
❑ Do the requirements provide an adequate basis for design and test?
❑ Is the implementation priority of each requirement included?
❑ Is each requirement in scope for the project, release, or iteration?

Correctness

❑ Do any requirements conflict with or duplicate other requirements?
❑ Is each requirement written in clear, concise, unambiguous, grammatically correct language?
❑ Is each requirement verifiable by testing, demonstration, review, or analysis?
❑ Are any specified error messages clear and meaningful?
❑ Are all requirements actually requirements, not solutions or constraints?
❑ Are the requirements technically feasible and implementable within known constraints?

Quality Attributes

❑ Are all usability, performance, security, and safety objectives properly specified?
❑ Are other quality attributes documented and quantified, with the acceptable trade-offs specified?
❑ Are the time-critical functions identified and timing criteria specified for them?
❑ Have internationalization and localization issues been adequately addressed?
❑ Are all of the quality requirements measurable?

Organization and Traceability

❑ Are the requirements organized in a logical and accessible way?
❑ Are all cross-references to other requirements and documents correct?
❑ Are all requirements written at a consistent and appropriate level of detail?
❑ Is each requirement uniquely and correctly labeled?
❑ Is each functional requirement traced back to its origin (e.g., system requirement, business rule)?

Other Issues

❑ Are any use cases or process flows missing?
❑ Are any alternative flows, exceptions, or other information missing from use cases?
❑ Are all of the business rules identified?
❑ Are there any missing visual models that would provide clarity or completeness?
❑ Are all necessary report specifications present and complete?

FIGURE 17-4 A defect checklist for reviewing requirements documents.

Requirements review tips

Chapter 8 of Karl Wiegers' *More About Software Requirements: Thorny Issues and Practical Advice* (Microsoft Press, 2006) offers suggestions to improve your requirements reviews. The following tips apply whether you are performing informal or formal reviews on your projects, and whether you're storing your requirements in traditional documents, in a requirements management tool, or in any other tangible form.

Plan the examination When someone asks you to review a document, the temptation is to begin at the top of page one and read it straight through. But you don't need to do that. The consumers of the requirements specification won't be reading it front-to-back like a book; reviewers don't have to, either. Invite certain reviewers to focus on specific sections of documents.

Start early   Begin reviewing sets of requirements when they are perhaps only 10 percent complete, not when you think they're "done." Detecting major defects early and spotting systemic problems in the way the requirements are being written is a powerful way to prevent—not just find—defects.

Allocate sufficient time   Give reviewers sufficient time to perform the reviews, both in terms of actual hours to review (effort) and calendar time. They have other important tasks that the review has to fit around.

Provide context   Give reviewers context for the document and perhaps for the project if they are not all working on the same project. Seek out reviewers who can provide a useful perspective based on their knowledge. For example, you might know a co-worker from another project who has a good eye for finding major requirement gaps even without being intimately familiar with the project.

Set review scope   Tell reviewers what material to examine, where to focus their attention, and what issues to look for. Suggest that they use a defect checklist like the one described in the preceding section. You might want to maximize availability and skills by asking different reviewers to review different sections or to use different parts of the checklists.

Limit re-reviews   Don't ask anyone to review the same material more than three times. He will be tired of looking at it and won't spot major issues after a third cycle because of "reviewer fatigue." If you do need someone to review it multiple times, highlight the changes so he can focus on those.

Prioritize review areas   Prioritize for review those portions of the requirements that are of high risk or have functionality that will be used frequently. Also, look for areas of the requirements that have few issues logged already. It might be the case that those sections have not yet been reviewed, not that they are problem-free.

Requirements review challenges

A peer review is both a technical activity and a social activity. Asking some colleagues to tell you what's wrong with your work is a learned—not instinctive—behavior. It takes time for a software organization to instill peer reviews into its culture. Following are some common challenges that organizations face regarding requirements reviews, some of which apply specifically to formal inspections, with suggestions for how to address each one (Wiegers 1998a; Wiegers 2002).

Large requirements documents   The prospect of thoroughly examining a several-hundred-page requirements document is daunting. You might be tempted to skip the review entirely and just proceed with construction—not a wise choice. Even given a document of moderate size, all reviewers might carefully examine the first part and a few stalwarts will study the middle, but it's unlikely that anyone will look at the last part.

To avoid overwhelming the review team, perform incremental reviews throughout requirements development. Identify high-risk areas that need a careful look through inspection, and use informal reviews for less risky material. Ask particular reviewers to start at different locations in the document to make certain that fresh eyes have looked at every page. To judge whether you really need to inspect the entire specification, examine a representative sample (Gilb and Graham 1993). The number and types of errors you find will help you determine whether investing in a full inspection is likely to pay off.

Large inspection teams   Many project participants and customers hold a stake in the requirements, so you might have a long list of potential participants for requirements inspections. However, large review teams increase the cost of the review, make it hard to schedule meetings, and have difficulty reaching agreement on issues. I once participated in a meeting with 13 other inspectors. Fourteen people cannot agree to leave a burning room, let alone agree on whether a particular requirement is correct. Try the following approaches to deal with a potentially large inspection team:

- Make sure every participant is there to find defects, not to be educated or to protect a position.

- Understand which perspective (such as customer, developer, or tester) each inspector represents. Several people who represent the same community can pool their input and send just one representative to the inspection meeting.

- Establish several small teams to inspect the requirements in parallel and combine their defect lists, removing any duplicates. Research has shown that multiple inspection teams find more requirements defects than does a single large group (Martin and Tsai 1990; Schneider, Martin, and Tsai 1992; Kosman 1997). The results of parallel inspections are primarily additive rather than redundant.

Geographically separated reviewers   Organizations often build products through the collaboration of geographically dispersed teams. This makes reviews more challenging. Teleconferencing doesn't reveal the body language and expressions of other reviewers like a face-to-face meeting does, but videoconferencing can be an effective solution. Web conferencing tools allow reviewers to ensure that they are all looking at the same material during the discussion.

Reviews of an electronic document placed in a shared network repository provide an alternative to a traditional review meeting. In this approach, reviewers use word-processor features to insert their comments into the text. (This is how Karl and Joy reviewed each other's work as we were writing this book.) Each comment is labeled with the reviewer's initials, and each reviewer can see what previous reviewers had to say. Web-based collaboration tools also can help. Some requirements management tools include components to facilitate distributed asynchronous reviews that do not involve live meetings. If you choose not to hold a meeting, recognize that this can reduce a review's effectiveness, but it's certainly better than not performing the review at all.

Unprepared reviewers   One of the prerequisites to a formal review meeting is that the participants have examined the material being reviewed ahead of time, individually identifying their initial sets of issues. Without this preparation, you risk people spending the meeting time doing all of their thinking on the spot and likely missing many important issues.

One project had a 50-page SRS to be reviewed by 15 people, far too many to be effective and efficient. Everyone had one week to review the document on their own and send issues back to the author. Not surprisingly, most people didn't look at it at all. So the lead BA scheduled a mandatory meeting for the reviewers to review the document together. He projected the SRS on the screen, dimmed the lights, and began reading through the requirements one by one. (The room had one very bright light shining down in the middle, directly on the lead BA—talk about being in the spotlight!) A couple of hours into the review meeting, the participants were yawning, their attention fading. Not surprisingly, the rate of issue detection decreased. Everyone longed for the meeting to end. This BA let the participants leave, suggesting that they review the document on their own time to speed up the next review meeting. Sure enough, being bored during the meeting triggered them to do their prep work. See the "Workshops" section in Chapter 7 for suggestions about how to keep participants engaged during review meetings.

Prototyping requirements

It's hard to visualize how a system will function under specific circumstances just by reading the requirements. Prototypes are validation tools that make the requirements real. They allow the user to experience some aspects of what a system based on the requirements would be like. Chapter 15, "Risk reduction through prototyping," has more information on different types of prototypes and how they improve requirements. Here we describe how prototypes can help stakeholders judge whether a product built according to the requirements would meet their needs, and whether the requirements are complete, feasible, and clearly communicated.

All kinds of prototypes allow you to find missing requirements before more expensive activities like development and testing take place. Something as simple as a paper mock-up can be used to walk through use cases, processes, or functions to detect any omitted or erroneous requirements. Prototypes also help confirm that stakeholders have a shared understanding of the requirements. Someone might implement a prototype based on his understanding of the requirements, only to learn that a requirement wasn't clear when prototype evaluators don't agree with his interpretation.

Proof-of-concept prototypes can demonstrate that the requirements are feasible. Evolutionary prototypes allow the users to see how the requirements would work when they are implemented, to validate that the result is what they expect. Additional levels of sophistication in prototypes, such as simulations, allow more precise validation of the requirements; however, building more sophisticated prototypes will also take more time.

Testing the requirements

Tests that are based on the functional requirements or derived from user requirements help make the expected system behaviors tangible to the project participants. The simple act of designing tests will reveal many problems with the requirements long before you can execute those tests on running software. Writing functional tests crystallizes your vision of how the system should behave under certain conditions. Vague and ambiguous requirements will jump out at you because you won't be able to describe the expected system response. When BAs, developers, and customers walk through tests together, they'll achieve a shared vision of how the product will work and increase their confidence that the requirements are correct. Testing is a powerful tool for both validating and verifying requirements.

> **Trap** Watch out for testers who claim they can't begin their work until the requirements are done, as well as for testers who claim they don't need requirements to test the software. Testing and requirements have a synergistic relationship; they represent complementary views of the system.

Making Charlie happy

I once asked my group's UNIX scripting guru, Charlie, to build a simple email interface extension for a commercial defect-tracking system we had adopted. I wrote a dozen functional requirements that described how the email interface should work. Charlie was thrilled. He'd written many scripts for people, but he'd never seen written requirements before.

Unfortunately, I waited two weeks before writing the tests for this email function. Sure enough, one of the requirements had an error. I found the mistake because my mental image of how I expected the function to work, represented in about 20 tests, conflicted with one requirement. Chagrined, I corrected the bad requirement before Charlie had completed his implementation, and when he delivered the script, it was defect-free. Finding the error before implementation was a small victory, but small victories add up.

You can begin deriving conceptual tests from user requirements early in the development process (Collard 1999; Armour and Miller 2001). Use the tests to evaluate functional requirements, analysis models, and prototypes. The tests should cover the normal flow of each use case, alternative flows, and the exceptions you identified during elicitation and analysis. Similarly, if you identified business process flows, the tests should cover the business process steps and all possible decision paths.

These conceptual tests are independent of implementation. For example, consider a use case called "View a Stored Order" for the Chemical Tracking System. Some conceptual tests are:

- User enters order number to view, order exists, user had placed the order. Expected result: show order details.

- User enters order number to view, order doesn't exist. Expected result: Display message "Sorry, I can't find that order."

- User enters order number to view, order exists, user hadn't placed the order. Expected result: Display message "Sorry, that's not your order."

Ideally, a BA will write the functional requirements and a tester will write the tests from a common starting point: the user requirements, as shown in Figure 17-5. Ambiguities in the user requirements and differences of interpretation will lead to inconsistencies between the views represented by the functional requirements, models, and tests. As developers translate requirements into user interface and technical designs, testers can elaborate the conceptual tests into detailed test procedures (Hsia, Kung, and Sell 1997).

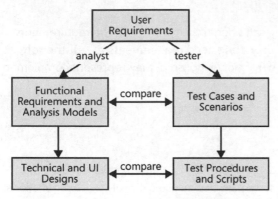

FIGURE 17-5 Development and testing work products are derived from a common source.

Let's see how the Chemical Tracking System team tied together requirements and visual models with early test thinking. Following are several pieces of requirements-related information, all of which pertain to the task of requesting a chemical.

Business requirement   As described in Chapter 5, "Establishing the business requirements," one of the primary business objectives for the Chemical Tracking System was to:

> *Reduce chemical purchasing expenses by 25% in the first year.*

Use case   A use case that aligns with this business requirement is "Request a Chemical." This use case includes a path that permits the user to request a chemical container that's already available in the chemical stockroom. Here's the use case description from Figure 8-3 in Chapter 8, "Understanding user requirements":

> *The Requester specifies the desired chemical to request by entering its name or chemical ID number or by importing its structure from a chemical drawing tool. The system either offers the Requester a container of the chemical from the chemical stockroom or lets the Requester order one from a vendor.*

Functional requirement   Here's a bit of functionality derived from this use case:

> *1. If the stockroom has containers of the chemical being requested, the system shall display a list of the available containers.*

> *2. The user shall either select one of the displayed containers or ask to place an order for a new container from a vendor.*

Dialog map   Figure 17-6 illustrates a portion of the dialog map for the "Request a Chemical" use case that pertains to this function. As was described in Chapter 12, "A picture is worth 1024 words," the boxes in this dialog map represent user interface displays, and the arrows represent possible navigation paths from one display to another. This dialog map was created far enough along in requirements development that the project participants were beginning to identify specific screens, menus, dialog boxes, and other dialog elements so they could give them names and contemplate a possible user interface architecture.

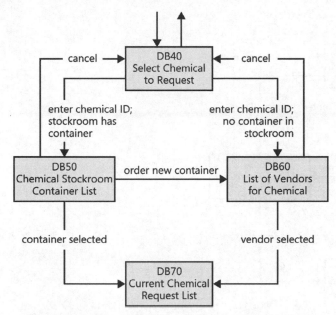

FIGURE 17-6 Portion of the dialog map for the "Request a Chemical" use case.

Test Because this use case has several possible execution paths, you can envision multiple tests to address the normal flow, alternative flows, and exceptions. The following is just one test, based on the flow that shows the user the available containers in the chemical stockroom.

> *At dialog box DB40, enter a valid chemical ID; the chemical stockroom has two containers of this chemical. Dialog box DB50 appears, showing the two containers. Select the second container. DB50 closes and container 2 is added to the bottom of the Current Chemical Request List in dialog box DB70.*

Ramesh, the test lead for the Chemical Tracking System, wrote several tests like this one based on his understanding of the use case. Such abstract tests are independent of implementation details. They don't discuss entering data into specific fields, clicking buttons, or other specific interaction techniques. As development progresses, the tester can refine such conceptual tests into specific test procedures.

Now comes the fun part—testing the requirements. Ramesh first mapped each test to the functional requirements. He checked to make certain that every test could be "executed" by going through a set of existing requirements. He also made sure that at least one test covered each functional requirement. Next, Ramesh traced the execution path for every test on the dialog map with a highlighter pen. The shaded line in Figure 17-7 shows how the preceding test traces onto the dialog map.

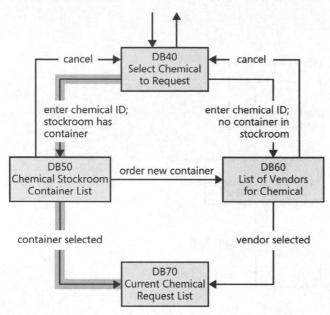

FIGURE 17-7 Tracing a test onto the dialog map for the "Request a Chemical" use case.

By tracing the execution path for each test, you can find incorrect or missing requirements, improve the user's navigation options, and refine the tests. Suppose that after "executing" all the tests in this fashion, the dialog map navigation line labeled "order new container" that goes from DB50 to DB60 in Figure 17-6 hasn't been highlighted. There are two possible interpretations:

- That navigation is not a permitted system behavior. The BA needs to remove that line from the dialog map. If the SRS contains a requirement that specifies the transition, that requirement must also be removed.

- The navigation is legitimate, but the test that demonstrates the behavior is missing.

In another scenario, suppose a tester wrote a test based on his interpretation of the use case that says the user can take some action to move directly from dialog box DB40 to DB70. However, the dialog map in Figure 17-6 doesn't contain such a navigation line, so that test can't be "executed" with the existing requirements set. Again, there are two possible interpretations. You'll need to determine which of the following is correct:

- The navigation from DB40 to DB70 is not a permitted system behavior, so the test is wrong.

- The navigation from DB40 to DB70 is legitimate, but the dialog map and perhaps the SRS are missing the requirement that is exercised by the test.

In these examples, the BA and the tester combined requirements, analysis models, and tests to detect missing, erroneous, or unnecessary requirements long before any code was written. Conceptual testing of software requirements is a powerful technique for controlling a project's cost and schedule by finding requirement ambiguities and errors early in the game. As Ross Collard (1999) pointed out,

Use cases and tests work well together in two ways: If the use cases for a system are complete, accurate, and clear, the process of deriving the tests is straightforward. And if the use cases are not in good shape, the attempt to derive tests will help to debug the use cases.

Validating requirements with acceptance criteria

Software developers might believe that they've built the perfect product, but the customer is the final arbiter. Customers need to assess whether a system satisfies its predefined *acceptance criteria*. Acceptance criteria—and hence acceptance testing—should evaluate whether the product satisfies its documented requirements and whether it is fit for use in the intended operating environment (Hsia, Kung, and Sell 1997; Leffingwell 2011; Pugh 2011). Having users devise acceptance tests is a valuable contributor to effective requirements development. The earlier that acceptance tests are written, the sooner they can help the team filter out defects in the requirements and, ultimately, in the implemented software.

Acceptance criteria

Working with customers to develop acceptance criteria provides a way to validate both the requirements and the solution itself. If a customer can't express how she would evaluate the system's satisfaction of a particular requirement, that requirement is not clear enough. Acceptance criteria define the minimum conditions for an application to be considered business-ready.

Thinking about acceptance criteria offers a shift in perspective from the elicitation question of "What do you need to do with the system?" to "How would you judge whether the solution meets your needs?" Encourage users to use the SMART mnemonic—*Specific, Measurable, Attainable, Relevant*, and *Time-sensitive*—when defining acceptance criteria. The criteria should be specified such that multiple objective observers would reach the same conclusion about whether they were satisfied. Acceptance criteria keep the focus on stakeholders' business objectives and the conditions that would allow the project sponsor to declare victory. This is more important than simply delivering on a requirements specification that might not really solve the stakeholders' business problems.

Defining acceptance criteria is more than just saying that all the requirements are implemented or all the tests passed. Acceptance tests constitute just a subset of acceptance criteria. Acceptance criteria could also encompass dimensions such as the following:

- Specific high-priority functionality that must be present and operating properly before the product could be accepted and used. (Other planned functionality could perhaps be delivered later, or capabilities that aren't working quite right could be fixed without delaying an initial release.)

- Essential nonfunctional criteria or quality metrics that must be satisfied. (Certain quality attributes must be at least minimally satisfied, although usability improvements, cosmetics, and performance tuning could be deferred. The product might have to meet quality metrics such as a certain minimum duration of operational usage without experiencing a failure.)

- Remaining open issues and defects. (You might stipulate that no defects exceeding a particular severity level remain open against high-priority requirements, although minor bugs could still be present.)

- Specific legal, regulatory, or contractual conditions. (These must be fully satisfied before the product is considered acceptable.)

- Supporting transition, infrastructure , or other project (not product) requirements. (Perhaps training materials must be available and data conversions completed before the solution can be released.)

It can also be valuable to think of "rejection criteria," conditions or assessment outcomes that would lead a stakeholder to deem the system not yet ready for delivery. Watch out for conflicting acceptance criteria, such that meeting one could block the satisfaction of another. In fact, looking for conflicting acceptance criteria early on is a way to discover conflicting requirements.

Agile projects create acceptance criteria based on user stories. As Dean Leffingwell (2011) put it,

> *Acceptance criteria are not functional or unit tests; rather, they are the conditions of satisfaction being placed on the system. Functional and unit tests go much deeper in testing all functional flows, exception flows, boundary conditions, and related functionality associated with the story.*

In principle, if all of the acceptance criteria for a user story are met, the product owner will accept the user story as being completed. Therefore, customers should be very specific in writing acceptance criteria that are important to them.

Acceptance tests

Acceptance tests constitute the largest portion of the acceptance criteria. Creators of acceptance tests should consider the most commonly performed and most important usage scenarios when deciding how to evaluate the software's acceptability. Focus on testing the normal flows of the use cases and their corresponding exceptions, devoting less attention to the less frequently used alternative flows. Ken Pugh (2011) offers a wealth of guidance for writing requirements-based acceptance tests.

Agile development approaches often create acceptance tests in lieu of writing precise functional requirements. Each test describes how a user story should function in the executable software. Because they are largely replacing detailed requirements, the acceptance tests on an agile project should cover all success and failure scenarios (Leffingwell 2011). The value in writing acceptance tests is that it guides users to think about how the system will behave following implementation. The problem with writing *only* acceptance tests is that the requirements exist only in people's minds. By not documenting and comparing alternate views of requirements—user requirements, functional requirements, analysis models, and tests—you can miss an opportunity to identify errors, inconsistencies, and gaps.

Automate the execution of acceptance tests whenever possible. This makes it easier to repeat the tests when changes are made and functionality is added in future iterations or releases. Acceptance tests must also address nonfunctional requirements. They should ensure that performance goals are achieved, that the system complies with usability standards, and that security expectations are fulfilled.

Some acceptance testing might be performed manually by users. The tests used in user acceptance testing (UAT) should be executed after a set of functionality is believed to be release-ready. This allows users to get their hands on the working software before it is officially delivered and permits users to familiarize themselves with the new software. The customer or product champion should select tests for UAT that represent the highest risk areas of the system. The acceptance tests will validate that the solution does what it is supposed to. Be sure to set up these tests using plausible test data. Suppose the test data used to generate a sales report isn't realistic for the application. A user who is performing UAT might incorrectly report a defect just because the report doesn't look right to him, or he might miss an erroneous calculation because the data is implausible.

> **Trap** Don't expect user acceptance testing to replace comprehensive requirements-based system testing, which covers all the normal and exception paths and a wide variety of data combinations, boundary values, and other places where defects might lurk.

Writing requirements isn't enough. You need to make sure that they're the *right* requirements and that they're *good enough* to serve as a foundation for design, construction, testing, and project management. Acceptance test planning, informal peer reviews, inspections, and requirements testing techniques will help you to build higher-quality systems faster and more inexpensively than you ever have before.

Next steps

- Choose a page of functional requirements at random from your project's SRS. Ask a group of people who represent different stakeholder perspectives to carefully examine that page of requirements for problems, using the defect checklist in Figure 17-4.

- If you found enough errors during the random sample review to make the team nervous about the overall quality of the requirements, persuade the user and development representatives to inspect the entire SRS. Train the team in the inspection process.

- Define conceptual tests for a use case or for a portion of the functionality that hasn't yet been coded. See whether the user representatives agree that the tests reflect the intended system behavior. Make sure you've defined all the functionality that will permit the tests to be passed and that there are no superfluous requirements.

- Work with your product champions to define the acceptance criteria that they and their colleagues will use to assess whether the system is acceptable to them. Have them define acceptance tests that could be used to judge completeness.

CHAPTER 18

Requirements reuse

Sylvia, the product manager at Tailspin Toys, was meeting with the development lead for their line of tablet apps for musicians. "Prasad, I just learned that Fabrikam, Inc., is going to release a larger version of their tablet, called a Substrate. Right now our guitar amplifier emulator runs on their smaller tablet, the ScratchPad. We need to come up with a version for the Substrate. We can do more with the larger screen. The Substrate will come with the new release of their operating system, which will run on both."

"Wow, this is great," said Prasad. "I'd like to be able to show more amp controls on the screen. We can make the controls bigger and easier to manipulate, too. We can reuse a lot of the core functionality from the ScratchPad emulator version. Unless Fabrikam changed the operating system APIs, we can reuse some of the code, too. We might want to drop some functionality in the ScratchPad version that our customers don't use. We can add the solid state/tube hybrid amp sounds from the web version, but we need to make some changes to suit the frequency response on the tablet. This should be fun!"

Reuse is an eternal goal for those seeking increased software productivity. People think most often in terms of code reuse, but many other software project components also have reuse potential. Reusing requirements can increase productivity and improve quality, as well as leading to greater consistency between related systems.

Reuse means taking advantage of work that has been done previously, whether on the same project or on an earlier project. Anytime you can avoid starting from scratch, you've got a running start on the project. The simplest way to reuse a requirement is to copy and paste it from an existing specification. The most sophisticated way is to reuse an entire functional component, from requirements through design, code, and tests. Numerous reuse options exist between these extremes.

Reuse is not free. It presents its own risks, both with respect to reusing existing items and to creating items with good reuse potential. It will likely take more time and effort to create high-quality reusable requirements than to write requirements you intend to use only on the current project. Despite the obvious merits, one study found that only about half of the organizations surveyed are actually practicing requirements reuse, primarily because of the poor quality of existing requirements (Chernak 2012). An organization that is serious about reuse needs to establish some infrastructure to make existing high-quality requirements knowledge accessible to future BAs and to foster a culture that values reuse.

This chapter describes several kinds of requirements reuse, identifies some classes of requirements information that have reuse potential in various contexts, and offers suggestions about how to perform requirements reuse. It presents some issues around making requirements reusable.

The chapter concludes with both barriers to effective reuse and success factors that can help your organization better take advantage of its existing body of requirements knowledge.

Why reuse requirements?

The benefits of effective requirements reuse include faster delivery, lower development costs, consistency both within and across applications, higher team productivity, fewer defects, and reduced rework. Reusing trusted requirements can save review time, accelerate the approval cycle, and speed up other project activities, such as testing. Reuse can improve your ability to estimate implementation effort if you have data available from implementing the same requirements on a previous project.

From the user's perspective, requirements reuse can improve functional consistency across related members of a product line or among a set of business applications. Consider the ability to format blocks of text by applying the same styling, spacing, and other properties in all members of a suite of related applications. Making this work in a uniform fashion involves reusing both functional and usability requirements. Such consistency can minimize the user's learning curve and frustration levels. It also saves time for stakeholders, who then will not need to specify similar requirements repeatedly.

Even if the implementation varies in different environments, the requirements might be the same. An airline's website might have a feature to let a passenger check in for a flight, pay for seat upgrades, and print boarding passes. The airline might also have self-service check-in kiosks at airports. The functionality for both check-in operations will be nearly identical, and hence reusable across the two products, even though the implementations and user experiences are dissimilar.

Dimensions of requirements reuse

We can imagine several types of requirements reuse. Sometimes a business analyst will recognize that a user-presented requirement resembles one from a previous project. Perhaps he can retrieve that existing requirement and adapt it for the new project. Such ad hoc reuse is most common with experienced BAs who have good memories and access to previous requirements collections. In other cases, a BA might use some existing requirements during elicitation to help users identify topics to consider for the new system. It's easier to modify something that exists than to create something new.

Table 18-1 describes three dimensions of requirements reuse: the extent of assets being reused, the extent to which an item must be modified for use in its new setting, and the mechanism being used to perform the reuse. When you're contemplating reusing requirements information, think about which option in each of these dimensions is most appropriate and practical for meeting your objectives.

TABLE 18-1 Three dimensions of requirements reuse

Dimension	Options
Extent of reuse	■ Individual requirement statement ■ Requirement plus its attributes ■ Requirement plus its attributes, context, and associated information such as data definitions, glossary definitions, acceptance tests, assumptions, constraints, and business rules ■ A set of related requirements ■ A set of requirements and their associated design elements ■ A set of requirements and their associated design, code, and test elements
Extent of modification	■ None ■ Associated requirement attributes (priority, rationale, origin, and so on) ■ Requirement statement itself ■ Related information (tests, design constraints, data definitions, and so on)
Reuse mechanism	■ Copy-and-paste from another specification ■ Copy from a library of reusable requirements ■ Refer to an original source

Extent of reuse

The first dimension has to do with the quantity of material that you are reusing. You might reuse just a single functional requirement. Or you might reuse such a statement along with any associated attributes, such as its rationale, origin, priority, and more if those are relevant to the target project. In some cases you can reuse not just the requirement but also associated artifacts: data definitions, acceptance tests, relevant business rules, constraints, assumptions, and so on. Often, a set of related requirements can be reused, such as all the functional requirements associated with a particular feature. Applications that run on similar platforms, such as different smartphone operating systems, could reuse requirements and design elements but perhaps not much code.

In the ideal scenario you can reuse a whole package of requirements, models, design components, code, and tests. That is, you reuse an entire chunk of implemented functionality essentially unchanged from a related product. This level of reuse can work when common operations are being employed across various projects on a common platform. Examples of such operations are error-handling strategies, internal data logging and reporting, communication protocol abstractions, and help systems. These functions must be developed for reuse with clear application programming interfaces (APIs) and all supporting documentation and test artifacts.

A reuse success tale

I once worked for a large retailer that was merging two online catalogs, one for consumers and one for corporations, into a single new system. The business objective was to reduce maintenance costs and make it easier to add new features that would appear in both catalogs. We developed the consumer catalog requirements first, based on the existing catalog functionality. For the corporate side, we started with those same consumer catalog requirements, then edited those that had to vary. Some new requirements were added for the new corporate catalog as well. The project delivered on schedule partly because of the time savings from reuse.

Extent of modification

The next dimension to consider is how much modification will be needed to make existing requirements reusable on the new project. In some cases, you'll be able to reuse a requirement unchanged. In the example given earlier about the airline's check-in kiosk, many of the functional requirements would be identical for the kiosk and for a website that offers passenger check-in. In other cases, you might reuse a requirement statement unchanged but have to modify some of its attributes, such as its priority or rationale as it applies to the new system. Often, you will start with an existing requirement but modify it to exactly suit the new purpose. Finally, whether or not you change the requirement, you might need to modify some designs and tests. An example is porting functionality from a PC to a tablet that has a touch screen rather than a mouse-and-keyboard interface.

Reuse mechanism

The most rudimentary form of reuse is simply a copy-and-paste of a piece of requirements information, either from another specification or from a library of reusable requirements. You don't retain a history of where the original information came from, and you can modify the copies you make. Copy-and-paste within a project increases the size of your specifications because you're duplicating information. If you find yourself populating a specification by doing a lot of copy-and-paste, a warning bell should ring. And just as when you copy code, copying and pasting requirements can introduce problems because of context issues, when the context isn't carried across with the paste operation.

In most cases, you're better off reusing existing content by referring to it instead of replicating it. This means that the original source of the information must be accessible to anyone who needs to view the requirement, and it must be persistent. If you're storing your requirements in a document and want the same requirement to appear in multiple places, you can use the cross-referencing feature of your word processor to link copies back to the master instance (Wiegers 2006). When the master instance is altered, the change is echoed everywhere you inserted a cross-reference link. This avoids the inconsistencies that can arise when one instance gets changed manually but others do not. However, it also runs the risk of all those requirements changing if someone else can alter the master instance.

Another copy-by-reference mechanism is to store not the actual requirement information but simply a pointer to it in your project documentation. Suppose you want to reuse descriptions of some user classes from other projects in your organization. First, collect such reusable information into a shared location. Possible forms for this collection include a word processing file, spreadsheet, HTML or XML file, database, and a specialized requirements tool. Give each object in that collection a unique identifier. To incorporate that information by reference, enter the identifier for each object you want to reuse in the appropriate section of your document. If technology allows, include a hyperlink directly to the reused object in the information collection. A reader who wants to view that user class description can simply follow the link to go to the master source. If you maintain that collection of reusable artifacts properly, those links and the destination information will always be current.

A much more effective way to reuse by reference is to store requirements in a requirements management tool, as described in Chapter 30, "Tools for requirements engineering." Depending on the tool's capabilities, you might be able to reuse a requirement that is already in the database without replicating it. Some such tools retain historical versions of individual requirements, which allows you to reuse a specific version of a requirement or set of related requirements. If someone modifies that requirement in the database, the older version that you are reusing still exists. You can then tailor your own version of that requirement to suit the needs of your project without disrupting other reusers.

Figure 18-1 illustrates this process. Project A creates the initial version of a particular requirement. Later on, Project B decides to reuse that same requirement, so the two projects share a common version. Then Project A modifies that requirement, thereby spawning version 2. However, version 1 still exists unchanged for use in Project B. If Project B needs to modify its copy later, it creates version 3, which does not affect any other project using any other version of that same requirement.

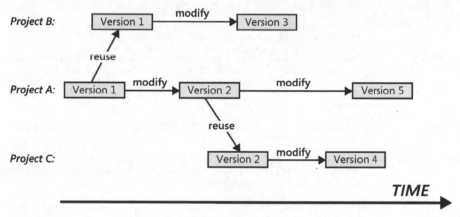

FIGURE 18-1 How a requirement can evolve through reuse in multiple projects.

Types of requirements information to reuse

Table 18-2 identifies some types of requirements-related assets that have good reuse potential for various scopes of applicability. Several of these assets appear in multiple scope categories. Some types of assets have very broad reusability, such as accessibility requirements (a subset of usability).

A set of related requirements in a specific functional area offers more reuse value than do single, isolated requirements. One example is around security (Firesmith 2004). There's no reason for every project team in an organization to reinvent requirements for user logon and authentication, changing and resetting passwords, and so forth. If you can write a set of comprehensive, well-specified requirements for these common capabilities, they can be reused many times to save time and provide consistency across applications. You might be able to reuse sets of constraints within a specific operating environment or delivery platform. For instance, developers of smartphone apps need to be aware of screen size, resolution, and user interaction constraints. Following are some other groupings of related requirements information to reuse in sets:

- Functionality plus associated exceptions and acceptance tests

- Data objects and their associated attributes and validations

- Compliance-related business rules, such as Sarbanes–Oxley, other regulatory constraints by industry, and organization policy-focused directives

- Symmetrical user functions such as undo/redo (if you reuse the requirements for an application's undo function, also reuse the corresponding redo requirements)

- Related operations to perform on data objects, such as create, read, update, and delete

TABLE 18-2 Some types of reusable requirements information

Scope of reuse	Potentially reusable requirements assets
Within a product or application	User requirements, specific functional requirements within use cases, performance requirements, usability requirements, business rules
Across a product line	Business objectives, business rules, business process models, context diagrams, ecosystem maps, user requirements, core product features, stakeholder profiles, user class descriptions, user personas, usability requirements, security requirements, compliance requirements, certification requirements, data models and definitions, acceptance tests, glossary
Across an enterprise	Business rules, stakeholder profiles, user class descriptions, user personas, glossary, security requirements
Across a business domain	Business process models, product features, user requirements, user class descriptions, user personas, acceptance tests, glossary, data models and definitions, business rules, security requirements, compliance requirements
Within an operating environment or platform	Constraints, interfaces, infrastructures of functionality needed to support certain types of requirements (such as a report generator)

Common reuse scenarios

Whether you are creating a family of products, building applications across an organization, or even developing a product having a feature that appears in multiple contexts, there are opportunities for reuse. Let's look at some scenarios where requirements reuse offers good potential.

Software product lines

Anytime you're creating a set of products in a family—a software product line—those products will have a lot of functionality in common. Sometimes you're producing variations of a base product for different customers or markets. Requirements you've incorporated into a specific variant for a particular customer might be folded into a common specification for the base product. Other product lines involve a family of related products that are based on a common architectural platform. For example, the vendor of a popular income tax preparation package offers a free version for online use as well as basic, deluxe, premier, home and business, and business versions for use on personal computers. Analyze the features in the software product line to see which ones are:

- Common, appearing in all members of the product line.

- Optional, appearing in certain family members but not others.

- Variants, with different versions of the feature appearing in different family members (Gomaa 2004; Dehlinger and Lutz 2008).

The common features offer the greatest opportunities for reusing not just certain requirements, but also their downstream work products, including architectural components, design elements, code, and tests. This is the most powerful form of reuse, but we don't often detect the opportunity to take advantage of it. Reusing the common functionality is far better than reimplementing it each time, perhaps making it slightly different without good reason. Be aware of any constraints that the operating environment or hardware platform of certain products might impose that could limit reuse options. If the implementation must be different in certain product-line members, you're limited to reusing only requirements, not designs and code.

Reengineered and replacement systems

Reengineered and replacement systems always reuse some requirements from the original incarnation, even if those "requirements" were never written down. If you have to reverse-engineer requirements knowledge from an older system for possible reuse, you might need to move your thinking up to a higher level of abstraction to get away from specific implementation characteristics. Often, you can harvest business rules that were embedded in an old system and reuse them on future projects, updating them as necessary, as in the case of regulatory or compliance rules.

> **Trap** Watch out for the temptation to reuse too much of an old system in the interest of saving time, thereby missing the opportunities offered by new platforms, architectures, and workflows.

Other likely reuse opportunities

Table 18-3 lists several other situations in which reusing requirements information is common. If you encounter any of these opportunities in your organization, contemplate whether it is worth accumulating the reusable artifacts into a shared repository and managing the information as an enterprise-level asset. If you previously worked on a project similar to the current one, consider whether you can use any artifacts from the earlier project again.

TABLE 18-3 Common opportunities where requirements reuse can be valuable

Reuse opportunity	Examples
Business processes	Often business processes are common across organizations and need to be commonly supported by software. Many institutions maintain a set of business process descriptions that are reused across IT projects.
Distributed deployments	Often the same system is deployed multiple times with slight variations. This is fairly typical for retail stores and warehouses. A common set of requirements is reused for each separate deployment.
Interfaces and integration	There is often a need to reuse requirements for interfaces and integration purposes. For example, in hospitals, most ancillary systems need interfaces to and from the admissions, discharge, and transfer system. This also applies to financial interfaces to an enterprise resource planning system.
Security	User authentication and security requirements are often the same across systems. For example, the systems might have a common requirement that all products must have a single sign-on using Active Directory for user authentication.
Common application features	Business applications often contain common functionality for which requirements—and perhaps even full implementations—can be reused. Possibilities include search operations, printing, file operations, user profiles, undo/redo, and text formatting.
Similar products for multiple platforms	The same core set of requirements is used even though there might be some detailed requirement and/or user interface design differences based on the platform. Examples include applications that run on both Mac and Windows or on both iOS and Android.
Standards, regulations, and legal compliance	Many organizations have developed a set of standards, often based on regulations, that are defined as a set of requirements. These are reused between projects. Examples are ADA Standards for Accessible Design and HIPAA privacy rules for healthcare companies.

Requirement patterns

Taking advantage of knowledge that makes the job of writing requirements easier can be regarded as reuse. That's the rationale behind requirement patterns: to package considerable knowledge about a particular type of requirement in a way that's convenient for a BA who wants to define such a requirement.

Pioneered by Stephen Withall (2007), a *requirement pattern* offers a systematic approach to specifying a particular type of requirement. A pattern defines a template with categories of information for each of the common types of requirements a project might encounter. Different types of requirement patterns will have their own sets of content categories. Populating the template will likely provide a more detailed specification of a requirement than if the BA simply wrote it in natural language. The structure and content of a requirement written according to a pattern facilitates reuse.

A requirement pattern contains several sections (Withall 2007):

1.   **Guidance**   Basic details about the pattern, including related patterns, situations to which it is (and is not) applicable, and a discussion of how to approach writing a requirement of this type.

2.   **Content**   A detailed explanation of the content that such a requirement ought to convey, item by item.

3. **Template**   A requirement definition with placeholders wherever variable pieces of information need to go. This can be used as a fill-in-the-blanks starting point for writing a specific requirement of that type.

4. **Examples**   One or more illustrative requirements of this type.

5. **Extra requirements**   Additional requirements that can define certain aspects of the topic, or an explanation of how to write a set of detailed requirements that spell out what must be done to satisfy an original, high-level requirement.

6. **Considerations for development and testing**   Factors for developers to keep in mind when implementing a requirement of the type specified by the pattern, and factors for testers to keep in mind when testing such requirements.

As an illustration, many software applications generate reports. Withall (2007) provides a pattern for specifying requirements that define reports. Withall's pattern includes a template that shows how to structure numerous report elements into a set of more detailed requirements that constitute a complete report specification. But the template is just one piece of the pattern. The pattern also contains an example of a reporting requirement, possible extra requirements to include, and considerable guidance about specifying, implementing, and testing such requirements.

You can create requirement patterns of your own that are ideally suited to your organization's style and projects. Following a pattern helps create consistency and will likely give you richer and more precise requirements. Simple templates like these remind you about important information that you might otherwise overlook. If you need to write a requirement on an unfamiliar topic, using a pattern is likely to be quicker than researching the topic yourself.

Tools to facilitate reuse

In an ideal world, your organization would store all of its software requirements in a requirements management tool with a complete set of traceability links. These links would tie each requirement back to a parent requirement or other origin, to other requirements it depends on, and to downstream development artifacts that are linked to it. Every historical version of each requirement would be available. This is the best way to enable effective reuse on a large scale across a whole application, product portfolio, or organization.

Few organizations have reached this level of sophistication, but storing your requirements in a tool will still enhance reuse in several ways (Akers 2008). Commercial requirements management tools provide various capabilities to facilitate reuse. Some even contain large libraries of requirements from certain domains available for ready reuse. When you're selecting a tool, include your expectations regarding how it will help you reuse requirements as part of the evaluation process. Chapter 30 describes typical capabilities of commercially available requirements management tools.

A tool might allow you to reuse a specific requirement by sharing it across multiple projects or baselines. If you do this, you need to think about what should happen if you change either the original requirement or its clones. Some tools let you lock the content so you can edit only the original instance of the requirement. This ensures that any places where that requirement is reused are also updated at the time of the editing. Of course, if you start with a reused requirement and then *do* want to modify it for use in its new setting, you don't want to keep that lock in place. In that case, you would like to copy it using a mode that permits you to change the copied requirement.

Similarly, when you copy a requirement that has associated traceability relationships, you might or might not want to carry along everything that is linked to it. Sometimes, you might want to pull just the requirement, plus its children and requirements on which it depends, into a new project. This would be the case if the function is the same but the delivery platforms differ, as is the case with applications that run on a web browser, tablet, smartphone, and kiosk.

> **Trap** If BAs can't find what they're looking for in the reuse repository, it doesn't matter how good the stored requirements are or how much time they might save: the BAs will write their own. Writing reusable requirements according to standard patterns provides a set of fields on which to search. Some people advocate adding meaningful keywords or requirement attributes to assist with searching.

Making requirements reusable

Just because a requirement exists doesn't mean it's reusable in its present form. It could be specific to a particular project. It might be written at too high a level because the BA could safely assume certain knowledge on the part of the development team or because some details were communicated only verbally. A requirement could be lacking information about how possible exceptions should be handled. You might have to tune up the original requirements to increase their value to future BAs.

Well-written requirements lend themselves to reuse. The steps you take to make requirements more reusable also increases their value to the project for which you originally write them; it simply makes them better requirements. Reusers need to know about dependencies each requirement has on others, as well as other requirements that go with it and that might also be reused, so that they can package sets of related requirements appropriately. Although *reuse* saves your team time and money, making something readily *reusable* is likely to cost time and money.

Reusable requirements must be written at the right level of abstraction and scope. Domain-specific requirements are written at a low level of abstraction. They are likely to be applicable only in their original domain (Shehata, Eberlein, and Hoover 2002). Generic requirements have broader applicability for reuse in a variety of systems. However, if you attempt to reuse requirements at too general a level, you won't save much effort because the BA will still have to elaborate the details. It's tricky to find the right balance between making reuse easier (with more abstract or generalized requirements) and making reuse pay off (with more detailed or specific requirements).

Figure 18-2 provides an example. Perhaps you're building an application that includes a user requirement to accept credit card payments. This user requirement would expand into a set of related functional and nonfunctional requirements around handling credit card payments. Other applications also might need to take payments by credit card, so that's a potentially reusable set of requirements.

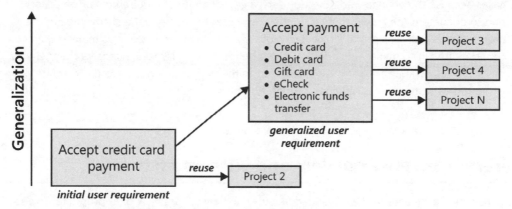

FIGURE 18-2 Generalized requirements offer greater reuse potential.

But suppose you could generalize that user requirement to encompass several payment mechanisms: credit card, debit card, gift card, eCheck, and electronic funds transfer. The resulting requirement offers greater reuse potential in a wider range of future projects. One project might need just credit card processing, whereas others require several of the payment processing methods. Generalizing an initial user requirement like this—from "accept credit card payment" to "accept payment"—could be valuable even on the current project. Even if the customer only asked to handle credit card payments initially, users might really like to accept multiple payment methods either now or in the future.

Choosing the right abstraction level for requirements can pay off during construction, as well. On one project that had exactly this need for multiple payment methods, generating clear requirements and rules for each case revealed both commonalities and distinctions. Independent from future reuse possibilities, building the higher-level abstractions contributed to easier design and construction.

That's the good news. The bad news is that it will take some effort to generalize the initially presented requirement. That's the investment you make in reusability, anticipating that you will recoup the investment—and more—through multiple, future reuse instances. It's up to you to decide whether to simply place today's requirements into a shared location for possible reuse or to invest effort to improve their reusability on future projects.

The "reusable requirements" explosion

A colleague offered a cautionary tale of how to reduce the potential value of reuse by writing excessively detailed requirements. A team tasked with writing requirements for a new project was obsessed with reuse. The BAs thought that if they documented all of the details for each requirement separately, then they could be reused. They ended up with more than 14,000 requirements! The repository contained entries that should have been just one requirement but had been structured as a parent with multiple child requirements, each giving a specific detail about the parent. Requirements this detailed were relevant only to that one application.

This volume of requirements also made the testing cycle much more difficult, leading to daily complaints from the testers. It was taking them much longer than expected to write test cases because they had to wade through such a vast quantity of requirements. The testers had to document the requirement ID in their test cases to ensure that test coverage of the requirements was achieved for traceability, but the number of traces on this many requirements became difficult to manage. In addition, the requirements underwent extensive change; they never did fully stabilize. All of these factors led to the project being deployed a year late, without producing the desired collection of reusable requirements.

Requirements reuse barriers and success factors

Requirements reuse sounds like a grand idea, but it isn't always practical or appropriate. This section describes some considerations to help your organization succeed with requirements reuse.

Reuse barriers

The first step to overcoming an obstacle is to recognize and understand it. Following are several barriers you might encounter when it comes to reusing requirements.

Missing or poor requirements   A common barrier is that the requirements developed on previous projects weren't documented, so it's impossible to reuse them. And even if you find a relevant requirement, it might be badly written, incomplete, or a poor fit for your present circumstances. Even if they're documented, the original requirements for an old application might not have been kept current as the application evolved over time, rendering them obsolete.

NIH and NAH   Two barriers to reuse are NIH and NAH syndromes. NIH means "not invented here." Some people are reluctant to reuse requirements from another organization or generic requirements found in a public collection. Requirements written elsewhere could be harder to understand: terminology could be different; the requirements might refer to documents that are unavailable; you might not be able to discern the context of the original requirements; and important background information could go unexplained. A BA might correctly decide that it takes less work to write new requirements than to understand and fix up the existing ones.

NAH, or "not applicable here," syndrome reveals itself when practitioners protest that a new process or approach does not apply to their project or organization. "We're different," they claim. The members might feel that their project is unique, so no existing requirements could possibly apply. Sometimes that's true, but often NIH and NAH indicate an inflexible attitude.

Writing style   The BAs on previous projects might have used a wide variety of requirements representation techniques and conventions. It's best to adopt some standard notations for documenting requirements to facilitate reuse, such as using patterns. If requirements are written at a common level of granularity, it's easier for future BAs to search for candidate requirements at the right level of detail. Consistent terminology is also important. You might overlook a potentially reusable requirement simply because some of the terminology involved is not the same as what your stakeholders are used to. Requirements written in natural language are notoriously prone to ambiguities, missing information, and hidden assumptions. These issues reduce their reuse potential.

Requirements that have embedded design constraints will offer little opportunity for reuse in a different environment. Think about the airport check-in kiosk described earlier. If user interface details about the kiosk were embedded in the requirements, you couldn't reuse those requirements for software having essentially the same functionality but running on a website.

Inconsistent organization   It can be difficult to find requirements to reuse because authors organize their requirements in many different ways: by project, process flow, business unit, product feature, category, subsystem or component, and so forth.

Project type   Requirements that are tightly coupled to specific implementation environments or platforms are less likely to generate reusable requirements or to benefit from an existing pool of requirements knowledge. Rapidly evolving domains don't yet have a pool of requirements information to reuse; requirements that are relevant today might be obsolete tomorrow.

Ownership   Another barrier has to do with ownership (Somerville and Sawyer 1997). If you're developing a software product for a specific customer, its requirements are likely the proprietary intellectual property of the customer. You might not have the legal right to reuse any of those requirements in a different system you develop for your own company or for other customers.

Reuse success factors

An organization that is serious about reuse should create mechanisms to make it easy to share and take advantage of existing information. This means pulling information that has the potential for reuse out of a specific project so others can access and reuse it. Keep the following success tips in mind.

Repository   You can't reuse something if you can't find it. An enabling tool for effective large-scale reuse, therefore, is a searchable repository in which to store requirements information. This repository could take several forms:

- A single network folder that contains previous requirements documents

- A collection of requirements stored in a requirements management tool that can be searched across projects

- A database that stores sets of requirements culled from projects for their reuse potential and enhanced with keywords to help future BAs know their origin, judge their suitability, and learn about their limitations

Consider giving someone the responsibility to manage the reusable requirements repository. This person would adapt existing requirements knowledge as necessary to represent and store the assets in a form suitable for efficient discovery, retrieval, and reuse. A scheme similar to that used to store and manage business rules as an enterprise asset could be adapted to handle reusable requirements.

Quality   No one wants to reuse junk. Potential reusers need confidence in the quality of the information. And even if a requirement you are reusing isn't perfect, you should try to make it better when you reuse it. This way you iteratively improve a requirement over time, increasing its reuse potential for future projects.

Interactions   Requirements often have logical links or dependencies on each other. Use traceability links in a tool to identify these dependencies so people know just what they're getting into when they select a requirement for reuse. Reused requirements must conform to existing business rules, constraints, standards, interfaces, and quality expectations.

Terminology   Establishing common terminology and definitions across your projects will be helpful for reusability. Terminology variations won't prevent you from reusing requirements, but you'll have to deal with the inconsistencies and take steps to prevent misunderstandings. Glossaries and data dictionaries are good sources of reusable information. Rather than incorporating an entire glossary into every requirements specification, create links from key terms to their definitions in the shared glossary.

Organizational culture   Management should encourage reuse from two perspectives: contributing high-quality components with real reuse potential, and effectively reusing existing artifacts. The individuals, project teams, and organizations that practice reuse most effectively are likely to enjoy the highest productivity. In a reuse culture, BAs look at the reusable requirements repository before creating their own requirements. They might start with a user story or other high-level requirement statement and see to what extent they can populate the details through reuse of existing information.

Your project requirements constitute valuable corporate information. To maximize the investment your teams make in requirements engineering, look for requirements knowledge that you can treat as an enterprise-level asset. The requirements you reuse do not have to be perfect to be valuable. Even if they just save you 20 percent of the work you might have otherwise spent writing new requirements, that's a big gain. A culture that encourages BAs to borrow first and create second, and that makes a little extra investment in making requirements reusable, can increase the productivity of both analysts and development teams and lead to higher-quality products.

Next steps

- Examine your current project to see if you can simplify requirements sets by reusing requirements knowledge from previous projects or other sources.

- Analyze your current project for requirements that are potentially reusable. Assess the scope of reuse from Table 18-2 for each requirement. Remember, you need to have a realistic chance of recouping the cost of extracting the reusable assets, packaging them, storing them, and making them accessible to others; otherwise, it's not a worthwhile investment.

- Think about what information you should store about your reusable requirements to make it easy for a future BA to search for them and judge whether they could be used on his project. Decide on a pragmatic repository in which to store requirements for reuse.

CHAPTER 19

Beyond requirements development

The Chemical Tracking System's project sponsor, Gerhard, had been skeptical of the need to spend time defining requirements. However, he joined the development team and product champions at a one-day training class on software requirements, which motivated him to support the requirements activities.

As the project progressed, Gerhard received excellent feedback from the user representatives about how well requirements development had gone. He even sponsored a luncheon for the analysts and product champions to celebrate reaching the significant milestone of baselined requirements for the first system release. At the luncheon, Gerhard thanked the participants for their effective teamwork. Then he said, "Now that the requirements are done, I look forward to seeing the final product."

"Please keep in mind, Gerhard, we won't have the final product for about a year," the project manager explained. "We plan to deliver the system through a series of bimonthly releases. If we take the time to think about design now, it will be easier for developers to add more functionality later. We'll also learn more about requirements as we go along. We will show you some working software at each release, though."

Gerhard was frustrated. It looked like the development team was stalling rather than getting down to the real work of programming. But was he jumping the gun?

Experienced project managers and developers understand the value of translating software requirements into rational project plans and robust designs. These steps are necessary whether the next release represents 1 percent or 100 percent of the final product. This chapter explores some approaches for bridging the gap between requirements development and a successful product release. Some of these activities are the business analyst's responsibility, whereas others fall within the project manager's domain. We'll look at several ways in which requirements influence project plans, designs, code, and tests, as shown in Figure 19-1. In addition to these connections, there is a link between the requirements for the software to be built and other project and transition requirements. Those include data migrations, training design and delivery, business process and organizational changes, infrastructure modifications, and others. Those activities aren't discussed further in this book.

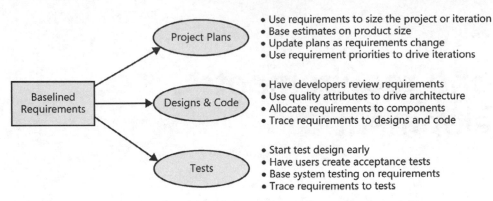

FIGURE 19-1 Requirements drive project planning, design, coding, and testing activities.

Estimating requirements effort

One of the earliest project planning activities is to judge how much of the project's schedule and effort should be devoted to requirements activities. Karl Wiegers (2006) suggests some ways to judge this and some factors that would lead you to spend either more or less time than you might otherwise expect. Small projects typically spend 15 to 18 percent of their total effort on requirements work (Wiegers 1996), but the appropriate percentage depends on the size and complexity of the project. Despite the fear that exploring requirements will slow down a project, considerable evidence shows that taking time to understand the requirements actually accelerates development, as the following examples illustrate:

- A study of 15 projects in the telecommunications and banking industries revealed that the most successful projects spent 28 percent of their resources on requirements elicitation, modeling, validation, and verification (Hofmann and Lehner 2001). The average project devoted 15.7 percent of its effort and 38.6 percent of its schedule to requirements engineering.

- NASA projects that invested more than 10 percent of their total resources on requirements development had substantially smaller cost and schedule overruns than projects that devoted less effort to requirements (Hooks and Farry 2001).

- In a European study, teams that developed products more quickly devoted more of their schedule and effort to requirements than did slower teams, as shown in Table 19-1 (Blackburn, Scudder, and Van Wassenhove 1996).

TABLE 19-1 Investing in requirements accelerates development

	Effort devoted to requirements	Schedule devoted to requirements
Faster projects	14%	17%
Slower projects	7%	9%

Requirements engineering activity is distributed throughout the project in different ways, depending on whether the project is following a sequential (waterfall), iterative, or incremental development life cycle, as was illustrated in Figure 3-3 in Chapter 3, "Good practices for requirements engineering."

> **Trap** Watch out for analysis paralysis. A project with massive up-front effort aimed at perfecting the requirements "once and for all" often delivers little useful functionality in an appropriate time frame. On the other hand, don't avoid requirements development because of the specter of analysis paralysis. As with so many issues in life, a sensible balance point lies somewhere between the two extremes.

When estimating the effort a project should devote to requirements development, let experience be your guide. Look back at the requirements effort from previous projects and judge how effective the requirements work on those projects was. If you can attribute issues to poor requirements, perhaps more emphasis on requirements work would pay off for you. Of course, this assessment demands that you retain some historical data from previous projects so you can better estimate future projects. You might not have any such data now, but if team members record how they spend their time on today's project, that becomes tomorrow's "historical data." It's not more complicated than that. Recording both estimated and actual effort allows you to think of how you can improve future estimates.

The requirements engineering consulting company Seilevel (Joy's company) developed an effective approach for estimating a project's requirements development effort, refined from work estimates and actual results from many projects. This approach involves three complementary estimates: percent of total work; a developer-to-BA ratio; and an activity breakdown that uses basic resource costs to generate a bottom-up estimate. Comparing the results from all three estimates and reconciling any significant disconnects allows the business analyst team to generate the most accurate estimates.

The first estimate is based on a percentage of the estimated total project work. Specifically, we consider that about 15 percent of the total project effort should be allocated to requirements work. This value is in line with the percentages cited earlier in this section. So if the full project is estimated at 1,000 hours, we estimate 150 hours of requirements work. Of course, the overall project estimate might change after the requirements are better understood.

The second type of estimate assumes a typical ratio of developers to business analysts. Our default value is 6:1, meaning that one BA can produce enough requirements to keep six developers busy. The BAs also will be working with quality assurance, project management, and the business itself, so this estimate encompasses all of the BA team's project work. For a packaged solution (COTS) project, this ratio changes to 3:1 (three developers per BA). There are still many selection, configuration, and transition requirements to be elicited and documented, but the development team is smaller because the code is largely purchased instead of developed new. So if we know the development team size, we can estimate an appropriate BA staffing level. This is a rule-of-thumb estimator, not a cast-in-concrete prediction of the future, so be sure to adjust for your organization and project type.

The third estimate considers the various activities a BA performs, based on estimates of the numbers of various artifacts that might be created on a specific project. The BA can estimate the number of process flows, user stories, screens, reports, and the like and then make reasonable assumptions of how many other requirements artifacts are needed. Based on time estimates per activity that we have accumulated from multiple projects, we can generate a total requirements effort estimate.

We created a spreadsheet tool for calculating all three of these requirements estimates, which is available with this book's companion content. Figure 19-2 illustrates a portion of the spreadsheet's results. The Summary Total Effort Comparison shows the estimates for the number of BAs and the BA budgets for both the requirements work and the entire project. These estimates serve as a starting point for reconciling the differences, negotiating resources, and planning the project's BA needs.

Input			
Quantity	Items	Quantity	Items
20	Existing pages of documentation for review	$ 750,000	Total project budget
0	Existing systems being updated or replaced	$125	BA blended hourly cost
5	Stakeholders	Standard	Type of project
1	Interfacing Systems - small systems	5	Number of developers
1	Interfacing Systems - medium systems	No	Is your team remote?
1	Interfacing Systems - large systems	52	Project duration? (weeks)
8	Process Flows	20	Requirements work duration? (weeks)
2	BDDs		
8	Screens		
1	Reports		

Summary Total Effort Comparison				
	% of total project	Ratio of dev to BAs	Activity based	
Number of BAs	1	0.8	0.8	*Excludes time off
BA budget for requirements work	$ 113,000	$ 83,000	$ 77,000	
BA budget for project duration	$ 293,000	$ 217,000	$ 200,000	

FIGURE 19-2 Partial output from the requirements effort estimation spreadsheet.

The requirements estimation tool has three worksheet tabs. First, there is a summary where you input several project characteristics. The tool will calculate various elements of the three types of estimates. Second, there is an assumptions tab where you can adjust items that vary from the provided assumptions. The third tab provides instructions about how to use the estimation tool.

The assumptions built into this estimation tool are based on Seilevel's extensive experience with actual projects. You'll need to tweak some of the assumptions for your own organization. For example, if your BAs are either novices or especially highly experienced, some of your estimates of the time needed per activity may vary from the defaults. To tailor the tool to best suit your reality, collect some data from your own projects and modify the adjustable parameters.

Important All estimates are based on the knowledge the estimator has available at the time and the assumptions he makes. Preliminary estimates based on limited information have large uncertainties. Refine your estimates as knowledge is gained and work is completed during the project. Record your assumptions so that it's clear what you were thinking when you came up with the numbers.

Betty's in a corner

Sridhar, the project manager of a million-dollar project, approached the BA, Betty, to discuss her initial estimate regarding how long requirements development would take. In an earlier email exchange she had estimated eight weeks. Sridhar asked, "Betty, is it really going to take you eight weeks to do the requirements for our shopping portal? Surely your team can have it done in four weeks; the system is just not that complex. I mean, really, people come to the website to search for and buy products. That's it! Heck, the development manager is thinking that his team can just develop the system without any requirements at all, so that's what they're planning to do if you don't have the requirements done in four weeks."

Betty is backed into a corner here. She can give in and agree to an unreasonable four-week deadline for this large project. Or, she can push back at the risk of looking ineffective because the project is supposed to be "simple." After all, Betty isn't actually sure how long it will take her to develop an adequate set of requirements, because she doesn't yet know the size of the system. Until she begins the analysis, she doesn't know what she doesn't know.

Variations on this story are a big part of why Seilevel developed the estimation tool described in this chapter. This tool aids Betty in her stressful conversation with Sridhar. She can say, "Well, if I only have four weeks, let me show you what I CAN do." She can tweak the numbers of reports or processes for which requirements are needed. Betty can effectively timebox the requirements effort. However, it's important for Sridhar to recognize that understanding the requirements for only the tip of the iceberg can lead to unpleasant surprises further down the road.

From requirements to project plans

Because requirements are the foundation for the project's intended work, you should base estimates, project plans, and schedules on those requirements. Remember, the most important project outcome is a system that meets its business objectives, not simply one that implements all the initial requirements according to the original project plan. The requirements and plans represent the team's assessment at a specific point in time of what it will take to achieve that outcome. But the project's scope might have been off target, or the initial plans might not have been realistic or well-aligned with the objectives. Business needs, business rules, and project constraints all can change. The project's business success will be problematic if you don't update your plans to align with evolving objectives and realities.

Estimating project size and effort from requirements

Making realistic estimates of the effort and time needed to complete a project depends on many factors, but it begins with estimating the size of the product to be built. You can base size estimates on functional requirements, user stories, analysis models, prototypes, or user interface designs. Although there's no perfect measure of software size, the following are some frequently used metrics:

- The number of individually testable requirements (Wilson 1995)

- Function points (Jones 1996b; IFPUG 2010)

- Story points (Cohn 2005; McConnell 2006) or use case points (Wiegers 2006)

- The number, type, and complexity of user interface elements

- Estimated lines of code needed to implement specific requirements

Base whatever approach you choose on your experience and on the nature of the software you're developing. Understanding what the development team has successfully achieved on similar projects using similar technologies lets you gauge team productivity. After you estimate size and productivity, you can estimate the total effort needed to implement the project. Effort estimates depend on the team size (multitasking people are less productive, and more communication interfaces slow things down) and planned schedule (compressed schedules actually increase the total effort needed).

One approach is to use commercial software estimation tools that suggest various feasible combinations of development effort and schedule. These tools let you adjust estimates based on factors such as the skill of the developers, project complexity, and the team's experience in the application domain. Complex, nonlinear relationships exist between product size, effort, development time, productivity, and staff buildup time (Putnam and Myers 1997). Understanding these relationships can keep you from being trapped in the "impossible region," combinations of product size, schedule, and team size where the probability of success is extremely low.

The best estimation processes acknowledge the early uncertainty and ongoing volatility of scope. People using such a process will express each estimate as a range, not a single value. They manage the accuracy of their estimate by widening the range based on the uncertainty and volatility of the data that fed into the estimate.

Agile projects estimate scope in units of *story points*, a measure of the relative effort that will be needed to implement a particular user story. Estimates of the size of a specific story depend on the knowledge you have—and lack—about the story, its complexity, and the functionality involved (Leffingwell 2011). Agile teams measure their team's *velocity*, the number of story points the team expects to complete in a standard iteration based on its previous experience and the results from early iterations on a new project. The team members combine the size of the product backlog with velocity to estimate the project's schedule, cost, and the number of iterations required. Dean Leffingwell (2011) describes several techniques for estimating and planning agile projects in this fashion.

If you don't compare your estimates to the actual project results and improve your estimating ability, your estimates will forever remain guesses. It takes time to accumulate enough data to correlate some measure of software size with requirements development effort and with total project effort. The early iterations on agile projects give the team an assessment of its velocity.

Even a good estimating process will be challenged if your project must cope with requirements that customers, managers, or lawmakers frequently change. If the changes are so great that the development team can't keep up with them, they can become paralyzed, unable to make meaningful progress. Agile development methods provide another way to deal with highly volatile requirements. These methods start by implementing a relatively solid portion of the requirements, knowing up front that changes will be made later. Teams then use customer feedback on the early increments to clarify the remaining product requirements.

A goal is not the same thing as an estimate. Anytime an imposed deadline and a thoughtfully estimated schedule don't agree, negotiation is in order. A project manager who can justify an estimate based on a well-thought-out process and historical data is in a better bargaining position than someone who simply makes her best guess. The project's business objectives should guide stakeholders to resolve the schedule conflict by stretching timelines, reducing scope, adding resources, or compromising on quality. These decisions aren't easy, but making them is the only way to maximize the delivered product value.

Got an hour?

A customer once asked our software group to adapt a small program that he had written for his personal use so that his colleagues could also access it on our network. "Got an hour?" my manager asked me, giving his top-of-the-head assessment of the project's size. When I spoke with the customer and his colleagues to understand what they really had in mind, the problem turned out to be a bit larger. I spent 100 hours writing the program they were looking for. The 100-fold expansion factor suggested that my manager's initial estimate of one hour was a trifle hasty. The team should perform a preliminary exploration of requirements, evaluate scope, and judge the product size *before* anyone makes estimates or commitments.

Uncertain requirements lead to uncertain estimates. Because requirements uncertainty is unavoidable early in the project and because estimates are usually optimistic, include contingency buffers in your schedule and budget to accommodate some requirements growth (Wiegers 2007). Scope growth takes place because business needs change, users and markets shift, and stakeholders reach a better understanding of what the software can or should do. On agile projects, scope growth typically leads to adding more iterations to the development cycle. Extensive requirements growth, however, often indicates that many requirements were missed during elicitation.

> **Important** Don't let your estimates be swayed by what you think someone else wants to hear. Your prediction of the future shouldn't change just because someone doesn't like it. Too large a mismatch in predictions indicates the need for negotiation, though.

Requirements and scheduling

Many projects practice "right-to-left scheduling": a delivery date is cast in concrete and then the product's requirements are defined. In such cases, it often proves impossible to meet the specified ship date while including all the demanded functionality at the expected quality level. It's more realistic to define the software requirements *before* making detailed plans and commitments. A design-to-schedule strategy can work if the project manager can negotiate what portion of the desired functionality can fit within the schedule constraints. Requirements prioritization is a key success factor.

For complex systems in which software is only a part of the final product, project managers generally establish high-level schedules after developing the product-level (system) requirements and a preliminary architecture. At this point, the key delivery dates can be established, based on input from sources including marketing, sales, customer service, and development.

Consider planning and funding the project in stages. An initial requirements exploration stage will provide enough information to let you make realistic plans and estimates for one or more construction stages. Projects that have uncertain requirements benefit from incremental and iterative development approaches. Incremental development lets the team begin delivering useful software long before the requirements become fully clear. Prioritization of requirements dictates the functionality to include in each construction timebox.

Software projects frequently fail to meet their goals because the developers and other project participants are optimistic estimators and poor planners, not because they're poor software engineers. Typical planning mistakes include overlooking common tasks, underestimating effort or time, failing to account for project risks, and not anticipating rework (McConnell 2006). Effective project scheduling requires the following elements:

- Estimated product size

- Known productivity of the development team, based on historical performance

- A list of the tasks needed to completely implement and verify a feature or use case

- Reasonably stable requirements, at least for the forthcoming development iteration

- Experience, which helps the project manager adjust for intangible factors and the unique aspects of each project

> **Trap** Don't succumb to pressure to make commitments that you know are unachievable. This is a recipe for a lose-lose outcome.

From requirements to designs and code

The boundary between requirements and design is not a sharp line but a gray, fuzzy area (Wiegers 2006). Try to keep requirements free from implementation bias, except when there's a compelling reason to intentionally constrain the design. Ideally, the descriptions of what the system is intended to do should not be slanted by design considerations. Practically speaking, though, projects often possess design constraints from prior products, product line standards, and user interface conventions. Because of this, a requirements specification almost always contains some design information. Try to avoid *inadvertent* design, needless or unintended restrictions on the design. Include designers in requirements reviews to make sure the requirements can serve as a solid foundation for design.

Architecture and allocation

A product's functionality, quality attributes, and constraints drive its architecture design (Bass, Clements, and Kazman 1998; Rozanski and Woods 2005). Analyzing a proposed architecture helps the analyst to verify the requirements and tune their precision, as does prototyping. Both methods use the following thought process: "If I understand the requirements correctly, this approach I'm reviewing is a good way to satisfy them. Now that I have a preliminary architecture (or a prototype) in hand, does it help me better understand the requirements and spot incorrect, missing, or conflicting requirements?"

Architecture is especially critical for systems that include both software and hardware components and for complex software-only systems. An essential step is to allocate the high-level system requirements to the various subsystems and components. An analyst, system engineer, or architect decomposes the system requirements into functional requirements for both software and hardware subsystems. Requirements trace information lets the development team track where each requirement is addressed in the design.

 Inappropriate allocation decisions can result in the software being expected to perform functions that should have been assigned to hardware components (or the reverse), in poor performance, or in the inability to replace one component easily with an improved version. On one project, the hardware engineer blatantly told my group that he expected our software to overcome all limitations of his hardware design! Although software is more malleable than hardware, engineers shouldn't use that flexibility as a reason to skimp on hardware design. Take a systems engineering approach to decide which capabilities each system component should deliver.

Allocation of system capabilities to subsystems and components must be done from the top down (Hooks and Farry 2001). Consider a Blu-ray Disc player. As illustrated in Figure 19-3, it includes motors to open and close the disc tray and to spin the disc, an optical subsystem to read the data on the disc, an image-rendering subsystem, a multifunction remote control, and more. The subsystems interact to control the behavior that results when, say, the user presses a button on the remote control to open the disc tray while the disc is playing. The system requirements drive the architecture design for such complex products, and the architecture influences the requirements allocation.

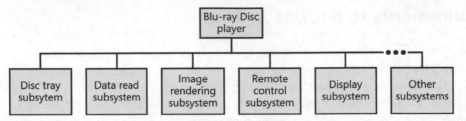

FIGURE 19-3 Complex products such as Blu-ray Disc players contain multiple software and hardware subsystems.

The incredible shrinking design

I once worked on a project that simulated the behavior of a photographic system with eight computational processes. After working hard on requirements analysis, the team was eager to start coding. Instead, we took the time to create a design model to think about how we'd build a solution. We quickly realized that three of the steps in the photographic simulation used identical computational algorithms, three more used another set, and the remaining two shared a third set. The design perspective simplified the problem from eight sets of complex calculations to just three. Had we skipped design, we likely would have noticed the code repetition at some point, but we saved a lot of time by detecting these simplifications early on. It's more efficient to revise design models than to rewrite code.

Software design

Software design receives short shrift on some projects, yet the time spent on design is an excellent investment. A variety of software designs will satisfy most products' requirements. These designs will vary in their performance, efficiency, robustness, and the technical methods employed. If you leap directly from requirements into code, you're essentially designing the software mentally and on the fly. You come up with *a* design but not necessarily with *an excellent* design. Poorly structured software is the likely result.

As with requirements, excellent designs result from iteration. Make multiple passes through the design to refine your initial concepts as you gain information and generate additional ideas. Shortcomings in design lead to products that are difficult to maintain and extend and that don't satisfy the customer's performance, usability, and reliability objectives. The time you spend translating requirements into designs is an excellent investment in building high-quality, robust products.

A project that's applying object-oriented development methods might begin with object-oriented analysis of requirements, using class diagrams and other UML models to represent and analyze requirements information. A designer can elaborate these conceptual class diagrams, which are free of implementation specifics, into more detailed object models for design and implementation.

You needn't develop a complete, detailed design for the entire product before you begin implementation, but you should design each component before you code it. Formal design is of most benefit to particularly difficult projects, projects involving systems with many internal component interfaces and interactions, and projects staffed with inexperienced developers (McConnell 1998). All projects, however, will benefit from the following strategies:

- Developing a solid architecture of subsystems and components that will permit enhancement over the product's life

- Identifying the key functional modules or object classes you need to build, as well as defining their interfaces, responsibilities, and collaborations with other units

- Ensuring that the design accommodates all the functional requirements and doesn't contain unnecessary functionality

- Defining each code unit's intended functionality, following the sound design principles of strong cohesion, loose coupling, and information hiding (McConnell 2004)

- Ensuring that the design addresses exception conditions that can arise

- Ensuring that the design will achieve stated performance, security, and other quality goals

- Identifying any existing components that can be reused

- Defining—and respecting—any limitations or constraints that have a significant impact on the design of the software components

As developers translate requirements into designs and code, they'll encounter points of ambiguity and confusion. Ideally, developers can route these issues back to customers or BAs for resolution through the project's issue-tracking process. If an issue can't be resolved immediately, any assumptions, guesses, or interpretations that a developer makes should be documented and reviewed with customer representatives.

User interface design

User interface design is an extensively studied domain that goes well beyond the scope of this book. Your requirements explorations probably took at least tentative steps into UI design. UI design is so closely related to requirements that you shouldn't just push it downstream to be done without end-user engagement. Chapter 15, "Risk reduction through prototyping," described how use cases lead to dialog maps, wireframes, or prototypes, and ultimately into detailed UI designs. A display-action-response (DAR) model is a useful tool for documenting the UI elements that appear in screens and how the system responds to user actions (Beatty and Chen 2012). A DAR model combines a visual screen layout with tables that describe the elements on the screen and their behaviors under different conditions. Figure 19-4 shows a sample page from a website, and Figure 19-5 shows a corresponding DAR model. The DAR model contains enough details about the screen layout and behavior that a developer should be able to implement it with confidence.

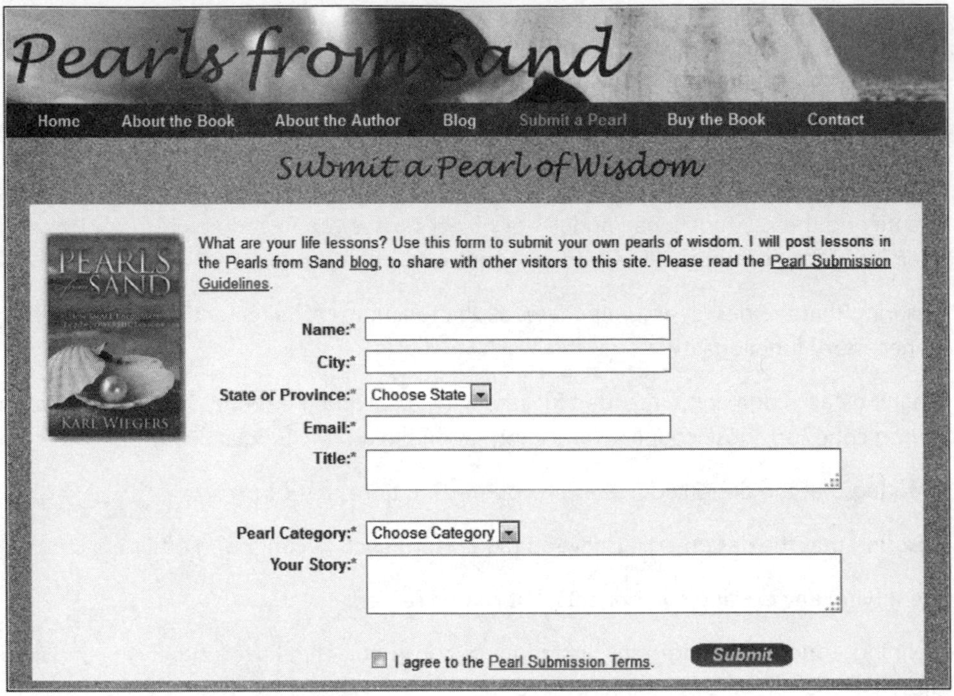

FIGURE 19-4 High-fidelity webpage design.

UI Element: Submit a Pearl Page at PearlsFromSand.com	
UI Element Description	
ID	submit.html
Description	Page where users can submit their own life lessons to be posted on the Pearls from Sand blog
UI Element Description	
Precondition	**Display**
Always	"Home" link "About the Book" link "About the Author" link "Blog" link "Submit a Pearl" link (inactive, different color because it's the current page) "Buy the Book" link "Contact" link "Name" text field "City" text field "State or Province" drop-down list "Email" text field "Title" text field "Pearl Category" drop-down list "Your Story" text field "I agree" check box, cleared "Submit" button "Pearl Submission Guidelines" link "Pearl Submission Terms" link
User just submitted a pearl	"Name," "City," "State or Province," and "Email" fields are populated with values from previous pearl. "Title," "Pearl Category," "Your Story," and "I agree" fields are reset to default values.

UI Element Behaviors		
Precondition	**User Action**	**Response**
Always	User clicks on navigation links: "Home," "About the Book," "About the Author," "Buy the Book," "Contact," "Pearl Submission Guidelines," "Pearl Submission Terms"	Corresponding page is displayed
Always	User clicks on either "Blog" link	Pearls from Sand blog opens in new browser tab
Always	User types or pastes text into a text field	User's text is displayed in field; for "Your Story" field, count of remaining characters is displayed
Always	User clicks on "I agree" check box	Check box toggles on/off
One or more invalid entries	User clicks on "Submit" link	Error message appears for any invalid text entry or length or for required fields that are blank
All fields have valid entries; "I agree" check box is selected	User clicks on "Submit" link	Pearl is submitted; pearl counter is incremented; email with pearl info is sent to Submitter and Administrator; successful submission acknowledgment message is displayed.
"I agree" box not checked	User clicks on "Submit" link	System displays error message on this page

FIGURE 19-5 Display-action-response (DAR) model for the webpage shown in Figure 19-4.

From requirements to tests

Requirements analysis and testing fit together beautifully. As consultant Dorothy Graham (2002) points out, "Good requirements engineering produces better tests; good test analysis produces better requirements." The requirements provide the foundation for system testing. The product should be tested against what it was intended to do as recorded in the requirements documentation, not against its design or code. System testing that's based on the code can become a self-fulfilling prophecy. The product might correctly exhibit all the behaviors described in tests based on the code, but that doesn't mean that it meets the customers' needs. Include testers in requirements reviews to make sure the requirements are verifiable and can serve as the basis for system testing.

Agile development teams typically write acceptance tests in lieu of precise requirements (Cohn 2004). Rather than specifying the capabilities the system must exhibit or the actions a user must be able to take, the acceptance tests flesh out the expected behavior of a user story. This conveys to developers the information they need to feel confident that they've correctly and completely implemented each story. As described in Chapter 17, "Validating the requirements," acceptance tests should cover:

- Expected behavior under normal conditions (good input data and valid user actions).

- How anticipated error conditions and expected failure scenarios should be handled (bad input data or invalid user actions).

- Whether quality expectations are satisfied (for example, response times, security protections, and the average time or number of user actions needed to accomplish a task).

What to test?

A seminar attendee once said, "I'm in our system testing group. We don't have written requirements, so we have to test what we think the software is supposed to do. Sometimes we're wrong, so we have to ask the developers what the software does and test it again."

Testing what the developers built isn't the same as testing what they were *supposed* to build. The requirements are the ultimate reference for system and user acceptance testing. If the system has poorly specified requirements, the testers will discover many requirements that developers inferred—rightly or wrongly—and implemented. The analyst should document legitimate implied requirements and their origins to make future regression testing more effective.

The testers or quality assurance staff should determine how they'd verify the implementation of each requirement. Possible methods include:

- Testing (executing the software to look for defects)
- Inspection (examining the code to ensure that it satisfies the requirements)
- Demonstration (showing that the product works as expected)
- Analysis (reasoning through how the system should work under certain circumstances)

Connecting testing back to requirements helps keep the testing effort prioritized and focused for maximum benefit. One colleague, a seasoned project manager and business analyst, related her experience along these lines: "A clearly articulated business need can drive user acceptance testing (UAT), which is typically the final hurdle a project undergoes prior to going live. On a recent web portal development project, we worked with the business sponsor to understand the real gains the web portal was expected to deliver. Understanding the critical requirements allowed the project manager to craft clear definitions of critical, moderate, and cosmetic defects. By tying defect criteria clearly to requirements, we guided our customers through UAT and successfully completed a major development effort without any ambiguity about quality or acceptance criteria."

The simple act of thinking about how you'll verify each requirement is a useful quality practice. Use analytical techniques such as cause-and-effect graphs to derive tests based on the logic described in a requirement. This will reveal ambiguities, missing or implied *else* conditions, and other problems. Each functional requirement should map to at least one test so that no expected system behavior goes unverified. Requirements-based testing applies several test design strategies: action-driven, data-driven (including boundary value analysis and equivalence class partitioning), logic-driven, event-driven, and state-driven (Poston 1996). Skillful testers will augment requirements-based testing with additional testing based on the product's history, intended usage scenarios, overall quality characteristics, service level agreements, boundary conditions, and quirks.

The effort invested in early test thinking isn't wasted, even if you plan a separate system testing effort before release. It's a matter of reallocating test effort that historically was weighted toward the latter project stages. Conceptual tests are readily transformed into specific test scenarios and automated, where feasible and appropriate. Moving test thinking up earlier in the development cycle will pay off with better requirements, clear communication and common expectations among stakeholders, and early defect removal.

As development progresses, the team will elaborate the requirements from the high level found in user requirements, through the functional requirements, and ultimately down to specifications for individual code modules. Testing authority Boris Beizer (1999) points out that testing against requirements must be performed at every level of software construction, not just the end-user level. Some application code isn't directly accessed by users but is needed for infrastructure operations. Each module must satisfy its own specification, even if that module's function is invisible to the user. Consequently, testing the system against user requirements is a necessary—but not sufficient— strategy for system testing.

From requirements to success

I once encountered a project in which a contract development team came on board to implement a very large application for which an earlier team had developed the requirements. The new team took one look at the dozen three-inch binders of requirements, shuddered in horror, and began coding. They didn't refer to the SRS during construction. Instead, they built what they thought they were supposed to build, based on an incomplete and inaccurate understanding of the project's goals. Not surprisingly, this project encountered a lot of problems. Trying to understand a huge volume of even excellent requirements is certainly hard, but ignoring them is a decisive step toward project failure.

It's faster to read the requirements, however extensive, before implementation than it is to build the wrong system and then have to build it again correctly. It's even faster to engage the development team early in the project so that they can participate in the requirements work and perform early prototyping or take an iterative development approach. The development team still has to read the entire specification eventually. However, they are spreading their reading time across the project, which alleviates some of the tedious nature of the activity.

A more successful team had a practice of listing all the requirements that were planned for a specific release. The project's quality assurance group evaluated each release by executing the tests for those requirements. A requirement that didn't satisfy its test criteria was counted as a defect. The QA group rejected the release if more than a predetermined number of requirements weren't met or if specific high-impact requirements weren't satisfied. This project was successful largely because it used its documented requirements to decide when a release was shippable.

The ultimate deliverable from a software development project is a solution that meets the customers' needs and expectations. Requirements are an essential step on the path from business need to satisfied customers. If you don't base your project plans, designs, and acceptance and system tests on a foundation of high-quality requirements, you're likely to waste a great deal of effort trying to deliver a solid product. Don't become a slave to your requirements processes, though. There's no point in spending time generating unnecessary documents and holding ritualized meetings. Strive for a sensible balance between rigorous specification and off-the-top-of-the-head coding that will reduce the risk of building the wrong product to an acceptable level.

Next steps

- Estimate the requirements work on your next project by using the requirements estimation tool from Figure 19-2. Track your time on the project and compare the results to your initial estimation. Adapt the estimation tool for your next project.

- Estimate the percentage of unplanned requirements growth on your last several projects. Can you build contingency buffers into your project schedules to accommodate a similar scope increase on future projects? Use the growth data from previous projects to justify the schedule contingency so that it doesn't look like arbitrary padding.

- Try to trace all the requirements in an implemented portion of your SRS to individual design elements. The design elements might be processes in design data flow diagrams, tables in data models, object classes or methods, or other design components. Are any design elements missing? Were any requirements overlooked?

- Record the number of lines of code, function points, story points, or UI elements that are needed to implement each feature or user requirement. Also record the actual effort needed to fully implement and verify each feature or use case. Look for correlations between size and effort that will help you make more accurate estimates in the future.

- Record your estimates of size and effort for the requirements development activities and deliverables on your project, and compare those to the actual results. Did you really do the 5 interviews planned, or did you end up doing 15? Did you create twice as many use cases as expected? How can you change your estimation process to be more accurate in the future?

PART III

Requirements for specific project classes

CHAPTER 20

Agile projects

Agile development refers to a set of software development methods that encourage continuous collaboration among stakeholders and rapid and frequent delivery of small increments of useful functionality. There are many different types of agile methods; some of the most popular are Scrum, Extreme Programming, Lean Software Development, Feature-Driven Development, and Kanban. The term "agile development" has gained popularity since the publication of the "Manifesto for Agile Software Development" (Beck et al. 2001). Agile methods are based on iterative and incremental approaches to software development, which have been around for many years (for example, see Boehm 1988; Gilb 1988; and Larman and Basili 2003).

The agile development approaches have characteristics that distinguish them from one another, but they all fundamentally champion an adaptive (sometimes called "change-driven") approach over a predictive (sometimes called "plan-driven") approach (Boehm and Turner 2004; IIBA 2009). A predictive approach, such as waterfall development, attempts to minimize the amount of risk in a project by doing extensive planning and documentation prior to initiating construction of the software. The project managers and business analysts make sure that all stakeholders understand exactly what will be delivered before it gets built. This can work well if the requirements are well understood at the outset and are likely to remain relatively stable during the project. Adaptive approaches such as agile methods are designed to accommodate the inevitable change that takes place on projects. They also work well for projects with highly uncertain or volatile requirements.

This chapter describes the characteristics of agile approaches as they relate to the requirements activities for a software project, the major adaptations of traditional requirements practices for an agile project, and a road map of where to find more detailed guidance throughout the rest of the book.

Agile requirements?

We do not use the term "agile requirements," because that implies that the requirements for an agile project are somehow qualitatively different from those for projects following other life cycles. Developers need to know the same information to be able to correctly implement the right functionality in the right way on all projects. However, agile and traditional projects do handle requirements differently in various respects, particularly with regard to the timing and depth of requirements activities and the extent of written requirements documentation. This is why we use the term "requirements for agile projects."

Limitations of the waterfall

Organizations often think of a waterfall development process as involving a linear sequence of activities, where project teams fully specify (and sometimes overspecify) the requirements, then create designs, then write code, and finally test the solution. In theory, this approach has several advantages. The team can catch any flaws in the application's requirements and design early on rather than during construction, testing, or maintenance, when fixing an error is much more costly. If the requirements are correct up front, it is easy to allocate budget and resources, to measure progress, and to estimate an accurate completion date. However, in practice, software development is rarely that straightforward.

Few projects follow a purely sequential waterfall approach. Even predictive projects expect a certain amount of change and put mechanisms in place to handle it. There is always some overlap and feedback between the phases. In general, though, on waterfall development projects the team puts considerable effort into trying to get the full requirements set "right" early on. There are many possible software development life cycles in addition to waterfall and agile approaches. They place varying degrees of emphasis on developing a complete set of requirements early in the project (McConnell 1996; Boehm and Turner 2004). A key differentiator across the spectrum between totally fixed, predictive projects and totally uncertain, adaptive projects is the amount of time that elapses between when a requirement is created and when software based on that requirement is delivered to customers.

Large projects that use a waterfall approach are often delivered late, lack necessary features, and fail to meet users' expectations. Waterfall projects are susceptible to this kind of failure because of the layers of dependency built upon the requirements. Stakeholders often change their requirements during the course of a long project, and projects struggle when the software development teams cannot respond to these changes effectively. The reality is that stakeholders *will* change requirements—because they don't know precisely what they want at the beginning of the project, because sometimes they can articulate their vision only after they see something that clearly doesn't match their vision, and because business needs sometimes change during the course of a project.

Although Winston Royce (1970) is often credited with being the first to publish the formal waterfall model (though not by that name), he actually presented it in the context of being an approach that is "risky and invites failure." He identified the exact problem that projects today still experience: errors in requirements likely aren't caught until testing, late in the project. He went on to explain that the steps *ideally* should be performed in the sequence of requirements, design, code, and test, but that projects *really* need to overlap some of these phases and iterate between them. Royce even proposed using simulations to prototype the requirements and designs as an experiment before committing to the full development effort. Modified waterfalls, though, are followed by many projects today, with varying degrees of success.

> ## Disruptive changes to business objectives
>
> A year into a large waterfall project, a new director of marketing took over as the executive sponsor. The team had already developed a lot of software, but they had not yet deployed anything that was useful to customers. Not surprisingly, the new sponsor had different business objectives than his predecessor. The business analysts shared the news with the development team that there were new business objectives, and consequently new user requirements, new functional requirements, and revised priorities on the old requirements.
>
> The development team had become accustomed to allocating all new requirements to a planned enhancement phase following the initial deployment. They lashed out, protesting that it was unacceptable to change course in the middle of the project. However, to continue to develop and deliver a product that fulfilled only the original requirements would have left the new sponsor dissatisfied. Had the team been using a development approach that anticipated and accommodated requirements changes, this shift in strategic direction would have been far less disruptive.

The agile development approach

Agile development methods attempt to address some limitations of the waterfall model. Agile methods focus on iterative and incremental development, breaking the development of software into short cycles called iterations (or, in the agile method known as Scrum, "sprints"). Iterations can be as short as one week or as long as a month. During each iteration, the development team adds a small set of functionality based on priorities established by the customer, tests it to make sure it works properly, and validates it with acceptance criteria established by the customer. Subsequent increments modify what already exists, enrich the initial features, add new ones, and correct defects that were discovered. Ongoing customer participation enables the team to spot problems and changes in direction early, thereby guiding developers to adjust their course before they are too far down the wrong path. The goal is to have a body of potentially shippable software at the end of each iteration, even if it constitutes just a small portion of the ultimately desired product.

Essential aspects of an agile approach to requirements

The following sections describe several differences in the ways that agile projects and traditional projects approach requirements. Many of the requirements practices applied on agile projects also work well on—and are a good idea for—projects following any other development life cycle.

Customer involvement

Collaborating with customers on software development projects always increases the chances of project success. This is true for waterfall projects as well as for agile projects. The main difference between the two approaches is in the timing of the customer involvement. On waterfall projects, customers typically dedicate considerable time up front, helping the BA understand, document, and validate requirements. Customers should also be involved later in the project during user acceptance testing, providing feedback on whether the product meets their needs. However, during the construction phase, there is generally little customer involvement, which makes it difficult for a project to adapt to changing customer needs.

On agile projects, customers (or a product owner who represents them) are engaged continuously throughout the project. During an initial planning iteration on some agile projects, customers work with the project team to identify and prioritize user stories that will serve as the preliminary road map for the development of the product. Because user stories are typically less detailed than traditional functional requirements, customers must be available during iterations to provide input and clarification during the design and construction activities. They should also test and provide feedback on the newly developed features when the construction phase of the iteration is complete.

It is common to have product owners, customers, and end users participate in writing user stories or other requirements, but these individuals might not all be trained in effective requirements methods. Inexpertly written user stories are likely not sufficient for clear communication of requirements. Regardless of who is writing the user stories, someone with solid business analysis skills should review and edit the stories before the team begins implementing them. Chapter 6, "Finding the voice of the user," further elaborates on customer involvement on agile projects.

Documentation detail

Because developers have little interaction with customers after construction begins on waterfall projects, the requirements must specify system behavior, data relationships, and user experience expectations in considerable detail. The close collaboration of customers with developers on agile projects generally means that requirements can be documented in less detail than on traditional projects. Instead, BAs or other people responsible for requirements will develop the necessary precision through conversations and documentation when it is needed (IIBA 2013).

People sometimes think that agile project teams are not supposed to write requirements. That is not accurate. Instead, agile methods encourage creating the minimum amount of documentation needed to accurately guide the developers and testers. Any documentation beyond what the development and test teams need (or that is required to satisfy regulations or standards) represents wasted effort. Certain user stories might have little detail provided, with only the riskiest or highest-impact functionality being specified in more detail, typically in the form of acceptance tests.

The backlog and prioritization

The product backlog on an agile project contains a list of requests for work that the team might perform (IIBA 2013). Product backlogs typically are composed of user stories, but some teams also populate the backlog with other requirements, business processes, and defects to be corrected. Each project should maintain only one backlog (Cohn 2010). Therefore, defects might need to be represented in the backlog for prioritization against new user stories. Some teams rewrite defects as new user stories or variants of old stories. Backlogs can be maintained on story cards or in tools. Agile purists might insist on using cards, but they are not practical for large projects or distributed teams. Chapter 27, "Requirements management practices," discusses the product backlog in more detail. Various tools for agile project management, including backlog management, are commercially available.

Prioritization of the backlog is an ongoing activity to select which work items go into upcoming iterations and which items are discarded from the backlog. The priorities assigned to backlog items don't have to remain constant forever, just for the next iteration (Leffingwell 2011). Tracing items in the backlog back to the business requirements facilitates prioritization. All projects, not just agile projects, ought to be managing priorities of the work remaining in their backlog.

Timing

Agile projects require fundamentally the same types of requirements activities as traditional development projects. Someone still needs to elicit requirements from user representatives, analyze them, document requirements of various kinds at appropriate levels of detail, and validate that the requirements will achieve the business objectives for the project. However, detailed requirements are not documented all at once at the beginning of an agile project. Instead, high-level requirements, typically in the form of user stories, are elicited to populate a product backlog early in a project for planning and prioritization.

As shown in Figure 20-1, user stories are allocated to specific iterations for implementation, and the details for each story are further clarified during that iteration. As was illustrated in Figure 3-3 in Chapter 3, "Good practices for requirements engineering," requirements might be developed in small portions throughout the entire project, even up until shortly before the product is released. However, it's important to learn about nonfunctional requirements early on so the system's architecture can be designed to achieve critical performance, usability, availability, and other quality goals.

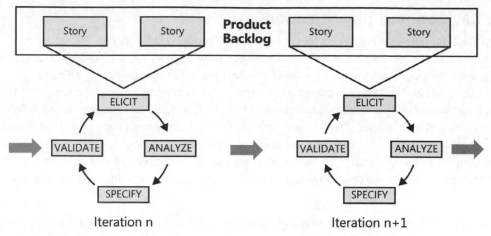

FIGURE 20-1 Standard requirements activities occur within each agile iteration.

Epics, user stories, and features, oh my!

As described in Chapter 8, "Understanding user requirements," a user story is a concise statement that articulates something a user needs and serves as a starting point for conversations to flesh out the details. User stories were created specifically to address the needs of agile developers. You might prefer to employ use case names, features, or process flows when exploring user requirements. The form you choose to describe these sorts of requirements is not important; this chapter primarily refers to them as user stories because they are so commonly used on agile projects.

User stories are sized so as to be fully implementable in a single iteration. Mike Cohn (2010) defines an *epic* as being a user story that is too large to fully implement in a single iteration. Because epics span iterations, they must be split into sets of smaller stories. Sometimes epics are large enough that they must be subdivided into multiple epics, each of which is then split into multiple stories until each resulting story can be reliably estimated and then implemented and tested within a single iteration (see Figure 20-2). Breaking epics down into smaller epics and then into user stories is often referred to as *story decomposition* (IIBA 2013).

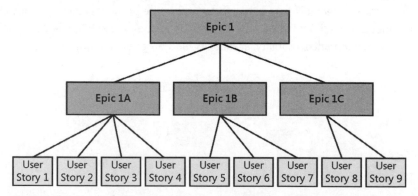

FIGURE 20-2 Epics can be subdivided into smaller epics and then into user stories.

A feature is a grouping of system capabilities that provides value to a user. In the context of an agile project, features could encompass an individual user story, multiple user stories, an individual epic, or multiple epics. For example, a zoom feature on a phone's camera might be developed to enable execution of the following two unrelated user stories:

- As a mother, I want to take recognizable pictures of my daughter during school performances so that I can share them with her grandparents.

- As a birdwatcher, I want to be able to take clear photographs of birds from a distance so that I can identify them.

Identifying the lowest level of stories that still aligns with the business requirements allows you to determine the smallest set of functionality that the team can deliver that provides value to the customer. This concept is often called a *minimum* (or minimal, or minimally) *marketable feature* (MMF), as described by Mark Denne and Jane Cleland-Huang (2003).

> **Important** When you develop requirements on agile projects, worry less about whether the thing is called a story, an epic, or a feature, and focus more on developing high-quality requirements that will guide the developer's ability to satisfy customer needs.

Expect change

Organizations know that change will happen on projects. Even business objectives can change. The biggest adaptation that BAs need to make when a requirement change arises on an agile project is to say not, "Wait, that's out of scope" or "We need to go through a formal process to incorporate that change," but rather, "Okay, let's talk about the change." This encourages customer collaboration to create or change user stories and prioritize each change request against everything else that's already in the backlog. As with all projects, agile project teams need to manage changes thoughtfully to reduce their negative impact, but they anticipate and even embrace the reality of change. See Chapter 28, "Change happens," for more information about managing requirements change on agile projects.

Knowing that you can handle changes doesn't mean you should blindly ignore the future and pay attention only to what's known now. It is still important to look ahead and see what might be coming farther down the road. The developers might not design for every possible future requirement. Given some glimpse of the future, though, they can create a more expandable and robust architecture or design hooks to make it easy to add new functionality.

Change also includes removing items from scope. Items can be removed from an iteration's scope for various reasons, including the following:

- Implementation issues prevent an item from being completed within the current time frame.

- Issues discovered by product owners or during testing make the implementation of a particular story unacceptable.

- Higher-priority items need to replace less important ones that were planned for an iteration.

Adapting requirements practices to agile projects

Most of the practices described throughout this book can easily be adapted to agile projects, perhaps by altering the timing when they're used, the degree to which they are applied, or who performs each practice. The International Institute of Business Analysis (IIBA) provides detailed suggestions regarding business analysis techniques to apply to agile projects (IIBA 2013). Many other chapters in this book address how to adapt the practices described in the chapter to suit an agile project. Table 20-1 provides a road map to the specific chapters that address agile projects directly.

TABLE 20-1 A road map to chapters that address agile development topics

Chapter	Topic
Chapter 2, "Requirements from the customer's perspective"	Reaching agreement on requirements
Chapter 4, "The business analyst"	The BA's role on agile projects and who is responsible for the requirements artifacts created
Chapter 5, "Establishing the business requirements"	Setting and managing the vision and scope
Chapter 6, "Finding the voice of the user"	User representation
Chapter 8, "Understanding user requirements"	User stories
Chapter 10, "Documenting the requirements"	Specifying requirements for agile development
Chapter 12, "A picture is worth 1024 words"	Modeling on agile projects
Chapter 14, "Beyond functionality"	Identifying quality attributes, especially those needed up front for architecture and design
Chapter 15, "Risk reduction through prototyping"	Agile projects and evolutionary prototyping
Chapter 16, "First things first: Setting requirement priorities"	Prioritization on agile projects
Chapter 17, "Validating the requirements"	Acceptance criteria and acceptance tests
Chapter 27, "Requirements management practices"	Managing requirements on agile projects through backlogs and burndown charts
Chapter 28, "Change happens"	Managing change on agile projects

Transitioning to agile: Now what?

If you're a business analyst who is new to agile development methods, don't worry: most of the practices you already use will still apply. After all, both agile and traditional project teams need to understand the requirements for the solutions they build. Following are a few suggestions to help you make the conversion to an agile approach:

- Determine what your role is on the team. As described in Chapter 4, some agile projects have a dedicated BA, whereas others have people with different titles who perform business analysis activities. Encourage all team members to focus on the goals of the project, not their individual roles or titles (Gorman and Gottesdiener 2011).

- Read a book on the agile product owner role so you understand user stories, acceptance tests, backlog prioritization, and why the agile BA is never "finished" until the end of the project or release. One suggested book is *Agile Product Management with Scrum* (Pichler 2010).

- Identify suggested agile practices that will work best in your organization. Consider what has worked well already with other development approaches in your organization, and carry on those practices. Collaborate with the people currently performing other team roles to determine how their practices will work in an agile environment.

- Implement a small project first as a pilot for agile methods, or implement only a few agile practices on your next project.

- If you decide to implement a hybrid model that adopts some agile practices but not others, select a few low-risk practices that can work well in any methodology to start. If you are new to agile, bring in an experienced coach for three or four iterations to help you avoid the temptation to revert to the historical practices with which you are comfortable.

- Don't be an agile purist just for the sake of being a purist.

Be agile when adopting agile practices

One organization I worked with decided to move from a traditional approach to agile development. The entire organization jumped in feet first, dogmatically trying to adapt agile practices across the entire organization at once. Many of the developers tried to be agile purists, writing story cards and incorrectly insisting that no other documentation was allowed.

This attempted implementation of agile approaches failed miserably. Not all of the stakeholders bought into the effort. Some of the practices the developers insisted on didn't scale up to their large projects. The customers didn't know how their role would be different on an agile project. The new projects failed so badly that the IT executive mandated that agile development must stop immediately. All projects would follow a waterfall model from that point forward. "Agile" became a bad word. This was like trying to fix one poor decision with another!

Something interesting happened in the IT organization. The development teams knew this mandate was also going to lead to disaster, so they adopted a hybrid development approach. They used backlogs to prioritize requirements, they developed in three-week iterations, and they specified detailed requirements just-in-time for each iteration. When the teams described their approach to their management, they just said they were using "standard waterfall approaches" in their development so they wouldn't get in trouble. Most of the agile practices actually worked well in their organization when they learned how to execute them properly. This organization initially tried to adopt agile methods in a way that didn't work in their organization and ended up giving agile an undeserved bad name.

CHAPTER 21

Enhancement and replacement projects

Most of this book describes requirements development as though you are beginning a new software or system development project, sometimes called a *green-field project*. However, many organizations devote much of their effort to enhancing or replacing existing information systems or building new releases of established commercial products. Most of the practices described in this book are appropriate for enhancement and replacement projects. This chapter provides specific suggestions as to which practices are most relevant and how to use them.

An *enhancement project* is one in which new capabilities are added to an existing system. Enhancement projects might also involve correcting defects, adding new reports, and modifying functionality to comply with revised business rules or needs.

A *replacement* (or *reengineering*) *project* replaces an existing application with a new custom-built system, a commercial off-the-shelf (COTS) system, or a hybrid of those. Replacement projects are most commonly implemented to improve performance, cut costs (such as maintenance costs or license fees), take advantage of modern technologies, or meet regulatory requirements. If your replacement project will involve a COTS solution, the guidance presented in Chapter 22, "Packaged solution projects," will also be helpful.

Replacement and enhancement projects face some particular requirements issues. The original developers who held all the critical information in their heads might be long gone. It's tempting to claim that a small enhancement doesn't warrant writing any requirements. Developers might believe that they don't need detailed requirements if they are replacing an existing system's functionality. The approaches described in this chapter can help you to deal with the challenges of enhancing or replacing an existing system to improve its ability to meet the organization's current business needs.

The case of the missing spec

The requirements specification for the next release of a mature system often says, essentially, "The new system should do everything the old system does, except add these new features and fix those bugs." A business analyst once received just such a specification for version 5 of a major product. To find out exactly what the current release did, she looked at the SRS for version 4. Unfortunately, it also said, in essence, "Version 4 should do everything that version 3 does, except add these new features and fix those bugs." She followed the trail back, but every

SRS described just the differences that the new version should exhibit compared to the previous version. Nowhere was there a description of the original system. Consequently, everyone had a different understanding of the current system's capabilities. If you're in this situation, document the requirements for your project more thoroughly so that all the stakeholders—both present and future—understand what the system does.

Expected challenges

The presence of an existing system leads to common challenges that both enhancement and replacement projects will face, including the following:

- The changes made could degrade the performance to which users are accustomed.

- Little or no requirements documentation might be available for the existing system.

- Users who are familiar with how the system works today might not like the changes they are about to encounter.

- You might unknowingly break or omit functionality that is vital to some stakeholder group.

- Stakeholders might take this opportunity to request new functionality that seems like a good idea but isn't really needed to meet the business objectives.

Even if there is existing documentation, it might not prove useful. For enhancement projects, the documentation might not be up to date. If the documentation doesn't match the existing application's reality, it is of limited use. For replacement systems, you also need to be wary of carrying forward *all* of the requirements, because some of the old functionality probably should not be migrated.

One of the major issues in replacement projects is validating that the reasons for the replacement are sound. There need to be justifiable business objectives for the change. When existing systems are being completely replaced, organizational processes might also have to change, which makes it harder for people to accept a new system. The change in business processes, change in the software system, and learning curve of a new system can disrupt current operations.

Requirements techniques when there is an existing system

Table 21-1 describes the most important requirements development techniques to consider when working on enhancement and replacement projects.

TABLE 21-1 Valuable requirements techniques for enhancement and replacement projects

Technique	Why it's relevant
Create a feature tree to show changes	■ Show features being added. ■ Identify features from the existing system that won't be in the new system.
Identify user classes	■ Assess who is affected by the changes. ■ Identify new user classes whose needs must be met.
Understand business processes	■ Understand how the current system is intertwined with stakeholders' daily jobs and the impacts of it changing. ■ Define new business processes that might need to be created to align with new features or a replacement system.
Document business rules	■ Record business rules that are currently embedded in code. ■ Look for new business rules that need to be honored. ■ Redesign the system to better handle volatile business rules that were expensive to maintain.
Create use cases or user stories	■ Understand what users must be able to do with the system. ■ Understand how users expect new features to work. ■ Prioritize functionality for the new system.
Create a context diagram	■ Identify and document external entities. ■ Extend existing interfaces to support new features. ■ Identify current interfaces that might need to be changed.
Create an ecosystem map	■ Look for other affected systems. ■ Look for new, modified, and obsolete interfaces between systems.
Create a dialog map	■ See how new screens fit into the existing user interface. ■ Show how the workflow screen navigation will change.
Create data models	■ Verify that the existing data model is sufficient or extend it for new features. ■ Verify that all of the data entities and attributes are still needed. ■ Consider what data has to be migrated, converted, corrected, archived, or discarded.
Specify quality attributes	■ Ensure that the new system is designed to fulfill quality expectations. ■ Improve satisfaction of quality attributes over the existing system.
Create report tables	■ Convert existing reports that are still needed. ■ Define new reports that aren't in the old system.
Build prototypes	■ Engage users in the redevelopment process. ■ Prototype major enhancements if there are uncertainties.
Inspect requirements specifications	■ Identify broken links in the traceability chain. ■ Determine if any previous requirements are obsolete or unnecessary in the replacement system.

Enhancement projects provide an opportunity to try new requirements methods in a small-scale and low-risk way. The pressure to get the next release out might make you think that you don't have time to experiment with requirements techniques, but enhancement projects let you tackle the learning curve in bite-sized chunks. When the next big project comes along, you'll have some experience and confidence in better requirements practices.

Suppose that a customer requests that a new feature be added to a mature product. If you haven't worked with user stories before, explore the new feature from the user-story perspective, discussing with the requester the tasks that users will perform with that feature. Practicing on this project reduces the risk compared to applying user stories for the first time on a green-field project, when your skill might mean the difference between success and high-profile failure.

Prioritizing by using business objectives

Enhancement projects are undertaken to add new capabilities to an existing application. It's easy to get caught up in the excitement and start adding unnecessary capabilities. To combat this risk of gold-plating, trace requirements back to business objectives to ensure that the new features are needed and to select the highest-impact features to implement first. You also might need to prioritize enhancement requests against the correction of defects that had been reported against the old system.

Also be wary of letting unnecessary new functionality slip into replacement projects. The main focus of replacement projects is to migrate existing functionality. However, customers might imagine that if you are developing a new system anyway, it is easy to add lots of new capabilities right away. Many replacement projects have collapsed because of the weight of uncontrolled scope growth. You're usually better off building a stable first release and adding more features through subsequent enhancement projects, provided the first release allows users to do their jobs.

Replacement projects often originate when stakeholders want to add functionality to an existing system that is too inflexible to support the growth or has technology limitations. However, there needs to be a clear business objective to justify implementing an expensive new system (Devine 2008). Use the anticipated cost savings from a new system (such as through reduced maintenance of an old, clunky system) plus the value of the new desired functionality to justify a system replacement project.

Also look for existing functionality that doesn't need to be retained in a replacement system. Don't replicate the existing system's shortcomings or miss an opportunity to update a system to suit new business needs and processes. For example, the BA might ask users, "Do you use *a particular menu option*?" If you consistently hear "I never do that," then maybe it isn't needed in the replacement system. Look for usage data that shows what screens, functions, or data entities are rarely accessed in the current system. Even the existing functionality has to map to current and anticipated business objectives to warrant re-implementing it in the new system.

> **Trap** Don't let stakeholders get away with saying "I have it today, so I need it in the new system" as a default method of justifying requirements.

Mind the gap

A *gap analysis* is a comparison of functionality between an existing system and a desired new system. A gap analysis can be expressed in different ways, including use cases, user stories, or features. When enhancing an existing system, perform a gap analysis to make sure you understand why it isn't currently meeting your business objectives.

Gap analysis for a replacement project entails understanding existing functionality and discovering the desired new functionality (see Figure 21-1). Identify user requirements for the existing system that stakeholders want to have re-implemented in the new system. Also, elicit new user requirements that the existing system does not address. Consider any change requests that were never implemented in the existing system. Prioritize the existing user requirements and the new ones together. Prioritize closing the gaps using business objectives as described in the previous section or the other prioritization techniques presented in Chapter 16, "First things first: Setting requirement priorities."

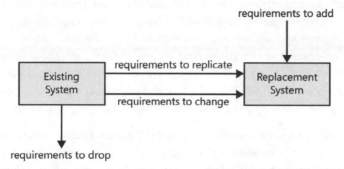

FIGURE 21-1 When you are replacing an existing system, some requirements will be implemented unchanged, some will be modified, some will be discarded, and some new requirements might be added.

Maintaining performance levels

Existing systems set user expectations for performance and throughput. Stakeholders almost always have key performance indicators (KPIs) for existing processes that they will want to maintain in the new system. A key performance indicator model (KPIM) can help you identify and specify these metrics for their corresponding business processes (Beatty and Chen 2012). The KPIM helps stakeholders see that even if the new system will be different, their business outcomes will be at least as good as before.

Unless you explicitly plan to maintain them, performance levels can be compromised as systems are enhanced. Stuffing new functionality into an existing system might slow it down. One data synchronization tool had a requirement to update a master data set from the day's transactions. It needed to run every 24 hours. In the initial release of the tool, the synchronization started at midnight and took about one hour to execute. After some enhancements to include additional attributes, merging, and synchronicity checks, the synchronization took 20 hours to execute. This was a problem, because users expected to have fully synchronized data from the night before available when they started their workday at 8:00 A.M. The maximum time to complete the synchronization was never explicitly specified, but the stakeholders assumed it could be done overnight in less than eight hours.

For replacement systems, prioritize the KPIs that are most important to maintain. Look for the business processes that trace to the most important KPIs and the requirements that enable those business processes; these are the requirements to implement first. For instance, if you're replacing a loan application system in which loan processors can enter 10 loans per day, it might be important to maintain at least that same throughput in the new system. The functionality that allows loan processers to enter loans should be some of the earliest implemented in the new system, so the loan processors can maintain their productivity.

When old requirements don't exist

Most older systems do not have documented—let alone accurate—requirements. In the absence of reliable documentation, teams might reverse-engineer an understanding of what the system does from the user interfaces, code, and database. We think of this as "software archaeology." To maximize the benefit from reverse engineering, the archaeology expedition should record what it learns in the form of requirements and design descriptions. Accumulating accurate information about certain portions of the current system positions the team to enhance a system with low risk, to replace a system without missing critical functionality, and to perform future enhancements efficiently. It halts the knowledge drain, so future maintainers better understand the changes that were just made.

If updating the requirements is overly burdensome, it will fall by the wayside as busy people rush on to the next change request. Obsolete requirements aren't helpful for future enhancements. There's a widespread fear in the software industry that writing documentation will consume too much time; the knee-jerk reaction is to neglect all opportunities to update requirements documentation. But what's the cost if you *don't* update the requirements and a future maintainer (perhaps you!) has to regenerate that information? The answer to this question will let you make a thoughtful business decision concerning whether to revise the requirements documentation when you change or re-create the software.

When the team performs additional enhancements and maintenance over time, it can extend these fractional knowledge representations, steadily improving the system documentation. The incremental cost of recording this newly found knowledge is small compared with the cost of someone having to rediscover it later on. Implementing enhancements almost always necessitates further requirements development, so add those new requirements to an existing requirements repository, if there is one. If you're replacing an old system, you have an opportunity to document the requirements for the new one and to keep the requirements up to date with what you learn throughout the project. Try to leave the requirements in better shape than you found them.

Which requirements should you specify?

It's not always worth taking the time to generate a complete set of requirements for an entire production system. Many options lie between the two extremes of continuing forever with no requirements documentation and reconstructing a perfect requirements set. Knowing why you'd like to have written requirements available lets you judge whether the cost of rebuilding all—or even part—of the specification is a sound investment.

Perhaps your current system is a shapeless mass of history and mystery like the one in Figure 21-2. Imagine that you've been asked to implement some new functionality in region A in this figure. Begin by recording the new requirements in a structured SRS or in a requirements management tool. When you add the new functionality, you'll have to figure out how it interfaces to or fits in with the existing system. The bridges in Figure 21-2 between region A and your current system represent these interfaces. This analysis provides insight into the white portion of the current system, region B. In addition to the requirements for region A, this insight is the new knowledge you need to capture.

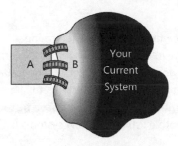

FIGURE 21-2 Adding enhancement A to an ill-documented existing system provides some visibility into the B area.

Rarely do you need to document the entire existing system. Focus detailed requirements efforts on the changes needed to meet the business objectives. If you're replacing a system, start by documenting the areas prioritized as most important to achieve the business objectives or those that pose the highest implementation risk. Any new requirements identified during the gap analysis will need to be specified at the same level of precision and using the same techniques as you would for a new system.

Level of detail

One of the biggest challenges is determining the appropriate level of detail at which to document requirements gleaned from the existing system. For enhancements, defining requirements for the new functionality alone might be sufficient. However, you will usually benefit from documenting all of the functionality that closely relates to the enhancement, to ensure that the change fits in seamlessly (region B in Figure 21-2). You might want to create business processes, user requirements, and/or functional requirements for those related areas. For example, let's say you are adding a discount code feature to an existing shopping cart function, but you don't have any documented requirements for the shopping cart. You might be tempted to write just a single user story: "As a customer, I need to be able to enter a discount code so I can get the cheapest price for the product." However, this user story alone lacks context, so consider capturing other user stories about shopping cart operations. That information could be valuable the next time you need to modify the shopping cart function.

I worked with one team that was just beginning to develop the requirements for version 2 of a major product with embedded software. They hadn't done a good job on the requirements for version 1, which was currently being implemented. The lead BA wondered, "Is it worth going back to improve the SRS for version 1?" The company anticipated that this product line would be a major revenue generator for at least 10 years. They also planned to reuse some of the core requirements in several spin-off products. In this case, it made sense to improve the requirements documentation for version 1 because it was the foundation for all subsequent development work in this product line. Had they been working on version 5.3 of a well-worn system that they expected to retire within a year, reconstructing a comprehensive set of requirements wouldn't have been a wise investment.

Trace Data

Requirements trace data for existing systems will help the enhancement developer determine which components she might have to modify because of a change in a specific requirement. In an ideal world, when you're replacing a system, the existing system would have a full set of functional requirements such that you could establish traceability between the old and new systems to avoid overlooking any requirements. However, a poorly documented old system won't have trace information available, and establishing rigorous traceability for both existing and new systems is time consuming.

As with any new development, it's a good practice to create a traceability matrix to link the new or changed requirements to the corresponding design elements, code, and test cases. Accumulating trace links as you perform the development work takes little effort, whereas it's a great deal of work to regenerate the links from a completed system. For replacement systems, perform requirements tracing at a high level: make a list of features and user stories for the existing system and prioritize to determine which of those will be implemented in the new system. See Chapter 29, "Links in the requirements chain," for more information on tracing requirements.

How to discover the requirements of an existing system

In enhancement and replacement projects, even if you don't have existing documentation, you do have a system to work from to discover the relevant requirements. During enhancement projects, consider drawing a dialog map for the new screens you have to add, showing the navigation connections to and from existing display elements. You might write use cases or user stories that span the new and existing functionality.

In replacement system projects, you need to understand all of the desired functionality, just as you do on any new development project. Study the user interface of the existing system to identify candidate functionality for the new system. Examine existing system interfaces to determine what data is exchanged between systems today. Understand how users use the current system. If no one understands the functionality and business rules behind the user interface, someone will need to look at the code or database to understand what's going on. Analyze any documentation that does exist—design documents, help screens, user manuals, training materials—to identify requirements.

You might not need to specify functional requirements for the existing system at all, instead creating models to fill the information void. Swimlane diagrams can describe how users do their jobs with the system today. Context diagrams, data flow diagrams, and entity-relationship diagrams are also useful. You might create user requirements, specifying them only at a high level without filling in all of the details. Another way to begin closing the information gap is to create data dictionary entries when you add new data elements to the system and modify existing definitions. The test suite might be useful as an initial source of information to recover the software requirements, because tests represent an alternative view of requirements.

Sometimes "good enough" is enough

A third-party assessment of current business analysis practices in one organization revealed that their teams did a fairly good job of writing requirements for new projects, but they failed to update the requirements as the products evolved through a series of enhancement releases. The BAs did create requirements for each enhancement project. However, they did not merge all of those revisions back into the requirements baseline. The organization's manager couldn't think of a measurable benefit from keeping the existing documentation 100 percent updated to reflect the implemented systems. He assumed that his requirements always reflected only 80 to 90 percent of the working software anyway, so there was little value in trying to perfect the requirements for an enhancement. This meant that future enhancement project teams would have to work with some uncertainty and close the gaps when needed, but that price was deemed acceptable.

Encouraging new system adoption

You're bound to run into resistance when changing or replacing an existing system. People are naturally reluctant to change. Introducing a new feature that will make users' jobs easier is a good thing. But users are accustomed to how the system works today, and you plan to modify that, which is not so good from the user's point of view. The issue is even bigger when you're replacing a system, because now you're changing more than just a bit of functionality. You're potentially changing the entire application's look and feel, its menus, the operating environment, and possibly the user's whole job. If you're a business analyst, project manager, or project sponsor, you have to anticipate the resistance and plan how you will overcome it, so the users will accept the new features or system.

An existing, established system is probably stable, fully integrated with surrounding systems, and well understood by users. A new system with all the same functionality might be none of these upon its initial release. Users might fear that the new system will disrupt their normal operations while they learn how to use it. Even worse, it might not support their current operations. Users might even be afraid of losing their jobs if the system automates tasks they perform manually today. It's not uncommon to hear users say that they will accept the new system only if it does everything the old system does—even if they don't personally use all of that functionality at present.

To mitigate the risk of user resistance, you first need to understand the business objectives and the user requirements. If either of these misses the mark, you will lose the users' trust quickly. During elicitation, focus on the benefits the new system or each feature will provide to the users. Help them understand the value of the proposed change to the organization as a whole. Keep in mind—even with enhancements—that just because something is new doesn't mean it will make the user's job easier. A poorly designed user interface can even make the system harder to use because the old features are harder to find, lost amidst a clutter of new options, or more cumbersome to access.

Our organization recently upgraded our document-repository tool to a new version to give us access to additional features and a more stable operating environment. During beta testing, I discovered that simple, common tasks such as checking out and downloading a file are now harder. In the previous version, you could check out a file in two clicks, but now it takes three or four, depending on the navigation path you choose. If our executive stakeholders thought these user interface changes were a big risk to user acceptance, they could invest in developing custom functionality to mimic the old system. Showing prototypes to users can help them get used to the new system or new features and reveal likely adoption issues early in the project.

One caveat with system replacements is that the key performance indicators for certain groups might be negatively affected, even if the system replacement provides a benefit for the organization as a whole. Let users know as soon as possible about features they might be losing or quality attributes that might degrade, so they can start to prepare for it. System adoption can involve as much emotion as logic, so expectation management is critical to lay the foundation for a successful rollout.

When you are migrating from an existing system, transition requirements are also important. Transition requirements describe the capabilities that the whole solution—not just the software application—must have to enable moving from the existing system to the new system (IIBA 2009). They can encompass data conversions, user training, organizational and business process changes, and the need to run both old and new systems in parallel for a period of time. Think about everything that will be required for stakeholders to comfortably and efficiently transition to the new way of working. Understanding transition requirements is part of assessing readiness and managing organizational change (IIBA 2009).

Can we iterate?

Enhancement projects are incremental by definition. Project teams can often adopt agile methods readily, by prioritizing enhancements using a product backlog as described in Chapter 20, "Agile projects." However, replacement projects do not always lend themselves to incremental delivery because you need a critical mass of functionality in the new application before users can begin using it to do their jobs. It's not practical for them to use the new system to do a small portion of their job and then have to go back to the old system to perform other functions. However, big-bang migrations are also challenging and unrealistic. It's difficult to replace in a single step an established system that has matured over many years and numerous releases.

One approach to implementing a replacement system incrementally is to identify functionality that can be isolated and begin by building just those pieces. We once helped a customer team to replace their current fulfillment system with a new custom-developed system. Inventory management represented about 10 percent of the total functionality of the entire fulfillment system. For the most part, the people who managed inventory were separate from the people who managed other parts of the fulfillment process. The initial strategy was to move just the inventory management functionality to a new system of its own. This was ideal functionality to isolate for the first release because it affected just a subset of users, who then would primarily work only in the new system. The one downside side to the approach is that a new software interface had to be developed so that the new inventory system could pass data to and from the existing fulfillment system.

We had no requirements documentation for the existing system. But retaining the original system and turning off its inventory management piece provided a clear boundary for the requirements effort. We primarily wrote use cases and functional requirements for the new inventory system, based on the most important functions of the existing system. We created an entity-relationship diagram and a data dictionary. We drew a context diagram for the entire existing fulfillment system to understand integration points that might be relevant when we split inventory out of it. Then we created a new context diagram to show how inventory management would exist as an external system that interacts with the truncated fulfillment system.

Not all enhancement or replacement projects will be this clean. Most of them will struggle to overcome the two biggest challenges: a lack of documentation for the existing system, and a potential battle to get users to adopt the new system or features. However, using the techniques described in this chapter can help you actively mitigate these risks.

CHAPTER 22

Packaged solution projects

Some organizations acquire and adapt purchased *packaged solutions* (also called *commercial off-the-shelf*, or *COTS*, products) to meet their software needs, instead of building new systems from scratch. *Software as a service* (*SaaS*), or *cloud*, solutions are becoming increasingly available to meet software needs as well. Whether you're purchasing a package as part or all of the solution for a new project or implementing a solution in the cloud, you still need requirements. Requirements let you evaluate solution candidates so that you can select the most appropriate package, and then they let you adapt the package to meet your needs.

As Figure 22-1 shows, COTS packages typically need to be configured, integrated, and extended to work in the target environment. Some COTS products can be deployed out of the box with no additional work needed to make them usable. Most, though, require some customization. This could take the form of configuring the default product, creating integrations to other systems, and/or developing extensions to provide additional functionality that is not included in the COTS package. These activities all demand requirements.

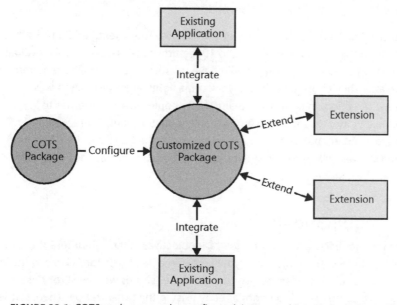

FIGURE 22-1 COTS packages can be configured, integrated into the existing application environment, and/or extended with new functionality.

This chapter discusses requirements for selecting and implementing packaged solutions. We do not distinguish between COTS and SaaS projects due to the similarity of the requirements activities involved. The decision to implement a packaged solution instead of custom developing a system is a matter of evaluating the cost-effectiveness of the two options and lies outside the scope of this book. If you're building a packaged solution to sell, the other chapters in the book are more relevant because those projects involve custom software development.

This chapter describes several ways to approach requirements definition when you plan to acquire a commercial package to meet your needs. We also provide suggestions for how to develop requirements to implement the packaged solution in your operating environment.

Requirements for selecting packaged solutions

COTS packages offer the acquiring organization less flexibility to meet requirements than custom (sometimes called *bespoke*) development does. You need to know which requested capabilities aren't negotiable and which you can adjust to fit within the package's constraints. The only way to choose the right packaged solution is to understand the business activities the package must let the users perform. Selecting packaged solutions entails identifying your requirements for the software, at least at a high level. The level of detail and effort you should put into specifying requirements for COTS selection depends on the expected package costs, the evaluation timeline, and the number of candidate solutions. Compare buying personal finance management software to buying a multimillion-dollar financial application for a 5,000-person company. You might only name the most important use cases in the first scenario, but write full use cases and develop data and quality requirements for a more extensive evaluation in the second.

One team needed to select packaged software to run a law office. They identified 20 tasks that users needed to perform using the software, which led to 10 features to be assessed while evaluating 4 candidate packages. The law partners knew they would have to create more detailed requirements to configure the software after they chose a package. However, a lightweight evaluation was appropriate for the package selection. In contrast, a team of 50 people worked together to develop detailed requirements for software to run a new semiconductor plant. There were only three candidate solutions to evaluate, but given the expected cost of the COTS software and its implementation, the company was willing to invest a lot in the selection process. They spent six months on the package selection alone.

Developing user requirements

Any package you choose must let users accomplish their task objectives, although different packaged solutions will do so in different ways. The majority of your requirements efforts for COTS acquisition should be focused at the user requirements level. Use cases and user stories work well for this purpose. Process models can also be used and might already exist in the organization. There's little point in specifying detailed functional requirements or designing a user interface, because the vendor (presumably) already did that.

It can also be helpful to list the features you need from the packaged solution. Identify the desired product features from an understanding of what users need to achieve with the solution and the business processes the package must enable. Suppose you have the following user story: "As a Research Manager, I need to review and approve new experiments before they are performed so that we don't waste time and supplies on poorly designed experiments." This user story helps identify the need for an approval workflow feature.

No packaged solution is likely to accommodate every use case you identify, so prioritize the user requirements or features. Trace them back to business requirements so you don't waste time on unnecessary evaluation criteria. Distinguish capabilities that must be available on day one from those that can wait for future extensions and those that your users can live without, perhaps forever.

Considering business rules

Your requirements exploration should identify pertinent business rules to which the COTS product must conform. Can you configure the package to comply with your corporate policies, industry standards, and relevant regulations? How easily can you modify the configured package when these rules change? Focus on the most important business rules, because it can be time consuming to evaluate the implementation of all of the pertinent rules.

Some packages incorporate widely applicable business rules, such as income tax withholding computations or printed tax forms. Do you trust that these are implemented correctly? Will the package vendor provide you with timely software updates when those rules and computations change? Will they charge you for the updates? Will the vendor supply a list of the business rules the package implements? If the product implements any intrinsic business rules that don't apply to you, can you disable, modify, or work around them? Does the vendor accept enhancement requests? If so, how are they prioritized?

Identifying data needs

You might need to define the data structures required to satisfy your user requirements and business rules, particularly if the new solution must be integrated into an ecosystem of existing applications. Look for major disconnects between your data model and the package vendor's data model. Do not be distracted by data entities and attributes that are simply named differently in the COTS solution. Instead, recognize where entities or their attributes don't exist in the packaged solution or have significantly different definitions from what you need, and then determine whether those entities can be handled in a different way for the solution to work.

Specify the reports that the COTS product must generate. Does it generate mandated reports in the correct formats? To what extent will the product let you customize its standard reports? Can you design new reports of your own to integrate with those that the vendor supplied?

Defining quality requirements

The quality attributes discussed in Chapter 14, "Beyond functionality," are another vital aspect of user requirements that feeds into packaged solution selection. Explore at least the following attributes:

- **Performance**   What maximum response times are acceptable for specific operations? Can the package handle the anticipated load of concurrent users and transaction throughput?

- **Usability**   Does the package conform to any established user interface conventions? Is the interface similar to what the users experience in other applications already? How easily can your users learn to use the new package? Is training provided by the vendor included as part of the package's cost?

- **Modifiability**   How hard will it be for your developers to modify or extend the package to meet your specific needs? Does the package provide appropriate "hooks" (connection and extension points) and application programming interfaces for adding extensions? Will all those extensions stay in place when you install a new version of the package?

- **Interoperability**   How easily can you integrate the package with your other enterprise applications? Does it use standard data interchange formats? Will it force you to upgrade any other third-party tools or infrastructure components because it doesn't handle backward compatibility?

- **Integrity**   Does the package safeguard data from loss, corruption, or unauthorized access?

- **Security**   Does the package permit control over which users are allowed to access the system or use specific functions? Can you define the necessary user privilege levels? Particularly for SaaS solutions, evaluate the service level agreements very carefully against your requirements.

Evaluating solutions

Many commercial packages purport to provide canned solutions for some portion of your enterprise information-processing needs. Do some initial market research to determine which packages are viable candidates deserving further consideration. Then you can use the requirements you identified as evaluation criteria in an informed COTS software selection process.

One evaluation approach includes the following sequence of activities (Lawlis et al. 2001):

1. Weight your requirements on a scale of 1 to 10 to distinguish their importance.

2. Rate each candidate package as to how well it satisfies each requirement. Use a rating of 1 for full satisfaction, 0.5 for partial satisfaction, and 0 for no coverage. You can find the information to make this assessment from product literature, a vendor's response to a request for proposal (RFP), or direct examination of the product. Keep in mind that an RFP is an invitation to bid on a project and might not provide information that reflects how you intend to use the product. Direct examination is necessary for high-priority requirements.

3. Calculate the score for each candidate based on the weight you gave each factor, to see which products appear to best fit your needs.

4. Evaluate product cost, vendor experience and viability, vendor support for the product, external interfaces that will enable extension and integration, and compliance with any technology requirements or constraints for your environment. Cost will be a selection factor, but evaluate the candidates initially without considering their cost.

You might consider which requirements are *not* met by any of the candidate packages and will require you to develop extensions. These can add significant costs to the COTS implementation and should be considered in the evaluation process.

 Recently, my organization wanted to select a requirements management tool that—among other capabilities—allowed users to work offline and synchronize to the master version of the requirements when the users went back online (Beatty and Ferrari 2011). We suspected that no tools on the market would offer a good solution for this. We included this capability in our evaluation to ensure that we uncovered any solutions that did offer it. If we didn't find one, we would know that it was a capability we'd have to implement as an extension to the selected package. Alternatively, we'd need to change our process for editing requirements.

Another evaluation approach is to determine whether—and how well—the package will let the users perform their tasks by deriving tests from the high-priority use cases. Include tests that explore how the system handles significant exception conditions that might arise. Walk through those tests to see how the candidate packages handle them. A similar approach is to run the COTS product through a suite of scenarios that represent the expected usage patterns, which is called an *operational profile* (Musa 1999).

> **Trap** If you don't have at least one person whose involvement spans all of the evaluations, there is no assurance that comparable interpretations of the features and scores were used.

The output of the evaluation process is typically an evaluation matrix with the selection requirements in the rows and various solutions' scores for each of those requirements in the columns. Figure 22-2 shows part of a sample evaluation matrix for a requirements management tool.

ID	Use Case	Feature	Priority	Tool 1	Tool 1 Comments
1	BA adds new requirements individually	Add new requirement	10	1	
2	BA adds new requirements individually	Automatically create unique ID for each requirement	10	1	
3	BA adds new requirements individually	Document a requirement with rich text formatting	3	0	Only supports text with no formatting.
5	BA models requirements	Describe a requirement with an image directly in the database	6	0.5	Need to do a workaround for this where you link to the resource outside the tool but store the link in the database.
6	BA models requirements	Describe a requirement with an embedded document in the database	8	1	
7	BA links existing documentation to requirements	Link requirements to actual documents in a SharePoint location	4	1	
9	BA adds a bulk of new requirements at once	Batch import structured data as new requirements from Excel	5	1	Batch import is supported and provides support for importing customized Excel files.

FIGURE 22-2 A sample of a packaged solution evaluation matrix for a requirements management tool.

Multi-stage evaluation

When I wrote the requirements for selecting a requirements management tool for our own consulting teams to use, I worked with the teams to identify the user classes and use cases for the tool. Although the primary users were business analysts, there were also a few use cases for managers, developers, and customers. I defined use cases by name and used my familiarity with the use cases to identify desired features. I created a traceability matrix to minimize the likelihood that any use cases or features would be missed.

We started with 200 features and 60 vendor choices, which were far too many for our evaluation timeline. We did a first-pass evaluation to eliminate most of the candidate tools. Our first pass considered only 30 features that we deemed the most important or most likely to distinguish tools from one another. This initial evaluation narrowed our search to 16 tool choices. Then we evaluated those 16 against the full set of 200 features. This detailed second-level evaluation resulted in a list of five closely ranked tools, all of which would clearly meet our needs.

In addition to an objective analysis, it's a good idea to evaluate candidate packages by using a real project, not just the tutorial project that comes with the product. We ended up adding a third level of evaluation to actually try each of those five tools on real projects so we could see which one most closely reflected the evaluation scores in practice. The third phase of the evaluation allowed us to select our favorite tool from the high-scoring ones.

Requirements for implementing packaged solutions

After you decide to implement a selected packaged solution, there is still more requirements work to do. Figure 22-3 shows that the spectrum of effort required to make a packaged solution useful ranges from using the package as is, right out of the box, to performing considerable requirements specification and software development for extensions. Table 22-1 describes these four types of COTS package implementations, which are not mutually exclusive. Any of these implementations might also require making infrastructure changes in the operating environment, such as upgrading operating systems or other software components that interact with the package.

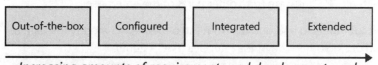

Increasing amounts of requirements and development work

FIGURE 22-3 A spectrum of implementation effort for packaged solutions.

TABLE 22-1 COTS package implementation approaches

Type of COTS implementation	Description
Out-of-the-box	Install the software and use it as is.
Configured	Adjust settings in the software to suit your needs without writing new code.
Integrated	Connect the package to existing systems in your application ecosystem; usually requires some custom code.
Extended	Develop additional functionality with custom code to enhance the package's capabilities to close needs gaps.

One advantage of purchasing a COTS solution is that it might provide useful capabilities that you hadn't originally sought. You typically select the package based on what you know you need. However, during implementation, you might discover valuable features that you hadn't even thought of. This can change the amount of work needed to install the package to exploit the additional features.

Configuration requirements

Sometimes you can use a package just as it comes from the vendor. More often, you'll need to adjust various configuration parameters in the package to better meet your needs. Configuration requirements are essential to most successful COTS implementations. One approach is to define configuration requirements for one process flow, use case, or user story at a time. Walk through user manuals for the purchased system to learn how to execute a specific task, looking for settings that need to be configured to suit your environment. Consider the full set of business rules when you are configuring the system, not just those you examined during the selection process. It might be helpful to create decision tables and decision trees to model these requirements. Many COTS solutions come with predefined mechanisms to specify roles and permissions. Use a roles and permissions matrix, such as the one shown in Figure 9-2 in Chapter 9, "Playing by the rules," to define which roles to create and what permissions those roles should have.

Integration requirements

Unless the packaged solution is used in a standalone mode, you'll need to integrate it into your application environment. This integration involves understanding the external interfaces the package will present to each of the other applications with which it must interact. Precisely specify the requirements for interchanging data and services between the package and other components in your environment. You will likely have to create some custom code to make all the parts fit together. This code could take the form of:

- Adapters that modify interfaces or add missing functionality.

- Firewalls that isolate the COTS software from other parts of the enterprise.

- Wrappers that intercept inputs to and outputs from the package and modify the data as necessary to be used on the other side of the interface (NASA 2009).

Extension requirements

One common goal of COTS implementations is to minimize customizations to the solution. Otherwise, you should just custom build the application yourself. In most COTS projects, though, there will be gaps between what the organization needs and what the package delivers. For each such gap, decide whether to ignore it (remove the requirement and just live with the tool); change how you do something outside the solution (modify the business process); or build something to bridge the gap (extend the solution). If you are extending the COTS solution, you'll need to fully specify the requirements for those new capabilities just as you would for any new product development. If you are implementing a COTS solution to replace an older system, look at the practices related to replacing a system that were discussed in Chapter 21, "Enhancement and replacement projects." While analyzing the requirements for any components to be added, assess whether they could negatively affect any existing elements or workflows in the package.

Data requirements

Begin with the data requirements used in the selection process. Map data entities and attributes from your existing data dictionary to the COTS entities and attributes. There will likely be areas where the solution doesn't handle some of your existing data entities or attributes. As with functional gaps, you'll need to decide how to handle data gaps, typically by adding attributes or repurposing an existing data structure in the COTS solution. Otherwise, when you convert data from any existing systems into the COTS solution, you will likely lose any data that was not properly mapped. Use report tables to specify requirements for deploying existing or new reports, as described in Chapter 13, "Specifying data requirements." Many COTS packages will provide some standard report templates to start with.

Business process changes

COTS packages are usually selected because implementing and maintaining them is expected to be less expensive than building custom software. Organizations need to be prepared to adapt their business processes to the package's workflow capabilities and limitations. This is different from most development projects where the software is designed specifically to accommodate existing or planned processes. In fact, a COTS solution that can be fully configured to meet your existing processes is likely to be expensive and complex. The more buttons and knobs you can adjust, the harder it is to configure. You need to strike a balance between implementing all of the desired user functionality and only what the COTS product offers out of the box (Chung, Hooper, and Huynh 2001).

Start with the user requirements identified during the selection process. Develop use cases or swimlane diagrams to understand how the tasks will change when users execute their tasks in the COTS solution. Users might resist the new packaged solution because it looks or behaves differently than their existing systems, so involve them early in this process. Users are more willing to accept the new solution if they contributed to shaping the necessary changes in their business processes.

 My team implemented a packaged solution for an insurance company to let them meet new compliance requirements. We started by modeling the as-is business processes. Then we studied the package's manuals to learn basic information about how to use the product. Based on the as-is models, we created to-be business processes to reflect how the users would complete their tasks using the COTS solution. We also created a data dictionary for their existing system and added a column to reflect the mapped field in the COTS solution. The users helped develop all of these work products, so they weren't surprised by the new system when it was deployed.

Common challenges with packaged solutions

The following are common challenges that you might encounter when selecting or implementing a packaged solution:

- **Too many candidates** There might be many solutions on the market that meet your needs at first glance. Select a short list of criteria to narrow the candidate list to a few top choices for a more refined evaluation.

- **Too many evaluation criteria** It might be hard to focus the evaluation criteria to only the most important ones without doing in-depth requirements specification. Use business objectives to help select the most important requirements as criteria. If you narrow the candidate package choices down to only a few, you can evaluate them against a long list of criteria.

- **Vendor misrepresents package capabilities** In the typical packaged software purchasing process, the vendor sales staff sells their solution to the customer organization's decision makers, and then engages a technical implementation team to provide in-depth knowledge about the product. That in-depth knowledge might prove to conflict somewhat with the customer's understanding of the product's capabilities based on the sales pitch. It's a good idea to ask to have a vendor technical specialist participate during the sales cycle. Determine whether you can have a healthy relationship with the vendor that enables both parties to be successful. The vendor is your business partner, so make sure they can play that role constructively.

- **Incorrect solution expectations** Sometimes a solution looks great during vendor demos, but it doesn't work like you expect after installation. To avoid this, during the selection process, have the vendor walk through your actual use cases so you can see how well the solution matches your expectations.

- **Users reject the solution** Just because an organization bought the software, there is no guarantee that the users will be receptive to it. As with all software development projects, engage users in the selection process or early in the implementation to make sure their needs are clearly understood and addressed to the extent possible. Expectation management is an important part of successful packaged solution implementation.

Buying, configuring, and extending a commercial software package often is a sensible business alternative to building a custom solution. Packages can provide a lot of flexibility, but at the same time they come with built-in limitations and constraints. You don't want to have to pay for a lot of features that your organization doesn't need. Nor do you want to build a fragile structure of extensions and integrations that might break with the next release of the package from the vendor. A careful package selection and implementation process will help you find the optimum balance of capability, usability, extensibility, and maintainability in a commercial packaged software solution.

CHAPTER 23

Outsourced projects

Rather than building systems by using their own staff, many organizations outsource their development efforts to contract development companies. They might outsource the work to take advantage of development skills they do not have available in-house, to augment their internal staff resources, to save money, or to accelerate development. The outsourced development supplier could be located physically nearby, on the other side of the world, or anywhere in between. Outsourced teams in other countries are typically referred to as being *offshore*. Offshoring is sometimes called *nearshoring* if the supplier's country is close by or shares a language and/or culture with the acquirer's country.

All outsourced projects involve distributed teams, with people working in two or more locations. The role of a business analyst is even more important on these projects than on a co-located project. Often, the BA's job is harder. If the team members are all in one location, developers can walk down the hall to ask the BA a question or to demonstrate newly developed functionality. This close collaboration can't happen in the same way with outsourced development, although modern communication tools certainly help. Compared to in-house development, outsourced—and particularly offshore—projects face requirements-related challenges such as the following:

- It's harder to get developer input on requirements and to pass along user feedback on delivered software to developers.

- A formal contractual definition of requirements is necessary, which can lead to contention if differences of interpretation are discovered late in the project.

- There might be a bigger gap between what the customers ultimately need and the product they get based on the initial requirements, because there are fewer opportunities to adjust the project's direction along the way.

- It might take longer to resolve requirements issues because of large time zone differences.

- Communicating the requirements is more difficult because of language and cultural barriers.

- Limited written requirements that might be adequate for in-house projects are insufficient for outsourced projects, because users and BAs are not readily available to answer developer questions, clarify ambiguities, and close gaps.

- Remote developers lack the organizational and business knowledge that in-house developers acquire with experience.

Although the original arguments for offshoring included anticipated cost savings based on hourly staff costs, many offshore projects actually experience a net *increase* in cost. Contributing factors include the additional effort required for more precise requirements, likely additional development iterations to close gaps because of unstated implied and assumed requirements, the additional overhead of the contractual arrangements, initial costs in developing effective norms of team behavior between the groups, and the costs of increased project communications and oversight throughout.

Software development work is the most common type of activity that is outsourced, but testing can also be outsourced. Outsourced testing presents the same challenges as outsourced development. Both types of activities rely on a solid foundation of clear requirements for success.

This chapter suggests techniques that are most important to enable successful requirements development and management on outsourced projects. This chapter does not discuss the decision process that leads to outsourcing the development or the process to select a vendor for the work.

Appropriate levels of requirements detail

Outsourcing product development to a separate company demands high-quality written requirements, because your direct interactions with the development team are likely to be minimal. As shown in Figure 23-1, you'll be sending the supplier a request for proposal (RFP), a requirements specification, and product acceptance criteria. Early on, both parties will engage in a review and will reach agreement, perhaps with negotiation and adjustments, before the supplier initiates development. The supplier will deliver the finished software product and supporting documentation.

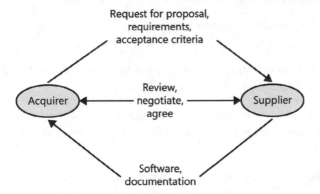

FIGURE 23-1 Requirements are the cornerstone of an outsourced project.

With outsourcing, you won't have the opportunities for day-to-day clarifications, decision making, and changes that you enjoy when developers and customers work in close proximity. Particularly with offshore development, you should anticipate that the supplier will build exactly what you ask them to build. You will get no more and no less, sometimes with no questions asked. The supplier won't implement the implicit and assumed requirements you thought were too obvious to write down. As a result, poorly defined and managed requirements are a common cause of outsourced project failure.

If you distribute an RFP, suppliers need to know exactly what you're requesting before they can produce realistic responses and estimates (Porter-Roth 2002). Because of the information that has to go into the RFP, you might have to develop more detailed requirements earlier in the project than on in-house development projects (Morgan 2009). At a minimum, specify a rich set of user requirements and nonfunctional requirements for the RFP. After the project is under way, you will likely need to specify all of the requirements with more precision than if an in-house team were building the same system, particularly if the outsourced team is offshore. If you are ever inclined to err on the side of overspecifying requirements, outsourced projects are the place to do so. It's the requirements author's responsibility to express the acquirer's expectations clearly. If certain deliverables must be produced for the acquirer to maintain a process certification or for compliance reasons, be sure to include those particulars as part of the RFP as well.

As with in-house development, visual requirements models augment functional and nonfunctional requirements for outsourced teams. Creating multiple representations of requirements increases the bandwidth of communication, so you might find it beneficial to create more models than if an in-house team were developing the software. Using representations like visual models to supplement written specifications is even more valuable if you are working across cultures and native languages, because it gives developers something to check their interpretations against. However, be sure the developers can understand the models you send them. If they aren't familiar with the models, that only raises the potential for confusion. One development manager was concerned that a written requirements specification plus mock-ups would not provide enough information for his offshore team to correctly implement a complex user interface (Beatty and Chen 2012). The display-action-response model described in Chapter 19, "Beyond requirements development," was developed specifically to meet the needs of this outsourced project.

Prototypes can also help clarify expectations for the supplier team. Similarly, the supplier can create prototypes to demonstrate to the acquirer their interpretation of the requirements and how they plan to respond to them. This is a way to create more customer-development interaction points to make course adjustments early in the project rather than late. Chapter 15, "Risk reduction through prototyping," has more information about creating and using prototypes.

Watch out for the ambiguous terms from Table 11-2 in Chapter 11, "Writing excellent requirements," that cause so much confusion. I once read an SRS intended for outsourcing that contained the word "support" in many places. The business analyst who wrote the SRS acknowledged that a contractor who was going to implement the software wouldn't know just what "support" meant in each case. A glossary is valuable when dealing with people who don't share the tacit knowledge held by those who are familiar with the acquiring company's environment. The structured keyword notation called Planguage (see Chapter 14, "Beyond functionality") can be used to describe requirements very explicitly for outsourced development (Gilb 2007).

Acquirer-supplier interactions

In the absence of real-time, face-to-face communication, you need other mechanisms to stay on top of what the supplier is doing, so arrange formal touch points between the acquirer and the supplier. In some outsourced projects, the supplier helps to write the functional requirements (Morgan 2009). This increases the initial costs associated with the outsourcing, but it also reduces the risk of misunderstandings.

Plan time for multiple review cycles of the requirements. Use collaboration tools to facilitate peer reviews with participants in multiple locations (Wiegers 2002). Be aware, though, that members of certain cultures find it difficult to offer even constructive criticism of another person's work. Authors in such a culture whose work is being reviewed could take review comments personally (Van Veenendaal 1999). The result is that the reviewers might sit politely during the peer review, saying nothing because they don't want to offend the author. This is courteous and considerate, but it does not contribute to a shared goal of discovering requirements defects as early as possible to make development cheaper and faster. Discover whether this cultural characteristic applies to your outsource partners so you can determine realistic expectations and strategies for your peer reviews.

The project schedule for one failed offshore project included a one-week task named "Hold requirements workshops," followed immediately by tasks to implement several subsystems (Wiegers 2003). The supplier forgot to include vital intermediate tasks to document, review, and revise the requirements specifications. The iterative and communication-intensive nature of requirements development dictates that you must allow sufficient time for these review cycles. The acquirer and the supplier on this project were in different countries, at opposite ends of the same continent. They experienced slow turnaround on the myriad questions that arose as the SRS cycled back and forth. Failure to resolve requirements issues in a timely way derailed the schedule and contributed to eventually sending the two parties into litigation.

Peer reviews and prototypes provide insight into how the supplier is interpreting the requirements. Incremental development is another risk-management technique that permits course corrections when a misunderstanding sends the supplier's developers in the wrong direction. If the supplier raises questions, document them and integrate the answers into the requirements (Gilb 2007). Monitor the resolution of the questions in an issue-tracking tool to which both supplier and acquirer teams have access, as described in Chapter 27, "Requirements management practices."

Contract development companies that work on many types of projects might lack the specific domain or company knowledge that is critical to making the right decisions. Consider delivering some training to the contractor staff about the project and application domain prior to requirements review, to try to bridge this knowledge gap.

Outsourced projects often involve teams with disparate company cultures and attitudes. Some suppliers will be so eager to please that they agree to outcomes they cannot deliver. When an error is brought to their attention, they might strive to save face by not fully accepting responsibility for the problems. Additional cultural differences arise with offshore suppliers. Some developers might hesitate to ask for help or clarification. They might be reluctant to say "no" or "I don't understand." This can lead to misinterpretations, unresolved issues, and unachievable commitments. To avoid these issues, employ elicitation and facilitation techniques such as reading between the lines for what isn't said and asking open-ended questions to gain accurate visibility into issues and status. Consider establishing ground rules with your team members, both local and remote, to expressly define how the team members should interact when they work together.

Developers whose first language is different than the language in which the requirements are written are likely to interpret requirements literally, not picking up nuances or fully appreciating the implications. They might make user interface design choices that you wouldn't expect. Things as diverse as date formats, systems of measurement (such as United States customary units, SI units, or imperial units), the symbolism of colors, and the order of people's given and family names can vary between countries. When interacting with people who have a different native language from yours, make your intentions and desires as clear as possible in simple language. Avoid the use of colloquialisms, jargon, idioms, and references to pop culture that could be misconstrued.

 One offshore team took a customer's requirements very literally. It was as though the developers translated each requirement from English into their own language, coded it, moved on to the next requirement, and continued until they reached the end of the list. The product that was delivered to the customer technically met the requirements, but it fell far short of meeting expectations. The developers weren't trying to be difficult. They just didn't understand the language of the requirements very well. Consequently, they never fully grasped the essence of what they were building. The customer brought most of the development work back in-house and effectively had to pay twice to have the software developed correctly.

> **Trap** Don't assume that suppliers will interpret ambiguous and incomplete requirements the same way that you do. The burden is on the acquirer to communicate all necessary information to the supplier, using frequent conversations to resolve requirements questions. But the burden is on the supplier to proactively ask clarifying questions instead of making assumptions that could be incorrect.

Change management

At the beginning of the project, establish a mutually acceptable change control process that all participants can use, no matter where they're located. Using a common set of web-based tools for handling change requests and tracking open issues is essential. Change always has a price, so using change management practices to control scope creep is vital in a contract-development situation. Identify the decision makers for proposed changes and the communication mechanisms you'll use to make sure the right people are kept informed. Most outsourced work has contractual agreements in place to describe exactly what the development team must deliver. The contract should specify who will pay for various kinds of changes, such as newly requested functionality or corrections made in the original requirements, and the process for incorporating the changes into the product. When there is misalignment between requirements and delivery, the arguments that ensue are consequently also contractual in nature. Unfortunately, often both parties lose (McConnell 1997).

Acceptance criteria

In keeping with Stephen Covey's recommendation to "begin with the end in mind" (Covey 2004), define in advance how you'll assess whether the contracted product is acceptable to you and your customers. How will you judge whether to make the final payment to the supplier? If the acceptance criteria are not fully satisfied, who is responsible for making corrections, and who pays for those? Include acceptance criteria in the RFP so the supplier knows up front what to expect. Validate the requirements before you give them to the outsourced team, to help ensure that the delivered product will be on target. Chapter 17, "Validating the requirements," suggested some approaches to defining acceptance criteria, as well as methods for reviewing and testing requirements.

Properly handled, outsourcing the development work can be an effective strategy to build your software system. Building collaborative relationships with outsourced development suppliers is challenging because of distance, language and cultural differences, and potentially competing interests. Suppliers might not be motivated to correct any requirement errors or ambiguities discovered along the way if they will be paid more to fix the problems following delivery of a release candidate. An essential starting point on a journey to a successful outsourced development experience is a set of high-quality, complete, and explicitly clear requirements. If the requirements you provide to the supplier are incomplete or misunderstood, failure of the project is probably at least as much your fault as theirs.

CHAPTER 24

Business process automation projects

Organizations often choose to fully or partially replace manual business processes with software to lower operational costs. In fact, most corporate IT projects involve some amount of business process automation, including the Chemical Tracking System and other projects we have mentioned in this book. Processes can be automated by building a new software system, extending an existing system, or buying a COTS package. If you're working on a business process automation project, there are several requirements techniques to consider using to mesh the new systems and updated business processes.

Because business process automation is so prevalent in software projects, many of the techniques described elsewhere in this book are relevant. This chapter presents a structure to help you tackle these sorts of projects and points out the techniques from the rest of the book that are most applicable. It also presents some additional techniques that aren't covered elsewhere in the book.

Here's an illustration of how business process automation projects sometimes go. One customer of ours had a spreadsheet that used approximately 300 inputs from different sources to calculate a risk profile for loans. The business stakeholders wanted software that would gather the data inputs and run the risk profile calculation, because it took a long time for their risk managers to execute this frequently repeated process. We analyzed where their users spent the bulk of their time on this process and quickly determined that assembling the data that fed into the spreadsheet took the most time. The calculations the spreadsheet performed were nearly instantaneous. The development team already had access to most of the data sources to populate the spreadsheet, so a manageable first phase of the project was to automatically pull that data into the spreadsheet. The business users would continue to manually assemble the rest of the inputs for awhile. In the second phase, development would automate the rest of the data inputs. The team decided they would not build software to replicate the spreadsheet calculations because the calculations were fast enough already.

This case study illustrates a typical business process automation project. The business identified a time-consuming, repetitive activity that they thought could be accelerated with the help of suitable software. Some analysis revealed the bottlenecks and identified possible efficiencies. This led to requirements and project plans for a partial solution that would save the business considerable time, reduce costs, and reduce data input errors.

Modeling business processes

Eliciting requirements to automate business processes begins by modeling those processes. By identifying tasks that users need to accomplish with the system, the business analyst can derive the necessary functional requirements that will let users perform those tasks. The processes that describe how the business currently works are called the *as-is processes*. Those that describe the envisioned future state of how the business will operate are called the *to-be processes*.

Business process acronyms galore

Extensive resources are available on business process analysis (BPA), business process reengineering (BPR), business process improvement (BPI), business process management (BPM), and business process model and notation (BPMN). This chapter is not a comprehensive resource on those topics. The following list provides some basic definitions of these concepts and their purposes, though you will find significant overlap in these definitions:

- Business process analysis (BPA) involves understanding the processes as a basis for improving them. It is similar to process modeling, as described in the Business Analysis Body of Knowledge (IIBA 2009).

- Business process reengineering (BPR) consists of analyzing and redesigning business processes for greater efficiency and effectiveness. BPR could target specific process areas, or it could involve a complete overhaul of an organization's processes from the ground up (Hammer and Champy 2006).

- Business process improvement (BPI) involves measuring and looking for opportunities for incremental process improvement (Harrington 1991). Tools from Six Sigma and lean management practices are often used for BPI efforts (Schonberger 2008).

- Business process management (BPM) encompasses understanding all of the enterprise's business processes, analyzing them to make them more efficient and effective, and working with organizations to make changes to the processes (Harmon 2007; Sharp and McDermott 2008). A BPM initiative might involve some combination of BPA, BPR, and BPI.

- Business process model and notation (BPMN) is a graphical notation for modeling business processes (OMG 2011). BPMN can be applied in any of these approaches to business process modeling. It is a robust language of symbols that can be useful when the basic syntax of a swimlane diagram doesn't suffice.

A variety of methods and tools implement BPA, BPR, BPI, and BPM, which are appropriate to employ if your project is undergoing major business process redesign. All four techniques are established approaches for understanding the business challenges and opportunities. After an organization decides that a software component is part of the solution for improving their business processes, the requirements engineering techniques described in this book become valuable.

Using current processes to derive requirements

The following steps will help you model a set of business processes and elicit requirements for an application that automates some or all of them. The sequence of these steps is not always the same, and you might not need all of them on every project. In some cases, the to-be process flows can come earlier in the sequence as a way of driving a gap analysis or to help ensure that the new system is more just than the old system dressed up in a new outfit. In general, though, consider following these steps:

1. As always with software development, start by understanding the business objectives, so you can link each objective to one or more processes.

2. Use organization charts to find all of the affected organizations and potential user classes for a future software solution.

3. Identify all of the relevant business processes involving participation of those user classes.

4. Document the as-is business processes by using flow charts, activity diagrams, or swimlane diagrams. Any of the three models is a practical choice for representing users' tasks. Users can quickly read them and point out any missing or incorrect steps, roles, or decision logic (Beatty and Chen 2012). You'll need to judge how far down into the as-is modeling you need to drill to get the necessary information to perform the remaining steps in this list.

5. Analyze the as-is processes to determine the biggest opportunities for improvement from automation. If this is not obvious, you will need to gather some data about how long it takes to execute individual steps or full processes. You can model these measures by using the key performance indicator model (KPIM) described later in this chapter. This step helps identify opportunities and, if a software solution is deemed appropriate, set the scope of the software development part of the project. Make sure you are addressing true bottlenecks in the process, so that accelerating them will speed up the overall process.

6. For the processes that are in scope for automation, walk through each as-is process flow with the appropriate stakeholders to elicit software requirements to support each step in the flow. The techniques described in Chapter 7, "Requirements elicitation," will be valuable during this activity. If applicable, you might also look for industry standards for the process you are modeling, to help you set improvement goals.

7. Trace the requirements to the process flow steps so that it is obvious if you are missing requirements for any specific steps. If you have process steps without requirements traced to them, confirm that those steps are not being automated as part of the project.

8. Document to-be process flows to help the business prepare for the new system and to identify any gaps that the new system might leave in their process. You might also create use cases to provide more detail about how users will interact with the new system. This information helps developers ensure that they create a system to meet the business's expectations and helps users understand what they are getting. The to-be process flows and use cases can be used to develop training materials for the new system and to identify any other transition

requirements. This step helps stakeholders to understand not only what is coming, but what manual activities and automated systems need to be unplugged.

When software isn't the solution

Sometimes you don't need to automate anything to improve business processes. One company had an internal website where it stored the names of people who worked on specific client projects: sales representative, implementation consultant, and so on. The sales representative data was nearly always accurate, but the implementation consultant data was wrong more than half the time. This resulted in people having to chase down who to contact. When you multiply the 2 or 3 minutes that each of the 200 people in the business unit spent on this activity at least once a week for a year's time, the cost ended up being enormous. The problem: there was no process in place between the sales and implementation teams to update the implementation project data after the project started. The solution: figure out who in sales would serve as the contact for gathering and manually updating contact information for the implementation team for each client. New software wouldn't have helped with this process shortcoming.

Designing future processes first

There is a chicken-and-egg problem with information systems and business processes. In some cases, people expect that building a new system will drive improvements or changes in the processes. However, the way the application is used in practice might not enable the desired business process changes. Process changes involve culture changes and user education that a software system cannot deliver. Some customers believe that the development team is responsible for a successful application rollout and for guiding the implementation of associated business processes. Users won't embrace a new system just because a developer says to, though.

In many cases, it's better to devise the new business processes first and then assess the needed changes in your information systems architecture. Properly supporting a new business process might involve changing multiple systems. Thinking about which users will use the system and how they will use it to do their jobs will help you define the correct user requirements, which in turn will maximize user adoption of the new system. Concurrent development of new processes and new applications helps ensure that the two merge nicely.

Modeling business performance metrics

It's important to understand which business performance metrics are most important to address with business process automation so that the development work can be prioritized. You might have success metrics to use as a starting point from the vision and scope document (see the "1.4 Success metrics" section in Chapter 5, "Establishing the business requirements"). If not, the business performance metrics developed here will help complete the vision and scope. For the spreadsheet example earlier in the chapter, you might care about how long it takes to populate the spreadsheet manually and how fast you need it to be in the automated solution.

KPIMs associate business processes with their important performance metrics. KPIMs are drawn as flowcharts, swimlane diagrams, or activity diagrams with key performance indicators (KPIs) overlaid on the related steps. Figure 24-1 shows an example KPIM (drawn as a flowchart) for the spreadsheet project to automate a risk profile calculation spreadsheet.

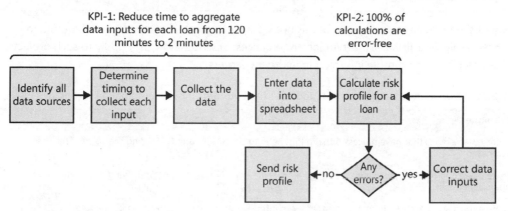

FIGURE 24-1 Example KPIM for a loan risk profile calculation process.

The most important processes to automate are those that have the most important metrics to maintain or improve. Determine a current baseline value for each metric, so that when you automate the process, you can tell if they are improving as desired. Keep in mind that you might degrade certain business performance metrics to improve others. Chapter 14, "Beyond functionality," discusses making trade-offs between quality attributes. The same concept applies here, but in this case the trade-offs are to favor one performance metric over another, perhaps in different parts of the business. Tracing requirements to the process flow steps, which in turn are mapped to KPIs, allows you to prioritize the requirements to be implemented.

You might need to build functionality into the system to periodically measure the relevant KPIs to evaluate the effectiveness of the newly automated solution, raising a warning flag if a KPI falls out of tolerance. In the spreadsheet example, the system could measure how much time it takes to aggregate data inputs to determine if the system is achieving the two-minute goal. If not, further changes might be needed.

Business users often think it's always best to automate a manual process if you can. However, there are costs associated with all development projects. Business analysis helps you determine which processes are worth automating and which are not. As an example, Seilevel (Joy's company) uses a COTS solution for managing the sales pipeline and another for managing human resource allocations. We run a report from the sales pipeline tool and manually input the upcoming projects into the resource allocation tool to forecast resource needs. Our consulting manager has to do this at least once a week. It takes him approximately 30 minutes each week to run the sales pipeline report, decide which projects from sales should be transferred, when those projects will start, and how many resources each one needs. We evaluated whether we should enable the integration feature to automatically transfer the data from one tool to the other. Although integrating the tools is as simple as enabling a feature, it would require custom development to automate the decision process our consulting manager goes through. Specifying and automating that decision logic would require more effort than we can justify.

Good practices for business process automation projects

Many of the practices from the rest of this book are important to business process automation projects. Table 24-1 lists the most important practices, describes how they apply to such projects, and indicates where to find more information in other chapters.

TABLE 24-1 A road map to chapters that address useful business process automation techniques

Technique	Chapter
Identify user classes that have processes that might need to be automated.	Chapter 6, "Finding the voice of the user"
Create or extend data models for information that is being handled manually.	Chapter 13, "Specifying data requirements"
Create a roles and permissions matrix to capture security requirements that previously were enforced manually.	Chapter 9, "Playing by the rules"
Identify business rules that must be automated when processes they affect are automated.	Chapter 9, "Playing by the rules"
Create flowcharts, swimlane diagrams, activity diagrams, or use cases to show how users currently perform tasks and how they will perform them after automation.	Chapter 8, "Understanding user requirements" and Chapter 12, "A picture is worth 1024 words"
Use data flow diagrams (DFDs) to identify processes that could be automated, and create new DFDs to show how newly automated processes interact with existing parts of the system.	Chapter 12, "A picture is worth 1024 words"
Adapt business processes to permit use of a COTS solution.	Chapter 22, "Packaged solution projects"
Create trace matrices to map process steps to requirements.	Chapter 29, "Links in the requirements chain"

You will likely apply the concepts from this chapter on almost every information systems project you work on. When you encounter part or all of a business process to be automated, use the framework in this chapter to ensure that you fully understand the goals of automating the process and the requirements to support it. This will help everyone understand user expectations so development can deliver a successful solution that yields the desired business benefits.

CHAPTER 25

Business analytics projects

Most normal people don't look at data sets just for fun. They study views of the data to make decisions about what to do, be it a decision to take some specific action or a decision to do nothing at all. In some cases, software systems automate the decision-making processes by interpreting data and taking actions based on predefined algorithms and rules. The main purpose of *business analytics* (also called *business intelligence* or *reporting*) projects is to develop systems that turn large and often highly complex data sets into meaningful information from which decisions can be made. Many other classes of projects might have business analytics components; the concepts presented in this chapter apply to those projects as well.

The decisions that people make using business analytics systems can be strategic, operational, or tactical. An executive might look at his sales team's global performance dashboard to decide who to promote (tactical), which products need different marketing strategies (operational), or which products to target by markets (strategic). Generally speaking, all software systems that include an analytics component should enable users to make decisions that improve organizational performance in some dimension.

There are many software applications commercially available to implement business analytics solutions. The business analyst who wants to use one of those applications might need to perform requirements activities for tool selection and implementation, using the process described in Chapter 22, "Packaged solution projects."

This chapter is meant only as an introduction to issues to consider when developing software requirements for business analytics projects. Bert Brijs (2013) authored an extensive resource for performing business analysis on these types of projects. He provides many definitions of the core concepts, specific domain examples, questions to ask, and issues you might encounter.

Overview of business analytics projects

For most information systems, reports represent a small portion of the functionality implemented. However, on business analytics projects, complex reports and the ability to manipulate their contents constitute the core functionality. Often, the output of analysis is embedded in applications that automate decision making. Business analytics projects have multiple layers, all of which might need to have software requirements defined for them. These projects must deal with understanding what data is required, the operations performed on the data, and the formatting and distribution of the data for use (Figure 25-1). There is no rigid sequence to these activities. A user might work with the data, then realize she needs different analysis performed on the data, and perhaps even different data sources.

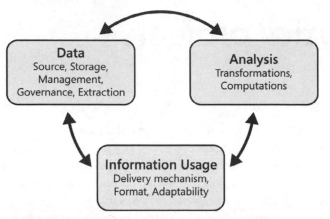

FIGURE 25-1 The components of a simple business analytics framework.

In the past, organizations that deployed analytics projects primarily focused on what the International Institute for Analytics (2013) calls "descriptive analytics." This includes looking at reports that tell stakeholders what is happening—or has happened—in their organization. Recent trends indicate a shift toward more organizations using "predictive analytics." Users organize, manipulate, and analyze information to predict what might happen in the future, as opposed to interpreting the past. Figure 25-2 shows where various applications of analytics fit on a spectrum ranging from more descriptive to more predictive.

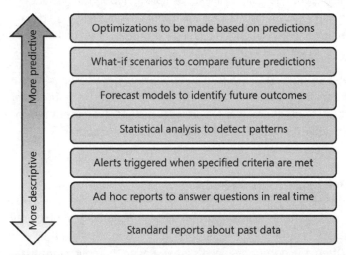

FIGURE 25-2 A spectrum of types of analytics (Patel and Taylor 2010; Davenport 2013).

As organizations embark on analytics projects, business analysts will find themselves tasked with eliciting and specifying requirements for these projects, but perhaps not knowing where to start. The strategic possibilities, the new analytics technologies, and the rapidly growing quantity of collected data can be intimidating. The end products of requirements development for a business analytics project will be similar to those for any other project: a set of business, user, functional, and nonfunctional requirements. However, many of the requirements practices described in this book are not sufficient to elicit and specify requirements for these types of projects. Process flows, use cases, and user stories can reveal that someone needs to generate analytics results, and performance requirements describe how quickly they need results, but none of these uncovers the complex knowledge required to implement the system.

If an organization is new to analytics, it should pilot a few small projects to demonstrate the value of analytics and to learn from the experience (Grochow 2012). Analytics projects are good candidates for incremental development if the team can identify the most important or most time-critical decisions that can be implemented in the next development iteration.

Another reason to consider incremental development is that business stakeholders sometimes have a hard time articulating and prioritizing the business problems they want to solve with an analytics project, particularly if it's their first. Some stakeholders might have had little practice thinking strategically. Others might find it hard to envision the possibilities that analytics technologies offer beyond their familiar spreadsheets. Users might get so excited about new analytics capabilities that they overwhelm the development team with features that sound potentially valuable. Elicitation might need to begin with some education about what new capabilities a business analytics solution can provide over traditional data reporting tools (Imhoff 2005). Developing the analytics solution in small chunks will give the users an opportunity to explore the initial capabilities and clarify their ideas of what they really need.

Requirements development for business analytics projects

As with other software projects, business analytics projects first need to have business objectives defined to establish and prioritize the scope of work. If stakeholders request an analytics project, they've already decided on that as a solution and might not have thought through their objectives carefully. Exploring the underlying business objectives might reveal that business analytics are not the right solution at all. To help stakeholders state their actual business objectives, you might ask the following questions:

- Why do you think an analytics solution will help you achieve the desired business outcomes?

- What do you want to accomplish by implementing analytics reporting?

- How do you expect to use analytics to improve your business outcomes?

- How are you hoping to use improved reporting capabilities or prediction results?

An effective subsequent elicitation strategy is to drive requirements specification based on the decisions that stakeholders need to make to achieve their business objectives. Try the following thought process (Taylor 2013):

1. Describe the business decisions that will be made using outputs of the system.

2. Link those decisions to the project's business objectives.

3. Decompose the decisions to discover the questions that need to be answered, the hierarchy of precursor questions that need to be answered to feed the main questions, and what role the analytics information plays in producing the answers to those questions.

4. Determine how analytics could be applied to assist in making these decisions.

Figure 25-3 outlines an approach to elicit and specify requirements for analytics projects. User requirements should be defined to describe how the analytics information will be used and what decisions will be made from it. Understanding the expected usage modes allows you to specify how the generated information should be distributed to end users and what information they need to see. This knowledge in turn allows you to define requirements for the data itself and for the analyses to be performed. The rest of the chapter describes each of these steps in more detail.

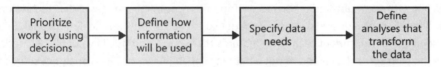

FIGURE 25-3 The process to define requirements for business analytics projects.

Prioritizing work by using decisions

On most types of projects, features can be prioritized by considering how they contribute to satisfying the business objectives. The same consideration is valid on analytics projects, except that there aren't discrete "features" to prioritize. Instead, you use the business objectives to prioritize the business decisions that the solution will enable, based on how much they contribute to achieving the objectives. For example, deciding which products to sell will have a greater impact on increasing revenue than making decisions about a sales team's vacation time. Therefore, you would likely implement the analytics and reports to determine which products to sell first.

Decisions should be stated as unambiguously as requirements. An example of a good decision statement is, "The vice president of marketing needs to decide each quarter how much marketing budget to allocate to each region based on current and targeted sales by region." As with requirements elicitation on other software projects, it's important to understand the underlying stakeholder need instead of just focusing on a presented solution. If stakeholders request certain data or reports, ask questions such as "Why do you need that information?" and "How will the recipient use that report?" Then work backward to identify their decisions and objectives.

Decision management techniques are available to help stakeholders identify the decisions they could or should make (Taylor 2012). A decision model that maps information (data) and knowledge (policies or regulations that constrain decisions) to related decisions can help organize the decisions to permit prioritization (Taylor 2013).

Defining how information will be used

The results of complex analytics must be delivered in a usable form to the stakeholders or systems that need to act on the information. The BA must also determine how smart the system is—that is, how much of the decision making is done by a human user and how much is automated in the system. This distinction will drive the type of elicitation questions the business analyst will ask.

 In one organization, the executive sales team wanted to see a dashboard report every morning showing multiple views of the data. This report had to include the previous day's sales by product line, quarterly sales by product line, total sales compared to competitors' sales, and sales volume by price band. They wanted 10 different filters (such as timeframe, increment, and region) that they could modify to see immediate changes in the reports. For example, if a user noticed a sales issue within a specific price band, she could change the filter to see a more precise view of the price band data by region. She could further drill down to look at another layer of detail that shows price band by region and by product line. This sort of flexibility is a common capability needed by business analytics systems.

Information usage by people

After you understand the decisions that users will need to make with the outputs of the analytics system, you can determine the best ways to deliver the information to them. The business analyst will need to consider the following three aspects of information delivery:

- **Delivery mechanism**   How is information physically made available to the end user? What tools can the user employ to view it: email applications, portals, mobile devices, others?

- **Format**   In what format is the information delivered: reports, dashboards, raw data, other?

- **Flexibility**   To what extent must the user be able to manipulate the information following delivery?

The spectrum of information delivery ranges from having each user create his personal view of the data (a local copy of a spreadsheet), to distributing a central aggregation of the data to users (emailed spreadsheets with standard dashboard views), to exposing data for users to manipulate on their own (a portal that permits ad hoc querying of a set of data).

As with requirements for other types of software systems, information usage on an analytics project is most commonly captured in the form of user requirements and report specifications. Techniques described elsewhere in the book—such as process flows, use cases, and user stories—apply for identifying how users plan to use the information in their daily tasks. Rather than focusing on specifying the data fields in the reports, though, use the decisions to be made to determine how users should receive the analytics output, how it should look, and how they need to be able to manipulate it.

Report tables, as described in Chapter 13, "Specifying data requirements," are useful on most analytics projects. You might have to extend these models for more complex options by using layers in the report specifications (Beatty and Chen 2012). Users of analytics data often like to see information presented in a dashboard view, with multiple charts and reports laid out in a single display. The "Dashboard reporting" section in Chapter 13 will help you specify such dashboard requirements. Some reports give the user the ability to manipulate views of the reports in predefined ways, such as with filters (Franks 2012). The display-action-response model described in Chapter 19, "Beyond requirements development," is valuable for specifying more comprehensive requirements for manipulating data in reports, when a simple report table structure won't suffice. These models capture complex interactive user interface elements on reports, such as filters or changes in display from drill-downs.

Beyond user requirements and reporting requirements, understanding information usage might also reveal new processes and security requirements that need to be defined. For example, the president of a small company might receive a weekly profit-and-loss report. If it looks correct, he will share it with his executive team—but only with his executive team, which implies the need for access controls. Security requirements, as described in Chapter 14, "Beyond functionality," might also be needed for data attributes, report views, or portal access. Perhaps regional sales vice presidents can see sales data for their region only, but a global vice president can view it for the entire organization. These sorts of quality attribute requirements apply to business analytics projects just as they do to any other software project.

Information usage in systems

It's important to note that the information from analytics projects might be used directly within software systems instead of being delivered to human users. The analytics might be embedded in the application as part of its daily operations. For example, some retail organizations use a customer's purchasing history to determine what products to apply personalized discounts to, in hopes of getting that customer to buy more from them. One retail chain determined that I was pregnant within a month of my knowing it, and they started sending email advertisements to me for baby products (this is obviously Joy's story!). Other examples include a system that prints coupons for a grocery shopper based on his current or prior purchases, customized ads displayed to website visitors, and call center applications that determine what offers to make to a particular customer who just called.

In these situations, the information delivery mechanism and format might be specified through external interface requirements. However, it is still important to understand how the information will be used so that the correct data is transformed as needed and delivered to the interfacing system in a usable form.

Specifying data needs

Data forms the core of all business analytics solutions. Many organizations employ data experts to develop and maintain their data solutions for these projects. BAs can define requirements for data sources, storage, management, and extraction mechanisms, although they might engage data specialists early in the requirements efforts to help. BAs can help explore what types of data need to be collected and analyzed, the total quantity of data the organization will be dealing with, and how much data they will accumulate over time. However, the data experts will be more familiar with what data is available, where it's located, what challenges it might present, and how it can best be exploited.

Because analytics projects often aim to discover new strategies for companies, these projects might involve identifying new data sources to analyze. It's important to fully understand the data requirements so technical teams can design the often complex infrastructures needed to support analytics. For example, architects might have to completely redesign an existing data storage solution to meet your project's needs.

Big data

The term *big data* typically describes a collection of data that is characterized as large volume (much data exists), high velocity (data flows rapidly into an organization), and/or highly complex (the data is diverse) (Franks 2012). Managing big data entails discovering, collecting, storing, and processing large quantities of data quickly and effectively. Jill Dyché (2012) provides a summary of what big data entails from the perspective of management and governance.

To really conceptualize big data, think about your personal data-based interactions from a single day: social media, email messages, videos, digital images, and electronic transactions. Consider that a commercial aircraft generates 10 *terabytes* of data during a 30-minute flight (Scalable Systems 2008). The nature of businesses today is that the data available to them is undergoing explosive growth. Applications that help users glean valuable knowledge from the mountains of data are therefore increasingly important.

The data models described in Chapter 13 are best suited to representing relational data stores. If the data objects relate to one another in some logical way, the BA can model those objects by using entity-relationship diagrams (ERDs). If the data attributes are known and consistent, data dictionaries also can be useful. Unfortunately, big data is often only semi-structured or even unstructured.

Unstructured data, exemplified by voice mails and text messages, doesn't lend itself to representation in traditional rows and columns. The challenge with unstructured data is that you have no idea where or how to begin looking for the information you seek (Davenport, Harris, and Morrison 2010). For instance, software operated by a security-related government agency might scan Internet traffic for instances of a word such as "bomb," but they need to see it in context to know the meaning of the word of interest. "Bomb" could indicate a terrorist threat, refer to an article on aerial combat in World War II, or describe a bad play's opening night.

The good news is that most data does possess some structure in the form of accompanying metadata, or data about the data (Franks 2012). Semi-structured data sources include email messages, image files, and video files. Because semi-structured data has associated metadata that provides some information about the data's structure and contents, you might be able to create entity-relationship diagrams and data dictionaries to represent what you do know about the data.

Data-based (not "database") requirements

Many of the data requirements that need to be specified for analytics projects are similar to those for other information systems projects. Although the nature of those requirements might not be the same, the questions you ask to elicit them are often similar. Keep in mind that most big data is generated by automated systems and usually represents a new data source for an organization, which means that it will take more work to determine the data requirements (Franks 2012). You can derive many data requirements from the decision-management criteria that you elicit from appropriate stakeholders. For example, decisions that need to be made hourly will likely have different underlying data needs from those that are made just once per calendar quarter. They might differ in terms of how frequently the source data is refreshed, when the data is extracted from the source, and how long the data must be retained.

Brijs (2013) provides a checklist of common expectations that stakeholders might have about business analytics and types of questions that can elicit those expectations. Following are some examples of questions a BA can ask to elicit data-related requirements:

Data sources

- What data objects and/or attributes do you need? From what sources will you get that data?

- Do you already have each of those data sources available? If not, where is the data? Do you need to develop requirements to populate those sources with the necessary data?

- What external or internal systems are providing data?

- How likely are these sources to change over time?

- Is there a need for an initial migration of historical data from an old to a new repository?

Data storage

- How much data is there today?

- How much is the data volume expected to grow and over what period of time?

- What types of data do you need to store?

- How long do you need to store the data? How securely must it be stored?

Data management and governance

- What are the structural characteristics of the data?

- How do you expect the data structure or values to change over time?

- What data transformations need to occur before the raw data is stored or analyzed?

- What transformations are needed to standardize the data from disparate systems?

- Under what conditions can old data be deleted? Does old data need to be archived? Destroyed?

- What integrity requirements apply to protecting the data from unauthorized access, loss, or corruption?

Data extraction

- How fast do users expect queries to return results?

- Do you need real-time or batched data? If not real-time, then at what frequency do you need it to be batched?

As with all requirements, ensure that the data-related requirements do not constrain developers with unnecessary design.

Defining analyses that transform the data

Analysis is the computational engine of the projects described in this chapter; it transforms the data and leads to answers to the questions posed (Franks 2012). A user defines a problem, receives data that he hopes will contain an answer, analyzes the data to find the answer, and decides on a solution to the problem. Or maybe the system analyzes the data to find the answer and then takes an action accordingly.

All of this is great, if you know what you are looking for. However, one challenging aspect of many business analytics projects is that the decision maker might not know just what he's looking for in the data. He might want to have certain data objects and attributes exposed in tools that allow him to explore, running different queries to ask what-if questions about the data. He literally doesn't know what he doesn't know, but he's hoping that by studying the data he'll glean something useful to act on. This is why it's important to start by understanding what decisions the stakeholders are trying to make. Even if he doesn't know exactly what he's looking for yet, a stakeholder should be able to define the type of problem he's trying to solve. Defining the necessary data analysis involves big-picture thinking (Davenport, Harris, and Morrison 2010). A BA with good creative-thinking skills can work with stakeholders to determine what new ideas might be explored with the analysis results.

As Figure 25-2 showed, analytics results lead to decision-making capabilities ranging from descriptive to predictive. To elicit the data analysis requirements, you might ask questions such as the following (Davenport, Harris, and Morrison 2010):

- What time frame are you trying to analyze: past, present, or future?

- If past, what kinds of insights about the past are you looking for?

- If present, what do you need to understand about the current situation so that you can take immediate actions?

- If future, what kinds of predictions or decisions do you want to make?

These questions will help you define functional requirements that specify the analyses the system must perform. Because analytics is a completely new capability for many organizations, you might do some research to discover how other organizations are using similar data to improve decision making.

A business analyst has the opportunity—perhaps even the responsibility—to help the stakeholders learn how analytics could be used in ways they hadn't previously envisioned.

Some analysis requires sophisticated algorithms to process, filter, and organize the data (Patel and Taylor 2010). Suppose a retail store wants to play targeted video ads when a customer walks in the store. A camera might scan her, perhaps by using facial recognition software, and the system will combine what it can learn about the customer (gender, age, attire, where she is looking) with logic built into the system to decide which ad to play. This type of decision logic can often be represented by using decision tables or decision trees, as described in Chapter 12, "A picture is worth 1024 words."

 It is important to understand the implications of automated decision making and be explicitly clear when defining the desired decision-logic system behaviors. A cautionary example is provided by systems that can scan social media and make stock trade movements accordingly. In 2013, a false piece of social media news reported that the president of the United States was injured in an explosion. The algorithms built into certain automated systems triggered them to start selling stocks, which led other systems to also sell stocks when they detected the market's decline, all within moments of the news release. Fortunately, the hoax was discovered quickly, and human decisions reversed the sudden sharp stock market drop caused by the automated trading systems. Perhaps the systems behaved exactly as intended, but maybe there was decision logic missing that could have limited the impact.

One of the most valuable aspects of business analytics systems is that they can enable future-state strategic analysis, such as exploring what-if scenarios. Consider questions such as, "If we offered our product on a new platform, what would we expect our future sales numbers to be?" or "If we offered our customers products targeted to their gender, how much more would they buy?" The system can run models and algorithms to enable these types of data extrapolations or predictions. Those models and algorithms need to be specified in the software requirements. If they are highly complex, a BA might enlist the help of data experts, statisticians, and mathematical modelers to help define them.

The analyses might require statistical or other computations to transform the data prior to it being presented to the user or delivered to a system for action. Either business rules in the organization or other industry standards could define these calculations. For instance, if analysis includes reporting gross profit margins by region, you need to specify exactly how that margin is calculated in your organization. The calculation formula requirement pattern described by Stephen Withall (2007) can be used to specify literally any calculation that is needed to transform the data. A specified formula should include a description of the value to be calculated, the formula itself, the variables used, and where their values come from. Also, specify any response time requirements for those calculations.

The evolutionary nature of analytics

Figure 25-1 illustrated the back-and-forth interactions between data, its analysis, and its usage (Franks 2012). Occasionally, the user receives a report and makes a decision, and then she's done. More commonly with business analytics applications, the user starts with a question and requests a report containing information relevant to the decision she must make. Someone extracts the requested data from available repositories, applies the relevant analytics processing, and delivers the report to the user. But after she sees the information, the user will think of new questions that require further analysis, which leads to requests for new reports and yet more analyses.

The key to defining requirements for analytics projects, therefore, is to start somewhere. Because the requirements might change over time, begin with what the stakeholders already know they want to learn from the available information, and plan for their questions to evolve. Also, understand how much the users expect their needs to evolve. For example, if they believe their needs from the business analytics solution will change significantly over time, they might require a solution that is easily adaptable and requires minimal additional development work.

An analytics solution should take into consideration the forms and conditions the data is in at the times it is extracted from a source, analyzed, and viewed by a user. For example, do users want certain raw data to be delivered to them so they can generate reports manually to examine? Or do they want a software application to organize that data for them and deliver it in a predefined, structured format? Do the users have a set of questions to which they want the answers every week for the next year? Or do they want to be able to ask new questions every day, rapidly developing new forms of data analysis and presentation to keep pace with rapidly changing business needs? The answers to these types of questions will tell your development team whether to make sets of data available for users to manipulate themselves or whether an analytics team will have to generate and format new information for those users to view (Franks 2012).

Your job as a BA on a business analytics project is to work with the project's stakeholders to understand their decision processes. Use those decisions to elicit the requirements that will access the necessary data, specify the analyses to be performed, and define the data presentation. You should understand what results stakeholders expect from an analytics solution, the decisions they hope the data will help them make, and how they want to dynamically modify the analyses or their presentation. Look for opportunities to help users be more successful by envisioning solutions that they might not have imagined were even possible.

CHAPTER 26

Embedded and other real-time systems projects

Most of the requirements examples and discussions in the book so far have dealt with business information systems. The world is also full of products that use software to control hardware devices, broadly called embedded systems. Among countless examples are cell phones, television remote controls, kiosks of all sorts, Internet routers, and robot cars. We've often used the term *system* in this book as a colloquial synonym for product, application, or solution, to refer to whatever software-containing thing you're building. In this chapter, though, *system* refers to a product that contains multiple, integrated software and hardware subsystems. The software that controls a real-time system can be embedded in the device in the form of a dedicated computer, or it can reside in a host computer separate from the hardware it controls. Embedded and other real-time systems have sensors, controllers, motors, power supplies, integrated circuits, and other mechanical, electrical, and electronic components that operate under software control.

Real-time systems can be classified as hard or soft. *Hard real-time systems* have rigid time constraints. The operations that the system performs must execute within specified deadlines or bad things happen. Life-critical and safety-critical control systems, such as air traffic control systems, are hard real-time systems. An operation that doesn't complete on time could result in a collision because of an undetected obstacle. *Soft real-time systems* also are subject to time constraints, but the consequences of missing the timing deadline during some operations are less severe. An ATM is a soft real-time system. If communication between the ATM and the bank doesn't complete in the allocated time interval, no one will die if the ATM has to try again or even if the operation terminates.

More than on most software development projects, it's important to have a good understanding of requirements before getting too far into development on embedded systems projects. Because software is more malleable than hardware, excessive requirements churn that dictates hardware changes is more expensive than comparable volatility on software-only projects. It's also essential to know about constraints that both hardware and software engineers must respect: physical object sizes; electrical components, connections, and voltages; standard communication protocols; the sequence in which certain operations must take place; and the like. Hardware components that have already been selected for the design impose constraints on those yet to be chosen.

The requirements elicitation techniques described elsewhere in this book are certainly applicable on real-time projects. The same modeling techniques can be used, with some refinements. This chapter addresses some of the special requirements considerations of embedded and other real-time systems.

System requirements, architecture, and allocation

When specifying a complex system, many teams first create a system requirements specification, abbreviated *SyRS* (ISO/IEC/IEEE 2011). The SyRS describes the capabilities of the system as a whole, including capabilities that could be provided by hardware components, software components, and/or humans. It also describes all of the inputs and outputs associated with the system. In addition to functionality, the SyRS should specify the critical performance, safety, and other quality requirements for the product. All this information feeds into the preliminary design analysis that will guide the team when it is choosing architectural components and allocating capabilities to them. The SyRS could be a separate deliverable from the software requirements specification, or the SRS could be embedded within the SyRS, particularly if most of the system complexity lies within the software.

Requirements analysis of a complex system is tightly intertwined with the system's architecture. Requirements thinking and design thinking become more commingled in real-time systems than in other types of software projects. The architecture represents the top level of design, often depicted by using simple box-and-arrow diagrams, although numerous other architecture modeling notations exist. A system's architecture consists of three elements:

- Components of the system, where a component could be a software object or module, a physical device, or a person

- Externally visible properties of the components

- Connections (interfaces) between the system components

The architecture is developed in a top-down, iterative fashion (Nelsen 1990; Hooks and Farry 2001). The person who takes the lead role in this type of analysis typically is a system analyst, requirements engineer, system engineer, or system architect with a strong technical background. The analyst partitions the system into appropriate software and hardware subsystems and components that will accommodate all of the inputs and produce all of the outputs. Certain system requirements might turn directly into software requirements if software is deemed to be the correct medium for providing a certain capability. In other cases, the analyst will decompose individual system requirements into numerous derived software, hardware, and/or manual requirements to be performed by humans (Figure 26-1). Deriving software requirements from system requirements can expand the volume of requirements several-fold, partly because that derivation generates interface requirements between the components. The analyst allocates the individual requirements to the most appropriate components, iteratively refining the architectural partitioning and the requirement allocations. The ultimate outcome is a set of requirements for each of the software, hardware, and human components that will collaborate to provide the necessary system services.

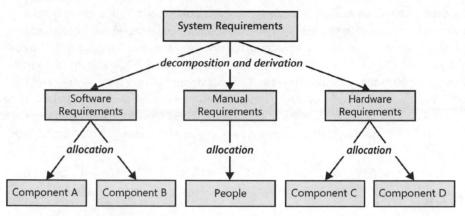

FIGURE 26-1 System requirements are decomposed into software, hardware, and manual requirements, then allocated to appropriate components.

It's a good idea to establish requirements trace links between system requirements, derived software and hardware requirements, and the architectural components to which they were allocated. Chapter 29, "Links in the requirements chain," discusses requirements traceability.

Poor allocation decisions can result in:

- The software being expected to perform functions that would have been easier or cheaper for hardware to perform (or the reverse).

- A person being expected to perform functions that would have been easier or cheaper for hardware or software to perform (or the reverse).

- Inadequate performance.

- The inability to easily upgrade or replace components.

For example, performing a certain function in software could require a faster processor than if a specialized piece of hardware were to perform that function. There are always trade-offs. Although software is easier to change than hardware, engineers shouldn't use that flexibility as a reason to skimp on hardware design. The people who perform the requirements allocation must understand the capabilities and limitations of the software and hardware components, as well as the costs and risks of implementing the functionality in each.

Modeling real-time systems

As with business information systems, visual modeling is a powerful analysis technique for specifying real-time systems. State-transition diagrams or their more sophisticated variants, such as state chart diagrams (Lavi and Kudish 2005) and UML state machine diagrams (Ambler 2005), are particularly relevant. Bruce Powel Douglass (2001) gives examples of how to employ use cases and other UML models to represent requirements for real-time systems.

Most real-time systems can exist in multiple states with defined conditions and events that permit transitions from one state to another. State tables and decision tables can be used to supplement or replace state-transition diagrams, often revealing errors in the diagrams. The context diagram (described in Chapter 5, "Establishing the business requirements") is also useful to show the environment in which the system operates and the boundaries between the system and the external entities with which it interfaces. Architecture diagrams show the partitioning of the system into subsystems with interfaces between them. This section shows some sample models (somewhat simplified, as usual) from an embedded system with which you might have personal experience: an exercise treadmill.

Context diagram

Figure 26-2 illustrates the context diagram for my home treadmill. This notation is slightly different from that used in Figure 5-6, shown earlier in Chapter 5, but the intent and the types of information displayed are the same (Lavi and Kudish 2005). Using the large square instead of a small circle to represent the system makes it easier to show multiple input and output flows between the system and a single external entity, such as the Exerciser (the person using the treadmill). The other two external entities are the website of the treadmill's manufacturer, from which the Exerciser can download various workout programs, and a sensor that measures the Exerciser's pulse rate. As usual with context diagrams, this model shows nothing of the treadmill's internals.

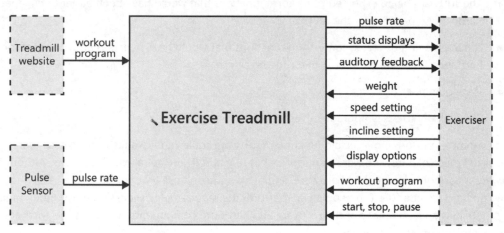

FIGURE 26-2 Context diagram for an exercise treadmill.

State-transition diagram

Figure 26-3 shows a state-transition diagram (STD) for the treadmill. Recall from Chapter 12, "A picture is worth 1024 words," that the boxes in an STD represent various states that the treadmill could be in, and the arrows represent allowed transitions from one state to another. The labels on the transition arrows indicate the conditions or events that trigger each state change. This diagram shows us more about how the treadmill functions. It also begins to provide some information about the user interface controls needed, such as controls labeled Speed, Incline, Start, Pause, and Stop. Figure 26-3 refers to "pressing" some control, but of course, those controls could be implemented in a variety of ways. Jonah Lavi and Joseph Kudish (2005) describe more sophisticated statechart diagrams for representing this kind of information in a richer way.

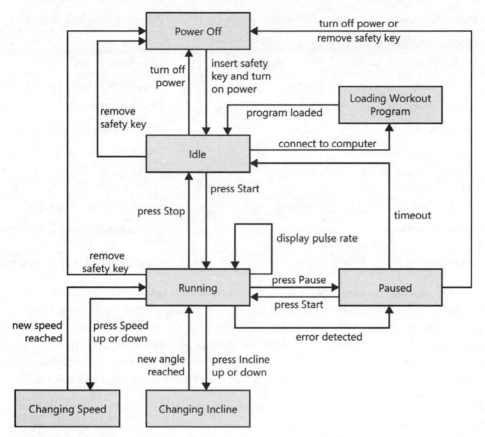

FIGURE 26-3 Partial state-transition diagram for an exercise treadmill.

Event-response table

Event-response analysis provides another way to think about the behavior of a real-time system and hence its functional requirements (Wiley 2000). As was described in Chapter 12, a system could respond to business events that trigger execution of a use case, signal events such as input from a sensor, and temporal events that cause something to happen after a specified time interval or at a specific point in time. Table 26-1 lists several events and their corresponding responses for the treadmill.

TABLE 26-1 Partial event-response table for an exercise treadmill

Event	Treadmill state	Response
Exerciser presses Incline Up button	Below maximum incline	Increase incline by 0.5 degree
Exerciser presses Incline Up button	At maximum incline	Generate "at limit" audio signal
Exerciser presses Speed Down button	Above minimum speed	Decrease speed by 0.1 mph
Exerciser presses Speed Down button	At minimum speed	Stop treadmill belt
Exerciser removes safety key	Running	Stop treadmill belt and turn power off
Exerciser removes safety key	Idle	Turn power off
Exerciser presses Pause button	Running	Stop treadmill belt; initiate timer
Exerciser presses Pause button	Paused or idle	Generate "error" audio signal
Timer for paused condition reaches timeout limit	Paused	Go to idle state
Exerciser presses Start button	Running	Generate "error" audio signal
Exerciser presses Start button	Paused	Start treadmill belt on current speed setting
Exerciser presses Start button	Idle	Start treadmill belt at lowest speed

This event list provides detailed requirements for the treadmill's functionality that flesh out the high-level view shown in the STD in Figure 26-3. It's also a great aid for conceiving tests. Even a complete event-response table still leaves plenty of design thinking to be done, such as how many degrees per minute the incline motor will change the belt's incline, and how quickly the treadmill belt will change from stopped to the set speed. Safety considerations will influence these decisions, too. It would be dangerous for the Exerciser if the belt started, accelerated, or stopped too abruptly.

Embedded systems must manage a combination of event-based functions (as shown in Table 26-1) and periodic control functions. Periodic functions are executed repeatedly while the system is in a particular state, rather than just once upon state entry. An example is monitoring the Exerciser's pulse rate once every second and adjusting the belt speed in response to maintain a preset pulse rate, if such an exercise program was being used.

 Drawing models like this is an excellent way to find missing requirements. I once reviewed a requirements specification for an embedded system that included a long table describing the various machine states, the functionality associated with each state, and possible navigation destinations from each state. I drew a state-transition diagram to represent that information at a higher level of abstraction. In the process of drawing the STD, I discovered two missing requirements. There was no requirement that allowed the machine to be turned off, and there was no provision for the possibility of entering an error state while the machine was running. As you've seen before, this example illustrates the value of creating multiple representations of requirements knowledge and verifying them against each other.

Architecture diagram

Another type of model that's useful for these types of systems is an architecture diagram, which is generally part of the high-level design. Figure 26-4 shows a portion of a simple architecture diagram for the treadmill. It identifies the major subsystems that will provide all of the treadmill's functions, as well as the data and control interfaces between them, at a high level of abstraction. Richer architecture description languages are available, and the Unified Modeling Language (UML) also works well for modeling architectures (Rozanski and Woods 2005). The subsystems shown in Figure 26-4 can be further elaborated into specific hardware components (motors and sensors) and software components as architectural analysis proceeds. A preliminary architecture analysis can reveal and refine functional, interface, and quality requirements that might not have been evident from other elicitation activities.

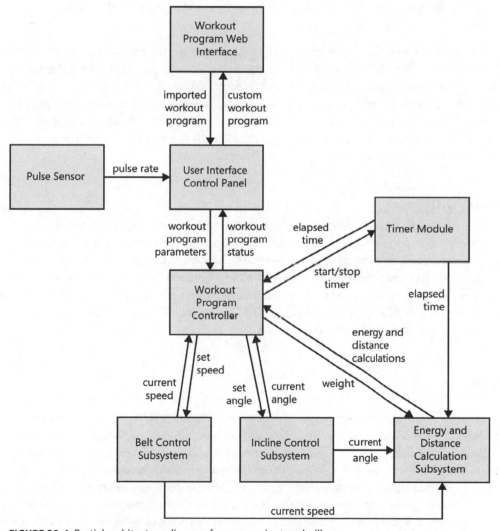

FIGURE 26-4 Partial architecture diagram for an exercise treadmill.

Drawing architecture models during requirements analysis is clearly taking a step into design. It's a necessary step. Iterating on the architectural partitioning and the allocation of system capabilities to subsystems and components is how an architect devises the most appropriate and effective solution. Further requirements elicitation is needed, though. Functional requirements such as the following will guide the developers in both choosing appropriate hardware components and designing user interface controls:

> **Incline.Angle.Range**   *The Exerciser shall be able to increase and decrease the incline angle of the treadmill from 0 degrees through 10 degrees, inclusive, in 0.5-degree increments.*

> **Incline.Angle.Limits**   *The treadmill shall stop changing its angle and provide audible feedback when it has reached the minimum or maximum limit of its incline range.*

In addition to the functionality represented by the architecture, the treadmill designers must know about the business rules that provide necessary algorithms. An example is calculating the number of calories the Exerciser has burned from the combination of his weight and the workout program, which is a series of segments of specified duration, incline angle, and belt speed. It might seem peculiar to speak of "business rules" in conjunction with an embedded system. However, virtually all of the requirements practices discussed elsewhere in this book apply to embedded and other real-time systems, just as they do to business information systems.

Prototyping

Prototyping and simulation are other powerful techniques for eliciting and validating the requirements for embedded systems. Because of the costs and time needed to build hardware (and perhaps to rebuild it if you discover requirement or design errors), you can use prototypes to test operational concepts and to explore both requirements and design options for the device. Simulations can help you better understand user interface displays and controls, network interactions, and hardware-software interfaces (Engblom 2007). Keep in mind, though, that the simulation will differ from the real product in numerous respects.

Interfaces

Interfaces are a critical aspect of embedded and other real-time systems. As you saw in Chapter 10, "Documenting the requirements," the SRS should address four classes of external interface requirements: user, software, hardware, and communications interfaces. In addition, the partitioning of complex systems into multiple subsystems creates numerous internal interfaces between components. Because embedded systems can be incorporated into other embedded systems as part of a larger product (such as a cell phone integrated into a motor vehicle's communication system), the interface issues become even more complex. Requirements analysis should concentrate on the external interface issues, leaving the internal interface specifications for architecture design.

If your external interfaces are relatively simple, you can specify them as described in section 5 of the SRS template illustrated in Figure 10-2, shown earlier in Chapter 10. Projects that are building complex systems often create a separate interface specification to document these critical aspects. Figure 26-5 suggests a template for an interface specification document that can accommodate both external and internal interfaces.

1. **Introduction**
    1.1   Document purpose
    1.2   Product overview
    1.3   Operating environment
    1.4   References
    1.5   Assumptions
2. **Interface diagrams**
3. **Data interfaces**
    3.x   <Interface ID x>
        3.x.1   Overview
        3.x.2   Data types
        3.x.3   Interface file formats
        3.x.4   Communication protocol
4. **Software interfaces**
    4.x   <Interface ID x>
        4.x.1   Overview
        4.x.2   Interface specification
        4.x.3   Timing issues
        4.x.4   Communication protocol
5. **Hardware interfaces**
    5.x   <Interface ID x>
        5.x.1   Overview
        5.x.2   Connection
        5.x.3   Data and control flow
6. **User interfaces**

FIGURE 26-5 Proposed template for an interface specification.

Timing requirements

Timing requirements lie at the heart of real-time control systems (Koopman 2010). Undesirable outcomes can result if signals are not received from sensors as scheduled, if the software cannot send control signals to the hardware when anticipated, or if the physical devices do not perform their actions on time. Timing requirements involve multiple dimensions:

- **Execution time**   The execution time for a specific task is the elapsed time from when it is initiated to when it completes. This can be measured as the duration between two specific events that bound the task's execution.

- **Latency**   Latency is the time lag between when a trigger event occurs and when the system begins to respond to it. Excessive latency poses a problem in, for example, music recording and production software, in which multiple prerecorded and live audio tracks must be precisely synchronized.

- **Predictability** Predictability refers to the repeated, consistent timing of a recurring event. Even if the timing is not especially "fast," events often have to be performed at precise intervals, as when sampling an incoming signal. Digitizing an audio waveform often is performed at 44,100 cycles per second. The sampling frequency must be predictable to avoid constructing a distorted digital representation of the analog waveform.

Some issues to explore regarding the timing and scheduling requirements for a system's real-time tasks are:

- Periodicity (frequency) of execution of the tasks and their tolerances.

- Deadlines and tolerances for execution of each task.

- Typical and worst-case execution time for each task.

- Consequences of missing a deadline.

- The minimum, average, and maximum arrival rate of data in each relevant component state.

- The maximum time before the first input or output is expected after a task initiates.

- What to do if data is not received within the maximum time before the expected first input (timeout).

- The sequence in which tasks must run.

- Tasks that must begin or end execution prior to other tasks beginning.

- Task prioritization, so you know which tasks can interrupt or preempt others, and on what basis.

- Functions that depend on what mode the system is in (normal mode versus firefighter service mode for an elevator, for example).

When specifying timing requirements, indicate any constraints and the acceptable timing tolerances. Understand the distinction between soft and hard real-time demands for your system so you don't specify overly stringent timing requirements. Those can lead to over-engineering the product at excessive cost and effort. If the timing tolerances are broader, you might be able to get away with using less expensive hardware. As Philip Koopman (2010) points out, "Real-time performance is seldom about being as fast as absolutely possible. Rather, it is about being just as fast as you need to be, and minimizing overall cost."

Specifying the timing requirements for the system involves understanding the deadlines for time-critical functions. It entails scheduling both sequential and concurrent functions to achieve the necessary performance within the constraints of processor capacity, input/output rates, and network communication rates. One team used a project-scheduling tool to model the timing requirements for an embedded product, working at the millisecond time scale rather than in the more traditional days and weeks. This creative and unconventional use of a modeling tool worked very well. In some cases, the timing and scheduling algorithms to be used might be imposed through requirements in the form of design constraints, but more frequently these will be design choices. Krishna Kavi, Robert Akl, and Ali Hurson (2009) offer a valuable overview of scheduling issues for real-time systems.

Quality attributes for embedded systems

Quality attribute requirements are especially critical for embedded and real-time systems. They can be vastly more complex and intertwined than those for other software applications. Business software is generally used in an office where there is not much variance in the environment. In contrast, the operating environment for embedded systems could involve temperature extremes, vibration, shock, and other factors that dictate specific quality considerations. Quality categories that are likely to be particularly important include performance, efficiency, reliability, robustness, safety, security, and usability. This section discusses some of the particular aspects of these quality attributes that you need to explore carefully during elicitation of requirements for such systems.

In addition to the software quality attributes that were discussed in Chapter 14, "Beyond functionality," embedded systems are subject to quality attributes and constraints that apply only to physical systems. These include size, shape, weight, materials, flammability, connectors, durability, cost, noise levels, and strength. All of these can dramatically increase the cost and effort needed to validate the requirements adequately. There could be business and political reasons to avoid using materials whose supply might be threatened by conflict or boycott, causing prices to skyrocket. Other materials are best avoided because of their environmental impacts. Avoiding the use of optimal materials could lead to trade-offs in performance, weight, cost, or other attributes.

It can be difficult and expensive to build in desired quality characteristics after the hardware design is complete, so address these requirements early during elicitation. Because quality characteristics often have a profound impact on a complex product's architecture, it's essential to perform the attribute prioritization and trade-off analysis before getting into design. Koopman (2010) presents a good discussion of nonfunctional requirements that are especially important for embedded systems development. Chapter 14 presented many examples of these and other quality attribute requirements.

Performance   The essence of a real-time system is that its performance must satisfy the timing needs and constraints of the operating environment. Therefore, all processing deadlines for specific operations must be included in the requirements. However, performance goes beyond operational response times. It includes startup and reset times, power consumption, battery life, battery recharge time (as with electric automobiles), and heat dissipation. Energy management alone has multiple dimensions. How should the system behave if the voltage drops momentarily, or under a particularly high current load during startup, or if external power is lost and the device must switch to battery backup power? And, unlike software, many of these components can degrade over time. What are the requirements for how long a battery maintains a given profile of power over time before it needs to be replaced?

Efficiency   Efficiency is the internal quality counterpart to the externally observable attribute of performance. Efficiency aspects of embedded systems focus on the consumption (and hence the remaining availability at any moment) of resources including processor capacity, memory, disk space, communication channels, electrical power, and network bandwidth. When you are dealing with these matters, requirements, architecture, and design become tightly coupled. For instance, if the total power demand of the device could exceed the power available, can the device be designed to cut power to components that don't need it all the time, thereby making more power available to other components or services?

The requirements should specify the maximum anticipated consumption of various system resources so designers can provide sufficient slack resources for future growth and unexpected operating conditions. This is one of those situations for which concurrent hardware and software design is vital. If the software is consuming too much of the available resources, the developers must resort to clever tricks to work around those limitations. Choosing more capable hardware up front offers a much less costly solution than fine-tuning the software components (Koopman 2010).

Reliability   Embedded and other real-time systems often have stringent reliability and availability requirements. Life-critical systems such as medical devices and airplane avionics offer little room for failure. An artificial cardiac pacemaker that's implanted into a patient's body must be expected to work reliably for years. If the product fails or the battery goes dead prematurely, the patient can die too. When you are specifying reliability requirements, realistically assess the likelihood and impact of failure so you don't over-engineer a product whose true reliability requirements aren't as demanding as you might think. Increasing reliability and availability comes at a price. Sometimes you need to pay that price; sometimes you do not.

An open-door policy

A door on a light-rail train car in a major American city recently failed to close when the train left the station. Sensors apparently failed to notify the train's driver of the malfunction. The train whizzed down the tracks at 55 miles an hour with an open door, a scary experience and an obvious safety hazard. The developers of the train software might have had a reliability or safety requirement stating that such an event could happen no more often than once every 100 million operating hours. You can't run a railway system for a few hundred million hours before you release it to test whether this requirement was satisfied. Instead, you need to design systems in such a way that the probability of experiencing a safety-critical failure is sufficiently low to meet the requirement. But things can still fail. In complex systems like this, it is usually the combinations of failures you didn't think of—corrosion on two switches, in this case—that cause such rare problems.

Robustness   Robustness has to do with how well the system responds to unexpected operating conditions. There are several aspects to robustness. One is survivability, which is often considered to apply to devices in use by the military but has everyday applications as well. A good example of embedded systems designed for high survivability are the aircraft "black boxes," electronic recording devices that are designed to survive the horrific trauma of an airplane crash. Actually bright orange and technically called the flight data recorder and the cockpit voice recorder, these devices are built to withstand an impact of 3,400 times the force of gravity, fires, immersion in water, and other hazards. Not only must the physical container retain its integrity under such extreme conditions, but the data recording devices inside must still be intact and readable.

Other aspects of robustness have to do with how the system deals with faults, or exceptions, that occur during execution and can lead to system failures. Both hardware and software faults can lead to failures. I once attempted to withdraw $140 from an ATM. The ATM gave me a receipt for $140, all right, but it only gave me $80 in cash. I waited 15 minutes while a bank employee rooted around in the back of the ATM; then she handed me my $60. Apparently there was a mechanical failure: several bills were stuck together and jammed the exit slot. Besides the fact that I wasted some time, I was concerned because the ATM thought the transaction had gone just fine—it never detected the problem.

There are four aspects to how systems handle faults (Koopman 2010):

- **Fault prevention** Ideally, the system will prevent many potential fault conditions before they can cause a failure. That's the idea behind having software systems test preconditions before initiating the execution of a use case.

- **Fault detection** The next-best course of action is to detect a fault as soon as it occurs. This is why requirements elicitation must explore exception conditions, so developers can anticipate possible errors and devise ways to look for them.

- **Fault recovery** If the system detects an anticipated fault, it should have mechanisms defined for responding to it. Requirements development should not only identify potential faults but also specify how they should be handled. Sometimes the system can retry an operation, as with an intermittent communication interruption or a timeout that might work fine the next time. Systems are sometimes designed with failover mechanisms. If a fault causes the system to fail, a backup system takes over the operation. In other cases, the system must terminate the operation, perhaps shutting down or restarting in some way that minimizes the negative impact on the user. As an example, if your car's antilock brake system (ABS) detects a faulty sensor, it might shut down the ABS, illuminate a warning light on the dashboard, and log that information in the car's computer for future diagnosis and repair. Which leads us to. . .

- **Fault logging** The system should retain a history of faults that it detects and what happened as a consequence. This information is useful for diagnosing what's wrong and can help a maintenance person detect patterns that lead to problems. For instance, a fault history might indicate a defective hardware component that should be replaced. Modern automobiles contain an on-board diagnostics system. A technician can plug a cable into this system and retrieve a history of events in the form of standardized codes that report what malfunctions occurred.

The designers of my treadmill recognized that under certain conditions the treadmill can be jammed in a position in which the incline angle cannot be lowered to zero. The user manual describes a (rather tricky) manual operation I can perform to reset the treadmill so it again has the full range of incline angles available. It would have been even better had the manufacturer designed the treadmill so that it was impossible for this jam to take place, if feasible. Sometimes, though, providing a workaround for a low-probability and low-impact failure is cheaper than designing the system to completely prevent the failure.

Safety   Any system that contains moving parts or uses electricity has the potential to cause injury or death to a human being. Safety requirements are vastly more significant for real-time systems than for information systems. Numerous books have been written on software and system safety engineering, so we will not attempt to recap all of that vital information here. Good sources are Nancy Leveson (1995), Debra Herrmann (1999), Philip Koopman (2010), and Terry Hardy (2011).

Begin your investigation of safety requirements by performing a *hazard analysis* (Ericson 2005; Ericson 2012). This will help you discover the potential risks that your product could present. You can rate them by their probability of occurrence and the severity of occurrence, so that you can focus on the most serious threats. (Chapter 32, "Software requirements and risk management," discusses risk analysis further.) A *fault tree analysis* is a graphical, root-cause analysis technique for thinking about safety threats and what factors could lead to them (Ericson 2011). This allows you to focus on how to avoid specific combinations of risk factors materializing when your product is in use. Safety requirements should address the risks and state what the system must do—or must not do—to avoid them.

Hardware devices often include some kind of emergency stop button or dead man's switch that will quickly turn the device off. The exercise treadmill had a safety requirement something like the following:

> **Stop.Emergency**   *The treadmill shall have an emergency stop mechanism that brings the belt to a halt within 1 second when activated.*

This requirement led to the design of a flat plastic key that must be inserted in the front of the treadmill before the treadmill can be powered up. Removing the key cuts the treadmill power, stopping the belt motion quickly. A lanyard attached to the key can be clipped to the Exerciser's clothing to pull out the key if the Exerciser slips or falls off the treadmill. It works!

Security   The security of embedded systems is under much discussion these days because of concerns about cyberattacks that could take over, disrupt, or disable power plants, railroad control systems, electrical distribution grids, and other critical infrastructure. Theft of intellectual property from the memory of embedded systems is also a risk. An attacker could potentially reverse engineer code to learn how the system works, either to copy it or to attack it. Protecting embedded systems involves some of the same security measures that host-based information systems need. These include the following (Koopman 2010):

- Secrecy, primarily through encryption

- Authentication, to ensure that only authorized users can access the system, typically provided through passwords (with all the human failings that involves)

- Data integrity checks, to try to discover whether the system has been tampered with

- Privacy of data, such as protecting against unauthorized tracking of users through their handheld GPS devices

In addition, though, embedded systems are subject to other types of specific attacks. These include attempts by users to take over control of the system; interception of electronic communications, particularly wireless communications; and the insertion of malicious software updates, sometimes through social engineering of gullible users (many of us fall for that trick from time to time). The full scope of security considerations for embedded systems is large, and it is a very serious concern (Anderson 2008). Koopman (2010) and David and Mike Kleidermacher (2012) offer many suggestions for how to make your embedded products more secure.

Usability   Many embedded systems include some kind of human-computer interface. The general principles of software usability apply, but other aspects of usability might be important when a person is using a physical device in the field as opposed to a keyboard in the office. Recently, I switched from using a mouse designed for right-handed users to a symmetrical one. I keep inadvertently hitting the right mouse button with the ring finger on my right hand. This wastes my time and can lead to undesired system responses.

Display screens on products to be used outdoors must accommodate different lighting situations. I once had an account at a bank whose drive-up ATM was located such that the LCD screen was completely unreadable when sunlight hit it at certain angles. As another example, I cannot read the display on my digital wristwatch when I'm wearing polarized sunglasses unless I rotate my wrist to just the right angle, because LCD displays are themselves polarized.

Some usability constraints are imposed by legislation such as the Americans with Disabilities Act, which requires certain systems to provide accessibility aids for people who have physical limitations. Embedded systems must accommodate users having different degrees of:

- Audio acuity and frequency response (consider when designing audio feedback and prompts).

- Visual acuity and color vision (consider the use of color and text size in visual displays).

- Handedness and manual dexterity (affects the user's ability to press small buttons accurately or to navigate using a touch screen).

- Body size and reach (keep the user profile in mind when establishing the physical positioning of controls, displays, and equipment).

- Native languages (important for devices controlled by speech recognition).

The challenges of embedded systems

Embedded and other real-time control systems offer a unique set of challenges that software-only applications do not. The basic principles and practices of requirements elicitation, analysis, specification, and validation apply to both classes of products. Embedded systems require taking a systems engineering approach so that developers do not optimize either software or hardware components at the expense of the other and to avoid ugly integration problems. Architecture and design choices are more tightly linked with requirements analysis than in software-only systems, partly because it is so much more expensive to change hardware after it has been designed or manufactured. Embedded systems present a different emphasis of constraints and quality attributes than do software-only systems, and often they are more interwoven with operating system considerations as well. Careful specification of system requirements, software requirements, hardware requirements, and interface requirements will go a long way toward making your embedded and other real-time development projects successful.

Requirements management

CHAPTER 27

Requirements management practices

"I finally finished implementing the multivendor catalog query feature," Shari reported at the Chemical Tracking System's weekly project status meeting. "Man, that was a lot of work!"

"Oh, the customers canceled that feature two weeks ago," the project manager, Dave, replied. "Didn't you get the revised SRS?"

Shari was confused. "What do you mean, it was canceled? Those requirements are at the top of page 6 of my latest SRS."

Dave said, "Hmmm, they're not in my copy. I've got version 1.5 of the SRS. What version are you looking at?"

"Mine says version 1.5 also," said Shari in disgust. "These documents should be identical, but obviously they're not. So, is this feature still needed, or did I just waste 30 hours of my life?"

If you've ever heard a conversation like this one, you know how frustrating it is when people waste time working from obsolete or inconsistent requirements specifications. Having great requirements gets you only partway to a solution; they also have to be well managed and effectively communicated among the project participants. Version control of individual requirements and sets of requirements is one of the core activities of requirements management.

Chapter 1, "The essential software requirement," divided the domain of software requirements engineering into requirements development and requirements management. (Some people refer to the entire domain as "requirements management," but we favor a narrower definition of that term.) This chapter addresses some principles and practices of requirements management. The other chapters in Part IV describe certain requirements management practices in more detail, including change control (Chapter 28, "Change happens"), change impact analysis (also Chapter 28), and requirements tracing (Chapter 29, "Links in the requirements chain"). Part IV concludes with a discussion of commercial tools that can help a project team develop and manage its requirements (Chapter 30, "Tools for requirements engineering"). Note that a project might be managing certain sets of agreed-upon requirements while concurrently performing requirements development activities on other portions of the product's requirements.

Requirements management process

Requirements management includes all activities that maintain the integrity, accuracy, and currency of requirements agreements throughout the project. Figure 27-1 shows the core activities of requirements management in four major categories: version control, change control, requirements status tracking, and requirements tracing.

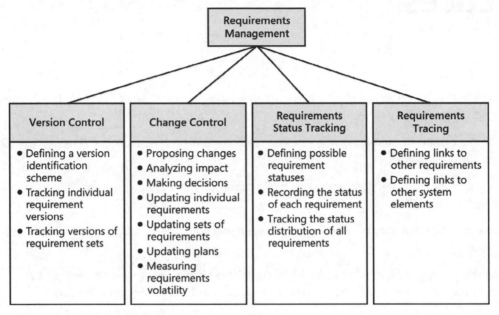

FIGURE 27-1 Major requirements management activities.

Your organization should define the activities that project teams are expected to perform to manage their requirements. Documenting these activities and training practitioners in their performance enables the members of the organization to conduct them consistently and effectively. Consider addressing the following topics:

- Tools, techniques, and conventions for distinguishing versions of individual requirements and of requirements sets

- The way that sets of requirements are approved and baselined (see Chapter 2, "Requirements from the customer's perspective")

- The ways that new requirements and changes to existing ones are proposed, evaluated, negotiated, and communicated

- How to assess the impact of a proposed change

- Requirement attributes and requirements status-tracking procedures, including the requirement statuses that you will use and who can change them

- Who is responsible for updating requirements trace information and when

- How to track and resolve requirements issues

- How the project's plans and commitments will reflect requirements changes

- How to use the requirements management (RM) tool effectively

You can include all this information in a single requirements management process description. Alternatively, you might prefer to write separate version control, change control, impact analysis, and status tracking procedures. These procedures should apply across your organization because they represent common functions that every project team ought to perform. Chapter 31, "Improving your requirements processes," describes several useful process assets for requirements management.

Your process descriptions should identify the team role that owns each of the requirements management activities. The project's business analyst typically has the lead responsibility for requirements management. The BA will set up the requirements storage mechanisms, define requirement attributes, coordinate requirement status and trace data updates, and monitor change activity as needed. The process description should also indicate who has authority to modify the requirements management process, how exceptions should be handled, and the escalation path for impediments encountered.

> **Trap** If no one on the project has responsibility for performing requirements management activities, don't expect them to get done. Similarly, if "everyone" has the responsibility, each person might expect that someone else is covering the necessary activities, so they can easily be overlooked.

The requirements baseline

Requirements development involves activities to elicit, analyze, specify, and validate a software project's requirements. Requirements development deliverables include business requirements, user requirements, functional and nonfunctional requirements, a data dictionary, and various analysis models. After they are reviewed and approved, any defined subset of these items constitutes a requirements baseline. As was described in Chapter 2, a requirements *baseline* is a set of requirements that stakeholders have agreed to, often defining the contents of a specific planned release or development iteration. The project might have additional agreements regarding deliverables, constraints, schedules, budgets, transition requirements, and contracts; those lie beyond the scope of this book.

At the time a set of requirements is baselined—typically following review and approval—the requirements are placed under configuration (or change) management. Subsequent changes can be made only through the project's defined change control procedure. Prior to baselining, the requirements are still evolving, so there's no point in imposing unnecessary process overhead on those modifications. A baseline could consist of some or all the requirements in a particular SRS (whether for an entire product or a single release), or a designated set of requirements stored in an RM tool, or an agreed-on set of user stories for a single iteration on an agile project.

If the scope of a release changes, update the requirements baseline accordingly. Distinguish the requirements in a particular baseline from others that were proposed but not accepted, are allocated to a different baseline, or remain unallocated in the product backlog. If the requirements are specified in the form of a document such as an SRS, clearly identify it as a baseline version to distinguish it from prior drafts. Storing requirements in an RM tool facilitates the identification of those that belong to a specific baseline and the management of changes to that baseline.

A development team that accepts proposed requirement changes or additions might not be able to fulfill its existing schedule and quality commitments. The project manager must negotiate changes to those commitments with affected managers, customers, and other stakeholders. The project can accommodate new or changed requirements in various ways:

- By deferring lower-priority requirements to later iterations or cutting them completely

- By obtaining additional staff or outsourcing some of the work

- By extending the delivery schedule or adding iterations to an agile project

- By sacrificing quality to ship by the original date

No single approach is universally correct, because projects differ in their flexibility of features, staff, budget, schedule, and quality (Wiegers 1996). The choice should be based on the project's business objectives and the priorities the key stakeholders established during project initiation. No matter how you respond to changing requirements, accept the reality of adjusting expectations and commitments when necessary. This is better than imagining that somehow all the new features will be incorporated by the original delivery date without budget overruns, team member burnout, or quality compromises.

Requirements version control

Version control—uniquely identifying different versions of an item—applies at the level of both individual requirements and requirements sets, most commonly represented in the form of documents. Begin version control as soon as you draft a requirement or a document so you can retain a history of changes made.

Every version of the requirements must be uniquely identified. Every team member must be able to access the current version of the requirements. Changes must be clearly documented and communicated to everyone affected. To minimize confusion and miscommunication, permit only designated individuals to update the requirements, and make sure that the version identifier changes whenever an update is made. Each circulated version of a requirements document or each requirement in a tool should include a revision history that identifies the changes made, the date of each change, the individual who made the change, and the reason for each change.

It's not a bug; it's a feature!

A contract development team received a flood of bug reports from the testers of the latest release they had just delivered to a customer. The contract team was perplexed—the system had passed all their own tests. After considerable investigation, it turned out that the customer was testing the new software against an obsolete version of the SRS. What the testers were reporting as bugs truly were features. Normally, this is just a little joke that software people like to make. The testers spent considerable time rewriting the tests against the correct version of the SRS and retesting the application, all because of a version control problem. Another colleague who once experienced the same kind of testing confusion because of an uncommunicated change said, "We probably wasted four to six hours of effort that our department had to absorb and couldn't spend on actual billable hours. I think software professionals would be shocked if they multiplied out these wasted hours times their bill rate to see what the loss in revenue is."

Similar confusion can arise when multiple BAs are working on a project. One BA begins to edit version 1.2 of the requirements specification. A few days later, another BA starts to work on some requirements and also labels his version 1.2, not knowing about the conflict. Pretty soon changes are lost, requirements are no longer up to date, work is overwritten, and confusion ensues.

The most robust approach to version control is to store the requirements in a requirements management tool, as described in Chapter 30. RM tools track the history of changes made to every requirement, which is valuable when you need to revert to an earlier version. Such a tool allows for comments describing the rationale behind a decision to add, modify, or delete a requirement. These comments are helpful if the requirement becomes a topic for discussion again in the future.

If you're storing requirements in documents, you can track changes by using the word processor's revision marks feature. This feature visually highlights changes made in the text with notations such as strikethrough highlighting for deletions and underscores for additions. When you baseline a document, first archive a marked-up version, then accept all the revisions, and then store the now clean version as the new baseline, ready for the next round of changes. Store requirements documents in a version control tool, such as the one your organization uses for controlling source code through check-out and check-in procedures. This will let you revert to earlier versions if necessary and to know who changed each document, when, and why. (Incidentally, this describes exactly how we wrote this book. We wrote the chapters in Microsoft Word, using revision marks as we iterated on the chapters. We had to refer back to previous versions on several occasions.)

I know of one project that stored several hundred use case documents written in Microsoft Word in a version control tool. The tool let the team members access all previous versions of every use case, and it logged the history of changes made to each one. The project's BA and her backup person had read-write access to the documents stored in the tool; the other team members had read-only access. This approach worked well for this team.

The simplest version control mechanism is to manually label each revision of a document according to a standard convention. Schemes that try to differentiate document versions based on dates are prone to confusion. I use a convention that labels the first version of any new document with its title and "Version 1.0 draft 1." The next draft keeps the same title but is identified as " Version 1.0 draft 2." The author increments the draft number with each iteration until the document is approved and baselined. At that time, the version identifier is changed to "Version 1.0 approved," again keeping the same document title. The next version is either "Version 1.1 draft 1" for a minor revision or "Version 2.0 draft 1" for a major change. (Of course, "major" and "minor" are subjective and depend on the context.) This scheme clearly distinguishes between draft and baselined document versions, but it does require manual discipline on the part of those who modify the documents.

Requirement attributes

Think of each requirement as an object with properties that distinguish it from other requirements. In addition to its textual description, each requirement should have supporting pieces of information or *attributes* associated with it. These attributes establish a context and background for each requirement. You can store attribute values in a document, a spreadsheet, a database, or—most effectively—a requirements management tool. It's cumbersome to use more than a couple of requirements attributes with documents.

RM tools typically provide several system-generated attributes in addition to letting you define others, some of which can be automatically populated. The tools let you query the database to view selected subsets of requirements based on their attribute values. For instance, you could list all high-priority requirements that were assigned to Shari for implementation in release 2.3 and have a status of Approved. Following is a list of potential requirement attributes to consider:

- Date the requirement was created

- Current version number of the requirement

- Author who wrote the requirement

- Priority

- Status

- Origin or source of the requirement

- Rationale behind the requirement

- Release number or iteration to which the requirement is allocated

- Stakeholder to contact with questions or to make decisions about proposed changes

- Validation method to be used or acceptance criteria

Wherefore this requirement?

The product manager at a company that makes electronic measurement devices wanted to track which requirements the team included simply because a competitor's product had the same capability. A good way to note such features is with a Rationale attribute, which indicates why a specific requirement is included in the product. Suppose you included some requirement because it meets the need of a particular user group. Later on, your marketing department decides they don't care about that user group any more. Having the justification present as a requirement attribute would help people decide whether that requirement could be omitted.

Another BA described his quandary with requirements that had no obvious justification. He said, "In my experience, many requirements exist without a real need behind them. They are introduced because the customer lacks an understanding of the technology, or because some key stakeholders get excited about the technology and want to show off, or because our sales team intentionally or unintentionally has misled the customer." If you can't provide a convincing rationale for a requirement and trace it back to a business need, the BA should question whether there's a real reason to devote effort to it.

Trap Selecting too many requirements attributes can overwhelm a team. They won't supply all attribute values for all requirements and won't use the attribute information effectively. Start with perhaps three or four key attributes. Add others only when you know how they will add value.

The requirements planned for a release will change as new requirements are added and existing ones are deleted or deferred. The team might be juggling separate requirements documents for multiple releases or iterations. Leaving obsolete requirements in the SRS can confuse readers as to whether those requirements are included in that baseline. A solution is to store the requirements in an RM tool and define a Release Number attribute. Deferring a requirement means changing its planned release, so simply updating the release number shifts the requirement into a different baseline. Handle deleted and rejected requirements by using a status attribute, as described in the next section.

Defining and updating these attribute values is part of the cost of requirements management, but that investment can yield a significant payback. One company periodically generated a requirements report that showed which of the 750 requirements from 3 related specifications were assigned to each designer. One designer discovered several requirements that she didn't realize were her responsibility. She estimated that she saved one to two months of engineering design rework that would have been required had she not found out about those requirements until later in the project. The larger the project, the easier it is to experience time-wasting miscommunications.

Tracking requirements status

"How are you coming on implementing that subsystem, Yvette?" asked the project manager, Dave.

"Pretty good, Dave. I'm about 90 percent done."

Dave was puzzled. "Didn't you say you were 90 percent done a couple of weeks ago?" he asked.

Yvette replied, "Yes, I thought I was, but now I'm really 90 percent done."

Like nearly everyone, software developers are sometimes overly optimistic when they report how much of a task is complete. The common "90 percent done" syndrome doesn't tell Dave much about how close Yvette really is to finishing the subsystem. But suppose Yvette had replied, "Pretty good, Dave. Of the 84 requirements for the subsystem, 61 are implemented and verified, 14 are implemented but not yet verified, and I haven't implemented the other 9 yet." Tracking the status of each functional requirement throughout development provides a more precise gauge of project progress.

Status was one of the requirement attributes proposed in the previous section. Tracking status means comparing where you really are at a particular time against the expectation of what "complete" means for this development cycle. You might have planned to implement only certain flows of a use case in the current release, leaving full implementation for a future release. Monitor the status of just those functional requirements that were committed for the current release, because that's the set that's supposed to be 100 percent done before you declare success and ship the release.

> **Trap** There's an old joke that the first half of a software project consumes the first 90 percent of the resources and the second half consumes the other 90 percent of the resources. Overoptimistic estimation and overgenerous status tracking constitute a reliable formula for project overruns.

Table 27-1 lists several possible requirement statuses. Some practitioners add others, such as Designed (the design elements that address the functional requirement have been created and reviewed) and Delivered (the software containing the requirement is in the hands of the users, as for acceptance or beta testing). It's valuable to keep a record of rejected requirements and the reasons they were rejected. Rejected requirements have a way of resurfacing later during development or on a future project. The Rejected status lets you keep a proposed requirement available for possible future reference without cluttering up a specific release's set of committed requirements. You don't need to monitor all of the possible statuses in Table 27-1; choose the ones that add value to your requirements activities.

TABLE 27-1 Suggested requirement statuses

Status	Definition
Proposed	The requirement has been requested by an authorized source.
In Progress	A business analyst is actively working on crafting the requirement.
Drafted	The initial version of the requirement has been written.
Approved	The requirement has been analyzed, its impact on the project has been estimated, and it has been allocated to the baseline for a specific release. The key stakeholders have agreed to incorporate the requirement, and the software development group has committed to implement it.
Implemented	The code that implements the requirement has been designed, written, and unit tested. The requirement has been traced to the pertinent design and code elements. The software that implemented the requirement is now ready for testing, review, or other verification.
Verified	The requirement has satisfied its acceptance criteria, meaning that the correct functioning of the implemented requirement has been confirmed. The requirement has been traced to pertinent tests. It is now considered complete.
Deferred	An approved requirement is now planned for implementation in a later release.
Deleted	An approved requirement has been removed from the baseline. Include an explanation of why and by whom the decision was made to delete it.
Rejected	The requirement was proposed but was never approved and is not planned for implementation in any upcoming release. Include an explanation of why and by whom the decision was made to reject it.

Classifying requirements into several status categories is more meaningful than trying to monitor the percent completion of each requirement or of the complete release baseline. Update a requirement's status only when specified transition conditions are satisfied. Certain status changes also require updates to the requirements trace data to indicate which design, code, and test elements addressed the requirement, as illustrated in Table 29-1 in Chapter 29.

Figure 27-2 illustrates how you can visually monitor the status of a set of requirements throughout a hypothetical 10-month project. It shows the percentage of all the system's requirements having each status value at the end of each month. Tracking the distribution by percentages doesn't show whether the number of requirements in the baseline is changing over time. The number of requirements increases as scope is added and decreases when functionality is removed from the baseline. The curves illustrate how the project is approaching its goal of complete verification of all approved requirements. A body of work is done when all requirements allocated to it have a status of Verified, Deleted, or Deferred.

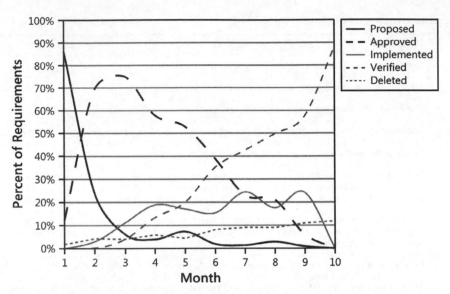

FIGURE 27-2 Tracking the distribution of requirements status throughout a project's development cycle.

Resolving requirements issues

Numerous questions, decisions, and issues related to requirements will arise during the course of a project. Potential issues include items flagged as TBD, pending decisions, information that is needed, and conflicts awaiting resolution. It's easy to lose sight of these open issues. Record issues in an issue-tracking tool so all affected stakeholders have access to them. Keep the issue-tracking and resolution process simple to ensure that nothing slips through the cracks. Some of the benefits of using an issue-tracking tool are:

- Issues from multiple requirements reviews are collected so that no issue ever gets lost.

- The project manager can easily see the current status of all issues.

- A single owner can be assigned to each issue.

- The history of discussion around an issue can be retained.

- The team can begin development earlier with a known set of open issues rather than having to wait until the SRS is complete.

Resolve requirements issues so they don't impede the timely baselining of a high-quality requirements set for your next release or iteration. A burndown chart that shows remaining issues and the rate at which they are being closed can help predict when all of the issues will be closed so you can accelerate issue resolution if necessary. (See "Managing requirements on agile projects" later in this chapter for a sample burndown chart.) Categorizing issues will help you determine which sections of requirements still need work. Few open issues on a section could mean either that the requirements haven't been reviewed yet or that the open issues are mostly resolved.

Nearly all of the defects logged early in a project are related to issues in the requirements, such as asking for clarification on a requirement, scope decisions, questions about development feasibility, and to-do items on the requirements themselves. All stakeholders can log questions as they review the requirements. Table 27-2 lists several common types of requirements issues that can arise.

TABLE 27-2 Common types of requirements issues

Issue type	Description
Requirement question	Something isn't understood or decided about a requirement.
Missing requirement	Developers uncovered a missed requirement during design or implementation.
Incorrect requirement	A requirement was wrong. It should be corrected or removed.
Implementation question	As developers implement requirements, they have questions about how something should work or about design alternatives.
Duplicate requirement	Two or more equivalent requirements are discovered. Delete all but one of them.
Unneeded requirement	A requirement simply isn't needed anymore.

Bad things can happen if you don't have an organized process for handling your requirements issues. On one project, a stakeholder mentioned very early on that we would handle something in "the portal." This was the first I had heard of a portal as part of the solution, so I asked about it. The stakeholder assured me that the COTS package being acquired included a portal component that simply had to be configured properly. We hadn't included any time for portal requirements in our plan, so I thought we might have a gap. I asked a teammate to record an issue about the portal so we wouldn't overlook that need. I left the project a few weeks later.

As it turned out, my teammate jotted the portal issue on a whiteboard that was later erased; she didn't record it in our issue-tracking tool. Six months into the project, our executive stakeholder came to me absolutely furious that no one had elicited requirements for the portal. I had to find out why we hadn't developed portal requirements: we simply forgot about it. Recording the issue in a tracking tool would have kept us from scrambling at the last minute and avoided upsetting the customer.

Measuring requirements effort

As with requirements development, your project plan should include tasks and resources for the requirements management activities described in this chapter. If you track how much effort you spend on requirements development and management activities, you can evaluate whether it was too little, about right, or too much, and adjust your future planning accordingly. Karl Wiegers (2006) discusses measuring various other aspects of the requirements work on a project.

Measuring effort requires a culture change and the individual discipline to record daily work activities (Wiegers 1996). Effort tracking isn't as time-consuming as people sometimes fear. Team members gain valuable insight from knowing how they *actually* spent their time, compared to how they *thought* they spent their time, compared to how they were *supposed* to spend their time. Effort tracking also indicates whether the team is performing the intended requirements-related activities.

Note that work effort is not the same as elapsed calendar time. Tasks can be interrupted; they might require interactions with other people that lead to delays. The total effort for a task, in units of labor hours, might not change because of such factors (although frequent interruptions do reduce an individual's productivity), but the calendar duration increases.

When tracking requirements development effort, you might find it valuable to separate the time spent by people in the BA role from time spent by other project participants. Tracking the BA's time will help you plan how much BA effort is needed on future projects (see Chapter 19, "Beyond requirements development," for more about estimating BA time). Measuring the total effort spent on requirements activities by all stakeholders gives you a sense of the total cost of requirements activities on a project. Record the number of hours spent on requirements development activities such as the following:

- Planning requirements-related activities for the project

- Holding workshops and interviews, analyzing documents, and performing other elicitation activities

- Writing requirements specifications, creating analysis models, and prioritizing requirements

- Creating and evaluating prototypes intended to assist with requirements development

- Reviewing requirements and performing other validation activities

Count the effort devoted to the following activities as requirements management effort:

- Configuring a requirements management tool for your project

- Submitting requirements changes and proposing new requirements

- Evaluating proposed changes, including performing impact analysis and making decisions

- Updating the requirements repository

- Communicating requirements changes to affected stakeholders

- Tracking and reporting requirements status

- Creating requirements trace information

Remember, the time you spend on these requirements-related activities is an investment in project success, not just a cost. To justify the activities, compare this time investment with the time the team spends dealing with issues that arose because these things were *not* done—the cost of poor quality.

Managing requirements on agile projects

Agile projects accommodate change by building the product through a series of development iterations and managing a dynamic product backlog of work remaining to be done. As described in Chapter 2, the stakeholders reach agreement on the stories to be implemented in each iteration. New stories that customers add while an iteration is under way are prioritized against the remaining backlog contents and allocated to future iterations. New stories might displace lower-priority stories if the team wants to keep the original delivery schedule. The goal—as it should be for all projects—is to always be working on the highest-priority stories to deliver the maximum value to customers as quickly as possible. See Chapter 28 for more information about handling requirement changes on agile projects.

Some agile teams, particularly large or distributed teams, use an agile project management tool to track the status of an iteration and the stories allocated to it. The stories and their associated acceptance criteria and acceptance tests might all be placed in a product backlog or user story–management tool. Story status can be monitored by using statuses analogous to those described earlier in Table 27-1 (Leffingwell 2011):

- In backlog (the story is not yet allocated to an iteration)

- Defined (details of the story were discussed and understood, and acceptance tests were written)

- In progress (the story is being implemented)

- Completed (the story is fully implemented)

- Accepted (acceptance tests were passed)

- Blocked (the developer is unable to proceed until something else is resolved)

Agile projects typically monitor their progress with an iteration burndown chart (Cohn 2004; Cohn 2005). The team estimates the total amount of work to do on the project, often sized in units of story points, which are derived from an understanding of the user stories in the product backlog (Cohn 2005; Leffingwell 2011). The story point total is thus proportional to the amount of effort the team must expend to implement the requirements. The team allocates certain user stories to each iteration based on their priority and their estimated size in story points. The team's past or average velocity dictates the number of story points the team plans to deliver in an iteration of a particular calendar duration.

The team charts the story points remaining in the product backlog at the end of each iteration. This total will change as work is completed, as current stories are better understood and re-estimated, as new stories are added, and as customers remove pending work from the backlog. That is, rather than monitoring the count and status of individual functional requirements or features (which can come in a variety of sizes), the burndown chart shows the total work remaining to be done at a specific time.

Figure 27-3 illustrates a burndown chart for a hypothetical project. Notice that the scope remaining, as measured in story points, actually increased in iterations 2, 3, and 5. This indicates that more new functionality was added to the backlog than was completed or removed during the course of the iteration. The burndown chart helps the team avoid the "90 percent done" syndrome by making visible the amount of work remaining, as opposed to the amount of work completed, which doesn't reflect the inevitable scope increases. The slope of the burndown chart also reveals the projected end date for the project, the point at which no work remains in the backlog.

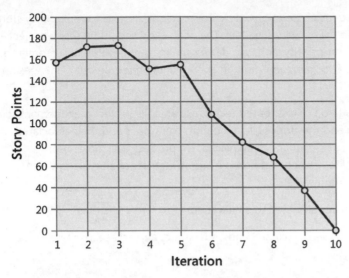

FIGURE 27-3 Sample iteration burndown chart for monitoring the product backlog on an agile project.

Why manage requirements?

Whether your project is following a sequential development life cycle, one of the various agile life cycles, or any other approach, managing the requirements is an essential activity. Requirements management helps to ensure that the effort you invest in requirements development isn't squandered. Effective requirements management reduces the expectation gap by keeping all project stakeholders informed about the current state of the requirements throughout the development process. It lets you know where you're headed, how the trip is going, and when you've arrived at your destination.

Next steps

- Document the processes your organization will follow to manage the requirements on each project. Engage several business analysts to draft, review, pilot, and approve the process activities and deliverables. The process steps you define must be practical and realistic, and they must add value to each affected project.

- If you're not using a requirements management tool, define a version labeling scheme to identify your requirements documents. Educate the BAs about this scheme.

- Select the statuses that you want to use to describe the life cycle of your functional requirements or user stories. Draw a state-transition diagram to show the conditions or events that trigger a change from one status to another.

- Define the current status for each requirement in your baseline. Keep the status current as development progresses.

CHAPTER 28

Change happens

"How's your development work coming, Glenn?" asked Dave, the Chemical Tracking System's project manager, during a status meeting.

"I'm not as far along as I'd planned to be," Glenn admitted. "I'm adding a new catalog query function for Harumi, and it's taking a lot longer than I expected."

Dave was puzzled. "I don't remember hearing about a new catalog query function. Did Harumi submit that request through the change process?"

"No, she approached me directly with the suggestion," said Glenn. "It seemed pretty simple, so I told her I'd work it in. It turned out not to be simple at all! Every time I think I'm done, I realize I missed a change needed in another file, so I have to fix that, rebuild the component, and test it again. I thought this would take about six hours, but I've spent almost three days on it so far. I know I'm holding up the next build. Should I finish adding this query function or go back to what I was working on before?"

Most developers have encountered an apparently simple change that turned out to be far more complicated than expected. Developers sometimes don't—or can't—produce realistic estimates of the cost and other ramifications of a proposed software change. Additionally, when developers who want to be accommodating agree to add enhancements that users request, requirements changes slip in through the back door instead of being approved by the right stakeholders. Such uncontrolled change is a common source of project chaos, schedule slips, quality problems, and hard feelings. This chapter describes both formal change control practices and how agile projects incorporate changes.

Why manage changes?

Software change isn't a bad thing; in fact, it's necessary. It's virtually impossible to define all of a product's requirements up front. The world changes as development progresses: new market opportunities arise, regulations and policies change, and business needs evolve. An effective software team can nimbly respond to necessary changes so that the product they build provides timely customer value. An organization that's serious about managing its software projects must ensure that:

- Proposed requirements changes are thoughtfully evaluated before being committed to.

- Appropriate individuals make informed business decisions about requested changes.

- Change activity is made visible to affected stakeholders.

- Approved changes are communicated to all affected participants.

- The project incorporates requirements changes in a consistent and effective fashion.

But change always has a price. Revising a simple webpage might be quick and easy; making a change in an integrated circuit design can cost tens of thousands of dollars. Even a rejected change request consumes the time needed to submit, evaluate, and decide to reject it. Unless project stakeholders manage changes during development, they won't really know what will be delivered, which ultimately leads to an expectation gap.

Problems can also arise if a developer implements a requirement change directly in the code without communicating with other team members. The documented requirements then become an inaccurate representation of what the product does. The code can become brittle if changes are made without respecting the architecture and design structure. On one project, developers introduced new and modified functionality that the rest of the team didn't discover until system testing. They didn't expect that functionality, and they didn't know how to test it. This required unplanned rework of test procedures and user documentation. Consistent change control practices help prevent such problems and the associated frustration, rework, and wasted time.

Beware subversive changes

A vendor and a customer once caused havoc when they bypassed the change process on a contracted project. The vendor (vetted by the IT department, but hired by the business area) was to develop a new mobile workstation application. Requirements were elicited collaboratively with 10 subject matter experts. Then the lead customer from the business area decided that she wanted more requirements changes. Not trusting that the revisions would be funded, she colluded with the vendor's developers to subvert the agreed-upon requirements. They rented a hotel room and worked in secret, making changes to the code on the fly. When testers found that the deliverable didn't match the requirements, the whole story came out. Backtracking the changes and expected outcomes cost the organization considerable time and effort.

By a strange twist of fate, that lead customer later became a business analyst. She took the time to apologize, because only then did she come to understand how her actions had undermined the rest of the team.

Managing scope creep

In an ideal world, you would document all of a new system's requirements before beginning construction, and they'd remain stable throughout the development effort. This is the premise behind the pure waterfall development model, but it doesn't work well in practice. At some point, you must freeze the requirements for a specific release or development iteration or you'll never finish it. However, stifling change prematurely ignores the realities that customers aren't always sure what they need, business needs change, and developers want to respond to those changes.

Requirements growth includes new functionality and significant modifications that are presented after a set of requirements has been baselined (see Chapter 2, "Requirements from the customer's perspective"). The longer a project goes on, the more growth it experiences. The requirements for software systems typically grow between 1 percent and 3 percent per calendar month (Jones 2006). Some requirements evolution is legitimate, unavoidable, and even advantageous. Scope creep, though, in which the project continuously incorporates more functionality without adjusting resources, schedules, or quality goals, is insidious. The problem is not that requirements change but that late changes can have a big impact on work already performed. If every proposed change is approved, it might appear to stakeholders that the software will never be delivered—and indeed, it might not.

The first step in managing scope creep is to document the business objectives, product vision, project scope, and limitations of the new system, as described in Chapter 5, "Establishing the business requirements." Evaluate every proposed requirement or feature against the business requirements. Engaging customers in elicitation reduces the number of requirements that are overlooked. Prototyping helps to control scope creep by helping developers and users share a clear understanding of user needs and prospective solutions. Using short development cycles to release a system incrementally provides frequent opportunities for adjustments.

The most effective technique for controlling scope creep is the ability to say "no" (Weinberg 1995). People don't like to say "no," and development teams can receive intense pressure to always say "yes." Philosophies such as "the customer is always right" or "we will achieve total customer satisfaction" are fine in the abstract, but you pay a price for them. Ignoring the price doesn't alter the fact that change is not free. The president of one software tool vendor is accustomed to hearing the development manager say "not now" when he suggests a new feature. "Not now" is more palatable than a simple rejection. It holds the promise of including the feature in a subsequent release.

> **Trap** Freezing the requirements for a new system too soon after initial elicitation activities is unwise and unrealistic. Instead, establish a baseline when you think a set of requirements is well enough defined for construction to begin, and then manage changes to minimize their adverse impact on the project.

Change control policy

Management should communicate a policy that states its expectations of how project teams will handle proposed changes in requirements and all other significant project artifacts. Policies are meaningful only if they are realistic, add value, and are enforced. The following change control policy statements can be helpful:

- All changes must follow the process. If a change request is not submitted in accordance with this process, it will not be considered.

- No design or implementation work other than feasibility exploration will be performed on unapproved changes.

- Simply requesting a change does not guarantee that it will be made. The project's change control board (CCB) will decide which changes to implement.

- The contents of the change database must be visible to all project stakeholders.

- Impact analysis must be performed for every change.

- Every incorporated change must be traceable to an approved change request.

- The rationale behind every approval or rejection of a change request must be recorded.

Of course, tiny changes will hardly affect the project, and big changes will have a significant impact. In practice, you might decide to leave certain requirements decisions to the developers' discretion, but no change affecting more than one individual's work should bypass your process. Include a "fast path" to expedite low-risk, low-investment change requests in a compressed decision cycle.

Basic concepts of the change control process

 When performing a software process assessment, I asked a project team how they handled requirements changes. After an awkward silence, one person said, "Whenever the marketing representative wants to make a change, he asks Bruce or Robin because they always say 'yes.' The rest of us push back about changes." This didn't strike me as a great change process.

A sensible change control process lets the project's leaders make informed business decisions that will provide the greatest customer and business value while controlling the product's life-cycle cost and the project's schedule. The process lets you track the status of all proposed changes, and it helps ensure that suggested changes aren't lost or overlooked. After you've baselined a set of requirements, you should follow this process for all proposed changes to that baseline.

Stakeholders sometimes balk at being asked to follow a new process, but a change control process is not an obstacle to making necessary modifications. It's a funneling and filtering mechanism to ensure that the project expeditiously incorporates the most appropriate changes. If a proposed change isn't important enough for a stakeholder to take just a couple of minutes to submit it through a standard, simple channel, then it's not worth considering for inclusion. Your change process should be well documented, as simple as possible, and—above all—effective.

> **Trap** If you ask your stakeholders to follow a new change control process that's ineffective, cumbersome, or too complicated, people will find ways to bypass the process—and they should.

Managing requirements changes is similar to the process for collecting and making decisions about defect reports. The same tools can support both activities. Remember, though: a tool is not a substitute for a documented process, and neither one is a substitute for appropriate discussions between stakeholders. Regard both a tool and a written process as ways to support these critical conversations.

When you need to incorporate a change, start at the highest level of abstraction that the change touches and cascade the change through affected system components. For example, a proposed change might affect a user requirement but not any business requirements. Modifying a high-level system requirement could affect numerous software and hardware requirements in multiple subsystems. Some changes pertain only to system internals, such as the way a communication service is implemented. These aren't user-visible requirements changes, but rather design or code changes.

A change control process description

Figure 28-1 illustrates a template for a change control process description to handle requirements modifications. A sample change control process description is available for downloading from this book's companion content website. If this template is too elaborate for your environment, scale it down for more informal projects. We find it helpful to include the following four components in all process descriptions:

- Entry criteria, the conditions that must be satisfied before the process execution can begin

- The various tasks involved in the process, the project role responsible for each task, and other participants in the task

- Steps to verify that the tasks were completed correctly

- Exit criteria, the conditions that indicate when the process is successfully completed

The rest of this section describes the various sections in the change control process description.

```
1.  Purpose and scope
2.  Roles and responsibilities
3.  Change request states
4.  Entry criteria
5.  Tasks
    5.1  Evaluate change request
    5.2  Make change decision
    5.3  Implement the change
    5.4  Verify the change
6.  Exit criteria
7.  Change control status reporting
Appendix: Attributes stored for each request
```

FIGURE 28-1 Sample template for a change control process description.

1. Purpose and scope

Describe the purpose of this process and the organizational scope to which it applies. Indicate whether any specific kinds of changes are exempted, such as changes in interim work products. Define any terms that are necessary for understanding the rest of the document.

2. Roles and responsibilities

List the project team roles that participate in the change control activities and describe their responsibilities. Table 28-1 suggests some pertinent roles; adapt these to each project situation. Different individuals need not be required for each role. For example, the CCB Chair might also receive submitted change requests. The same person can fill several—perhaps all—roles on a small project. As one experienced project manager put it, "What I find important is that the representation of the CCB needs to be able to speak to the needs of the diverse stakeholders, including the end users, the business, and the development community: do we need it, can we sell it, can we build it?"

TABLE 28-1 Possible project roles in change-management activities

Role	Description and responsibilities
CCB Chair	Chairperson of the change control board; generally has final decision-making authority if the CCB does not reach agreement; identifies the Evaluator and the Modifier for each change request
CCB	The group that decides to approve or reject proposed changes for a specific project
Evaluator	Person whom the CCB Chair asks to analyze the impact of a proposed change
Modifier	Person who is responsible for making changes in a work product in response to an approved change request
Originator	Person who submits a new change request
Request Receiver	Person who initially receives newly submitted change requests
Verifier	Person who determines whether the change was made correctly

3. Change request status

A change request passes through a defined life cycle of states. You can represent these states by using a state-transition diagram (see Chapter 12," A picture is worth 1024 words"), as illustrated in Figure 28-2. Update a request's status only when the specified transition criteria are met. For instance, you can set the state to "Change Made" after all affected work products have been modified to implement the change, whether that is just a single requirement statement or a set of related development work products.

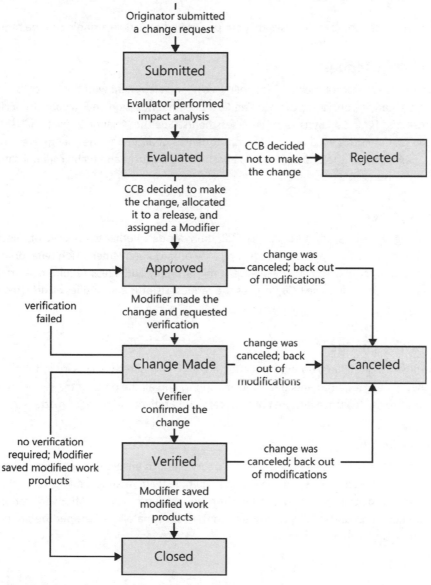

FIGURE 28-2 State-transition diagram for a change request.

4. Entry criteria

The basic entry criterion for your change control process is that a change request with all the necessary information has been received through an approved channel. All potential originators should know how to submit a change request. Your change tool should assign a unique identifier to each request and route all changes to the Request Receiver.

5. Tasks

This section of the process describes the tasks that are performed to handle a single change request.

5.1 Evaluate change request

Begin by evaluating the request for technical feasibility, cost, and alignment with the project's business requirements and resource constraints. The CCB Chair might assign an Evaluator to perform impact analysis, risk and hazard analysis, or other assessments. (See the "Change impact analysis" section later in this chapter.) This ensures that the consequences of accepting the change are understood. The Evaluator and the CCB should also consider the business and technical implications, if any, of rejecting the request.

5.2 Make change decision

The appropriate decision makers, chartered as the CCB, then decide whether to approve or reject the change. The CCB gives each approved change a priority or target implementation date, or it allocates the change to a specific iteration or release. It might simply add a new requirement to the product backlog of pending work. The CCB updates the request's status and notifies all affected team members.

5.3 Implement the change

The assigned Modifier (or Modifiers) updates the affected work products as necessary to fully implement the change. Use requirements trace information to find all the parts of the system that the change touches, and revise the trace information if necessary to reflect the changes made.

5.4 Verify the change

Requirements changes typically are verified through a peer review to ensure that modified deliverables correctly address all aspects of the change. Multiple team members might verify the changes made in various downstream work products through testing or review. After verification is complete, the Modifier stores updated work products in the appropriate locations per the project's document and code management conventions.

6. Exit criteria

Satisfying the following exit criteria indicates that an execution of your change control process was properly completed:

- ❑ The status of the request is Rejected, Closed, or Canceled.

- ❑ All modified work products are updated and stored in the correct locations.

- ❑ The relevant stakeholders have been notified of the change details and the status of the change request.

7. Change control status reporting

Identify the charts and reports you'll use to summarize the contents of the change database. These charts might show the number of change requests in each state as a function of time, or trends in the average time that a change request is unresolved. Describe the procedures for producing the charts and reports. The project manager uses these reports when tracking the project's status.

Appendix: Attributes stored for each request

Table 28-2 lists some data attributes to consider storing for each change request. Some of these items are supplied by the Originator and some by the CCB. In your change control process, indicate which attributes are required and which are optional. Don't define more attributes than you really need. Your change tool should handle some of these (ID, date submitted, date updated) automatically.

TABLE 28-2 Suggested change request attributes

Item	Description
Change origin	Functional area that requested the change; possible groups include marketing, management, customer, development, and testing
Change request ID	Unique identifier assigned to the request
Change type	Type of change request, such as requirement change, proposed enhancement, or defect report
Date submitted	Date the Originator submitted the change request
Date updated	Date the change request was most recently modified
Description	Free-form text description of the change being requested
Implementation priority	The relative importance of making the change as determined by the CCB: low, medium, or high
Modifier	Person who is primarily responsible for implementing the change
Originator	Person who submitted this change request
Originator priority	The relative importance of making the change from the Originator's point of view: low, medium, or high
Planned release	Product release or iteration for which an approved change is scheduled
Project	Name of the project in which a change is being requested

Item	Description
Response	Free-form text of responses made to the change request; multiple responses can be made over time; do not change existing responses when entering a new one
Status	The current status of the change request, selected from the options in Figure 28-2
Title	One-line summary of the proposed change
Verifier	Person who is responsible for determining whether the change was made correctly

The change control board

The *change control board* is the body of people—whether it is one individual or a diverse group—that decides which proposed changes and new requirements to accept, which to accept with revisions, and which to reject. The CCB also decides which reported defects to correct and when to correct them. Some CCBs are empowered to make decisions, whereas others can only make recommendations for management decision. Projects always have some de facto group that makes change decisions. Establishing a CCB formalizes this group's composition and authority and defines its operating procedures.

To some people, the term "change control board" conjures an image of wasteful bureaucratic overhead. Instead, think of the CCB as providing a valuable structure to help manage even a small project. On a small project, it makes sense to have only one or two people make the change decisions. Very large projects or programs might have several levels of CCBs, some responsible for business decisions, such as requirements changes, and some for technical changes. A large program that encompasses multiple projects would establish a program-level CCB and an individual CCB for each project. Each project CCB resolves issues and changes that affect only that project. Issues that affect multiple projects and changes that exceed a specified cost or schedule impact are escalated to the program-level CCB.

CCB composition

The CCB membership should represent all groups who need to participate in making decisions within the scope of that CCB's authority. Consider selecting representatives from the following areas:

- Project or program management

- Business analysis or product management

- Development

- Testing or quality assurance

- Marketing, the business for which the application is being built, or customer representatives

- Technical support or help desk

Only the subset of these people who need to make the decisions will be part of the CCB, although all stakeholders must be informed of decisions that affect their work. The CCB for a project with both software and hardware components might also include representatives from hardware engineering, systems engineering, and/or manufacturing. Keep the CCB small so the group can respond promptly and efficiently to change requests. Make sure the CCB members understand and accept their responsibilities. Invite other individuals to CCB meetings as necessary to ensure that the group has adequate technical and business information.

CCB charter

All of the project teams in an organization can follow the same change control process. However, their CCBs might function in different ways. Each project should create a brief charter (which could be part of the project management plan) that describes its CCB's purpose, scope of authority, membership, operating procedures, and decision-making process (Sorensen 1999). A template for a CCB charter is available for downloading from this book's companion content website. The charter should state the frequency of regularly scheduled CCB meetings and the conditions that trigger a special meeting or decision. The scope of the CCB's authority indicates which decisions it can make and which ones it must escalate.

Making decisions

Each CCB needs to define its decision-making process, which should indicate:

- The number of CCB members or the key roles that constitute a decision-making quorum.

- The decision rules to be used (see Chapter 2 for more about decision rules).

- Whether the CCB Chair can overrule the CCB's collective decision.

- Whether a higher level of CCB or management must ratify the group's decision.

The CCB balances the anticipated benefits against the estimated impact of accepting a proposed change. Benefits from improving the product could include financial savings, increased revenue, higher customer satisfaction, and competitive advantage. Possible negative impacts include increased development and support costs, delayed delivery, and degraded product quality.

> **Trap** Because people don't like to say "no," it's easy to accumulate a huge backlog of approved change requests that will never get done. Before accepting a proposed change, make sure you understand the rationale behind it and the business value the change will provide.

Communicating status

After the CCB makes its decision, a designated individual updates the request's status in the change database. Some tools automatically generate an email message to communicate the new status to the Originator who proposed the change and to others affected by the change. If an email message is not generated automatically, inform the affected people so they can respond to the change.

Renegotiating commitments

Stakeholders can't stuff more and more functionality into a project that has schedule, staff, budget, or quality constraints and still expect to succeed. Before accepting a significant requirement change, renegotiate commitments with management and customers to accommodate the change. You might ask for more time or to defer lower-priority requirements. If you don't obtain some commitment adjustments, document the threats to success in your project's risk list so people aren't surprised if there are negative outcomes.

Change control tools

Many teams use commercial issue-tracking tools to collect, store, and manage requirements changes. A report of recently submitted change requests extracted from the tool can serve as the agenda for a CCB meeting. Issue-tracking tools can report the number of requests having each state at any given time. Because the available tools, their vendors, and their features frequently change, we don't provide specific tool recommendations here. To support your change process, look for a tool that:

- Allows you to define the attributes that constitute a change request.

- Allows you to implement a change request life cycle with multiple change request statuses.

- Enforces the state-transition model so that only authorized users can make specific status changes.

- Records the date of each status change and the identity of the person who made it.

- Provides customizable, automatic email notification when an Originator submits a new request or when a request's status is updated.

- Produces both standard and custom reports and charts.

Some commercial requirements management tools have a change-request system built in. These systems can link a proposed change to a specific requirement so that the individual responsible for each requirement is notified by email whenever someone submits a pertinent change request.

Tooling up a process

When I worked on a web development team, one of our first process improvements was to implement a change control process to manage our huge backlog of change requests (Wiegers 1999). We began with a process like the one described in this chapter. We piloted it for a few weeks by using paper forms while I evaluated several issue-tracking tools. During the pilot process we discovered ways to improve the process and additional data attributes for the change requests. We selected a highly configurable tool and tailored it to match our process. The team used this process and tool to handle requirements changes in systems under development, defect reports and suggested enhancements for production systems, and requests for new projects. Change control was one of our most successful process improvement initiatives.

Measuring change activity

Measuring change activity is a way to assess the stability of the requirements. It also reveals opportunities for process improvements that might lead to fewer changes in the future. Consider tracking the following aspects of your requirements change activity:

- The total number of change requests received, currently open, and closed

- The cumulative number of added, deleted, and modified requirements

- The number of requests that originated from each change origin

- The number of changes received against each requirement since it was baselined

- The total effort devoted to processing and implementing change requests

You don't necessarily need to monitor your requirements change activities to this degree. As with all software metrics, understand your goals and how you'll use the data before you decide what to measure (Wiegers 2007). Start with simple metrics to begin establishing a measurement culture in your organization and to collect the data you need to manage your projects effectively.

Figure 28-3 illustrates a way to track the amount of requirements change your project experiences during development (Wiegers 2006). This requirements volatility chart tracks the rate at which new proposals for requirements changes arrive after a baseline was established. This chart should trend toward zero as you approach release. A sustained high frequency of changes implies a risk of failing to meet your schedule commitments. It probably also indicates that the original requirements set was incomplete; better elicitation practices might be in order.

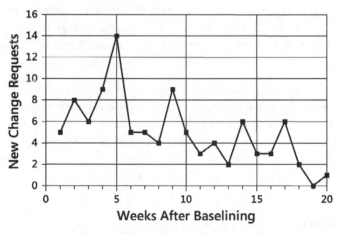

FIGURE 28-3 Sample chart of requirements change activity.

Tracking the requirements change origins is also illuminating. Figure 28-4 shows a way to represent the number of change requests that came from different sources. The project manager could discuss a chart like this with the marketing manager and point out that marketing has requested the most requirements changes. This might lead to a fruitful discussion about actions the team could take to reduce the number of changes received from marketing in the future or better ways to handle them. Using data as a starting point for such discussions is more constructive than holding a confrontational debate fueled by emotion. Come up with your own list of possible requirements change origins.

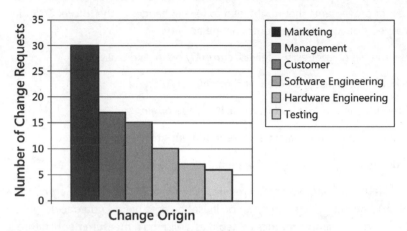

FIGURE 28-4 Sample chart of requirement change origins.

Change impact analysis

 The need for impact analysis is obvious for major enhancements. However, unexpected complications can lurk below the surface of even minor change requests. A company once had to change the text of one error message in its product. What could be simpler? The product was available in both English-language and German-language versions. There were no problems in English, but in German the new message exceeded the maximum character length allocated for error message displays in both the message box and a database. Coping with this seemingly simple change request turned out to be much more work than the developer had anticipated when he promised a quick turnaround.

Impact analysis is a key aspect of responsible requirements management (Arnold and Bohner 1996). It provides an accurate understanding of the implications of a proposed change, which helps the team make informed business decisions about which proposals to approve. The analysis examines the request to identify components that might have to be created, modified, or discarded, and to estimate the effort required to implement the change. Before a developer says, "Sure, no problem" in response to a change request, he should spend a little time on impact analysis.

Impact analysis procedure

The CCB Chair will ask one or more technical people (business analysts, developers, and/or testers) to perform the impact analysis for a specific change proposal. Impact analysis involves three steps:

1. Understand the possible implications of making the change. A requirement change often produces a large ripple effect, leading to modifications in other requirements, architectures,

designs, code, and tests. Changes can lead to conflicts with other requirements or can compromise quality attributes, such as performance or security.

2. Identify all the requirements, files, models, and documents that might have to be modified if the team incorporates the requested change.

3. Identify the tasks required to implement the change, and estimate the effort needed to complete those tasks.

> **Important** Skipping impact analysis doesn't change the size of the task. It just turns the size into a surprise. Software surprises are rarely good news.

Figure 28-5 presents a checklist of questions to help the evaluator understand the implications of accepting a proposed change. The checklist in Figure 28-6 contains questions to help identify all software elements and other work products that the change might affect. Requirements trace information that links the affected requirement to other downstream deliverables helps greatly with impact analysis. As you gain experience in using these checklists, modify them to suit your own projects. (Note: Figures 28-5 through 28-8 are available for downloading from this book's companion content website.)

❑ Will the change enhance or impair the ability to satisfy any business requirements?

❑ Do any existing requirements in the baseline conflict with the proposed change?

❑ Do any other pending requirements changes conflict with the proposed change?

❑ What are the business or technical consequences of not making the change?

❑ What are possible adverse side effects or other risks of making the proposed change?

❑ Will the proposed change adversely affect performance or other quality attributes?

❑ Is the proposed change feasible within known technical constraints and current staff skills?

❑ Will the proposed change place unacceptable demands on any resources required for the development, test, or operating environments?

❑ Must any tools be acquired to implement and test the change?

❑ How will the proposed change affect the sequence, dependencies, effort, or duration of any tasks currently in the project plan?

❑ Will prototyping or other user input be required to validate the change?

❑ How much effort that has already been invested in the project will be lost if this change is accepted?

❑ Will the proposed change cause an increase in product unit cost, such as by increasing third-party product licensing fees?

❑ Will the change affect any marketing, manufacturing, training, or customer support plans?

FIGURE 28-5 Questions to understand the possible implications of a proposed change.

> ❑ Identify any user interface changes, additions, or deletions required.
>
> ❑ Identify any changes, additions, or deletions required in reports, databases, or files.
>
> ❑ Identify the design components that must be created, modified, or deleted.
>
> ❑ Identify the source code files that must be created, modified, or deleted.
>
> ❑ Identify any changes required in build files or procedures.
>
> ❑ Identify existing unit, integration, and system tests to be modified or deleted.
>
> ❑ Estimate the number of new unit, integration, and system tests needed.
>
> ❑ Identify help screens, training or support materials, or other user documentation that must be created or modified.
>
> ❑ Identify other applications, libraries, or hardware components affected by the change.
>
> ❑ Identify any third-party software to be acquired or modified.
>
> ❑ Identify any impact the proposed change will have on the project management plan, quality assurance plan, configuration management plan, or other plans.

FIGURE 28-6 Checklist to determine work products that might be affected by a proposed change.

Many estimation problems arise because the estimator doesn't think of all the work required to complete an activity. Therefore, this impact analysis approach emphasizes thorough task identification. For substantial changes, use a small team—not just one developer—to do the analysis and effort estimation to avoid overlooking important tasks. Following is a simple procedure for evaluating the impact of a proposed requirement change:

1. Work through the checklist in Figure 28-5.

2. Work through the checklist in Figure 28-6. Some requirements management tools include an impact analysis report that follows traceability links and finds the system elements that depend on the requirements affected by a change request.

3. Use the worksheet in Figure 28-7 to estimate the effort required for the anticipated tasks. Most change requests will require only a portion of the tasks on the worksheet.

4. Sum the effort estimates.

5. Identify the sequence in which the tasks must be performed and how they can be interleaved with currently planned tasks.

6. Estimate the impact of the proposed change on the project's schedule and cost.

7. Evaluate the change's priority compared to other pending requirements.

8. Report the impact analysis results to the CCB.

Hours	Task
_____	Update the SRS or requirements repository
_____	Develop and evaluate a prototype
_____	Create new design components
_____	Modify existing design components
_____	Develop new user interface components
_____	Modify existing user interface components
_____	Develop new user documentation and help screens
_____	Modify existing user documentation and help screens
_____	Develop new source code
_____	Modify existing source code
_____	License and integrate third-party software
_____	Modify build files and procedures
_____	Write new unit and integration tests
_____	Modify existing unit and integration tests
_____	Perform unit and integration testing after implementation
_____	Write new system and acceptance tests
_____	Modify existing system and acceptance tests
_____	Modify automated test suites
_____	Perform regression testing
_____	Develop new reports
_____	Modify existing reports
_____	Develop new database elements
_____	Modify existing database elements
_____	Develop new data files
_____	Modify existing data files
_____	Modify various project plans
_____	Update other documentation
_____	Update the requirements traceability matrix
_____	Review modified work products
_____	Perform rework following reviews and testing
_____	Other tasks
_____	**Total Estimated Effort**

FIGURE 28-7 Worksheet for estimating effort of a requirement change.

In most cases, this procedure shouldn't take more than a couple of hours to complete for a single change request. This seems like a lot of time to a busy developer, but it's a small investment in making sure the project wisely invests its limited resources. To improve your future impact analysis, compare the actual effort needed to implement each change with the estimated effort. Understand the reasons for any differences, and modify the impact estimation checklists and worksheet to help ensure that future impact analyses are more accurate.

Money down the drain

Two developers at the A. Datum Corporation estimated that it would take four weeks to add an enhancement to one of their information systems. The customer approved the estimate, and the developers set to work. After two months, the enhancement was only about half done and the customer lost patience: "If I'd known how long this was really going to take and how much it was going to cost, I wouldn't have approved it. Let's forget the whole thing." In the rush to begin implementation, the developers didn't do enough impact analysis to develop a reliable estimate that would let the customer make a good business decision. Consequently, the company wasted several hundred hours of work that could have been avoided with a few hours of impact analysis.

Impact analysis template

Figure 28-8 suggests a template for reporting the results from analyzing the impact of a requirement change. The people who will implement the change will need the analysis details and the effort planning worksheet, but the CCB needs only the summary of analysis results. As with all templates, try it and then adjust it to meet your project needs.

```
Change request ID: _____
Title: _____
Description: _____
           _____
Evaluator: _____
Date prepared: _____
Estimated total effort:          _____ labor hours
Estimated schedule impact: _____ days
Additional cost impact:          _____ dollars
Quality impact: _____
           _____
Other components affected: _____
           _____
Other tasks affected: _____
Life-cycle cost issues: _____
```

FIGURE 28-8 Impact analysis template.

Change management on agile projects

Agile projects are specifically structured to respond to—and even welcome—scope changes. One of the 12 principles of agile software development is "Welcome changing requirements, even late in development. Agile processes harness change for the customer's competitive advantage" (*www.agilemanifesto.org/principles.html*). This principle acknowledges the reality that requirements changes are inevitable, necessary, and often valuable. Accepting change helps to meet evolving business objectives and priorities and to accommodate the limitations of human plans and foresight.

Agile projects manage change by maintaining a dynamic backlog of work to be done (see Figure 28-9). "Work" includes user stories yet to be implemented, defects to be corrected, business process changes to be addressed, training to be developed and delivered, and the myriad other activities involved with any software project. Each iteration implements the set of work items in the backlog that have the highest priority at that time. As stakeholders request new work, it goes into the backlog and is prioritized against the other backlog contents. Work that has not yet been allocated can be reprioritized or removed from the backlog at any time. A new, high-priority story could be allocated to the forthcoming iteration, forcing a lower-priority story of about the same size to be deferred to a later iteration. Carefully managing the scope of each iteration ensures that it is completed on time and with high quality.

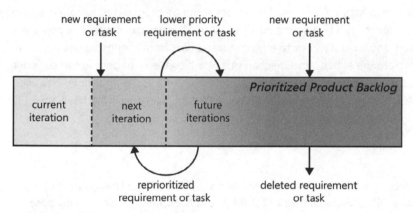

FIGURE 28-9 Agile projects manage change with a dynamic product backlog.

Because of the iterative nature of agile projects, every few weeks there will be an opportunity to select a set of work items from the backlog for the next development iteration. Agile teams vary as to whether new work that arrives during an iteration is always deferred to a future iteration, or whether they can modify the contents of the current iteration. Keeping the contents of an iteration frozen while it is under way provides stability for developers and predictability regarding what stakeholders can expect out of the iteration. On the other hand, adjusting the iteration's contents makes the team more responsive to customer needs.

Agile methods vary as to their philosophy on this point; there is no single "correct" approach. Either freeze the baseline for an iteration once it is under way or introduce high-priority changes as soon as you learn about them, whatever you think will work best for your team and the project's business objectives. The basic principle is to avoid both excessive change (churning requirements) and excessive rigidity (frozen requirements) within an iteration. One solution is to set the iteration length to the right duration for keeping most change out of the current iteration. That is, if changes need to be introduced too often, the standard iteration length might need to be shortened.

All agile methods define a role representing the end-user and customer constituencies. In Scrum this is the product owner role; in Extreme Programming this is the customer role. The customer or product owner has primary responsibility for prioritizing the contents of the product backlog.

He also makes decisions to accept proposed requirements changes, based on their alignment with the overarching product vision and the business value they will enable (Cohn 2010).

Because an agile team is a collaborative and cross-functional group of developers, testers, a business analyst, a project manager, and others, the team is already configured like the change control board discussed earlier in the chapter. The short duration of agile iterations and the small increment of product delivered in each iteration allows agile teams to perform change control frequently but on a limited scale. However, even agile projects must evaluate the potential cost of changes in requirements and their impact on product components. Scope changes that could affect the overall cost or duration of the project need to be escalated to a higher-level change authority, such as the project sponsor (Thomas 2008).

No matter what kind of project you're working on or what development life cycle your team is following, change is going to happen. You need to expect it and be prepared to handle it. Disciplined change-management practices can reduce the disruption that changes can cause. The purpose of change control is not to inhibit change, nor to inhibit stakeholders from proposing changes. It is to provide visibility into change activity and mechanisms by which the right people can consider proposed changes and incorporate appropriate ones into the project at the right time. This will maximize the business value and minimize the negative impact of changes on the team.

Next steps

- Identify the decision makers on your project, and set them up as a change control board. Have the CCB adopt a charter to establish and document the board's purpose, composition, and decision-making process.

- Define a state-transition diagram for the life cycle of proposed requirements changes in your project, starting with the diagram in Figure 28-2. Write a process to describe how your team will handle proposed requirements changes. Use the process manually until you're convinced that it's practical and effective.

- Select an issue-tracking tool that's compatible with your development environment. Tailor it to align with the process you created in the previous step.

- The next time you evaluate a requirement change request, first estimate the effort using your old method. Then estimate it again using the impact analysis approach described in this chapter. If you implement the change, compare the two estimates to see which agrees more closely with the actual effort required. Modify the impact analysis checklists and worksheet based on your experience to improve their future value.

CHAPTER 29

Links in the requirements chain

"We just learned that the new union contract is changing how overtime pay and shift bonuses are calculated," Justin reported at the weekly team meeting. "It's also changing how the seniority rules affect priority for vacation scheduling and shift preferences. We have to update the payroll and staff scheduling systems to handle all these changes right away. How long do you think it will take to get this done, Chris?"

"Man, that's going to be a lot of work," said Chris. "The logic for the seniority rules is sprinkled throughout the scheduling system. I can't give you a decent estimate yet. It's going to take hours just to scan through the code and try to find all the places where those rules show up."

Software changes that seem simple often have far-reaching impacts, necessitating modification of many parts of the system. It's hard to find all the system elements that might be affected by an altered requirement. Chapter 28, "Change happens," discussed the importance of performing an impact analysis to make sure the team knows what it's getting into before it commits to implementing a proposed change. Change impact analysis is easier if you have a road map that shows where each requirement or business rule was implemented in the software.

This chapter addresses the subject of requirements tracing (or traceability). Requirements trace information documents the dependencies and logical links between individual requirements and other system elements. These elements include other requirements of various types, business rules, architecture and other design components, source code modules, tests, and help files. Trace information facilitates impact analysis by helping you identify all the work products you might have to modify to implement a proposed requirement change.

Tracing requirements

Trace links allow you to follow the life of a requirement both forward and backward, from origin through implementation. Chapter 11, "Writing excellent requirements," identified traceability as one of the characteristics of excellent requirements. (Note that being *traceable*—having the properties to facilitate tracing—is not the same as being *traced*—actually having logical links between requirements and other elements recorded.) For requirements to be traceable, each one must be uniquely and persistently labeled so that you can refer to it unambiguously throughout the project. Write the requirements in a fine-grained fashion, rather than creating large paragraphs containing many individual functional requirements that readers have to parse out.

Figure 29-1 illustrates four types of requirements trace links (Jarke 1998). Customer needs are traced *forward to requirements*, so you can tell which requirements will be affected if those needs change during or after development. Customer needs could be articulated in the form of business objectives, market demands, and/or user requirements. A complete set of forward traces also gives you confidence that the requirements set has addressed all stated customer needs. Conversely, you can trace *backward from requirements* to customer needs to identify the origin of each software requirement. If you choose to represent customer needs in the form of use cases, the top half of Figure 29-1 illustrates tracing between use cases and functional requirements.

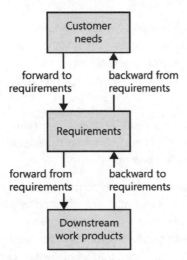

FIGURE 29-1 Four types of requirements tracing.

The bottom half of Figure 29-1 indicates that, as requirements flow into downstream deliverables during development, you can trace *forward from requirements* by defining links between individual functional and nonfunctional requirements and specific system elements. This type of link allows you to determine that you've satisfied every requirement because you know which design components and code elements address each one. The fourth type of link traces specific product elements *backward to requirements* so that you know why each element was created. Most applications include some scaffolding or enabling code, such as for testing, that doesn't relate directly to user-specified requirements, but you should know why each line of code was written.

Suppose a tester encounters unexpected functionality with no corresponding written requirement. This code could indicate that a developer implemented a legitimate implied or verbally communicated requirement that the business analyst can now add to the requirements set. Alternatively, it might be "orphan code," an instance of gold-plating that doesn't belong in the product. Trace links can help you sort out these kinds of situations and build a more complete picture of how the pieces of your system fit together. Conversely, tests that are derived from—and traced back to—individual requirements provide a mechanism for detecting unimplemented requirements, because the expected functionality will be missing from the system being tested. Trace links also help you keep track of parentage, interconnections, and dependencies among individual requirements.

This information reveals the propagation of change that can result when a particular requirement is deleted or modified.

Figure 29-2 illustrates many kinds of traceability relationships that can be defined on a project. Of course, you don't need to define and manage all these trace link types. On many projects, you can gain most of the traceability benefits you want for just a fraction of the potential effort. Maybe you only need to trace system tests back to functional requirements or user requirements. Perform a cost-benefit analysis to decide which links will contribute to the success of your project, both in terms of development and long-term maintenance effort. Don't ask team members to spend time recording information unless you know how they can use it.

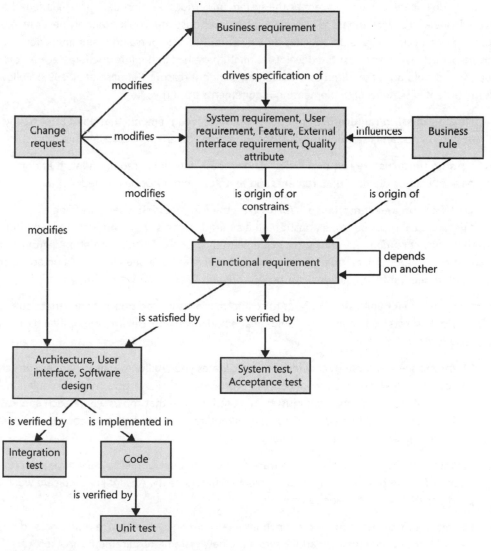

FIGURE 29-2 Some possible requirements trace links.

Motivations for tracing requirements

 I've had the embarrassing experience of writing a program and then realizing that I had inadvertently overlooked a requirement. It was in the SRS—I simply missed it. I had to go back and write additional code after I thought I was done programming. Overlooking a requirement is more than an embarrassment if it means a customer isn't satisfied or a product is missing a critical function. Requirements tracing provides a way to demonstrate compliance with a specification, contract, or regulation. At an organization level, implementing requirements tracing can improve the quality of your products, reduce maintenance costs, and facilitate reuse.

Keeping the link information current as the system undergoes development and maintenance takes discipline and time. If the trace information becomes obsolete, you'll probably never reconstruct it. Obsolete or inaccurate trace data wastes time by sending developers and maintainers down the wrong path, destroying any trust the developers might have had in the information. Because of these realities, you should adopt requirements tracing for the right reasons (Ramesh et al. 1995). Following are some potential benefits of implementing requirements tracing:

- **Finding missing requirements**   Look for business requirements that don't trace to any user requirements, and user requirements that don't trace to any functional requirements.

- **Finding unnecessary requirements**   Look for any functional requirements that don't trace back to user or business requirements and therefore might not be needed.

- **Certification and compliance**   You can use trace information when certifying a safety-critical product, to demonstrate that all requirements were implemented—although that doesn't confirm that they were implemented correctly! Trace information demonstrates that requirements demanded for regulatory compliance have been included and addressed, as is often needed for applications for health care and financial services companies.

- **Change impact analysis**   Without trace information, there's a good chance that you'll overlook a system element that would be affected if you add, delete, or modify a particular requirement.

- **Maintenance**   Reliable trace information facilitates your ability to make changes correctly and completely during maintenance. When corporate policies or government regulations change, software systems often must be updated. A table that shows where each applicable business rule was addressed in the functional requirements, designs, and code makes it easier to make the necessary changes properly.

- **Project tracking**   If you record the trace data during development, you'll have an accurate record of the implementation status of planned functionality. Absent links indicate work products that have not yet been created.

- **Reengineering**   You can list the functions in an existing system you're replacing and trace them to where they are addressed in the new system's requirements and software components.

- **Reuse**   Trace information facilitates the reuse of product components by identifying packages of related requirements, designs, code, and tests.

- **Testing**   When a test fails, the links between tests, requirements, and code point developers toward likely areas to examine for the defect.

Many of these are long-term benefits, reducing overall product life-cycle costs but increasing the development cost by the effort expended to accumulate and manage the trace information. View requirements tracing as an investment that increases your chances of delivering a maintainable product that satisfies all the stated customer requirements. This investment will pay dividends anytime you have to modify, extend, or replace the product. Establishing traces is not much work if you collect the information as development proceeds, but it's tedious and expensive to do on a completed system.

The requirements traceability matrix

The most common way to represent the links between requirements and other system elements is in a *requirements traceability matrix*, also called a *requirements trace matrix* or a *traceability table*. Joy Beatty and Anthony Chen (2012) describe a similar tool called a *requirements mapping matrix* that shows the relationships between multiple types of objects. Table 29-1 illustrates a portion of a requirements traceability matrix, drawn from the Chemical Tracking System. When I've set up such matrices in the past, I started with a copy of the baselined SRS and deleted everything except the labels for the functional requirements. Then I set up a table laid out like Table 29-1 with only the "Functional requirement" column populated. As fellow team members and I worked on the project, we gradually filled in the blank cells in the matrix.

TABLE 29-1 One kind of requirements traceability matrix

User requirement	Functional requirement	Design element	Code element	Test
UC 28	catalog.query.sort	Class catalog	CatalogSort()	search./ search.8
UC-29	catalog.query.import	Class catalog	CatalogImport() CatalogValidate()	search.12 search.13 search.14

Table 29-1 shows how each functional requirement is linked backward to a specific use case and forward to one or more design, code, and test elements. A design element can be something like an architectural component, a table in a relational data model, or an object class. Code references can be class methods, stored procedures, source code file names, or modules within a source file. Including more trace detail takes more work, but it gives you the precise locations of the related software elements.

Fill in the information as the work gets done, not as it gets planned. That is, enter **CatalogSort()** in the "Code element" column of the first row in Table 29-1 only when the code in that function has been written. That way a reader knows that populated cells in the requirements traceability matrix indicate work that's been completed.

> **Important** Listing the test cases for each requirement does *not* indicate that the software has passed those tests. It simply indicates that certain tests have been written to verify the requirement at the appropriate time. Tracking testing status is a separate matter.

Another way to represent trace information is through a set of matrices that define links between pairs of system elements, such as these:

- One type of requirement to other requirements of that same type

- One type of requirement to requirements of another type

- One type of requirement to tests

You can use these matrices to define various relationships that are possible between pairs of requirements, such as "specifies/is specified by," "is dependent on," "is parent of," and "constrains/is constrained by" (Sommerville and Sawyer 1997).

Table 29-2 illustrates a two-way traceability matrix. Most cells in the matrix are empty. Each cell at the intersection of two linked components contains a symbol to indicate the connection. Table 29-2 uses an arrow to indicate that a certain functional requirement is traced from a particular use case. For instance, FR-2 is traced from UC-1, and FR-5 is traced from both UC-2 and UC-4. This indicates that the functional requirement FR-5 is reused across two use cases, UC-2 and UC-4.

TABLE 29-2 Requirements traceability matrix showing links between use cases and functional requirements

Functional requirement	Use case			
	UC-1	UC-2	UC-3	UC-4
FR-1	↵			
FR-2	↵			
FR-3			↵	
FR-4			↵	
FR-5		↵		↵
FR-6			↵	

Trace links can define one-to-one, one-to-many, or many-to-many relationships between system elements. The format in Table 29-1 accommodates these cardinalities by letting you enter several items in each table cell. Here are some examples of the possible link cardinalities:

- **One-to-one** One design element is implemented in one code module.

- **One-to-many** One functional requirement is verified by multiple tests.

- **Many-to-many** Each use case leads to multiple functional requirements, and certain functional requirements are common to several use cases. Similarly, a shared or repeated design element might satisfy several functional requirements. Ideally, you'll capture all these interconnections, but in practice, many-to-many trace relationships become complex and difficult to manage.

Nonfunctional requirements such as quality attributes often do not trace directly into code. A response-time requirement might dictate the use of certain hardware, algorithms, database structures, and architectural approaches. A portability requirement could restrict the language features that the programmer uses but might not result in specific code segments that enable portability. Other quality attributes are indeed implemented in code. Security requirements for user authentication lead to derived functional requirements that might be implemented through passwords or biometrics functionality. In those cases, you can trace the corresponding functional requirements backward to their parent nonfunctional requirement and forward into downstream deliverables as usual. Figure 29-3 illustrates a possible traceability chain involving nonfunctional requirements.

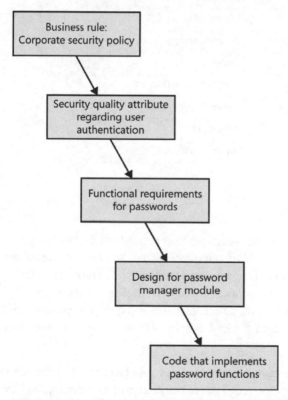

FIGURE 29-3 Sample traceability chain for requirements dealing with application security.

Trace links should be defined by whomever has the appropriate information available. Table 29-3 identifies some typical sources of knowledge about links between various types of source and target objects. Determine the roles and individuals who should supply each type of trace information for your project. Expect some pushback from busy people whom the analyst or project manager asks to provide this data. Those practitioners are entitled to an explanation of requirements tracing, why it provides value, and why they're being asked to contribute to the process. Point out that the incremental cost of capturing trace information at the time the work is done is small; it's primarily a matter of habit, discipline, and having the storage mechanism established.

> **Trap** Gathering and managing requirements trace data must be made the explicit responsibility of certain individuals or it won't happen. Typically, a business analyst or a quality assurance engineer collects, stores, and reports on the trace information.

TABLE 29-3 Likely sources of trace link information

Link source object type	Link target object type	Information source
System requirement	Functional requirement	System engineer
User requirement	Functional requirement	Business analyst
Business requirement	User requirement	Business analyst
Functional requirement	Functional requirement	Business analyst
Functional requirement	Test	Tester
Functional requirement	Architecture element	Architect or developer
Functional requirement	Other design elements	Designer or developer
Design element	Code	Developer
Business rule	Functional requirement	Business analyst

Tools for requirements tracing

As Chapter 30, "Tools for requirements engineering," describes, commercial requirements management tools often have powerful requirements-tracing capabilities. You can store requirements and other information in a tool's database and define links between the various types of stored objects, including peer links between two requirements of the same kind. Some tools let you differentiate traced-to and traced-from relationships, automatically defining the complementary links. That is, if you indicate that requirement R is *traced to* test T, the tool will also show the symmetrical relationship in which T is *traced from* R.

Some tools automatically flag a trace link as being *suspect* whenever the object on either end of the link is modified. A suspect link displays a visual indicator (such as a red question mark or a diagonal red line) in the corresponding cell in the requirements traceability matrix. For example, if you changed Use Case 3, the requirements traceability matrix in Table 29-2 might look like Table 29-4 the next time you see it. The suspect link indicators (in this case, question marks) tell you to check whether functional requirements 3, 4, and 6 need to be changed to remain consistent with the modified UC-3. After making any necessary changes, you clear the suspect link indicators manually. This process helps ensure that you've accounted for the known ripple effects of a change.

TABLE 29-4 Suspect links in a requirements traceability matrix

Functional requirement	Use case			
	UC-1	UC-2	UC-3	UC-4
FR-1	↵			
FR-2	↵			
FR-3			↵?	
FR-4			↵?	
FR-5		↵		↵
FR-6			↵?	

Requirements management tools also let you define cross-project or cross-subsystem links. I know of one large software product that had 20 major subsystems, with certain high-level system requirements apportioned among multiple subsystems. In some cases, a requirement that was allocated to one subsystem was actually implemented through a service that another subsystem provided. This project used a requirements management tool to successfully track these complex trace relationships.

It's impossible to perform requirements tracing manually for any but very small applications. You can use a spreadsheet to maintain trace data for up to a couple hundred requirements, but larger systems demand a more robust solution. Requirements tracing can't be fully automated because the knowledge of the links originates in the development team members' minds. However, after you've identified the links, tools can help you manage the vast quantity of trace information.

A requirements tracing procedure

Consider following this sequence of steps when you begin to implement requirements tracing on a specific project:

1. Educate the team and your management about the concepts and importance of requirements tracing, your objectives for this activity, where the trace data is stored, and the techniques for defining the links. Ask all participants to commit to their responsibilities.

2. Select the link relationships you want to define from the possibilities shown in Figure 29-2. Don't try to do all of these at once! You'll be overwhelmed.

3. Choose the type of traceability matrix you want to use: the single-matrix style shown in Table 29-1 or several matrices like the one illustrated in Table 29-2. Select a mechanism for

storing the data: a table in a text document, a spreadsheet, or (much better) a requirements management tool.

4. Identify the parts of the product for which you want to maintain traceability information. Start with the critical core functions, the high-risk portions, or the portions that you expect will undergo the most maintenance and evolution over the product's life.

5. Identify the individuals who will supply each type of link information and the person (most likely a BA) who will coordinate the tracing activities and manage the data.

6. Modify your development procedures to remind developers to update the links after implementing a requirement or an approved change. The trace data should be updated soon after someone completes a task that creates or changes a link in the requirements chain.

7. Define the labeling conventions you will use to give each system element a unique identifier so that the elements can be linked together. Chapter 10, "Documenting the requirements," described several ways to label requirements.

8. As development proceeds, have each participant provide the requested trace information as they complete small bodies of work. Stress the advantage of ongoing accumulation of the trace data over assembling it at a major milestone or at the end of the project.

9. Audit the trace information periodically to make sure it's being kept current. If a requirement is reported as implemented and verified, yet its trace data is incomplete or inaccurate, your requirements tracing process isn't working as intended.

I've described this procedure as though you were starting to collect trace information at the outset of a new project. If you're maintaining an existing system, you probably don't have trace data available. There's no time like the present to begin accumulating this information. The next time you add an enhancement or make a modification, write down what you discover about connections between code, tests, designs, and requirements. You'll never reconstruct a complete requirements traceability matrix, but this small amount of effort might make it easier the next time someone needs to work on that same part of the system.

Best approached with caffeine and music

My friend Sonoko, a highly experienced software developer who works on credit-card transaction processing systems, recently sent me an email message. "I thought you'd be amused to know that I've spent the afternoon creating a requirements traceability matrix for one of my projects, and I'm about to die of tedium," Sonoko said. "The requirements spec was 30 pages long, my technical design is 100 pages long, and the matrix is therefore hefty. I know that we have to do them, but I fell asleep two hours ago."

I asked Sonoko some follow-up questions to better understand what she was doing. "Since I make my technical designs available to the business analyst, affected business areas, and project manager, the traceability matrix proves to them that I addressed every requirement they gave me," she replied. "In my design review, I present the design by walking through the traceability matrix, which is logically sequenced by requirement." I asked Sonoko why she was taking the time to create this traceability matrix. She said, "I create it because it ensures that I cover everything, and it provides a quick way for me to see all of the system elements that a given requirement affects."

After working for decades in the software industry, Sonoko clearly understands the value that linking requirements to affected design elements can provide. But, as she points out, it's not a fun chore to wade through such a large volume of information and link the bits together. If the way she approaches technical design permits, it would save time to begin aggregating the trace information as her design begins to stabilize, instead of at the end.

Is requirements tracing feasible? Is it necessary?

You might conclude that accumulating requirements trace information is more expensive than it's worth or that it's not feasible for your project. That's entirely possible. Acquiring a tool with the necessary capabilities, setting it up, entering the data, and keeping it current is expensive and time consuming. You might not need to construct a group memory like this if members of your team possess the necessary knowledge and share it with others when it's needed. Only your team can decide whether requirements tracing—be it just requirements-to-tests or something more elaborate—adds value to your project above its cost.

Consider the following example, though. A conference attendee who worked at an aircraft manufacturer told me that the SRS for his team's part of the company's latest jetliner was a stack of paper six feet thick. They had a complete requirements traceability matrix. I've flown on that very model of airplane, and I was happy to hear that the developers had managed their software requirements so carefully. Managing traces on a huge product with many interrelated subsystems is a lot of work. This aircraft manufacturer knows it is essential. The U.S. Federal Aviation Administration agrees: traceability from requirements to designs is required for certification of aviation software. Similarly, the U.S. Food and Drug Administration advocates that medical device manufacturers demonstrate traceability of a product's requirements into downstream deliverables as part of the validation process for the device.

Even if your products won't cause loss of life or limb if they fail, you should take requirements tracing seriously. At a minimum, consider tracing between business requirements and user requirements to look for alignment, omissions, and unnecessary requirements. The CEO of a major corporation who was present when I described requirements tracing at a seminar asked, "Why *wouldn't* you do this for your strategic business systems?" That's an excellent question. You should decide to use any improved requirements engineering practice based on both the costs of applying the technique and the risks of *not* using it. As with all software processes, make an economic decision to invest your valuable time where you expect the greatest payback.

Next steps

- Set up a trace matrix for 15 or 20 requirements from an important portion of the system you're currently developing. Try the approaches shown in both Tables 29-1 and 29-2. Populate the matrix as the project progresses for a few weeks. Evaluate which method seems most effective and what procedures for collecting and storing traceability information will work for your team.

- The next time you perform maintenance on a poorly documented system, record what you learn from reverse engineering the part of the product you're modifying. Build a fragment of a requirements traceability matrix for the piece of the puzzle you're manipulating so that the next time someone has to work on it they have a head start. Grow the matrix as your team continues to maintain the product.

- Trace your functional requirements back to user requirements, and trace your user requirements to business requirements. Count the requirements that you could cut because they don't link back to a business requirement. Count the requirements that were missing until the trace matrix revealed their absence. Estimate the costs had you not discovered these requirements errors until much later in the project. This analysis will help you judge whether requirements tracing will pay off in your environment.

CHAPTER 30

Tools for requirements engineering

Estelle finally got her SRS document completed and approved. Now James wants to add a requirement, but it messes up the numbering scheme, incrementing the labels for requirements that follow it in that section of the document. Estelle hopes that changing the requirement identifiers won't cause problems for anyone already working from those requirements. Sean requests to delete a requirement. Estelle suspects that the requirement might come back into scope in the future, so she wonders where to put it and how to keep the developers from working on it now. Antonio asked Estelle yesterday why a specific requirement was included, but she didn't have any way to answer that question.

One of the developers, Rahm, asked for a list of all the requirements that he was responsible for on the next release, but Estelle doesn't have any easy way to generate such a list. In fact, it's not easy to keep track of which requirements are scheduled for which release, because they are all stored in the same document. Estelle would like to know the status of requirements that are already under development, but she doesn't have an easy way to find that information either.

Estelle's document-based requirements approach is falling short of her requirements management needs. She needs a tool.

In earlier chapters, we discussed the creation of a natural-language software requirements specification to contain the functional and nonfunctional requirements, as well as documents that contain the business requirements and user requirements. We pointed out that these deliverables are just containers for sets of requirements information; they need not be traditional word-processing documents. Although still widely used, a document-based approach to developing and managing requirements has numerous limitations, including the following:

- It's difficult to keep the documents current and synchronized.

- Communicating changes to all affected team members is a manual process.

- It's not easy to store supplementary information—attributes—about each requirement.

- It's hard to define links between requirements and other system elements.

- Tracking the status of both individual requirements and the entire set of requirements is cumbersome.

- Concurrently managing sets of requirements that are planned for different releases or for related products is tricky. When a requirement is deferred from one release to a later one, a BA needs to manually move it from one requirements specification to another.

- Reusing a requirement generally means that the business analyst must copy the text from the original document into another document for each other system or product where the requirement is to be used.

- It's difficult for multiple project participants to modify the requirements, particularly if the participants are geographically separated.

- There's no convenient place to store proposed requirements that were considered but rejected and requirements that were deleted from a baseline.

- It's hard to create, trace, and track edits to analysis models in the same location as requirements.

- Identifying missing, duplicate, and unnecessary requirements is difficult.

Requirements development (RD) tools and requirements management (RM) tools provide solutions to all of these limitations. RD tools can help you elicit the right requirements for your project and judge whether those requirements are well-written. RM tools help you manage changes to those requirements, track status, and trace requirements to other project deliverables.

A team working on a small project might be able to get away without using any requirements tools, instead using documents, spreadsheets, or simple databases to manage their requirements. Teams working on large projects will benefit from commercial requirements engineering tools. None of these tools replaces a defined process that your team members follow to develop and manage their requirements. Use a tool when you already have an approach that works but that requires greater efficiency. Don't expect a tool to compensate for a lack of business analysis and requirements engineering process, training, discipline, or experience.

> **Trap** Avoid the temptation to develop your own requirements tools or to cobble together general-purpose automation products in an attempt to mimic the commercial requirements products. This initially looks like an easy solution, but it can quickly overwhelm a team that doesn't have the resources to build the tools it really needs.

This chapter presents several benefits of using requirements tools and identifies some general capabilities you can expect to find in such products. Dozens of commercial requirements tools are available. This chapter doesn't contain a feature-by-feature tool comparison, because the products are constantly evolving and their capabilities (and sometimes their vendors) change with each release. RD and RM tools often aren't cheap, but the high cost of requirements-related problems can justify your investment in them. Recognize that the cost of a tool is not simply what you pay for the initial license. The cost also includes annual maintenance fees and periodic upgrades, software installation and configuration, administration, vendor support and consulting, and training for users. Cloud-based solutions eliminate some of these additional support activities and costs. Your cost-benefit analysis should take into account all of the expenses before you make a purchase decision.

Requirements development tools

Requirements development (RD) tools are used by business analysts to work with stakeholders to elicit and document requirements more effectively and more efficiently than with manual methods. Stakeholders will vary in how they best consume and share information: textually, visually, or audibly. RD tools can improve stakeholder collaboration by accommodating a variety of communication methods (Frye 2009). This section subdivides the development tools into elicitation, prototyping, and modeling tools. Some of the tools in the RD category provide all of these services. Some of them also offer requirements management capabilities. In general, RD tools are not as mature as RM tools, and their overall impact on projects is typically less than that of RM tools.

Elicitation tools

Elicitation tools include those used for recording notes during elicitation sessions. These enable the BA to quickly organize ideas and to annotate follow-up questions, action items, core terms, and the like. Mind-mapping tools facilitate brainstorming as well as organizing the information produced. Audio pens and other recording tools allow playback of conversations or provide visual reminders of what happened during an elicitation session. Some recording devices also tie the audio directly to the text that was written at the same time, enabling you to hear specific portions of the audio conversation as needed. Tools that support quality checks, such as scanning a requirements document for vague and ambiguous words, help a BA write clearer requirements. Some elicitation tools convert requirements from text to auto-generated diagrams. Certain tools also enable collaborative voting to help a team prioritize requirements.

Prototyping tools

Prototyping tools facilitate the creation of work products that range from electronic mock-ups to full application simulations. Simple prototyping tools come with basic shapes and designs to create low-fidelity wireframes (Garmahis 2009). Common applications such as Microsoft PowerPoint can be used to quickly mock up screens and the navigations between them or to annotate existing screen shots. Sophisticated tools might enable mocked-up functionality that a user can click through to see just how the application would work. Some prototyping tools support version control, feedback management, requirements linking, and code generation. See the cautions in Chapter 15, "Risk reduction through prototyping," to avoid investing more effort in creating prototypes than is needed to achieve your goals. If you use a tool to create high-fidelity prototypes, make it clear to customers that the prototypes are just possible models and that the final product might be different. Some prototyping tools can show screen mock-ups in a "hand-drawn" style to help manage customer expectations.

Modeling tools

Requirements modeling tools help the BA create diagrams like those described in Chapter 5, "Establishing the business requirements," Chapter 12, "A picture is worth 1024 words," and Chapter 13, "Specifying data requirements." These tools support the use of standard shapes, notations, and syntax for drawing diagrams according to established conventions. They might provide templates as starting points and examples to help the BA learn more about each model. Often these tools automatically connect shapes in diagrams to accelerate the drawing process and to help ensure that the diagrams are drawn correctly. They also enable you to create diagrams that look cleaner and more consistent than if you draw them manually. Specialized software modeling tools facilitate iteration by dragging along connected arrows and labels whenever you move a symbol in the diagram; general-purpose drawing tools might not provide that capability.

Many requirements management tools also provide some modeling capability. The most sophisticated tools allow you to trace individual requirements to models or even to specific elements of models. For example, analysts can create swimlane diagrams in the tool, and then after they write requirements, they can trace those requirements back to specific steps in the diagrams.

Keep in mind that no tool will be able to tell you if a requirement or a model element is missing, logically incorrect, or unnecessary. These tools enable BAs to represent information in multiple ways and to spot certain types of errors and omissions, but they don't eliminate the need for thinking and peer review.

Requirements management tools

An RM tool that stores information in a multiuser database provides a robust solution to the limitations of storing requirements in documents. Small project teams can get away with just entering the requirements text and several attributes of each requirement. Larger project teams will benefit from letting users import requirements from source documents, define attribute values, filter and display the database contents, export requirements in various formats, define traceability links, and connect requirements to items stored in other software development tools.

Requirements management tools have been available for many years. They are both more plentiful and more mature than requirements development tools. To be fair, the problem they solve is more tractable. It's easier to create a database in which to store requirements and provide some capabilities to manipulate them than to help a BA discover new knowledge, craft that knowledge into precise requirement statements and diagrams, and ensure that the resulting information representations are correct. Some tools combine both RD and RM capabilities into a powerful solution aid.

Benefits of using an RM tool

Even if you do a magnificent job of eliciting and specifying your project's requirements, you can lose control of them as development progresses. An RM tool becomes most valuable as time passes and the team members' memories of the requirements details fade. The following sections describe some of the tasks such a tool can help you perform.

Manage versions and changes   Your project should define one or more requirements baselines, each identifying a specific collection of requirements allocated to a particular release or iteration. Some RM tools provide baselining functions. The tools also maintain a history of the changes made to each requirement. You can record the rationale behind each change decision and revert to a previous version of a requirement if necessary. Some tools contain a change-proposal system that links change requests directly to the affected requirements.

Store requirements attributes   You should record several descriptive attributes for each requirement, as discussed in Chapter 27, "Requirements management practices." Everyone working on the project must be able to view the attributes, and selected individuals will be permitted to update attribute values. RM tools generate several system-defined attributes, such as the date a requirement was created and its current version number, and they let you define additional attributes of various data types. Thoughtful definition of attributes allows stakeholders to select subsets of the requirements based on specific combinations of attribute values. A Release Number attribute is one way to keep track of the requirements allocated to various releases.

Facilitate impact analysis   RM tools enable requirements tracing by letting you define links between different types of requirements, between requirements in different subsystems, and between individual requirements and related system components (for example, designs, code modules, tests, and user documentation). These links help you analyze the impact that a proposed change to a specific requirement will have on other system elements. It's also a good idea to trace each functional requirement back to its origin or parent so that you know where it came from. For instance, you might ask to see a list of all the requirements originating from a specific business rule so that you can judge the consequences of a change in that rule. Chapter 28, "Change happens," describes impact analysis, and Chapter 29, "Links in the requirements chain," addresses requirements tracing.

Identify missing and extraneous requirements   The tracing functionality in RM tools helps stakeholders identify requirements that are missing, such as user requirements that have no mapped functional requirements. Similarly, they can reveal requirements that cannot be traced back to a reasonable origin, raising the question of whether those requirements are necessary. If a business requirement is cut from scope, then all the requirements that trace from it can also be cut quickly.

Track requirements status   Collecting requirements in a database lets you know how many discrete requirements you've specified for the product. As Chapter 27 described, tracking the status of each requirement during development supports the overall status tracking of the project.

Control access   RM tools let you define access permissions for individuals or groups of users and share information with a geographically dispersed team through a web interface to the database. Some tools permit multiple users to update the database contents concurrently.

Communicate with stakeholders   An RM tool serves as a master repository so that all stakeholders work from the same set of requirements. Some tools permit team members to discuss requirements issues electronically through threaded conversations. Automatically triggered email messages notify affected individuals when a new discussion entry is made or when a specific requirement is modified. This is a convenient method for visibly tracking decisions made about requirements. Making the requirements accessible online can minimize document proliferation and version confusion.

Reuse requirements   Storing requirements in a database facilitates the reuse of them in multiple projects or subprojects. Requirements that logically fit into multiple parts of the product description can be stored once and referenced whenever necessary, to avoid duplicating requirements. Chapter 18, "Requirements reuse," describes important concepts regarding effectively reusing requirements.

Track issue status   Some RM tools have functionality for tracking open issues and linking each issue to its related requirements. As issues are resolved, it's easy to determine whether any requirements must be updated. You can also quickly find a history of the issue and its resolution. Tracking issues in a tool enables automatic reporting on the status of the issues.

Generate tailored subsets   RM tools allow you to extract and view a set of requirements that fits a particular purpose. For example, you might want a report that contains all of the requirements for a specific development iteration, all of the requirements that relate to a particular feature, or a set of requirements that needs to be inspected.

RM tool capabilities

The feature tree in Figure 30-1 presents a summary of the types of capabilities commonly found in RM tools. You can find detailed feature comparisons of many RM tools online (for example, see Seilevel 2011; INCOSE 2010; Volere 2013).

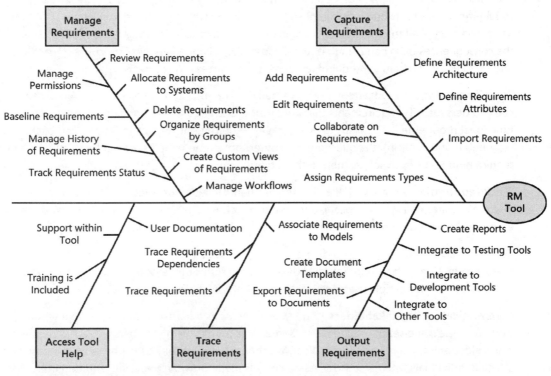

FIGURE 30-1 Common RM tool features.

RM tools let you define different requirement types, such as business requirements, use cases, functional requirements, hardware requirements, and constraints. This lets you differentiate all the types of information that are typically contained in an SRS. Many tools allow you to configure an information architecture (which defines how requirements types and other objects relate to one another) that is customized to your practices. Chapter 29 shows common traceability links that can be defined in the information architecture. Most of the tools provide strong capabilities for defining attributes for each requirement type, a great advantage over the typical document-based approach.

RM tools typically support hierarchical numeric requirement labels, in addition to maintaining a unique internal identifier for each requirement. These identifiers often consist of a short text prefix that indicates the requirement type—such as UR for a user requirement—followed by a unique integer. Some tools provide displays to let you manipulate the hierarchical requirements tree.

Requirements can be imported into an RM tool from various source document formats. The textual description of a requirement is treated simply as a required attribute. Several products let you incorporate nontextual objects such as graphics and spreadsheets into the requirements repository. Other products let you link individual requirements to external files (such as Microsoft Word files, graphics files, and so on) that provide supplementary information that augments the contents of the requirements repository.

Output capabilities from the tools generally include the ability to generate a requirements document in a variety of formats, including predefined or user-specified documents, spreadsheets, and webpages. Some tools allow significant customization for creating templates, allowing you to specify page layout, boilerplate text, attributes to extract from the database, and the text styles to use. Specification documents are then simply reports that are generated from the tool according to certain query criteria, formatted to look like a typical SRS. For example, you could create an SRS that contains all the functional requirements that are allocated to a specific release and assigned to a particular developer. Some tools provide functionality that lets users make changes in exported documents offline, which are then synchronized with the tool's database when the user is back online.

Most tools enable different views of the requirements to be generated within the tool or exported from the tool. Features typically include the ability to set up user groups and define permissions for selected users or groups to create, read, update, and delete projects, requirements, attributes, and attribute values. Setting up appropriate views and permissions facilitates the review of requirements and collaboration to improve those requirements. Some tools also include learning aids, such as tutorials or sample projects, to help users get up to speed.

Requirements management tools generally have robust tracing features. Tracing is handled by defining links between two types of objects or objects of the same type. Some requirements management tools include modeling capabilities that also allow the models to be linked at an element level to individual requirements or to other model elements.

Some agile project management tools also provide RM capabilities. These tools are used to manage and prioritize backlogs, allocate requirements to iterations, and generate test cases directly from requirements.

RM tools often integrate with other tools used in application development, as illustrated in Figure 30-2. Chapter 29 describes how individual requirements can be linked to objects that might reside in these other tools. For instance, you might be able to trace specific requirements to individual design elements stored in a design modeling tool, or to tests stored in a test management tool.

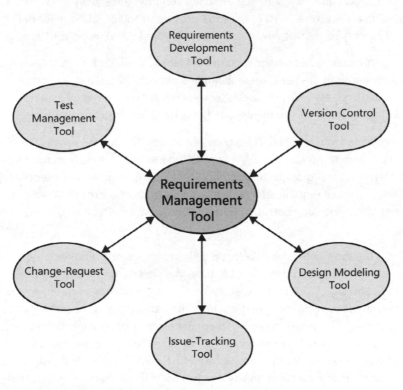

FIGURE 30-2 RM tools integrate with other kinds of software tools.

When you are selecting an RM product, determine whether the tool will be able to exchange data with the other tools you use. Think about how you'll take advantage of these product integrations as you perform your requirements engineering, testing, project tracking, and other processes. For example, consider how you would define trace links between functional requirements and specific design or code elements, and how you would verify that all tests linked back to specific functional requirements have been successfully executed.

Selecting and implementing a requirements tool

Any of these requirements tools can move your requirements practices to a higher plane of sophistication and capability. However, success depends upon selecting the most appropriate tool for your organization and getting your teams to adopt it as part of their routine practices.

Selecting a tool

Select a tool based on the combination of desired features, platform, and pricing that best fits your development environment and culture. Business analysts should lead the selection efforts by defining the evaluation criteria and performing the actual assessment. Some companies outsource tool evaluations to consultants who can assess a company's needs comprehensively and make recommendations from the available tool candidates. If you do the evaluation yourself, the suggestions described in Chapter 22, "Packaged solution projects," for choosing a COTS package also can be applied to selecting a requirements tool. Chapter 22 also offers a real story from one requirements tool evaluation. To summarize the selection process:

1. Identify your organization's requirements for the tool to serve as evaluation criteria.

2. Prioritize and weight the criteria according to what capabilities or other factors matter most to your organization.

3. Set up demos or acquire evaluation copies of the tools you want to consider.

4. Score each tool against the criteria in a consistent manner.

5. Calculate a total score for each tool by using your criteria scores and the weights you assigned to them.

6. For each tool that scored well, use it on an actual project to see if it behaves as you anticipated from the objective scores.

7. To make a final selection, combine the scores, licensing costs, and ongoing costs with information on vendor support, input from current users, and your team's subjective impressions of the products. Two good final questions to ask people who evaluate the tools are, "Which tool would you most want to use?" and, "Which tool would you be most upset about being forced to use?"

Setting up the tool and processes

Recognize that it will take effort to install a tool, load a project's requirements into it, define attributes and trace links, keep the contents current, define access groups and their privileges, and adapt your processes to use the tool. Configuring the tool can be complex; there is a steep learning curve just to set up a sophisticated requirements tool. Management must allocate the resources needed for these operations. Make an organization-wide commitment to actually use the product you select, instead of letting it become expensive shelfware.

 There's little point in using a requirements tool if you don't take advantage of its capabilities. I encountered one project team that had diligently stored all its requirements in an RM tool but hadn't defined any requirement attributes or trace links. Nor did they provide online access for all the stakeholders. The fact that the requirements were stored in a different form didn't provide significant benefits, although it consumed the effort needed to get the requirements into the tool. Another team stored hundreds of requirements in a high-end tool and defined many trace links. Their only use of the information was to generate massive printed traceability reports that were supposed to be reviewed manually for problems. No one actually examined the reports, and no one regarded the database as the authoritative repository of the project's requirements. Neither of these organizations reaped the full benefits of their considerable investments of time and money in the tools.

Even if you select the best available tool, it won't necessarily provide every capability that your organization wants or needs. It might not support your existing requirements templates or processes. You'll still likely need to adapt some of your existing processes to incorporate the tool in them. Expect to have to make some changes to templates, attribute names, and the sequencing of requirements development activities. Consider the following suggestions to overcome process issues as you strive to maximize your return on investment from a requirements tool:

- Assign an experienced BA to own the tool setup and process adaptations. She will understand the impact of configuration choices and process changes.

- Think carefully about the various requirement types that you define. Don't treat every section of your current SRS template as a separate requirement type, but don't simply stuff all of the SRS contents into a single requirement type either.

- Use the tool to facilitate communication with project stakeholders in various locations. Set the access and change privileges to permit sufficient input to the requirements by various people without giving everyone complete freedom to change everything in the database.

- Don't try to capture requirements directly in an RM tool during your early elicitation workshops. As the requirements begin to stabilize, though, storing them in the tool makes them visible to the workshop participants for refinement.

- Use RD tools during elicitation activities only if you are confident that they will not slow down the discovery process and waste your stakeholders' time.

- Don't define trace links until the requirements stabilize. Otherwise, you can count on doing a lot of work to revise the links as requirements continue to evolve.

- To accelerate the movement from a document-based paradigm to the use of the tool, set a date after which the tool's database will be regarded as the definitive repository of the project's requirements. After that date, requirements residing only in word-processing documents won't be recognized as valid requirements.

Provided you remember that a tool can't overcome process deficiencies, you're likely to find that requirements tools greatly enhance the control you have over your software requirements.

Important Don't even pilot the use of an RM tool until your organization can create a reasonable software requirements specification on paper. If your biggest problems are with eliciting and writing clear, high-quality requirements, an RM tool won't help you (although an RD tool might).

Facilitating user adoption

The diligence of the users of your requirements tools is a critical success factor. Dedicated, disciplined, and knowledgeable people will make progress even with mediocre tools, whereas the best tools won't pay for themselves in the hands of unmotivated or ill-trained users. Don't write a check for a tool unless you're willing to respect the learning curve and make the time investment.

Buying a tool is easy; changing your culture and processes to accept the tool and take best advantage of it is much harder. Most organizations already are comfortable with taking elicitation notes in a word-processing document or by hand, and with storing their requirements in documents. Changing to use software-based tools requires a different way of thinking. Using RD tools requires breaking old habits for running elicitation sessions. An RM tool makes the requirements visible to any stakeholder who has access to the database. Some stakeholders interpret this visibility as reducing the control they have over the requirements, the requirements engineering process, or both. Some people prefer not to share an incomplete or imperfect set of requirements with the world, yet the database contents are there for all to see. Keeping the requirements private until they're "done" means you miss an opportunity to have other pairs of eyes scan the requirements frequently for possible problems.

People are often resistant to change things that they're familiar with, and they usually have a comfort level with working on requirements in documents. They might have a perception—even if incorrect—that using a requirements tool will be harder for them. Also, don't forget that most of the tool users are already busy. Time must be allocated to let them get used to using the tool in their daily jobs. Eventually, the tool probably won't actually require more time from users, but they first need to get over the learning curve and develop new work habits using the tool. Following are some suggestions to help you deal with issues regarding user adoption and culture change:

- Identify a tool advocate, a local enthusiast who learns the tool's ins and outs, mentors other users, and sees that it gets employed as intended. This person should be an experienced business analyst who can be the single owner for ensuring tool adoption. This initial tool advocate will work with other users on their projects to ingrain the tool into their daily activities. Then he'll train and mentor others to support the tool as other projects adopt it.

- One of the biggest adoption challenges to overcome is that users don't believe the tool will actually add any value. Perhaps they haven't recognized the pain from limitations of their existing manual approaches. Share stories with them about where the lack of a tool caused a negative impact and ask them to think of their own examples.

- Your team members are smart, but it's better to train them than to expect them to figure out how best to use the tool on their own. They can undoubtedly deduce the basic operations, but they won't learn about the full set of tool capabilities and how to exploit them efficiently.

- Because you can't expect instantaneous results, don't base a project's success on a tool you're using for the first time. Begin with a pilot application of the tool on a noncritical project. This will help the organization learn how much effort it takes to administer and support the tool. Chapter 31, "Improving your requirements processes," describes the learning curve associated with adopting new tools and techniques.

The proliferation and increased usage of tools to assist with requirements development and management represents a significant trend in software engineering that will undoubtedly continue. Too many organizations, though, fail to reap the benefits of their investment in such tools. They do not adequately consider their organization's culture and processes and the effort needed to shift from a document-based requirements paradigm to a tool-based approach. The guidance in this chapter will help you choose appropriate tools and use them effectively. Just remember, a tool cannot replace a solid requirements process or team members with suitable skills and knowledge. A fool with a tool is an amplified fool.

Next steps

- Analyze shortcomings in your current requirements process to see whether a requirements development or requirements management tool is likely to provide sufficient value to justify the investment. Make sure you understand the causes of your current shortcomings; don't simply assume that a tool will magically correct them.

- Before launching a comparative evaluation, assess your organization's readiness for adopting a tool. Reflect on previous attempts to incorporate new tools into your development process. Understand why they succeeded or failed so that you can position yourselves for success this time.

PART V

Implementing requirements engineering

CHAPTER 31

Improving your requirements processes

Everyone agreed that the last few projects had not gone smoothly. As the lead business analyst, Joanne knew that requirements issues had caused at least some of the problems. The BAs on the various projects varied greatly in their education and experience levels. They each used different approaches for developing and managing requirements, just doing the best they could based on what they knew. They each organized their requirements in different ways. Some teams followed effective requirements change processes, which reduced the turmoil in their projects, whereas others reacted to every change request that came along in a knee-jerk fashion. The frustration level was high all around.

Joanne had tried mentoring her less experienced BAs; some were more receptive to her input than others. Some of the teams in Joanne's organization did do a good job on their requirements, and those projects suffered fewer headaches than those of the other teams. Joanne realized that it would be great to bring all of the teams up to a higher level of requirements performance. Maybe now the time was right to get serious about improving their requirements practices. But would the other BAs and their fellow team members play along? Was management truly committed to reducing the pain points? Would anything really change this time, or would this improvement initiative founder on the rocks of indifference, as the earlier ones had?

Previous chapters have described several dozen requirements engineering "good practices" to consider applying in your organization. Putting better practices into action is the essence of software process improvement. In a nutshell, process improvement consists of using more of the approaches that work well for you and avoiding those that have given you headaches in the past. However, the path to improved performance is paved with false starts, resistance from those who are affected, and the challenge of having too little time to handle improvement activities in addition to current tasks.

The ultimate objective of process improvement is to reduce the cost of creating and maintaining software, thereby increasing the value delivered by projects. Ways to accomplish this include:

- Correcting problems encountered on previous projects that arose from process shortcomings.

- Anticipating and preventing problems that you might encounter on future projects.

- Adopting practices that are more efficient and effective than those currently being used.

If your team's current methods seem to work well—or if people insist that they do, despite evidence to the contrary—people might not see the need to change their approach. However, even successful software organizations can struggle when confronted with larger or more complex projects than they are used to, different customers, long-distance collaborations, tighter schedules, or new business domains. Approaches that worked for a team of 5 people with a single customer don't scale up to 100 people located in 3 time zones who are serving 50 corporate customers. At the least, you should be aware of other approaches to requirements engineering that could be valuable additions to your tool kit.

This chapter describes how requirements relate to various other project processes and stakeholders. We present some basic concepts about software process improvement and a suggested process improvement cycle. We also list several useful requirements "process assets" that your organization should have available. The chapter concludes by describing a process improvement road map for implementing improved requirements engineering processes.

How requirements relate to other project processes

Requirements lie at the heart of every well-run software project, supporting and enabling the other technical and management activities. Changes that you make in your requirements development and management approaches will affect these other project processes, and vice versa. Figure 31-1 illustrates some connections between requirements and other project processes; the sections that follow briefly describe these process interfaces.

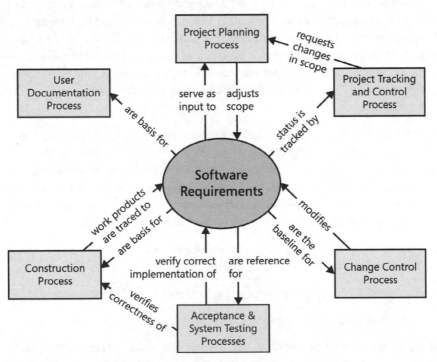

FIGURE 31-1 Relationship of requirements to other project processes.

Project planning   Requirements serve as the foundation of the project planning process. The planners select an appropriate software development life cycle and create resource and schedule estimates based on the requirements. Project planning might indicate that it's not possible to deliver the entire desired feature set within the available bounds of resources and time. The planning process can lead to reductions in the project scope or to the selection of an incremental or staged-release approach to deliver functionality in phases. On an agile project, scope is defined through the set of user stories in the product or release backlog and is incrementally implemented in each iteration. The scope planned for future iterations is based on the velocity measurements from earlier iterations.

Project tracking and control   Project tracking includes monitoring the project's status so the project manager can see whether construction and verification are proceeding as intended. If they are not, management, customers, or other stakeholders might need to request scope modification through the planning process. This would change the requirements set being worked on. On an agile project, scope is adjusted by moving lower-priority items to future iterations if necessary to complete each iteration on schedule.

Change control   After a set of requirements has been baselined, all subsequent changes and additions should be made through a defined change control process. Requirements changes modify the backlog of remaining work to be done and the priorities of the work items in the backlog. Requirements tracing helps you assess the impact of scope changes. As described in Chapter 28, "Change happens," the change control process helps ensure that the right people make informed and well-communicated decisions to accept appropriate requirements changes.

Acceptance and system testing   User requirements and functional requirements are essential inputs to acceptance testing and system testing, respectively. If the expected behavior of the software under various conditions isn't clearly specified, the testers will be hard-pressed to verify that all planned functionality has been implemented as intended. A colleague related her recent experience: "I was assigned to write a test plan for an SRS from another analyst. I ended up going way over the estimated time because I had to wade around to figure out what the functionality was. The related functionality was sometimes in unexpected sections of the SRS. Other times, the analyst who wrote the SRS talked us through the full description of options that were *not* chosen before finally getting to the one that was. It was painful."

Construction   Requirements are the basis for the design and implementation work, and they tie together the various construction work products. Use design reviews to ensure that the designs correctly address all of the requirements. Unit testing can determine whether the code satisfies the design specifications and the pertinent requirements. Requirements tracing lets you identify the software design and code elements that were derived from each requirement.

User documentation   I once worked in an office area that also housed the technical writers who prepared user documentation for complex software products. I asked one of the writers why they worked such long hours. "We're at the end of the food chain," she replied. "We have to respond to the final changes in user interface displays and the features that got dropped or added at the last minute." The product's requirements provide input to the user documentation, so poorly written or late-breaking requirements lead to documentation problems. It's not surprising that the people at the end of the requirements chain, such as technical writers and testers, are often enthusiastic supporters of improved requirements engineering practices and of being engaged earlier in the process.

Requirements and various stakeholder groups

Figure 31-2 shows some of the project stakeholders who might interact with a software development group and some of the contributions they make to a project's requirements activities. If you're the business analyst or project manager, explain to stakeholders in each area the information and participation you need from them if the product development effort is to succeed. Agree on the communication interfaces between the development group and other functional areas, such as a system requirements specification, a market requirements document, or a set of user stories.

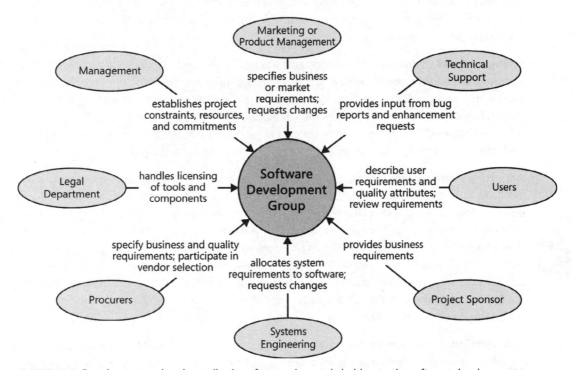

FIGURE 31-2 Requirements-related contributions from various stakeholders to the software development team.

On the flip side, the BA and project manager should ask the other stakeholders what they need from the development team to make their jobs easier. What input about requirements feasibility will help marketing plan their product concepts better? What feedback about requirements status will give the sponsor adequate visibility into project progress? What collaboration with systems engineering will ensure that system requirements are properly partitioned among software and hardware subsystems? The business analyst and project manager should strive to build collaborative relationships between the development team and the other stakeholders of the requirements process.

Gaining commitment to change

When a software organization changes its requirements processes, the interactions it has with other stakeholder communities change as well. People don't like to be forced out of their comfort zone, so expect some resistance to the process changes you propose. Understand the origins of the resistance so you can both respect it and defuse it.

Much resistance comes from fear of the unknown. To reduce this fear, communicate your process improvement rationale. Explain the benefits that the other groups will receive from the new process. Begin from this viewpoint: "Here are the problems we've all experienced. What are the issues from your perspective? Can we put our heads together to figure out a better way to do things here?" Engaging other stakeholders in the improvement initiative leads to shared ownership of the solutions.

Following are some forms of resistance that you might encounter:

- People who are already too busy to get their project work done don't think they have time to invest in adopting better practices. But if you don't invest that time, there's no reason to expect the next project to go more smoothly than the last one.

- A change control process might be viewed as a barrier thrown up by development to make it harder to get changes made. In reality, it is a structure, not a barrier. It permits well-informed people to make good business decisions and to communicate those decisions. The software team must ensure that the requirements change process really does work. If new processes don't yield better results, people will naturally find ways to work around them.

- Some developers and managers view writing and reviewing requirements as bureaucratic time-wasters that delay the "real work" of coding. If you can explain the high cost of continually rewriting the code while the team tries to figure out what the system should do, developers and managers will better appreciate the need for good requirements. Overlooked requirements can reduce profitability during the operational lifetime of a software product, because effort must continually be invested in producing upgrades.

Any time people are asked to change the way they work, the natural reaction is to ask, "What's in it for me?" However, process changes don't always result in fabulous, immediate benefits for each person involved. A better question—and one that deserves a good answer—is "What's in it for *us*?" Every process change should offer clear benefits to the project team, the development organization, the company, and/or the customer. Stakeholders who are asked to spend more time helping to create better requirements just see this as more work for them to do today. But suppose they understand that this investment on their part can pay off significantly with reduced rework later in the project, reduced support costs, and increased value for the customers. This understanding might make them more willing to spend the time now.

It's common for some project stakeholders to be unaware of the requirement-related impacts from the organization's current ways of working. Therefore, an important method for gaining commitment to process change is to make the problems visible in a nonjudgmental and constructive fashion. Suppose the development team builds an application that requires considerable customer support because of user interface problems. If a support team separate from development has to deal with those issues, the development team might not even be aware of the problems. Or suppose management has outsourced development in an attempt to save costs or time, but has not dealt with the resulting communication barriers and cultural differences. If management is not aware of these consequences, they won't have any reason to change their approach to correct the shortcomings.

We've often heard business analysts and other practitioners say that they can't make some process change in their organization without "management support." Too often, management support translates merely into permission to do something different. But as an intelligent professional, you don't need management's permission to work in the best way you know how: that's your job. However, you definitely do need management *commitment* for a project-wide or organization-wide improvement effort to be sustained and successful. Without management commitment, only those practitioners who think that better requirements are important will get on board. It doesn't help if your senior people say they "support" the improvements but then revert to the same old processes as soon as problems arise. Behaviors—not pronouncements—constitute evidence of commitment to quality. Figure 31-3 lists 10 signs that your organization's management is truly committed to excellent requirements processes.

1. Asking that requirements for a project be documented in an appropriate form.
2. Working with the business analyst to provide business requirements for each project.
3. Expecting requirements to be reviewed by appropriate stakeholders, including themselves when appropriate.
4. Asking stakeholders to agree on requirements before implementing each portion of the solution.
5. Ensuring that project plans include time and resources for requirements tasks.
6. Collaborating with other key stakeholders to gain their participation in requirements activities.
7. Establishing effective mechanisms and policies to handle requirements changes.
8. Investing in training, tools, books, and other resources for those involved in requirements activities.
9. Funding and staffing activities to improve the organization's requirements processes.
10. Making the time available for team members to spend on requirements process improvement activities.

FIGURE 31-3 Some behaviors that indicate management's commitment to excellent requirements processes.

Fundamentals of software process improvement

Because you're reading this chapter, presumably you intend to change some of the approaches your organization currently uses for requirements engineering. As you begin your journey, keep in mind the following principles of software process improvement (Wiegers 1996):

1. **Process improvement should be evolutionary and continuous.** Instead of aiming for perfection, develop a few improved templates and procedures and get started with implementation. Adjust your approaches as the team gains experience with the new techniques. Sometimes simple and easy changes can lead to substantial gains, so look for the

low-hanging fruit, problem areas that everyone involved agrees are ripe for improvement. See Table 3-2 in Chapter 3, "Good practices for requirements engineering," for some suggestions of effective practices to implement.

2. **People and organizations change only when they have an incentive to do so.** The strongest incentive for change is pain. Not artificially induced pain, such as management-imposed schedule pressure to make teams work harder, but rather the very real pain people have experienced on previous projects. Following are some examples of problems that can provide compelling drivers for changing your requirements processes:

   - The project missed deadlines because requirements were more extensive than expected.

   - Developers worked a lot of overtime because of misunderstood or ambiguous requirements.

   - System test effort was wasted because the testers didn't understand what the product was supposed to do.

   - The right functionality was present, but users were dissatisfied because of sluggish performance, poor usability, or other quality shortcomings.

   - The organization experienced high maintenance costs because customers requested many enhancements that could have been identified during requirements elicitation.

   - Requirement changes weren't implemented appropriately during the course of the project, so the delivered solution did not meet the customer needs.

   - Edits to requirements were lost or overwritten because multiple BAs were working on them concurrently without a version control process.

   - Customers were not available to clarify and flesh out requirements.

   - Requirements-related issues were not resolved in a timely fashion, causing rework.

3. **Process changes should be goal-oriented.** Before you begin the journey to superior processes, make sure you know your objectives (Potter and Sakry 2002). Do you want to reduce the amount of work that is redone because of requirements problems? Do you want to overlook fewer requirements during implementation? Do you want to cut unneeded features sooner? A road map that defines pathways to your objectives greatly improves your chances of successful improvement.

4. **Treat your improvement activities as mini-projects.** Many improvement initiatives founder because they're poorly planned or because resources never materialize. Include process improvement resources and tasks in an overall project plan. Perform the planning, tracking, measurement, and reporting that you'd do for any project, scaled for the size of the improvement project. Write a simple action plan for each improvement area you tackle.

> **Trap** The single biggest threat to a software process improvement program is lack of management commitment, followed closely by reorganizations that shuffle the program's participants and priorities.

All team members have the opportunity—and the responsibility—to improve how they do their work. If you address something obvious on your own, your fellow team members might well see the merit and adopt the new way of working without fuss. However, a broad process improvement effort can succeed only if management is motivated to commit resources, set expectations, and hold team members accountable for contributing to the change initiative.

Process improvement one-liners

The experienced software process improvement leader accumulates a list of short, pithy observations about this difficult domain. Here are some that we have picked up over the years:

- Take chewable bites. (If you bite into too large a process change, the team might choke on it.)

- Take a lot of satisfaction from small victories. (You won't have many big victories.)

- Use gentle pressure, relentlessly applied. (Steer the team toward a better future by keeping the change initiative visible and continually chipping away at it.)

- Focus, focus, focus. (A busy software team can work on only three, or two, or perhaps just one improvement initiative at a time. But always work on at least one.)

- Look for allies. (Every team has its early adopters who will try out new approaches and give the improvement leaders feedback. Cultivate them. Thank them. Reward them.)

- Action plans that don't turn into actions are not useful. (It's easy to perform a process assessment and to write an action plan. It's hard to get people to work in new ways that hold the promise of better results, yet that's the only useful outcome of process improvement.)

- Everyone has to play. (Get buy-in from team members who have to implement the change by involving them through the assessment and solution discovery parts of the improvement activities.)

Root cause analysis

It's important to focus your limited time and budget for process improvement efforts where they will do the most good. If you can identify the causes of any process shortcomings you've experienced, you can home in on those as high-yield improvement opportunities.

Root cause analysis seeks to identify the underlying factors that contribute to an observed problem, distinguishing symptoms from their causes. Root cause analysis involves asking "why" the problem exists several times in succession, each time probing for the reason that underlies the answer to the previous "why" question. Perform root cause analysis before adopting process changes, to determine why your current approaches aren't already achieving your desired outcomes. Otherwise, it's easy to run around blindly, trying new methods without any confidence that they'll address the real problems.

Sometimes it's not clear which is the problem and which is the root cause. Certain symptoms and root causes chain together, with one symptom being the root cause of another symptom. Suppose you're experiencing a symptom of too many requirements being missed during elicitation. One possible root cause is that the business analysts didn't ask the right questions. This root cause is itself a symptom of another problem, that the people performing the BA role don't know how to do it well.

A *cause-and-effect diagram*—also called a *fishbone diagram* or *Ishikawa diagram*, after its inventor, Kaoru Ishikawa—is a useful way to depict the results of a root cause analysis. Figure 31-4 illustrates a cause and effect diagram that partially analyzes a problem in which an organization's project teams repeatedly fail to complete projects on time. The "bones" in the diagram that branch off the main "backbone" show the answers to the question "Why don't teams finish projects on time?" Additional bones show the answers to subsequent "why" questions. Eventually this analysis reveals fundamental root causes in the most highly branched bones.

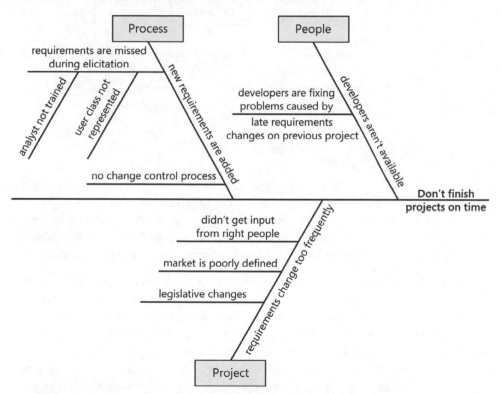

FIGURE 31-4 A cause-and-effect diagram identifying root causes for identified problem symptoms.

You won't have to tackle every root cause you identify by using this type of analysis. The Pareto principle states the familiar 80/20 rule, which suggests that perhaps 20 percent of the vital root causes lead to approximately 80 percent of the observed problems. Even a simple root cause analysis will likely reveal the high-leverage causes that your requirements improvement actions should target.

The process improvement cycle

Figure 31-5 illustrates an effective process improvement cycle. This cycle reflects the importance of knowing where you are before you take off for someplace else, the need to chart your course, and the value of learning from your experiences as part of continuous improvement.

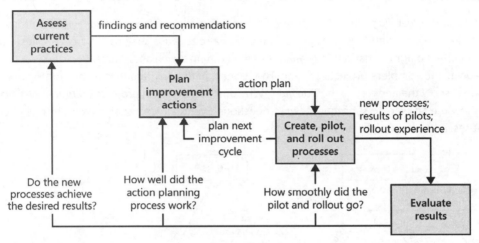

FIGURE 31-5 The software process improvement cycle.

Assess current practices

Step 1 of any improvement activity is to assess the practices currently being used to identify their strengths and shortcomings. The assessment lays the foundation for selecting the changes you should make. It also brings visibility to the processes actually being used in the organization, which are frequently different from the stated or documented processes. And you'll find that different team members often have rather different perspectives as to what processes the team is actually using.

You can evaluate your current requirements processes in several ways. If you tried any of the "Next steps" at the end of previous chapters, you've already begun an informal evaluation of your requirements practices and their results. Appendix B, "Requirements troubleshooting guide," offers dozens of symptoms of common requirements problems, along with possible root causes and possible solutions. Structured questionnaires can reveal insights about your current processes at a low cost. Interviews and discussions with team members provide a more accurate and comprehensive understanding than questionnaires reveal. Formal evaluations by outside consultants produce a list of findings—statements of both strengths and weaknesses in the current processes—and recommendations for addressing the improvement opportunities.

For a simple do-it-yourself approach, use the questionnaire in Appendix A, "Current requirements practice self-assessment," to calibrate your organization's current requirements engineering practices. This self-assessment helps you decide which of your requirements processes are most in need of improvement. Just because you give yourself a low rating on a particular question isn't reason enough to address it immediately or perhaps at all. Focus your energy on improving those practice areas that cause your projects the most difficulties and those that pose risks to the success of your future projects.

Plan improvement actions

In keeping with the philosophy of treating process improvement activities as projects, write an action plan following your current-practices assessment (Potter and Sakry 2002). Tactical action plans target specific improvement areas, such as the ways you elicit or prioritize requirements. Each action plan should identify measurable improvement goals, the participants, and the individual action items that must be completed to implement the plan. Without a plan, it's easy to overlook important tasks. The plan also lets you monitor progress as you track the completion of individual action items.

Figure 31-6 illustrates a process improvement action plan template we've used many times. Include no more than about 10 items in each action plan, scoped such that the plan can be completed in 2 or 3 months. As an example, I saw a plan for requirements management improvements that included these action items:

1. Draft a requirements change control process.

2. Review and revise the change control process.

3. Pilot the change control process with Project A.

4. Revise the change control process based on feedback from the pilot.

5. Evaluate problem-tracking tools, and select one to support the change control process.

6. Procure the problem-tracking tool, and customize it to support the change control process.

7. Roll out the new change control process and tool to the organization.

Assign each action item to a specific individual who is responsible for seeing that the item is completed. Don't assign "the team" as an action item owner. Teams don't do work; individuals do.

If you need more than about 10 action items, focus the initial activity cycle on the most important issues and address the rest later in a separate action plan. Remember, process change is incremental and ongoing. The process improvement road map described later in this chapter illustrates how you can group multiple improvement actions into an overall software process improvement plan.

Action Plan for Requirements Process Improvement

Project: _____   Date: _____

<your project name here>   *<date plan was written>*

Goals:
<State a few goals you wish to accomplish by successfully executing this plan. State the goals in terms of business value, not process changes.>

Measures of Success:
<Describe how you will determine if the process changes are yielding the desired results.>

Scope of Organizational Impact:
<Describe the breadth of impact of the process changes described in this plan.>

Staffing and Participants:
<Identify the individuals who will implement this plan, their roles, and their time commitment on an hours per week or percentage basis.>

Tracking and Reporting Process:
<Describe how progress on the action items in this plan will be tracked and to whom status, results, and issues will be reported.>

Dependencies, Risks, and Barriers:
<Identify any external factors that are required for this plan to succeed or which could prevent successful implementation of the plan.>

Estimated Completion Date for All Activities:
<When do you expect this plan to be fully implemented?>

Action Items:
<Write 3 to 10 action items for each action plan.>

Action Item	Owner	Due Date	Activities	Deliverables	Resources Needed
<Sequence number>	*<Responsible individual>*	*<Target date>*	*<Activities that will be performed to implement this action item>*	*<Procedures, templates, or other process assets that will be created>*	*<Any external resources needed, including materials, tools, documents, or other people>*

FIGURE 31-6 Action plan template for software process improvement.

Create, pilot, and roll out processes

So far, you've evaluated your current requirements practices and crafted a plan for addressing the areas you think are most likely to yield benefits. Now comes the hard part: implementing the plan.

Implementing an action plan means developing processes that you believe will yield better results than your current ways of working do. Don't expect to get the new processes perfect on the first try. Many approaches that seem like a good idea in the abstract turn out to be less pragmatic or less effective than anticipated. Therefore, pilot most of the new procedures or templates you create on a small scale before implementing them for real. Use the knowledge gained from the pilot to adjust the new process. This improves the chance that it will be effective and well received when you roll it out to the affected community. Keep the following suggestions in mind for your process pilots:

- Select pilot participants who will give the new approaches a fair try and provide helpful feedback. These participants could be either allies or skeptics, but they shouldn't strongly oppose the improvement effort.

- Quantify the criteria the team will use to evaluate the pilot's results.

- Identify the stakeholders who need to be informed about the pilot and why it is being performed.

- Consider piloting portions of the new processes on different projects. This engages more people in trying new approaches, which increases awareness, feedback, and buy-in.

- As part of the evaluation, ask pilot participants how they would feel if they had to go back to their former ways of working.

If the pilot was successful, you're ready to make any final adjustments to the process and roll it out to the affected community for implementation. Even motivated and receptive teams have a limited capacity to absorb change, so don't place too many new expectations on a project team at once. Craft a roll-out plan that defines how you'll distribute the new methods and materials to the project teams, and provide sufficient training, coaching, and assistance. Also consider how management will set and communicate their expectations about the new processes.

Evaluate results

The final step of a process improvement cycle is to evaluate the activities performed and the results achieved. This evaluation will help the team do an even better job on future improvement activities. Assess how smoothly the pilots ran. How effective were they in resolving the uncertainties about the new processes? Would you change anything the next time you conduct a process pilot?

Consider how well the rollout of the new processes went. Was the availability of the new processes or templates communicated to everyone affected? Did participants understand and successfully apply the new processes? Would you change anything about how you handle the next rollout?

A critical step is to assess whether the new processes are yielding the desired results. Some new practices deliver visible improvements quickly, but others take time to demonstrate their full value. For example, you should be able to tell quickly whether a new requirements change control process is effective. However, a new document template can take some time to prove its worth as business analysts and other stakeholders get used to it. Give new approaches adequate time to work, and select measures early on that will demonstrate the success of each change.

Accept the reality of the learning curve, the productivity drop that takes place as practitioners take time to assimilate new ways of working, as illustrated in Figure 31-7. This short-term productivity drop—sometimes called the "valley of despair"—is part of the investment your organization is making in process improvement. People who don't understand this might be tempted to abandon the improvement effort before it begins to pay off, thereby achieving a zero—or worse—return on their investment. Educate your managers and peers about the learning curve, and commit to seeing the change initiative through.

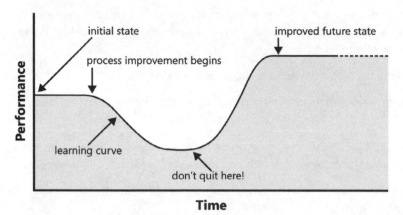

FIGURE 31-7 The learning curve, an unavoidable aspect of process improvement.

Requirements engineering process assets

High-performance projects have effective processes for all of the requirements engineering components: elicitation, analysis, specification, validation, and management. To facilitate the performance of these processes, every organization needs a collection of requirements *process assets* (Wiegers 1998b). A process encompasses the actions you take and the deliverables you produce; process assets help the team members perform processes consistently and effectively. These process assets will help those involved in the project understand the steps they should follow and the work products they're expected to create. Process assets include the types of documents described in Table 31-1.

TABLE 31-1 Types of process assets

Type	Description
Checklist	A list that enumerates activities, deliverables, or other items to be noted or verified. Checklists are memory joggers. They help ensure that busy people don't overlook important details.
Example	A representative of a specific type of work product. Accumulate and share good examples as your project teams create them.
Plan	An outline of how an objective will be accomplished and what is needed to accomplish it.
Policy	A guiding principle that sets a management expectation of behaviors, actions, and deliverables. Processes should enable satisfaction of the policies.
Procedure	A step-by-step description of the sequence of tasks that accomplishes an activity. Describe the tasks to be performed and identify the project roles that perform them. Guidance documents can support a process or procedure with tutorial information and helpful tips.

Type	Description
Process description	A documented definition of a set of activities performed for some purpose. A process description might include the process objective, key milestones, participants, communication steps, inputs and outputs, deliverables, and how to tailor the process to different project situations.
Template	A pattern to be used as a guide for producing a work product. Templates for key project documents provide many "slots" for capturing and organizing information. Guidance text embedded in the template will help the document author use it effectively. Other templates define a structure that is useful for writing a specific type of information, such as a functional requirement, quality attribute, business rule, or user story.

Figure 31-8 identifies some valuable process assets for requirements engineering. These items should be no larger than they need to be to let team members use them consistently and effectively. They need not be separate documents; an overall requirements management process could include the status tracking procedure, change control process, and impact analysis checklist. Store these items in a shared process assets library for ease of access and ready availability, and establish mechanisms for improving them with experience (Wiegers 1998b). Many of the process assets in Figure 31-8 are available with the companion content for this book.

Requirements Development Process Assets

- Requirements development process
- Requirements allocation procedure
- Requirements prioritization procedure
- Vision and scope template
- Use case template
- Software requirements specification template
- Requirements review checklist

Requirements Management Process Assets

- Requirements management process
- Requirements status tracking procedure
- Change control process
- Change control board charter template
- Requirements change impact analysis checklist
- Requirements tracing procedure

FIGURE 31-8 Key process assets for requirements development and requirements management.

Following are brief descriptions of each of the process assets listed in Figure 31-8, along with references to the chapters in which they are discussed further. Each project should plan how it will perform its requirements activities, drawing from and tailoring the contents of the organization's process assets to best suit its needs. For instance, a large project that involves numerous user classes and other stakeholders in multiple locations would benefit from a written elicitation plan that identifies the techniques to be used for eliciting requirements, who will perform them, when, and where. A project that has co-located and highly engaged stakeholders can use a simpler, more agile process.

Requirements development process assets

The items listed here will help your teams do a better job of eliciting, analyzing, specifying, and validating requirements for their projects.

Requirements development process This process describes how to identify and classify stakeholders in your domain and how to plan the elicitation activities. The process describes the requirements deliverables each project is expected to create and the requirements analysis and validation activities to perform. Chapter 7, "Requirements elicitation," describes the contents of an elicitation plan.

Requirements allocation procedure This procedure describes how to allocate high-level product requirements to specific subsystems when you are developing systems that contain both hardware and software components or multiple software subsystems. See Chapter 26, "Embedded and other real-time systems projects," for more about requirements allocation.

Requirements prioritization procedure This procedure describes techniques and tools to be used for prioritizing requirements and dynamically adjusting the backlog contents throughout the project. Chapter 16, "First things first: Setting requirement priorities," describes several prioritization techniques.

Vision and scope template This template guides the project sponsor and the business analyst in thinking through the business objectives, success metrics, product vision, and other elements of the business requirements. Chapter 5, "Establishing the business requirements," recommends a template.

Use case template As described in Chapter 8, "Understanding user requirements," the use case template provides a structured format for describing tasks that users need to perform with a system.

Software requirements specification template The SRS template provides a structured, consistent way to organize the product's functional and nonfunctional requirements. Consider adopting more than one template to accommodate the various types or sizes of projects your organization undertakes. Chapter 10, "Documenting the requirements," describes a sample SRS template.

Requirements review checklist Peer review of requirements documents constitutes a powerful software quality technique. A review checklist identifies the types of errors commonly found in requirements documents, which helps the reviewer to focus his attention on common problem areas. Chapter 17, "Validating the requirements," contains a sample requirements review checklist.

Requirements management process assets

The following items can assist your teams in managing sets of documented requirements.

Requirements management process This process describes the actions a team takes to distinguish versions of the requirements, define baselines, deal with changes, track requirements status, and accumulate traceability information (see Chapter 27, "Requirements management practices"). For a sample requirements management process description, see Appendix J of *CMM Implementation Guide* (Caputo 1998).

Requirements status tracking procedure Requirements management includes monitoring and reporting the status of each functional requirement. See Chapter 27 for more about requirements status tracking.

Change control process   The change control process defines the way that a new requirement or a modification to an existing requirement is proposed, communicated, evaluated, and resolved. Chapter 28 describes the change control process.

Change control board charter template   As described in Chapter 28, the change control board (CCB) charter describes the composition, function, and operating procedures of the CCB.

Requirements change impact analysis checklist   As illustrated in Chapter 28, an impact analysis checklist helps you contemplate the possible tasks, side effects, and risks associated with implementing a specific requirement change, as well as estimating the effort for the tasks.

Requirements tracing procedure   This procedure describes who provides the trace data that connects each requirement to other project artifacts, who collects and manages the data, and how and where it is stored. Chapter 29, "Links in the requirements chain," addresses requirements tracing.

Are we there yet?

As with other journeys, a process improvement initiative should have a goal. If you don't define specific improvement goals, people might not work in alignment, you can't tell whether you're making progress, you can't prioritize improvement efforts, and you can't tell if you've reached your destination. *Metrics* are quantifiable aspects of a software project, product, or process. *Key performance indicators*, or KPIs, are metrics that are tied to a target and reveal your progress toward achieving a specific goal or outcome. A set of KPIs can be displayed in a measurement dashboard that shows how you are approaching meeting your goals.

Keep two considerations in mind when setting process improvement goals. First, remember that process improvement for its own sake is meaningless. Therefore, ask yourself whether achieving that goal would in fact deliver the business value improvements that you seek. Second, you don't want the team members to get frustrated trying to reach a target they cannot realistically attain, so ask yourself whether the goal is achievable in your environment. The answer to both questions must be "yes" for an improvement goal to be appropriate.

Numerous aspects of requirements work on a project can be measured, including product size, requirements quality, requirements status, change activity, and the effort devoted to requirements engineering and management (Wiegers 2006). In addition, measurements of whether the project achieved its business objectives will reflect whether the requirements activities were on target. For process improvement activities, though, you need to select measurement targets that will tell you whether your improvement investments are paying off in the ways you hope they will. We mentioned earlier in this chapter that process improvement should be goal-oriented, and that a great motivator for process change is pain the organization has experienced on previous projects. So select your KPIs by defining quantitative improvement goals and then determining how you could judge whether the pain that led you to choose those goals is lessening.

Note that you can't measure quantitative progress unless you've established a baseline, a reference starting point of how things are working for you today. Ideally, you would measure the current value of some indicator, then set a desired target value you'd like to reach after a certain period of time, and direct your process improvement activities toward achieving that outcome. In reality, many software organizations lack a measurement culture, so they will have difficulty establishing such a quantitative baseline. Nonetheless, it's hard to tell how close you're getting to your objective if you have neither a starting point nor a yardstick.

Table 31-2 lists several possible requirements process improvement goals you might have. For conciseness, we've omitted the suffix "by X <amount> in Y <period of time>" that should be applied to each of these. For each goal, the table suggests possible indicators that would tell whether the changes you're making are paying off as intended. Most measurements of software are lagging indicators. It takes a while for new approaches to demonstrate sustained benefits, so give the new ways of working a chance to take hold and begin to yield benefits.

TABLE 31-2 Possible key performance indicators for certain requirements process improvement goals

Improvement goal	Suggested indicators
Reduce rework performed because of requirements errors	■ Hours of rework at all life-cycle stages attributable to an erroneous, ambiguous, unnecessary, or missing requirement ■ Percentage of requirements that have errors discovered following baselining
Reduce the negative impact of requirements changes	■ Number of new requirements presented after baselining that could have been known beforehand ■ Percentage of requirements that are modified after baselining ■ Number of hours per release or iteration needed to modify deliverables because of requirement changes ■ Distribution of change requests by origin
Reduce the time needed to clarify requirements during development	■ Number of requirements questions and issues raised after baselining ■ Average time needed to resolve each question or issue
Improve estimation accuracy for total requirements development effort	■ Estimated and actual labor hours spent on requirements development activities per release and for the total project
Reduce the number of unneeded features implemented	■ Percentage of committed features that are removed before their implementation begins ■ Percentage of committed features that are removed before delivering a release or iteration

If you're not sure what indicators to select, follow a simple thought process called goal-question-metric or GQM (Basili and Rombach 1988; Wiegers 2007). GQM is a way of thinking backward to figure out what metrics would be valuable. First, state the improvement goals. For each goal, think of questions you would have to answer to judge whether the team is reaching that goal. Finally, identify metrics that will provide an answer for each question. These metrics, or combinations of them, will serve as your key performance indicators.

If you select realistic KPIs for your goals but don't see signs of progress after a reasonable period, you need to investigate:

■ Were the problems correctly analyzed and root causes identified?

■ Did you select improvement actions that directly addressed those root causes?

- Was the plan created to implement those improvement actions realistic? Was the plan executed as intended?

- Has something changed since your original analysis that should lead you to redirect the team's improvement activities?

- Have team members actually adopted new ways of working and pushed through the learning curve to begin applying them in practice?

- Did you set realistic targets that the team had a chance of achieving?

Many points of failure are on the path to improved requirements practices; make sure that your improvement initiative doesn't get caught in one of those traps.

Creating a requirements process improvement road map

Haphazard approaches to process improvement rarely lead to sustainable success. Rather than just diving in, consider developing a road map for implementing improved requirements practices in your organization. If you tried any of the requirements process assessment approaches described in this chapter, you have some ideas about the practices and process assets that would be most helpful to your organization. The process improvement road map sequences improvement actions to yield the greatest and quickest benefits with the smallest investment.

Because every situation is different, there is no one-size-fits-all road map. Formulaic approaches to process improvement don't replace careful thinking, good judgment, and common sense. Figure 31-9 illustrates one organization's road map for improving its requirements processes. The desired business goals are shown (in simplified form) in the boxes on the right side of the figure, and the major improvement activities are shown in the other boxes. The circles indicate intermediate milestones along the paths toward the business goals. *M1* means *milestone 1*. Implement each threaded set of improvement activities from left to right. After you've created a road map, give ownership of each milestone to an individual, who can then write an action plan for achieving that milestone. Then turn those action plans into actions!

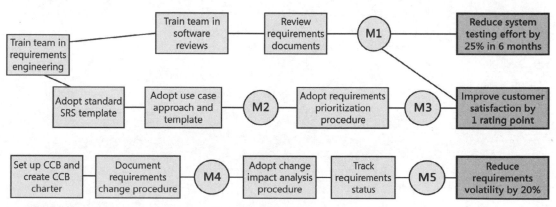

FIGURE 31-9 Sample requirements process improvement road map.

Next steps

- Complete the "Current requirements practice self-assessment" in Appendix A. Identify your top three improvement opportunities for requirements practices, based on the consequences of shortcomings in your current practices.

- Determine which of the process assets listed in Figure 31-8 are not presently available in your organization but would be useful to have.

- Based on the two preceding steps, develop a requirements process improvement road map patterned after that shown in Figure 31-9. Persuade someone in your organization to take responsibility for each milestone. Have each milestone owner use the template in Figure 31-6 to write an action plan for implementing the recommendations leading up to his or her milestone. Track the progress of the action items in the plan as they are implemented.

- Select one new requirements engineering practice from this book to learn more about and try to apply it starting next week—literally! Select two or three additional practices to begin applying within a month. Choose others as long-term improvements, five or six months from now. Identify the situation to which you want to apply each new practice, the benefits that you hope it will provide, and any help or additional information you might need. Think about whose cooperation you'll need to use the new techniques. Identify any barriers that might impede your ability to use the practice and consider who could help you break down those barriers.

CHAPTER 32

Software requirements and risk management

Dave, the project manager for the Chemical Tracking System at Contoso Pharmaceuticals, is meeting with his lead programmer, Helen, and the lead tester, Ramesh. All are excited about the new project, but they remember the problems they ran into on an earlier project called the Pharm Simulator.

"Remember how we didn't find out that the users hated the Simulator's user interface until beta testing?" Helen asked. "It took us four weeks to rebuild it and retest it. I sure don't want to go through that death march again."

"That was awful," Dave agreed. "It was also annoying that the users we talked to swore they needed a lot of features that no one has used so far. That drug interaction modeling feature took three times longer to code than we expected, and we wound up throwing it out. What a waste!"

Ramesh had a suggestion. "Maybe we should list these problems from the Simulator so we can try to avoid them on the Chemical Tracking System. I read an article on software risk management that said we should identify risks up front and figure out how to prevent them from hurting the project."

"I don't know about that," Dave protested. "We probably won't have those same problems again. If we write down things that could go wrong on the Chemical Tracking System, it'll look like I don't know how to run a software project. I don't want any negative thinkers on this project. We have to plan for success!"

As Dave's final comment suggests, software engineers and project managers are eternal optimists. We often expect our next project to run smoothly, despite the history of problems on earlier projects. The reality is that dozens of potential pitfalls can delay or derail a software project. Contrary to Dave's beliefs, software teams *must* identify and control their project risks, beginning with those related to requirements.

A *risk* is a condition that could cause some loss or otherwise threaten the success of a project. This condition hasn't actually caused a problem yet—and you'd like to keep it that way. These potential problems might have an adverse impact on the project's cost, schedule, or technical success; the product's quality; or the team's effectiveness. *Risk management* is the process of identifying, evaluating, and controlling risks before they harm your project. If something untoward has already happened on the project, it's an issue, not a risk. Deal with current problems and issues through your project's ongoing status tracking and corrective action processes.

Because no one can predict the future with certainty, risk management is used to minimize the likelihood or impact of potential problems. Risk management means dealing with a concern before it becomes a crisis. This improves the chance of project success and reduces the financial or other consequences of those risks that you can't avoid. Risks that lie outside the team's sphere of control should be directed to the appropriate level of management for attention.

Because requirements play such a central role in software projects, the prudent project manager will identify requirements-related risks early and control them aggressively. Typical requirements risks include misunderstanding the requirements, inadequate user involvement, uncertain or changing project scope and objectives, and continually changing requirements. Project managers can control requirements risks only through collaboration with customers and other stakeholders. Jointly documenting requirements risks and planning mitigation actions reinforces the customer-development partnership that was discussed in Chapter 2, "Requirements from the customer's perspective."

Simply knowing about the risks doesn't make them go away, so this chapter presents a brief tutorial on software risk management (Wiegers 2007). Later in the chapter, we also describe a number of risk factors that can raise their ugly heads during requirements engineering activities. Use this information to launch an attack on your requirements risks before they attack your project.

Fundamentals of software risk management

Projects face many kinds of risks besides those related to requirements. Dependence on an external entity, such as a subcontractor or another project that is providing components to be reused, is a common source of risk. Project management is fraught with risks from poor estimation, rejection of accurate estimates by managers, insufficient visibility into project status, and staff turnover. Technology risks threaten highly complex and leading-edge development projects. Lack of knowledge is another source of risk, such as with practitioners who have insufficient experience with the technologies being used or with the application domain. Transitioning to a new development method introduces a raft of new risks. And ever-changing, imposed government regulations can disrupt the best-laid project plans.

Scary! This is why all projects need to take risk management seriously. Risk management involves scanning the horizon for icebergs, rather than steaming full speed ahead with great confidence that your ship is unsinkable. As with other processes, scale your risk management activities to your project's size. Small projects can get by with a simple risk list, but formal risk management planning is a key element of a successful large-scale project.

Elements of risk management

Risk management involves the application of tools and procedures to contain project risk within acceptable limits. It provides a standard approach to identify and document risk factors, evaluate their potential severity, and propose strategies for mitigating them (Williams, Walker, and Dorofee 1997). Risk management includes the activities shown in Figure 32-1 (adapted from McConnell [1996]).

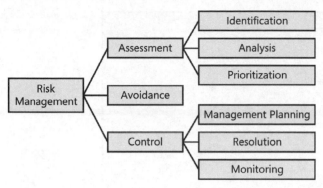

FIGURE 32-1 Elements of risk management.

Risk assessment is the process of examining a project to identify potential threats. Facilitate *risk identification* with lists of common risk factors such as those described in the "Requirements-related risks" section later in this chapter or with other public lists of typical risks (for example, Carr et al. 1993; McConnell 1996). During *risk analysis*, you'll examine the potential consequences of specific risks to your project. *Risk prioritization* helps you focus on the most severe risks by assessing the potential *risk exposure* from each. Risk exposure is a function of both the probability of incurring a loss due to the risk and the potential magnitude of that loss.

Risk avoidance is one way to deal with a risk: don't do the risky thing. You can avoid some risks by not undertaking certain projects, by relying on proven rather than cutting-edge technologies and development methods, or by excluding features that will be especially difficult to implement. Software development is intrinsically risky, though, so avoiding risk might also mean losing opportunities.

Most of the time you'll have to perform *risk control* activities to manage the top-priority risks you identified. *Risk management planning* produces a plan for dealing with each significant risk, including mitigation approaches, contingency plans, owners, and timelines. Mitigation actions try either to prevent the risk from becoming a problem at all or to reduce the adverse impact if it does. The risks won't control themselves, so *risk resolution* involves executing the plans for mitigating each risk. Finally, track your progress toward resolving each risk item through *risk monitoring*, which should become part of your routine project status tracking. Monitor how well your risk mitigation actions are working, look for new risks that have popped up, retire risks whose threat has passed, and update the priorities of your risk list periodically.

Documenting project risks

It's not enough to simply recognize the risks that face your project. You need to manage them in a way that lets you communicate risk issues and status to stakeholders throughout the project's duration. Figure 32-2 shows a template for documenting an individual risk statement. You might find it more convenient to store this information in tabular form, such as a spreadsheet, which makes it easy to sort the list of risks in various ways, or in a database. Keep the risk list separate from project plans so that it's easy to update throughout the project's duration.

```
ID:
<sequence number>

Submitter:
<individual who brought this risk to the team's attention>

Date Opened:
<date the risk was identified>

Date Closed:
<date the risk was closed out>

Risk Statement:
<statement of the risk in the form "condition-consequence">

Scope of Impact:
<project teams, business areas, and functional areas the risk could affect>

Probability:
<the likelihood of the risk becoming a problem>

Impact:
<numerical rating of the potential damage if the risk does become a problem>

Exposure:
<probability multiplied by impact>

Risk Management Plan:
<one or more approaches to control, avoid, minimize, or otherwise mitigate the risk>

Contingency Plan:
<course of action to follow if the risk management plan is not effective>

Owner:
<individual responsible for resolving the risk>

Date Due:
<date by which the mitigation actions are to be implemented>
```

FIGURE 32-2 Risk item tracking template.

Use a *condition-consequence* format when you document risk statements. That is, state the risk condition that you are concerned about, followed by the potential adverse outcome—the consequence—from that condition. Often, people who suggest risks state only the condition ("the customers don't agree on the product requirements") or the consequence ("we can satisfy only one of our major customers"). Pull these statements together into the condition-consequence structure: "If the customers don't agree on the product requirements, then we might be able to satisfy only one of our major customers." One condition might lead to several consequences, and several conditions can result in the same consequence.

The template provides spaces to record the probability of a risk materializing into a problem, the negative impact on the project as a result of that problem, and the overall risk exposure. I like to estimate the probability on a scale from 0.1 (highly unlikely) to 1.0 (certain to happen), and the impact on a relative scale of 1 (no problem) to 10 (big trouble). Even better, try to rate the potential impact in units of lost time or money. Multiply the probability by the impact to estimate the exposure from each risk.

Don't try to quantify risks too precisely. Your goal is to differentiate the most threatening risks from those you don't need to tackle immediately. You might find it easier simply to estimate both probability and impact as high, medium, or low. Those items that have at least one *high* rating demand your early attention.

Use the Risk Management Plan field to identify the actions you intend to take to control the risk. Some mitigation strategies work to reduce the risk probability, others to reduce the impact. Consider the cost of mitigation when planning. It doesn't make sense to spend $20,000 to control a risk with a maximum estimated impact of only $10,000 if it materialized into a problem. You might also devise contingency plans for the most severe risks to anticipate what actions to take if, despite your efforts, the risk does affect your project. Assign every risk that you plan to control to an individual owner, and set a target date for completing the mitigation actions. Long-term or complex risks might require a multistep mitigation strategy.

Figure 32-3 illustrates a risk that the Chemical Tracking System team leaders discussed at the beginning of this chapter. The team estimated the probability and impact on the basis of their previous experience. Until they evaluate other risks, they won't know how serious a risk exposure of 4.2 is—risk exposures are relative. The first two mitigation approaches reduce the probability of this risk becoming a problem by increasing user involvement in the requirements process. Prototyping reduces the potential impact by seeking early feedback on the user interface.

ID: 1   **Submitter:** Yuhong Li

Date Opened: 8/22/13   **Date Closed:** (open)

Risk Statement:
If we have insufficient user involvement in requirements elicitation, then we might need to perform extensive user interface rework after beta testing.

Scope of Impact:
Could affect entire system, including any customizations done on integrated COTS components.

Probability: 0.6   **Impact:** 7   **Exposure:** 4.2

Risk Management Plan:
1. Specify usability requirements during early elicitation activities.
2. Hold facilitated workshops with product champions to develop the requirements.
3. Develop a throwaway mock-up prototype of core functionality with input from product champions.
4. Have members of several user classes evaluate the prototype.

Contingency Plan:
Bring in an expert usability consultant to ensure that the UI conforms to established best practices for human-computer interface design.

Owner: Reina Cabatana   **Date Due:** 2/13/14

FIGURE 32-3 Sample risk item from the Chemical Tracking System.

Planning for risk management

A risk list is not the same as a risk management plan. For a small project, you can include your plans for controlling risks in the software project management plan. A large project should write a separate risk management plan that spells out the approaches it intends to take to identify, evaluate, document, and track risks. This plan should include the roles and responsibilities for the risk management activities. A risk management plan template is available with this book's companion content. Many projects appoint a project risk manager to be responsible for staying on top of the things that could go wrong. One company dubbed their risk manager "Eeyore," after the gloomy Winnie-the-Pooh character who constantly bemoaned how bad things could become.

> **Trap** Don't assume that risks are under control just because you identified them and selected mitigation actions. Follow through on the risk management actions. Include enough time for risk management in the project schedule so that you don't waste your investment in risk planning. Include risk mitigation activities, risk status reporting, and updating the risk list in your project's task list.

Establish a rhythm of periodic risk monitoring. Keep the 10 or so risks that have the highest risk exposure visible, and track the effectiveness of your mitigation approaches regularly. When a mitigation action is completed, reevaluate the probability and impact for that risk item and then update the risk list and any other pending mitigation plans accordingly. A risk is not necessarily under control simply because the mitigation actions have been completed. You need to judge whether your mitigation approaches have reduced the exposure to an acceptable level or whether the opportunity for a specific risk to become a problem has passed.

Out of control

A project manager once asked me what to do if the same items remained on his top-five risk list week after week. This suggests that the mitigation actions for those risks aren't being implemented, that they aren't effective, or that there's no way for the team to control those risks. If your mitigation actions are effective, the exposure from risks that you are attempting to control will decrease. This lets other risks that were less threatening than the initial top five float up to the top of the risk list and engage your attention. Periodically reassess the probability of each risk materializing, and the potential loss if it does, to see whether your risk mitigation activities are getting the job done.

Requirements-related risks

The risk factors described on the following pages are organized by the five requirements engineering subdisciplines of elicitation, analysis, specification, validation, and management. Techniques are suggested that can reduce each risk's probability or impact. This list is just a starting point;

accumulate your own list of risk factors and mitigation strategies based on the lessons you learn from each project. Theron Leishman and David Cook (2002) describe additional risks related to software requirements. Be sure to write your risk statements in the condition-consequence format.

Requirements elicitation

Numerous factors can conspire to hamper your requirements elicitation efforts. Following are several areas of potential elicitation risk and suggestions for how to avoid them.

Product vision and project scope   Scope creep is more likely if the stakeholders lack a shared understanding of what the product is supposed to be (and not be) and do. Early in the project, write a vision and scope document that contains your business requirements, and use it to guide decisions about new or modified requirements.

Time spent on requirements development   Tight project schedules often pressure managers and customers into glossing over the requirements because they believe that if the developers don't start coding immediately, they won't finish on time. Record how much effort you actually spend on requirements development for each project so that you can judge whether it was sufficient and improve your planning for future projects. Agile development approaches allow construction to begin earlier than on projects following a waterfall life cycle.

Customer engagement   Insufficient customer involvement during the project increases the chance of an expectation gap. Identify stakeholders, customers, and user classes early in the project. Determine who will serve as the literal voice of the user for each user class. Engage key stakeholders as product champions. Make sure product champions fulfill their commitments so you elicit the correct needs.

Completeness and correctness of requirements specifications   Elicit user requirements that map to business requirements to ensure that the solution will deliver what the customers really need. Devise usage scenarios, write tests from the requirements, and have customers define their acceptance criteria. Create prototypes to make the requirements more meaningful for users and to elicit specific feedback from them. Enlist customer representatives to review the requirements and analysis models.

Requirements for innovative products   It's easy to misgauge market response to products that are the first of their kind. Emphasize market research, build prototypes, and use focus groups to obtain early and frequent customer feedback about your innovative product visions.

Defining nonfunctional requirements   Because of the natural emphasis on product functionality, it's easy to neglect nonfunctional requirements. Query customers about quality characteristics such as performance, usability, security, and reliability. Document these nonfunctional requirements and their acceptance criteria as precisely as you can.

Customer agreement on requirements   If the diverse customers for your system don't agree on what you should build, someone will be unhappy with the result. Determine who the primary customers are, and use the product champion approach to get adequate customer representation and involvement. Make sure you're relying on the right people for making decisions about requirements. Have appropriate stakeholder representatives review the requirements.

Unstated requirements   Customers often hold implicit expectations that are neither communicated nor documented. Try to identify any assumptions the customers might be making. Use open-ended questions to encourage customers to share more of their thoughts, wishes, ideas, information, and concerns than you might otherwise hear. Asking customers what would make them reject the product might reveal some topics that have not yet been explored.

Existing product used as the requirements reference   Requirements development might not be deemed important on next-generation or replacement projects. Developers are sometimes told to use the existing product as their source for requirements, with a list of changes and additions. Chapter 21, "Enhancement and replacement projects," suggested some ways to reverse-engineer requirements from an existing application.

Solutions presented as needs   User-proposed solutions can mask the users' actual needs, lead to automating ineffective business processes, and overconstrain the developers' design options. The analyst must drill down to understand the intent—the real requirement—behind a solution the customer has presented.

Distrust between the business and the development team   As you have seen throughout this book, effective requirements engineering demands close collaboration among various stakeholders, particularly customer communities (the business side for IT projects) and developers. If these parties do not feel that their counterparts are working in good faith toward a mutually beneficial outcome, conflicts can arise and requirements elicitation can be threatened.

Requirements analysis

It isn't prudent to just record whatever the customer tells you and dive into development. Requirements analysis poses its own threat areas, as described below.

Requirements prioritization   Ensure that every functional requirement, feature, or user requirement is prioritized and allocated to a specific system release or iteration. Evaluate the priority of new requirements against the backlog of work remaining to be done, so that you can make appropriate trade-off decisions and iteration plans.

Technically difficult features   Evaluate the feasibility of each requirement to identify those that might take longer than anticipated to implement. Use status tracking to watch for requirements that are falling behind their implementation schedule. Take corrective action as early as possible. Prototype the novel or risky requirements to select effective approaches.

Unfamiliar technologies, methods, languages, tools, or hardware   Don't underestimate the learning curve of getting up to speed with new techniques that are needed to satisfy certain requirements. Identify those high-risk requirements early on, and work with the development team to allow sufficient time for false starts, learning, and experimentation.

Requirements specification

Requirements are all about communication. Just because requirements are communicated on paper or in writing doesn't mean they are actually understood.

Requirements understanding   Different interpretations of the requirements by developers and customers lead to expectation gaps, in which the delivered product fails to satisfy customer needs. Peer review of requirements by developers, testers, and customers can mitigate this risk. Trained and experienced business analysts will acquire the right information and write high-quality specifications. Creating models and prototypes that represent the requirements from multiple perspectives can reveal fuzzy, ambiguous requirements.

Time pressure to proceed despite open issues   It is a good idea to mark areas of the requirements that need further work with TBD (to be determined) or as issues, but it's risky to proceed with construction if these haven't been resolved. Record who is responsible for closing each open issue and the target date for resolution.

Ambiguous terminology   Create a glossary to define business and technical terms that might be interpreted differently by different readers. Requirements reviews can help participants reach a common understanding of terms and concepts.

Design included in requirements   Design elements that are included in the requirements place constraints on the options available to developers. Unnecessary constraints inhibit the creation of optimal designs. Review the requirements to make sure they emphasize what needs to be done to solve the business problem, rather than dictating the solution.

Requirements validation

Even if you've done a good job on requirements elicitation, it's important to confirm the quality and validity of the solution that the requirements specify. Validation offers the following pitfalls.

Unvalidated requirements   The prospect of reviewing a lengthy requirements specification is daunting, as is the idea of writing tests very early in the development process. However, if you confirm the correctness and quality of each set of requirements before their implementation, you can avoid considerable expensive rework later. Include time and resources for these quality activities in the project plan. Gain commitment from your customer representatives to participate in requirements reviews. Perform incremental, informal reviews to find problems as early and cheaply as possible.

Inspection proficiency   If inspection participants do not know how to inspect requirements effectively, they might miss serious defects. Train all team members who will participate in inspections of requirements documents. Invite an experienced inspector from your organization or an outside consultant to observe your early inspections to coach the participants.

Requirements management

Much of the requirements-related risk on a software project comes from how changes are handled. Those and other requirements management risks are mentioned below.

Changing requirements   You can control rampant scope creep by using documented business requirements and scope definitions as the benchmark for approving changes. A collaborative elicitation process with extensive user involvement can cut requirements creep nearly in half (Jones 1996a). Detecting requirements errors early reduces the number of modifications requested later on. Design the system for easy modifiability, particularly when you are following an iterative life cycle.

Requirements change process   Risks related to how requirements changes are handled include not having a defined change process, using ineffective change mechanisms, failing to incorporate valuable changes efficiently, and incorporating changes that bypass the process. A requirements change process that includes impact analysis, a change control board, and a tool to support the process is an important starting point. Clear communication of changes to the affected stakeholders is essential.

Unimplemented requirements   Requirements tracing helps you avoid overlooking any requirements during design, construction, or testing.

Expanding project scope   If requirements are poorly defined initially, further clarification can expand the scope of the project. Vaguely specified areas of the product will consume more effort than anticipated. The project resources that were allocated according to the initial incomplete requirements might be insufficient to implement the full scope of user needs. To mitigate this risk, plan on a phased or incremental delivery life cycle. Implement the top priority functionality in the early releases, and elaborate the system's capabilities in later iterations.

Risk management is your friend

A project manager can use risk management to raise the awareness of conditions that could cause the project to suffer. Consider the manager of a new project who's concerned about getting appropriate users involved in requirements elicitation. The astute manager will realize that this condition poses a risk and will document it in the risk list, estimating the probability and impact based on previous experience. If time passes and users still are not involved, the risk exposure for this item will increase, perhaps to the point where it compromises the project's success. I've been able to convince managers to postpone a project that could not engage sufficient user representatives by arguing that we shouldn't waste the company's money on a doomed project.

Periodic risk tracking keeps the project manager apprised of the threat from identified risks. Escalate risks that aren't adequately controlled to senior managers, who can either initiate corrective actions or make a conscious business decision to proceed despite the risks. Risk management helps you keep your eyes open and make informed decisions, even if you can't control or avoid every adversity your project might encounter.

Next steps

- Identify several requirements-related risks facing your current project. Don't identify known problems as risks, only things that haven't happened yet. Document the risks by using the template in Figure 32-2. Suggest at least one possible mitigation approach for each risk that you choose to control. Are there any risks that you are going to simply accept and hope they don't bite you?

- Hold a risk brainstorming session with key project stakeholders. Identify as many requirements-related risks as you can. Evaluate each for its probability of occurrence and relative impact, and multiply these together to calculate the risk exposure. Sort the risk list in descending order by risk exposure to identify your top five requirements-related risks. For each one, identify actions that can be taken to mitigate the risk. Assign each action to an individual to implement.

- Build your own list of potential requirements risks facing your organization. Start with the ones in this chapter, then augment the list based on actual project experiences. This rich risk list will help each future project manager identify his own risks early on.

Epilogue

Nothing is more important to a software project's success than understanding what problems it needs to solve. Requirements provide the foundation for that success. If the development team and its customers don't agree on the product's capabilities and characteristics, the most likely outcome is one of those unpleasant software surprises that we'd all prefer to avoid. If your current requirements practices aren't giving you the results you need, selectively and thoughtfully apply the techniques presented in this book that you think might help. Effective requirements engineering involves:

- Engaging customer representatives early and extensively.

- Developing requirements iteratively and incrementally.

- Representing the requirements in various ways to make sure everyone understands them.

- Assuring the requirements' completeness and correctness with all stakeholder groups.

- Finding the right supporting technology and practices to enable a shared view and ensure requirements integrity.

- Controlling the way that requirements changes are made.

Changing the way an organization works is difficult. It's hard to acknowledge that your current approaches aren't working as well as you'd like and to figure out what to try next. It's hard to find the time to learn about new techniques, develop improved processes, pilot and adjust them, and roll them out to the rest of the organization. And it can be difficult to convince the various stakeholders that change is needed. However, if you don't change the way your teams work, there's no reason to believe that the next project will go any better than the last one.

Success in software process improvement depends on:

- Focusing on a few clear pain points at a time.

- Setting clear goals and defining action plans for your improvement activities.

- Addressing the human and cultural factors associated with organizational change.

- Persuading everyone to view process improvement as a strategic investment in business success.

Keep these process improvement principles in mind as you define a road map to improved requirements engineering performance. Stay grounded in practical approaches that are appropriate for your organization and team. If you actively apply known good practices and rely on common sense, you can significantly improve how you handle your project's requirements, with all the advantages and benefits that brings. And remember that without excellent requirements, software is like a box of chocolates: you never know what you're going to get.

Current requirements practice self-assessment

This appendix contains 20 questions that you can use to calibrate your team's current requirements engineering practices and to identify areas to reinforce. You can download a copy of this assessment and a spreadsheet to help you analyze the responses from the companion content website for this book. More comprehensive assessments are available if you want to get a more precise understanding of what aspects of your current practices and documents would benefit most from improvement. Seilevel (2012) offers a thorough project assessment that can be adapted to evaluate your organization's requirements practices and deliverables.

To complete the quick assessment in this appendix, select the response for each question that most closely describes the way your team currently deals with that requirements issue. If you want to quantify the self-assessment, give yourself 0 points for each (a) response, 1 point for each (b), 3 points for each (c), and 5 points for each (d) response [except for question 16, where both (c) and (d) are worth 5 points]. The maximum possible score is 100 points. Generally speaking, the higher the score, the more mature—and likely more effective—your requirements practices are. Each question refers you to the chapter or chapters that address the topic of the question.

Instead of just trying to achieve a high score, use this self-assessment to spot opportunities to apply new practices that might benefit your organization. Some questions might not pertain to the kind of software your organization develops. Also, situations are different; not every project needs the most rigorous approaches. Recognize, though, that informal approaches to requirements increase the likelihood that your team will end up doing excessive rework. Most organizations will benefit from following the practices represented by the "c" and "d" responses.

The people you select to complete the assessment could influence the results. Watch out for respondents who, rather than describing what's really going on in the organization, might bias their responses based on politics, on what they wish was being done, or on what they think the "correct" answers should be. Asking multiple people to complete the self-assessment independently will help remove some of that bias and provide a more realistic representation of your current practices than asking just one person. Multiple responders might also reveal different understandings of how certain practices are being performed at present. You can use the spreadsheet tool provided on the companion content website to accumulate multiple sets of responses and view the distribution.

1. How are the project's business requirements defined, communicated, and used? [Chapter 5]

   a. We sometimes write a high-level product description early on, but we don't refer back to it.

   b. The person who conceives the product knows the business requirements and discusses them verbally with the development team.

   c. We record business requirements in a vision and scope, project charter, or similar document according to a standard template. All project stakeholders have access to this document.

   d. We actively use the documented business requirements on our project, evaluating proposed product features and requirement changes to see whether they lie within the documented scope, and adjusting scope as needed based on business objectives.

2. How are the user communities for the product identified and characterized? [Chapter 6]

   a. The developers think they know who our users will be.

   b. Marketing or the project sponsor believes that they know who the users are.

   c. Target user groups or market segments are identified by management or marketing from some combination of market research, our existing user base, and input from other stakeholders.

   d. The project stakeholders identify distinct user classes, whose characteristics are summarized in the software requirements specification.

3. How do you elicit customer input on the requirements? [Chapter 7]

   a. The developers are confident that they already know what to build.

   b. Typical users are surveyed with questionnaires or interviewed in focus groups.

   c. We meet with people, sometimes one on one and sometimes in groups, and they tell us what they want.

   d. A variety of elicitation techniques are used, including interviews and workshops with user class representatives, document analysis, and system interface analysis.

4. How well trained and how experienced are your business analysts? [Chapter 4]

   a. They are developers or former users who have little experience and no specific training in software requirements engineering.

   b. Developers, experienced users, or project managers who have had some previous exposure to requirements engineering perform the BA role.

   c. The BAs have had several days of training and considerable experience in collaborating with users.

d. We have professional business analysts or requirements engineers who are trained and proficient in interviewing techniques, the facilitation of group sessions, technical writing, and modeling. They understand both the application domain and the software development process.

5. How are the high-level system requirements allocated to the software portions of the product? [Chapters 19 and 26]

   a. Software is expected to overcome any shortcomings in the hardware.

   b. Software and hardware engineers discuss which subsystems should perform which functions.

   c. A system engineer or an architect analyzes the system requirements and decides which ones will be implemented in each software subsystem.

   d. Knowledgeable team members collaborate to allocate portions of the system requirements to software subsystems and components and to trace them into specific software requirements. Component interfaces are explicitly defined and documented.

6. To what extent are requirements reused on your projects? [Chapter 18]

   a. We do not reuse requirements.

   b. A business analyst who is familiar with previous projects sometimes knows of requirements that can be reused on a new project, so she copies and pastes the requirements into the new specification.

   c. A business analyst can search through the previous projects stored in our requirements management tool for requirements that are relevant to his new project. He can reuse specific versions of those requirements by using the functions built into the tool.

   d. We have established a repository of potentially reusable requirements, which have been adapted and improved from previous projects. BAs routinely check this repository for requirements that might be usable on their current projects. We use trace links to pull in child requirements, dependent requirements, design elements, and tests when possible when we are reusing a requirement.

7. What approaches are used when working with stakeholders to identify the specific software requirements? [Chapters 7, 8, 12, and 13]

   a. We begin with a general understanding, write some code, show the software to some users, and modify the code until they're happy.

   b. Management or marketing provides a product concept, and the developers write the requirements. Customer stakeholders tell the development team if they've missed anything.

    c.   Marketing or customer representatives tell the development team what features and functions the product should contain. Sometimes marketing tells the development team when the product direction changes.

    d.   We hold structured requirements elicitation interviews or workshops with representatives from the different user classes for the product. We employ use cases or user stories to understand the users' goals, and we create analysis models to help ensure we identify all the functional requirements. We flesh out the requirements incrementally and iteratively, giving the customers numerous opportunities to improve them.

8. How are the software requirements documented? [Chapters 10, 11, 12, and 30]

    a.   We piece together oral history, email and voice mail messages, interview notes, and meeting notes.

    b.   We write unstructured narrative textual documents, or we create simple requirements lists, or we draw some diagrams.

    c.   We write requirements in structured natural language according to a standard template. Sometimes we augment these requirements with visual analysis models that use standard notations.

    d.   We create requirements and visual analysis models and store them all in a requirements management tool. Several attributes are stored along with each requirement.

9. How are nonfunctional requirements, such as software quality attributes, elicited and documented? [Chapter 14]

    a.   What are "software quality attributes"?

    b.   We do beta testing to get feedback about how the users like the product.

    c.   We document certain attributes, such as performance, usability, and security requirements.

    d.   We work with customers to identify the important quality attributes for each product, which we then document in a precise and verifiable way.

10. How are the individual functional requirements labeled? [Chapter 10]

    a.   We write paragraphs of narrative text or short user stories; specific requirements are not explicitly identified.

    b.   We use bulleted or numbered lists.

    c.   We use a hierarchical numbering scheme, such as "3.1.2.4."

    d.   Each discrete requirement has a unique, meaningful label that is not disrupted when other requirements are added, moved, or deleted.

11. How are priorities for the requirements established? [Chapter 16]

    a. All of the requirements are important, so we don't need to prioritize them.

    b. The customers tell us which requirements are most important to them. If the customers don't tell us or don't agree, the developers decide.

    c. Each requirement is labeled as high, medium, or low priority by customer consensus.

    d. To help us make priority decisions, we use an analytical process to rate the value, the cost, and the technical risk of each requirement, or we use a similar structured prioritization technique.

12. What techniques are used to prepare a partial solution and verify a mutual understanding of the problem? [Chapter 15]

    a. We just build the system and then fix it if we need to.

    b. We build some simple prototypes and ask users for feedback. Sometimes we're pressured to deliver prototype code.

    c. We create prototypes for both user interface mock-ups and technical proofs of concept when appropriate.

    d. Our project plans include tasks to create electronic or paper throwaway prototypes to help us refine the requirements. Sometimes we build evolutionary prototypes. We use evaluation scripts to obtain customer feedback on our prototypes.

13. How are the requirements validated? [Chapter 17]

    a. We think our requirements are pretty good when we first write them.

    b. We pass the specified requirements around to people to get their feedback.

    c. The BA and some stakeholders hold informal reviews when they have time.

    d. We inspect our requirements documents and models, with participants that include customers, developers, and testers. We write tests against the requirements and use them to validate the requirements and models.

14. How are different versions of the requirements documents distinguished? [Chapters 27 and 30]

    a. The document shows the auto-generated date that the document was printed.

    b. We use a sequence number—like 1.0, 1.1, and so on—for each document version.

    c. We have a manual identification scheme that distinguishes draft versions from baselined versions and major revisions from minor revisions.

    d. The requirements documents are stored under version control in a document management system, or requirements are stored in a requirements management tool that maintains a revision history for each requirement.

15. How are software requirements traced back to their origin? [Chapter 29]

   a. They aren't.

   b. We know where many of the requirements came from but don't document the knowledge.

   c. Each requirement has an identified origin.

   d. We have full two-way tracing between business requirements, system requirements, user requirements, functional requirements, and nonfunctional requirements.

16. How are requirements used as the basis for developing project plans? [Chapter 19]

   a. The delivery date is set before we begin requirements development. We can't change either the project schedule or the scope. Sometimes we go through a rapid descoping phase to drop features just before the delivery date.

   b. The first iteration of the project plan addresses the schedule needed to gather requirements. The rest of the project plan is developed after we have a preliminary understanding of the requirements. We can't change the plan much thereafter, however.

   c. We start with just enough information about requirements to prioritize them, then estimate the effort needed to implement the top-priority requirements. We develop our requirements and our software incrementally, planning the requirements for each iteration based on their priority and size. If we need to accommodate more requirements than our plan allowed, we add more iterations.

   d. We base the schedules and plans on the estimated effort needed to implement the required functionality, starting with the highest-priority requirements. These plans are updated as the requirements change. If we must drop features or adjust resources to meet schedule commitments, we do so as early as possible. We plan to deliver multiple releases to accommodate requirements changes and growth. [Note: (c) and (d) are equally good responses for this question.]

17. How are the requirements used as a basis for design? [Chapter 19]

   a. When we have written requirements, we refer to them during development.

   b. The requirements documents describe the solution we intend to implement.

   c. Each functional requirement is traced to a design element.

   d. Developers inspect the requirements to make sure they can be used as the basis for design. We have full two-way traceability between individual functional requirements and design elements.

18. How are the requirements used as the basis for testing? [Chapter 19]

   a. The testers test the software based on how they think it should function.

   b. The testers test what the developers said they implemented.

   c. We write system tests against the user requirements and functional requirements.

   d. Testers inspect the requirements to make sure they are verifiable and to begin their test planning. We trace system tests to specific functional requirements. System testing progress is measured in part by requirements coverage.

19. How is a software requirements baseline defined and managed for each project? [Chapters 2 and 27]

   a. We don't have to think about baselines because we are on an agile project.

   b. The customers and managers sign off on the requirements, but the development team still gets a lot of changes and complaints.

   c. We define an initial requirements baseline, but we don't always keep it current as changes are made over time.

   d. The requirements are stored in a requirements management tool when an initial baseline is defined. The requirements repository is updated as requirements changes are approved. We maintain a change history for each requirement after it's baselined. On an agile project, the team agrees on a requirements baseline for each iteration.

20. How are changes to the requirements managed? [Chapter 28]

   a. The requirements change whenever someone has a new idea or realizes that he forgot something.

   b. We discourage change by freezing the requirements after the requirements phase is complete, but informal change agreements are still made.

   c. We use a defined format for submitting change requests and a central submission point. The project manager decides which changes to incorporate.

   d. Changes are made according to our documented change control process. We use a tool to collect, store, and communicate change requests. The impact of each change is evaluated before the change control board decides whether to approve it.

Requirements troubleshooting guide

With perseverance and the cooperation of the various stakeholders, you can successfully implement improved requirements development and management practices in your organization. You should select practices that will solve or prevent specific requirements-related problems that your projects experience. After you've identified the most pressing issues you're going to address, it's important to determine the root causes that contribute to each observed problem. Effective solutions confront root causes, not just superficially observed symptoms.

This appendix lists many symptoms of requirements-related problems that you might encounter. The symptoms are accompanied by related possible root causes and suggestions for dealing with each problem. Of course, these aren't the only possible problems, so extend this table with your own experiences as you encounter—and handle—symptoms that aren't listed here. Sometimes observed symptoms are themselves root causes of other problems. For instance, the process symptom "People performing the BA role don't know how to do it well" is a root cause of numerous elicitation symptoms you might observe. These things chain together; not all of the possible links are shown here.

Unfortunately, there's no guarantee that a proposed solution will cure your specific symptom, especially if the underlying problems are political or cultural in nature or if the root causes lie outside the development team's sphere of control. As we've cautioned before, none of these solutions will work if you're dealing with unreasonable people.

Common signs of requirements problems

Problems are conditions that lead to a negative impact on your project. Signs that indicate that your projects might be suffering from requirements-related problems include:

- A product that doesn't satisfy user needs or meet user expectations.

- A product that requires corrections and updates immediately following release.

- A delivered solution that doesn't help the organization achieve its business objectives.

- Project schedule and budget overruns.

- Team member frustration, loss of morale, loss of motivation, and staff turnover.

- Extensive rework during development of the solution.

- A missed market window or delayed business benefit.

- Loss of market share or revenue.

- Product returns, market rejection of the product, and poor reviews.

Common barriers to implementing solutions

Any attempt to change the way people work or the way an organization operates might encounter resistance. As you identify corrective actions that could address the root causes of your requirements problems, also think about the obstacles that might make it difficult to implement those actions, and possible ways to get around those obstacles. Common barriers to implementing changes in requirements practices include:

- Lack of recognition of the problems that current requirements practices cause.

- Lack of time—everyone is already too busy.

- Market or management pressure to deliver quickly.

- Lack of management commitment to investing in a requirements engineering process.

- Skepticism about the value of requirements engineering.

- Reluctance to follow a new or more structured requirements or software development process.

- Politics and entrenched corporate culture.

- Conflicts between stakeholders.

- Inadequately trained and skilled team members.

- Unclear project roles and responsibilities.

- Lack of ownership and accountability for requirements activities.

Notice that these are people-oriented and communication-oriented issues, not technical impediments. There are no easy ways to overcome most of these barriers, but the first step is to recognize them.

Requirements troubleshooting guide

To use this section, identify symptoms that suggest that requirements activities aren't going as well as you'd like on your project. Then search the "Symptoms" columns in the tables for something that resembles your observation. Alternatively, scan through the "Symptoms" columns for conditions that describe your project or organization. Next, study the "Possible root causes" column for each symptom to see which factors might be contributing to the problem in your environment. Finally, select practices and approaches from the "Possible solutions" column that you think would effectively address those root causes, thereby—if all goes well—resolving the problem.

Process issues

The symptoms described in this section suggest that your requirements development and management processes are in need of a tune-up.

Symptoms	Possible root causes	Possible solutions
■ Requirements processes and document templates are inconsistent across projects. ■ Requirements processes aren't effective. ■ Document templates aren't fully fleshed out or used as intended.	■ Lack of common understanding of the requirements process. ■ No mechanism for sharing process experiences and materials. ■ Lack of good examples of templates and requirements documents. ■ No requirements processes defined. ■ BAs don't understand how to use all the sections in the templates appropriately.	■ Use project retrospectives to learn about current problems and their impacts on projects. ■ Document the current requirements process and create a proposed description of the desired process. ■ Train all team members in requirements engineering. ■ Adopt one or more standard templates for requirements deliverables. Provide guidance to help project teams tailor the templates as appropriate. ■ Collect and share good examples of templates and actual requirements documents in a shared repository. ■ Consider whether the templates are too complex for all projects; simplify them if you can.
■ People performing the BA role don't know how to do it well.	■ Lack of education about or experience with requirements engineering and the BA role. ■ Management expects that any user, developer, or other team member can automatically be a good BA, so people are assigned to the role without training or guidance.	■ Train prospective BAs in both requirements engineering and associated soft skills. ■ Write a job description and a skills list for your BAs. ■ Set up a mentoring program for new BAs. ■ Provide management with descriptions of the BA role as found in many organizations. ■ Develop a professional BA career path in the organization.

Symptoms	Possible root causes	Possible solutions
■ Requirements management tools are underutilized.	■ Inadequate training in tool capabilities. ■ Processes and culture haven't been modified to take full advantage of tools. ■ No one is responsible for leading the use of the tool. ■ Amount of time needed to configure, learn how to use, and employ the tool is underestimated.	■ Send some BAs to a tool vendor training class. ■ Establish a tool advocate to administer the tool and mentor other tool users. ■ Identify and address the process and culture issues that impede full exploitation of the tool.

Product issues

Certain problems with the products you build indicate that improved requirements practices might be advisable.

Symptoms	Possible root causes	Possible solutions
■ Dissatisfied customers. ■ Customers reject the product. ■ Poor product reviews. ■ Low sales, loss of market share. ■ Excessive number of enhancement requests received.	■ Inadequate user involvement in requirements development. ■ Unrealistic customer expectations. ■ Mismatch between customer's and developer's perception of specific requirements. ■ Insufficient market research. ■ Poor problem definition. ■ Necessary changes are not incorporated during development. ■ Developers implemented what they thought they should, not what the requirements specified.	■ Define user classes. ■ Identify product champions. ■ Convene focus groups. ■ Use collaborative requirements elicitation approaches. ■ Build prototypes and have users evaluate them. ■ Have customer representatives review requirements. ■ Use incremental and iterative development methods to adapt to customer needs.
■ Product doesn't achieve business objectives.	■ Lack of clear, accurate business requirements, including business objectives and success metrics.	■ Develop business requirements with key stakeholders. ■ Understand which success metrics are important to the project's business stakeholders. ■ Communicate business objectives to other stakeholders to achieve alignment.

Planning issues

The symptoms listed in this section suggest that the ways in which requirements and project planning intertwine are not being handled optimally.

Symptoms	Possible root causes	Possible solutions
■ Requirements are incomplete. ■ Requirements are insufficiently detailed. ■ Construction begins before the requirements for a development iteration or enhancement cycle are sufficiently understood.	■ Inadequate user involvement in requirements development. ■ Insufficient time spent on requirements development. ■ Release date set before requirements are understood. ■ Key marketing or business stakeholders are not engaged in the requirements process. ■ Management or customers don't understand the need for requirements. ■ BAs and developers don't agree on what constitutes adequate requirements. ■ Requirements tracing is not used to identify gaps. ■ Too many open requirements issues.	■ Don't commit to a delivery schedule before requirements are sufficiently understood. ■ On an agile project, expect to cut scope or add iterations as precision in the requirements develops. ■ Involve developers early in the project to ensure that they understand requirements. ■ Define business requirements, especially scope, carefully. ■ Educate stakeholders about the risks of hasty construction. ■ Build a collaborative relationship between BAs, developers, and customers to set realistic goals. ■ Use incremental development approaches to begin delivering customer value quickly. ■ Have developers review requirements before they begin implementing them. ■ Trace functional requirements to business requirements and user requirements to look for missing requirements. ■ Manage and track requirements issue status.
■ Schedule is cut after project starts but scope is not reduced.	■ Stakeholders don't understand the impact of reduced time on achievable project scope.	■ Build a collaborative relationship between project management and customers to set realistic goals. ■ Negotiate trade-offs when project constraints change. ■ Use better estimation techniques.
■ Some necessary and planned requirements work isn't performed. ■ Multiple people perform the same requirements activities.	■ Unclear roles and responsibilities for requirements activities. ■ Requirements tasks are not incorporated into project plans. ■ No one has responsibility for managing requirements.	■ Define roles and responsibilities for requirements activities on each project. ■ Commit the resources needed for effective requirements development and management. ■ Build requirements activities and deliverables into project plans and schedules.
■ More requirements are planned than can be implemented with available time and resources.	■ Schedule is set before requirements are defined. ■ Project is committed to before scope is accurately assessed. ■ Scope growth is uncontrolled. ■ The learning curve for unfamiliar technologies or tools isn't taken into account. ■ Insufficient staff is allocated to project. ■ Stakeholders are afraid they will have only one release opportunity.	■ Document vision and scope, aligned with business objectives, before making commitments. ■ Derive development schedule from requirements. ■ Plan for multiple delivery cycles to accommodate lower-priority requirements. ■ Incorporate training time and learning curve time in schedule. ■ Prioritize requirements based on business objectives. ■ Timebox the development or deliver product features incrementally. ■ Adjust priorities dynamically as project realities dictate.

Symptoms	Possible root causes	Possible solutions
■ Undocumented or poorly defined scope. ■ Releases or iterations are poorly planned.	■ Unclear business objectives. ■ Haste to begin construction. ■ Lack of understanding of the importance of scope definition. ■ Lack of agreement on scope among stakeholders. ■ Volatile market or rapidly changing business needs.	■ Don't begin a project without clear business objectives. ■ Write a vision and scope document and obtain buy-in from key stakeholders. ■ Postpone or cancel the project if sponsorship and scope definition are not achieved. ■ Use shorter development iterations to adapt to rapidly changing requirements.

Communication issues

Many problems, including those in the following table, arise because of ineffective communication among project stakeholders.

Symptoms	Possible root causes	Possible solutions
■ Duplication of effort as multiple people implement the same requirement.	■ Responsibilities for implementing requirements are not clear. ■ Inadequate communication among subgroups working on the project.	■ Define clear roles and responsibilities for software implementation. ■ Provide visible status tracking of individual requirements. ■ Introduce more effective communication techniques and practices among team members.
■ Revisiting decisions made previously.	■ Lack of clear recognition and empowerment of appropriate decision makers. ■ Failure to record how and why decisions are made.	■ Identify the project's requirements decision makers and define their decision-making process. ■ Identify and empower product champions. ■ Document why requirements were added, rejected, deferred, or canceled.
■ Requirements questions and issues are not resolved.	■ Lack of coordination of questions and issues that arise about requirements. ■ Responsibilities for resolving issues are not clear. ■ No one is responsible for tracking issues and their status. ■ Team is unable to obtain necessary information from a vendor, client, contractor, or other stakeholder.	■ Assign each open issue to an individual for resolution. ■ Use an issue-tracking tool for tracking requirements issues to closure. ■ Monitor open issues as part of project tracking. ■ Obtain commitment from all stakeholders early on for open and timely information exchange and for answering questions and resolving issues.
■ Project participants don't share the same vocabulary.	■ Assuming that everyone has the same and the correct interpretation of key terms.	■ Define terms in a glossary. ■ Define data structures and elements in a data dictionary. ■ Train development team in the business domain. ■ Train user representatives in requirements engineering.

Elicitation issues

Many symptoms suggest that those team members who are engaged in requirements elicitation are not performing as well as they could be.

Symptoms	Possible root causes	Possible solutions
■ The team can't get customer representatives to participate in elicitation. ■ Developers make many guesses about what to implement. ■ Developers have to resolve requirements questions that arise.	■ Customer representatives don't have time to participate in requirements development. ■ Customers don't understand the need to participate. ■ Customers don't know what BAs need from them. ■ Customers aren't committed to the project. ■ Customers think that developers should already know what the customers need. ■ BAs don't know who the customers are. ■ BAs don't have access to actual users. ■ Resistance to following a requirements development process. ■ No BA is dedicated to the project.	■ Educate customers and managers about requirements and the need for their participation. ■ Describe the risks from insufficient user involvement to customers and managers. ■ Build a collaborative relationship between development teams and their customers. ■ Define user classes or market segments. ■ Identify a product champion for each user class. ■ Obtain development and customer management commitment to an effective requirements process. ■ Define clear roles and responsibilities. ■ Hold regular customer meetings with defined agendas.
■ Wrong user representatives are involved.	■ Managers, the marketing team, or other surrogates do not speak accurately for end users. ■ Managers don't make qualified actual users available to work with BAs.	■ Define user classes. ■ Identify and empower appropriate and effective product champions. ■ Develop user personas as stand-ins for real users. ■ Decline requirement requests from unauthorized or inappropriate sources.
■ Users are unsure about their needs.	■ Users don't understand or can't describe their business process well. ■ System is being built to support a new, incompletely defined business process. ■ Users aren't committed to the project, perhaps are threatened by it. ■ Business objectives are not well defined or communicated.	■ Clarify the intended outcomes of a successful project for the stakeholders affected by it. ■ Identify product champions or product owners. ■ Model the user's business process. ■ Develop an elicitation plan to define requirements sources and select appropriate elicitation techniques. ■ Compile a list of generic questions as a starting point for elicitation activities. ■ Develop use cases or user stories. ■ Build prototypes and have users evaluate them. ■ Use incremental development to clarify requirements a bit at a time.
■ Project manager or business analyst doesn't know who the users are.	■ Ill-defined product vision. ■ Poorly understood marketplace needs.	■ Create a product vision statement. ■ Perform sufficient market research. ■ Identify users of current or competing products. ■ Establish focus groups. ■ Create user personas. ■ Use an organization chart to look for likely users.

Symptoms	Possible root causes	Possible solutions
■ Too many people are involved in requirements elicitation.	■ Everyone wants to be represented for political reasons. ■ User classes aren't clearly defined. ■ Lack of delegation to specific user representatives. ■ There really are a lot of different user classes.	■ Define user classes. ■ Identify product champions or product owners. ■ Identify requirements decision makers. ■ Distinguish political priorities from business and technical priorities. ■ Focus on the needs of favored user classes.
■ Implemented "requirements" don't meet user needs. ■ Requirements are overconstrained.	■ Requirements contain unnecessary or premature design constraints. ■ Solutions are presented as needs, and requirements have to be deduced from the presented solutions. ■ New software must conform to existing application standards and user interface constraints. ■ Customers don't know what information constitutes "the requirements." ■ Requirements discussions focus on user interface design.	■ Ask "why" several times to understand the real user needs behind the presented requirements and the rationale behind design constraints. ■ Understand user requirements before addressing user interface specifics. ■ Develop skilled BAs who can ask the right questions and elicit true needs. ■ Educate customers about requirements development. ■ Document business rules and constraints.
■ Needed requirements are missed.	■ Users don't know what they need. ■ BA didn't ask the right questions. ■ Insufficient time was provided for elicitation. ■ Some user classes aren't represented. ■ Appropriate, knowledgeable user representatives did not participate in elicitation. ■ Elicitation participants make incorrect assumptions. ■ Insufficient communication between developers and customers. ■ Users don't express their implicit and assumed requirements.	■ Develop skilled BAs who can ask the right questions. ■ Elicit use cases or user stories. ■ Use multiple elicitation techniques. ■ Represent requirements in multiple ways, emphasizing visual models, to look for gaps. ■ Conduct requirements reviews. Use multiple, incremental reviews. ■ Analyze requirements by using a CRUD matrix. ■ Build prototypes and have users evaluate them. ■ Build the product incrementally and incorporate new requirements in later iterations. ■ Create and use a requirements traceability matrix to find missing requirements.
■ Requirements specified are incorrect or inappropriate.	■ The wrong user representatives or inappropriate surrogates are involved. ■ User representatives speak for themselves, not for those they represent. ■ Managers do not provide access to user representatives. ■ Business requirements are not clearly established. ■ User and functional requirements are not aligned with business objectives.	■ Determine what was wrong with the flawed requirements and why they were specified. ■ Define user classes. ■ Identify appropriate product champions, educate them, and empower them. ■ Have a multifunctional team review requirements. ■ Communicate the risks of inaccurate requirements to high-authority stakeholders. ■ Explain the importance of good user representation to high-level stakeholders.

Analysis issues

The symptoms described in the following table indicate that more effective requirements analysis is advisable.

Symptoms	Possible root causes	Possible solutions
■ Unnecessary requirements are specified. ■ Unexpected functionality becomes apparent during testing. ■ Functionality is specified and built, but not used.	■ Ineffective requirement approval process. ■ Developers incorporate functionality without input from users. ■ Users request complex solutions instead of expressing business needs. ■ Elicitation focuses on system functions instead of user goals. ■ Developers and customers interpret requirements differently. ■ Requirements don't trace back to business objectives.	■ Record the origin and rationale for each requirement. ■ Employ use cases to focus on the users' business objectives. Derive functional requirements from the use cases or user stories. ■ Prioritize requirements to deliver high-value functionality early. ■ Have a multifunctional team review requirements.
■ Testers aren't able to write good tests from requirements.	■ Requirements are ambiguous, incomplete, or lack sufficient detail.	■ Have testers review requirements early on for verifiability and other quality issues.
■ All requirements seem to be equally important. ■ All requirements have high priority. ■ BAs can't make informed trade-off decisions when new requirements appear.	■ Fear that low-priority requirements will never be implemented. ■ Insufficient or evolving knowledge about the business and its needs. ■ Information on the value and cost of requirements is not known, communicated, or discussed. ■ The product isn't usable unless a large, critical set of functionality is implemented. ■ Unreasonable customer or developer expectations. ■ Only customers provide input regarding priorities.	■ Develop a collaborative process for prioritizing requirements to balance customer value against implementation cost and technical risk. ■ Prioritize requirements early. ■ Develop detailed specifications of high-priority requirements. ■ Use incremental development or staged releases to deliver maximum value as early as possible. ■ Dynamically adjust the priorities of requirements remaining in the backlog.
■ Changing requirements priorities.	■ Decision makers are not identified or empowered. ■ Internal political pressure. ■ Unclear business objectives, or lack of agreement on business objectives. ■ External forces, such as regulatory or legislative issues. ■ Requirements and their priorities are not agreed to by the appropriate people.	■ Document the project's business objectives, scope, and priorities. ■ Align requirements priorities to business objectives. ■ Identify and empower requirements decision makers. ■ Track the impact of changes in terms of cost, revenue, and schedule slippage. ■ Use incremental development and dynamically adjust the priorities of requirements remaining in the backlog.

Symptoms	Possible root causes	Possible solutions
■ Conflicting requirements priorities among stakeholders.	■ Different user classes have conflicting needs. ■ Lack of focus on the original product vision, or the vision evolves during the project. ■ Unclear business objectives, or lack of agreement on business objectives. ■ Changing business objectives. ■ It's not clear who the requirements decision makers are.	■ Perform sufficient market research. ■ Establish and communicate business objectives. ■ Base priorities on vision, scope, and business objectives. ■ Identify favored user classes or market segments. ■ Identify product champions to represent different user classes. ■ Identify and empower requirements decision makers.
■ Rapid descoping late in the project.	■ Unrealistic optimism about developer productivity. ■ Insufficient early and ongoing prioritization. ■ Not relying on priorities to define implementation sequence and to make controlled scope changes.	■ Define priorities early on. ■ Use priorities to guide decisions about what to work on now and what to defer. ■ Reprioritize when new requirements are incorporated. ■ Adjust scope periodically, not just late in the project. ■ Use incremental development or staged releases to stay focused on delivering customer value.
■ Developers find requirements vague and ambiguous. ■ Developers have to track down missing information. ■ Developers misunderstand requirements and have to rework their implementations.	■ BAs and customers don't understand the level of requirements detail developers need. ■ Customers don't know what they need or can't articulate it clearly. ■ Insufficient time is spent on elicitation. ■ Business rules aren't identified, communicated, or understood. ■ Requirements contain vague and ambiguous words. ■ Stakeholders interpret terms, concepts, and data definitions differently. ■ Customers assume that developers already know enough about the business domain and their needs.	■ Train BAs in writing good requirements. ■ Avoid using subjective, ambiguous words in requirements specifications. ■ Have developers and customers review requirements early for clarity and appropriate detail. ■ Model requirements to find missing information and enhance details. ■ Build prototypes and have users evaluate them. ■ Refine requirements in progressive levels of detail. ■ Document business rules. ■ Define terms in a glossary. ■ Define data items in a data dictionary. ■ Facilitate effective communication among all project participants.
■ Some requirements aren't technically feasible.	■ Requirements are not analyzed sufficiently. ■ Customers don't accept feasibility analysis results. ■ Lack of understanding of the limitations of tools, technologies, and the operating environment.	■ Perform feasibility analysis. ■ Create proof-of-concept prototypes. ■ Have a developer participate in elicitation. ■ Have developers review requirements for feasibility. ■ Conduct a separate research or exploratory mini-project or pilot to assess feasibility.

Symptoms	Possible root causes	Possible solutions
■ Requirements from different sources or user classes conflict. ■ Difficulty in reaching agreement on requirements among stakeholders.	■ Lack of shared product vision. ■ Requirements decision makers are not identified. ■ Business processes are not understood in the same way by different stakeholders. ■ Politics drive requirements input. ■ Diverse users or market segments have differing needs, expectations, and objectives. ■ Product isn't sufficiently focused on a specific target market. ■ Some user groups already have a useful system in place that they're attached to.	■ Develop, approve, and communicate a unified set of business requirements. ■ Understand target market segments and user classes. ■ Identify favored user classes to resolve conflicts. ■ Identify product champions to resolve conflicts within each user class. ■ Identify and empower requirements decision makers. ■ Focus on shared business interests instead of emotional and political positions.
■ Requirements contain TBDs, information gaps, and open issues.	■ No one is assigned to resolve TBDs or open issues before requirements are baselined. ■ No time is available to resolve TBDs or open issues before beginning implementation.	■ Review requirements to identify information gaps. ■ Assign responsibility for resolving each TBD or open issue to an individual. ■ Prioritize TBDs to be resolved if time is tight. ■ Track each TBD or open issue to closure before baselining a set of requirements.
■ BAs spend too much time on requirements analysis.	■ Reluctance to proceed until the requirements are "perfect" (analysis paralysis). ■ An intent to develop a complete specification rather than one that is good enough. ■ Inappropriate selection of analysis techniques for the project.	■ Focus analysis and modeling on the complex, novel, or uncertain portions of the requirements. ■ Use peer reviews to judge when requirements are good enough for development to proceed at acceptable risk.

Specification issues

The symptoms in the following table indicate shortcomings in the way that requirements are being specified for the project.

Symptoms	Possible root causes	Possible solutions
■ Requirements are not documented. ■ Developers create the requirements. ■ Customers provide requirements details to developers verbally. ■ Developers do a lot of exploratory programming as they try to figure out what customers want.	■ No one is sure what to build. ■ Insufficient time is provided to elicit and document requirements. ■ There's a perception that writing requirements slows down the project. ■ Individuals responsible for specification aren't clearly identified and committed. ■ No defined requirements development process or templates in place. ■ Development management doesn't value and expect requirements specifications. ■ Developers think they know what customers need.	■ Point out risks of inadequately specified requirements. ■ Define and follow a requirements development process. ■ Establish team role definitions, and obtain commitment from individuals to perform their roles. ■ Train other team members and customers in the requirements process. ■ Build requirements effort, resources, tasks, and deliverables into project plans and schedules. ■ Have standard templates and good examples of requirements specifications available to share.

Symptoms	Possible root causes	Possible solutions
■ Stakeholders assume that functionality in the existing system will be replicated in a new system.	■ Requirements for a new system are specified as deltas from a poorly documented existing system. ■ Business objectives aren't clear.	■ Reverse engineer the existing system to understand its full capabilities. ■ Write a requirements specification that includes all the desired functionality for the new system. ■ Build as-is and to-be process models so that stakeholders are clear on what the future system will and won't do. ■ Don't replicate old functionality that might not be needed.
■ Requirements documentation doesn't accurately describe the system.	■ Changes made during development are not incorporated into requirements documentation.	■ Follow a change control process that includes updating requirements when changes are accepted. ■ Pass all change requests through the change control board. ■ Have key stakeholders review modified requirements.
■ Different, conflicting versions of the requirements exist.	■ Poor version control practices. ■ Multiple "master" copies of requirements documents. ■ Requirements are maintained separately in a tool and in documents; people aren't sure which is the definitive source.	■ Define and follow good version control practices for requirements documents. ■ Store requirements in a requirements management tool. ■ Assign a requirements manager to be responsible for making changes to requirements.

Validation issues

It's difficult to know for sure if the requirements you've developed will in fact achieve the intended business objectives. The symptoms in this section are indicative of requirements validation shortcomings.

Symptoms	Possible root causes	Possible solutions
■ Product doesn't achieve business objectives or meet user expectations. ■ Customers have unstated, assumed, or implicit requirements that weren't satisfied.	■ Customers didn't accurately present their needs. ■ Market or business needs changed and mechanisms were not in place to revise requirements accordingly. ■ The BA didn't ask the right questions. ■ Inadequate customer participation in requirements development. ■ Wrong customer representatives involved, such as surrogates who don't represent the real users' real needs. ■ Market needs were not accurately assessed, especially for innovative products with uncertain requirements. ■ Project participants made incorrect assumptions.	■ Perform market research to understand market segments and their needs. ■ Engage product champions representing each user class throughout the duration of the project. ■ Train BAs in how to elicit requirements. ■ Develop use cases to make sure business tasks are understood. ■ Have customers participate in requirements reviews. ■ Build prototypes and have users evaluate them. ■ Have users write acceptance tests and acceptance criteria. ■ Establish effective change mechanisms to allow requirements to adapt to business realities.

Symptoms	Possible root causes	Possible solutions
■ Product does not achieve performance goals or satisfy other quality expectations that users have.	■ Quality attribute requirements were not elicited and specified. ■ Stakeholders don't understand nonfunctional requirements and their importance. ■ The requirements template or tool being used doesn't have sections for nonfunctional requirements. ■ Users don't state their assumptions about the system's quality characteristics. ■ Quality attributes weren't specified precisely enough to give all stakeholders the same understanding.	■ Educate BAs and customers about nonfunctional requirements and how to specify them. ■ Have BAs explore nonfunctional requirements during elicitation. ■ Use an SRS template that includes sections for nonfunctional requirements. ■ Use Planguage to specify quality attributes precisely.

Requirements management issues

One sign that requirements are not being managed well is that not all of the intended requirements are implemented.

Symptoms	Possible root causes	Possible solutions
■ Some planned requirements were not implemented.	■ SRS was not well organized or well written. ■ Individual requirements were not discretely identified and labeled. ■ Developers didn't follow the SRS. ■ SRS was not communicated to everyone. ■ Changes were not communicated to all those affected. ■ Requirements were inadvertently overlooked during implementation. ■ Responsibilities for implementing requirements were not assigned. ■ The status of individual requirements was not tracked accurately.	■ Keep requirements current and make them available to the whole team. ■ Make sure the change control process includes communication to stakeholders. ■ Store requirements in a requirements management tool. ■ Track the status of individual requirements. ■ Create and use a requirements traceability matrix. ■ Define clear responsibilities for software construction. ■ Train BAs in writing clear, concise requirements.

Change management issues

There are many indicators that a software project is not handling change requests well, several of which are itemized in the following table.

Symptoms	Possible root causes	Possible solutions
■ Requirements change frequently. ■ Many requirements changes are made late in the development cycle. ■ Changes cause missed delivery targets.	■ Customers aren't sure what they need. ■ Changing business processes or market demands. ■ Not all the right people were involved in eliciting and approving the requirements. ■ Requirements weren't adequately defined initially. ■ Requirements baseline wasn't defined or agreed to. ■ External sources, such as the government or political issues, dictate changes. ■ The initial requirements contained many solution ideas, which did not satisfy the real needs. ■ Market needs weren't well understood.	■ Improve requirements elicitation practices. ■ Implement and follow a change control process. ■ Establish a change control board to make decisions on proposed changes. ■ Perform impact analysis before accepting changes. ■ Have stakeholders review requirements before baselining them. ■ Design software for high modifiability to accommodate change. ■ Include contingency buffers in the project schedule to accommodate some change. ■ Use incremental development approaches to respond quickly to changing requirements. ■ Protect the schedule and negotiate to deliver reduced scope, planning a follow-on release.
■ New requirements are added frequently. ■ Increased scope causes missed delivery targets.	■ Requirements elicitation was incomplete. ■ Insufficient customer participation in requirements development. ■ Business needs or environment are changing rapidly. ■ Business domain is not well understood. ■ Stakeholders don't understand or respect project scope. ■ Management, marketing, or customers demand new features without considering their impact on the project.	■ Improve requirements elicitation practices. ■ Define and communicate scope. ■ Have the right people make explicit business decisions to change scope. ■ Perform root cause analysis to see where new requirements come from and why. ■ Perform change impact analysis before accepting new requirements. ■ Ensure that all user classes have provided input. ■ Include contingency buffers in the project schedule to accommodate some growth. ■ Use incremental development approaches to respond quickly to new requirements.

Symptoms	Possible root causes	Possible solutions
■ Requirements move in and out of scope.	■ Vision and scope are not clearly defined. ■ Business objectives are not clearly understood and communicated. ■ Scope is volatile, perhaps in response to changing market demands. ■ Requirements priorities are poorly defined. ■ Decision makers don't agree on project scope.	■ Clearly define the business objectives, vision, and scope. ■ Use the scope statement to decide whether proposed requirements are in or out of scope. ■ Record the rationale for rejecting a proposed requirement. ■ Ensure that the change control board has the appropriate members and a shared understanding of project scope. ■ Use incremental development to adapt flexibly to a changing scope boundary. ■ Focus on implementing the stable requirements.
■ Scope definition changes after development is underway.	■ Poorly defined, poorly understood, or changing business objectives. ■ Market segments and market needs aren't well understood. ■ Competing products become available. ■ Key stakeholders did not review and approve requirements. ■ Changes in key stakeholders partway through the project.	■ Define business objectives and align vision and scope with them. ■ Identify decision-making stakeholders at the business requirements level. ■ Have decision makers review the vision and scope document. ■ Follow a change control process to incorporate changes. ■ Renegotiate schedules, resources, and commitments when project direction changes.
■ People don't know the scope or understand scope changes.	■ Requirements changes aren't communicated to all affected stakeholders. ■ Requirements specifications aren't updated when requirements change. ■ Customers request changes directly from developers. ■ Not everyone has ready access to the requirements documentation. ■ Informal communication pathways exclude some project participants. ■ It's not clear who needs to be informed of changes. ■ No established change control process. ■ Lack of understanding of interrelationships between requirements.	■ Define an owner for each requirement. ■ Define trace links between requirements and other artifacts. ■ Include all affected areas in requirements communications. ■ Establish a change control process that includes the communication mechanisms. ■ Handle all requirements changes through the change control process. ■ Use a requirements management tool to make current requirements available to stakeholders. ■ Improve collaboration and communication among project participants and other stakeholders.
■ Proposed requirements changes are lost. ■ The status of each change request isn't known.	■ Ineffective or undefined change control process. ■ Change control process isn't followed.	■ Adopt a practical, effective change control process and educate stakeholders about it. ■ Assign responsibilities for performing the change control process steps. ■ Ensure that the change control process is followed. ■ Use requirements management tools to track changes and track each requirement's status.

Symptoms	Possible root causes	Possible solutions
■ Stakeholders bypass the change control process. ■ Customers request changes directly from developers.	■ Change control process isn't practical and effective. ■ Change control board is ineffective. ■ Stakeholders don't understand or accept the change control process. ■ Management doesn't require that the change control process be followed.	■ Ensure that the change control process is pragmatic, effective, efficient, and accessible to all stakeholders. ■ Make the change control process flexible in how it handles small versus large changes. ■ Establish and charter an appropriate change control board. ■ Enlist management to commit to and champion the change control process. ■ Enforce a policy that requirements changes are made only through the change control process.
■ Requirements changes take much more effort than planned. ■ Changes affect more system components than expected. ■ Changes conflict with other requirements. ■ Changes degrade system quality.	■ Insufficient impact analysis of proposed requirements changes. ■ Developers underestimate the impact of requirements changes. ■ The wrong people make decisions to accept changes. ■ Team members are afraid to be honest about the impact of proposed changes. ■ Change requests do not provide enough information to permit good impact analysis.	■ Adopt a change impact analysis procedure and checklist. ■ Incorporate impact analysis into the change control process. ■ Use requirements trace information to evaluate the impact of proposed changes. ■ Communicate changes to all affected stakeholders. ■ Renegotiate project commitments as needed and make necessary trade-offs when changes are proposed.

Sample requirements documents

This appendix illustrates some of the requirements documents and diagrams described in this book, using a hypothetical project called the Cafeteria Ordering System (COS). This appendix includes:

- A vision and scope document.

- A list of use cases and several use case specifications, showing different degrees of detail.

- A portion of a software requirements specification.

- Several partial analysis models, including a feature tree, context diagram, entity-relationship diagram, and state-transition diagram.

- A partial data dictionary.

- Several business rules.

Because this is just an example, these deliverables aren't intended to be complete. Instead, they are meant to illustrate how the various types of requirements information relate to each other and how you might write the contents of each document section. The information in these examples could be organized and grouped in many other reasonable ways, including combining it into a single document on a small project or storing it in a requirements management tool. Clarity, completeness, and usability of the requirements information are the essential objectives. The examples conform to the templates described in previous chapters. Because this is a small project, some template sections have been combined. Every project should consider how to adapt the organization's standard templates to best suit the size and nature of the project.

Vision and Scope Document

1. Business Requirements

1.1 Background

Employees at the company Process Impact presently spend an average of 65 minutes per day going to the cafeteria to select, purchase, and eat lunch. About 20 minutes of this time is spent walking to and from the cafeteria, selecting their meals, and paying by cash or credit card. When employees go out for lunch, they spend an average of 90 minutes off-site. Some employees phone the cafeteria in advance to order a meal to be ready for them to pick up. Employees don't always get the selections they want because the cafeteria runs out of certain items. The cafeteria wastes a significant quantity of food that is not purchased and must be thrown away. These same issues apply to breakfast and supper, although far fewer employees use the cafeteria for those meals than for lunch.

1.2 Business Opportunity

Many employees have requested a system that would permit a cafeteria user to order meals (defined as a set of one or more food items selected from the cafeteria menu) online, to be picked up at the cafeteria or delivered to a company location at a specified time and date. Such a system would save employees time, and it would increase their chance of getting the items they prefer. Knowing what food items customers want in advance would reduce waste in the cafeteria and would improve the efficiency of cafeteria staff. The future ability for employees to order meals for delivery from local restaurants would make a wide range of choices available to employees and provide the possibility of cost savings through volume discount agreements with the restaurants.

1.3 Business Objectives

BO-1: Reduce the cost of cafeteria food wastage by 40% within 6 months following initial release. *[This example shows the use of Planguage to precisely state a business objective.]*

> Scale: Cost of food thrown away each week by cafeteria staff
>
> Meter: Examination of Cafeteria Inventory System logs
>
> Past: 33% (2013, initial study)
>
> Goal: Less than 20%
>
> Stretch: Less than 15%

BO-2: Reduce cafeteria operating costs by 15% within 12 months following initial release.

BO-3: Increase average effective work time by 15 minutes per cafeteria-using employee per day within 6 months following initial release.

1.4 Success Metrics

SM-1: 75% of employees who used the cafeteria at least 3 times per week during Q3 2013 use the COS at least once a week within 6 months following initial release.

SM-2: The average rating on the quarterly cafeteria satisfaction survey increases by 0.5 on a scale of 1 to 6 from the Q3 2013 rating within 3 months following initial release and by 1.0 within 12 months.

1.5 Vision Statement

For employees who want to order meals from the company cafeteria or from local restaurants online, the Cafeteria Ordering System is an Internet-based and smartphone-enabled application that will accept individual or group meal orders, process payments, and trigger delivery of the prepared meals to a designated location on the Process Impact campus. Unlike the current telephone and manual ordering processes, employees who use the Cafeteria Ordering System will not have to go to the cafeteria to get their meals, which will save them time and will increase the food choices available to them.

1.6 Business Risks

RI-1: The Cafeteria Employees Union might require that their contract be renegotiated to reflect the new employee roles and cafeteria hours of operation. (Probability = 0.6; Impact = 3)

RI-2: Too few employees might use the system, reducing the return on investment from the system development and the changes in cafeteria operating procedures. (Probability = 0.3; Impact = 9)

RI-3: Local restaurants might not agree to offer delivery, which would reduce employee satisfaction with the system and possibly their usage of it. (Probability = 0.3; Impact = 3)

RI-4: Sufficient delivery capacity might not be available, which means that employees might not always receive their meals on time and could not always request delivery for the desired times. (Probability = 0.5; Impact = 6)

1.7 Business Assumptions and Dependencies

AS-1: Systems with appropriate user interfaces will be available for cafeteria employees to process the expected volume of meals ordered.

AS-2: Cafeteria staff and vehicles will be available to deliver all meals for specified delivery time slots within 15 minutes of the requested delivery time.

DE-1: If a restaurant has its own online ordering system, the Cafeteria Ordering System must be able to communicate with it bidirectionally.

2. Scope and Limitations

2.1 Major Features

FE-1: Order and pay for meals from the cafeteria menu to be picked up or delivered.

FE-2: Order and pay for meals from local restaurants to be delivered.

FE-3: Create, view, modify, and cancel meal subscriptions for standing or recurring meal orders, or for daily special meals.

FE-4: Create, view, modify, delete, and archive cafeteria menus.

FE-5: View ingredient lists and nutritional information for cafeteria menu items.

FE-6: Provide system access through corporate intranet, smartphone, tablet, and outside Internet access by authorized employees.

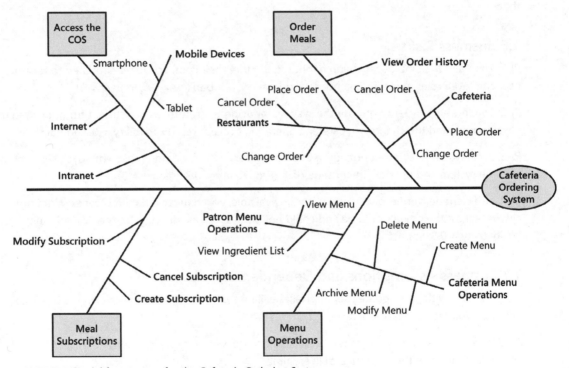

FIGURE C-1 Partial feature tree for the Cafeteria Ordering System.

2.2 Scope of Initial and Subsequent Releases

Feature	Release 1	Release 2	Release 3
FE-1, Order from cafeteria	Standard meals from lunch menu only; meal orders for delivery can be paid for by payroll deduction only	Accept credit and debit card payments	Accept meal orders for breakfasts and suppers
FE-2, Order from restaurants	Not implemented	Delivery to campus locations only	Fully implemented
FE-3, Meal subscriptions	Not implemented	Implemented if time permits	Fully implemented
FE-4, Menus	Create and view menus	Modify, delete, and archive menus	
FE-5, Ingredient lists	Not implemented	Fully implemented	
FE-6, System access	Intranet and outside Internet access	iOS and Android phone and tablet apps	Windows Phone and tablet apps

2.3 Limitations and Exclusions

LI-1: Some food items that are available from the cafeteria will not be suitable for delivery, so the delivery menus available to patrons of the COS must be a subset of the full cafeteria menus.

LI-2: The COS shall be used only for the cafeteria at the Process Impact campus in Clackamas, Oregon.

3. Business Context

3.1 Stakeholder Profiles

Stakeholder	Major value	Attitudes	Major interests	Constraints
Corporate Management	Improved employee productivity; cost savings for cafeteria	Strong commitment through release 2; support for release 3 contingent on earlier results	Cost and employee time savings must exceed development and usage costs	None identified
Cafeteria Staff	More efficient use of staff time throughout the day; higher customer satisfaction	Concern about union relationships and possible downsizing; otherwise receptive	Job preservation	Training for staff in Internet usage needed; delivery staff and vehicles needed
Patrons	Better food selection; time savings; convenience	Strong enthusiasm, but might not use it as much as expected because of social value of eating lunches in cafeteria and restaurants	Simplicity of use; reliability of delivery; availability of food choices	Corporate intranet access, Internet access, or a mobile device is needed
Payroll Department	No benefit; needs to set up payroll deduction registration scheme	Not happy about the software work needed, but recognizes the value to the company and employees	Minimal changes in current payroll applications	No resources yet committed to make software changes

Stakeholder	Major value	Attitudes	Major interests	Constraints
Restaurant Managers	Increased sales; marketing exposure to generate new customers	Receptive but cautious	Minimal new technology needed; concern about resources and costs of delivering meals	Might not have capacity to handle order levels; might not all have menus online

3.2 Project Priorities

Dimension	Constraint	Driver	Degree of freedom
Features	All features scheduled for release 1.0 must be fully operational		
Quality	95% of user acceptance tests must pass; all security tests must pass		
Schedule			Release 1 planned to be available by end of Q1 of next year, release 2 by end of Q2; overrun of up to 2 weeks acceptable without sponsor review
Cost			Budget overrun up to 15% acceptable without sponsor review
Staff		Team size is half-time project manager, half-time BA, 3 developers, and 1 tester; additional developer and half-time tester available if necessary	

3.3 Deployment Considerations

The web server software will need to be upgraded to the latest version. Apps will have to be developed for iOS and Android smartphones and tablets as part of the second release, with corresponding apps for Windows Phone and tablets to follow for the third release. Any corresponding infrastructure changes must be in place at the time of the second release. Videos no more than five minutes in length shall be developed to train users in both the Internet-based and app-based versions of COS.

Use Cases

The various user classes identified the following primary actors and use cases for the COS:

Primary actor	Use cases
Patron	1. Order a Meal 2. Change Meal Order 3. Cancel Meal Order 4. View Menu 5. Register for Payroll Deduction 6. Unregister for Payroll Deduction 7. Manage Meal Subscription
Menu Manager	8. Create a Menu 9. Modify a Menu 10. Delete a Menu 11. Archive Menus 12. Define a Meal Special
Cafeteria Staff	13. Prepare Meal 14. Generate a Payment Request 15. Request Meal Delivery 16. Generate System Usage Reports
Meal Deliverer	17. Record Meal Delivery 18. Print Delivery Instructions

ID and Name:	UC-1: Order a Meal		
Created By:	Prithvi Raj	Date Created:	October 4, 2013
Primary Actor:	Patron	Secondary Actors:	Cafeteria Inventory System
Description:	A Patron accesses the Cafeteria Ordering System from either the corporate intranet or external Internet, views the menu for a specific date, selects food items, and places an order for a meal to be picked up in the cafeteria or delivered to a specified location within a specified 15-minute time window.		
Trigger:	A Patron indicates that he wants to order a meal.		
Preconditions:	PRE-1. Patron is logged into COS. PRE-2. Patron is registered for meal payments by payroll deduction.		
Postconditions:	POST-1. Meal order is stored in COS with a status of "Accepted." POST-2. Inventory of available food items is updated to reflect items in this order. POST-3. Remaining delivery capacity for the requested time window is updated.		
Normal Flow:	**1.0 Order a Single Meal** 1. Patron asks to view menu for a specific date. (see 1.0.E1, 1.0.E2) 2. COS displays menu of available food items and the daily special. 3. Patron selects one or more food items from menu. (see 1.1) 4. Patron indicates that meal order is complete. (see 1.2) 5. COS displays ordered menu items, individual prices, and total price, including taxes and delivery charge. 6. Patron either confirms meal order (continue normal flow) or requests to modify meal order (return to step 2). 7. COS displays available delivery times for the delivery date. 8. Patron selects a delivery time and specifies the delivery location. 9. Patron specifies payment method. 10. COS confirms acceptance of the order. 11. COS sends Patron an email message confirming order details, price, and delivery instructions. 12. COS stores order, sends food item information to Cafeteria Inventory System, and updates available delivery times.		

Alternative Flows:	**1.1 Order multiple identical meals** 1. Patron requests a specified number of identical meals. (see 1.1.E1) 2. Return to step 4 of normal flow. **1.2 Order multiple meals** 1. Patron asks to order another meal. 2. Return to step 1 of normal flow.
Exceptions:	**1.0.E1 Requested date is today and current time is after today's order cutoff time** 1. COS informs Patron that it's too late to place an order for today. 2a. If Patron cancels the meal ordering process, then COS terminates use case. 2b. Else if Patron requests another date, then COS restarts use case. **1.0.E2 No delivery times left** 1. COS informs Patron that no delivery times are available for the meal date. 2a. If Patron cancels the meal ordering process, then COS terminates use case. 2b. Else if Patron requests to pick the order up at the cafeteria, then continue with normal flow, but skip steps 7 and 8. **1.1.E1 Insufficient inventory to fulfill multiple meal order** 1. COS informs Patron of the maximum number of identical meals he can order, based on current available inventory. 2a. If Patron modifies number of meals ordered, then return to step 4 of normal flow. 2b. Else if Patron cancels the meal ordering process, then COS terminates use case.
Priority:	High
Frequency of Use:	Approximately 300 users, average of one usage per day. Peak usage load for this use case is between 9:00 A.M. and 10:00 A.M. local time.
Business Rules:	BR-1, BR-2, BR-3, BR-4, BR-11, BR-12, BR-33
Other Information:	1. Patron shall be able to cancel the meal ordering process at any time prior to confirming it. 2. Patron shall be able to view all meals he ordered within the previous six months and repeat one of those meals as the new order, provided that all food items are available on the menu for the requested delivery date. (Priority = medium) *[Note: You could also show this as an alternative flow for the use case.]* 3. The default date is the current date if the Patron is using the system before today's order cutoff time. Otherwise, the default date is the next day that the cafeteria is open.
Assumptions:	Assume that 15 percent of Patrons will order the daily special (Source: previous 6 months of cafeteria data).

[Note: the following use case is written in less detail than UC-1, to illustrate that it isn't always necessary to fully specify every detail of the use case, provided developers have the necessary information available from some other source.]

ID and Name:	**UC-5 Register for Payroll Deduction**		
Created By:	Nancy Anderson	Date Created:	September 15, 2013
Primary Actor:	Patron	Secondary Actors:	Payroll System
Description:	Cafeteria patrons who use the COS and have meals delivered must be registered for payroll deduction. For noncash purchases made through the COS, the cafeteria will issue a payment request to the Payroll System, which will deduct the meal costs from the next scheduled employee payday direct deposit.		
Trigger:	Patron requests to register for payroll deduction, or Patron says yes when COS asks if he wants to register.		
Preconditions:	PRE-1. Patron is logged into COS.		
Postconditions:	POST-1. Patron is registered for payroll deduction.		
Normal Flow:	**5.0 Register for Payroll Deduction** 1. COS asks Payroll System if Patron is eligible to register for payroll deduction. 2. Payroll System confirms that Patron is eligible to register for payroll deduction. 3. COS asks Patron to confirm his desire to register for payroll deduction. 4. If so, COS asks Payroll System to establish payroll deduction for Patron. 5. Payroll System confirms that payroll deduction is established. 6. COS informs Patron that payroll deduction is established.		
Alternative Flows:	None		
Exceptions:	5.0.E1 Patron is not eligible for payroll deduction. 5.0.E2 Patron is already enrolled for payroll deduction.		
Priority:	High		
Business Rules:	BR-86 and BR-88 govern an employee's eligibility to enroll for payroll deduction.		
Other Information:	Expect high frequency of executing this use case within first 2 weeks after system is released.		

[Note: the following use case is written in a very brief form, to illustrate that it is not always necessary to fully complete the use case template, provided developers have the necessary information available from some other source. It's a good idea to plan out which use cases require detailing and which do not.]

ID and Name:	**UC-9 Modify a Menu**		
Created By:	Mark Hassall	Date Created:	October 7, 2013
Description:	The cafeteria Menu Manager may retrieve the menu for a specific date in the future, modify it to add new food items, remove or change food items, create or change a meal special, or change prices, and save the modified menu.		
Exceptions:	No menu exists for the specified date; show an error message and let the Menu Manager enter a new date.		
Priority:	High		
Business Rules:	BR-24		
Other Information:	Certain food items will not be deliverable, so the menu presented to the Patrons of the COS for delivery will not always exactly match the menu available for pickup in the cafeteria. The Menu Manager can set which items are not deliverable.		

Software Requirements Specification

1. Introduction

1.1 Purpose

This SRS describes the functional and nonfunctional requirements for software release 1.0 of the Cafeteria Ordering System (COS). This document is intended to be used by the members of the project team who will implement and verify the correct functioning of the system. Unless otherwise noted, all requirements specified here are committed for release 1.0.

1.2 Document Conventions

No special typographical conventions are used in this SRS.

1.3 Project Scope

The COS will permit Process Impact employees to order meals from the company cafeteria online to be delivered to specified campus locations. A detailed description is available in the *Cafeteria Ordering System Vision and Scope Document* [1], along with the features that are scheduled for full or partial implementation in this release.

1.4 References

1.   Wiegers, Karl. *Cafeteria Ordering System Vision and Scope Document, www.processimpact.com/ projects/COS/COS Vision and Scope.docx*

2.   Beatty, Joy. *Process Impact Intranet Development Standard, Version 1.3, www.processimpact.com/ corporate/standards/PI Intranet Development Standard.pdf*

3.   Rath, Andrew. *Process Impact Internet Application User Interface Standard, Version 2.0, www.processimpact.com/corporate/standards/PI Internet UI Standard.pdf*

2. Overall Description

2.1 Product Perspective

The Cafeteria Ordering System is a new software system that replaces the current manual and telephone processes for ordering and picking up meals in the Process Impact cafeteria. The context diagram in Figure C-2 illustrates the external entities and system interfaces for release 1.0. The system is expected to evolve over several releases, ultimately connecting to the Internet ordering services for several local restaurants and to credit and debit card authorization services.

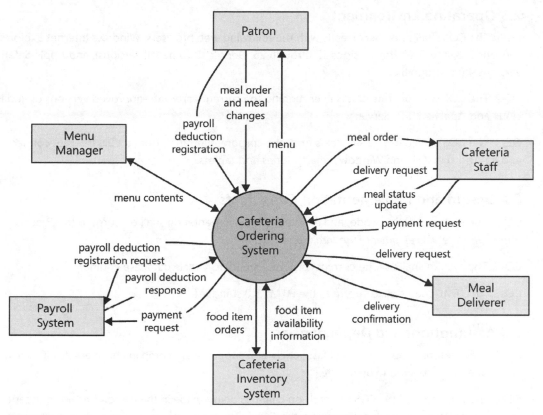

FIGURE C-2 Context diagram for release 1.0 of the Cafeteria Ordering System.

2.2 User Classes and Characteristics

User class	Description
Patron (favored)	A Patron is a Process Impact employee who wants to order meals to be delivered from the company cafeteria. There are about 600 potential Patrons, of which 300 are expected to use the COS an average of 5 times per week each. Patrons will sometimes order multiple meals for group events or guests. An estimated 60 percent of orders will be placed using the corporate intranet, with 40 percent of orders being placed from home or by smartphone or tablet apps.
Cafeteria Staff	The Process Impact cafeteria employs about 20 Cafeteria Staff who will receive orders from the COS, prepare meals, package them for delivery, and request delivery. Most of the Cafeteria Staff will need training in the use of the hardware and software for the COS.
Menu Manager	The Menu Manager is a cafeteria employee who establishes and maintains daily menus of the food items available from the cafeteria. Some menu items may not be available for delivery. The Menu Manager will also define the cafeteria's daily specials. The Menu Manager will need to edit existing menus periodically.
Meal Deliverer	As the Cafeteria Staff prepare orders for delivery, they will issue delivery requests to a Meal Deliverer's smartphone. The Meal Deliverer will pick up the food and deliver it to the Patron. A Meal Deliverer's other interactions with the COS will be to confirm that a meal was (or was not) delivered.

2.3 Operating Environment

OE-1: The COS shall operate correctly with the following web browsers: Windows Internet Explorer versions 7, 8, and 9; Firefox versions 12 through 26; Google Chrome (all versions); and Apple Safari versions 4.0 through 8.0.

OE-2: The COS shall operate on a server running the current corporate-approved versions of Red Hat Linux and Apache HTTP Server.

OE-3: The COS shall permit user access from the corporate intranet; from a VPN Internet connection; and by Android, iOS, and Windows smartphones and tablets.

2.4 Design and Implementation Constraints

CO-1: The system's design, code, and maintenance documentation shall conform to the *Process Impact Intranet Development Standard, Version 1.3* [2].

CO-2: The system shall use the current corporate standard Oracle database engine.

CO-3: All HTML code shall conform to the HTML 5.0 standard.

2.5 Assumptions and Dependencies

AS-1: The cafeteria is open for breakfast, lunch, and supper every company business day in which employees are expected to be on site.

DE-1: The operation of the COS depends on changes being made in the Payroll System to accept payment requests for meals ordered with the COS.

DE-2: The operation of the COS depends on changes being made in the Cafeteria Inventory System to update the availability of food items as COS accepts meal orders.

3. System Features

3.1 Order Meals from Cafeteria

3.1.1 Description

A cafeteria Patron whose identity has been verified can order meals either to be delivered to a specified company location or to be picked up in the cafeteria. A Patron can cancel or change a meal order if it has not yet been prepared. Priority = High.

3.1.2 Functional Requirements

Order.Place:	**Placing a meal order**
.Register:	The COS shall confirm that the Patron is registered for payroll deduction.
.No:	If the Patron is not registered for payroll deduction, the COS shall give the Patron options to register now and continue placing an order, to place an order for pickup in the cafeteria (but not for delivery), or to exit.
.Date:	The COS shall prompt the Patron for the meal date (see BR-8).
.Cutoff:	If the meal date is the current date and the current time is after the order cutoff time, the COS shall inform the Patron that it's too late to place an order for today. The Patron can either change the meal date or cancel the order.
Order.Deliver:	**Delivery or pickup**
.Select:	The Patron shall specify whether the order is to be picked up or delivered.
.Location:	If the order is to be delivered and there are still available delivery times for the meal date, the Patron shall provide a valid delivery location.
.Notimes:	The COS shall notify the Patron if there are no available delivery times for the meal date. The Patron shall either cancel the order or indicate that he will pick up the order in the cafeteria.
.Times:	The COS shall display the remaining available delivery times for the meal date. The COS shall allow the Patron to request one of the delivery times shown, to change the order to be picked up in the cafeteria, or to cancel the order.
Order.Menu:	**Viewing a menu**
.Date:	The COS shall display a menu for the date that the Patron specified.
.Available:	The menu for the specified date shall display only those food items for which at least one unit is available in the cafeteria's inventory and which can be delivered.
Order.Units:	**Ordering multiple meals and multiple food items**
.Multiple:	The COS shall permit the user to order multiple identical meals, up to the fewest available units of any menu item in the order.
.TooMany:	If the Patron orders more units of a menu item than are presently in the cafeteria's inventory, the COS shall inform the Patron of the maximum number of units of that food item that he can order.
Order.Confirm:	**Confirming an order**
.Display:	When the Patron indicates that he does not wish to order any more food items, the COS shall display the food items ordered, the individual food item prices, and the payment amount calculated per BR-12.
.Prompt:	The COS shall prompt the Patron to confirm the meal order.
.Response:	The Patron can confirm, edit, or cancel the order.
.More:	The COS shall let the Patron order additional meals for the same or for a different date. BR-3 and BR-4 pertain to multiple meals in a single order.

Order.Pay:	**Meal order payment**
.Method:	When the Patron indicates that he is done placing orders, the COS shall ask the user to select a payment method.
.Deliver:	See BR-11.
.Pickup:	If the meal is to be picked up in the cafeteria, the Patron shall choose to pay by payroll deduction or by cash at the time of pickup.
.Deduct:	If the Patron selected payroll deduction, the COS shall issue a payment request to the Payroll System.
.OK:	If the payment request is accepted, the COS shall display a message confirming acceptance of the order with a transaction number.
.NG:	If the payment request is rejected, the COS shall display the reason for the rejection. The Patron shall either cancel the order, or change the payment method to cash and request to pick up the order at the cafeteria.

Order.Done:	**When the Patron has confirmed the order, the COS shall do the following as a single transaction.**
.Store:	Assign the next available meal order number to the meal and store the meal order with a status of "Accepted."
.Inventory:	Send a message to the Cafeteria Inventory System with the number of units of each food item in the order.
.Menu:	Update the menu for the current order's order date to reflect any items that are now out of stock in the cafeteria inventory.
.Times:	Update the remaining available delivery times for the date of this order.
.Patron:	Send an email message or text message (depending on the Patron's profile setting) to the Patron with the meal order and meal payment information.
.Cafeteria:	Send an email message to the Cafeteria Staff with the meal order information.
.Failure:	If any step of Order.Done fails, the COS shall roll back the transaction and notify the user that the order was unsuccessful, along with the reason for failure.

[Note: Functional requirements for reordering a meal and for changing and canceling meal orders are not provided in this example.]

3.2 Order Meals from Restaurants

[Details are not provided in this example. Quite a lot of the functionality described under 3.1 Order Meals from Cafeteria could likely be reused, so this section should just specify the additional functionality that addresses the restaurant interface.]

3.3 Create, View, Modify, and Delete Meal Subscriptions

[Details are not provided in this example.]

3.4 Create, View, Modify, and Delete Cafeteria Menus

[Details are not provided in this example.]

4. Data Requirements

4.1 Logical Data Model

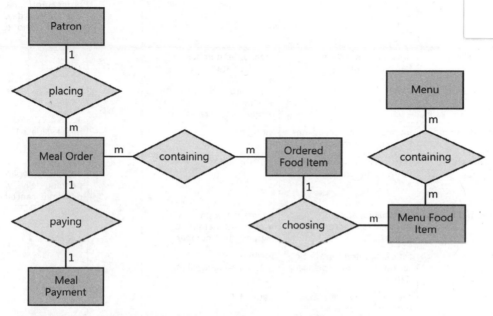

FIGURE C-3 Partial data model for release 1.0 of the Cafeteria Ordering System.

4.2 Data Dictionary

Data element	Description	Composition or data type	Length	Values
delivery instruction	where and to whom a meal is to be delivered, if it isn't being picked up in the cafeteria	patron name + patron phone number + meal date + delivery location + delivery time window		
delivery location	building and room to which an ordered meal is to be delivered	alphanumeric	50	hyphens and commas permitted
delivery time window	beginning time of a 15-minute range on the meal date during which an ordered meal is to be delivered	time	hh:mm	local time; hh = 0-23 inclusive; mm = 00, 15, 30, or 45
employee ID	company ID number of the employee who placed a meal order	integer	6	
food item description	description of a food item on a menu	alphabetic	100	
food item price	pre-tax cost of a single unit of a menu food item	numeric, dollars and cents	dd.cc	

Data element	Description	Composition or data type	Length	Values
meal date	the date the meal is to be delivered or picked up	date, MM/DD/YYYY	10	default = current date if the current time is before the order cutoff time, else the next day; cannot be prior to current date
meal order	details about a meal a Patron ordered	meal order number + order date + meal date + 1:m{ordered food item} + delivery instruction + meal order status		
meal order number	unique ID that COS assigns to each accepted meal order	integer	7	Initial value is 1
meal order status	status of a meal order that a Patron initiated	alphabetic	16	Incomplete, accepted, prepared, pending delivery, delivered, canceled
meal payment	information about a payment COS accepted for a meal	payment amount + payment method + transaction number		
menu	list of food items available for purchase on a specific date	menu date + 1:m{menu food item}		
menu date	the date for which a specific menu is available	date, MM/DD/YYYY	10	
menu food item	description of a menu item	food item description + food item price		
order cutoff time	the time of day before which all meal orders for that date must be placed	time, HH:MM	5	
order date	the date on which a Patron placed a meal order	date, MM/DD/YYYY	10	
ordered food item	one menu food item that a Patron requested as part of a meal order	menu food item + quantity ordered		
patron	a Process Impact employee who is authorized to order a meal	patron name + employee ID + patron phone number + patron location + patron email		
patron email	email address of the employee who placed a meal order	alphanumeric	50	
patron location	building and room numbers of the employee who placed a meal order	alphanumeric	50	hyphens and commas permitted
patron name	name of the employee who placed a meal order	alphabetic	30	
patron phone number	telephone number of the employee who placed a meal order	AAA-EEE-NNNN xXXXX for area code (A), exchange (E), number (N), and extension (X)	18	

Data element	Description	Composition or data type	Length	Values
payment amount	total price of an order in dollars and cents, calculated per BR-12	numeric, dollars and cents	dddd.cc	
payment method	how the Patron is paying for a meal he ordered	alphabetic	16	payroll deduction, cash, credit card, debit card
quantity ordered	the number of units of each food item that the Patron is ordering in a single meal order	integer	4	default = 1; maximum = quantity presently in inventory
transaction number	unique sequence number that COS assigns to each payment transaction	integer	12	

4.3 Reports

4.3.1 Ordered Meal History Report

Report ID	COS-RPT-1
Report Title	Ordered Meal History
Report Purpose	Patron wants to see a list of all meals that he had previously ordered from the Process Impact cafeteria or local restaurants over a specified time period up to 6 months prior to the current date, so he can reorder a particular meal he liked.
Priority	Medium
Report Users	Patrons
Data Sources	Database of previously placed meal orders
Frequency and Disposition	Report is generated on demand by a Patron. Data in the report is static. Report is displayed on user's web browser screen on a computer, tablet, or smartphone. It can be printed if the display device permits printing.
Latency	Complete report must be displayed to Patron within 3 seconds after it is requested.
Visual Layout	Landscape mode
Header and Footer	Report header shall contain the report title, Patron's name, and date range specified. If printed, report footer shall show the page number.
Report Body	Fields shown and column headings: ■ Order Number ■ Meal Date ■ Ordered From ("Cafeteria" or restaurant name) ■ Items Ordered (list all items in the meal order, their quantity, and their prices) ■ Total Food Price ■ Tax ■ Delivery Charge ■ Total Price (sum of food item prices, tax, and delivery charge) Selection Criteria: date range specified by Patron, inclusive of end points Sort Criteria: reverse chronological order
End-of-Report Indicator	None
Interactivity	Patron can drill down to see ingredients and nutritional information for each item in the order.
Security Access Restrictions	A Patron may retrieve only his own meal order history.

[Note: Other COS reports are not provided in this example.]

4.4 Data Integrity, Retention, and Disposal

DI-1: The COS shall retain individual Patron meal orders for 6 months following the meal's delivery date.

DI-2: The COS shall retain menus for 1 year following the menu date.

5. External Interface Requirements

5.1 User Interfaces

UI-1: The Cafeteria Ordering System screen displays shall conform to the *Process Impact Internet Application User Interface Standard, Version 2.0* [3].

UI-2: The system shall provide a help link from each displayed webpage to explain how to use that page.

UI-3: The webpages shall permit complete navigation and food item selection by using the keyboard alone, in addition to using mouse and keyboard combinations.

5.2 Software Interfaces

SI-1: Cafeteria Inventory System

> SI-1.1: The COS shall transmit the quantities of food items ordered to the Cafeteria Inventory System through a programmatic interface.
>
> SI-1.2: The COS shall poll the Cafeteria Inventory System to determine whether a requested food item is available.
>
> SI-1.3: When the Cafeteria Inventory System notifies the COS that a specific food item is no longer available, the COS shall remove that food item from the menu for the current date.

SI-2: Payroll System

> The COS shall communicate with the Payroll System through a programmatic interface for the following operations:
>
> SI-2.1: To allow a Patron to register and unregister for payroll deduction.
>
> SI-2.2: To inquire whether a Patron is registered for payroll deduction.
>
> SI-2.3: To inquire whether a Patron is eligible to register for payroll deduction.
>
> SI-2.4: To submit a payment request for a purchased meal.
>
> SI-2.5: To reverse a previous charge because a patron rejected a meal or wasn't satisfied with it, or because the meal was not delivered per the delivery instructions.

5.3 Hardware Interfaces

No hardware interfaces have been identified.

5.4 Communications Interfaces

CI-1: The COS shall send an email or text message (based on user account settings) to the Patron to confirm acceptance of an order, price, and delivery instructions.

CI-2: The COS shall send an email or text message (based on user account settings) to the Patron to report any problems with a meal order or delivery.

6. Quality Attributes

6.1 Usability Requirements

USE-1: The COS shall allow a Patron to retrieve the previous meal ordered with a single interaction.

USE-2: 95% of new users shall be able to successfully order a meal without errors on their first try.

6.2 Performance Requirements

PER-1: The system shall accommodate a total of 400 users and a maximum of 100 concurrent users during the peak usage time window of 9:00 A.M. to 10:00 A.M. local time, with an estimated average session duration of 8 minutes.

PER-2: 95% of webpages generated by the COS shall download completely within 4 seconds from the time the user requests the page over a 20 Mbps or faster Internet connection.

PER-3: The system shall display confirmation messages to users within an average of 3 seconds and a maximum of 6 seconds after the user submits information to the system.

6.3 Security Requirements

SEC-1: All network transactions that involve financial information or personally identifiable information shall be encrypted per BR-33.

SEC-2: Users shall be required to log on to the COS for all operations except viewing a menu.

SEC-3: Only authorized Menu Managers shall be permitted to work with menus, per BR-24.

SEC-4: The system shall permit Patrons to view only orders that they placed.

6.4 Safety Requirements

SAF-1: The user shall be able to see a list of all ingredients in any menu items, with ingredients highlighted that are known to cause allergic reactions in more than 0.5 percent of the North American population.

6.5 Availability Requirements

AVL-1: The COS shall be available at least 98% of the time between 5:00 A.M. and midnight local time and at least 90% of the time between midnight and 5:00 A.M. local time, excluding scheduled maintenance windows.

6.6 Robustness Requirements

ROB-1: If the connection between the user and the COS is broken prior to a new order being either confirmed or terminated, the COS shall enable the user to recover an incomplete order and continue working on it.

Appendix A: Analysis Models

Figure C-4 is a state-transition diagram that shows the possible meal order statuses and the allowed changes in status.

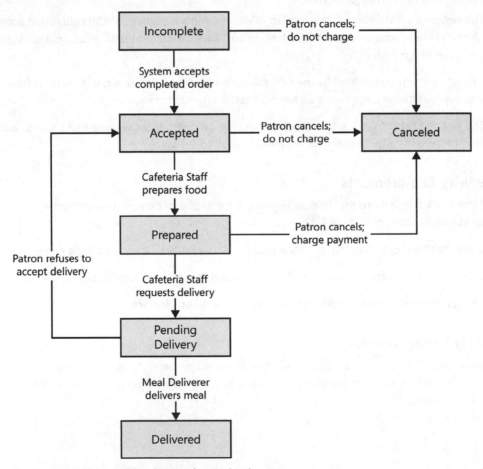

FIGURE C-4 State-transition diagram for meal order status.

Business Rules

[Note: The following illustrates a portion of a separate business rules catalog.]

ID	Rule definition	Type of rule	Static or dynamic	Source
BR-1	Delivery time windows are 15 minutes, beginning on each quarter hour.	Fact	Dynamic	Cafeteria Manager
BR-2	Deliveries must be completed between 11:00 A.M. and 2:00 P.M. local time, inclusive.	Constraint	Dynamic	Cafeteria Manager
BR-3	All meals in a single order must be delivered to the same location.	Constraint	Static	Cafeteria Manager
BR-4	All meals in a single order must be paid for by using the same payment method.	Constraint	Static	Cafeteria Manager
BR-8	Meals must be ordered within 14 calendar days of the meal date.	Constraint	Dynamic	Cafeteria Manager
BR-11	If an order is to be delivered, the patron must pay by payroll deduction.	Constraint	Dynamic	Cafeteria Manager
BR-12	Order price is calculated as the sum of each food item price times the quantity of that food item ordered, plus applicable sales tax, plus a delivery charge if a meal is delivered outside the free delivery zone.	Computation	Dynamic	cafeteria policy; state tax code
BR-24	Only cafeteria employees who are designated as Menu Managers by the Cafeteria Manager can create, modify, or delete cafeteria menus.	Constraint	Static	cafeteria policy
BR-33	Network transmissions that involve financial information or personally identifiable information require 256-bit encryption.	Constraint	Static	corporate security policy
BR-86	Only regular employees can register for payroll deduction for any company purchase.	Constraint	Static	Corporate Accounting Manager
BR-88	An employee can register for payroll deduction payment of cafeteria meals if no more than 40 percent of his gross pay is currently being deducted for other reasons.	Constraint	Dynamic	Corporate Accounting Manager

Glossary

acceptance criteria Conditions that a software product must satisfy to be accepted by a user, customer, or other stakeholder.

acceptance test A test that evaluates anticipated usage scenarios to determine the software's acceptability. Used in agile development both to express details about a user story and to determine whether a user story is fully and correctly implemented.

activity diagram An analysis model that depicts a process flow proceeding from one activity to another. Similar to a flowchart.

actor A person performing a specific role, a software system, or a hardware device that interacts with a system to achieve a useful goal. Also called a *user role*.

agile development A term used for software development methods characterized by continuous collaboration between developers and customers, limited documentation of requirements in the form of user stories and corresponding acceptance tests, and rapid and frequent delivery of small increments of useful functionality. Agile development methods include Extreme Programming, Scrum, Feature-Driven Development, Lean Software Development, and Kanban.

allocation See *requirements allocation*.

alternative flow A path through a use case that leads to success but that involves a variation from the normal flow in the specifics of the task or in the actor's interaction with the system.

analysis, requirements The process of classifying requirements information into various categories, evaluating requirements for desirable qualities, representing requirements in different forms, deriving detailed requirements from high-level requirements, negotiating priorities, and related activities.

analyst See *business analyst*.

application See *product*.

architecture The structure of a system, including any software, hardware, and human components that make up the system, the interfaces and relationships between those components, and the component behaviors that are visible to other components.

assumption A statement that is believed to be true in the absence of proof or definitive knowledge.

attribute, quality See *quality attribute*.

attribute, requirement See *requirement attribute*.

BA See *business analyst*.

backlog, product On an agile project, the prioritized list of work remaining for the project. A backlog can contain user stories, business processes, change requests, infrastructure development, and defect stories. Work items from the backlog are allocated to upcoming iterations based on their priority.

baseline, requirements A snapshot in time that represents the current agreed-upon, reviewed, and approved set of requirements, often defining the contents of a specific product release or development iteration. Serves as the basis for further development work.

big data A collection of data that is characterized as large volume (much data exists), high velocity (data flows rapidly into an organization), and/or highly complex (the data is diverse). Managing big data entails understanding how to discover, collect, store, and process the data quickly and effectively.

business analyst (BA) The role on a project team that has primary responsibility for working with stakeholder representatives to elicit, analyze, specify, validate, and manage the project's requirements. Also called a *requirements analyst, system analyst, requirements engineer, requirements manager, business systems analyst,* and simply *analyst.*

business analytics system A software system used to convert large and complex data sets into meaningful information from which to make decisions.

business objective A financial or nonfinancial business benefit that an organization expects to receive as a result of a project or some other initiative.

business objectives model A visual representation of a hierarchy of business problems and business objectives.

business requirements A set of information that describes a business need that leads to one or more projects to deliver a solution and the desired ultimate business outcomes. The business requirements include business opportunities, business objectives, success metrics, a vision statement, and scope and limitations.

business rule A policy, guideline, standard, regulation, or computational formula that defines or constrains some aspect of the business.

cardinality The number of instances of a particular data entity that logically relate to an instance of another entity. Possibilities are one-to-one, one-to-many, and many-to-many.

change control board (CCB) The group of people responsible for deciding to accept or reject proposed changes on a software project, including changes in requirements.

class A description of a set of objects having common properties and behaviors, which typically correspond to real-world items (persons, places, or things) in the business or problem domain.

class diagram An analysis model that shows a set of system or problem domain classes, their interfaces, and their relationships.

constraint A restriction that is imposed on the choices available to the developer for the design and construction of a product. Other types of constraints can restrict the options available to project managers. Business rules often impose constraints on business operations and hence on software systems.

context diagram An analysis model that depicts a system at a high level of abstraction. The context diagram identifies objects outside the system that exchange data with the system, but it shows nothing about the system's internal structure or behavior.

COTS (commercial off-the-shelf) product A software package purchased from a vendor and either used as a self-contained solution to a problem or integrated, customized, and/or extended to satisfy customer needs.

CRUD matrix A table that correlates system actions with data entities to show where each data item is created, read, updated, and deleted.

customer An individual or organization that derives either direct or indirect benefit from a product. Software customers might request, pay for, select, specify, use, or receive the output generated by a software product.

dashboard report A screen display or printed report that uses multiple textual and/or graphical representations of data to provide a consolidated, multidimensional view of what is going on in an organization or a process.

data dictionary A collection of definitions for the data elements and data structures that are relevant to the problem domain.

data flow diagram An analysis model that depicts the processes, data stores, external entities, and flows among them that characterize the behavior of data flowing through business processes or software systems.

decision rule An agreed-upon way by which a body of people arrives at a decision.

decision table An analysis model in the form of a matrix that shows all combinations of values for a set of conditions and indicates the expected system action in response to each combination.

decision tree An analysis model that visually depicts the actions a system takes in response to specific combinations of a set of conditions.

dependency As used in requirements specification, a reliance that a project has on a factor, event, or group outside its control.

dialog map An analysis model that depicts a user interface architecture, showing the dialog elements with which the user can interact and the navigations permitted between them.

ecosystem map An analysis model that shows a set of systems that interact with each other and the nature of their relationships. Unlike a context diagram, an ecosystem map shows systems that have a relationship even if there is no direct interface between them.

elicitation, requirements The process of identifying requirements from various sources through interviews, workshops, focus groups, observations, document analysis, and other mechanisms.

embedded system A system that contains hardware components controlled by software running on a dedicated computer that is incorporated as part of a larger product.

entity An item in the business domain about which data is collected and stored.

entity-relationship diagram An analysis model that identifies the logical relationships between pairs of entities. Used for modeling data.

epic A user story on an agile project that is too large to implement in one development iteration. It is subdivided into smaller stories that each can be fully implemented in a single iteration.

event A trigger or stimulus that takes place in a system's environment that leads to a system response, such as a functional behavior or a change in state.

event-response table A list of the external or time-triggered events that could affect the system and a description of how the system is to respond to each event.

evolutionary prototype A fully functional prototype created as a skeleton or an initial increment of the final product, which is fleshed out and extended incrementally as requirements become clear and ready for implementation.

exception A condition that can prevent a use case from concluding successfully. Unless some recovery mechanism is possible, the use case's postconditions are not reached and the actor's goal is not achieved.

extend relationship A construct in which an alternative flow in a use case branches off from the normal flow into a separate extension use case.

external entity An object in a context diagram or a data flow diagram that represents a user class, actor, software system, or hardware device that is external to the system being described but interfaces to it in some fashion. Also called a *terminator*.

external interface requirement A description of a connection between a software system and a user, another software system, or a hardware device.

facilitator A person who is responsible for planning and leading a group activity, such as a requirements elicitation workshop.

feature One or more logically related system capabilities that provide value to a user and are described by a set of functional requirements.

feature tree An analysis model that depicts the features planned for a product in a hierarchical tree, showing up to two levels of subfeatures beneath each main feature.

flowchart An analysis model that shows the processing steps and decision points in the logic of a process. Similar to an activity diagram.

function point A measure of software size, based on the number and complexity of internal logical files, external interface files, external inputs, outputs, and queries.

functional requirement A description of a behavior that a software system will exhibit under specific conditions.

gap analysis A comparison of the current state to an alternative or potential state for a system, process, or other aspect of a business situation, to identify significant differences between them.

gold-plating Unnecessary or excessively complex functionality that is specified or built into a product, sometimes without customer approval.

green-field project A project in which new software or a new system is developed.

horizontal prototype See *mock-up*.

include relationship A construct in which several steps that recur in multiple use cases are factored out into a separate sub-use case, which the other use cases then invoke when needed.

inspection A type of formal peer review that involves a trained team of individuals who follow a well-defined process to examine a work product carefully for defects.

issue, requirement A defect, open question, or decision regarding a requirement. Examples include items flagged as TBD, pending decisions, information that is needed, and conflicts awaiting resolution.

iteration An uninterrupted development period, typically one to four weeks in duration, during which a development team implements a defined set of functionality selected from the product backlog or baselined requirements for the product.

mock-up A partial or possible representation of a user interface for a software system. Used to evaluate usability and to assess the completeness and correctness of requirements. Could be executable or could be in the form of a paper prototype. Also called a *horizontal prototype*.

navigation map See *dialog map*.

nonfunctional requirement A description of a property or characteristic that a system must exhibit or a constraint that it must respect.

normal flow The default sequence of steps in a use case, which leads to satisfying the use case's postconditions and letting the user achieve his goal. Also known as the *normal course, main course, basic flow, normal sequence, main success scenario*, and *happy path*.

operational profile A suite of scenarios that represents the expected usage pattern of a software product.

paper prototype A non-executable mock-up of a software system's user interface using low-tech screen sketches.

peer review An activity in which one or more persons other than the author of a work product examine that product with the intent of finding defects and improvement opportunities.

pilot A controlled execution of a new solution (such as a process, tool, software system, or training course) with the objective of evaluating the solution under real conditions to assess its readiness for general deployment.

Planguage A keyword-oriented language developed by Tom Gilb that enables precise and quantitative specification of requirements, particularly nonfunctional requirements.

postcondition A condition that describes the state of a system after a use case is successfully completed.

precondition A condition that must be satisfied or a state the system must be in before a use case can begin.

prioritization The act of determining which requirements for a software product are the most important for achieving business success and the sequence in which requirements should be implemented.

procedure A step-by-step description of a course of action to be taken to perform a specified activity, describing how the activity is to be accomplished.

process A sequence of activities performed for a particular purpose. A *process description* is a documented definition of those activities.

process assets Items such as templates, forms, checklists, policies, procedures, process descriptions, and sample work products that are collected to assist an organization's effective application of software development practices.

process flow The sequential steps of a business process or the operations of a proposed software system. Often represented by using an activity diagram, flowchart, swimlane diagram, or other modeling notation.

product Whatever ultimate deliverable a project is developing. In this book, *product*, *application*, *system*, and *solution* are used interchangeably.

product backlog See *backlog, product*.

product champion A designated representative of a specific user class who supplies the user requirements for the group that he or she represents.

product owner A role, typically on an agile project team, that represents the customer and that is responsible for setting the product vision, providing project boundaries and constraints, prioritizing the contents of the product backlog, and making product decisions.

proof of concept A prototype that implements a portion of a software-containing system that slices through multiple layers of the architecture. Used to evaluate technical feasibility and performance. Also called a *vertical prototype*.

prototype A partial, preliminary, or possible implementation of a software system. Used to explore and validate requirements and design approaches. Types of prototypes are *evolutionary* and *throwaway; paper* and *electronic;* and *mock-up* and *proof-of-concept*.

quality attribute A nonfunctional requirement that describes a service or performance characteristic of a product. Types of quality attributes include usability, portability, maintainability, integrity, efficiency, reliability, and robustness. Quality attribute requirements describe the extent to which a software product must demonstrate desired characteristics.

quality-of-service requirement See *quality attribute*.

real-time system A hardware and software system that must produce a response within a specified time after an initiating event.

requirement A statement of a customer need or objective, or of a condition or capability that a product must possess to satisfy such a need or objective. A property that a product must have to provide value to a stakeholder.

requirement attribute Descriptive information about a requirement that enriches its definition beyond the statement of intended functionality. Example attribute types are origin, rationale, priority, owner, release number, and version number.

requirement pattern A systematic approach to specifying a particular type of requirement.

requirements allocation The process of apportioning system requirements among various architectural subsystems and components.

requirements analysis See *analysis, requirements*.

requirements analyst See *business analyst*.

requirements development The process of defining a project's scope, identifying user classes and user representatives, and eliciting, analyzing, specifying, and validating requirements. The product of requirements development is a set of documented requirements that defines some portion of the product to be built.

requirements engineer See *business analyst*.

requirements engineering The subdiscipline of systems engineering and software engineering that encompasses all project activities associated with understanding a product's necessary capabilities and attributes. Includes both requirements development and requirements management.

requirements management The process of working with a defined set of requirements throughout the product's development process and its operational life. Includes tracking requirements status, managing changes to requirements, controlling versions of requirements specifications, and tracing individual requirements to other requirements and system elements.

requirements specification See *software requirements specification* and *specification, requirements*.

requirements traceability matrix A table that depicts logical links between individual functional requirements and other system artifacts, including other functional requirements, user requirements, business requirements, architecture and design elements, code modules, tests, and business rules.

retrospective A review in which project participants reflect on the project's activities and outcomes with the intent of identifying ways to make the next project be even more successful.

reuse, requirements The act of using existing requirements knowledge in multiple systems that share some similar functionality.

review See *peer review*.

risk A condition that could cause some loss or otherwise threaten the success of a project.

root cause analysis An activity that seeks to understand the underlying factors that contribute to an observed problem.

scenario A description of a specific interaction between a user and a system to accomplish some goal. Alternatively, an instance of usage of the system, or a specific path through a use case.

scope The portion of the ultimate product vision that the current project will address. The scope draws the boundary between what's in and what's out for a project that creates a specific release or for a single development iteration.

scope creep A condition in which the scope of a project continues to increase in an uncontrolled fashion throughout the development process.

software development life cycle A sequence of activities by which a software product is defined, designed, built, and verified.

software requirements specification (SRS) A collection of the functional and nonfunctional requirements for a software product.

solution All of the components delivered by a project to achieve a set of business objectives specified by an organization, including software, hardware, business processes, user manuals, and training.

specification, requirements The process of documenting a software application's requirements in a structured, shareable, and manageable form. Also, the product from this process (see *software requirements specification*).

sprint See *iteration*.

SRS See *software requirements specification*.

stakeholder An individual, group, or organization that is actively involved in a project, is affected by its process or outcome, or can influence its process or outcome.

state machine diagram An analysis model that shows the sequence of states that an object in a system goes through during its lifetime in response to specific events that take place, or that shows the possible states of the system as a whole. Similar to a state-transition diagram.

state table An analysis model that shows in matrix form the various states that a system, or an object in the system, can be in, and which of the possible transitions between states are allowed.

state-transition diagram An analysis model that visually depicts the various states in which a system or an object in the system can exist, the permitted transitions that can take place between states, and the conditions and/or events that trigger each transition. Similar to a state machine or statechart diagram.

story See *user story*.

subject matter expert An individual who has extensive experience and knowledge in a domain and who is recognized as an authoritative source of information about the domain.

swimlane diagram An analysis model that shows the sequential steps of a business process flow or the operations of a proposed software system. The process is subdivided into visual components called lanes, which show the systems or actors that execute the steps.

system A product that contains multiple software and/or hardware subsystems. Colloquially, *system* also is used interchangeably in this book with *application*, *product*, and *solution* to refer to whatever software-containing deliverable a team is building.

system requirement A high-level requirement for a product that contains multiple subsystems, which could be all software or software and hardware.

TBD Abbreviation for *to be determined*. TBD serves as a placeholder when you know you are missing some requirements information. See *issue, requirement*.

template A pattern to be used as a guide for producing a complete document or other item.

throwaway prototype A prototype that is created with the intent of discarding it after it has served its purpose of clarifying and validating requirements and/or design alternatives.

tracing The process of defining logical links between one system element (user requirement, functional requirement, business rule, design component, code module, test, and the like) and another. Also called *traceability*.

UML An abbreviation for the Unified Modeling Language, which describes a set of standard notations for creating various visual models of systems, particularly for object-oriented software development.

usage scenario See *scenario*.

use case A description of a set of logically related possible interactions between an actor and a system that results in an outcome that provides value to the actor. Can encompass multiple scenarios.

use case diagram An analysis model that identifies the actors who can interact with a system to accomplish valuable goals and the various use cases that each actor might be involved with.

user A customer who will interact with a system either directly or indirectly (for example, by using outputs from the system but not generating those outputs personally). Also called *end user*.

user class A group of users for a system who have similar characteristics and requirements for the system. Members of a user class function as *actors* when interacting with the system through use cases.

user requirement A goal or task that specific classes of users must be able to perform with a system, or a desired product attribute. Use cases, user stories, and scenarios are common ways to represent user requirements.

user role See *actor*.

user story A format to capture user requirements on agile projects in the form of one or two sentences that articulate a user need or describe a unit of desired functionality, as well as stating the benefit of the functionality to the user.

validation The process of evaluating a project deliverable to determine whether it satisfies customer needs. Often stated as "Are we building the right product?"

verification The process of evaluating a project deliverable to determine whether it satisfies the specifications on which it was based. Often stated as "Are we building the product right?"

vertical prototype See *proof of concept*.

vision A statement that describes the strategic concept or the ultimate purpose and form of a new system.

vision and scope document A collection of the business requirements for a new system, including business objectives, success metrics, a product vision statement, and a project scope description.

waterfall development life cycle A model of the software development process in which the various activities of requirements, design, coding, testing, and deployment are performed sequentially with little overlap or iteration.

wireframe A kind of throwaway mock-up prototype that is often used for preliminary webpage design.

work product Any interim or final deliverable created for a software project.

References

Abran, Alain, James W. Moore, Pierre Bourque, and Robert Dupuis, eds. 2004. *Guide to the Software Engineering Body of Knowledge, 2004 Version.* Los Alamitos, CA: IEEE Computer Society Press.

Akers, Doug. 2008. "Real Reuse for Requirements." *Methods & Tools* 16(1):33–40.

Alexander, Ian F., and Ljerka Beus-Dukic. 2009. *Discovering Requirements: How to Specify Products and Services.* Chichester, England: John Wiley & Sons Ltd.

Alexander, Ian F., and Nell Maiden. 2004. *Scenarios, Stories, Use Cases: Through the Systems Development Life-Cycle.* Chichester, England: John Wiley & Sons Ltd.

Alexander, Ian F., and Richard Stevens. 2002. *Writing Better Requirements.* London: Addison-Wesley.

Ambler, Scott. 2005. *The Elements of UML 2.0 Style.* New York: Cambridge University Press.

Anderson, Ross J. 2008. *Security Engineering: A Guide to Building Dependable Distributed Systems,* 2nd ed. Indianapolis, IN: Wiley Publishing, Inc.

Arlow, Jim. 1998. "Use Cases, UML Visual Modeling and the Trivialisation of Business Requirements." *Requirements Engineering* 3(2):150–152.

Armour, Frank, and Granville Miller. 2001. *Advanced Use Case Modeling: Software Systems.* Boston: Addison-Wesley.

Arnold, Robert S., and Shawn A. Bohner. 1996. *Software Change Impact Analysis.* Los Alamitos, CA: IEEE Computer Society Press.

Basili, Victor R., and H. Dieter Rombach. 1988. "The TAME Project: Towards Improvement-Oriented Software Environments." *IEEE Transactions on Software Engineering.* 14(6):758–773.

Bass, Len, Paul Clements, and Rick Kazman. 1998. *Software Architecture in Practice.* Reading, MA: Addison-Wesley.

Beatty, Joy, and Anthony Chen. 2012. *Visual Models for Software Requirements.* Redmond, WA: Microsoft Press.

Beatty, Joy, and Remo Ferrari. 2011. "How to Evaluate and Select a Requirements Management Tool." *http://www.seilevel.com/wp-content/uploads/RequirementsManagementToolWhitepaper_1.pdf.*

Beck, Kent, et al. 2001. "Manifesto for Agile Software Development." *http://www.agilemanifesto.org.*

Beizer, Boris. 1999. "Best and Worst Testing Practices: A Baker's Dozen." *Cutter IT Journal* 12(2):32–38.

Beyer, Hugh, and Karen Holtzblatt. 1998. *Contextual Design: Defining Customer-Centered Systems*. San Francisco, CA: Morgan Kaufmann Publishers, Inc.

Blackburn, Joseph D., Gary D. Scudder, and Luk N. Van Wassenhove. 1996. "Improving Speed and Productivity of Software Development: A Global Survey of Software Developers." *IEEE Transactions on Software Engineering* 22(12):875–885.

Boehm, Barry W. 1981. *Software Engineering Economics*. Upper Saddle River, NJ: Prentice Hall.

_____. 1988. "A Spiral Model of Software Development and Enhancement." *IEEE Computer* 21(5):61–72.

_____. 2000. "Requirements that Handle IKIWISI, COTS, and Rapid Change." *IEEE Computer* 33(7):99–102.

Boehm, Barry W., Chris Abts, A. Winsor Brown, Sunita Chulani, Bradford K. Clark, Ellis Horowitz, Ray Madachy, Donald J. Reifer, and Bert Steece. 2000. *Software Cost Estimation with Cocomo II*. Upper Saddle River, NJ: Prentice Hall PTR.

Boehm, Barry W., and Philip N. Papaccio. 1988. "Understanding and Controlling Software Costs." *IEEE Transactions on Software Engineering* 14(10):1462–1477.

Boehm, Barry, and Richard Turner. 2004. *Balancing Agility and Discipline: A Guide for the Perplexed*. Boston: Addison-Wesley.

Booch, Grady, James Rumbaugh, and Ivar Jacobson. 1999. *The Unified Modeling Language User Guide*. Reading, MA: Addison-Wesley.

Box, George E. P., and Norman R. Draper. 1987. *Empirical Model-Building and Response Surfaces*. New York: John Wiley & Sons, Inc.

Boyer, Jérôme, and Hafedh Mili. 2011. *Agile Business Rule Development: Process, Architecture, and JRules Examples*. Heidelberg, Germany: Springer.

Bradshaw, Jeffrey M. 1997. *Software Agents*. Menlo Park, CA: The AAAI Press.

Brijs, Bert. 2013. *Business Analysis for Business Intelligence*. Boca Raton, FL: CRC Press.

Brooks, Frederick P., Jr. 1987. "No Silver Bullet: Essence and Accidents of Software Engineering." *IEEE Computer* 20(4):10–19.

Brosseau, Jim. 2010. "Software Quality Attributes: Following All the Steps." *http://www.clarrus.com/ resources/articles/software-quality-attributes*.

Brown, Norm. 1996. "Industrial-Strength Management Strategies." *IEEE Software* 13(4):94–103.

Business Rules Group. 2012. *http://www.businessrulesgroup.org*.

Callele, David, Eric Neufeld, and Kevin Schneider. 2008. "Emotional Requirements." *IEEE Software* 25(1):43–45.

Caputo, Kim. 1998. *CMM Implementation Guide: Choreographing Software Process Improvement*. Reading, MA: Addison-Wesley.

Carr, Marvin J., Suresh L. Konda, Ira Monarch, F. Carol Ulrich, and Clay F. Walker. 1993. *Taxonomy-Based Risk Identification* (CMU/ SEI-93-TR-6). Pittsburgh, PA: Software Engineering Institute, Carnegie Mellon University.

Cavano, J. P., and J. A. McCall. 1978. "A Framework for the Measurement of Software Quality." *ACM SIGSOFT Software Engineering Notes* 3(5):133–139.

Charette, Robert N. 1990. *Applications Strategies for Risk Analysis*. New York: McGraw Hill.

Chernak, Yuri. 2012. "Requirements Reuse: The State of the Practice." In *Proceedings of the 2012 IEEE International Conference on Software Science, Technology and Engineering*, 46–53. Los Alamitos, CA: IEEE Computer Society Press.

Chung, Lawrence, Kendra Cooper, and D.T. Huynh. 2001. "COTS-Aware Requirements Engineering Techniques." In *Proceedings of the 2001 Workshop on Embedded Software Technology (WEST'01)*.

Cockburn, Alistair. 2001. *Writing Effective Use Cases*. Boston: Addison-Wesley.

Cohen, Lou. 1995. *Quality Function Deployment: How to Make QFD Work for You*. Reading, MA: Addison-Wesley.

Cohn, Mike. 2004. *User Stories Applied: For Agile Software Development*. Boston: Addison-Wesley.

_____. 2005. *Agile Estimating and Planning*. Upper Saddle River, NJ: Prentice Hall.

_____. 2010. *Succeeding with Agile: Software Development Using Scrum*. Upper Saddle River, NJ: Addison-Wesley.

Collard, Ross. 1999. "Test Design." *Software Testing & Quality Engineering* 1(4):30–37.

Colorado State University. 2013. "Writing@CSU." *http://writing.colostate.edu/guides/guide .cfm?guideid=68*.

Constantine, Larry. 1998. "Prototyping from the User's Viewpoint." *Software Development* 6(11):51–57.

Constantine, Larry L., and Lucy A. D. Lockwood. 1999. *Software for Use: A Practical Guide to the Models and Methods of Usage-Centered Design*. Reading, MA: Addison-Wesley.

Cooper, Alan. 2004. *The Inmates Are Running the Asylum: Why High-Tech Products Drive Us Crazy and How to Restore the Sanity*. Indianapolis, IN: Sams Publishing.

Covey, Stephen R. 2004. *The 7 Habits of Highly Effective People*. New York: Free Press.

Davenport, Thomas H., ed. 2013. *Enterprise Analytics: Optimize Performance, Process, and Decisions through Big Data*. Upper Saddle River, NJ: Pearson Education, Inc.

Davenport, Thomas H., Jeanne G. Harris, and Robert Morrison. 2010. *Analytics at Work: Smarter Decisions, Better Results*. Boston: Harvard Business Review Press.

Davis, Alan M. 1993. *Software Requirements: Objects, Functions, and States, Revised Edition*. Englewood Cliffs, NJ: Prentice Hall PTR.

_____. 1995. *201 Principles of Software Development*. New York: McGraw-Hill.

_____. 2005. *Just Enough Requirements Management: Where Software Development Meets Marketing*. New York: Dorset House Publishing.

DeGrace, Peter, and Leslie Hulet Stahl. 1993. *The Olduvai Imperative: CASE and the State of Software Engineering Practice*. Englewood Cliffs, NJ: Yourdon Press/Prentice Hall.

Dehlinger, Josh, and Robyn R. Lutz. 2008. "Supporting Requirements Reuse in Multi-Agent System Product Line Design and Evolution." In *Proceedings of the 24th IEEE International Conference on Software Maintenance*, 207–216. Los Alamitos, CA: IEEE Computer Society Press.

DeMarco, Tom. 1979. *Structured Analysis and System Specification*. Upper Saddle River, NJ: Prentice Hall PTR.

DeMarco, Tom, and Timothy Lister. 1999. *Peopleware: Productive Projects and Teams*, 2nd ed. New York: Dorset House Publishing.

Denne, Mark, and Jane Cleland-Huang. 2003. *Software by Numbers: Low-Risk, High-Return Development*. Santa Clara, CA: Sun Microsystems Press/Prentice Hall.

Derby, Esther, and Diana Larsen. 2006. *Agile Retrospectives: Making Good Teams Great*. Raleigh, NC: The Pragmatic Bookshelf.

Devine, Tom. 2008. "Replacing a Legacy System." *http://www.richconsulting.com/our/pdfs/ RichConsulting_ReplacingLegacy.pdf*.

Douglass, Bruce Powel. 2001. "Capturing Real-Time Requirements." *Embedded Systems Programming* (November 2001). *http://www.embedded.com/story/OEG20011016S0126*.

Dyché, Jill. 2012. "The 7 Steps in Big Data Delivery." *http://www.networkworld.com/news/ tech/2012/071112-big-data-delivery-260813.html*.

Engblom, Jakob. 2007. "Using Simulation Tools For Embedded Systems Software Development: Part 1." *Embedded Systems Programming* (May 2007). *http://www.embedded.com/ design/real-time-and-performance/4007090/Using-simulation-tools-for-embedded- systems-software-development-Part-1*.

Ericson II, Clifton A. 2005. *Hazard Analysis Techniques for System Safety*. Hoboken, NJ: John Wiley & Sons, Inc.

_____. 2011. *Fault Tree Analysis Primer*. Charleston, NC: CreateSpace.

_____. 2012. *Hazard Analysis Primer*. Charleston, NC: CreateSpace.

Fagan, Michael E. 1976. "Design and Code Inspections to Reduce Errors in Program Development." *IBM Systems Journal* 15(3):182–211.

Ferdinandi, Patricia L. 2002. *A Requirements Pattern: Succeeding in the Internet Economy*. Boston: Addison-Wesley.

Firesmith, Donald. 2004. "Specifying Reusable Security Requirements." *Journal of Object Technology* 3(1):61–75.

Fisher, Roger, William Ury, and Bruce Patton. 2011. *Getting to Yes: Negotiating Agreement Without Giving In*. New York: Penguin Books.

Florence, Al. 2002. "Reducing Risks Through Proper Specification of Software Requirements." *CrossTalk* 15(4):13–15.

Fowler, Martin. 1999. *Refactoring: Improving the Design of Existing Code*. Reading, MA: Addison-Wesley.

———. 2003. *UML Distilled: A Brief Guide to the Standard Object Modeling Language*, 3rd ed. Boston: Addison-Wesley.

Franks, Bill. 2012. *Taming the Big Data Tidal Wave: Finding Opportunities in Huge Data Streams with Advanced Analytics*. Hoboken, NJ: John Wiley & Sons, Inc.

Frye, Colleen. 2009. "New Requirements Definition Tools Focus on Chronic Flaws." TechTarget. *http://searchsoftwarequality.techtarget.com/news/1354455/New-requirements-definition-tools-focus-on-chronic-flaws*.

GAO (Government Accounting Office). 2004. "Stronger Management Practices Are Needed to Improve DOD's Software-Intensive Weapon Acquisitions." GAO-04-393, *http://www.gao .gov/products/GAO-04-393*.

Garmahis, Michael. 2009. "Top 20 Wireframe Tools." *http://garmahis.com/reviews/wireframe-tools*.

Gause, Donald C., and Brian Lawrence. 1999. "User-Driven Design." *Software Testing & Quality Engineering* 1(1):22–28.

Gause, Donald C., and Gerald M. Weinberg. 1989. *Exploring Requirements: Quality Before Design*. New York: Dorset House Publishing.

Gilb, Tom. 1988. *Principles of Software Engineering Management*. Harlow, England: Addison-Wesley.

———. 1997. "Quantifying the Qualitative: How to Avoid Vague Requirements by Clear Specification Language." *Requirenautics Quarterly* 12:9–13.

———. 2005. *Competitive Engineering: A Handbook for Systems Engineering, Requirements Engineering, and Software Engineering Using Planguage*. Oxford, England: Elsevier Butterworth-Heinemann.

———. 2007. "Requirements for Outsourcing." *Methods and Tools* (Winter 2007).

Gilb, Tom, and Kai Gilb. 2011. "User Stories: A Skeptical View." *Agile Record* 6:52–54.

Gilb, Tom, and Dorothy Graham. 1993. *Software Inspection*. Wokingham, England: Addison-Wesley.

Glass, Robert L. 1992. *Building Quality Software*. Englewood Cliffs, NJ: Prentice Hall.

Gomaa, Hassan. 2004. *Designing Software Product Lines with UML: From Use Cases to Pattern-Based Software Architectures*. Boston: Addison-Wesley.

Gorman, Mary, and Ellen Gottesdiener. 2011. "It's the Goal, Not the Role: The Value of Business Analysis in Scrum." *http://www.stickyminds.com/s.asp?F=S16902_COL_2*.

Gottesdiener, Ellen. 2001. "Decide How to Decide." *Software Development* 9(1):65–70.

_____. 2002. *Requirements by Collaboration: Workshops for Defining Needs*. Boston: Addison-Wesley.

_____. 2005. *The Software Requirements Memory Jogger*. Salem, NH: Goal/QPC.

_____. 2009. "Agile Business Analysis in Flow: The Work of the Agile Analyst (Part 2)." *http://ebgconsulting.com/Pubs/Articles*.

Grady, Robert B. 1999. "An Economic Release Decision Model: Insights into Software Project Management." In *Proceedings of the Applications of Software Measurement Conference*, 227–239. Orange Park, FL: Software Quality Engineering.

Grady, Robert B., and Tom Van Slack. 1994. "Key Lessons in Achieving Widespread Inspection Use." *IEEE Software* 11(4):46–57.

Graham, Dorothy. 2002. "Requirements and Testing: Seven Missing-Link Myths." *IEEE Software* 19(5):15–17.

Grochow, Jerrold M. 2012. "IT Planning for Business Analytics." International Institute for Analytics Brief.

Ham, Gary A. 1998. "Four Roads to Use Case Discovery: There Is a Use (and a Case) for Each One." *CrossTalk* 11(12):17–19.

Hammer, Michael, and Graham Champy. 2006. *Reengineering the Corporation: A Manifesto for Business Revolution*. New York: HarperCollins.

Hardy, Terry L. 2011. *Essential Questions in System Safety: A Guide for Safety Decision Makers*. Bloomington, IN: AuthorHouse.

Harmon, Paul. 2007. *Business Process Change: A Guide for Business Managers and BPM and Six Sigma Professionals*, 2nd ed. Burlington, MA: Morgan Kaufmann Publishers, Inc.

Harrington, H. James. 1991. *Business Process Improvement: The Breakthrough Strategy for Total Quality, Productivity, and Competitiveness*. New York: McGraw-Hill.

Haskins, B., J. Stecklein, D. Brandon, G. Moroney, R. Lovell, and J. Dabney. 2004. "Error Cost Escalation through the Project Life Cycle." In *Proceedings of the 14th Annual International Symposium of INCOSE*. Toulouse, France. International Council on Systems Engineering.

Hatley, Derek, Peter Hruschka, and Imtiaz Pirbhai. 2000. *Process for System Architecture and Requirements Engineering*. New York: Dorset House Publishing.

Herrmann, Debra S. 1999. *Software Safety and Reliability: Techniques, Approaches, and Standards of Key Industrial Sectors*. Los Alamitos, CA: IEEE Computer Society Press.

Hoffman, Cecilie, and Rebecca Burgess. 2009. "Use and Profit from Peer Reviews on Business Requirements Documents." *Business Analyst Times* (September–December 2009).

Hofmann, Hubert F., and Franz Lehner. 2001. "Requirements Engineering as a Success Factor in Software Projects." *IEEE Software* 18(4):58–66.

Hooks, Ivy F., and Kristin A. Farry. 2001. *Customer-Centered Products: Creating Successful Products Through Smart Requirements Management*. New York: AMACOM.

Hsia, Pei, David Kung, and Chris Sell. 1997. "Software Requirements and Acceptance Testing." In *Annals of Software Engineering*. 3:291–317.

Humphrey, Watts S. 1989. *Managing the Software Process*. Reading, MA: Addison-Wesley.

IEEE. 1998. "IEEE Std 1061-1998: IEEE Standard for a Software Quality Metrics Methodology." Los Alamitos, CA: IEEE Computer Society Press.

IFPUG. 2010. *Function Point Counting Practices Manual, Version 4.3.1*. Princeton Junction, NJ: International Function Point Users Group.

IIBA. 2009. *A Guide to the Business Analysis Body of Knowledge (BABOK Guide), Version 2.0*. Toronto: International Institute of Business Analysis.

_____. 2010. *IIBA Business Analysis Self-Assessment*. Toronto: International Institute of Business Analysis.

_____. 2011. *IIBA Business Analysis Competency Model, Version 3.0*. Toronto: International Institute of Business Analysis.

_____. 2013. *IIBA Agile Extension to the BABOK Guide, Version 1.0*. Toronto: International Institute of Business Analysis.

Imhoff, Claudia. 2005. "Charting a Smooth Course to BI Implementation." Intelligent Solutions, Inc. *http://www.sas.com/reg/wp/corp/3529*.

INCOSE. 2010. "INCOSE Requirements Management Tools Survey." *http://www.incose.org/productspubs/products/rmsurvey.aspx*.

International Institute for Analytics. 2013. "Analytics 3.0." International Institute for Analytics. *http://iianalytics.com/a3*.

ISO/IEC. 2007. "ISO/IEC 25030:2007, Software engineering—Software product Quality Requirements and Evaluation (SQuaRE)—Quality Requirements." Geneva, Switzerland: International Organization for Standardization.

_____. 2011. "ISO/IEC 25010:2011, Systems and software engineering—Systems and software Quality Requirements and Evaluation (SQuaRE)—System and software quality models." Geneva, Switzerland: International Organization for Standardization.

ISO/IEC/IEEE. 2011. "ISO/IEC/IEEE 29148:2011(E), Systems and software engineering—Life cycle processes—Requirements engineering." Geneva, Switzerland: International Organization for Standardization.

Jacobson, Ivar, Grady Booch, and James Rumbaugh. 1999. *The Unified Software Development Process*. Reading, MA: Addison-Wesley.

Jacobson, Ivar, Magnus Christerson, Patrik Jonsson, and Gunnar Övergaard. 1992. *Object-Oriented Software Engineering: A Use Case Driven Approach*. Harlow, England: Addison-Wesley.

Jarke, Matthias. 1998. "Requirements Tracing." *Communications of the ACM* 41(12):32–36.

Jeffries, Ron, Ann Anderson, and Chet Hendrickson. 2001. *Extreme Programming Installed*. Boston: Addison-Wesley.

Johnson, Jeff. 2010. *Designing with the Mind in Mind: Simple Guide to Understanding User Interface Design Rule*s. San Francisco, CA: Morgan Kaufmann Publishers, Inc.

Jones, Capers. 1994. *Assessment and Control of Software Risks*. Englewood Cliffs, NJ: Prentice Hall PTR.

_____. 1996a. "Strategies for Managing Requirements Creep." *IEEE Computer* 29(6):92–94.

_____. 1996b. *Applied Software Measurement,* 2nd ed. New York: McGraw-Hill.

_____. 2006. "Social and Technical Reasons for Software Project Failures." *CrossTalk* 19(6):4–9.

Jung, Ho-Won. 1998. "Optimizing Value and Cost in Requirements Analysis." *IEEE Software* 15(4):74–78.

Karlsson, Joachim, and Kevin Ryan. 1997. "A Cost-Value Approach for Prioritizing Requirements." *IEEE Software* 14(5):67–74.

Kavi, Krishna M., Robert Akl, and Ali R. Hurson. 2009. "Real-Time Systems: An Introduction and the State-of-the-Art." *Wiley Encyclopedia of Computer Science and Engineering*, 2369–2377.

Keil, Mark, and Erran Carmel. 1995. "Customer-Developer Links in Software Development." *Communications of the ACM* 38(5):33–44.

Kelly, John C., Joseph S. Sherif, and Jonathon Hops. 1992. "An Analysis of Defect Densities Found During Software Inspections." *Journal of Systems and Software* 17(2):111–117.

Kerth, Norman L. 2001. *Project Retrospectives: A Handbook for Team Reviews*. New York: Dorset House Publishing.

Kleidermacher, David, and Mike Kleidermacher. 2012. *Embedded Systems Security: Practical Methods for Safe and Secure Software and Systems Development*. Waltham, MA: Elsevier Inc.

Koopman, Philip. 2010. *Better Embedded Systems Software*. Pittsburgh, PA: Drumnadrochit Press.

Kosman, Robert J. 1997. "A Two-Step Methodology to Reduce Requirement Defects." In *Annals of Software Engineering*. 3:477–494.

Kovitz, Benjamin L. 1999. *Practical Software Requirements: A Manual of Content and Style*. Greenwich, CT: Manning Publications Co.

Krug, Steve. 2006. *Don't Make Me Think: A Common Sense Approach to Web Usability,* 2nd ed. Berkeley, CA: New Riders Publishing.

Kukreja, Nupul, Sheetal Swaroop Payyavula, Barry Boehm, and Srinivas Padmanabhuni. 2012. "Selecting an Appropriate Framework for Value-Based Requirements Prioritization: A Case Study." In *Proceedings of the 20th IEEE International Requirements Engineering Conference*, 303–308. Los Alamitos, CA: IEEE Computer Society Press.

Kulak, Daryl, and Eamonn Guiney. 2004. *Use Cases: Requirements in Context,* 2nd ed. Boston: Addison-Wesley.

Larman, Craig. 1998. "The Use Case Model: What Are the Processes?" *Java Report* 3(8):62–72.

_____. 2004. *Agile and Iterative Development: A Manager's Guide.* Boston: Addison-Wesley.

Larman, Craig, and Victor R. Basili. 2003. "Iterative and Incremental Development: A Brief History." *IEEE Computer* 36(6):47–56.

Lauesen, Soren. 2002. *Software Requirements: Styles and Techniques.* London: Addison-Wesley.

Lavi, Jonah Z., and Joseph Kudish. 2005. *Systems Modeling & Requirements Specification Using ECSAM: An Analysis Method for Embedded and Computer-Based Systems.* New York: Dorset House Publishing.

Lawlis, Patricia K., Kathryn E. Mark, Deborah A. Thomas, and Terry Courtheyn. 2001. "A Formal Process for Evaluating COTS Software Products." *IEEE Computer* 34(5):58–63.

Lawrence, Brian. 1996. "Unresolved Ambiguity." *American Programmer* 9(5):17–22.

_____. 1997. "Requirements Happens. . ." *American Programmer* 10(4):3–9.

Lazar, Jonathan. 2001. *User-Centered Web Development.* Sudbury, MA: Jones and Bartlett Publishers.

Leffingwell, Dean. 1997. "Calculating the Return on Investment from More Effective Requirements Management." *American Programmer* 10(4):13–16.

_____. 2011. *Agile Software Requirements: Lean Requirements Practices for Teams, Programs, and the Enterprise.* Upper Saddle River, NJ: Addison-Wesley.

Leffingwell, Dean, and Don Widrig. 2000. *Managing Software Requirements: A Unified Approach.* Reading, MA: Addison-Wesley.

Leishman, Theron R., and David A. Cook. 2002. "Requirements Risks Can Drown Software Projects." *CrossTalk* 15(4):4–8.

Leveson, Nancy. 1995. *Safeware: System Safety and Computers.* Reading, MA: Addison-Wesley.

Lilly, Susan. 2000. "How to Avoid Use-Case Pitfalls." *Software Development* 8(1):40–44.

Martin, Johnny, and W. T. Tsai. 1990. "N-fold Inspection: A Requirements Analysis Technique." *Communications of the ACM* 33(2):225–232.

Mavin, Alistair, Philip Wilkinson, Adrian Harwood, and Mark Novak. 2009. "EARS (Easy Approach to Requirements Syntax)." In *Proceedings of the 17th International Conference on Requirements Engineering,* 317–322. Los Alamitos, CA: IEEE Computer Society Press.

McConnell, Steve. 1996. *Rapid Development: Taming Wild Software Schedules.* Redmond, WA: Microsoft Press.

_____. 1997. "Managing Outsourced Projects." *Software Development* 5(12):80, 78–79.

_____. 1998. *Software Project Survival Guide.* Redmond, WA: Microsoft Press.

_____. 2004. *Code Complete: A Practical Handbook of Software Construction,* 2nd ed. Redmond, WA: Microsoft Press.

_____. 2006. *Software Estimation: Demystifying the Black Art.* Redmond, WA: Microsoft Press.

McGraw, Karen L., and Karan Harbison. 1997. *User-Centered Requirements: The Scenario-Based Engineering Process.* Mahwah, NJ: Lawrence Erlbaum Associates.

Miller, Roxanne E. 2009. *The Quest for Software Requirements.* Milwaukee, WI: MavenMark Books.

Moore, Geoffrey A. 2002. *Crossing the Chasm: Marketing and Selling High-Tech Products to Mainstream Customers.* New York: HarperBusiness.

Morgan, Matthew. 2009. "Requirements Definition for Outsourced Teams." *Business Analyst Times. http://www.batimes.com/articles/requirements-definition-for-outsourced-teams .html.*

Morgan, Tony. 2002. *Business Rules and Information Systems: Aligning IT with Business Goals.* Boston: Addison-Wesley.

Musa, John D. 1996. "Software-Reliability-Engineered Testing." *IEEE Computer* 29(11):61–68.

_____. 1999. *Software Reliability Engineering.* New York: McGraw-Hill.

NASA. 2009. "NPR 7150.2A: NASA Software Engineering Requirements." *http://nodis3.gsfc .nasa.gov/displayDir.cfm?Internal_ID=N_PR_7150_002A_&page_name=AppendixA.*

Nejmeh, Brian A., and Ian Thomas. 2002. "Business-Driven Product Planning Using Feature Vectors and Increments." *IEEE Software* 19(6):34–42.

Nelsen, E. Dale. 1990. "System Engineering and Requirement Allocation." In *System and Software Requirements Engineering,* Richard H. Thayer and Merlin Dorfman, eds. Los Alamitos, CA: IEEE Computer Society Press.

Nielsen, Jakob. 2000. *Designing Web Usability.* Indianapolis, IN: New Riders Publishing.

OMG. 2011. *Business Process Model and Notation (BPMN) version 2.0.* Object Management Group. *http://www.omg.org/spec/BPMN/2.0.*

Pardee, William J. 1996. *To Satisfy & Delight Your Customer: How to Manage for Customer Value.* New York: Dorset House Publishing.

Patel, T., and James Taylor. 2010. "Business Analytics 101: Unlock the Business Intelligence Hidden in Company Databases." *http://www.sas.com/resources/whitepaper/wp_28372.pdf.*

Patterson, Kelly, Joseph Grenny, Ron McMillan, and Al Switzler. 2011. *Crucial Conversations: Tools for Talking When Stakes are High,* 2nd ed. New York: McGraw-Hill.

Peterson, Gary. 2002. "Risqué Requirements." *CrossTalk* 15(4):31.

Pichler, Roman. 2010. *Agile Product Management with Scrum: Creating Products that Customers Love.* Upper Saddle River, NJ: Addison-Wesley.

PMI. 2013. *A Guide to the Project Management Body of Knowledge: PMBOK Guide,* 5th ed. Newtown Square, PA: Project Management Institute.

Podeswa, Howard. 2009. *The Business Analyst's Handbook.* Boston: Course Technology.

_____. 2010. *UML for the IT Business Analyst: A Practical Guide to Requirements Gathering Using the Unified Modeling Language,* 2nd ed. Boston: Course Technology.

Porter, Adam A., Lawrence G. Votta, Jr., and Victor R. Basili. 1995. "Comparing Detection Methods for Software Requirements Inspections: A Replicated Experiment." *IEEE Transactions on Software Engineering* 21(6):563–575.

Porter-Roth, Bud. 2002. *Request for Proposal: A Guide to Effective RFP Development.* Boston: Addison-Wesley.

Poston, Robert M. 1996. *Automating Specification-Based Software Testing.* Los Alamitos, CA: IEEE Computer Society Press.

Potter, Neil S., and Mary E. Sakry. 2002. *Making Process Improvement Work: A Concise Action Guide for Software Managers and Practitioners.* Boston: Addison-Wesley.

Pugh, Ken. 2011. *Lean-Agile Acceptance Test-Driven Development: Better Software Through Collaboration.* Upper Saddle River, NJ: Addison-Wesley.

Putnam, Lawrence H., and Ware Myers. 1997. *Industrial Strength Software: Effective Management Using Measurement.* Los Alamitos, CA: IEEE Computer Society Press.

Radice, Ronald A. 2002. *High Quality Low Cost Software Inspections.* Andover, MA: Paradoxicon Publishing.

Ramesh, Bala, Curtis Stubbs, Timothy Powers, and Michael Edwards. 1995. "Lessons Learned from Implementing Requirements Traceability." *CrossTalk* 8(4):11–15, 20.

Rettig, Marc. 1994. "Prototyping for Tiny Fingers." *Communications of the ACM* 37(4):21–27.

Rierson, Leanna. 2013. *Developing Safety-Critical Software: A Practical Guide for Aviation Software and DO-178C Compliance.* Boca Raton, FL: CRC Press.

Robertson, James. 2002. "Eureka! Why Analysts Should Invent Requirements." *IEEE Software* 19(4):20–22.

Robertson, James, and Suzanne Robertson. 1994. *Complete Systems Analysis: The Workbook, the Textbook, the Answers.* New York: Dorset House Publishing.

Robertson, Suzanne, and James Robertson. 2013. *Mastering the Requirements Process: Getting Requirements Right,* 3rd ed. Upper Saddle River, NJ: Addison-Wesley.

Rose-Coutré, Robert. 2007. "Capturing Implied Requirements." *http://www.stickyminds.com/s .asp?F=S12998_ART_2.*

Ross, Ronald G. 1997. *The Business Rule Book: Classifying, Defining, and Modeling Rules, Version 4.0,* 2nd ed. Houston: Business Rule Solutions, LLC.

_____. 2001. "The Business Rules Classification Scheme." *DataToKnowledge Newsletter* 29(5).

Ross, Ronald G., and Gladys S. W. Lam. 2011. *Building Business Solutions: Business Analysis with Business Rules*. Houston: Business Rule Solutions, LLC.

Rothman, Johanna. 2000. *Reflections Newsletter* 3(1).

Royce, Winston. 1970. "Managing the Development of Large Software Systems." In *Proceedings of IEEE WESCON* 26, 1–9.

Rozanski, Nick, and Eoin Woods. 2005. *Software Systems Architecture: Working with Stakeholders Using Viewpoints and Perspectives*. Upper Saddle River, NJ: Pearson Education, Inc.

Rubin, Jeffrey, and Dana Chisnell. 2008. *Handbook of Usability Testing: How to Plan, Design, and Conduct Effective Tests,* 2nd ed. Indianapolis, IN: Wiley Publishing, Inc.

Scalable Systems. 2008. "How Big is Your Data?" *http://www.scalable-systems.com/whitepaper/ Scalable_WhitePaper_Big_Data.pdf*.

Schneider, G. Michael, Johnny Martin, and W. T. Tsai. 1992. "An Experimental Study of Fault Detection in User Requirements Documents." *ACM Transactions on Software Engineering and Methodology* 1(2):188–204.

Schonberger, Richard. J. 2008. *Best Practices in Lean Six Sigma Process Improvement: A Deeper Look*. Hoboken, NJ: John Wiley & Sons, Inc.

Schwaber, Ken. 2004. *Agile Project Management with Scrum*. Redmond, WA: Microsoft Press.

Schwarz, Roger. 2002. *The Skilled Facilitator: A Comprehensive Resource for Consultants, Facilitators, Managers, Trainers, and Coaches*. San Francisco, CA: Jossey-Bass.

Seilevel. 2011. "Seilevel Requirements Management Tool Evaluation Results." *http://www.seilevel .com/wp-content/uploads/2011/09/Seilevel-RequirementsManagementToolEvalResults2.xls*.

———. 2012. "Seilevel Project Assessment." *http://www.seilevel.com/wp-content/uploads/ Project_Assessments_Template.xls*.

Sharp, Alec, and Patrick McDermott. 2008. *Workflow Modeling: Tools for Process Improvement and Application Development*. Norwood, Massachusetts: Artec, Inc.

Shehata, Mohammed S., Armin Eberlein, and H. James Hoover. 2002. "Requirements Reuse and Feature Interaction Management." In *Proceedings of the 15th International Conference on Software & Systems Engineering and their Applications*. Paris.

Shull, F., V. Basili, B. Boehm., A. W. Brown, A. Costa, M. Lindvall, D. Port, I. Rus, R. Tesoriero, and M. Zelkowitz. 2002. "What We Have Learned About Fighting Defects." In *Proceedings of the Eighth IEEE Symposium on Software Metrics*, 249–258. Ottawa, Canada. IEEE Computer Society Press.

Sibbet, David. 1994. *Effective Facilitation: Achieving Results with Groups*. San Francisco, CA: The Grove Consultants International.

Simmons, Erik. 2001. "From Requirements to Release Criteria: Specifying, Demonstrating, and Monitoring Product Quality." In *Proceedings of the 2001 Pacific Northwest Software Quality Conference*, 155–165. Portland, OR: Pacific Northwest Software Quality Conference.

Smith, Larry W. 2000. "Project Clarity Through Stakeholder Analysis." *CrossTalk* 13(12):4–9.

Sommerville, Ian, and Pete Sawyer. 1997. *Requirements Engineering: A Good Practice Guide*. Chichester, England: John Wiley & Sons Ltd.

Sorensen, Reed. 1999. "CCB—An Acronym for 'Chocolate Chip Brownies'? A Tutorial on Control Boards." *CrossTalk* 12(3):3–6.

The Standish Group. 2009. "Chaos Summary 2009." West Yarmouth, MA: The Standish Group International, Inc.

Stevens, Richard, Peter Brook, Ken Jackson, and Stuart Arnold. 1998. *Systems Engineering: Coping with Complexity*. London: Prentice Hall.

Taylor, James. 2012. "Decision Discovery for a Major Business Function." International Institute for Analytics Research Brief.

_____. 2013. "Using Decision Discovery to Manage Analytic Project Requirements." International Institute for Analytics Research Brief.

Thayer, Richard H. 2002. "Software System Engineering: A Tutorial." *IEEE Computer* 35(4):68–73.

Thomas, Steven. 2008. "Agile Change Management." *http://itsadeliverything.com/agile-change-management*.

Thompson, Bruce, and Karl Wiegers. 1995. "Creative Client/ Server for Evolving Enterprises." *Software Development* 3(2):34–44.

Van Veenendaal, Erik P. W. M. 1999. "Practical Quality Assurance for Embedded Software." *Software Quality Professional* 1(3):7–18.

Voas, Jeffrey. 1999. "Protecting Against What? The Achilles Heel of Information Assurance." *IEEE Software* 16(1):28–29.

Volere. 2013. "Requirements Tools." *http://www.volere.co.uk/tools.htm*.

von Halle, Barbara. 2002. *Business Rules Applied: Building Better Systems Using the Business Rules Approach*. New York: John Wiley & Sons, Inc.

von Halle, Barbara, and Larry Goldberg. 2010. *The Decision Model: A Business Logic Framework Linking Business and Technology*. Boca Raton, FL: Auerbach Publications.

Wallace, Dolores R., and Laura M. Ippolito. 1997. "Verifying and Validating Software Requirements Specifications." In *Software Requirements Engineering*, 2nd ed., Richard H. Thayer and Merlin Dorfman, eds., 389–404. Los Alamitos, CA: IEEE Computer Society Press.

Wasserman, Anthony I. 1985. "Extending State Transition Diagrams for the Specification of Human-Computer Interaction." *IEEE Transactions on Software Engineering* SE-11(8):699–713.

Weinberg, Gerald M. 1995. "Just Say No! Improving the Requirements Process." *American Programmer* 8(10):19–23.

Wiegers, Karl E. 1996. *Creating a Software Engineering Culture*. New York: Dorset House Publishing.

_____. 1998a. "The Seven Deadly Sins of Software Reviews." *Software Development* 6(3):44–47.

_____. 1998b. "Improve Your Process With Online 'Good Practices'." *Software Development* 6(12):45–50.

_____. 1999. "Software Process Improvement in Web Time." *IEEE Software* 16(4):78–86.

_____. 2000. "The Habits of Effective Analysts." *Software Development* 8(10):62–65.

_____. 2002. *Peer Reviews in Software: A Practical Guide*. Boston: Addison-Wesley.

_____. 2003. "See You in Court." *Software Development* 11(1):36–40.

_____. 2006. *More About Software Requirements: Thorny Issues and Practical Advice*. Redmond, WA: Microsoft Press.

_____. 2007. *Practical Project Initiation: A Handbook with Tools*. Redmond, WA: Microsoft Press.

_____. 2011. *Pearls from Sand: How Small Encounters Lead to Powerful Lessons*. New York: Morgan James Publishing.

Wiley, Bill. 2000. *Essential System Requirements: A Practical Guide to Event-Driven Methods*. Reading, MA: Addison-Wesley.

Williams, Ray C., Julie A. Walker, and Audrey J. Dorofee. 1997. "Putting Risk Management into Practice." *IEEE Software* 14(3):75–82.

Wilson, Peter B. 1995. "Testable Requirements—An Alternative Sizing Measure." *The Journal of the Quality Assurance Institute* 9(4):3–11.

Withall, Stephen. 2007. *Software Requirement Patterns*. Redmond, WA: Microsoft Press.

Wood, Jane, and Denise Silver. 1995. *Joint Application Development*, 2nd ed. New York: John Wiley & Sons, Inc.

Young, Ralph R. 2001. *Effective Requirements Practices*. Boston: Addison-Wesley.

_____. 2004. *The Requirements Engineering Handbook*. Norwood, MA: Artech House.

Index

A

B

About the authors

KARL WIEGERS is principal consultant with Process Impact, a software process consulting and education company in Portland, Oregon. His interests include requirements engineering, peer reviews, project management, and process improvement. Previously, he spent 18 years at Eastman Kodak Company as a photographic research scientist, software developer, software manager, and software process and quality improvement leader. Karl received a PhD degree in organic chemistry from the University of Illinois. When he's not on the computer, Karl enjoys wine tasting, playing guitar, writing and recording songs, and doing volunteer work.

Karl is the author of numerous books and articles on software development, chemistry, self-help, and military history. His books include the two previous editions of *Software Requirements* (Microsoft Press, 1999 and 2003), *More About Software Requirements* (Microsoft Press, 2006), *Practical Project Initiation* (Microsoft Press, 2007), *Peer Reviews in Software* (Addison-Wesley, 2002), and *Creating a Software Engineering Culture* (Dorset House Publishing, 1996). He is also the author of a memoir of life lessons, *Pearls from Sand* (Morgan James Publishing, 2011). Karl has served on the editorial board for *IEEE Software* magazine and as a contributing editor for *Software Development* magazine. He has delivered more than 300 seminars and training courses on software requirements. You can reach Karl at *www.processimpact .com* and *www.karlwiegers.com*. (Photo credit: Emily Down, Jama Software)

JOY BEATTY is a vice president at Seilevel, a professional services and training company in Austin, Texas, that helps redefine the way customers create software requirements. With 15 years of experience in business analysis, Joy evolves new methods and helps customers implement best practices that improve requirements elicitation and modeling. She assists Fortune 500 companies as they build business analysis centers of excellence. Joy has provided training to thousands of business analysts and is a Certified Business Analysis Professional (CBAP). Joy graduated from Purdue University with BS degrees in both computer science and mathematics. Joy's passions beyond requirements include rowing, swimming, and being outside with her family.

Joy is actively involved as a leader in the requirements community. She has worked with the International Institute of Business Analysis (IIBA) on *A Guide to the Business Analysis Body of Knowledge (BABOK Guide)*. Additionally, she writes about requirements methodologies in journals, white papers, and blog posts and presents at requirements-related conferences. She also co-authored *Visual Models for Software Requirements* (Microsoft Press, 2012). Joy can be reached at *www.seilevel.com* and *joy.beatty@seilevel.com*.

Now that you've read the book...

Tell us what you think!

Was it useful?
Did it teach you what you wanted to learn?
Was there room for improvement?

Let us know at http://aka.ms/tellpress

Your feedback goes directly to the staff at Microsoft Press,
and we read every one of your responses. Thanks in advance!

 Microsoft